FERRANTI: A HISTORY

The Jagger portrait of Dr S. Z. de Ferranti in his doctoral robes. This protrait now hangs in the IEE's main lecture hall.
(Museum of Science and Industry at Manchester.)

Ferranti: A History

*Building a Family Business,
1882–1975*

by
John F. Wilson

Carnegie Publishing Ltd

This book is dedicated to Sebastian Ziani de Ferranti (1864–1930)
and his son, Vincent, and grandson, Sebastian, without whose
vision and enterprise the firm would never have emerged and
expanded so impressively.

Published by Carnegie Publishing Ltd
Carnegie House, Chatsworth Road
Lancaster LA1 4SL

in association with
The Dr Sebastian de Ferranti Centenary Fund

Copyright © The Dr Sebastian de Ferranti Centenary Fund

All rights reserved

British Library Cataloguing-in-Publication data
A CIP record for this book is available from the British Library

ISBN 1-85936-080-7

Typeset in Minion by Carnegie Publishing
Printed and bound in the UK by
Biddles Ltd, Guildford

Contents

Tables, Figures and Illustrations	ix
Abbreviations	xiv
Foreword by Sebastian de Ferranti	xv
Author's Preface	xvii
Ferranti: an introduction	1
1. Early evolution and company culture	3
2. Organisational capabilities and cultural perspectives under the second generation	8
3. Labour management and the human approach	16
4. Conclusion	19

Part One: The First Generation

1	Family Background and Formative Years	23
	1.1 The Ziani de Ferranti family	21
	1.2 The Scott family	26
	1.3 The young Ferranti	30
	1.4 The young engineer	34
	1.5 A new career plan	37
	1.6 The research engineer	40
	1.7 A business proposition	42
	1.8 The 'Brush Bubble'	45
	1.9 The business scene	49
	1.10 The first business	51
	1.11 The man by 1885	56
2	The Deptford Experience	59
	2.1 The meter business	60
	2.2 Contact with Sir Coutts Lindsay	63
	2.3 The Grosvenor Gallery contract	68
	2.4 Progress and achievement	73
	2.5 Marriage and litigation	79
	2.6 Deptford under construction	84

	2.7	The 'Bold Conception'	92
3	Lessons in Management and Finance		95
	3.1	Extra-Deptford activities	96
	3.2	Business worries	101
	3.3	Rebuilding the business	105
	3.4	The move to Hollinwood	113
	3.5	Industrial relations at Hollinwood	116
	3.6	Management Structure at Hollinwood	118
	3.7	The expanding market and new competition	125
	3.8	New company; new beginning?	132
	3.9	Crisis and change in the company	135
4	The Independent Engineer		143
	4.1	Textile machinery	144
	4.2	Turbines and valves	150
	4.3	Motor-bikes, automobiles and aeroplanes	156
	4.4	The senior statesman	161
	4.5	A market-led strategy for recovery	164
	4.6	Products and prices	172
5	The Return from Exile		179
	5.1	The munitions business and Ferranti at war	180
	5.2	Rationalisation and transformer expansion	187
	5.3	A family firm again	199
	5.4	The 1920s electrical industry	202
	5.5	The construction of a grid network	207
	5.6	Domestic appliances	212
	5.7	The venture into radio	215
	5.8	Ferranti by 1930	222
6	The Elder Statesman		227
	6.1	The electrical engineer and electrical publicist	228
	6.2	The innovator	231
	6.3	The paternalist	232
	6.4	The 'Ferranti Spirit'	235
	6.5	Dr Ferranti	236

Part Two: The Second Generation

7	Electronics and Defence, 1930–1945		241
	7.1	New Regime; New Environment	242
	7.2	The move into electronics	250

	7.3	Television	262
	7.4	Finances and fuzes	265
	7.5	The venture into radar	271
	7.6	Off to Edinburgh	278
	7.7	War and Ferranti	282
8	Post-war Reconstruction	287
	8.1	The third generation and new appointments	288
	8.2	Meters and transformers	293
	8.3	Consumer goods	309
	8.4	Rationalisation	316
	8.5	Avionics at Moston and Bracknell	318
	8.6	The Crewe Toll Adventure	322
	8.7	Maintaining the balance	334
9	The Computer Story	341
	9.1	The emergence of computing	342
	9.2	Ferranti and the first computer trials	346
	9.3	The Mark I, Mark I* and Relations with the NRDC	349
	9.4	Pegasus and progress	356
	9.5	Marketing, sales and innovation	361
	9.6	Commercial computers and punched-cards	368
	9.7	Scientific computers	375
	9.8	Completing the range: Sirius and Orion	380
	9.9	The Bracknell story	384
	9.10	Computer finances and computer mergers	387
	9.11	Conclusion	396
10	Bloodhound and Wythenshawe	399
	10.1	The first guided weapons contract	400
	10.2	Early progress and trials	405
	10.3	The move to Wythenshawe	408
	10.4	Into production of Mark I	411
	10.5	Progress to Bloodhound Mark II	414
	10.6	The Bloodhound revelations	417
	10.7	Lang and its consequences	424
	10.8	Automation systems	429
	10.9	Conclusion	438
11.	The Ferranti Dilemma	439
	11.1	Sebastian and his team	441
	11.2	Semiconductor experiments and products	449

	11.3	Starting up in microelectronics	457
	11.4	Looking for state support	464
	11.5	Edinburgh and the TSR-2	471
	11.6	Numerical control	480
	11.7	Digital systems	485
	11.8	Prospects and proposals	489
12.	The End of Family Control		497
	12.1	Meters and transformers	499
	12.2	Finances and organisation in the early-1970s	514
	12.3	Negotiations with the bank and goverment involvement	522
	12.4	Conclusions	529
13.	The Ferranti Traditions: A Test of Durability		533
	Notes		537

Appendix A: The Ferranti Family Genealogy	575
Appendix B: List of Patents taken out by Sebastian Ziani de Ferranti, 1882-1930	577
Appendix C: The Financing of Ferranti, 1890-1993	585
Appendix D: Chairmen and Directors of Ferranti Ltd., 1905-93	594
Appendix E: Shareholdings of the Ferranti family	596
Appendix F: The Ferranti Product Range, 1882–1975	598
Sources and Bibliography	603
Index	611

Tables, Figures and Illustrations

Tables

1.	Finance and Labour-Force at Ferranti, 1907–82	14
7.1.	Ferranti radio sales and profits, 1930–1938	257
9.1.	The Number of Ferranti computer sales from the West Gorton computer department, 1951–63	368
9.2.	The financial performance of the computer department, 1952–1964	389
9.3.	The share of computer sales in the UK, 1950–59	390
10.1.	The actual and agreed costs of the Bloodhound Mark I production contract up to 31 March 1961	419
10.2.	Financial performance of the Wythenshawe Division, 1959–1963	420
11.1.	Ferranti integrated circuit sales and R & D expenditure, 1961–71	460
11.2.	The financial performance of Crewe Toll, 1960–70	479
11.3.	Performance of the Digital Systems Department, 1961–70	488
12.1.	Cash inflow and cash outflow, 1961–75	517
12.2.	The financial performance of Ferranti Ltd compared with its major divisions, 1971–72 to 1974–75	520
1.	Company capital, 1890–1990	585
2.	Profitability and return on capital employed, 1892–1993	591
3.	Turnover and employment at Ferranti, 1890–1993	595

Figures

1.	The Ferranti Organisation in 1960	11
2.	Ferranti Turnover and Capital Employed at Constant Prices, 1906–1975 (1980=100)	15
3.1.	The structure of S.Z.de Ferranti Ltd in 1900	121
5.1.	Ferranti Ltd Turnover, 1914–39	206

7.1. *Wartime Turnover at Ferranti Ltd, 1938–46*	282
7.2. *The Ferranti Structure in 1945*	285
8.1. *Evolution of Departments*	290
8.2. *Turnover Growth at Ferranti Ltd, 1945–63*	291
9.1. *Mergers in the British computer industry, 1959–68*	396
11.1. *Ferranti Turnover in Constant and Current Prices, 1906–75*	442
11.2. *Main Ferranti locations in the UK by 1975*	443
12.1. *The Ferranti Overdraft, 1945–75*	523
Family Tree from 1801	576

Illustrations

Dr S. Z. de Ferranti, 1930	ii
Doge Sebastian Ziani	24
Cesare Ziani de Ferranti	28
Juliana Ziani de Ferranti	29
130–2 Bold St, Liverpool	31
St Augustine's, Ramsgate	33
A railway engine drawn by Sebastian Ziani de Ferranti, 1875	35
S. Z. de Ferranti, 1882	38
Appold St works	44
Ferranti-Thomson alternator, 1882	47
Ferranti-Thomson alternator, 1882	53
S. Z. de Ferranti, 1882	56
Ferranti Meter Catalogue, 1885	61
Ferranti DC Meter, 1885	63
Grosvenor Gallery	64
Sir Coutts Lindsay	65
Ferranti-Addenbrook telephony transformer, 1885	68
Ferranti transformer, 1886	70
Deptford workers, 1889	72
Charles Pratt Sparks, 1916	73
Ferranti alternators, 1887	74

Lord Wantage, VC	77
LESCo advertisement, 1889	78
Ferranti 10,000V mains, 1890	86
Deptford chisel test, 1890	87
Deptford engines, 1889	88
Deptford station, 1889	89
Ferranti 10,000 hp alternator, 1890	90
Charterhouse Sq. works, 1890	98
Ferranti steam-alternator, 1890	99
Gertrude Ince, 1882	100
Ferranti-Wright AC meter, 1890	107
Ferranti steam-alternator and Parsons turbine, 1894	109
Ferranti transformer, 1894	112
Ferranti steam-alternator, 1895	114
Ferranti frame in the shop, 1899	122
Ferranti switchgear, 1894	124
Ferranti switchgear, 1899	126
Arthur Whittaker, 1943	136
Ferranti AC meter, 1905	138
Textile machinery, 1923	146
Ferranti steam turbine, 1902	148
Ferranti steam turbine, 1911	151
Ferranti steam turbine, 1912	152
Hopkinson-Ferranti steam valve, 1906	155
The de Ferranti family, 1913	156
Ferranti product range, 1911	166
Ferranti Canada advertisement, 1913	170
Ferranti female employees, 1916	183
Ferranti munitions workers, 1918	185
Ferranti transformer, 1919	191
One million volt arc test at Hollinwood, 1925	193
Ferranti Canada	195
Ferranti Canada	196

Vincent de Ferranti, 1930	200
Ferranti grid transformer, 1932	210
Ferranti meter assembly line, Hollinwood	211
Baslow Hall, 1925	213
Ferranti AF3 audio transformer, 1925	218
Ferranti AF3 audio transformer, 1925	218
Hollinwood factory, 1931	223
Dr S. Z. de Ferranti, 1925	229
J. W. Davies, 1945	234
Sir Vincent de Ferranti, 1945	243
Ferranti staff dinner, 1936	249
Ferranti thermionic emission valves, 1945	254
Sebastian de Ferranti, 1966	289
Sir Vincent and Lady de Ferranti, 1948	292
Ferranti pre-payment meter, 1968	295
Denis de Ferranti, 1950	296
Ferranti grid transformer, 1955	299
Ferranti grid transformer, 1965	300
Ferranti Canada	303
Ferranti fridge-heater, 1960	315
Ferranti digital computer, 1968	324
Ferranti AIRPASS radar	327
Ferranti Mk IV numerical control machine	337
First Manchester computer, 1948	343
Professor F. C. Williams and staff, 1949	345
Ferranti Mark I* computer, 1951	350
Ferranti Mark I* computer, 1953	352
Ferranti Pegasus computer, 1957	355
Ferranti Pegasus circuits, 1957	358
Ferranti Mercury computer, 1957	376
Ferranti Atlas computer, 1962	378
Ferranti Sirius computer, 1959	381
Ferranti CAAIS digital computer, 1972	387

Denis Best, 1968	403
Dr Norman Searby and Bob Grove, 1968	404
Wythenshawe factory, 1960	409
Bloodhound test-bed	412
Argus computer circuits, 1966	431
Argus computer, 1970	432
Argus computer, 1969	433
Argus system at Manchester Airport, 1967	434
Ferranti helicopter simulator, 1970	435
Argus computers, 1980	437
MK I Bristol/Ferranti Bloodhound Missiles, 1962	438
Sir Vincent de Ferranti, 1963	440
Sir Vincent de Ferranti, 1958	444
Silicon semiconductor production process, 1956	450
Ferranti semiconductor products, 1956–1970	454
Transistor production line, 1970	457
Integrated circuit production line, 1965	459
Testing equipment for Integrated circuits, 1970	461
Ferranti F100-L microcircuit, 1973	462
The Ferranti ULA, 1973	468
Concorde, 1970	476
Ferranti laser-powered cutting machine, 1970	481
Sebastian de Ferranti, 1963	493
High voltage laboratory, Chadderton, 1965	498
The Avenue works, Chadderton, 1970	499
Ferranti meters, 1970	505
Ferranti power transformers, 1966	506
Transformer testing facility, Chadderton, 1968	508
Ferranti testing transformer, 1972	509
Ferranti board of directors, 1973	514
Sebastian de Ferranti, 1968	518

Abbreviations

AC	alternating current
AF	audio frequency
AEI	Associated Electric Industries Ltd
BEAMA	British Electrical & Allied Manufacturers' Association
BZF	Basil Ziani de Ferranti
CEB	Central Electricity Board
CEGB	Central Electricity Generating Board
CPS	Charles Pratt Sparks
CZF	Cesar Ziani de Ferranti
DC	direct current
DTI	Department of Trade & Industry
EAW	Electrical Association for Women
EDA	Electrical Development Association
FBM	Ferranti Board Minutes
FEL	Ferranti Engineering Ltd
GE	General Electric (of the USA)
GEC	General Electric Company Ltd (of the UK)
gWh	gigawatt-hours
hp	horse power
IEE	Institution of Electrical Engineering
JSB	Juliana's scrap-book
JZF	Juliana Ziani de Ferranti
kVA	kilovolt-amperes
kWh	kilowatt-hour
LESCo.	London Electricity Supply Co.
MoA	Ministry of Aviation
MoD	Ministry of Defence
NEB	National Enterprise Board
NEMA	National Electrical Manufacturers' Association
NESCo.	Newcastle Electricity Supply Co.
rpm	revolutions per minute
SZF	Sebastian Ziani de Ferranti
VZF	Vincent Zinai de Ferranti

Foreword

The history of the Ferranti company is fading from living memory. I would like my grandchildren, and anyone else who is interested, to have some of the facts laid out by a scholar so that any history that might later be written could be based on what I believe to be an accurate academic account.

The company's reputation was all out of proportion to its size, and as a centre of engineering excellence and innovation it was known worldwide. My grandfather's renown, on the other hand, will live on as an outstanding engineer whose engineering authority was principally made between the ages of nineteen and twenty-four.

In the 110 years of its existence until near the end it was owned and controlled by three people. In the years 1956 to 1975, with my brother Basil, I had over fifty-one per cent of the voting equity. My father between the years 1930–63 owned fifty-one per cent, and my grandfather, in turn, owned the vast majority of the equity.

John Wilson has been working on the project for twenty years, absorbing himself in the archival collection. It took just over 100 years to build the company, and by Alun-Jones's unfortunate judgement, and that of his board of directors, it went into receivership in the same number of months.

I hope in looking at this detailed account the reader will bear in mind that it cannot give any idea of the excitement and sense of achievement that we had day by day in the company. My father said that there was no point in doing a job unless you got fun out of it. He was right. He also said he was not prepared always to do the logical thing. I agree with that too. Wealth without responsibility was of little interest to him or to me. This was less true for my brother, who took a different view.

Ferranti was an unusual firm, and its ethos so distinctive that often its organisation and strategies were unconventional. John Wilson, as an academic steeped in the business and economics literature, does not wholly capture what is the very essence of the Ferranti drive for engineering achievement and excellence.

Above all, my grandfather, father and I had a long-term commitment to engineering vision. All too often this defied conventional methods simply because we were not driven by stock market valuations.

My grandfather established the firm in 1882 after introducing a novel form of armature for the early alternators, as opposed to the engineering cul-de-sac, the DC system, which others advocated. He went on to build the world's first high voltage AC power station at Deptford, again defying contemporary practice and comment that his ideas were ahead of his time. That indifferent engineer, Edison, called it the foolhardiness of youth. It is now the world's standard practice. It was an approach which he followed relentlessly throughout a career spanning forty-nine years, during which he took out 176 patents covering a highly diverse range of products, from alternating current generators, high voltage cables and transformers through to meters, radio components, gyroscopes and domestic appliances. This engineering-led approach provided the foundations for a business culture which was carried on by my father, Vincent, under whose first-class management it expanded dramatically into new technologies like computing, avionics and semiconductors. I was absorbed into this family ethos from being a child, learning at home, and later working with my father reminding managers that because he owned fifty-one per cent of the equity he was prepared to take a long-term view on engineering projects, provided the company remained profitable. This philosophy I followed as Chairman and Managing Director of the company between 1963 and 1982, encouraging departments to take risks on exciting new ideas where they saw a commercial opportunity and eventual profit. This eventual profit was the danger in some divisions, given the cash outlay and inevitable bank borrowings. Our activities were limited by the profit we generated.

So, the company was not institutionalised and this free-booting spirit of enterprise is difficult to capture in an orthodox history written by a professional academic bound by the rules of university research and with little regard to the all important personalities involved. By definition, the unconventional defies orthodoxy. This is why the reader should remember what was the driving force behind the firm's evolution when trawling through the mountains of detail accumulated by Professor Wilson. One cannot blame him for adhering to academic conventions when analysing key events in history: it would be remiss of a professional historian to do otherwise. Crucially, though, the Ferranti spirit lived through the actions and thoughts of engineers who worked for the firm over those 111 years. It is their achievements which best reflect the meaning behind the engineering-led ethos established by my family as we wished to bring new engineering ideas to the world. Ferranti existed to convert this dream into reality, a message not to forget when reading this academic account.

Sebastian de Ferranti
Henbury, December 1999.

Preface

When I first visited the Ferranti Archives in March 1978 there was no thought in my mind that the project would still be flourishing over twenty years later. It has been a career-long commitment full of fascinating research opportunities. Few business historians could have been given such access to both people and records in charting the rise (and fall) of a major company.

In consequence, I have naturally accumulated an enormous backlog of debts, given the substantial amount of time certain people have devoted to helping me. First and foremost, one must start by noting that there would have been no project (and no company!) without the de Ferranti family. In particular, without the support of Sebastian de Ferranti the research would never have progressed from a dry doctorate into a full-blown corporate history without the encouragement and funding provided by this remarkable man. Not only does he have a true sense of history, but he is also willing to back his instincts. From the provision of a Research Fellowship at the University of Manchester to his continued support for the present project, he has backed the historical research just as robustly as he backed work on semiconductors or transformers. Just as Sebastian's grandfather pleaded for more men like Matthew Boulton to support technological innovation, I would like to state that with more men like Sebastian de Ferranti British business history would be in a position to match American efforts. Similarly, his brother Basil was a great help when consulted on any aspect of the company's history.

The respective Ferranti archivists – Charles Somers, Bob Campbell and Cliff Wimpenny – have also assisted me enormously. While none have been professional archivists, as I note in the Bibliography each in his own distinctive way has contributed to the collection of an impressive array of documents and artefacts. In addition, their assistants, respectively, Edith Walsh, Doreen Scott and Chris Pennington, were equally important in supplying everything I wanted. I will always cherish the memories of those trips to the archives, because I was always made so welcome.

Apart from the archivists, a legion of Ferranti employees either agreed to be interviewed or wrote copious notes on my stumbling efforts. While it would be invidious to describe the help of all of these kind people, a special mention must be given to Tom Lunt, the former Staff Manager, whose easy charm and affinity with academic life provided an ideal introduction to the complexities of a firm with which he has been associated for over fifty years. In addition, two of the trustees of the Dr. Ferranti Centenary Memorial Fund, Tom Grime and Albert Dodd, have been unstinting in the amount of advice they have provided. I would also like to thank several senior people who provided information, including: Maurice Gribble, Dr. Alan Shepherd, Denis Best, Dr. Norman Searby, Sir Donald McCallum, Sir Richard H. Davies, Peter Dorey, Tony Thomas, Harry Kirkham, Lester George, Harry Johnson, Peter Hall, and Sir Derek Alun-Jones.

While owners and employees have been extremely helpful, I should also note that over the years many academic colleagues have directed me effectively. In this context, Professor A. E. (Ted) Musson was an inspiration during both my time as a postgraduate student and as a colleague. My debt to him is enormous. Other scholars who have helped me include Les Hannah, Geoff Tweedale, Tetsuro Nakaoka, John Hendry, Andrew Marrison, Martin Campbell-Kelly, Sir Geoffrey Owen, Richard Coopey, and Jonathan Zeitlin.

This preface would not be complete without thanking the many librarians and professional archivists who have assisted me over the years, especially in Preston and Manchester. Thanks especially to Stephen Forshaw at the Manchester Museum of Science and Industry for helping to select the photographs. Inevitably, though, the Worcester Oracle has woven her magic spell once again, enlightening me on the many intricacies of life. Thank you Watsons! My personal dedication of this book goes to you for the wonderful support provided over the last year.

Finally, I can only repeat previous expressions of gratitude to the patience and support of Barbara and Anthony. You make it all worthwhile.

JFW, Preston 1999

Ferranti: an introduction

Writing the history of a firm like Ferranti presents a substantial challenge. In the first place, one must remember that until 1975 Ferranti was run by the eponymous owning family, giving it a distinctive culture which owed all to the fascination with engineering invention and innovation. This culture was the driving force behind the firm's growth and diversification for over a century, spilling over even into the era (1975–93) when non-family managers determined policy, and some would say drove it into bankruptcy. In the period covered by this book (1882–1975), we shall see how three key members of the de Ferranti family, Sebastian (1864–1930), Vincent (1893–1980) and Sebastian (1927–), developed an engineering-led business which prided itself on a widely-renowned ability to pioneer a range of new ideas and products. Crucially, because this drive often conflicted with orthodox business methods, it is impossible to assess the Ferranti story according to conventional yardsticks. The family owner-managers chose to risk their resources on exciting new ideas, ignoring the pressures imposed on professional managers because it was their funds which were at risk. 'There is no substitute for fifty-one per cent', as Sir Vincent de Ferranti would frequently tell his staff during his period as chairman and managing director of Ferranti which saw the firm expand remarkably in scale and scope.

In a business world which was increasingly dominated by the desire for short-term gain over long-term planning and innovation, Ferranti would consequently appear to have been an enigma, eschewing the conventional in favour of excitement and engineering achievement. As a direct result of this drive, Ferranti gained and nurtured a reputation as one of the most innovative engineering firms in Britain. The following chapters will describe how over its 111 year history (1882–1993) a succession of new concepts and products emerged from its proprietors and engineers, from massive generators and transformers, meters, steam valves, high-voltage cables and switchgear prior to the First World War, to more recently airborne navigation systems, computers and automation, and microelectronic chips. These innovations were an essential feature of the corporate image Ferranti built successfully after its launch in 1882, providing the dynamic behind a story full of excitement. At times, this dynamic created insuperable financial problems for the firm, especially when market conditions did not prove as profitable as the family anticipated. Here again, though, successive generations were willing to support ventures irrespective of conventional business considerations, reflecting a long-term commitment to the firm which defies orthodox analysis. This is the dilemma which faces us when relating the history of Ferranti.

Before embarking on this history, it is consequently important to ask a series of more fundamental questions about the company and its culture. Practitioners and academics alike now recognise how crucial this factor often becomes in determining organisational success, particularly if that culture is positioned accurately in relation to both the firm's resources and the environment in which it functions.[1] In particular, we need an insight into the ethos which prevailed at Ferranti, examining such crucial issues as the founder's hopes in ensuring the enterprise's survival and how later generations of the family sustained this ethos. It would also be interesting to examine the degree of cooperation received from employees, because we shall see how the family placed considerable emphasis on delegating responsibility down the line to managers and engineers. It is a truism that firms are composed of people, and at Ferranti from the earliest days the family was above all concerned with motivating staff and encouraging enterprise at all levels in the organisation, the aim being to reinforce engineering innovation. The inauguration of Inventors' Dinners by Sebastian de Ferranti in the 1960s reflected this commitment, by celebrating both individual and corporate contributions to improving engineering standards in a wide range of fields. It was a culture which pervaded the firm right up to the 1980s, demonstrating how Ferranti operated in ways which were radically different from the standard practices adopted in much of British business. In particular, the firm was never institutionalised through the establishment of myriad levels of committees and management ranks.

This introductory chapter will provide an outline of the Ferranti ethos as an essential background to the chronological coverage which follows, emphasising in particular the role of the de Ferranti family up to the 1970s, and the traditions they passed on to later variants of the firm. Family firms like Ferranti have often been criticised for imposing a baleful influence on British industrial competitiveness, allegedly because they lacked both adequate organisational depth and sophistication and failed to invest in long-term growth strategies.[2] Of course, these views have been widely criticised as overly simplistic and generalised, and in examining the Ferranti ethos it is possible to illustrate how critics have failed to assess whether the family firm's structure and strategy was appropriate to both its resources and environment.[3] These are by no means easy issues to discuss, especially in the case of the unorthodox firm of Ferranti, providing a fascinating challenge for the business historian.

1. Early evolution and company culture

Over the 111 years of its corporate existence (1882–1993), Ferranti experienced what can only be described as a roller-coaster existence: it evolved from a small workshop in 1882 into one of Britain's leading high technology ventures; yet in 1903 and in 1975 the firm experienced two major crises which had remarkably similar causes and consequences. Finally in 1987, when the firm was no longer family-owned and managed, it was the victim of a massive fraud which ultimately led to bankruptcy and liquidation by 1993. The expansion up to 1975 was all the more dramatic because it occurred in spite of the alleged disadvantages associated with family firms, namely, the reliance on self-generated funds and a reluctance to delegate responsibility for strategic decision-making to professional managers. In fact, in organisational terms Ferranti was a most unusual family firm, because considerable autonomy was bestowed on departmental (and later, divisional) managers, establishing a system which was central to the general ethos. One must note that the crises in 1903 and 1975 were precipitated by the first of these characteristics, posing serious questions about this form of industrial capitalism. On the other hand, inconsistent decision-making at the firm's bankers, as well as intervention by politicians pursuing job-saving agendas, were equally important in deciding the company's fate, especially in the 1970s. Throughout its history, however, and especially up to the 1970s, Ferranti remained committed to a mission based on engineering innovation which provided the strategic direction for what by all accounts was an exciting business.

Founder's role

Of seminal importance when discussing this mission was the role of the company's founder, Sebastian Ziani de Ferranti (1864–1930). In this context, one can only agree with Schein's view that founders are instrumental in shaping 'the basic assumptions and beliefs shared by members of an organisation'.[4] It was Sebastian's commitment to establishing the 'All Electric' age, by improving and pioneering ideas related to electrical engineering (and any other engineering with which he came into contact), which provided the basic assumptions and beliefs shared within the firm. In addition, he also wanted to provide for his family, given the financial crisis arising from his father's illness in 1881–82. This approach was instrumental in establishing a company culture which endured for several generations, providing the principal focus of this book. Even at the tender age of fourteen (see section 1.5), he was informing his parents that 'the best thing for me to be will be a Manufacturing Engineer as then everything I invented I will be able to carry out with advantage'. Innovatory instincts and artistic feelings were consequently apparent from an early age, providing a working philosophy for a career spanning forty-eight years as a 'Manufacturing Engineer'. He was also a very persuasive individual, extolling the value in his ideas with flair and enthusiasm. Using his distinctive presence and good looks, he was also capable of convincing potential supporters and customers that the products were worth backing. By the time he was eighteen, two experienced businessmen had consequently agreed to fund the establishment of his first company (see section 1.7), establishing an individual who was to have a major influence on British power station practice.

It will become clear when reading the early chapters that Ferranti was above all a practical innovator. For example, as a result of work on high-tension AC (alternating current) generation and distribution systems, within ten years of starting in business he was known across Europe and the USA for designing and building what is now recognised as the world's first modern power station, at Deptford (see section 2.5). Unfortunately, though, because of restrictive legislation and powerful competition from gas and steam, the British electrical market failed to grow significantly until the late 1890s, providing few opportunities for Ferranti and his Deptford backers to expand both the scale and scope of their businesses (see section 2.6). The reasons behind, and implications of, these developments will be examined in the first three chapters. Of critical importance here, though, is the inference that innovative engineers like Ferranti were often forced to compromise between a stark commercial reality and engineering excellence. At no time, however, was Ferranti put off by this environment, insisting that because he was technically correct it was worth persisting in the face of often overwhelming odds.

In general terms up to the late 1890s, British progress in the field of electrical engineering remained sluggish, demonstrating how the commercial environment acted as a major constraint on the ability of Ferranti to expand his product base. On the other hand, it is important to stress that this was by no means the only reason why the firm remained relatively small-scale, access to finance being another reason why limited progress was made at that time. Of course, Ferranti was by no means unusual in this respect, because the whole culture of 'personal capitalism' revolved around the intrinsic belief in self-finance, eschewing the need to rely on outsiders who might interfere in the firm's management.[5] Nevertheless, given the rapid rate of technological progress in electrical engineering, not to mention the intensifying competition from much larger American and German multinationals, the refusal to accept equity capital from professional investors severely constrained the firm's expansion up to 1903 (see section 3.7). By the 1890s, then, two of the firm's enduring characteristics had already become well-established norms, namely, a technology-led strategy and dogged financial self-reliance. It is also important to note that they were intrinsically linked, financial independence ensuring complete control over strategy and structure, an aim the family worked hard to achieve over the following eighty years. As Sir Vincent de Ferranti would often say to anyone who questioned his propensity to take what he always described as 'sporting swipes' at new products: 'There is no substitute for fifty-one per cent'.

Having noted these essential characteristics of the Ferranti ethos up to the 1890s, it is vital to remember that on several occasions there were violent internal disagreements over strategy and finance, in particular between the founder and one of his first partners, Francis Ince. As a solicitor and experienced businessman, Ince constantly chided Ferranti for pursuing commercially dangerous practices, arguing in one case (see section 1.9) that 'we shall be improved off the face of the earth, and others with a less perfect machine will do all the work and laugh at us while we are theorising'. The reference to 'theorising' should here be heavily qualified, of course, because the early chapters will illustrate that, apart from a brief spell at University College, London, Ferranti was essentially self-taught and preferred practical work to academic investigations. As the Deptford power station backers also discovered, the excessive development of products as they passed through the workshop materially affected commercial viability (see section 2.5), especially when funds were tight and demand limited. Nevertheless, Ferranti stubbornly refused to change his approach, establishing a technology-led strategy as the firm's central philosophy. Ironically, he was only able to survive in business because of an ingenious DC electricity meter first developed in 1885, the manufacture of which made possible his drive for engineering excellence in other areas.

Organisational ethos

When in the late 1890s the British electrical market finally started to offer significant prospects for expansion, as a result of pursuing a technology-led strategy Ferranti was consequently well-placed to exploit the new openings. As the firm's flagship product at this time was the large steam-alternator, their cramped London factory soon limited expansion, an obstacle which prompted a move north in 1896, when the first factory in Hollinwood was rented and equipped (see section 3.4). It was a well-timed move, funded largely from meter profits. At the same time, it is also vital to note that the expansion forced the firm to introduce some significant organisational developments which were to become consistent features of the company ethos. Although Charles Sparks had been recruited in 1885 as a junior partner who would take responsibility for production, and in 1890 a manager was given sole charge of meter manufacture, the firm was largely run by the two main partners, Sebastian de Ferranti and Francis Ince (see section 3.6). This simple structure worked because the firm remained essentially small-scale. However, the move into larger premises in Hollinwood, and the considerable expansion in both the scale and scope of production, meant that a new system had to be devised which would free the partners from routine management. Ferranti was also convinced that once appropriate departmental managers had been found, they should be given sufficient autonomy, in order to encourage an entrepreneurial approach towards product development. In effect, this laid the foundations of an organisational culture which survived in various guises right up to the 1980s.

Of course, one of the great dangers associated with the devolved structure which emerged at Ferranti after 1896 was the possibility that inadequate control over finance would lead to serious liquidity problems when one or more departments struggled to achieve a profit. This possibility was all the more evident when a technology-led strategy was pursued relentlessly in the drive to fashion a comprehensive product range. Even though A. B. Anderson was recruited into the senior management team, largely because Francis Ince refused to move north to Hollinwood, and in 1899 improved departmental reporting procedures were introduced after a series of organisational reforms, the firm struggled to improve its financial status. It was at this time that Ferranti established a heavy reliance on bank overdrafts, Parr's Bank acting as the main source of cash until its acquisition by the Westminster Bank in 1919. Ferranti realised that his firm was financially weak, leading in 1901 to a capital reconstruction, when non-voting preference shares were floated on the Manchester Stock Exchange (see section 3.8). However, because the founder insisted on retaining ninety per cent of the equity and only engineers sat on the board of directors, this scheme failed to generate sufficient interest. Although further changes were made to the organisation, largely as a result of advice from the prominent Manchester company promoter, Scott Lings, by 1903 the firm was in deep financial trouble, leading ultimately to receivers being appointed by Parr's Bank.

The 1903 crisis came as a big shock to Ferranti and his team of departmental managers, particularly after they had succeeded in developing what many contemporaries regarded as a product range which matched technically anything the American or European competition could offer. Unfortunately, though, this competition had precipitated a drastic reduction in the prices of virtually all electrical engineering goods, and in spite of the organisational reforms introduced by A. B. Anderson by 1903 Parr's Bank was obliged to act decisively because there was simply insufficient money coming into Ferranti. Section 3.9 will provide further details on this crisis, demonstrating how it was essentially caused by a combination of lack of profit and an intensely competitive external environment. As a consequence, and like many of its British counterparts, Ferranti was obliged to undergo a period of retrenchment. In fact, in 1903 Parr's Bank appointed two chartered accountants as receiver-managers to run Ferranti, resulting in a major rationalisation of the product range and the refloating of Ferranti Ltd in 1905.

The key differences between the Ferranti businesses which existed either side of 1905 revolved largely around the senior personnel and their policies: while Sebastian de Ferranti had been more interested in an engineering-led strategy and departmental autonomy, the new regime insisted on a much more conservative approach. The two receiver-managers, A. W. Tait and Arthur Whittaker, were actually given complete control of the new company in 1905, and as a result of introducing a complicated shareholding scheme they were able to demote the founder to a position as technical director, excluding him from the Hollinwood factory for much of the following decade. In addition, they also tightened up the financial controls over departmental managers which Anderson had attempted to introduce in the late 1890s. Furthermore, as well as negotiating price agreements among leading meter producers, they initiated a market-led strategy built around the creation of an extensive agency network in both home and overseas countries. This was a very different regime to the ethos instilled by the firm's founder up to 1903. Of course, the need for product improvement was not forgotten, especially in the key product areas of meters and instruments. More importantly, the introduction of much more orthodox commercial practices proved successful in reestablishing the Ferranti name in what was a highly competitive market (see section 4.5).

Tait and Whittaker had clearly been more adept than Sebastian de Ferranti in matching the firm's values and ethos to its resources and environment. Indeed, by the First World War a viable business had been established which was based on achieving a balance between market-led, financial and engineering-led strategies. This balance was of necessity heavily skewed towards the first two aims in the period 1905–14, when intense competition limited the opportunities for relatively small manufacturers like Ferranti. However, after securing several large munitions contracts at the beginning of the First World War, the founder, by then known as Dr Ferranti,[6] forced his way back into the firm, leading ultimately to greater interest in his technology-led aims. The munitions contracts were actually vital in restoring Ferranti to full financial health, providing Dr Ferranti with the funds to diversify the product range into a series of high growth markets (see sections 5.2–5.7). So influential did Dr Ferranti become, indeed, that by 1928 he was once again chairman of the company he founded, while after several reconstructions the equity capital had been transferred back to the family (see section 5.8).

Although by 1928 Ferranti was once again a family firm, it is important to emphasise that organisationally it was very different from the business which had operated up to 1903. The commitment to engineering innovation was still very much at the heart of its mission, and as departmental managers were encouraged to take autonomous decisions about product development the range had been extended from meters and instruments into power transformers, radio components and domestic electrical appliances. On the other hand, as a result of the receiver-managers' work these tendencies were balanced by the imposition of tight financial reporting procedures and the pursuit of ambitious marketing and sales strategies. When in 1930 Dr Ferranti died suddenly and prematurely, his company was consequently in much better shape to cope with both the financial strains of remaining a family firm and the organisational consequences of diversification. Although this legacy was no doubt the result of a compromise between engineering ideals and business necessity, it is clear that by the 1930s the Ferranti culture had developed a durability which allowed senior management to maintain this balance, leading the firm into a period of even more rapid expansion.

2. Organisational capabilities and cultural perspectives under the second generation

Management style

One of the major tests faced by family firms in general is ensuring an adequate succession, in order to maintain strategic direction and organisational continuity. In this context, Ferranti was fortunate that on the death of Dr Ferranti his eldest surviving son, Vincent (later, Sir Vincent), was ready to build on the first generation's achievements. It is vital to stress that Vincent's formative years coincided with the dark years surrounding the 1903 crisis, providing a harsh business lesson for the family. Vincent was consequently highly motivated by the desire not to plunge Ferranti into such a period of uncertainty again. He certainly shared his father's love of engineering, a reflection of which was his role as transformer department manager since 1921, when Ferranti became known as one of the country's leading designers and producers of large transformers and testing equipment. At the same time, Vincent regarded financial solvency as a central guiding principle, giving managers the simple rule that while they could develop new products, it was essential that year-on-year their departments were profitable (see section 7.1). Some latitude in this approach was allowed at times, as we shall see with the radio and television ventures. Occasionally, funds were also provided from a central pool for promising ideas, for example in the case of avionics and semiconductors. In general, though, Vincent kept a careful watch over departmental performance throughout his period as chairman, reminding managers through his powerful personal presence that financial discipline was essential.

The style of management adopted by Vincent was clearly an essential means of preventing a recurrence of the problems which had undermined the company in 1903, particularly in view of what was a considerable expansion and diversification of the Ferranti product range between the 1920s and 1960s (see Figure 8.1, p. 290). It is important to stress the informal nature of this style, indicating how throughout his time as chairman (1930–63) Vincent was so confident of his own ability to make the most suitable decisions that he rejected the need for an institutionalised approach towards decision-making. His main fear was that a top-heavy organisation characterised by meetings, memos and administrative systems would stifle the firm's ability to innovate. At the same time, he personally monitored the financial well-being of his firm, constructing a series of graphs which charted crucial indicators like output, capital employed and profitability (see section 7.1). Departmental reports were also read scrupulously by the chairman, while he was by no means averse to visiting factories at a moment's notice if he felt that personal attention to a particular problem was required. In addition, to reinforce the reporting procedures introduced in the late 1890s, in 1936 a cost & works (or management) accounting department was established, and the latest Hollerith comptometers were installed, substantially improving the flow of financial information to senior management. These organisational capabilities were also augmented further in the late 1940s, when (by then, Sir) Vincent recruited a mathematician and an economist to advise him personally on performance indicators, leading ultimately to the introduction of forecasting techniques as further tools of financial management.[7]

Having noted the essential features of Sir Vincent's style, one must always remember that it was effected not as a constraint on departmental operations, but as a backup system. As Figure 8.1 reveals, having been in 1914 principally a meter producer with interests in transformers, instruments and domestic appliances, Ferranti diversified into a range of technologies during the interwar years, while from the 1940s especially the firm emerged as a major player in an even wider range of new markets. This substantiates the claim that under Sir Vincent the engineering-led strategy so beloved of his father was still very much to the fore, giving departmental managers the opportunity to venture into related products whenever they felt it was appropriate. Although a family company dominated by one person, Ferranti clearly operated as a highly devolved, 'organic' type of organisation, placing managers in positions of real responsibility, technologically and financially.[8] Naturally, Sir Vincent and his team kept a careful eye on financial performance, but the heavy hand of central control was held in abeyance, facilitating the development of a participatory culture in which engineers' and managers' instincts could flourish.

Diversification and control

The story related in Figure 8.1 provides adequate testimony to the claim that an engineering-led strategy continued to be at the heart of Ferranti activities right up to the 1980s. At the same time, while Sir Vincent was able to create a financial reporting system which oversaw this proliferation, he was also faced with the growing problem of coordinating what increasingly amounted to a series of unrelated businesses. While Ferranti had exploited the era's technological opportunities as well as many electrical companies, its diversification was conducted in a non-sequential manner which lacked any element of planning. In effect, the general approach was to encourage managers to develop lines which they might be able to exploit, yet frequently new departments were established to produce and sell the concept, compounding the challenge for management. This proliferation was particularly pronounced after 1945, forcing Sir Vincent and his eldest son, Sebastian, to restructure the business along divisional lines during the late 1950s, by grouping product departments under a single manager who could be trusted (see sections 8.1 and 8.7). Figure 1 illustrates how the new organisation worked in practice, with the divisional and functional managers reporting directly to the managing director. Clearly, though, substantial limits would have been imposed on the managing director's ability to follow everything which was happening in such a diverse and geographically-dispersed company like Ferranti in the 1950s and 1960s. Indeed, the divisional managers soon came to be known as 'barons' who ran their own 'fiefdoms' far from the centre at Hollinwood, an organisational characteristic which would play a central role in the pattern of decision-making over that period.

In developing the divisional structure, Sir Vincent and Sebastian had clearly responded imaginatively to the challenges of running a highly diversified firm like Ferranti. Sebastian had actually taken over as managing director in 1957, sharing the load of running such a dispersed organisation. As he soon discovered when his father retired in 1963, however, problems would later emerge when the board of directors tried to balance divisional against

Figure 1. *The Ferranti Organisation in 1960*

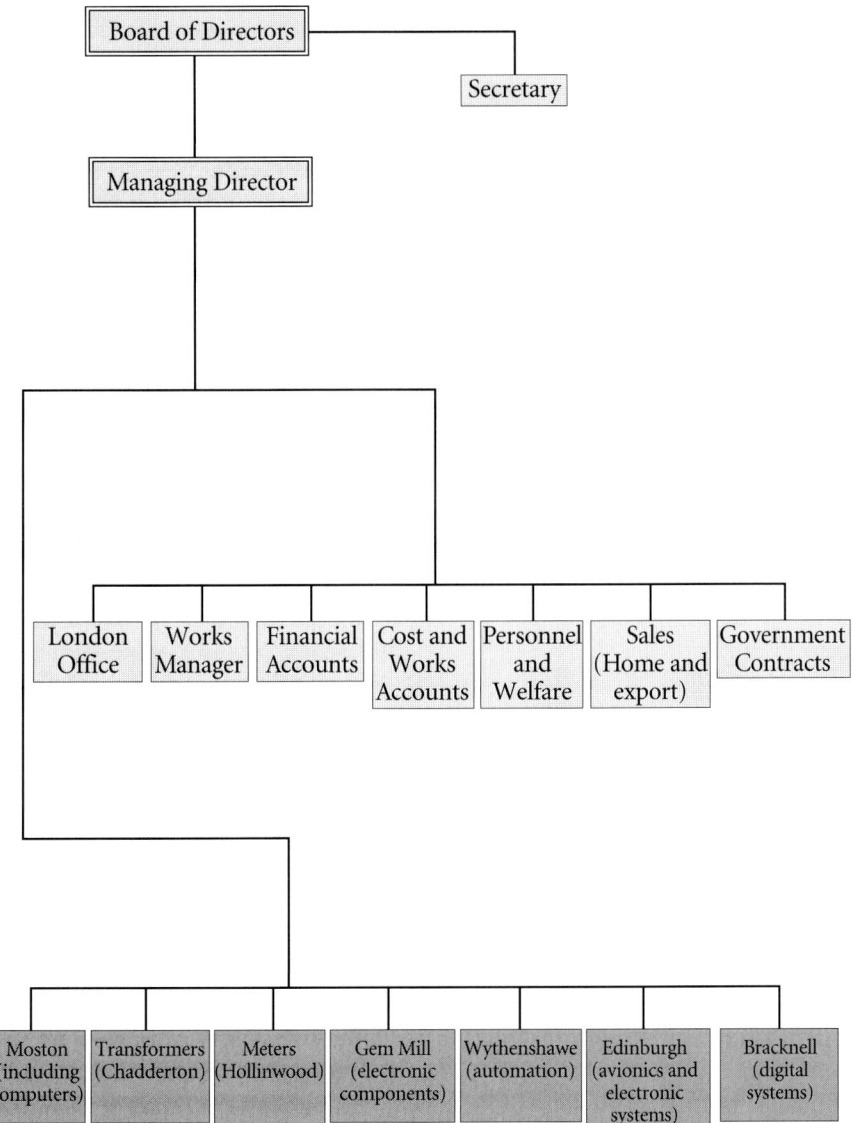

corporate aims, especially as most of the senior managers were brought on to the board. Reflecting the family's reluctance to formalise arrangements within the organisation, though, it is vital to remember that the system was by no means as formalised as Figure 1 implies. It is especially important to note that rarely did the board discuss strategy, given the preference of both Vincent and Sebastian for either instinctive judgements or intimate discussons with a small group of managers or engineers.

In the first place, Sir Vincent, and later Sebastian, were in almost daily contact with the cost & works accountants, monitoring vital indicators like cash-flow, departmental profitability and general financial performance. This would be followed on the next day by meetings with both divisional and departmental managers, in order to check up on progress or discuss new developments, ascertaining exactly when cash would be required. This indicates how the family preferred a non-institutionalised structure which would limit the levels of bureaucracy required. The geographical proximity of most divisions also allowed the retention of sales and other functional services at the headquarters in Hollinwood. The Edinburgh and Bracknell divisions, on the other hand, were given much greater autonomy than the other divisions in view of both their rapid growth and desire for independence (see sections 8.6 and 9.9). Overall, though, while the structure might well have lacked the sophistication of a multidivisional form of organisation, it provided the balance between centralised and autonomous control which the family regarded as fundamental to creating a freebooting culture capable of encouraging innovation.

Defence bias

The post-1930 proliferation of Ferranti activities will be a principal theme of chapters 7–10, when startling new ventures like mainframe computers, guided weapons, airborne radar and guidance systems and microelectronics will be described in great detail. Judging from this diversification, Sir Vincent and Sebastian clearly succeeded in fashioning a conducive environment in which employees could develop their own ideas. As owners of over fifty per cent of the equity, they always felt free to encourage managers to take 'sporting swipes' at promising new technologies, resulting in some striking innovations which put Ferranti at the forefront of Britain's drive to compete with American and European rivals in these markets. However, several commentators also criticised them for preferring to focus excessively on what they mistakenly regarded as the relatively non-competitive defence markets, introducing another key feature of the firm's growth over that period. Of course, defence markets have always been highly competitive, especially given the common view that the services should never be dependent upon a single supplier, not to mention the difficulties experienced when dealing with some of the research establishments. Sir Vincent has also been quoted as commenting that defence contracts were analogous to fluff on a jacket which could so easily be blown away.

Reflecting the immediate post-1945 market environment, Sir Vincent attempted to develop a balance between civil and defence businesses, largely because he felt that an excessive reliance on the latter was dangerous (see section 8.7). This strategy was best manifested in the expansion of domestic appliance production at Moston, particularly radio and television, and of power transformers at Hollinwood. Nevertheless, the firm recorded considerable technological successes in defence markets as varied as aircraft navigation and radar equipment (see sections 8.5 and 8.6), guided weaponry (section 10.5) and naval computers (section 9.9), establishing substantial businesses which inevitably swamped the less successful civil efforts.

In spite of Sir Vincent's intention to achieve a balance between civil and defence businesses, it is clear that the engineering-led strategy flourished more effectively when engineering principles took precedence over the need to mass-produce for the civil market. The meter department remained an exception to this rule right up to the 1960s, generating significant profits through its use of mass-production techniques. In this context, though, one must remember that not only was the meter market controlled by organisations which were more familiar with engineering priorities than the typical consumer, but Ferranti engineers were also well equipped to cater for their demands. Ferranti rightly complained that even when successful civil technologies were developed, for example mainframe computers and numerical control equipment, the domestic markets for such products were so limited that it was financially precarious to risk too much on these businesses (see sections 8.7 and 9.10). Substantial sums were actually spent on these technologies by their respective divisions, largely because Vincent and Sebastian de Ferranti were keen to venture into such novel technologies. However, in view of the guiding principle that departments must be self-financing, their sale (in 1963 and 1969, respectively) became inevitable, swinging the balance even further in favour of defence markets. Ferranti developed a consistent policy of selling off unprofitable departments, a tradition which can be traced back to the decision in 1891 to transfer all high-voltage cable patents to the British Insulated Wire Co. (see section 3.2). For example, in the late 1950s Sir Vincent and Sebastian were obliged to sell off the loss-making radio, television and cathode-ray tube businesses (see section 8.4). Only transformers and meters remained consistent features of the civil product portfolio, where Ferranti found it easier to compete along technical lines by exploiting its long-established name as British leader in markets dominated by engineering-led customers like electricity authorities.

In view of the market difficulties experienced when commercialising high technology innovations, and the Ferranti failure to develop a market-driven approach in its domestic appliance departments, Sir Vincent was acting rationally in encouraging his divisional and departmental managers to build strong positions in a variety of defence markets. After all, the defence market remained buoyant right up to the late 1960s. Table 1 charts the financial implications of this strategy, indicating how especially after becoming a major defence supplier in the mid-1930s the business expanded rapidly.

Table 1. *Finance and Labour-Force at Ferranti, 1907–82*

	SZF 1907	SZF 1928	VZF 1935	VZF 1955	SZF 1963	SZF 1982
Labour	762	4,009	5,394	9,392	20,489	17,983
Issued capital*	0.12	0.21	0.8	3.0	4.5	58.0
Capital employed*	0.25	0.61	1.1	11.1	24.0	107.7
Return on capital employed†	N.A.	12.6	4.0	10.8	7.0	22.1
Output*	0.13	1.1	1.4	13.8	33.4	306.9

Key: * in £ million

† This is calculated by dividing the capital employed by gross profits expressed as a percentage.

Sources: see Appendix C.

Figure 2 reflects this growth up to the 1960s even more accurately, indicating how when one deflates the data by reference to retail price movements Ferranti was a much larger company compared to 1906 and to 1930. One must not be misled by the increase in issued capital into believing that Sir Vincent raised money on the open market to fund this expansion, because the new shares were created by capitalising ploughed-back profits which had accumulated in a reserve account (see Appendix C, Table 1). This ensured that not only would the family remain sole owners of the firm, but also that internal resources would be the principal source of expansion capital for the developments described in Figure 8.1. At the same time, Westminster (later, National Westminster) Bank continued to provide adequate liquidity up to the early 1970s, indicating how frequent recourse to overdrafts was made by Ferranti when internal resources were overstretched. Indeed, over the post-War years crucial decisions were heavily influenced by the Bank's

Figure 2. *Ferranti Turnover and Capital Employed at Constant Prices, 1906–1975 (1980=100)*

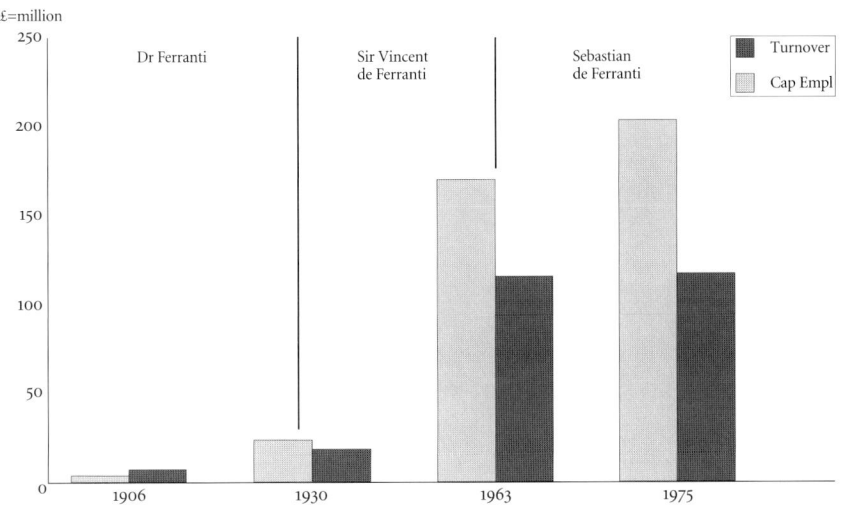

attitude towards the company's general financial health (see section 8.4). It is important to remember, though, that the Bank provided this support because it was convinced that Ferranti had developed both a strong product base and an effective internal accounting system, assuring the family of extensive latitude in taking 'sporting swipes' at new ideas.

An innovation culture had clearly been imbued into the organisation by Dr Ferranti, a culture which over succeeding generations both Sir Vincent and Sebastian de Ferranti were keen to maintain and develop in determining both the manner in which their firm evolved and the product range which emerged. Clearly, the external environment had played an important role in this process, particularly in the way a limited market for high technology goods had forced Ferranti to seek customers for its expertise in the defence sector. Above all, though, the de Ferranti family was interested in technological innovation, preferring to channel its limited financial resources into projects which looked both interesting, exciting and potentially rewarding. They were able to take this approach because the City institutions were not looking over their shoulders and pressing for better financial rewards. Of course, the Westminster Bank at times influenced the actions of both Sir Vincent and Sebastian (see sections 8.4 and 12.2). Overall, though, they were free to spend the fruits of previous endeavours on long-term development programmes. This was in stark contrast to the general scene in British business from the 1940s, where, as a result of the growing influence of financial institutions over strategy and structure, short-termism was coming to dominate planning procedures.[9] Ferranti took great pride in its independence from this pervasive trend, leading the family to argue publicly that it was only by taking a long-term view of engineering and commercial opportunities that the company could prosper.

3. Labour management and the human approach

The combination of an innovation culture and extensive financial reporting procedures had clearly benefited Ferranti enormously in the twentieth century, facilitating the rapid expansion reflected in both Figure 2 and Figure 8.1. It was on these twin pillars that Sir Vincent especially built a durable organisation which was well equipped to exploit the era's many technological opportunities, confirming the viability of a culture which was well suited to the firm's resources and environment. One feature of this expansion which has still not been examined, however, is how Sebastian, Vincent and Sebastian were able to generate the degree of commitment from its employees, because for the innovation culture to work effectively high levels of cooperation were required from all levels of the workforce before practical results could be achieved. Ferranti has never been associated with the great paternalistic firms like Rowntree, Cadbury or Lever Bros,[10] largely because it never reached their size. However, from what we have implied in the previous two sections it is clear that the family instilled great loyalty into its workforce, building a positive relationship which provided the basis for a distinctive approach towards personnel management.

The human approach

It would be fair to say that when assessing the founder's attitude towards his workforce he was a mass of apparent contradictions. In the first place, it is vital to stress that Dr Ferranti was always courteous to employees. Indeed, as he often worked on the shopfloor they affectionately referred to him as 'The Guv'nor'. Reflecting the loyalty he had already built up in London, over one-quarter of his workforce moved north with him in 1896 (see section 3.5), where he often voiced disdain at the way in which cotton firms adopted a hire-and-fire policy. He was generally described as a good employer who treated all staff to an annual 'bean feast', paying the standard rates for all jobs, and attempting to provide greater continuity of employment than many of his counterparts in the cotton industry. On the other hand, Dr Ferranti was virulently opposed to trade unionism. Section 3.5 will reveal how he was at the forefront of the 1897 engineering dispute, fought over the long-running issue of 'The Right to Manage'. Not only did he participate in the lock-out of all Amalgamated Society of Engineers' members from his works, he also hired a private police force to protect both his property and the skilled artisans recruited in from other parts of the country, contributing extensively to the employers' victory.

In production matters Dr Ferranti was clearly just as determined to ensure complete control as he was over issues related to the ownership of his firm. Although both conditions of employment and rates of pay remained comparable to those in union-dominated shops, Ferranti actually remained a union-free stronghold until the First World War, giving senior management the opportunity to run the workshop as they thought fit. After 1915, however, a more realistic and sensitive approach started to emerge, partly because the workforce was growing in both size and sophistication, and partly because women were employed in greater numbers. The first significant step was the appointment of a Lady Supervisor in 1915, following which in 1917 a works committee was established as a means of airing industrial grievances before management. These efforts were also matched by the construction of a modern canteen and sports and recreation club at the end of the War, while over thirty cottages were purchased close by the works to house foremen and other employees.

During the 1930s, Sir Vincent appointed R. J. Hebbert to what in most respects amounted to being a military secretary. Hebbert's duties, nominally coming under the umbrella term of staff manager, were mainly concerned with monitoring staff potential, as well as providing the chairman with a list of suitable people when new posts appeared. Clearly, Sir Vincent came to rely heavily upon the advice of this highly personable and wise, yet tough, individual. It was also in the 1930s when Ferranti started its staff pension scheme, offering the significant inducement of post-employment support for those who remained with the firm. Sebastian de Ferranti remained doubtful of the benefits arising from works committees and the restoration in 1917 of the right to join a union. On the other hand, they were anxious to develop a human approach towards labour management where at all possible, establishing a tradition in the firm which lasted right up to its dissolution.

In pursuing this human approach, Ferranti was clearly trying to come to terms with the challenges posed by its expansion. A further refinement was the establishment in 1925 of a new post of general works manager. The first incumbent, J. W. Davies, was appointed to provide the family owner-managers with a direct line to the shopfloor. Sir Vincent always felt that people from his social background would never be capable of understanding the dynamics of working class life, leading to the appointment of Davies as his 'eyes and ears' on the shopfloor. Davies had also built up extensive local links with both trade union leaders and employers' associations, giving him a direct link with other sources of information on employment trends. Reflecting the success with which Ferranti adopted this more professional approach towards labour management, it is interesting to note that, apart from the 1922 engineering dispute and the General Strike of 1926, the firm experienced only minor industrial disputes after 1918. Of course, one must remember that, as a result of cotton's difficulties, the spectre of unemployment haunted the Hollinwood area throughout the inter-war years, helping to create a workforce willing to acquiesce in management's policies. On the other hand, one could never accuse Ferranti of exploiting this situation, because by pursuing the human approach outlined earlier the family provided a firm basis for effective cooperation between workers and employers. The continued presence of men like Sebastian, Vincent and Sebastian de Ferranti in senior positions also helped to cement this bond, providing the kind of healthy atmosphere which was essential if the firm was going to exploit any competitive advantage it gained by pursuing product development strategies.

Although the earlier antipathy towards trade unions had clearly created some difficulties at Ferranti, by the 1920s a more harmonious base had been established which Sir Vincent built on successfully over the following decades. Ferranti was never able to create the kind of internal labour market firms like Rowntree and Cadbury had achieved by that time, even though successive generations of workers followed each other into the firm. Crucially, though, the human approach was regarded as central to creating a harmonious relationship within the business. Sir Vincent's habit, especially at the beginning of his time as chairman, of standing by clocking-on machines at the start of a working day, often unbeknown to departmental managers, was a means of reinforcing the point that he wanted to be seen. In particular, he was always concerned that management decisions would not adversely affect significant numbers of employees. For example, in the late 1950s he ensured that as many as possible of those made redundant by the termination of television and radio production would be immediately re-engaged on guided weapons production. His son, Sebastian, adopted a similar approach when negotiating the sale of West Gorton (mainframe computers), insisting that it was a major condition of any deal that the purchasers (ICT) would keep on all the workforce (see section 9.10). Indeed, this policy position was one of the reasons why, as we shall see in chapter 12, Ferranti failed to take the hard decision and close the transformer division when it started making heavy losses after 1970.

Sebastian and Vincent de Ferranti had evidently been instrumental in developing a healthy working relationship with its expanding workforce, a tradition continued by Sebastian in the 1960s and 1970s. It is important to stress, however, that apart from the monitoring function performed by R. J. Hebbert, and later by T. J. Lunt, little was done in the area of formal management training. Ferranti did start to recruit a few graduates into the company during the late 1930s, principally to act as salesmen. However, as a reflection of contemporary attitudes the family continued to believe that 'Managers are born, not made'. Sir Vincent often reflected that all his officers in the Royal Engineers would have made good works managers, an attitude which coloured his approach to appointing managers who could lead well. In addition, he placed considerable faith in engineers as the major source of managerial talent, emphasising how internal networking and training were far more important in the development of managers. Indeed, the family regarded this as a virtue of an organisational culture which they felt would generate the required talent organically. The logic behind this strategy was based on the premise that by creating a freebooting environment engineers would be encouraged to try new ideas. These ideas would then be passed on to the managing director for his approval, often resulting in the engineer responsible being converted into the new venture's manager.

As Figure 8.1 (p. 290) reveals, it was also a system which apparently worked, leading to the proliferation of departments described in the last section. It was an innovation culture which proved successful because especially under Sir Vincent it was well matched to both the firm's managerial and financial resources and its environment. As we shall see in chapters 10 and 11, Sebastian was faced with a host of different challenges once he became chairman in 1963, leading to serious liquidity problems. At the same time, in spite of these circumstances Ferranti continued to invest in new products, reflecting the traditions which had been at work since the 1880s.

4. Conclusion

The three key members of the de Ferranti family who will feature in this story so prominently had clearly succeeded in creating and developing a firm which manifested its commitment to engineering innovation. Over the following chapters we shall see how this culture supported the emergence of one of Britain's most enterprising firms. Liquidity problems at times limited managerial actions, for example after the 1903 crisis and again in the mid-1950s. Nevertheless, Sebastian, Vincent and Sebastian clung firmly to their belief in financial independence as the foundation-stone on which long-term planning could be based. It was a philosophy which extended their freedom to take what Sir Vincent also referred to as 'punts' on new ideas, leading to the expansion described in Figure 8.1. While Sebastian stuck to the engineering-led strategy which gave rise to significant achievements in microelectronics and avionics, at the same time he was faced with the challenge of returning some of the profit made on the *Bloodhound* guided missile system. It was this payment which initiated serious liquidity problems at Ferranti. Whether or not this equipped the firm with the capabilities to survive the changing conditions of the 1960s and 1970s, we shall see in the last two chapters. Above all, though, one must remember that the family was committed to its engineering-led strategy, pursuing at every opportunity new and exciting projects on the frontiers of a range of technologies. This drive might well have defied orthodox business principles, leading to much debate throughout the text concerning the rationale behind various decisions. On the other hand, the firm followed both what interested the family and looked like generating profits, because they owned the firm and believed fundamentally in their mission.

Part One

The First Generation

1

Family Background and Formative Years

It is fascinating to speculate on the sources of genius. Even though the subject of genetically transmitting talent must be left to the scientists, one can say with certainty that an examination of the ancestry of the de Ferranti family reveals a succession of colourful, talented and highly original characters. Indeed, at least part of Sebastian Ziani de Ferranti's character and motivation must have come from stories of his Italian forebears, who can be traced back as far as the ninth century. By the nineteenth century, moreover, the family included a varied collection of artists, musicians and photographers, each with a fascinating and innovative approach towards their work. It was into this invigorating family background that the founder of Ferranti was born, providing a formative influence on the thought pattern which emerged in the young man's mind. In addition, by the time he was a teenager, the family's finances had been badly dented by illness, as well as various other problems, creating a powerful motivating force behind his emerging ambition to become a 'Manufacturing Engineer'. It is important above all, though, to emphasise the role played by practical interests, personal study and contacts with knowledgeable people in sustaining career ambitions which were pursued relentlessly, revealing an inner drive in the man which provided an exceptional, and in some ways naive, motivation. As we shall see, he developed an intuitive ability and desire to change the world by the application of engineering concepts, and his wish not just to dream, but to succeed in putting ideas into practice, makes the story so absorbing and eventful.

1.1 The Ziani de Ferranti family

In 1905 Sebastian Ziani de Ferranti commissioned a Venetian scholar, Dr Auguste Negri, to conduct a genealogical investigation (reproduced in Appendix A) into the Italian side of his family. Negri confirmed that the Ziani (or Zani) name could be traced back as far as the eighth century, with the earliest recorded evidence referring to the Vipzani of Rome and Padua.[1]

Pope Alexander III bestowing on Doge Sebastian Ziani a ring wedding Venice to the sea,
a gift arising from the city's role in repelling Barbarossa's attentions.
(Museum of Science and Industry at Manchester.)

Part of the Vipzani family fled to Venice in the early ninth century, after Attila the Hun had destroyed Padua. In their new home, after modifying Vipzani to Ziani, they soon established themselves as one of the leading families. The Ziani name can be found among the twenty-four houses which formed the Patrician nobility, while in 1172 Sebastian Ziani was elected Doge of Venice, to be followed in that position by his son, Peter. Although Sebastian only reigned as Doge for five years – he had been seventy-one on his accession – this 'eminent captain' was able to extend the influence Venice was already accumulating in European affairs.[2] It was to Venice, for example, that Pope Alexander III turned for sanctuary from the attentions of Frederic Barbarossa. Indeed, the city's formidable military forces proved so effective that the enemy was obliged to sue for peace. In return for this assistance, the Pope conferred a myriad of prizes on Venice, most notably a ring which wedded the city to the sea in recognition of its status as one of the major Mediterranean powers. As Doge between 1205 and 1229, Peter Ziani maintained this position, helping the leaders of the Fourth Crusade to crush Venice's great rival, Constantinople. Sebastian had also been responsible for a series of architectural embellishments to the city, installing granite columns looted from Constantinople in the Piazzetta between the Campanille and the Doge's Palace, as well as building the Rialto Bridge.

Some time in the thirteenth or fourteenth century a branch of the Ziani family left Venice to settle in Bologna, from which strain the de Ferranti family originates. The Bolognan Zianis were of no less note than their Venetian relatives, as Appendix A reveals, continuing the tradition of statesmanship already apparent from Negri's research. There is also evidence of considerable musical achievement in the family, one seventeenth century Ziani becoming a prominent Venetian composer.[3] It was in the early nineteenth century that, as a result of an inheritance, Giovanni Battista Ziani (born 1783) adopted the de Ferranti suffix. The first to inherit the Ziani de Ferranti name was Marco Aurelio (born 1801), who was to become a musician of international renown. Marco was so greatly influenced by the famous violinist Paganini that music became his passion. Under the guidance of Gerli of Lucca, by the age of sixteen Marco had become a virtuoso violinist, playing a series of concerts in the principal European cities. Early in his musical career, he also developed an interest in the guitar, and it was with this increasingly popular instrument that he became associated.[4]

Marco was clearly a highly talented individual, because apart from his musical skills he was also endowed with considerable literary powers. He had published poems written in Latin at the age of twelve, while later in life went on to produce a veritable library of books. These literary skills took him in 1820 to St Petersburg, as librarian to a Senator Meitleiff. During his stay in Russia, as well as moving on to become private secretary to Prince Varischkin, a cousin to the Czar, he managed to write a four volume commentary on Dante's *Inferno* and 290 essays on multifarious subjects. More importantly, it was at that time that he developed further an innovatory method of playing the guitar which was to be demonstrated on a tour of Europe in the mid-1820s. He finally settled in Brussels, when in 1827 the King of Belgium bestowed on the twenty-six year old the polymath title of Professor of Italian Language, Literature and the Guitar, at the Royal Conservatoire. His technique of sustaining notes and playing an independent accompaniment was said to be enchanting, the *Echo de Bruxelles* reporting:

> What Paganini is on the violin, Thalberg on the piano, Servois on the cello, Godefried on the harp, Ferranti is on the guitar. He is a discoverer ... in his hands the guitar is no more the instrument you know – it becomes possessed of a voice and a soul.[5]

On concert tours of Europe, Britain and America, often accompanied by Paganini, Marco Aurelio was praised as the world's finest guitarist. In his newly-adopted country of Belgium, he was given the title of Guitarist to the King, providing a good living for his expanding family.

1.2 The Scott family

Stories of the Ziani de Ferranti line were clearly to be a source of inspiration to later generations of the family. At the same time, it is also important to note that Sebastian was to inherit a particularly important asset from his mother's family. William Scott (1797–1862) was an artist of some repute in mid-nineteenth century Britain, having run a studio in London which was attended for a time by such prominent names as Millais and Tenniel. His commissions clearly came from a wide area, because each time he travelled to a subject's home a pencil sketch of the locality was made, and the surviving scenes are from counties all over England.[6] Scott also provided his eight children with artistic instruction, four of which were to use these skills in a professional capacity. William Montagu Scott (born 1820) was perhaps the most successful, having been trained alongside Millais and Tenniel before entering the Royal Academy and later emigrating to New Rochelle, New York, to extend his reputation as a portrait and daguerrotype painter. Eugene Montagu Scott (born 1834) also emigrated, to Australia, where he worked as an artist for the Sydney and Melbourne editions of *Punch*. Edwin Augustine (born 1832), on the other hand, stayed in the British Isles, working mainly for the Earl of Carlisle. Of the Scott girls, only Emily (born 1827) became a professional artist, specialising successfully in miniature paintings. She later married Charles Seymour, the lead violinist of the Halle orchestra, further extending the family's links with the arts.[7]

The principal Scott family character with whom we are concerned is Juliana (born 1825), 'a tall handsome woman, of a most gracious presence, with masses of dark hair, a high complexion, strong features and dark eyes, large and glowing'.[8] She was also an obstinate and quarrelsome young woman who was to cause her family some concern, especially after insisting on marrying a young Polish man, 'a guitarist of rare ability', Stanislas Szczepanowski.[9] Before this tragic decision was made, however, Juliana had devoted much of her bountiful energy to becoming a concert pianist, playing professionally from the age of nineteen. After her first concert, in Manchester, one critic stated that:

> She has been trained in a good school, for, despite some little evidence of timidity and nervousness, she displayed great power of touch and an extraordinary brilliance of execution, mingled with much delicacy and feeling.[10]

She also longed for the excitement and freedom of a musician's life. After meeting Szczepanowski at one of his concerts, Juliana was also not going to be held back by the natural caution expressed by William Scott in a series of emotional, yet reasonable, appeals he drafted to his headstrong daughter.[11]

Apart from being a talented guitarist, Szczepanowski was a political exile from his home country. Poland was a much troubled nation during the nineteenth century, having been divided between Austria, Prussia and Russia in the post-Napoleonic War negotiations. By 1830, such was the resentment of Russian misrule that a popular revolt had been sparked, during which Szczepanowski, who was at that time just seventeen, was ejected from the country for his part in the uprising. He consequently decided to travel around Europe as an itinerant musician, and after acquiring some skills from one of the most important influences on guitar design at that time, the Spanish guitarist Ferdinand Sor,[12] he generated a wide reputation as a guitarist of genuine flair. Juliana first met Szczepanowski at one of his concerts in London, impetuously falling in love with this romantic character in spite of her father's protestations.

William Scott was naturally suspicious of this relationship between his daughter and a man who was twelve years her senior, a widower and a refugee. Nevertheless, his heart-tugging letters failed to dissuade Juliana from marrying her lover in August 1845. An indication of the life-style enjoyed by the Szczepanowskis is the fact that each of their four children was born in different cities, Emilka (1846) in Edinburgh, Wladziu (1848) in Dresden, Vanda (1850) in London, and Vincent (1852) in Leipzig. Unfortunately, however, the call of the Polish cause was too strong for Szczepanowski, because in 1852 he deserted his young family in Ostend, after having been

Sebastian's father, Cesare Ziani de Ferranti with guitar, serenading a portrait of his wife. *(Museum of Science and Industry at Manchester.)*

lured into a dissident organisation dedicated to liberating their country. Szczepanowski eventually returned to England after fighting in the Crimean War, living in London until his death in 1877.[13] However, Juliana had officially divorced him in 1860, having fallen in love with a young photographer she had met in 1857.

The awful misery caused by the disappearance of her husband naturally cut deep into Juliana as she struggled to bring up four young children. After waiting several months in Ostend, she returned to England, settling in Manchester where teaching piano and intermittent concerts provided the bulk of her income. It was after one of her concerts, ironically in Ostend, that she met Guilio Cesare Ziani de Ferranti (born 1831), the son of the internationally famous guitarist, Marco Aurelio Ziani de Ferranti. The combination of his good looks, pleasant disposition and connections in the musical world proved extremely attractive to Juliana, resulting in a close

Sebastian's mother, Juliana Ziani de Ferranti.
(Museum of Science and Industry at Manchester.)

relationship which soon blossomed into love. Although just as artistic and inventive as his father, Cesar (as Juliana always called him) had not followed a musical calling, having instead become one of the new breed of photographers who were developing what had been a laboratory play-thing into a new art form. Juliana described his work, no doubt with some element of bias, as 'fully as good as the specimens he has from the first artists in Paris or Brussels',[14] a compliment reflected in the expanding business he was building in Belgium. His talents also impressed Juliana's father, William Scott, who in 1854 had moved to Liverpool and established himself as a portrait painter to the wealthy middle classes of the industrial north.[15] Although Scott might well have viewed photography as a direct threat to his own business, after a meeting with his prospective son-in-law in 1860 the two men decided to establish a partnership which would offer both art-forms to potential clients, marking the start of the Ferranti links with British business.

By the Matrimonial Causes Act of 1857, a marriage could be annulled if one of the spouses had not seen, nor heard from, his/her partner for seven years. After a trip to Hungary in 1860 to allay her conscience, Juliana was to take advantage of this law to divorce Szczepanowski. In preparation for her impending marriage to Cesar, she was also received into the Roman Catholic Church in May 1859, following which on 4 November 1860 Juliana took her second husband. She had actually already given birth to his daughter, Juliet, in May 1858. In typical Victorian fashion, though, it was decided that the child should be placed in a convent out of William Scott's sight, on the grounds that the shock of such a revelation would have destroyed the happiness he now felt after seeing his business partner become his son-in-law.

1.3 The young Ferranti

When William Scott died in 1862, he was content in the knowledge that Juliana was a more settled person. Certainly, Cesar's successful photographic business was able to support his newly-acquired family, especially after he received a commission from Queen Victoria to photograph the Princes Leopold and Arthur. In thanking the Queen for the commission, Cesar reported that it had brought him a rush of orders. Certainly, there is evidence that some of the leading local figures passed through his studio in Havelock Buildings,[16] allowing the family the luxury of purchasing a second home, across the Mersey in Egremont. By 1872, he was even patenting improvements to the process of colouring photographic plates,[17] continuing the innovatory tradition for which the Ziani de Ferranti family had already become well-known in other fields, as well as providing an example for later generations to follow.

130-2 Bold Street, Liverpool in 1963, where S. Z. de Ferranti was born in 1864. *(Museum of Science and Industry at Manchester.)*

It was while the photographic business was beginning to expand that on 9 April 1864 Juliana gave birth to their second child, a son who was christened Sebastian Pietro Innocenzo Adhemar Ziani de Ferranti. Apart from being a rather weak child, constantly prone to coughs and colds, the young Sebastian (or Basti, as his mother usually referred to him) enjoyed a pleasant ten years at Egremont. He was obviously very much the baby of the family, while as a result of his two step-brothers (Wladziu and Vincent) joining the merchant navy in 1866 Juliana was able to indulge her youngest son, building up a very intimate relationship which provided a secure family base. The family also hired a nanny, Elizabeth (or Bysshe, as her charge nicknamed her),[18] who frequently took Sebastian down to the beaches at the head of the Mersey estuary, where he watched with intense fascination the ships visiting Liverpool docks. He filled a series of sketch-books with drawings of ships, some as large as six-masters,[19] demonstrating a natural artistic flair which Juliana felt had been inherited from her father. Vincent would also often write home to his step-brother, relating all the most exciting episodes in each voyage on his ship, the S.S. *Culmore*, and sending newspaper cuttings which described maritime dramas. In 1877, Sebastian was even treated to a trip to Spain on the *Culmore*, an experience the young boy thoroughly enjoyed.[20]

Vincent's influence upon the young Ferranti would appear to have been of crucial significance in converting a fascination with ships into an instinctive inquisitiveness regarding the reasons why and how prime movers worked. Ferranti later recalled that his step-brother had provided the initial spur to his technical interests, because in order to progress in the merchant navy – he passed his First Officer's examination in January 1873 – Vincent had collected a selection of books on steam engines which he passed on to Sebastian.[21] They would often converse on the subject, leading Sebastian later to ask his parents for books 'something like Vincent's', as well as sketch-books to fill with drawings of steam engines and locomotives.[22] Juliana might well have hoped that her youngest son would use the undoubted artistic skills he possessed to follow in her father's footsteps. However, there were already signs that Sebastian was moving in an entirely different direction, because by the mid-1870s it was apparent that he was utilising the knowledge derived from conversations with Vincent to develop a growing fascination with things-mechanical.

By the time Sebastian was wrenched from the cosy family environment of Egremont and sent to a preparatory boarding school in Hampstead, in March 1874, the ten-year-old's fascination with steam engines was extending from the written word to practical experiments. He already possessed 'a turbine engine consisting of a rotating spherical boiler, from the upper part of which emerged a tube fitted with two oppositely pointing nozzles'.[23] This would seem to have been a Heron wheel. It was in 1875 that Cesar also received a request from his son for 'a littel model of a steme fire ingun wakein by stime [sic]'.[24] The spelling in this quotation reveals the urgent need for more formal tuition in 'the three Rs', a point Cesar constantly made to his son.[25] At the same time, though, a model steam engine was provided which Sebastian regarded as extremely impressive, largely because it was a self-assembly model with a working piston movement. Books like *The Life of the Stephensons* by Samuel Smiles and R Routledge's *Discoveries and Inventions of the Nineteenth Century*, as well as copies of the *Engineer*, *Engineering* and the *Illustrated News*, were also purchased for his immediate consumption. This demonstrates how supportive Juliana and Cesar proved to be, even though neither could understand why their son should be pursuing such interests.

As a budding engineer, Sebastian was clearly provided with a good deal of encouragement from his family. Notwithstanding this fact, it is important to note that he was not spoilt. Indeed, even after his move to the Benedictine school of St Augustine's (in Ramsgate) in September 1877, the letters from his parents often scolded him for the phonetic approach he took towards spelling. Juliana wrote that she was 'very sorry Pa should see what little use you appear to make of the instruction he is paying so very much for you

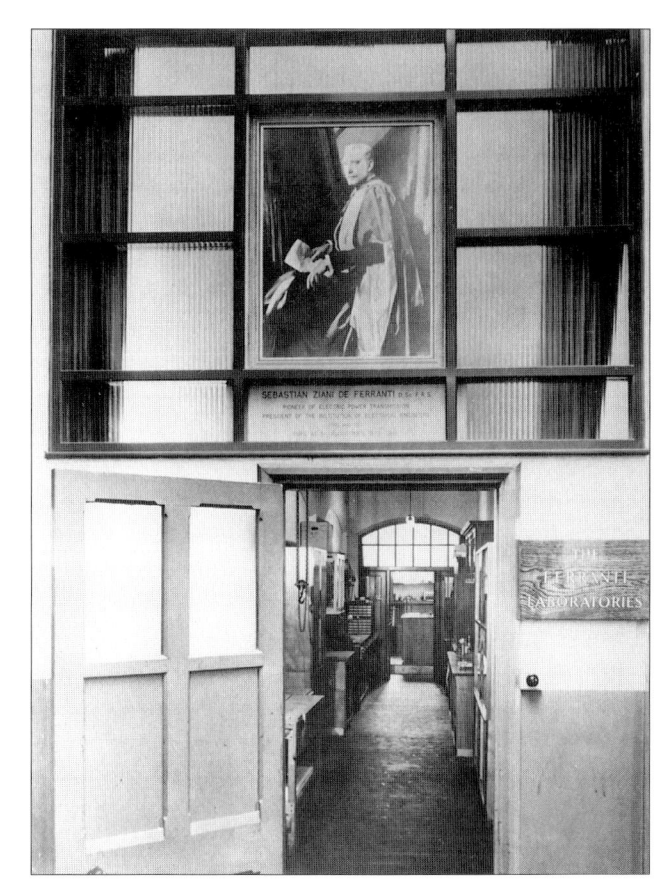

The Ferranti Laboratories at St Augustine's, Ramsgate, opened in 1963 to commemorate the achievements of their most celebrated 'old boy'. *(Museum of Science and Industry at Manchester.)*

to receive'.[26] Cesar was even more scathing, pointing out how 'you ought to make sure that you deserve [holidays] before enjoying the leisure hours'.[27] Of course, Ferranti is not the only inventor-entrepreneur who has incurred the wrath of his superiors over such matters: Elmer Sperry was warned by one teacher that a poor speller might only attain the dignity of a grocer's clerk;[28] while Thomas A. Edison was called an 'addled youth' by one dissatisfied teacher.[29] Sebastian attempted to deflect this criticism by quoting Smiles: 'N.B. Remember that Stephenson began as a cowherd and yet look what he came to. He also made what all the educated men put together could not do'.[30] Not surprisingly, though, Cesar was not convinced by such comments, frequently reminding the young man of the need to raise his academic standards.

Although there does appear to have been some family friction over the rate of Sebastian's academic progress, the choice of St Augustine's as his senior school proved to be extremely fortuitous. Of course, even though the Benedictine order has a general commitment towards providing an education of true value to the individual, several commentators have argued that British public schools were more concerned with a liberal arts education which imbued in the pupil a 'distinctive English view' of the world.[31] In St Augustine's case, though, the teachers adopted a more open approach towards both curriculum and pupil development. For example, because the headmaster, Abbot Egan, realised that Sebastian's interests lay more outside the classroom, a workroom was provided in which the pupil could continue his practical-experimental interests. Although the room was actually the school kitchen, Abbot Egan was at least partly correct when he claimed that the 'freedom from the ordinary routine and the valuable use he made of his time laid the foundation of his brilliant success as one of the most eminent [electrical engineers] of the century'.[32] The Ferranti company later repaid this debt by paying for a new laboratory block at the school. The science teacher, Fr Bergh, had given Sebastian liberal access to the St Augustine's laboratory, primitive though it was. Crucially, in recognising his own inadequacies in technical instruction, in 1880 Fr Bergh also put his most promising pupil in touch with a local photographer and amateur electrical engineer, A. J. Jarman. It was this contact with the new field of electrical engineering that marked a watershed in the life of Ferranti, because thereafter his attentions were focused almost exclusively on developing a source of energy which he felt even at that early stage 'would be a blessing to the world'.[33]

1.4 The young engineer

Throughout the late 1870s, Sebastian continued to immerse himself in the world of engineering, pursuing a *dilettante* form of technical education which was typical for his era. Most significantly, it was in March 1876 that he first showed an ability to think originally, informing his parents that: 'I have made a picture of a water heater and condenser combined which I have invented so that hot water from the condenser combined will run into the boiler instead of the steam coming out of the funnel'.[34] Although the sketch is certainly not of a device which would have revolutionised steam engine design, the underlying principle of economy in steam generation was sound. As we shall see in section 4.2, it is also interesting to link these embryonic ideas with his later work on steam turbines.[35] Thereafter, a constant stream of ideas was reported, one letter describing how he had 'thought of three new inventions. One for coupling the three wheels of an express engine which are of different size for starting it with a heavy strain and can be

S. Z. de Ferranti's drawing of a railway engine, 1875.
(*Museum of Science and Industry at Manchester.*)

disconnected at a moment's notice'.[36] Unfortunately, these drawings have not survived. Scholey, on the other hand, has commented that a locomotive drawn by Sebastian in 1876 was similar to the high-speed trains of the 1890s.[37] This indicates how the hobby was no longer a simple matter of collecting information and pictures, for the material was being used to fire Sebastian's intuitive spirit. It was in this period that, by using his artistic skills to draft solutions from which others could work, Ferranti was beginning to develop the intellectual capacity for grappling with the mechanics of a problem, revealing an ability to understand the total engineering problem.

This passion for things-mechanical was clearly beginning to dominate Sebastian's life. Naturally, although willing to supply appropriate material for the passion, his artistic parents were still struggling to come to terms with this development. Over Christmas in 1878, however, they were left in no doubt about what was driving on their son. For a present that year, Juliana had given him a pictorial storybook. With all the arrogance of youth, and much to his mother's amazement, he replied: 'I am going to have *no more* tale-books'. Instead, he requested a book on compound steam engines.[38] Cesar replied by questioning whether his son could understand such a complicated subject, a letter which was greeted with the comment that all Vincent's books had been memorised and more detailed information 'no matter how complicated or difficult to understand' was now required in order to broaden his knowledge.[39] In an aside of momentous importance, Sebastian also comforted his parents by noting that all his ideas 'seemed to come to me naturally'.[40] No-one in the family ever sent him a present again without receiving express orders. During school holidays, which were often spent with his step-brother Wladziu in London, Sebastian also spent much of his time either visiting the South Kensington Museum (the forerunner of the Science Museum) or attending lectures at the Royal Polytechnic.[41] Furthermore, on the regular day-breaks Sebastian received for good behaviour at St Augustine's, the Abbot of Canterbury monastery allowed him access to what Sebastian described as 'the king of tools', the lathe,[42] providing some practical tuition which would complement the theoretical knowledge already accumulated.

It was consequently with great anticipation that Sebastian went to meet A. J. Jarman in the early months of 1880. Electricity had already come to the attention of young Ferranti, because he had read both Professor Pepper's *Boy's Playbook of Science* and Ganot's *Treatise on Physics*.[43] We also know that by March 1879 a book entitled *Electricity and Magnetism* had come into his possession. Substantial parts of this were also being memorised 'so that when I have finished I will know a good deal about the science and I expect it will be very useful to me'.[44] Unfortunately, though, Sebastian allowed his enthusiasm for electricity's potential to misdirect his thinking,[45] because after reading a section on the properties of magnets he thought he had invented a perpetual-motion machine. As he reported to his parents:

> When I think of what a wonderful thing it is that I whilst only a boy should bring so many theories together and out of them make so wonderful a machine (yet so simple) it quite takes me aback and makes me think what strange and wonderful changes in commerce and manufacture would occur through its success.[46]

Here can be seen the unbounded enthusiasm which Ferranti always possessed, as well as the supreme, if at times misplaced, confidence in his own ability. Most significantly, the experiments with magnets transferred his interests from steam engines to electricity, giving the introduction to Jarman added note in the context of Sebastian's development.

In fact, in 1879 Fr Bergh had already helped Ferranti build crude arc lamps and connect them to a galvanic battery.[47] During that year's Christmas vacation, the youth had also visited the offices of the Anglo-American Brush Electric Light Co. to inspect for himself what was generally regarded as the best generator on the market.[48] In his description of this visit, Ferranti reported to Juliana that 'I went away so delighted that I lost my way twice with thinking of it', such was the grip electricity was taking of the young man's thought processes. Jarman, who was later to form an electrical engineering business himself,[49] at that time was copying a Siemens dynamo which had won the prestigious Trinity House tests for the Lizard lighthouse in 1876. Ferranti was allowed to assist in the 'experiments ... to improve and render the machines cheaper than they are at present'.[50] The two enthusiasts also devised an electric bell for use at St Augustine's, following which Ferranti was able to produce his own arc lamp capable of producing 'a beautiful little electric light'.[51]

Electrical engineering in 1880 was still in an embryonic state, even though Sir Humphrey Davy had demonstrated an arc lamp as long ago as 1812 and Michael Faraday had announced his pioneering discovery of electro-magnetic induction in 1831.[52] Even standard terminology had yet to be devised, one authority remembering that 'there was no generally recognised ohm. I have heard seventy feet of bell wire specified as a kind of unit of resistance'.[53] A conference at the 1881 International Exposition of Electric Lighting in Paris was to settle upon a standard terminology, but much work still needed to be done if all the hopes of many scientists and self-trained electrical engineers were to be fulfilled. At the same time, one should note that the sheer romance of this new technology was attracting bright, inventive people, such was the growing belief in its prospects as a significant contribution to society.

The main obstacle to faster progress was the development of an effective generator. In 1867, the independent discovery of the principle of self-excitation by Werner Siemens, Henry Wilde and S. A. Varley had facilitated progress, by dispensing with the need for cumbersome and inefficient magnets.[54] Even so, in 1880 electric lighting was only being used extensively in lighthouses. Those electrical firms which did exist were confined to acting, in R. E. Crompton's words, as simply a collection of 'scientific travelling showmen'.[55] It was at this time, though, that another inventor made his first tentative steps by copying a Siemens dynamo, using a wooden pattern provided by A. J. Jarman. Although it was to be eighteen months before Ferranti was able to patent his own design, Jarman had managed to convert the youth's unbounded enthusiasm and correct any misunderstandings about electro-magnetic theory, providing the opportunity to encourage the development of a latent talent which was bursting with ideas.

1.5 A new career plan

It was becoming increasingly apparent to Juliana and Cesar that any artistic aspirations they might have harboured for their son were being overwhelmed by his unswerving desire to pursue what to them would have seemed like a bewildering range of technical studies. In fact, as early as January 1879, in a remarkable letter from a fourteen-year-old to his mother, he mapped out his future. First, contemptuously dismissing any thought of trying for the London matriculation examination, he expressed a desire to enter the University of London, which he had read in the *Daily Telegraph* was 'the great place for engineering'. What most attracted him to this idea was the comment that 'through it an extensive field was opened to manufacturing engineers'. He then went on to explain, prophetically, that: 'I think that the best thing

A sketch of S. Z. de Ferranti by Vanda Szczepanowska, 1882. (*Museum of Science and Industry at Manchester.*)

for me to be will be a Manufacturing Engineer as then everything I invented I will be able to carry out with advantage'.[56] Of course, it is not unusual for one so young to have great plans for the future. In this case, though, what is remarkable about this letter, apart from its predictive powers, was the rationality of the ambitions and the complete confidence with which they were expressed. Cesar would have preferred it had his son taken the matriculation examination, even though Abbot Egan predicted a preparation time of eighteen, rather than the usual twelve, months. In any case, the young Ferranti felt that he already possessed the necessary qualifications for his chosen career – an inventive mind, a mechanical aptitude, artistic ability, and eternal optimism.

It was during the 1880 summer vacation that Cesar finally relented and agreed to pay the registration fee of thirty guineas for a course in engineering at University College, London.[57] Juliana also gave him permission to give up piano lessons, explaining to his sister, Juliet, that 'his mind is so full of science and inventions and he is longing to be occupied with some construction or another'.[58] Unfortunately, though, it is unlikely that Ferranti derived much benefit from his brief sojourn in the academic world, even though University College had recently been expanded and the engineering laboratories were staffed by some of the leading figures in that field.[59] The head of engineering, for example, was Sir Alexander Kennedy, the man who 'virtually created engineering as a modern university subject in England, especially the laboratory training of students'.[60] Other prominent figures like Dr Oliver Lodge and Professor Carey Foster also lectured there at that time.[61] Sadly, though, as Ferranti himself confessed:

> I always found it difficult to learn ... I was wanting the whole time to get on to something of a practical nature in the industry for myself. I am afraid that this interfered with everything else that I attempted to do.[62]

This illustrates the practical orientation of his achievements in a career dedicated to innovation. Indeed, it is fair to say that Ferranti is best remembered as an inventive engineer and manufacturer, rather than as a theoretician, focusing more on devising a total engineering solution to problems which baffled more myopic individuals. Whether this lack of academic application acted as an obstacle to progress must be debated later (see section 2.6), but in the early 1880s the justification for remaining at university was dwindling as Ferranti made more progress with his own designs and experiments.

Tragically, it was not his yearning 'to get on to something of a practical nature' which jettisoned Ferranti out of academia, but Cesar's cerebral thrombosis in February 1881. Cesar was afflicted with serious mental disorders for the rest of his life as a result of this illness, precipitating such a major decline in the prosperity of his photographic business that a university education became a luxury the family could no longer afford. In the spring of 1881, for the first time in his life, Ferranti was consequently wrested from the cocoon of domestic tranquility; no longer would a note to his parents procure all the necessary working materials or books. Indeed, Cesar fell heavily into debt at this time, after borrowing several hundred pounds from friends. As organisational psychologists like Cox and Cooper emphasise, because many successful businessmen have experienced similar traumas in childhood, it is apparent that such events motivate some individuals into devising means of supporting their families.[63] Certainly in the case of Ferranti, it would be accurate to say that over the next few years he was motivated as much by the financial insolvency of the family as the desire to make a real contribution to electrical technology.

Cesar's medical and financial problems clearly played a major role in the early 1880s scenario, especially with regard to his son's activities. However, before passing on to describe these events it is important to note that another aspect of the family background was to exacerbate these difficulties. In fact, Juliana had been separated from her husband since December 1879. The marriage had for some time been in difficulties, not least because Juliana still longed for the social and intellectual stimulation of life in the musical world, while Cesar preferred to concentrate his attentions on the photographic business in Liverpool. This conflict was compounded by Juliana's discovery in 1870 that her first husband was still alive, souring the marriage irreparably.[64] By 1872, such was the atmosphere in the Egremont home that Cesar had taken a mistress. Although it was 1879 before Juliana left her husband to go and live with Wladziu in London, the atmosphere at home deteriorated badly. This was the main reason why Sebastian spent so many of his school vacations in London, providing him with the opportunity to visit museums and works of technical interest.

It was in this context that the young Ferranti was forced to leave University College, largely because he was obliged to help support both of his parents. Typically, though, he was by no means overawed by the changed situation, informing his father that: 'I know that I have the *strength*, the *ability* and the *determination* to overcome all difficulties'.[65] This is a measure of the confidence possessed by the seventeen-year-old, an attribute which, along with a cheerful personality, was always to see him through the moments of adversity which were to feature frequently during his career as an electrical engineer. More importantly, as we noted earlier, the family's dire financial position provided a very strong source of motivation, and in assessing Sebastian's early career one must never forget this factor as one of the more important influences behind his drive to become a 'Manufacturing Engineer'.

1.6 The research engineer

Leaving University College, of course, would have been only a minor setback to the non-academic, prospective 'Manufacturing Engineer', allowing him greater freedom to concentrate on a range of electrical experiments. His friend and mentor from Ramsgate, A. J. Jarman, had also recently moved to London, in order to expand his photographic business. The two were consequently able to meet regularly to discuss their ideas on generator design.[66] Ferranti was at this time working on a form of armature coil first devised by Paccinotti in 1860 and copied by Z. T. Gramme in 1870 when producing one of the earliest commercially viable dynamos.[67] This coil, composed of soft iron wire, allowed the generation of such unprecedented outputs that many were beginning to incorporate it into their own generators.

In the case of Ferranti, he had decided to use it in what was nicknamed his 'Rabbit' dynamo.[68] He even managed to sell the 'Rabbit' to a London dealer in electrical apparatus, Caplatzi's in Euston Rd. However, the machine had taken almost a year to perfect, and the price of £5 10s. was hardly going to solve the family's pressing financial problems. Notwithstanding this point, although it will become apparent as the story unfolds that commercial viability was not always a prime consideration behind some of the projects Ferranti initiated, it is important to stress that his design had passed the acid test of market sensitivity.

By the summer of 1881, with Cesar's plight deteriorating badly, it was becoming ever more imperative that Ferranti should find paid employment of a more secure kind. He had already made a number of contacts in the emerging electrical industry, prompting him to enquire into the possibility of combining innate interest with financial necessity. One of these contacts was the chief electrician to the South Kensington Museum, a Mr Grout, who was so impressed with the young man's knowledge of electrical engineering that he provided a letter of introduction to Alexander Siemens, the head of research at the London branch of the German electrical and cable giant, Siemens.[69] Ferranti was not actually successful in his first bid, Siemens refusing even to interview him. Typically, though, this did not deter him, because after returning a week later with an order for carbon rods he managed to persuade Alexander Siemens to employ him as a research assistant.[70] Here, again, one is struck by the impression Ferranti made on older, more experienced engineers, an asset which was to prove useful throughout a career spent persuading others to back his projects. In this case, it provided him with the opportunity to enter one of the most progressive firms in the industry, at a time when few openings of this kind existed. As Juliana noted: 'If we were ever so rich instead of being as we are, almost penniless, we could not procure a place for Sebastian where he could have greater advantages'.[71]

Although Ferranti had already worked on a Siemens dynamo in Jarman's workshop, as one of the firm's research assistants he was placed right at the heart of British electrical engineering. His principal responsibilities were to assist Alexander Siemens and the firm's chief research engineer, Dr E. Obach, in the development of a new range of generators, providing direct access to what would have been at that time the world's most advanced facilities. Siemens, of course, was a subsidiary of the German firm of the same name whose product strategy was firmly based on that country's dedication to research as an essential ingredient in company survival and growth.[72] As Ferranti himself reported, the job was 'as good for me as if I was spending piles of money weekly on experiments',[73] indicating how the young engineer was to derive great benefit from working with Siemens. Not only was Ferranti given an invaluable insight into many aspects of the early 1880s electrical industry, he was also fortunate to work directly with one of the most eminent men in the field, William Siemens. Indeed, Ferranti was seconded to carry out a series of experiments at King's College on the arc furnace William Siemens had developed in 1879, while in July 1882 he was sent to Owen's College, Manchester, to demonstrate the product.[74]

Clearly, Ferranti made a good impression on his employers. Indeed, such was their faith in him that within three months of joining the company he was given the responsibility for installing a dynamo and eight arc lamps at the Sanitary Exhibition held in the Ironmasters' Exchange, Wolverhampton. Electrical apologists expounded the healthier properties of electric lighting, compared to its gas counterpart,[75] making it imperative that at such exhibitions the Siemens product should create a favourable impression on the public. It consequently says much for this seventeen-year-old's ability that they were willing to place so much trust in him. The exhibition certainly seems to have been a success, leading to further spells out of the laboratory installing a dynamo in the Crown Point Printing Works, Leeds, and at the 1881 Smoke Abatement Exhibition in London. This was invaluable experience, broadening his knowledge of the practical problems facing electrical engineers, as well as making fresh contacts in the industry which were soon to prove extremely fruitful.

1.7 A business proposition

The Siemens job had evidently been a lucky break for the young Ferranti, because not only did it provide invaluable experience of electrical engineering, he was also able to contribute consistently to family income from his weekly salary of £1 and additional payments made for working on installation contracts. The financial rewards were crucial in those most difficult of times, helping to support both of his parents. However, to some he met such a salary was regarded as a poor reward for his ability and originality. While working on the Wolverhampton exhibition in September 1881, Ferranti met one of his father's professional acquaintances, Alfred Thompson. As both were electrical enthusiasts, their conversation was animated and lengthy, leading Thompson to the view that the young Siemens employee had more to offer the nascent industry than simply working for another firm.[76] He consequently introduced Ferranti to a lawyer, Francis Ince, who was also keen to see much greater progress in electrical engineering. Both Thompson and Ince agreed that Ferranti was wasting his time at Siemens, the latter warning that they would 'rob your brains. You'll do the inventing and they'll collect the cash'. Ferranti naively asked if he should ask for a raise in salary, a question which lead Ince to proclaim in no uncertain terms: 'You must start right away on your own'. This was the opportunity for which Ferranti had been waiting to fulfil his ambition of becoming a 'Manufacturing Engineer'. Although several difficult years were to pass before one could say Ferranti had established himself in that position, the meetings with Thompson and Ince had clearly been of central importance in channelling his efforts.

The main reason why Ferranti was able to interest these two men, apart from the obvious enthusiasm and confidence he demonstrated, was the work which he was doing in Jarman's workshop on an improvement to the form of armature used in the Siemens alternator. Although it was to take several months before Ferranti could demonstrate the effectiveness of his design, by May 1882 Thompson was promising 'to undertake the promotion of your inventions when they are practicable'.[77] Of course, Ferranti was still a minor, and before any legal contract drawn up by Ince could be signed Cesar had to be induced to travel down to London to sign an agreement on his son's behalf. This contract stated that

> the said S. Z. de Ferranti claims to be the Inventor of an Electric Generator ... which has hitherto neither in part or in whole been patented or practically applied. And being desirous of having working machines made therefrom and the said invention patented and brought into practical working has applied to the said Alfred Thompson to advance money for that purpose and the said Alfred Thompson has agreed to do so ... that in consideration of the payment to the said S. Z. de Ferranti of the sum of £2 per week for a period not exceeding two months during the time he is engaged in perfecting the said Invention ... and of the payment by the said Alfred Thompson of all further working expenses incurred in constructing the said working machine and forming a Company to undertake the practical working.

There were later to be problems over the first sentence in this agreement, leading to an acrimonious exchange of letters in *The Times* when Ferranti left Siemens on 12 July 1882.[78] No legal challenge actually ensued, though, leaving the young engineer free to embark on a new and challenging phase in his life. It is not known why two months elapsed between Thompson's initial promise of support and Ferranti leaving Siemens, other than to note that the interim period was evidently spent productively. By 18 July, the provisional specification for a generator had been lodged with the Patent Office by the patent agents Marks & Clerk, allowing work to begin on producing a marketable version.

Machine floor of the Appold St, Finsbury works of Ferranti, Thompson and Ince Ltd, 1882. *(Museum of Science and Industry at Manchester.)*

Although it had been Alfred Thompson who first recognised the young engineer's potential, and put up the first tranche of development finance, one must above all stress how by 1882 Francis Ince was becoming the guiding hand on which Ferranti constantly relied over the next twenty years. Ince was a successful solicitor specialising in company law, having first entered the profession in partnership with J. P. Ingledew in 1865.[79] They soon expanded from an original base in Cardiff into larger premises in Benet's Chambers, Fenchurch St, London, counting among their clients the Coal Depot Owners' Association and the Falkland Islands Co. Reflecting a link with the new electrical industry, Ince also advised the Hammond Electric Light & Power Co., one of the most dynamic firms in this sector. Ince was a man of many interests who liked to tax his mind with a wide range of pursuits, being a far-sighted optimist, yet a person who insisted upon orderliness and businesslike behaviour in all aspects of life. This innate caution was later to create some friction between Ferranti and Ince, because the two differed in fundamental ways: while Ferranti was usually expansive and eager to improve a product until it approached perfection, Ince acted as the counter-balance, urging profitable practices and sound, natural growth. It was a relationship not unlike that between Hugo Hirst and Gustav Byng, the German founders of GEC,[80] another marriage of, respectively, the ambitious and the conservative. For Ferranti, acquiring the support of a man like Francis Ince was indeed of great significance, creating a partnership which over the following eighteen years resulted in the emergence of one of the country's major electrical engineering concerns.

1.8 The 'Brush Bubble'

It was to take several decades before contemporaries disregarded the 'luxury' label applied to electric lighting by William Siemens in 1882.[81] In that year, though, many contemporaries felt that they were at the dawn of 'The Electrical Age'. Four years earlier, Thomas A. Edison had announced the development of an incandescent bulb, creating panic among gas shareholders.[82] Unfortunately, the American inventor had been typically over-optimistic in his claims, leading to 'growing popular incredulity' about the Edison bulb.[83] In the meantime, J. W. Swan, working independently in Newcastle, had patented a similar device which sold well in Britain. Edison's bulb was eventually developed into a commercially viable form, leading to intense competition in a small market. Finally, although the two inventors never met, by 1882 the Edison & Swan Electric Light Co. had been formed to exploit the growing potential in electric lighting. For two reasons, the incandescent bulb was undoubtedly essential if the new medium was to make any significant progress at this time: firstly, the arc light was far too bright and excessively hot for domestic use;[84] while secondly, at this stage no more than sixty arc lamps could be connected to one generator, making it economically uncompetitive. As the *Electrician* stated in 1881, 'it must take many years before even a perfect light will supersede gas'.[85] Clearly, the mountainous problems of interrelatedness and the sunken investment in gas-lighting and steam power were to provide enormous challenges to the first generation of electrical pioneers.

Undaunted by these obstacles, in the early 1880s tremendous efforts were being made to persuade a sceptical world that electric lighting had a viable future. Edison was actually the first to develop a complete central electricity supply system, equipping in 1882 what is generally accepted to be the world's first power station at the Holborn Viaduct in London.[86] This was closely followed by the Brighton station, equipped by a man who was to play an important part in the early career of Sebastian de Ferranti, Robert Hammond. Concurrently, there was also a whole series of exhibitions and lighting experiments arranged to publicise the medium's potential. As early as January 1881, the *Electrician* was claiming that 'there has been great progress in every stage of electric lighting: apparatus has been improved, extension has been great, and public opinion has been educated'.[87] In that year, Brush sales had totalled £80,000, but as a result of the burst of activity in the following twelve months in 1882 they soared to over £200,000, while Siemens' sales rose from £35,846 to £83,780,[88] and Crompton's firm was clearly very busy.[89]

By the spring of 1882, the electrical industry was finally beginning to shed the impression that it was merely a laboratory plaything. Unfortunately, though, this feeling of anticipation was to be excessively exploited by some dubious financial interests working on the London stock exchange. As Kennedy has noted, this institution had failed to develop a floor in industrial securities,[90] leading to substantial ignorance of industrial and technical matters amongst financiers. In consequence, when many engineers spoke in over-optimistic tones about the new illuminant, this proved too great a lure for the less scrupulous promoters, all too many of whom were anxious to capitalise on the ignorance of investors. The chief culprit was the Anglo-American Brush Electric Light Co., a firm which floated fourteen subsidiaries in May 1882 which the *Statist* felt had monopolised the attentions of investors by making a series of outlandish claims concerning the potential market for their goods.[91] The Brush £10 ordinary shares shot up to £68 and a 100% dividend was announced on their half-yearly results, further cultivating the feeling that electrical investments were a definite 'buy'. The 'Brush Bubble', as contemporaries were to name the event, eventually raised £7,000,000 for electrical ventures as promoters rushed to exploit the complete state of ignorance about the real prospects for electric lighting.[92] As we shall see later, this proved to be a highly damaging event for the embryonic industry, even though it created a conducive environment for the launch of new ventures headed by promising young inventors.

Obviously, the £2 per week provided by Thompson for Ferranti was rather modest when compared to the scale of investment others were indulging in during the spring and summer of 1882. Clearly, though, Ferranti was well placed to benefit from the general interest shown in electric lighting. During the two months following his departure from Siemens, he worked hard and long in Jarman's workshop to prove that his ideas were practicable. Such was the faith his two new associates placed in these efforts that on 15 September the firm of Ferranti, Thompson & Ince Ltd was registered. A day earlier, the three 'went to meet some gentlemen in the City',[93] in order to discuss the prospects of raising the new company's £250,000 capital. It is probable that among these 'gentlemen' was Robert Hammond, the managing director of the firm for which Ince acted as company solicitor, the Hammond

Electric Light & Power Supply Co., bringing another key individual into the Ferranti orbit at a highly opportune time.

Having been involved in the iron trade up to 1881, after visiting London in July of that year to inquire into the most effective method of lighting an iron works Hammond contracted with the Brush firm to sell their generators in the north of England through the newly-created Hammond Electric Light & Power Supply Co.[94] A flourishing business was soon established, and by the time of the 'Brush Bubble' Hammond was so well known in the industry that Brush invited him to head four of their newly-floated subsidiaries. Hammond soon recognised, however, that if electric lighting was to compete with gas, a system of bulk supply was required. Brush, though, were reluctant to produce machines with a capacity to supply more than 200 lights,[95] leading to some disagreement between the two firms. Furthermore, by September there were already rumours that Brush were in difficulties. Indeed, the Brush £10 share, having reached £68 in May, had plummeted to £24 by September, largely because sales had been extremely disappointing. Later, in January 1883, wholesale changes to the management structure were effected after widespread accusations of poor decision-making.[96] The *Statist* had also noted in September 1882 that 'Brush shares have suffered from the attention given to a new economical dynamo ... of which the Hammond Company have obtained the right of use'.[97] The *Financier* similarly reported that this machine

Ferranti-Thomson Alternator No. 8, 1882. *(Museum of Science and Industry at Manchester.)*

might place another nail in the Brush coffin.[98] This provided an early indication of the impact Ferranti was about to make on the industry, providing Hammond with the incentive to acquire a major interest in Ferranti, Thompson & Ince Ltd.

When launched in November 1882, many contemporaries were agreed that the Ferranti generator was one of the few capable of providing sufficient power for bulk supply purposes. In fact, in the use of two crowns of fixed coils with iron cores, the Ferranti machine looked remarkably similar to those produced by engineers like Siemens and Wilde.[99] Beneath the surface, however, there was a significant innovation in the form of a novel armature, the idea for which was based on the general principle that this part of a generator must be as light as possible, in order that it might revolve at high speeds and produce more current.[100] Many of his contemporaries were at that time manufacturing much larger machines, because of the belief in the link between size and power. However, as the *Engineer* noted: 'Mr Ferranti goes on the assumption that speed is ... cheaper and better than wire, and we are not prepared to dispute the point'.[101] The Ferranti armature, made of copper strip only one inch wide and moulded into the requisite zig-zag shape, was also much cheaper to manufacture than those made by Siemens, giving his company a competitive edge in the price-conscious market of the 1880s which few could rival.[102]

The commercial viability of the Ferranti zig-zag alternator was generally recognised by the end of 1882, especially after Hammond was introduced into the operation. Unfortunately, though, just as the first machine was being produced it was discovered that Ferranti had not been the first to propose the use of such a design. Juliana mentions 'a great trouble' in August, when Thompson and Ince heard of the problem after a chance meeting between Ferranti and Sir William Thomson (later Lord Kelvin) at the patent office.[103] It transpired that Sir William had already patented a form of armature which in most respects resembled the Ferranti version, leading to a series of hurried negotiations. It was finally agreed that, in return for an annual royalty payment of £500, the distinguished scientist was willing to sign over all rights to the invention.[104] Indeed, the coincidental patenting of the zig-zag armature proved to have tremendous benefits, because not only were they able to attach one of the leading scientific names to the venture, by using the marketing name of 'Ferranti-Thomson' for the alternator, the two patentees also struck up a friendship which provided a source of technical expertise unsurpassed at that time. One must also note that to have been working along the same lines as the future Lord Kelvin must surely confirm the feelings expressed by a growing number of people, from A. J. Jarman to William Siemens and Robert Hammond, that Ferranti was a gifted individual who possessed the remarkable ability to visualise an engineering solution to problems which would have previously troubled many of his rivals.

1.9 The business scene

After having been successful in raising sufficient financial support from Robert Hammond, and ninety-two other investors,[105] Ferranti, Thompson & Ince Ltd looked set to exploit the growing interest in electric lighting. The first public trial of the Ferranti-Thomson alternator demonstrated just how much progress had been achieved, the *Electrician* proving that it could light 12.4 incandescent lamps per horse power, compared to just eight for the Siemens machine.[106] Hammond had earlier made the foolish claim that the Ferranti generator 'would give about five times as much power as any machine in existence',[107] sparking a flurry of letters and articles which highlighted the physical impossibility of such a feat. As 'Secretary of a Brush Co.' pointed out, Hammond was implying that 'in reality … the new machine gives out at least three horse power for each horse power put into it'.[108] The authoritative *Engineer* also devoted a long piece to explaining the mistake.[109] By November, however, the same journal was prepared to admit that the Ferranti generator could do more work per horsepower than 'any other good machine already in the market',[110] providing technical approbation for the alternator at a crucial time.

While technical acclaim was clearly of great importance to the new company, and Ferranti must have been gratified by the way in which the trade journals generally praised his design, towards the close of 1882 people like Robert Hammond were much more concerned about the commercial prospects for electric lighting. Indeed, in retrospect, it is clear that 1882 was very much a false start to the history of British electrical engineering, with much of the money raised during the 'Brush Bubble' either written off as a bad investment or creamed off by unscrupulous company promoters. The industry became firmly established as a 'lemon' in the minds of investors, a point we shall examine further in chapter 3, when it will be demonstrated that the bitter experiences of the 'Brush Bubble' remained long in the memories of investors.[111] Moreover, the demand for generators collapsed at the end of the year. As a result, at the small workshop established by Ferranti, Thompson & Ince Ltd in Appold St, London, like the industry as a whole they suffered from 'a year of promise unfulfilled'.[112]

There are several reasons why the electrical industry experienced such a dramatic change in fortunes at that time, not the least of which, according to many contemporaries, was the 1882 Electric Lighting Act.[113] As early as

1878, a Select Committee chaired by Sir Lyon Playfair had investigated the need to impose controls on the new industry. This committee wisely concluded that statutory intervention would stifle the innovatory process. Four years later, though, with the arch-'Municipal Socialist' Joseph Chamberlain as President of the Board of Trade, the government was prompted to introduce legislation to establish public welfare safeguards, placing electric lighting in the same category as water and gas supply and public transport. The general approach towards such utilities by the late-nineteenth century was to encourage local authority control and ownership, the 1870 Tramways Act having established the principle that after twenty-one years of private enterprise undertakings could be compulsorily purchased at the 'fair market value', regardless of goodwill and without compensation for loss of earnings.[114] Although the gas and water supply industries were never subjected to such compulsory purchase legislation, companies in these sectors had been falling under municipal control for several decades,[115] a trend further accelerated by the 1875 Public Health Act.

It was in this context that the 1882 Electric Lighting Act was passed. Three of its clauses deserve special mention: firstly, a lighting company had to seek the permission of a municipality before the Board of Trade would sanction a provisional order to light a prescribed area; secondly, the company's lease could only last a maximum of twenty-one years, after which the system could be purchased by a local authority, without providing compensation for goodwill or loss of earnings; and thirdly, no systems were allowed to supply electricity over more than one municipality. Influential contemporaries like Emil Garcke (by 1883, managing director of Brush) regarded such restrictions as 'pernicious'.[116] Indeed, there is little doubt that psychologically the 1882 Act further blunted confidence in electric lighting. It is fair to argue that twenty-one years was sufficient time in which to make a good return on the investment required for a public supply system, while only in the 1890s did electrical engineers begin to build inter-municipal networks, minimising the immediate impact of the Act.[117] On the other hand, the power vested in local authorities was to become a permanent feature of the British electrical scene, limiting the willingness of private enterprise to risk funds on a venture which in the 1880s had yet to establish a firm footing in the energy markets.

The combination of such legislation with the 'Brush Bubble' were two of the main factors which explain the more difficult conditions of late 1882. Furthermore, one must also remember that this period marked the beginning of a severe slump in the economy as a whole, when the position deteriorated to such an extent that in an unprecedented move the government initiated a Royal Commission on the Depression in Trade and Industry. This body reported in 1885 that 'in consequence of the unremunerative character of the trade of the country [there was] less inducement to the capitalist to embark his capital in productive enterprise'.[118] If this was so of trade in general, then the electrical industry would have been even harder pressed to raise support after having induced significant losses in 1882. Unlike older industries, as a new industry it also had few resources on which to rely in difficult times. The depression had also affected house-building, limiting the prospects for a new illuminant which was trying to break into the market already dominated by several standing competitors, severely denting the hopes of Ferranti and Hammond that bulk supply systems could be sold to new estates.

1.10 The first business

Clearly, within twelve months of the 'Brush Bubble', market conditions had changed beyond all recognition. Ferranti may well have achieved his ambition of becoming a 'Manufacturing Engineer', but there seemed little hope that, for the foreseeable future, the business would expand from its modest premises in Appold St, London. Indeed, by November 1883 Ferranti, Thompson & Ince Ltd had been voluntarily liquidated and a new business formed, the Ferranti Hammond Electric Light Co., which merged all their interests in order to reduce any unnecessary duplication of overheads and focus company strategy more clearly.[119] This ended Thompson's brief connection with Ferranti and the electrical industry, while Francis Ince continued to act only in an advisory capacity to the new business. In the meantime, Ferranti was occupied as technical consultant to Hammond in the desperate search for customers willing to invest in electric lighting, starting two years in which the young engineer was to learn much about the realities of commercial life.

While in retrospect Hammond's decision to sell the Ferranti alternator as a suitable generator for bulk supply systems might appear to have been over-ambitious in the context of early 1880s British electrical developments, it was only what the Americans were attempting. Edison, for example, was already installing central supply stations in New York and other American towns.[120] In Britain, on the other hand, the pioneers were faced with a highly cautious market carefully controlled by parliament and lacking financial support. In this context, it is also important to remember that as Ferranti had chosen to manufacture alternators, which produced alternating current (AC), he was in conflict with distinguished engineers like Edison, Crompton and Brush who believed in the early 1880s that only direct current (DC) dynamos could be sold.[121] Sir Charles Young, the chairman of Hammond's, diplomatically noted that many customers were reluctant to commit themselves until one system had attained dominance.[122] The *Engineer* was more truthful, though, when it argued that AC machines were not yet required in the British electricity supply industry.[123]

The struggle between the AC and DC camps, or the 'Battle of the Systems' as it came to be known, belongs to the next chapter. It is worth emphasising at this stage, though, how Ferranti had placed his faith in a method of generating electricity which he advocated, in word and deed, throughout his life, and which eventually became standard practice around the world. In the early 1880s, however, when most British and American installations were of an isolated nature, intended simply as a means of lighting individual locations, rather than providing a public supply, Ferranti and Hammond were committing themselves to a system which appeared to possess little commercial potential. Of course, this demonstrates the visionary nature of their strategy, emphasising how far ahead of contemporary thinking they were beginning to move. Their first catalogue even talked of a 'Ferranti System' capable of distributing electricity over an area of four square miles, a claim no other contemporary enterprise was making. DC systems, on the other hand, were cheaper and easier to install, providing intense competition. Irrespective of this commercial risk, though, Ferranti remained totally committed to AC, encouraging Hammond to back his instinctive belief in the system by investing heavily in an extensive marketing drive which covered Britain, France and Belgium.

Although the Hammond and Ferranti companies had been merged in November 1883 as an economy measure, this was not accompanied by a period of retrenchment. In fact, by the end of the year two new branches had been added to compliment the aim of supplying bulk distribution systems. A crucial feature of this expansion was the establishment of the Hammond Electrical Engineering College, as a means of supplying the pool of technical talent the company would require if the market did expand. Technical education was at that time poorly developed in Britain, as Ferranti himself had discovered, and in order 'to supply a want which was felt throughout the electrical world' Hammond argued that the provision of 'skilled electricians combining practice with theory' would bring enormous benefits.[124] To this end, the courses at the Hammond Electrical Engineering College, run by H. E. Harrison, were divided into a first year of theoretical training, followed by a practical year at the Appold St works or on installation work. This also reduced the need for heavy expenditure on staff training, because the students paid their own fees. In general, there is little doubt about the pioneering nature of Hammond's achievement in establishing this College at a time when formal technical education had hardly begun to develop.[125] Even after the Hammond company folded in 1885, this institution survived in the form of Faraday House.

Feranti-Thomson alternator (drawing issued to the press 1882). *(Museum of Science and Industry at Manchester.)*

Although the Hammond Electrical Engineering College was undoubtedly a sound feature of the company's strategy, when it was decided to add the manufacture of incandescent bulbs to the firm's range of activities it would appear that they overextended themselves. As we noted earlier, EdiSwan bulbs dominated that particular market, after the merger of the two leading patent-holders in 1883. Hammond decided to compete with this firm by purchasing the rights to make the Wright & Mackie bulb, which differed only marginally from the EdiSwan product, renting a factory in Bermondsey St, London, where he hoped to build up a rival to the market leaders.[126] Ferranti was also closely associated with this project, designing a bulb manufacturing plant and installing two alternators for testing purposes. Unfortunately, though, it was almost a year before saleable bulbs could be produced,[127] and when one considers the price of 3s. 6d., 1s. 6d. lower than EdiSwan, one is left with the clear impression that the venture proved to be a considerable drain on company resources.

While the bulb business proved to be a commercial failure, one must remember that the key to Hammond's strategy had always been the Ferranti alternator. Indeed, the duo invested a considerable amount of time visiting potential customers and distributing catalogues on the machine. They also demonstrated at several of the leading publicity events, resulting in the Ferranti alternator being awarded a Gold Medal at the 1884 International

Health Exhibition for their 1,000-light alternator which illuminated the entire west wing. This machine was later sold to the First Avenue Hotel, Holborn, an installation the *Engineer* regarded as a fine example of the potential in Ferranti machines.[128] Other orders gained at this time included a 500-lighter from J. & J. Colman of Norwich, while in 1884 Sir William Thomson commissioned a 100-lighter as a bequest to his former college, Peterhouse, Cambridge. The latter also marked a substantial improvement in design, as a result of Sir William's frequent visits to the Appold St works.[129] It is also interesting to note that this machine was still being used in the university's laboratories seventy years later, testimony to the durability of the Ferranti-Thomson combination. Nevertheless, in spite of securing a provisional order to light the vestry of Hampstead, they were frustrated in their hope of building bulk distribution systems to serve large-scale markets. Even with this provisional order, because it would have required substantial support from his shareholders, Hammond experienced the full backlash from the 'Brush Bubble'. As he reported to the company meeting in 1885: 'Every shareholder gave the same answer, that they had lost enough money by electric lighting, that they had been too soon in it, and did not care to put more money in it. Outsiders also said that it was a too risky thing. There was none who would risk £100 in it'.[130]

Ferranti Hammond's failure to secure any orders for large-scale projects seriously undermined the commercial viability of the whole strategy formulated by these two pioneers. At the same time, it is also doubtful whether the contracts for isolated installations made much profit. There were two main reasons behind this trend: firstly, the one-off nature of each order prevented Ferranti from standardising design and production; while, secondly, each product was developed and perfected so extensively that delivery dates were often missed, a problem which recurred frequently in later years. The latter was a particularly serious problem, Ince warning his partner in 1883 that such an approach towards manufacturing could have disastrous consequences:

> It is of great importance that no machines should ever stand for improvement and if you insist on this we shall be improved off the face of the earth, and others with a less perfect machine will do all the work and laugh at us while we are theorising ... Constant tinkering and alterations in the machines now in hand simply means great expense in finishing them; and a future sale no one knows when, without an atom of profit.[131]

That Ferranti had been allowed to pursue such intensive development programmes supports the view that the firm was a highly personalised organisation reliant to a significant extent on the engineering skills of its leading partner. Of course, this managerial style was typical for that era, and given the sluggish development of a market for electrical goods there was little need to build a more sophisticated organisation. Nevertheless, it is vital to emphasise how at an early stage a technology-led strategy became the hallmark of the Ferranti philosophy, laying the foundation-stone for an ethos which remained the key feature of the firm's culture.

The technology-led strategy pursued by Ferranti will be analysed in much greater detail as we progress through the next few chapters. As far as the early 1880s were concerned, however, the combination of a stagnant market, especially for bulk supply systems, the over-ambitious investment in bulb making, and inefficient manufacturing practices were undoubtedly responsible for the troubles experienced by Ferranti Hammond between 1883 and 1885. An added complication was that, having been forced to sign a long-term contract with Brush in 1881, when market prospects seemed much brighter, by 1885 Ferranti Hammond had stock-piled machines worth over £10,000 which could not be sold at profitable prices.[132] The company had already been forced to reduce expenditure on both advertising and product development in 1884, after having to come 'face to face with the considerable loss of £30,000'.[133] This provided Ferranti with a harsh lesson in business management, because once Hammond had failed to raise any support for his projected lighting of Hampstead there seemed to be very little prospect of surviving such a deep recession. Although Ferranti Hammond had fought vigorously against both the vagaries of the market and the caution of financiers, in June 1885 it was finally decided to liquidate the company and bring to a temporary halt the career for which Ferranti had yearned. It had been a severe baptism of fire for him, albeit one which was to provide many lessons for a career largely spent struggling against adverse circumstances. Furthermore, one suspects Ferranti would not have wanted to do anything else with his life.

When one considers the reasons why Ferranti Hammond failed to take off as a commercially viable operation, it is important to remember that even by 1888 only one public electricity supply company was operating in Britain, ironically from the Brighton station first built by Hammond with Brush equipment in 1882. Naturally, in this context the strategy of manufacturing alternators for bulk supply systems can be questioned. On the other hand, in 1882 it would have been impossible to predict the sudden and calamitous downturn in demand for all types of generator. Siemens, Brush and Crompton all experienced hard times after 1882,[134] demonstrating how market conditions remained unconducive even for dynamo producers. This depressed state also contrasts sharply with the prevailing economic and technical climate in countries like Germany and the USA, where vibrant electrical industries emerged which were later able to swamp their British

Portrait of S. Z. de Ferranti in 1882. *(Museum of Science and Industry at Manchester.)*

counterparts. 1882 had indeed been a false start for the British electrical industry. Moreover, with the 'Brush Bubble' acting as a psychological deterrent to greater financial involvement in the technology, not to mention a legal system which gave local authorities wide-ranging powers over electricity supply, it was not surprising that gas lighting and steam power went largely unchallenged in their respective fields for at least another decade. British electrical engineering remained in a state of suspended animation between 1882 and 1888, a situation which had serious consequences for the industry's ability to compete both in the energy markets and against much larger foreign rivals, creating few opportunities for entrepreneurs like Ferranti.

1.11 The man by 1885

To a less motivated person, one might expect this baptism of fire to have had a moderating impact on any preconceived career plans. However, one of the strongest characteristics Ferranti always demonstrated was an indomitable spirit which refused to bend in the face of any problem. To compound the commercial difficulties, Ferranti was also still supporting his parents, as well as his sister and two step-sisters, all of whom had moved to London after Cesar's thrombosis. In addition to these commitments, with sketch books brimming over with ideas and inventions (see Appendix B) he felt he had much to contribute to the ailing electrical industry, a spirit inherited by later generations of the family. The collapse of Ferranti Hammond was consequently used as an opportunity to venture off on his own again, with Francis Ince and the aptly-named Charles Sparks as partners.[135] Indeed, within a month new premises at 57B Hatton Gardens, London, had been taken as a base for operations. Nowhere is the family's pioneering spirit better illustrated than in this new venture, which under the trading name of 'S. Z. de Ferranti' provided the young engineer with the vehicle by which he could immediately regain a position in an industry which had initially proved so hostile to all the hopes of the previous seven years.

By 1885, at the age of just twenty-one, it is clear that Ferranti had already established himself as an important member of the British electrical fraternity. His reputation was based on a widely-acknowledged ability to design alternators which proved to be more efficient than those of his rivals. While many criticised his commitment to AC, few challenged the desire to make electricity cheaper and more readily available. Ferranti was convinced that electrical technology would be a force for improvement, leading him to draw up a vision of an 'All-Electric Age' which drove him on, albeit in a naive and intuitive manner. Stories of the achievements of the Ziani family must have provided some inspiration, and the artistic talents derived from the Scott connection were also of great use. Of more immediate relevance, though, apart from his family's financial plight, was the confidence and enthusiasm expressed about both the potential in electricity and his own ability to design equipment capable of fulfilling that potential. This was the motivation driving Sebastian Ziani de Ferranti on to bolder deeds which were to make him internationally famous by the age of twenty-four. It is also apparent from what we have seen so far that through practical interests, personal study and good contacts Ferranti had striven industriously to become a 'Manufacturing Engineer', overcoming a range of unfortunate events which failed to quench his thirst for discovery and achievement.

2

The Deptford Experience

Having established himself as the leading AC generator designer and producer in the early 1880s, Ferranti had made rapid strides towards achieving his designated goal of becoming a 'Manufacturing Engineer'. Although by 1885 his operation was a shadow of its earlier form, he remained optimistic of both the prospects for electricity and confident of his own ability to exploit this opening. Over the following six years, Ferranti was to go on and enhance his reputation by diversifying away from simply the manufacture of equipment into designing and constructing power stations. Indeed, his work between 1885 and 1891 has been described as 'one of the boldest conceptions in the whole history of central station work',[1] laying down the basic principles of a modern supply system which were described as a prophetic vision of present day practice. One must note that, because the venture was commercially calamitous, Ferranti has been heavily criticised for pushing the frontiers of technology too far for the prevailing levels of knowledge and the existing market conditions. In particular, the prominent American historian, T. P. Hughes, has argued that the enterprise of Ferranti and his backers was misplaced,[2] while in an earlier publication he expressed the view that they had been 'overloading an entire engineering-human complex'.[3] On the other hand, it is perhaps ironic that such criticism should be levelled at Ferranti, because Hughes had also devalued the general level of enterprise within the British electrical fraternity during the 1880s.[4]

In examining this crucial engineering development, we shall test the validity of these arguments. The British electrical industry still faced enormous obstacles which severely constrained its effective emergence during the 1880s,[5] indicating how Ferranti was simply attempting to remove some of these hurdles by exhibiting the tremendous potential in this new source of energy. Once again, we shall see how he experienced little difficulty in raising the necessary finance, at a time when others were still suffering from the 'Brush Bubble' backlash. Of course, questions were asked at the time about the manner in which those funds were employed. Nevertheless, there is little doubt that in the medium- to long-term his ideas had a substantial impact on thinking about bulk electricity supply. The whole project was yet another challenge to Ferranti, testing his personal qualities to the absolute limit as he tried to push electrical engineering forward at what many regarded as an alarming rate, producing a remarkable event in the industry's history.

2.1 The meter business

Meter designs

As we noted at the end of the last chapter, creating 'S. Z. de Ferranti' was a clear illustration of the young engineer's obstinate refusal to bow before the early 1880s problems. It provided the necessary vehicle for extending both his influence upon electrical engineering and an emerging reputation as a pioneering designer. Just as crucially, he was now in charge of his own destiny, rather than part of somebody else's venture. This independence was to become an important theme of his career over the following twenty years, reflecting the highly individualistic Victorian business culture.[6] To date, his reputation had been based on the zig-zag armature devised in 1882. From 1885, however, Ferranti was able to extend his interests enormously into every facet of electrical engineering. He already possessed a range of patents (see Appendix B), and one in particular, 5926 of 1883 for 'Mercury Disc Dynamos and Meters', was to provide the commercial basis for his new partnership. Indeed, Francis Ince had only been persuaded to join the business after Ferranti had sold the rights to market his novel design for a meter in Belgium and France to the Compagnie Generale d'Electricitie (CGE) of Antwerp.

The humble meter had actually received little attention from electrical engineers up to the mid-1880s, pioneering efforts having ranged from a clock mechanism to measure the length of time electricity had been used, to Edison's electrolytic device. Typically, Ferranti was convinced that a more suitable solution could be produced. As contemporaries were used to reading reliable gas meters, it was especially important that consumers should learn to trust electricity if it was to be used more widely. Although patenting his idea in 1883, it was actually only in the latter months of 1884 that Ferranti started his experiments, using a bath of mercury in which a fan was placed to convert the flow of electro-magnetic pulses into a mechanical movement which would activate a readout mechanism.[7] It is interesting to note that the germ of this first Ferranti meter was born out of his childhood bible, Ganot's *Treatise on Physics*, demonstrating how his grasp of electro-magnetic theory had improved significantly since the early stumbling efforts with a perpetual motion machine.[8] The vital breakthrough came, however, when Ferranti consulted Sir William Thomson on this device, because initially progress was thwarted by a failure to immerse the fan completely in the

The first Ferranti meter catalogue, distributed in 1885.
Note the description 'Inventor and manufacturer'.

mercury. Sir William explained that the surface tension of the mercury prevented the fan from turning, using the analogy of trying to sail a boat on a frozen loch. This lead Ferranti to immerse the fan completely, following which after some further improvements he finally produced what was claimed to be 'the only commercial meter up to the present time', the mercury-motor meter.[9]

Technical recognition

Ferranti later admitted that these early meters were 'at first very incorrect, did not give at all proportionate readings, and would therefore have been of no use from a commercial point of view'. In fact, they could only measure currents down to as low as three amperes.[10] Further development work ensued, resulting by the end of 1885 in the meter's ability to register loads as low as 0.3 amperes, an accuracy unrivalled by any contemporary design. One Ferranti employee remembered that these early meters 'tended to become hot and were not an unqualified success'.[11] However, this hindsight view ignores the impact they made on the industry: at the International Inventions Exhibition of 1885 the meter was awarded a Silver Medal, and at the Antwerp Exhibition a Diploma of Honour. In 1892, the *Electrician* tested two of these meters after seven years of service for the Kensington Court Supply Co., and reported that the wear and tear on the mechanism was negligible, while its constancy 'was by no means unsatisfactory when we take into account the date of the meters; 1885 is almost in the dark ages as far as electricity supply meters are concerned'.[12] By November 1885 over £200 worth of lathes and drilling machines had consequently been installed in his Hatton Gardens workshop to boost production.[13]

The diversification into meter production was to have momentous consequences for future Ferranti businesses. One must note, though, that the first products were to serve DC electricity supplies, rather than his preferred AC system. This was a wise move, because the commercial reality of having to cope with a market dominated by DC had clearly influenced his strategy. Indeed, commercial success did accompany this venture, because not only was he able to negotiate the agreement with CGE of Antwerp, worth £5,000 over the next three years, orders from a large number of export and domestic customers were received. Among these customers was the Berlin Edison Co. (the forerunner of the German electrical giant, AEG), HMS Vernon, the Electrical Power & Storage Co., and individuals like J. W. Swan, R. E. Crompton and Sir William Thomson.[14] These orders provided a solid foundation for the young business, giving meter production a special place in the Ferranti business, as we shall see in the next chapter,

One of the early Ferranti DC meters which provided a reliable source of business while generator sales in the 1880s failed to expand. *(Museum of Science and Industry at Manchester.)*

especially as over the following decades this provided the funds for experimentation and innovation in a wide range of fields. Crucially, establishing the vital meter department allowed Ferranti to restart his career as a 'Manufacturing Engineer'.

2.2 Contact with Sir Coutts Lindsay

1885 was consequently a crucial year in the company's history. Moreover, not only does this mark the beginning of a long and successful association with the meter, it was also when Ferranti established contact with Sir Coutts Lindsay & Co., one of the most enterprising electricity supply companies in the country. This venture had been formed in 1884 by Sir Coutts Lindsay, the owner of the Grosvenor Gallery, initially to provide electric lighting for both his own use and in the neighbouring businesses in New Bond St. More importantly, over the following seven years it was to act as the nucleus of an organisation which symbolised the reawakening of the British electrical industry.[15] Although a rather incongruous marriage of art and industry, the common denominator was romance and vision, both of which Sir Coutts Lindsay and Ferranti possessed in abundance.

The Grosvenor Gallery had started life in 1877 as a sanctuary for Pre-Raphaelite painters, after a period of considerable conflict within the art world between on the one hand what might be regarded as 'the establishment',

Entrance of Grovesnor Art Gallery where Sir Coutts Lindsay started his power supply business *(Museum of Science and Industry at Manchester.)*

represented by the Royal Academy, and on the other hand artists like Sir Coutts Lindsay, Whistler and Millais.[16] Surtees describes Sir Coutts Lindsay as 'a talented painter and loving son, fatally attractive to women and a faithless husband ... His hair is thick with curls ... Byronic in appearance and romantic in effect'.[17] This reflects a rather mercurial type of character, but crucially he was also adventurous by nature and usually attempted to innovate where possible. The head of the Lindsay family was the Earl of Crawford, a prominent amateur scientist who had been instrumental in founding the Society of Telegraph Engineers, the forerunner of the Institution of Electrical Engineers.[18] Crawford had also been British Commissioner to the momentous Paris Electrical Exhibition of 1881, when great strides towards establishing a standardised electrical terminology had been made. On his return from Paris, he recommended the use of electric lighting to his nephew, Sir Coutts Lindsay, to improve the ambience at the Grosvenor Gallery. The first generators were installed in the Gallery's backyard in 1883, providing a

Sir Coutts Lindsay at the time he opened the Grovesnor Gallery (1877).

limited service. After several neighbours requested a supply, however, Sir Coutts Lindsay & Co. was formed a year later to convert this system into a fully-fledged supply operation.[19]

Legal difficulties and Gaulard and Gibbs

The creation of a supply company by itself was a bold move, given the state of the British electrical industry at that time. What is even more remarkable about the new plan was Sir Coutts's decision to use high-tension AC to distribute electricity. In ordinary circumstances, the 1882 Electric Lighting Act dictated that supply companies had to negotiate with their local authority for permission to lay mains in the roads to connect up customers from a central supply source. However, Sir Coutts realised that if he employed high-tension AC he could hang cables from the roofs of his customers and avoid all the statutory controls. Had he chosen DC, the weight of the hanging cable would have precluded an extensive system, because it operated at such low voltages that a very good conductor was required in order to prevent the loss of pressure. AC, on the other hand, could be transmitted at high voltages, thereby reducing substantially the amount of copper needed in the cable. Foreseeing a potentially enormous demand for electric lighting from the West End clubs, theatres and wealthy residents, it seemed sensible to utilise this cheaper method.

While Sir Coutts experienced no difficulty in acquiring a Siemens alternator (said to be the largest produced to date [20]) capable of generating the 1200 volts required by the service, the key problem his operation faced, like all AC proponents in the early days, was converting this high transmission voltage down to a level which could be safely used. Although Kennedy, Jablochkoff, Fuller and Gordon had each designed theoretical high-tension AC systems, until 1883 'no one could be said to have any definite knowledge on the subject of the efficiency of an induction coil as an appliance for transforming energy'.[21] It was just at that time that a French engineer, Lucien Gaulard, with backing from an Englishman, John Gibbs, were developing what they called 'secondary generators'.[22] They first exhibited their ideas in 1883 at the Royal Aquarium Exhibition, Westminster, following which an experimental fifteen mile AC network was installed along part of the line owned by the Metropolitan Railway Co. A year later, such was the faith expressed in the secondary generators by a growing number of authorities after winning a prize at the Turin Electrical Exhibition for a system which was said to operate at the incredibly high efficiency of ninety-one per cent at full load, they had secured contracts in Rome, Tours, Aschersleben and for the Grosvenor Gallery.[23]

Technical problems

The first trial of the Grosvenor Gallery installation took place in March 1885. It soon became apparent, though, that the Gaulard & Gibbs secondary generators were incapable of living up to the expectations of 1884. With the benefit of hindsight, we now know that Gaulard had made two basic errors when designing his devices: the secondary generators were built with an 'open' magnetic circuit, giving them a prejudicial electrostatic capacity; and they had been placed in series along the circuit, preventing the use of automatic regulation during operation.[24] Towards the end of 1885, Gaulard did actually provide his secondary generators with 'closed' magnetic circuits. However, although Kennedy had demonstrated as early as 1883 that transformers should be connected in parallel, in order to make their operation self-regulating, Gaulard had ignored this well-publicised discovery, leading to major faults on the line and many bulbs blowing when the circuit was overloaded.[25] Furthermore, the local telephone and telegraph companies complained about interference caused by induction from the cables. Although Dr John Hopkinson, of Owen's College, Manchester,[26] was brought in to solve this problem (by placing the incoming and outgoing mains nine inches apart), major faults continued to hamper progress, giving Sir Coutts Lindsay & Co. an extremely poor reputation amongst its customers.

By the end of 1885, Sir Coutts Lindsay and his customers were beginning to despair of ever being able to use the Gaulard & Gibbs system. The key faults were:

1. No two secondary generators gave the same electromotive force.
2. Regulation by hand resistance was so bad that lights were jumping, and many broken.
3. The closed magnetic circuit made it impossible to shift the core … therefore forcing the consumer to burn all the lights or none at all.
4. Poor insulation between primary and secondary circuits.[27]

It was publicity the early electrical engineers could have well done without, particularly as the supply had to be suspended owing to mounting complaints from customers. The decision to use AC had consequently back-fired on Sir Coutts. Indeed, such were the difficulties that the Grosvenor Gallery proved incapable of generating enough money to cover its expenses.[28] Fortunately, though, it was the mounting financial problems which prompted the Earl of Crawford to take charge in January 1886, a move which proved decisive. In particular, it was Crawford who was better able to assess the technical failings of the Gaulard & Gibbs system, leading him to hire a bright young engineer whose ideas seemed to promise a brighter future for the beleaguered station.

2.3 The Grosvenor Gallery contract

The first Ferranti transformer

Ferranti had evidently kept a close watch on developments at the Grosvenor Gallery, because not only had he supplied some meters to the operation, the use of AC was also a reflection of his own ideas on electricity supply. Typically, he informed G. L. Addenbrook, the chief test engineer of the United Telephone Co., in October 1885 that the Gaulard & Gibbs secondary generators needed completely redesigning, commenting that 'the mechanical construction of both these types of transformers was very poor and that a more satisfactory one could be devised'.[29] He had heard that the work of three Hungarian engineers, Zipernowski, Deri and Blathy, seemed to promise a more enduring solution to the system's problems.[30] Addenbrook was naturally interested in these comments, especially because he had been experiencing some difficulties with the speech transformer induction coils employed in his firm's system. Ferranti had actually used induction coils in an earlier electrolytic meter (patent 4596 of 1882), and within a day of meeting Addenbrook, using some florists's iron wire and a shunt coil from a mercury-motor meter, an improved audio transformer had been produced

Telephony transformer patented by G. L. Addenbrooke and S. Z. de Ferranti, 1885.
(Museum of Science and Industry at Manchester.)

which solved the United Telephone Co.'s problems. While underestimating the intuitive skills of his young collaborator, Addenbrook remembered:

> Somewhat to his surprise, I think, considering how little we had to go on in winding this transformer and in estimating the quantity of iron to put in the magnetic circuit, not only did the lamp glow, but the light was hardly perceptibly less than that given by other lamps connected across the circuit.[31]

The speech transformer was then patented jointly by Ferranti and Addenbrook (14917 of 1885), pushing the new electrical engineering firm into another area which was to have even wider ramifications than the venture into meter production. As we shall see in chapter five, in the 1920s Ferranti was also to return to this work when developing an improved type of audio frequency transformer for radio sets, indicating how the 1885 patent set him on two tracks which were to prove extremely beneficial to his company.

During the five days following the speech transformer patent, between 4 and 9 December, Ferranti made further rapid strides by developing a transformer capable of stepping up 100 V to 2400 V, and *vice versa*. In the construction of the experimental model, he used hoop iron ordinarily placed on carriage wheels, such was the rudimentary nature of the technology. In terms of its construction, insulation and efficiency, however, the end-product was regarded as 'a considerable improvement on existing forms'.[32] He then followed this a day later with a patent (15251 of 1885) which incorporated four features which were to become fundamental to modern power station practice: step-up transformers at the power station; the use of tubular concentric mains; automatic control of transformer sub-stations; and cut-out devices for phasing out equipment as demand falls away. Having already established a reputation as an alternator designer of note, Ferranti was now equipped with the basic products and systems for a major assault on the market. Unfortunately, though, there still remained the problem of a stagnant level of demand, forcing him to push his ideas more aggressively if any progress was to be made after the faltering start of the previous three years.

A new contract

The opportunity to extend his interests came when the Grosvenor Gallery plant was finally closed down at the end of 1885, at which point Ferranti offered his services to the Earl of Crawford and Sir Coutts Lindsay. Juliana de Ferranti noted hopefully in her diary that 'things seem to promise well for him'.[33] Indeed, after a series of dinners and a demonstration of the Ferranti transformer, by 13 January 1886 Ferranti had been offered the post

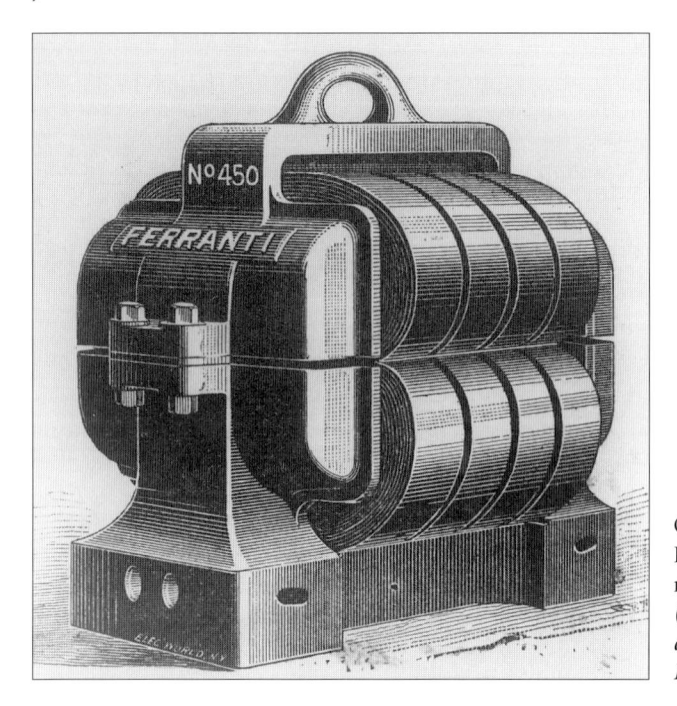

One of the first Ferranti transformers, made in 1886. *(Museum of Science and Industry at Manchester.)*

of chief engineer to Sir Coutts Lindsay & Co., at an annual salary of £500. It was an appointment which could not have come at a more fortunate time for the young engineer, because although his meter business was beginning to expand, stagnation in the generator market had badly affected the industry generally. The Grosvenor Gallery was to provide an excellent shop-window for what was advertised as the 'Ferranti System'. Furthermore, not only did the station become the showpiece of the British electrical industry, at the tender age of twenty-three Ferranti was also able to claim that he had become one of the world's foremost authorities on high tension AC supply systems.

Ferranti had been extremely fortunate to acquire the contract to run the Grosvenor Gallery station. Apart from the Brighton station equipped by Hammond in 1882, not one of the eighty-one provisional orders granted under the 1882 Electric Lighting Act had resulted in a public supply.[34] The Americans, on the other hand, had been making significant progress, Edison alone having installed generating equipment in 149 central stations by 1888.[35] While Hughes has argued that this British lag was largely caused by the absence of what he called 'the American spirit of go-aheadness',[36] it is apparent from what we have seen so far that British electrical entrepreneurs were severely handicapped by an unresponsive environment. One could never argue that Crompton, Siemens, Brush, Hammond and Ferranti had not made every effort to overcome the fundamental problem of competing with highly efficient and well-established standing competitors like gas in the lighting market and steam for the provision of power. Illustrating just how obstructive the British scene proved to be, this difficulty had been compounded by the legal restrictions imposed in 1882, the unwillingness of financiers to support electrical ventures after the debacle of the 'Brush Bubble', and the severe trade depression starting in 1883. Even the powerful German firm of Siemens was forced to concentrate its British subsidiary's attentions on cables, while Brush experienced a period of severe retrenchment, and Crompton looked to Europe for orders.[37] In contrast, American pioneers like Edison and Westinghouse were provided with a much more conducive environment. This demonstrates how valuable time had been lost in developing a competitive electrical industry which would have the financial resources and technological capabilities to withstand the later incursions of foreign businesses. It was also a story later paralleled in computing, as chapter nine will relate.

The engineering team

In contrast to the problems experienced elsewhere in the British electrical industry, by 1886 Ferranti was clearly able to see an end to the damaging stagnation of the previous three years. Although it was August before permission was granted to replace all the old Grosvenor Gallery equipment, at least his team was kept busy keeping the station operative. At the head of this team was C. P. Sparks, a former pupil at the Hammond Electrical Engineering College who was later to enjoy such a highly successful career as a consulting engineer that he was given the honour of being elected President of the IEE for two consecutive years, in 1915 and 1916, only the second person after Ferranti himself to have achieved this distinction. At the College, Sparks had 'proved himself to be a diligent and accurate worker and at the examinations … showed himself to have made most satisfactory progress'.[38] This prompted Ferranti to bring him into the partnership in 1885, albeit as a very junior member,[39] to perform the crucial role of supervising the manufacture and installation of plant, leaving the senior partner free to concentrate on the design and development of new products. Francis Ince took overall charge of general business matters, creating a functional division of responsibilities which provided the organisational basis for a period of significant expansion.

To augment this small operation, Ferranti also decided to recruit additional staff to assist in the running of the Grosvenor Gallery plant. The first to arrive as installation engineer was his step-brother, Vincent Szczepanowski, the man who had been largely responsible for developing the early Ferranti interest in steam engines. Another relative employed was a cousin, Herman Donner, who acted as draughtsman, copying the sketches and translating

Workers at Deptford, including S. Z. de Ferranti (centre with bowler hat and long coat), Kolle and Elphinstone c. 1889. *(Museum of Science and Industry at Manchester.)*

them into working drawings from which Sparks and Szczepanowski could work. On the distribution side, G. L. Addenbrook was hired for his experience of cable-laying, while the former chief engineer to the Brighton operation, H. W. Kolle, was also persuaded to bring his considerable, if not unique, knowledge of running a power station to the Grosvenor Gallery. This demonstrates how Ferranti was learning the advantages of delegating responsibility for the more routine tasks associated with his business. While he always remained quietly in charge of broad strategy, in future decades Ferranti was to develop a cohesive approach towards team-work which became one of the hallmarks of company research and product development strategy. What is also interesting about this team is its youth: in 1886 Ferranti was still only twenty-two, Sparks was twenty-one, Kolle twenty-two, Donner twenty-one, Addenbrook was twenty-six, while Szczepanowski was by far the senior at thirty-six. Perhaps one might argue that their youthful exuberance could well have blinded them to the problems ahead. Notwithstanding this comment, under the intuitive leadership of Ferranti they were to venture into new technological territory over the next five years, ignoring the advice of more conservative authorities who warned against such pioneering work.

2.4 Progress and achievement

Grosvenor Gallery reorganisation

Although Ferranti was evidently in a better commercial position than many of his British counterparts in 1886, in the first six months at the Grosvenor Gallery he was sorely tested by the directors' refusal to scrap the old plant. Together with Sparks, he did manage to restart the supply by modifying the Gaulard & Gibbs secondary generators. However, such were the mounting problems that the team 'worked harder to keep things going and to maintain the prestige of electric lighting … than we had to at any later date'. This point is well substantiated by the frequent comments Juliana de Ferranti made in her diary about how her son rarely came home before midnight. Sparks also noted that 'anyone having seen, heard or smelt the [devices] would never have thought of using such apparatus'.[40] Other tasks imposed on the young team were the reorganisation of the distribution system, converting the circuits from series to parallel operation, while the engines and alternator were also rebedded to ensure that any increase in demand would not result in excess noise and friction. Such was his commitment to the station that Ferranti did not apply for a single patent in 1886, one of only six barren years in a career spanning almost half a century.[41] It was becoming

C. P. Sparks *c.* 1916, partner to Ferranti between 1885 and 1900, and later President of the IEE (1915–16). *(Museum of Science and Industry at Manchester.)*

increasingly apparent, however, that any further extension of the network would stretch both his abilities and the equipment to breaking-point, especially as more consumers were requesting a supply. Ferranti consequently lobbied the directors for permission to redesign the entire station. He even recommended building an entirely new facility, taking several of the directors 'in a boat to look at different places where there was land to sell',[42] including the Stowage Wharf at Deptford.[43] After much deliberation, it was finally decided that the chief engineer should prove the viability of his system at the Grosvenor Gallery before larger sums were risked in a bigger project.

The Grosvenor Gallery reorganisation was the first real test of the young engineer's abilities as an electrical engineer. The board had given him a generous budget of £20,000, the bulk of which was used to install new machinery. A new boiler house was first constructed on the other side of New Bond St from the Gallery, as well as a subway through which the steam would be supplied from four Babcock & Wilcox boilers. New instruments were also designed by Ferranti for regulating the water levels and ratio pressures in the pumps, in order to work the boiler house automatically.[44] The steam would be used to work the 500 hp Corliss valve engine supplied by Hick, Hargreaves of Bolton, as well as the three existing Marshall engines. Hick Hargreaves also fabricated the larger parts of the new Ferranti alternators, the design of which differed markedly from the machines first made in 1882. The principal change was to replace the zig-zag armature with

Artist's drawing of two 520 kW Ferranti alternators at the Grosvenor Gallery.
(Museum of Science and Industry at Manchester.)

independent coils bolted on to an iron core, in order to increase their power, establishing a new design which others were later to copy.[45] These alternators, installed in February 1887, were the largest generators built in the world to date, standing nine feet six inches high, occupying a floor space of nine feet by eleven, weighing 33.5 tons, and producing an unprecedented output of 2400 volts.[46] Even more significantly, although designed to light 10,000 lamps, they each proved to have a capacity of 19,500 lamps at peak load, far exceeding attempts by other engineers to produce machines which supplied in bulk.[47]

Ferranti was clearly making great strides as a power station engineer after 1886. Not only were some features of the new station innovatory, the task of installing all the equipment, while maintaining a continuous supply, was a testimony to the team's organisational skills. Due to local circumstances, the end wall of the engine room could not be opened, forcing them to bring all the new machinery in over the existing plant. As one contemporary stated:

> That a large building could be underpinned, foundations lowered to forty-six feet below street level, over 100 tons of machinery put in place, and some forty tons of machinery removed ... without interruption in the regular supply of electricity reflects the highest credit on Mr Ferranti and his efficient engineering staff.[48]

There was an increasing sense of urgency about this, because while great care was taken not to rush the job, lest mistakes should creep into the work, coils were frequently burning out on the old Siemens machines as the demand increased.[49]

Station reopened

The new station was actually completed in August 1887, after five main circuits emanating from an iron lattice tower placed on the Gallery roof had been built into the revised distribution system.[50] Their success in overcoming the bad start provided by Gaulard & Gibbs in 1885 can also be confirmed by looking at the growing business generated from the fashionable districts of West End London. Fewer than 300 lamps had been connected to the circuit when Ferranti had taken over as chief engineer in January 1886. By October 1887, however, over 11,000 were being supplied, and new consumers were constantly signing up over the next two years.[51] The list of installations reads like an address book of the most fashionable clubs, theatres and residential districts around the Grosvenor Gallery. A crucial development was the acquisition of the Prince of Wales's custom, because when he commissioned them to light Marlborough House electricity became fashionable and the status-conscious classes rushed to acquire a supply. By the end of 1887, the Grosvenor Gallery network covered an area from Regent's Park in the north to the Thames in the south, and from the Royal Courts of Justice in the east to Knightsbridge in the west. Another factor of importance was the mix of both domestic and commercial premises among the consumers, spreading the demand throughout the day and making the station more economical to run at a time when it was vital to reduce costs in order to compete more effectively with gas.

LESCo. created

The whole project must clearly have been a source of great pride to Ferranti. Crucially, because it established the viability of high-tension AC as a means of supplying electricity in bulk Sir Coutts Lindsay & Co. was now ready to implement the more ambitious plans first mooted in August 1886. Another factor prompting this reconsideration was the growing threat from a number of new London electricity supply companies which wanted a share of the lucrative West End market,[52] prompting the Lindsay family to create the London Electricity Supply Co. on 26 August 1887. The most remarkable feature of this new venture, hereafter referred to as LESCo., was what to many contemporaries seemed to be a massive nominal capital of one million pounds, because nothing on this scale had ever been attempted before. In fact, only the construction of the power station at Niagara in the 1890s exceeded LESCo.'s plans.[53] However, such was the board's complete confidence in their 23 year old engineer that they were willing to support this bold enterprise, venturing into a scheme which was to make the Grosvenor Gallery look paltry by comparison.

Ferranti was later to admit that his inspiration for the Deptford project was one of electricity's arch rivals, the Gas Light & Coke Co., a business which supplied much of the North Thames district of London from a centralised plant at Beckton.[54] This model of rationalised production and distribution could well be applied to electricity supply, according to Ferranti, providing a model for the rest of the industry.[55] Indeed, it was a scheme which made even the most pessimistic take notice: the first stage was intended to provide plant capable of lighting 250,000 lamps, and a second stage would expand this capacity to two million lamps, in the hope that LESCo. would continue to dominate the London market. 'There is an air almost of necromancy, an Aladdin's lamp kind of effect, upon the public and untechnical mind on learning the details ...' is how one source described the anticipation and incredulity surrounding Deptford.[56] Certainly, the details were quite remarkable for their day. For example, the 'small' engine room – a misnomer,

Lord Wantage, VC, the chairman and principal financier of LESCo. from the time of its establishment until 1906.

given that the average engine room of that era would have been one-quarter its size [57] – was to house two 1500 hp engines which were belt-connected to a 1,000 kW Ferranti alternator. The 'large' engine room was to have four 3,000 kW alternators powered by 10,000 hp engines. Ferranti also intended to distribute electricity at the unprecedented pressure of 10,000 V, challenging many of the preconceived ideas about safety.

Wantage and Forbes

There were, of course, many who shared his optimism, not least the twenty-eight shareholders who by September 1888 had purchased LESCo.'s issued

THE MODERN COLOSSUS
STEPS FROM THE GROSVENOR GALLERY TO DEPTFORD.
(SEE PROSPECTUS OF LONDON ELECTRIC SUPPLY CORPORATION LD.)

LESCo advert/drawing in *Electrical Plant*, May 1889.

capital of £535,000. In fact, Sir Coutts Lindsay's involvement in LESCo. was minimal, given his relatively paltry financial resources.[58] At the same time, other members of his family invested heavily in the scheme, including the Earl of Crawford, who took up £50,000 worth of LESCo. shares. By far the most important investor, though, was Sir Coutts's brother, Lord Wantage. Married to the daughter of Baron Overstone, one of the wealthiest and most influential bankers of the period, Lord Wantage (formerly Robert Loyd-Lindsay) agreed to invest £220,000 in LESCo., reflecting the courage of a man who had been awarded the Victoria Cross for his gallantry at the Battle of the Alma and on the Inkerman Heights during the Crimean War. In addition to his money, Lord Wantage was also responsible for recruiting James S. Forbes as chairman of LESCo., largely because Sir Coutts Lindsay's business acumen had been brought into question after the troubles at the Grosvenor Gallery.[59] Forbes, described as 'an industrial diplomat of a high order',[60] had initially established his reputation in the railway sector, later moving on to become chairman of the Edison & Swan United Electric Light Co. and the National Telephone Co. In fact, because he had become an enthusiastic supporter of the electrical industry, Forbes was keen to join Lord Wantage and steer LESCo. through its first few difficult years.

2.5 Marriage and litigation

Marriage to Gertrude

In retrospect, it seems strange that, just as the Deptford station was about to go up, Ferranti somehow found time to marry. Having spent much of the previous six years in the company of Francis Ince, such was the intimate relationship which developed between the two men that Ferranti was often invited to dine with the solicitor's family and even spend summer holidays with them.[61] This brought the young engineer into close contact with Ince's youngest daughter, Gertrude, sparking off what soon blossomed into romance. As a member of the Anglican church, Francis Ince was disturbed at the prospect of a daughter marrying into the Roman Catholic religion. Nevertheless, he was so fond of his young business partner that in spite of a few grumbles about the choice of church, St Dominic's in Hampstead, he gladly gave them his blessing on their wedding day, 24 April 1888.

Typically, demonstrating how Gertrude had soon to acclimatise to the kind of life they would lead, Ferranti used his honeymoon (in France and Switzerland) as an opportunity to generate new engineering and business contacts. At one stage, they stayed with the Brown family, one of the driving forces behind the major Swiss engineering firm of Brown, Boveri. Francis Ince also kept him informed of progress at Deptford.[62] Most importantly, the close affection between the newly-weds proved to be a great source of strength in the trials that lay ahead. Over the next three years especially, Gertrude provided the domestic tranquility which was essential in supporting her husband's work. Predictably, it was Deptford that dragged Ferranti and his wife back from Europe. Indeed, as Gertrude has noted: 'The principal thing I remember during those first months of married life was Deptford, and again Deptford. We talked Deptford and dreamed Deptford'.[63] They even lived on site for much of the period, hiring a cottage which acted as office, draughtsman's workroom and dormitory. There, apart from entertaining the team on the piano or making a rushed meal, Gertrude would even trace or paint technical sketches, illustrating how the married couple worked harmoniously at this most difficult time.

The Gaulard and Gibbs case

Unfortunately, though, as a result of his involvement in two important legal cases, Ferranti was unable to devote himself completely to the Deptford project. The first was a *cause célèbre* in the electrical industry during 1888, when Gaulard & Gibbs petitioned for the revocation of the Ferranti patent covering the use of transformers in a distribution system.[64] Had they succeeded in this case, then Gaulard & Gibbs would have gained a monopoly which could have severely constrained the development of high tension AC, because their master-patent, first taken out in 1882 and changed by disclaimer in 1887, claimed the sole right to use the transformer. Naturally, electrical enthusiasts watched the case with great interest, particularly after Francis Ince skilfully counter-petitioned for the revocation of the Gaulard & Gibbs patent, arguing that not only had it been preceded by the work of other engineers and scientists, but also that their claim was not the proper subject matter for a patent.

There was clearly a good deal of acrimony between the two camps, particularly after discovering that the French engineer had been secretly testing a new 'secondary generator'.[65] Ferranti had consequently refused to grant Gaulard access to the Grosvenor Gallery station. The legal position was soon clarified, however, when in July 1888 Mr Justice Kekewich ruled that the 1887 Gaulard & Gibbs disclaimer, in withdrawing rights to a special form of induction coil and claiming a monopoly of transformer distribution systems in general, was unacceptable.[66] Gaulard & Gibbs pursued their case through the Court of Appeal and on to the House of Lords, but the original ruling was upheld, a conclusion widely supported in the industry.[67] To Gaulard it was a death-blow, following which in 1889 he died in a Paris hospital afflicted by what his partner described as 'ungenerous infringement following so closely in the wake of absolute incredulity'.[68] To Ferranti and Ince, on the other hand, vanquishing the patent now made the transformer, not the AC distribution system, the legitimate object of legal protection, freeing LESCo. and its increasing number of counterparts from the threat of royalty payments.

'Battle of the Systems' and the Marindin Inquiry

It was the proliferation of these counterparts in London, however, which was to distract Ferranti and LESCo. further from the essential task of ensuring that Deptford worked effectively, particularly after the Board of Trade renewed its interest in the industry. Deptford's success naturally depended upon being granted unrestricted access to the London lighting market, in order to exploit the economies of scale possible with such large-scale generating plant and high tension AC distribution techniques. Inevitably, though, this posed legal problems which required special investigation. The restrictive 1882 Electric Lighting Act was actually repealed in 1888, to be replaced by an Act which doubled the operating lease for private companies to forty-two years and gave the Board of Trade greater discretionary powers to overrule obstructive local authorities. However, the clause which prevented suppliers distributing over two or more boroughs was retained, forcing the Board of Trade to intervene in allocating rights to the competitors who wanted to supply the many London boroughs.[69] LESCo. had actually applied for permission to supply twenty-four London boroughs, while other companies (using both AC and DC systems) were also lobbying for rights in overlapping areas, causing some confusion at the Board of Trade.

It is interesting to see how the situation in London resurrected the 'Battle of the Systems', a debate which, as we noted in the last chapter, had raged in 1882 when both AC and DC camps had competed for the available business by decrying each other's technology. This debate reached a crescendo when in 1888 R. E. Crompton gave a paper to the IEE on 'Central Station Lighting: Transformers versus Accumulators', discussion of which lasted four sessions.[70] Crompton, as a manufacturer of DC dynamos, was a fierce critic of the high tension AC system, arguing that low tension DC equipment was much more cost-effective. He admitted that the latter was more expensive to install, because batteries (accumulators) were required to provide a back-up supply, while current was supplied at such a low voltage that the cable had to be composed of a high quality conducting material. On the other hand, not only were running costs lower using DC, dynamos could also be used to recharge the batteries during off-peak periods. Furthermore, Crompton criticised Deptford directly for its reliance on a single set of generators, arguing that consumers would be too vulnerable to a breakdown. Another fundamental problem for the AC camp was the failure of any engineer to develop a motor which would run on this system, implying that even if an AC supplier did win a franchise to supply a borough then a DC system would also have to be made available for those wanting to use electric power.

Edison's visit

Ferranti was clearly still being attacked in the same way that the *Engineer* had criticised his alternator in 1883.[71] In spite of his collaboration on the zig-zag alternator in 1882–83, even Sir William Thomson argued in 1888 that 'the DC system, with its great simplicity, and its thoroughly convenient and economical use of power, as well as light, is destined to predominate'.[72] This reveals how an authoritative body of opinion still felt that AC was inappropriate to the British context. Ferranti even had to contend with American criticism, when reflecting the world-wide interest aroused by the scheme, the doyen of the DC camp, Thomas A. Edison, visited Deptford in September 1889. Not even a bad cold could put the American inventor off making his inspection. When questioned by journalists about the pace of progress in

Britain, he asserted that: 'You may be slow to begin, but I must say that when you do go ahead you may even beat us'.[73] Not surprisingly, though, as a committed advocate of DC, he was very critical of both the scale envisaged at Deptford and the use of 10,000 volts, arguing that the former was unnecessary, while the latter was dangerous. Ferranti naturally refused to accept all these claims, producing a pamphlet with Francis Ince in which he quoted the significant fact that at the Grosvenor Gallery no accidents had yet occurred arising from the 2,400V system, while New York had the highest mortality rate from electric shocks, even though DC was used.[74]

This trans-Atlantic debate served to highlight further just how innovative the Deptford project was perceived to be by contemporaries. It also coincided with the growing confusion concerning which London boroughs each supply company would be allowed to supply, bearing in mind the large number of applications presented to the Board of Trade. It was finally decided in April 1889 to depute the Board's electrical specialist, Major Marindin, to examine the situation and report on how the areas should be allocated. LESCo. had already pulled off a significant coup in 1888, using Forbes's influence with the major railway companies to negotiate rights to lay cables along their lines and obviate the need to seek the permission of each local authority to dig up the streets for this purpose.[75] Notwithstanding this achievement, the Marindin Inquiry would materially affect any prospects LESCo. might have had of exploiting its potential scale advantages, even though Forbes tried every means to influence the civil servant in favour of their scheme.

Steam-pipe explosion and Marindin's findings

Certainly, LESCo. spared no expense in presenting their case, hiring a QC, Sir John Pember, to speak in front of the Inquiry. Cleverly, no doubt after discussing the project with Ferranti, Pember linked the potential advantages of high tension AC with one of the major issues affecting all London citizens at that time, severe road congestion.[76] Pember informed Major Marindin that if a low tension DC system was to light an area with 200,000 lamps, then 408 tons of coal would have to be delivered each day by cart, adding further to existing jams. Alternatively, one could supply high tension AC into central London from places like Deptford, where coal could be landed from colliers at a saving of up to thirteen shillings per ton.[77] Marindin accepted this point, commenting that LESCo.'s station possessed 'the undoubted advantage over any others' in locational terms. However, of much greater concern to the Inquiry was the 'experimental nature' of the scheme, an opinion Marindin formed after an explosion occurred when a bend in one of the pipes supplying steam to the 1,500 hp engines burst, killing one man and seriously scalding three more. As Marindin had only just finished his tour of inspection when this accident occurred,[78] although clearly it was a failure in established steam power technology, rather than one associated with high tension AC, it convinced him that the station was over-ambitious. Ferranti later dealt with this problem by designing an improved form of steam pipe bend, using a number of solid-drawn copper tubes, which the *Engineer* described as being 'beyond reproach so far as safely withstanding any [contemporary] working pressures'.[79] Nevertheless, the damage had already been done and LESCo. was to suffer the consequences.

The steam-pipe explosion was undoubtedly to have a major influence on the Inquiry. When Marindin also considered the need to have a DC supply in order to overcome the well-known deficiencies of the existing AC motor design, this ensured that LESCo. were not going to secure all the territory they required. Pember had stated that the company was not afraid of competing with DC systems, arguing that Deptford was technically superior to anything this camp had to offer. Unfortunately, though, in most of the twenty-four areas for which they had applied it was the AC system of the Metropolitan Electricity Supply Co. which was the only direct alternative, leading Marindin to divide up the market between them. Although the Earl of Crawford claimed that LESCo. was 'perfectly well satisfied with what he offered us' when Marindin published his report,[80] clearly he was putting a gloss on what was a gloomy outcome. In the first place, LESCo. was authorised to supply only thirteen, not twenty-four, areas, the majority of which were in commercially unattractive areas south of the Thames where DC suppliers had already established a strong foothold. Even more damagingly, Marindin deprived the company of customers already supplied from the Grosvenor Gallery in the more lucrative West End markets, transferring them to the Metropolitan Co. Furthermore, the Board of Trade also ruled that the 'large' engine room should be restricted to two of the four 10,000 hp units planned, insisting on the provision of adequate reserve capacity to ensure an unbroken supply to consumers.

The Marindin report was clearly to have an important bearing on the commercial viability of Deptford in the following years as electricity struggled to compete against gas for the large London lighting market. By depriving LESCo. of existing customers and restricting expansion opportunities to the commercially unattractive southern London boroughs, the Board of Trade was preventing the exploitation of generation and distribution economies of scale which were the hallmarks of the high tension AC system. It is a moot point, however, whether the report had much of a bearing on LESCo.'s short-term commercial viability. Crucially, Marindin's concern about the 'experimental nature' of the project was equally relevant, because not only were there accidents to deal with, many of the engineering issues had also not yet been tackled in the field, providing Ferranti and his team with a series of challenges which had to be overcome before electricity could be supplied. Marindin was important, and the Inquiry no doubt provided an unwanted distraction for Ferranti and the management team. Above all, though, it was the success with which technical matters were solved that would determine LESCo.'s short-term viability.

2.6 Deptford under construction

Technical challenges

Construction work began on the four-acre site at Deptford in April 1888.[81] Poor weather hindered progress at first,[82] forcing Ferranti to buy some Thomson-Houston arc-lighters and initiate a night shift.[83] The first task was to lay a concrete raft four feet thick and 405 feet long, which acted both as a dock and as the station's foundations. A tramway was also installed, to facilitate the movement of machinery and later to convey fuel from river to boiler house. These early parts of the project were completed by October 1888, along with the installation of twenty-four Babcock & Wilcox boilers which exhausted through a highly innovatory multi-flue system into two chimneys.[84] Ferranti was actually dubbed 'the Michael Angelo' of the scheme,[85] because he alone was responsible for designing every aspect, from the station itself to all the prime movers, generators, switchgear, cabling and meters. This by itself was a remarkable achievement, indicating the extent to which Deptford was the manifestation of his engineering genius. At the same time, it is important to stress that the scheme was by no means a one-man effort, because not only did his engineering team work long and hard to ensure that the system would work, the Lindsay family also continued to pump in much-needed capital, illustrating how Ferranti was given all the support necessary when embarking on this fascinating technical adventure.

To give some idea of the challenges facing this team, it is interesting to note that the steel ingots for the 10,000 hp steam engines were the largest cast in Scotland to date. Hick, Hargreaves of Bolton were once again commissioned to supply both sets of reciprocating engines, after agreeing to reduce their prices,[86] sustaining this firm's competitiveness in this sector. Largely because his workshop was too small for the job, Ferranti also tried to subcontract the manufacture of the 1,000 kW and 3,000 kW alternators. However, after being told by two of the largest engineering companies in Europe, Krupps and Creusot, that delivery would take up to three years, he installed his own production plant at Deptford at a cost of £6,000. The lathe for turning the 3000 kW alternator rims was said to have been as big as anything in use at the Woolwich Arsenal at that time,[87] such was the magnitude of the engineering task. Indeed, there is little doubt that the Deptford generators were at that time the largest in the world.[88]

The scale of this generating equipment was consequently the most impressive feature of the Deptford station, leading contemporaries to marvel at the finished product when completed by March 1889. Of course, Ferranti had benefited from his experience in manufacturing the large Grosvenor Gallery generators, patenting several improvements to his design in 1888 (see Appendix B) which were to provide the technical basis for the larger machines. This reflected his incremental approach towards product development, allowing steady progress in the design stage which was willingly funded by LESCo. On the other hand, when Ferranti decided to take on the design and production of a cable to transmit unprecedented distribution voltages, he came across major difficulties which created some friction in this relationship. One must remember, though, that no alternative sources of 10,000 volt cable were available, forcing Ferranti to take on the challenge at a crucial time for LESCo.

The 10 kV cable

Although a cable design had actually featured in two Ferranti patents (4596 of 1882 and 15251 of 1885), he had always purchased this component of the distribution system from specialist suppliers like the India Rubber & Gutta Percha Co. At Deptford, however, Ferranti decided to test out his own ideas, using the expertise of C. P. Sparks and G. L. Addenbrook to design by July 1887 a tubular concentric type of cable which built on his earlier patents.[89] Sir William Thomson, persisting in his sceptical approach towards high tension AC, asked him: 'Are you really going up to 10,000 volts? Have you any practical trials up to such high potentials?'.[90] Although the distinguished scientist agreed to provide some technical data on insulating materials for such a high tension cable, it was to be in the field that Ferranti had to tackle a range of unprecedented problems, providing a fascinating case-study in technological innovation.

The first attempt at producing a high tension cable began in July 1887, when C. P. Sparks and G. L. Addenbrook were deputed to help Ferranti with the task.[91] The innovatory feature of this first cable was its insulating medium, composed of paper soaked in ozokerite (paraffin wax), which Sir William Thomson had advised was more effective and cheaper than the conventional dielectric, rubber. After a series of trials which lasted until 1889, the first

The Ferranti 10,000 volt main showing the various layers of copper and insulation. *(Museum of Science and Industry at Manchester.)*

Ferranti cable was laid between Deptford and the Grosvenor Gallery. Unfortunately, though, because the cable consisted simply of two copper concentric tubes separated by a layer of ozokerite-soaked paper, by the end of 1889 it had to be replaced because of the severe induction problems it caused in the system.[92] Although the prominent cable firm of Fowler-Waring agreed to supply a replacement, this proved no more capable of carrying 10,000 volts. Furthermore, as it was laid along railway lines, its outer coating of jute was susceptible to catching fire when hit by sparks from the passing trains.[93] As a result, tests on the Ferranti main were continued, resulting early in 1890 in a simple refinement which Ferranti had actually tried as early as 1888,[94] placing the concentric cable in an iron sheath which obviated all the induction problems and proved capable of carrying the full load. Thus was born the first viable high tension cable, establishing Ferranti as a leading authority in the field which, as we shall see in the next chapter, he was later able to exploit commercially.

Owing to the lack of space at the works of 'S. Z. de Ferranti', the new cable was actually manufactured in the Deptford station, under the supervision of H. W. Kolle. It was a laborious process, because copper tubes of the requisite thickness could only be purchased in twenty feet lengths, and as

The famous chisel test on a live 10,000V Ferranti cable at Deptford, with H. W. Kolle holding the chisel and de Ferranti standing above the hammer-wielding Henty.
(Museum of Science and Industry at Manchester.)

four seven-mile trunk mains were required it was not until the summer of 1890 before the job had been completed. The laying process was evidently successful, however, because of the 7,000 joints needed only twenty-eight were found to be faulty.[95] The Board of Trade, on the other hand, remained sceptical, forcing Ferranti to stage a most remarkable experiment. In the Deptford station yard, H. W. Kolle was asked to stand on an earthed copper plate holding an uninsulated chisel to the cable, while one of the foremen, H. W. Henty, struck the chisel with a sledge-hammer, thus breaking the cable and activating the main fuse. 'Frightened? I was scared out of my life', quipped Kolle later, 'Young Henty had never used a sledge-hammer before'.[96] Joking aside, though, Deptford was now able to operate at its full potential, because with the Grosvenor Gallery plant being phased out the full 10,000 volts could be transmitted directly to the sub-stations for the first time.

Commercial problems and the Grosvenor Gallery fire

Although by October 1890 the new station was reported to be 'working in a highly satisfactory manner',[97] progress had evidently been slow. In fact, only the 'small' engine room had been completed by that time, leading

J. S. Forbes to state in his annual report that he hoped that Deptford had 'turned the corner', after a total of £390,000 had been spent on land, buildings and equipment.[98] At the company's next annual meeting, though, one shareholder complained bitterly about the £3,000 salary paid to Ferranti, bearing in mind his failure to complete the contract.[99] £3,000 was indeed a high salary for the electrical industry at that time, although Forbes defended it by noting that it was common for some chief engineers (principally in the railway industry) to be paid a commission based on the total cost of a project. One must also remember that Ferranti had to pay his team himself out of the fee. This successfully deflected some of the criticism. However, as expenditure continued to mount, many were beginning to question the wisdom of embarking on such an adventurous scheme.[100] For example, the cable had cost almost £150,000 for the 3.4 square mile distribution area, while LESCo.'s rival, the Metropolitan Co., with a distribution area of 4.6 miles, had only spent £106,000 on this aspect of their scheme.[101]

Clearly, pioneering was proving to be a financial burden to LESCo. Just at the time when Ferranti and LESCo. thought that they had actually 'turned the corner', in the autumn of 1890, they also were to suffer a major setback as a result of simple human error. The Grosvenor Gallery station was finally closed down on 1 November 1890, when the alternators were shipped out to

10,000hp engines for Deptford at Hick Hargreaves works in Bolton.
(Museum of Science and Industry at Manchester.)

Deptford to act as a reserve. During the removals, though, in an act which tempted fate just too much, the transformers which were to be put in their place were housed in a wood-lined room above the boiler house. Sure enough, disaster was to strike, when on the morning of 15 November a linesman created a 5,000 volt arc at the plug switch when bringing a fresh bank of transformers into service. Not only could he have stopped the arc as soon as he had caused it by pulling the switch, he could also have cut off the supply from Deptford by using the nearby circuit-breaker. Sadly, though, as a result of his panic a fire ensued which cost LESCo. £20,000 in damaged equipment.[102] Ferranti rushed through the replacements, in order to bring the key sub-station back into service, but the haste with which the new transformers had been made was responsible for a major failure on 3 December, resulting in a complete cessation of supply to the 38,272 lamps connected to the LESCo. circuits.[103] In such a competitive atmosphere, the closedown was a loss of goodwill which they could ill afford after the delays in bringing Deptford on stream.

In a limited sense, the Grosvenor Gallery failure actually proved to be a blessing in disguise, because in the five weeks it took Ferranti to rebuild and equip the sub-station his team was able to complete a series of jobs which had been causing some consternation. One of these problems was

Electrical Industries drawing of the interior of the Deptford Station, 19 July, 1889.
(Museum of Science and Industry at Manchester.)

the discovery that, when using step-up transformers at Deptford, the voltage at the London end was actually higher than that transmitted from the station. This phenomenon is now known as the 'Ferranti Effect', although Oliver Heaviside, a prominent theoretician, had postulated in 1887 that operating both step-up and step-down transformers could induce the increase in voltage.[104] J. A. Fleming was brought in to advise Ferranti on what was yet another unforeseen practical constraint, after which the generators were rewound so that they could generate at 10,000 volts, dispensing with the need for step-up transformers. Condensers and fuses were also fitted to the circuit, as a further means of compensating for this problem. This indicates how Deptford was operating very much on the frontiers of knowledge, because only prominent theoreticians like Heaviside and Fleming had ever considered phenomena like the 'Ferranti Effect'. It also highlights the struggle Ferranti had always had with the theoretical side of electrical engineering, a point to which we shall return later when examining the overall achievement at Deptford.

In practical terms, of course, the Grosvenor Gallery failure was naturally a disaster for both Ferranti and LESCo. Only 4,800 lamps remained on the circuits when supply recommenced in February 1891, and although this had risen to almost 24,000 by May only just over a quarter of the 90,000 lamp capacity at Deptford was being used.[105] Ferranti was confident that the future

The flywheel ring of a Ferranti 10,000hp alternator under construction at Deptford in 1890.
(Museum of Science and Industry at Manchester.)

looked much brighter now that the 'small' engine room had been completed, reporting in 1891 that:

> I desire to call attention to the fact that from the commencement of your operations to the present time, no engineering or electrical difficulties whatever have arisen which I have not been able to overcome, and at the present moment I know of no weak point in your system, and consider success to be assured.[106]

This confident, if over-optimistic, assertion, which must never be misconstrued as boastfulness, was aimed at persuading the LESCo. board to provide funds to complete the 'large' engine room, equipment for which was nearing completion in Bolton and at Deptford. The board, on the other hand, was naturally rather more cautious, having sanctioned expenditure to date of almost £650,000 on a station only working at one-quarter capacity. 'We had, for good or evil, launched ourselves on a new path; we had no beaten path to follow', is how Forbes justified this expense at the LESCo. AGM in March 1891.[107] Even contemporary enthusiasts like the *Electrician*, however, were convinced that 'severe economies were to be effected'.[108]

Disagreements with Forbes

The commissioning of the 'large' engine room was, indeed, postponed indefinitely soon after the 1891 AGM, the board having decided that sufficient capacity had already been installed at Deptford to cater for the foreseeable future. Ferranti was naturally annoyed at this decision, allegedly initiating fiery exchanges with his chairman. Forbes is reported to have said: 'You are a very clever man, Mr Ferranti, but I'm thinking you're sadly lacking in pre-vision',[109] an argument many within LESCo. could not refute. At no point in the evidence is it suggested that Ferranti was fired by LESCo. However, by July 1891 he had severed his contract with the venture, bringing to an end 'by effluxion of time' what must have developed into a turbulent relationship.[110] There can be no doubt that Forbes had taken the correct commercial decision not to complete the 'large' engine room, especially when one considers the problems experienced at Deptford during the early 1890s. It is vital to note that most of the difficulties did not arise from its pioneering nature, a long spell of frost and fog putting the whole system under such a strain in November 1891 that, as Forbes reported: 'The whole thing came to a collapse: the dynamos, mains and everything went wrong, and for four days or more we were without light'.[111] At a time of general economic difficulties, and in view of the station's earlier technical and legal problems, it is consequently not surprising that confidence in LESCo. did not inspire a steady increase in demand. Indeed, in 1894 LESCo. was in such dire financial straits that Lord Wantage was obliged to call in the receiver to institute a financial reorganisation. Not until 1905 did the business pay its first ordinary share dividend.

Over this period, though, Deptford continued to operate according to the Ferranti design, in spite of a claim by two of the most eminent electrical engineers of the day, J. A. Fleming and John Hopkinson, that the system was surviving 'on very thin ice'.[112] All the Ferranti equipment remained in service for many years to come, in the case of the cables for over forty years. Ferranti was even commissioned to supply another 1,000 kW alternator in 1896, such was the growth in demand after the problems of the early 1890s. Substantiating Parson's claim that 'Ferranti's instincts were right', Deptford was to become a symbol of the way forward in electricity supply under the guiding hand of its chief engineer between 1892 and 1939, G. W. Partridge.[113] Notwithstanding these achievements, a question mark still hangs over the commercial acumen shown by LESCo. and Ferranti in starting such a project at a time when the market for electricity was only just beginning to expand after the early 1880s difficulties had nearly strangled the industry at birth.

2.7 The 'Bold Conception'

Had what Parsons calls 'one of the boldest conceptions in the whole history of central station work' been over-ambitious?[114] Had Ferranti, in the case of the first Grosvenor Gallery fire, been guilty of what Hughes describes as 'overloading more than a switch; he was overloading an entire engineering-human complex. He was asking for more from the personnel than training and experience allowed'?[115] Obviously, one might reply by asking Hughes how long it takes to train an operator to pull a switch correctly. At the same time, when he also argues that Ferranti was 'pursuing a course that briefly appeared to be the mainstream but took him out of the rising tide of technological change',[116] clearly there is a case to answer. Hughes is here alluding to the use by Ferranti of single-phase AC, which by 1891 had been supplanted by the more efficient polyphase AC system developed roughly at the same time by Nikola Tesla in the USA and by Sidney Brown of Brown, Boveri in Europe. Clearly, though, such a judgement employs excessive hindsight in expecting Deptford to utilise a method of transmitting electricity which was only effectively demonstrated in the year Ferranti resigned from LESCo. One should also note that the general principles of both systems were very similar, based on the need to build high tension AC power stations where land was cheap and fuel and water readily available at relatively low prices.

Ferranti, at a remarkably young age, was undoubtedly in the mainstream of electrical engineering when Deptford was designed and built. In another respect, though, the project was extremely risky, given the financial burden it imposed on LESCo. Again, the Lindsay family had been willing to sponsor his ideas, in the hope of capturing a larger share of the burgeoning London electric lighting market. In return, they were faced with a range of unique problems which prevented more rapid progress in fulfilling that aim. As Hannah claims, while being 'a futuristic vision of engineering genius [Deptford] was well in advance of its time and LESCo. paid the price of backing an unsuccessful project on the frontiers of technology'.[117] Byatt also suggests that 'Ferranti was moving in the right direction, but tried to go much too far too early', pointing out how only by 1890 were there a million lamps in use across London.[118] On the other hand, this view purposely diminishes the impact Marindin had in severely restricting the potential size of LESCo.'s market,[119] while some of the areas already being supplied from the Grosvenor Gallery were actually given to their rivals. Overall, though, and with the benefit of hindsight, one cannot disagree too much with the conventional view that Deptford was a high-risk gamble reflecting intuitive engineering with little commercial rationale, particularly when one examines the legal, technological and commercial prospects of electricity supply in Britain at that time.

One of the crucial points arising from this debate is clearly the restrictive environment in which Ferranti and other British electrical entrepreneurs continued to operate throughout the 1880s and early 1890s. In this context, both the role of the state in restricting the potential scale of operations, and the existence of well-entrenched rivals like steam and gas, severely limited the opportunities for expansion. As Hannah notes, the industry's progress up to the First World War hardly amounted to a major leap forward of a Schumpeterian nature, in sharp contrast to the booming conditions prevailing across the Atlantic.[120] While Hughes and other prominent American historians might well castigate British electrical engineers for their lack of boldness, they are clearly ignoring the poor domestic prospects for electricity supply.[121] Another American scholar, A. D. Chandler, claims that there were no rational reasons why British electrical engineering firms should not have been as aggressive as their American and German counterparts in building up large-scale production and distribution facilities. He is particularly interested in how firms established 'first-mover' advantages in new technologies, criticising the small-scale British firms for failing to exploit new openings on the grounds that: 'The market was there; the workers were as skilled as those in Germany and the United States; and London investors were eager to profit from the new technology'.[122] After assessing the early career of

Ferranti, however, it seems clear that few such incentives existed to establish large-scale British firms at that time, limiting any opportunities to capture the 'first-mover' advantages which American and German entrepreneurs were exploiting at that time.

In this context, it is interesting to note that Hughes's article, aimed at disparaging the 'Bold Conception' of Deptford,[123] comes but a year after he had criticised British electrical engineers for being unenterprising. Surely, there is a double standard here, because in one breath he is guilty of condemning them for failing to keep up with the Americans, and in the next he castigates Ferranti for trying too hard. As the *Western Electric* said at the time, when reviewing an *Electrical Review* article ridiculing what it called *The Dream of Ferranti*: 'We hardly know what to think of the *Review*. Can it be that Mr Ferranti incurred its displeasure by his bold and daring display of that characteristic so distinctly American', that of enterprise?[124] Ferranti was rightly regarded by his contemporaries as one of the leading electrical engineers of that era. Deptford was also certainly the symbol of a reawakening in the British electrical industry which, as we shall see in the next chapter, was to spark a much higher level of activity in the following decades. Problems remained with the scale of demand and the size of British electrical manufacturers, just as Deptford continued to drain funds away from the Lindsay family. Nevertheless, in 1890 greater optimism pervaded the industry than at any other time since the heady days of 1882, giving engineers like Ferranti the opportunity to push forward the frontiers of electrical technology. Whether they were able to go on and exploit this potential was debatable, because such was the lag in progress, when compared with that in the USA and Germany during the 1880s and 1890s, that most British firms proved to be uncompetitive in both home and overseas markets. As we shall now go on to examine, this was yet another challenge to Ferranti as he transferred his attentions once again to the business of manufacturing electrical equipment, providing historians with further interesting insights into a career which had already proved extraordinarily eventful.

3

Lessons in Management and Finance

Having left LESCo. after six years as its chief engineer, the man dubbed the 'English Edison'[1] was in 1891 obliged to revert to his original role as a 'Manufacturing Engineer'. It was a transition he found extremely difficult and frustrating, not simply because after the boom years of 1888–91 demand tapered off badly, but also because the structural characteristics of British electrical equipment markets severely inhibited a manufacturer's freedom to design and produce. These problems were compounded by the distinct disadvantage at which the industry was placed by this time, when compared to its American and German counterparts, leading to acute crises when a series of multinational subsidiaries were implanted in the UK after the resurgence in demand from 1897.

In trying to assess the manner in which Ferranti dealt with this difficult domestic environment, it is important to balance out the internal and external constraints affecting the young engineer's business. Chandler, as we noted at the end of the last chapter, was wrong to expect British manufacturers to have made the substantial investments in production and distribution which their foreign rivals were undertaking from the late 1880s,[2] because neither the market stimulus had been as conducive, nor the level of financial support as encouraging after the embarrassments of 1882. On the other hand, Chandler is correct when stressing the importance of 'personal capitalism' as a key ingredient of the British business scene.[3] In the Ferranti case, the independent stand he always took regarding the ownership and control of his firm undoubtedly accentuated the external constraints. It is difficult to argue which of these internal and external factors created more problems, because each seemed to accentuate the other. Nevertheless, the dilemma of choosing between personal control and raising external finance posed major difficulties for Ferranti over the period 1885–1903, contributing significantly to the firm's troubles.

3.1 Extra-Deptford activities

The Niagara Scheme

Before going on to analyse his return to electrical manufacturing, it is interesting to stress that, even while he was working on the designs for Deptford, Ferranti actually embarked on the even more ambitious project of harnessing the enormous potential of the Niagara Falls on the USA-Canada border.[4] In retrospect, this might seem foolhardy, particularly in view of the difficulties he experienced at Deptford. Yet again, though, this venture reflects the confidence Ferranti had in his own ability to design equipment for the most ambitious electricity supply projects. By 1888, working with Francis Ince and a prominent member of the IEE, Colonel Shaw, he had even negotiated the concession to build a power station on the Canadian side of the Falls, having filled a succession of sketch-books with designs and specifications.[5] Unfortunately, though, little interest from British financiers was forthcoming, resulting in a group of American engineers and financiers led by S. Evershed and his Cataract Construction Co. taking on the project.[6]

Ferranti was naturally annoyed that the caution of British financiers should result in such a situation. Furthermore, when the Cataract Construction Co. initiated a competition for the best equipment designs, he publicly expressed disdain at the manner in which these designs were employed by the Americans. Ferranti naturally submitted some plans. However, although the competition was supervised by the International Niagara Commission, and such authoritative names as Sir William Thomson, Professor W. C. Unwin of London, and Professor E. Mascart of Paris were drafted in to award prizes of up to $22,000 for the best tenders, it is clear that Evershed simply intended to draft the best ideas into an American-built station.[7] This caused great indignation in European electrical circles, leading prominent engineers like Ferranti to complain publicly at an IEE debate on the subject in 1893 that 'the designs were based on the unrecompensed work of the world'.[8]

Of course, had British financiers been as supportive as Evershed's New York associates, then Ferranti would have been able to steal a march on his rivals. Unfortunately, though, nothing like as much interest was shown on this side of the Atlantic in a project which seemed technologically (and commercially) precarious. British investors were not known for their willingness to engage in risky ventures, a point we shall return to later, giving Evershed's syndicate the opportunity to build one of the world's most impressive hydro-electric power stations. More importantly for Ferranti, with designs languishing on the drawing board, the Niagara Falls project was an inauspicious start to a vital decade for the British electrical engineering industry. Not only had he failed to raise any money from British financiers, his American rivals had also been bolstered by substantial financial support from their domestic institutions, providing the conducive market to develop such advanced systems as polyphase AC distribution which were slow to appear in Britain.[9]

On to Laufenburg

Undeterred by this lack of success, characteristically Ferranti turned his attentions to another large-scale project, to harness the rapids on the Rhine at Laufenburg.[10] Although the scheme had been initiated by J. Dierden of the Stroud Waterworks, in July 1891, after an initial investigation Ferranti decided that where the river dropped through a steep, narrow gorge a cost-effective hydro-electric power station could be constructed to produce the cheapest electricity in Europe. A Swiss consortium, the Compressed Air Co., backed by the German electrical giant AEG, had already tendered plans for a scheme, revealing some similarities with the Niagara Falls episode. Moreover, once again the lack of financial resources at his disposal became the main problem Ferranti had to tackle. In this case, though, he was able to interest a major German cable company, Felten & Guillaume, whose links with Ferranti will become clearer later.[11] Indeed, by 1892 a complete tender had been submitted which would have incorporated all the most advanced features of electrical technology available at that time, including polyphase AC. However, after much bureaucratic wrangling and political machinations, it was 1905 before the Berne authorities decided on which scheme to adopt, by which time Ferranti had sold his plans to Felten & Guillaume for £5,500.

Charterhouse Square

The failure to win either of these contracts was a blow to the commercial prospects of S. Z. de Ferranti, especially after the LESCo. contract had been terminated and demand for electrical machinery fell off badly in Britain after 1891. That Ferranti was considered as a serious contender for the Niagara Falls and Laufenburg schemes indicates how he had built up an extensive reputation by 1890. However, reputations do not necessarily produce business, and in the following years he suffered just as much as his British counterparts from the collapse in demand. This was particularly problematical at S. Z. de Ferranti because in March 1888 the firm had actually moved into much larger premises, at 46 Charterhouse Square, London, having outgrown the limited capacity of the Hatton Gardens works. With five floors now at his disposal, Ferranti was able to invest some time planning the

The works of S. Z. Ferranti Ltd at Chaterhouse Square, c. 1890. (Museum of Science and Industry at Manchester.)

layout, especially for the booming meter department.[12] Of central importance to his deliberations, however, was the establishment of an experimental department, typifying the technology-led strategy which was always close to his heart. As we noted at the end of chapter 1, because Ferranti was more interested in engineering development, as opposed to producing for the market, the Charterhouse Square experimental department provided the facilities for pursuing a much more ambitious approach towards research and development. It was a culture which he instilled into the very fabric of the company he founded, giving the pursuit of engineering excellence a key position at the core of the organisation.

The organisational dynamics of the Ferranti business will be examined further when we assess the 1896 move into even larger premises (see section 3.4). At this stage, it is essential to chart how the venture coped with the changing market prospects of the period. Charterhouse Square was, of course, initially kept extremely busy with the Deptford equipment contracts. At the same time, several export contracts were also secured as a result of the partnership's imaginative approach towards marketing. As Ferranti was too busy to exploit the growing reputation his firm was earning as a result of the Grosvenor Gallery and Deptford projects, in 1888 he negotiated a series of agency agreements in what were seen as potentially lucrative markets. One of the business deals negotiated on his honeymoon was with Oliver Patin,[13] resulting in the creation of Ferranti, Patin et Cie. as an agency for the French and Belgian markets.[14] Similar arrangements were also made with John Haskins in Boston, to exploit the American market, and with The River Plate Trust, Loan & Agency Co., which had the exclusive right to sell Ferranti equipment in South America.[15] Although British businessmen have been heavily criticised for failing to develop an aggressive approach towards overseas marketing,[16] the decision to link up with agencies was growing in popularity in the 1880s and '90s, providing Ferranti and Ince with the opportunity to maximise the sales opportunities created by the wide publicity surrounding Deptford. Indeed, up to 1891 this proved reasonably successful, with contracts worth approximately £15,000 coming from the agents. Haskins did not in fact manage to sell any Ferranti products in the American market, but the River Plate Trust, Loan and Agency Co. sold two alternators, in La Plata and Rosario, while Patin supplied generating equipment to stations in Paris, Nancy, Le Havre, Melun, Troyes, Nimes, Dijon, Sens and St Cere.[17]

Establishing a reputation in overseas markets was clearly an effective way for S. Z. de Ferranti to keep its new Charterhouse Square works busy. Another significant feature of these overseas contracts was the standard size of all the alternators sold, because the agents were instructed only to sell 3,000-lighter

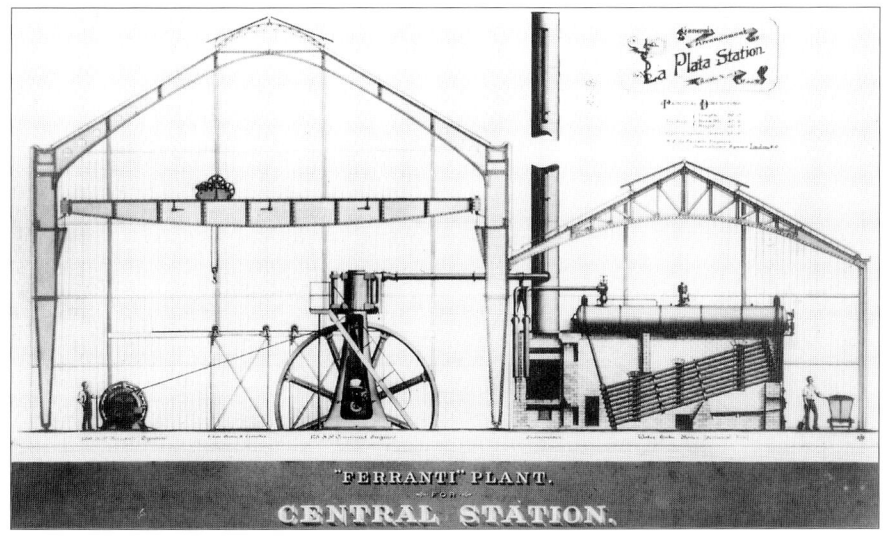

La Plata Station elevation drawing of Ferranti plant, two 175hp engines and two 150 dynamos, installed in 1890. (*Museum of Science and Industry at Manchester.*)

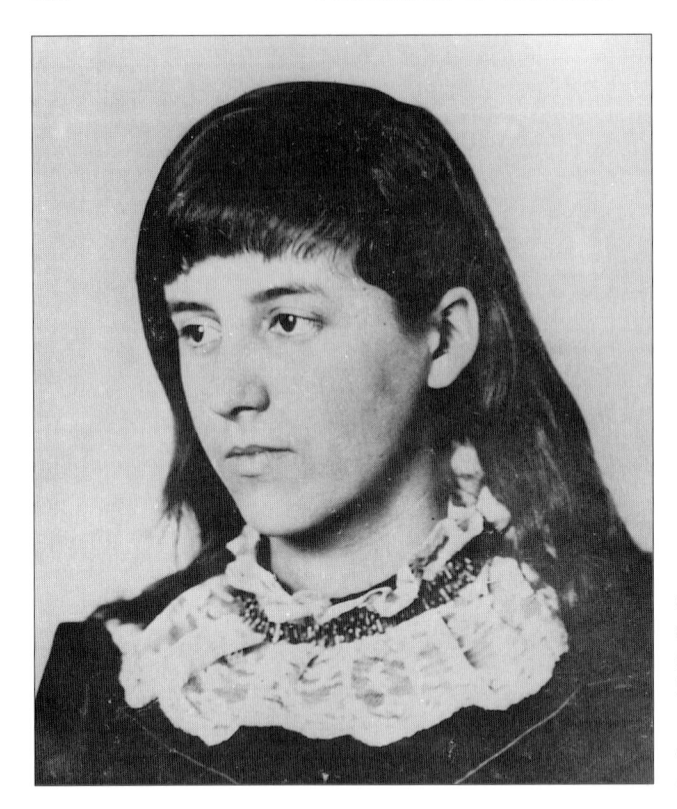

Gertrude Ruth Ince, aged 12 at the time she first met her future husband, S. Z. Ferranti. *(Museum of Science and Industry at Manchester.)*

machines. As we shall see later, this was a degree of standardisation which manufacturers found difficult to achieve when selling in the home market, allowing Charles Sparks as works manager to operate Charterhouse Square at a high level of efficiency. It is also noticeable that the alternators were of the flywheel type, namely, that they were connected up to the steam engine as if they were the flywheel, as in the 10,000 hp units supplied to Deptford's 'large' engine room. This design was eventually to become one of the distinguishing hallmarks of the Ferranti business in generators up to 1905, indicating how the export orders allowed him the opportunity to perfect a design which was later to become popular in British power station practice. The machines supplied to France and Belgium also worked without reserve plant, such was the confidence in Ferranti designs, indicating how abroad different operating standards were employed.[18] However, having successfully established an overseas marketing operation, in 1891 Ferranti and Ince decided to dispense with the agents' services, preferring instead to conduct their own selling operations.[19] This would prove to be a short-sighted decision, because the depression in demand at home certainly put the firm's finances under tremendous strain over the following four years.

3.2 Business worries

Individualism and business

As a private partnership, S. Z. de Ferranti had limited access to capital resources, relying largely on reinvested profits for the bulk of the finance for fixed investment in plant and facilities. Although by 1890 a total of £18,500 in unclaimed profits had been ploughed back into the firm, Ferranti accounting for fifty-six per cent, Ince thirty-four per cent, and Sparks ten per cent, and a further £10,000 had been borrowed from LESCo., this capital base proved woefully inadequate. The manufacturing plant at Deptford alone had cost over £17,000, while the fixed assets at Charterhouse Square stood at £21,000 by 1890. Only generous progress payments from LESCo. would appear to have kept the business afloat up to 1891, especially as stocks amounted to over £16,800. Francis Ince had also invested £5,420 in LESCo., limiting his ability to fund the manufacturing firm, and even though S. Z. de Ferranti actually made a profit of £6,474 in 1889,[20] none of the partners was going to enjoy the full fruits of their labours.

Ince was especially worried about this illiquidity, lobbying Ferranti to convert the partnership into a joint stock company in order 'to mend the mess we are in'.[21] Typically, however, Ferranti complained to his wife that such a solution would 'take all my interest out of the work',[22] reflecting the widespread feeling among British businessmen that ownership and control ought to be vested in the same person, or family, to ensure that firms were run efficiently.[23] Ince chided Ferranti for what he called 'the wonderful idea you have always had of your own desire for freedom of action'.[24] At the same time, one must remember that this attitude was fundamental to the firm's long-term success, because even though it was often dogged by financial shortages, independence of thought and action was considered crucial to pursuing exciting engineering projects.

Of course, Ferranti was well aware of the financial predicament. His solution was to solicit the support of 'sleeping' partners who might provide fresh capital, without interfering in the formulation of management strategy. He even tried to interest Lord Wantage in taking on this role,[25] an offer the principal shareholder in LESCo. was only too keen to reject. Ferranti then consulted an old friend, Alfred Cook, the Leeds printer whom he had met when installing a Siemens dynamo in his works back in 1881. Again, though, nothing other than advice was forthcoming. The next port of call was Hick, Hargreaves of Bolton, where after travelling third-class he was 'practically speaking, begging' for money from the engineering firm which had supplied steam engines to the Grosvenor Gallery and Deptford projects. Although as a private partnership (until 1892) the senior executives at Hick, Hargreaves would have empathised with the Ferranti predicament, it was two years before they agreed to invest £2,000 in S. Z. de Ferranti. Clearly, the 'desire for freedom of action' was seriously jeopardising the business's future, highlighting the potentially severe financial constraints which such an individualistic approach imposed. Furthermore, the Ferranti family was inevitably affected by these difficulties. As Gertrude remembered: 'There was little money coming in and it became essential to economise'.[26] They already had a daughter, Zoe, who was born in 1889, followed by Basil in 1891, while both Juliana and Juliet de Ferranti still lived with the young family and Cesar was also being supported in Liverpool.

S. Z. de Ferranti Ltd

Ferranti was to experience few more trying periods in his life, indicating how the financial status of his family remained a major motivation when building up the business. The need to support his family would also have been one of the main reasons why in 1891 Ferranti finally agreed to the conversion of S. Z. de Ferranti into a joint stock company. In fact, Ince had actually managed to persuade a group of financiers to invest in the company,[27] arguing that divorcing control and ownership provided the most realistic means of keeping the business afloat. Ferranti, on the other hand, was so fiercely opposed to their proposed role in managing the business that he refused to cooperate, arguing that personal control was essential if engineering excellence and innovation were to be pursed. This established at an early stage what became a cornerstone of the Ferranti philosophy, because continually over the following eighty years the family rejected the advice proffered by professional advisors who wanted to dilute their influence over company strategy. It was this preference for unfettered control which consequently resulted in the registration of S. Z. de Ferranti Ltd in June 1890 as a 'private' company.

In fact, this form of company was not legally recognised until 1907, the architects of British limited liability legislation having intended the joint stock company to have been a vehicle for injecting a range of capital sources into business. However, with a business culture which remained heavily individualistic, the vast majority of companies registered were private bodies which simply sought to exploit for the owners the advantages of limited liability.[28] The £100,000 nominal capital of S. Z. de Ferranti Ltd was composed of 8,000 £10 ordinary shares and 2,000 £10 preference shares, with the former representing the voting stock. Not surprisingly, then, Ferranti insisted on being allocated seventy-five per cent of the ordinary shares, giving him complete control of the business. Ince was actually given the remaining twenty-five per cent, while Sparks received only 250 preference shares.[29]

It is important to stress that the solution adopted by Ferranti to the mounting financial difficulties experienced as a result of expansion was actually a common feature of the British business scene.[30] The private company has actually been described as 'a typical British compromise',[31] because in becoming a joint stock company firms were simply acquiring the legal protection of limited liability, while preventing the separation of management and ownership common in such organisations. In effect, though, the move simply perpetuated the mounting financial problems which so badly affected S. Z. de Ferranti Ltd in the 1890s, because no fresh capital was raised in 1890. At the same time, it is vital to stress how to Ferranti retaining personal control of the firm he established was central to sustaining the technology-led strategy which was its central driving philosophy. He regarded the imposition of outside interference as an inevitable threat to his wish for complete freedom of action in product development, an attitude which pervaded the Ferranti organisation for decades.

Ferranti and British Insulated Wire Co.

The outlook for S. Z. de Ferranti Ltd must have consequently been bleak by the time LESCo. had parted with its services in July 1891. It was just at that time, however, that a Liverpool entrepreneur, J. B. Atherton, was trying to break into the cable industry, a move which was to have important ramifications for Ferranti and his colleagues. The British cable industry was extremely successful, manufacturers having gained a competitive advantage over European and American rivals as a result of the technological superiority gained during the earlier expansion of telegraphy. However, because it had developed much earlier during the telegraphic boom of the 1840s and 1850s, only rarely was there much integration with electrical engineering concerns.[32] Atherton had recognised the potential in cable production, creating in the summer of 1891 the British Insulated Wire Co., with premises in Prescot, Merseyside. However, the technical press was extremely dubious about his proposed use of American patents for a paper-insulated variant which had been manufactured by the Norwich Insulated Wire Co. of New Jersey.[33] Indeed, not only was there general scepticism about the firm's products, W. H. Preece, chief electrician to the General Post Office, also advised the British Insulated Wire Co. that the American patents contravened those held by Ferranti. This forced Atherton to rush down to Charterhouse Square and negotiate an agreement with the struggling young engineer, providing the patentee with a much-needed injection of capital at an extremely pertinent point in his business career.

The agreement between Ferranti and British Insulated Wire (hereafter B. I. Wire) was signed on 2 August 1891. It stipulated that, in return for the exclusive use of five cable patents, the former would receive £6,210 in cash and £20,915 in shares.[34] As this represented almost one-quarter of B. I. Wire's equity, Ferranti was also made a director of the firm, while apart from insuring his life for the next five years he was given the right to purchase one-quarter of any further increase in its capital.[35] This proved to be a mutually-beneficial deal, because not only did Ferranti take out a further five cable patents (see Appendix B) between 1892 and 1897, B. I. Wire managed to establish a firm footing in the industry. By 1896, they were offering the first flexible high-voltage concentric cable, fifteen miles of which was supplied to LESCo., boosting sales considerably over the rest of the decade. Such was B. I. Wire's growing reputation that in 1900 an issue of £300,000 was over-subscribed, largely because the firm had paid average annual dividends of fifteen per cent over the previous five years.[36]

S. Z. de Ferranti Ltd had consequently been thrown a much-needed lifeline by B. I. Wire. Apart from the regular dividend income which helped to sort out some of the family's finances, the B. I. Wire shares owned by Ferranti actually increased in value to almost £50,000 by 1899, providing a valuable source of collateral for the many short-term loans upon which his company relied. Furthermore, through B. I. Wire Ferranti also came into contact with a wider group of business associates to whom he was able to sell £20,000 worth of preference shares (viz., non-voting stock) in S. Z. de Ferranti Ltd, injecting capital into the firm at a crucial time. Among these investors were E. K. Muspratt, a leading chemical manufacturer, Prince, Smith of Keighley, suppliers of plant to B. I. Wire, and the German cable company mentioned earlier with regard to the Laufenburg project, Felten & Guillaume.[37] It took until 1893 before all this money could be raised, forcing Ferranti to continue the 'most unpleasant business [of] begging' associates to purchase the non-voting shares.[38] Eventually, though, S. Z. de Ferranti Ltd was placed in a much stronger position as a direct result of the cable contract,[39] giving him the freedom to maintain the independent stance which remained one of the organisation's strongest characteristics over the following decades.

3.3 Rebuilding the business

Market difficulties

Although the additional funds raised from B. I. Wire and its associates proved extremely useful, it is important to remember that the vital context within which these deals were brokered was a troublesome market for electrical engineering. In the first place, after a significant boom in activity between 1888 and 1891, orders for generating equipment slumped badly in the early 1890s. This predicament was also exacerbated for S. Z. de Ferranti Ltd by the standard British convention of potential equipment purchasers inspecting plant before placing an order. Given the problems experienced at Deptford, few potential customers were willing to place much faith in the firm's ability to provide equipment for the normally much smaller power stations which were being built at that time. In fact, of the fifty British central power stations in operation by 1892, and of the fifteen under construction, Ferranti equipment was being used at only three, Deptford, Rochester and Glasgow.[40] As five other firms (Siemens, Brush, Crompton, Mather & Platt, and the Electric Construction Co.) accounted for over three-quarters of the generator market,[41] this left Ferranti with a considerable mountain to climb if he was to make an impact on the domestic market.

As Appendix C reveals, the company's output fell alarmingly over this period. One of the major reasons behind this trend was clearly the sharp downturn in demand for electrical products during the early 1890s. At the same time, another factor to consider was a fall in prices. The electrical engineering slump actually coincided with a general depression in the economy, when engineering manufacturers were taking the opportunity afforded by the standardisation of generator design to diversify into the new sector in order to utilise spare capacity. This dangerous trend precipitated a sharp deflation in the price of electrical goods, because the usual practice for newcomers to an industry was to tender at low prices until enough goodwill had been built up in the marketplace.[42] In addition, intense price competition was also accentuated by the nature of the early electrical market, because contracts for the entire power station, from generators to switchgear, were placed with one firm. This would mean that for the typically small British electrical manufacturer expensive spare capacity would be left idle as the contract progressed through the works, tempting firms into further price-cuts when tendering for new business.[43] It was a vicious downward spiral, the most severe impact of which was the inability of British firms to accumulate sufficient funds to invest in the new technologies (polyphase AC machinery and electric traction, for example) which their American and German rivals were developing at this time.[44]

This combination of increased competition, scarce business and falling prices was naturally damaging to the short- and long-term prospects of British electrical engineering, extending the technological gap between the emerging industries. Ferranti complained in a speech to the IEE in 1894 that as there was no rival in Britain to giants like General Electric and Westinghouse in the USA and Siemens and AEG in Germany, the ruinous domestic competition was undermining competitiveness.[45] The British industry still contained a large number of relatively small firms, creating an atomistic structure which prevented the necessary degree of integration pursued relentlessly by their foreign rivals. To give but one indicator of the growing differences, in the mid-1890s the average British electrical manufacturers were reporting sales of c. £100,000, while in 1898 General Electric produced a net profit of $4 million.[46] At the same time, though, one must also remember that an intense individualism had prevented S. Z. de Ferranti Ltd from growing more rapidly after 1890. Furthermore, in the industry as a whole cooperation proved to be an impossible dream at this time, indicating how self-imposed constraints proved to be just as significant in holding up progress as the external factors like a small domestic market.

Meter expansion

Ferranti was consequently faced with a difficult transition period in the early 1890s, especially with regard to the heavy side of the business (generators and transformers). In this context, it is vital to emphasise how, just as in 1885 when Ferranti and Ince had started their second partnership, the company's meter business would appear to have provided a solid base for the later expansion of activities. Indeed, meter production was the foundation on which the business rested initially, consistently providing the finance for some of the company's riskier ventures. Certainly, it was less susceptible to the cyclical fluctuations which periodically affected the generator department, because even though electricity supply undertakings usually only placed bulk orders in the autumn, with the expansion in customers during the 1890s manufacturers could at least rely on regular meter contracts. Ironically, though, while Ferranti was regarded as the leading British protagonist of AC electricity supply, in the 1890s he still sold more DC meters, such was the technological state of the home market at that time.[47] An AC meter had been developed in 1888, the production of which was based on the methods licensed from two Swiss engineers, E. Paccaud and F. Borel.[48] In 1890, Ferranti also cooperated with Arthur Wright, later chief engineer to the Brighton

The Ferranti-Wright AC meter, first produced in 1890 and largely used in power stations. *(Museum of Science and Industry at Manchester.)*

power station, on a further refinement to his design which was said to result in 'an ingenious form of AC meter'.[49] Nevertheless, the Ferranti reputation was built on producing what one contemporary described as a DC meter which was 'the result of a patient endeavour to produce in their most perfect forms instruments possessing the three essentials, simplicity, accuracy and reliability'.[50]

Ferranti clearly regarded the meter department as one of the most important parts of his business. Indeed, relocating the business in Charterhouse Square, close by the Clerkenwell watch-making district, provided ready access to a highly skilled workforce capable of assembling these intricate instruments efficiently. Meter production actually occupied the top two floors of the five-storey Charterhouse Square premises, in which American machine tools were installed to aid the mass-production of a standardised and interchangeable product.[51] Most importantly, a manager was appointed to run this department, Ferranti deciding to delegate responsibility to a professional engineer, W. F. Hegarty, in order to ensure that the investment in designs and production techniques proved remunerative. This was a significant managerial development in the company, because not only was this the first time Ferranti had delegated responsibility to a professional manager, Hegarty was also given a profit-sharing incentive scheme, bringing an attention to departmental profitability which had hitherto been unnecessary in the company. This indicates how, even though Ferranti refused to dilute his controlling interest, he was never slow to hire professional managers to undertake the more routine aspects of production. Indeed, as we shall see in the next section, a distinct managerial style emerged within S. Z. de Ferranti Ltd, based on the family's willingness to encourage initiative at departmental level, facilitating the process of diversification (and later, expansion) on which they were embarked.

In the meter, Ferranti had recognised a staple source of income which was not as susceptible to the sharp fluctuations in demand for capital equipment like generators and transformers. By 1895, meter sales had exceeded £25,000 per annum, or almost forty per cent of total output, on which an average annual profit of £12,000 was recouped between 1891 and 1895, accounting for all the company's surplus over that period (see Appendix C). It is important to note that Appendix C gives only the net profit for this period, because the annual balance sheet never recorded the gross profit, emphasising how this information ought to be treated cautiously. Nevertheless, the profit figures illustrate the value of having a bulk business to subsidise the more volatile departments, a strategy most of the larger electrical manufacturers also pursued. In most cases, electric bulb production was used in this way, often accompanied by the negotiation of extensive price-fixing agreements which provided a consistent level of profitability.[52] Ferranti chose not to venture into what was a 'closed shop' dominated by the main patent-holders like EdiSwan and GEC. However, the meter proved to be a viable alternative in this respect, especially with the number of customers increasing significantly as a result of the investment in generating plant since 1887.[53] We shall also see over the following chapters how price-fixing became an important feature of the meter business, reinforcing the drive towards market dominance which Ferranti continued to enjoy for many decades.

The Portsmouth contract

While the meter department gathered strength during the early 1890s, the heavier departments were slow to generate a good flow of business in a heavily-depressed market. It was actually 1893 before S. Z. de Ferranti Ltd managed to win its first power station contract since Deptford, when Portsmouth Corporation placed what was vitally important business. Originally, acting on the advice of Bradford Corporation's chief engineer, J. S. Shoolbred, Portsmouth had intended to install a low tension DC system, appointing Professor Garnett of Tynemouth Polytechnic to choose the best tender.[54] This seemed like a retrograde step to Ferranti, and on one of his 'begging' errands in the north he decided to visit Garnett and persuade him that a high tension AC system would prove more efficient. Although the academic was at first sceptical, after six months of lobbying the Corporation was finally convinced that the Ferranti scheme would work, illustrating once again how the young engineer was able to use his forceful personality to good effect.

The Portsmouth contract, while on a much smaller scale than Deptford, was actually to be just as innovative, particularly in the way that Ferranti proposed to operate the generators. We have already seen how with respect to the generators installed in the 'large' engine room at Deptford, and those exported to France, Belgium and South America, Ferranti had attached wide diameter alternators to the flywheel of a slow-speed engine. This flywheel-alternator design generated some controversy among his contemporaries, because the standard practice was to attach low-capacity generators by belt to high-speed engines. Garnett, however, was willing to pin his faith on the young engineer's projections of efficiency, persuading the Portsmouth councillors to accept the Ferranti system. Ferranti was also successful in silencing his critics, because the two 212 kW alternators supplied to the station, driven by Yates & Thom engines which operated at just ninety-six rpm, produced the record low figure of 3*d.* per kW for the price of electricity generation.[55] The average cost of electricity in Britain as a whole even as late as 1900 was actually 4*d.* per kW,[56] demonstrating the radical advance in efficiency Ferranti had achieved with his flywheel-alternator. By March 1895,

Parsons turbine and Ferranti alternator at the Portsmouth power station, 1894. (*Museum of Science and Industry at Manchester.*)

a third 212 kW set had also been supplied to Portsmouth, such was the rapid growth in demand for electricity, again confirming the efficacy of installing the Ferranti equipment.

Portsmouth, rather than the LESCo. project, can consequently lay claim to be the first major contract which started Ferranti off as a general supplier of central station equipment. While the flywheel-alternator (later renamed the 'steam alternator') was the most successful feature of the Portsmouth contract, in two further respects Ferranti was also able to use this opportunity as a launching pad for new products. One of the factors holding up AC's progress at this time was the continued use of arc lamps for street lighting, because DC was over twice as effective for this purpose.[57] Although several engineers had attempted a variety of ingenious solutions to this problem, for example, Hutin & Leblanc's alternating current transformer, at Portsmouth Ferranti was able to introduce what he called a rectifier to effect a solution which proved extremely popular. The rectifier allowed a station to generate AC and have the alternations in its flux damped down to provide an unidirectional current for arc-lighting. It proved to be a major breakthrough for both the AC camp and S. Z. de Ferranti Ltd, because by 1897 not only were Ferranti rectifiers rapidly replacing the popular Brush and Thomson-Houston arc-lighters formerly used for street lighting,[58] they were also substantially improving the attractiveness of this form of electricity supply. Naturally, once more powerful incandescent bulbs were developed early in the twentieth century, the life of the rectifier business was limited. In the meantime, though, Ferranti was able to sell large numbers of these machines to stations all over the British Isles, supplementing the meter and expanding generator businesses after a difficult couple of years.

Another new product range which was boosted substantially by the publicity it received at Portsmouth was switchgear. A remarkable feature of the new station was that no fire insurance was taken out by the Corporation to cover the kind of accident that had happened at the Grosvenor Gallery in 1890. This might seem foolhardy, but as the *Electrician* reported in May 1894, it was 'almost impossible for a fire to occur at the station', such were the advances Ferranti had made in switchboard design.[59] His key innovation was to contain the switch, cable receiver, fuse, ammeter and 'bus-bar of each generating unit in a cell of granite or marble, wiring them together into a single circuit which quite simply established 'the basic principles of high voltage switchgear'.[60] This view was expressed by H. W. Clothier, an electrical engineer who was later to make significant advances in switchgear design himself while working for Reyrolle. Clothier actually learnt his trade under Ferranti at Charterhouse Square, rising to the post of switchgear department manager and helping to extend the company's reputation as one of the leading suppliers in this industry.[61] A further advance in high voltage switchgear was also achieved in 1896, when Ferranti introduced the use of oil as a means of insulating the primary contacts, ensuring the total safety of this vital feature of power stations. By May 1900, the *Electrical Engineer* claimed that Ferranti switchgear was standard equipment for all high-tension AC installations,[62] providing the firm with yet another successful product which after the Portsmouth installation sold in substantial numbers.

Business expansion

The successes recorded at Portsmouth were indeed most opportune. In fact, the opening ceremony in June 1894 coincided with a resurgence in demand for generating and associated equipment for which S. Z de Ferranti Ltd was apparently well equipped. At the Portsmouth celebratory dinner, in a speech of true Victorian grandiloquence, Professor Garnett suggested that the generators should be inscribed with three 'Fs', because 'they represent the fortissimo of electricity, and I think the names of Franklin, Faraday and Ferranti ought to be placed upon them'.[63] This was excellent publicity for the company, especially as the merits of each new product were widely publicised in the trade press, bringing their capabilities to the attention of what was after 1894 an increasing number of prospective power station constructors and promoters. The *Electrician*'s annual survey for 1896 revealed that Ferranti alternators were being used in fifteen stations,[64] compared to just three in 1892, while Byatt calculates that the company accounted for fourteen per cent of an expanding power station generator market between 1893 and 1898.[65] This was a major advance for S. Z. de Ferranti Ltd, because only Siemens held a larger share of the market (thirty per cent) at this time, while other British manufacturers like Brush, Crompton, Mather & Platt, and the Electric Construction Co. were falling behind, after having dominated up to the early 1890s.

S. Z. de Ferranti Ltd had clearly made substantial progress since the bleak days of 1891, when no domestic power station contracts could be secured and financial reserves were being stretched to the limit. Appendix C illustrates how sales leapt by over sixty per cent between 1893 and 1895, while by 1896 they stood at an all-time record of almost £100,000 (after several years of falling prices). While the meter department continued to play a vital role in this success, it was generator, rectifier and switchgear sales which provided the main boost after 1894 as investment in British generating capacity surged to unprecedented levels.[66] Ferranti also again built what were the largest generators in the world to date, when supplying two 1500 kW units to the City of London Electric Light Co. in 1896. A year earlier, a 1,000 kW unit

A Ferranti transformer (now in the Science Museum), used at a LESCo. Substation. *(Museum of Science and Industry at Manchester.)*

was made for LESCo., reflecting the reputation Ferranti had established in this market. It was also for the Bankside station of the City Co. that oil-insulated high-voltage switchgear was developed, confirming his position as one of the leading designers in this field.[67] This firm eventually purchased sixty of these devices, giving S. Z. de Ferranti Ltd the opportunity to mass produce them to a standard design.

The 'All-Electric' ideal

1894 had clearly been an important year for Ferranti, especially in publicising his new range of products. In another respect, this year also provided him with the opportunity to publicise widely his wholehearted commitment to the 'All-Electric Age', when speaking in front of the Royal Scottish Society of Arts. He chose as his title the topic 'Electrical Developments of the Future and their Effect on Everyday Life', laying out the basic tenets of a committed belief in the potential of electricity to revolutionise every aspect of home-life and work. One of his main points was the need to use energy resources more efficiently, after explaining that only one-twenty-fifth of the energy latent in coal was actually transformed into electricity. He looked forward to the day when machines like the Parsons turbine (see section 4.2) or the internal combustion engine would supplant the reciprocating engine, a development which in turn would stimulate the wider use of electricity by reducing the cost of generation. One might also add that this speech inspired Colonel Peebles, of Bruce, Peebles & Co., to enter electrical engineering, such was its inspirational tone.

The 1894 speech illustrates how Ferranti was keen to back up his practical achievements as an electrical engineer with bold public statements of his belief in the 'All-Electric' age. His infectious enthusiasm was able to convey the message effectively, advertising both the Ferranti name and the products of his firm to a much wider audience. As the *Electrical Review* noted in 1910:

> There has always run this thread of thought – how to shape the project in hand to the economic needs of the future. It is this that has made him incessant in his endeavours to improve whatever came under his hand – to redesign, where a more commercial agent would have been content with the thing that was; to spend, on further inventing, the cash earned by some earlier manufacture; to throw himself with the vigour of unabated youth into developments of which he himself scarcely dreamed of a quarter-century before.

As we shall see in later chapters, progressively from the 1890s Ferranti used his reputation as one of the most prominent names in the industry to spread the gospel of an 'All-Electric Age' to all who would listen, providing publicity for his firm and its products which was an essential ingredient in its evolution as a major part of the British electrical industry. His son, Vincent, was also to preach exactly the same gospel during a term as President of the IEE, continuing a tradition which was in turn taken up by the third generation, Sebastian, in the 1970s.

3.4 The move to Hollinwood

The steam-alternator

The company's reputation as a competitive supplier of power station equipment had clearly become widely accepted by 1895, stimulating a significant surge in activity at the Charterhouse Square works. In turn, this growth was also to prompt Ferranti into a further diversification of his product range which had major implications for the firm's development. This diversification arose principally out of his growing frustration over the difficulties experienced when fitting his flywheel-alternator to the steam engines supplied by specialist manufacturers. Few firms were actually capable of supplying the slow-speed engines required by Ferranti, prompting him to design his own machine and dispense with all the delays and imperfections attendant on the subcontractor system.

As we saw in sections 1.3 and 1.4, Ferranti had been fascinated by steam engines ever since his early conversations with Vincent Szczepanowski, the step-brother who provided him with books on the subject. Now, he had the opportunity to apply his own ideas on their design to a machine which would power the flywheel-alternators. This resulted in the development of a cross-compound, vertical, slow-speed engine which was widely regarded as one of the most efficient of its type in the 1890s. The reciprocating parts were all thoroughly enclosed to prevent oil leakage, and to reduce maintenance time he used forced lubrication through an oil filter in the bed-frame. Ferranti also employed roller bearings for the flywheel, resulting in less friction and a balanced movement which was essential in a machine expected to work for long periods.[68] Thus was conceived the Ferranti 'steam alternator', as the flywheel-alternator was marketed, substantially improving the firm's competitive position in the power station market at a time when demand was increasing substantially.

Ferranti steam-alternator No. 244, 300kW, for Huddersfield, 1895. (*Museum of Science and Industry at Manchester.*)

The move to Hollinwood

The commercial viability of this diversification into engine production will be examined later, but coming at a time when the Charterhouse Square works was already bursting at the seams, with orders for three of the largest generators in the world and meter, rectifier and switchgear production increasing significantly, it created a problem which could only be solved by finding larger premises. Accompanied by Gertrude, Ferranti consequently set off on a tour of suitable sites which would provide both the space for an expanding business and cheaper rents, rates and labour than in the capital.[69] Furthermore, while London had to date been the only major British centre of electrical activity, power stations were beginning to appear in most of the provincial towns after 1890, giving electrical manufacturers greater scope when choosing their locations. Sites in the Midlands were first inspected, including a factory later used by Rolls Royce. Finally, though, at the end of 1895 a four acre plot in Hollinwood was chosen, on which the Crown Iron Works had been trading until recently, providing S. Z. de Ferranti Ltd with a base which for the following seventy years acted as the firm's headquarters.

Unfortunately, however, the plans had to be shelved temporarily, because Ferranti was obliged to undergo what was at the time a serious operation, to have his appendix removed. As his wife remembered, he was 'never a decidedly robust man', frequently succumbing to a range of illnesses and physical problems. Throughout 1895, severe abdominal pains had interrupted his work, forcing him to hire the distinguished surgeon, Sir Frederick Treves, to cure the problem.[70] The operation took place in January 1896, but such was the relatively primitive state of anaesthetics and surgery techniques in the 1890s that it was March before Ferranti could resume his manufacturing work. Typically, though, during the convalescence, he wasted little time in planning the move into what has since become known as the Crown Works at Hollinwood. In that time, he prepared the workshop layout and designed special machine tools to manufacture engine components so that production would be affected as little as possible by the move.[71]

At first sight, the appearance and amenities of Hollinwood must not have seemed very promising to the senior employees who made the move from London. Situated between Oldham and Manchester, the town had a population of 9,000, most of whom lived in drab rows of terraced housing which had been built for workers in the local cotton mills and coal mine. Superficial impressions can, however, be extremely misleading, because from a commercial point of view the new premises offered substantial advantages. The Crown Works, consisting of two buildings, was located next to the Lancashire & Yorkshire Railway Co. line, providing an effective transport link with not only Manchester and surrounding districts, but also export markets via the newly-constructed Manchester Ship Canal. There was also ample space on the adjoining common for any expansion of capacity, an essential element in the Ferranti plans and something which would have been prohibitively expensive at Charterhouse Square. Skilled labour was also plentiful in the region, while unskilled labour was thirty per cent cheaper than in London, providing strong inducements to a cash-conscious family firm.[72] At the same time, the local economy would derive substantial benefits from attracting a firm competing in what was to be one of the high-growth sectors of world trade over the next eighty years. The staple cotton and coal trades of northeast Lancashire dwindled away over the next forty years, as a result of overcapacity and intense competition. In contrast, the Ferranti business provided a substantial cushion against the worst effects of this depression, relieving the problems felt in many other east Lancashire towns.

The move to Hollinwood had substantial mutual advantages to both the locality and S. Z. de Ferranti Ltd. Although it was decided that the meter department should remain at Charterhouse Square, for the heavier parts of the business the Crown Works provided much more space. In particular, Ferranti was able to start a pattern shop, and later a foundry, in order to make the works more self-dependent. American equipment was also imported to equip the toolroom, where the special production plant was fabricated for use in manufacturing rectifiers, transformers, generators and engines. This self-sufficient approach was typical of the British engineering industry in general, because the standardised production of interchangeable parts was regarded as alien to the conventional practice of designing and making high-quality equipment on a one-off basis. Of course, as we shall see later, the ubiquitous influence of the consulting engineer also prevented any tendency towards standardisation. On the other hand, engineering manufacturers themselves were just as loath to introduce what was regarded dismissively as 'American' methods of mass-production,[73] creating a tradition which Ferranti perpetuated in his desire to produce machinery of the highest possible quality.

3.5 Industrial relations at Hollinwood

By the time Ferranti had moved the heavy electrical engineering departments to Hollinwood, it was clear that both his business philosophy and approach towards production were symptomatic of all the principal features of Britain's entrepreneurial class. He was, above all, an individualist, extolling the virtues of self-determination and quality production as the route to business success.

In this context, it is important to stress that Ferranti disliked employee interference on the shopfloor just as much as he loathed the potential intrusions of shareholders in running the business. He was evidently regarded as a good employer, having persuaded one-quarter of the 400 Charterhouse Square workers to take up the offer of a job in the Crown Works. He and Gertrude organised a yearly 'bean feast' and sports day, while the *Echo* noted how: 'He believes in the wisdom of short hours, especially as a means, not only of efficient work, but also of intellectual recreation'.[74] One ex-Charterhouse Square employee remembered that Ferranti was 'a most courteous man' when dealing with workers, providing pleasant and comfortable working conditions,[75] indicating how he was steeped in the moral and ethical preachings of Victorian philanthropy. On the other hand, he expected complete cooperation and obedience in return, acting promptly to stifle any attempts to interfere in his management of the shopfloor.

An excellent example of the lengths Ferranti was willing to go in abolishing restrictive practices in his firm can be see in his actions during the 1897 Engineers' Lockout. There had been rumblings of a serious dispute between engineering employers and the powerful Amalgamated Society of Engineers (ASE) throughout the early 1890s. Indeed, when the Engineering Employers' Federation (EEF) was formed in 1896 'every circumstance was leading towards the clash of forces'.[76] This tension was to culminate in the lock-out of 1897, the principal issues of which were the demand for an eight-hour day from the ASE, while employers wanted more flexibility over the machine-manning question. Engineering was at that time a bastion of union control, with workshop practice largely dictated by members of the ASE. Employers, on the other hand, were keen to replace these anachronistic practices, especially in view of both the increased levels of fixed investment in plant and machinery committed at that time, as well as the increasing competition from American and German manufacturers.[77] Melling describes how a multirole supervisory system was being introduced by the leading engineering firms during the 1890s, replacing the control exercised by skilled artisans with foremen, draughtsmen and cost accountants.[78] This had antagonised the ASE, the members of which were unwilling to accept the termination of their traditional hegemony over workshop practices without a struggle. It was in these circumstances that the 1897 lock-out began, initiating what was generally called the 'Right to Manage' dispute which involved over 700 firms employing 48,000 workers.[79]

As a member of the EEF, S. Z. de Ferranti Ltd was anxious to ensure that the ASE was forced to accept the right of management to determine production methods. For Ferranti himself, it was also an opportunity to demonstrate to his new employees what was a fierce commitment to self-determination.

In the Hollinwood area, Ferranti actually emerged as something of a local figurehead on the employers' side, delivering a fiery anti-union speech to the Manchester Employers' Association in which he outlined his ideas on 'How to Win a Lock-Out'.[80] He denounced what he described as 'socialism', arguing that it 'would ruin the country' and encouraging fellow-employers to hire non-union labour as a means of keeping their works going. The Crown Works was even provided with a private police force, in order to protect this 'scab' labour. As a result, Francis Ince described Hollinwood as being 'very warm', largely because of the provocative stance Ferranti took with regard to showing 'the ASE that they are not the masters'.[81] Ferranti not only put the workers up in his works, or found them houses in safe areas of the town, and paid their travelling expenses, he also guaranteed them a job when the dispute ended. Even night-school students were hired and trained to use the machine tools, ensuring that production was hardly disrupted as the dispute dragged on into early 1898.

The doggedness Ferranti exhibited in 1897–8 was absolutely typical of the man, such was the fierce streak of individualism which dominated his attitude to life in general. He was even willing to take the disapproval of local newspapers, who were critical of his heavy-handed tactics in hiring private police to protect the replacement labour.[82] This criticism he regarded as a price worth paying if it meant an end to union domination in the workshop. Again, one must not forget our earlier description of Ferranti as a paternalistic employer who took a great interest in the welfare of his workforce, because even after the EEF had secured a victory over the ASE he maintained conditions of employment and rates of pay which were comparable to those in union-dominated shops.[83] On the other hand, he insisted on absolute control over all aspects of his business. When the ASE finally bowed to the pressures exerted by the EEF in January 1898, an agreement was signed which provided management with much greater influence over workshop practices. This vindicated to men like Ferranti all that they had done over the previous six months, especially as the Crown Works was actually to remain union-free until the First World War, securing for management complete mastery of the shopfloor.

3.6 Management Structure at Hollinwood

Liquidity and Parr's Bank

Although the 1897 lock-out had achieved all the employers' aims, for a firm which was only just recovering from earlier financial difficulties, not to mention the problems associated with acquiring much bigger premises, the dispute obviously happened at just the wrong time. In the first place, fully equipping the Crown Works had cost £62,000 by 1900, exceeding by 210 per cent the initial estimates Ferranti had submitted to his partners.[84] Running two factories, in Hollinwood and at Charterhouse Square, was also resulting in a considerable duplication of overhead expenditure. This forced them to decide in May 1898 that the meter department should be moved north, especially after Sparks reported that this would save the firm over £3,700 per annum.[85] The need to supervise finances was by then imperative, because even though business continued to expand after the successes at Portsmouth, capital remained in short supply. Sparks was informed by one of the clerks working in the London office that: 'I am either interviewing creditors or adopting means to keep out of their way nearly all day, which is very serious'.[86] The India Rubber & Gutta Percha Co. was actually threatening to issue a writ for the non-payment of a bill for £200, while Thomas Bolton & Sons temporarily stopped delivering much-needed copper until a debt of £1,500 had been paid.

This illiquidity revived all the worries Ferranti and Ince had been expressing during the early 1890s, albeit in the changed circumstances of a booming market. However, the solution they found to this problem would prove to have crucial long-term implications for the manner in which S. Z. de Ferranti Ltd was funded over the following seventy years. Clearly, raising money from professional investors was excluded from the discussions, because of the founder's refusal to dilute his control of the business. At the same time, it proved difficult to generate adequate profits, especially from the heavy departments. In this context, Ferranti decided to take out an overdraft of £12,000 with Parr's Bank, using as collateral the B. I. Wire shares acquired since 1891. British banks have been heavily criticised for their cautious and liquidity-conscious approach,[87] frequently with good reason. Parr's, on the other hand, was very much an exception to this rule, participating extensively in the funding of north west industrial activity, albeit on a short- to medium-term basis. As we shall see in the case of Ferranti, the bank overdraft certainly proved vital in providing liquidity at crucial times in the company's history, allowing the family to maintain control of the firm when adequate funds could not be generated from the business.

Organisational changes

Although the bank overdraft proved to be a safety valve for the cash-starved business, another factor compounding the problems Ferranti was experiencing at this time was the refusal of Francis Ince to move away from his

London legal practice in St Benet's Chambers. Although the registered office of S. Z. de Ferranti Ltd stayed there, even after the meter department had been transferred to Hollinwood, in effect the company was by 1898 completely divorced from its London roots. Eventually, such an arrangement was to cause a rift within the partnership, especially after Ince discovered that he was being excluded from major policy discussions. In the meantime, though, as a direct result of Ince's remoteness, the firm's organisational capabilities were substantially enhanced, in order to keep him informed about the financial position. His first innovation was the establishment of an accounts department at the Crown Works, the principal functions of which were to provide weekly ways-and-means reports on output, costs, stocks and departmental profitability. Ince also ensured that a competent manager was recruited to run this department, resulting in the appointment of A. B. Anderson as the intermediary between London and Hollinwood.

In response to both its financial difficulties and substantial expansion, S. Z. de Ferranti Ltd was clearly evolving into a more sophisticated organisation after its move to Hollinwood. Just as significant was the changing relationship between the two senior partners, because largely as a result of the distances involved Anderson progressively usurped Ince's former position as business adviser to Ferranti. Having joined the company in 1894, at the age of twenty-four, Anderson swiftly rose from cashier to chief accountant. He impressed his fellow-managers and the workforce not only with an immaculate dress sense, which he regarded as an essential prerequisite for all executives, but also a firm grasp of detail. Recognising the problems of communicating between London and Hollinwood, opportunistically he soon managed to become the chairman's principal source of advice on how the firm should be managed. While this pushiness did not endear him to some members of the de Ferranti family, as we shall see later it is clear that his work for both the company and the industry as a whole marks him out as one of the era's leading electrical figures.

The introduction of an accounts department in 1896 was a vital managerial innovation, building on the first steps made in this direction when W. F. Hegarty was appointed to run the meter department in 1891. The substantial expansion of output after 1896 had also obliged him to departmentalise the business, appointing professional managers to supervise the production of each main range. In consequence, as Figure 3.1 reveals, by 1897 there were five trading departments, as well as departments devoted to functional activities like accounting, sales, patents and research and development. This resulted in a marked change in organisational culture, because Ferranti and Sparks were no longer expected to maintain a heavy involvement in each product range, as managers took on the roles of designing and making the products. We noted earlier how while Ferranti insisted on retaining complete control over the company, he was keen to instil entrepreneurial instincts into his senior employees, delegating to a significant extent the tasks of bringing a product to the market. To complement this organisational innovation, new internal accounting procedures were also introduced, obliging departmental managers to submit weekly reports to the accounts department on key indicators like output, stocks and gross profitability. Although these records no longer exist, they clearly would have allowed Ince and Anderson to make a realistic assessment of the company's financial status and monitor departmental trends.

Figure 3.1. *The structure of S. Z. de Ferranti Ltd in 1900*

```
                    Senior partners
                (Ferranti, Ince and Sparks)
                            |
   ┌────────┬───────────┬───┴────────┬────────┬──────────┐
Accounts  Patents/   Installations  Sales   Secretary
          R & D           |
                  General Works Manager
                            |
   ┌────────┬───────────┬───┴────────┬────────┬──────────┐
 Meter   Engines    Alternators  Instruments  Rectifiers/
                                              Transformers
```

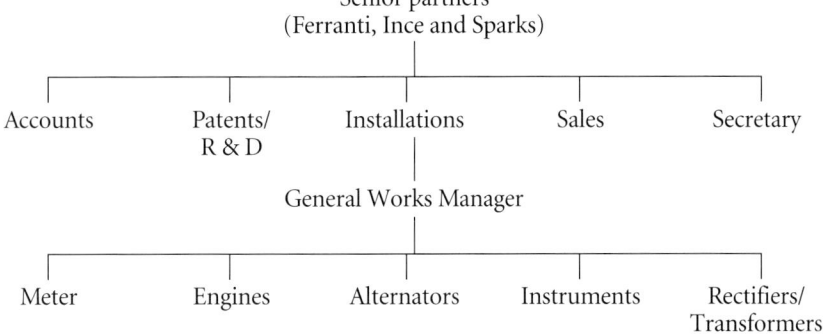

S. Z. de Ferranti Ltd was consequently making some effort to introduce new methods of managing an expanding business. Figure 3.1 provides some indication of how it was structured by 1900, reflecting the departmentalisation of both the functional and trading activities at that time. Of course, it is vital to stress how this managerial hierarchy was not as advanced as those developed by the company's American and German counterparts at this time. Indeed, as Chandler observes of the British electrical industry as a whole, neither were the kind of investments in mass-production and mass-distribution facilities being made.[88] In this context, it is vital to stress that in spite of its organisational evolution S. Z. de Ferranti Ltd continued to operate as an engineering-led business. For example, all the departmental managers were recruited from the engineering team built up by Ferranti since the mid-1880s. C. P. Sparks was general works manager, while George del Rivo replaced Hegarty in the meter department, Charles Day took responsibility for engines, H. W. Clothier for switchgear, and A. E. Hadley for installations. As we shall see later, this characteristic would also have an important bearing on the financial market's attitude towards such a company,

A Ferranti 600kW frame in the shop in September 1899. *(Museum of Science and Industry at Manchester.)*

because at that time few investors believed that a business dominated by engineers could be effectively managed.

Another crucial point to remember is the control exercised by Ferranti over all key decisions, from directing product strategy to determining sales activities. The departmental managers were certainly encouraged to take initiatives with respect to their own product ranges. On the other hand, their independence was severely proscribed by the founder's propensity to become involved in every facet of the business. In addition, this centralisation of decision-making would have limited the impact of the financial reporting procedures introduced in 1896. Of course, the combination of a small British market and the extensive use of consulting engineers made the elaboration of extensive managerial hierarchies commercially unsound, indicating how Chandler is expecting too much of firms like S. Z. de Ferranti Ltd to have developed in the same way as American rivals like General Electric and Westinghouse.[89] Nevertheless, the highly personalised managerial style adopted by Ferranti would have limited the impact of any organisational innovations. Furthermore, privately-owned firms like S. Z. de Ferranti Ltd were imposing their own financial constraints on expansion, a point highlighted by the inability to keep pace with the rate of progress in the USA and Germany. For example, few British firms had developed the new range of technologies (polyphase AC and electric traction) which were coming on stream at that time, resulting in such a technological lag that imports were beginning to eat deeply into the home market once demand started to increase after 1894.[90] Ferranti himself was so preoccupied with business matters between 1896 and 1901 that he took out only sixteen patents in that period (see Appendix B), a paltry record for one so prolific.

More financial worries

As in 1890, Ferranti was naturally well aware of these financial difficulties, informing his wife in August 1898 that 'the money problem … has given me the greatest possible anxiety'.[91] Much to Ince's amazement, Ferranti had recommended a year earlier that the company should borrow money to purchase the Crown Works, expand capacity and open a foundry. Ince complained to Sparks that Ferranti seemed to want 'works that would be bigger than Palmers [the shipbuilders] at Jarrow',[92] replying to the senior partner by noting that:

> When I come to think over your propositions I am very sorry that you should have made them because I had thought that the experience we have had had taught you by this time that the only way to make a business was to exercise diligence and economy and to allow natural growth.[93]

This reveals the huge gulf which existed between Ferranti and Ince by this time on basic issues like managing and financing the business. Above all, it is clear that the former had failed to heed any of the advice proferred by the latter since 1882. As Appendix C reveals, net profits were actually rising after the labour relations problems of 1897, while the overdraft from Parr's relieved some of the strain associated with expanding the business. However, one can also see how capital employed was rising inexorably, more than doubling between 1894 and 1900, to reach almost £250,000, posing a major challenge to this family firm.

Although in 1897 Ince had rejected the notion that the company should extend its capital, by September 1898 an extraordinary general meeting of S. Z. de Ferranti Ltd had agreed to sanction the issue of 80,000 £1 preference shares and £100,000 in debentures. In fact, because the preference shares were never issued, the firm was obliged to rely on the £79,600 in debentures which had been sold through Parr's Bank by the end of 1899. This not only placed the millstone of fixed-interest payments around the company's neck, it would also have serious implications when the firm's finances later reached crisis point.[94] The problem here is that interest payments on debentures

200V Ferranti switchgear at Bankside, c. 1894. (Museum of Science and Industry at Manchester.)

(nominally a mortgage on the firm's assets) must be made each year regardless of profitability, while ordinary shareholders only receive a return when the company has the funds. This pattern of fund-raising was actually typical of the British electrical industry as a whole, because fixed-interest securities were the only type of capital manufacturers were able to sell successfully to a financial world still deeply suspicious of their prospects after the embarrassments of 1882.[95] Even in the more expansive climate of the mid-1890s, when investors were much more willing to purchase domestic securities after the Baring Crisis of 1890 had severely dented confidence in overseas activity, prominent firms like Cromptons were unable to sell all the debentures they issued.[96] This again contrasts sharply with the extensive support American manufacturers received from Wall St financiers, while the German industrial banks worked closely with their domestic electrical firms to ensure that they had the funds to remain competitive.[97]

One cannot say that all the blame for the lack of funding in Britain lay with financiers, the highly personalised approach of entrepreneurs like Ferranti having resisted greater professional involvement in firms. On the other hand, British investors' preference for fixed-interest securities and overseas investments did not help matters, while the failure of a floor in industrial securities to emerge on the London stock exchange simply perpetuated the degree of ignorance most displayed when assessing domestic prospects.[98] In the case of S. Z. de Ferranti Ltd, of the firm's £224,771 capital employed by 1900, forty-seven per cent represented either debentures or the overdraft, while reserves accumulated since 1890 stood at only £40,000. This highlights the precarious state of its finances, creating a persistent sense of illiquidity throughout this period and forcing the firm to live a hand-to-mouth existence which did little for the already frail nerves of Francis Ince.

3.5 The expanding market and new competition

Market prospects and muncipal control

The one consolation for Ferranti in this challenging situation was the flourishing state of the electrical market, especially as both private and municipal ventures started to invest substantially in electricity supply for domestic, industrial and traction purposes. Byatt has estimated that total domestic purchases of electrical machinery rose by a factor of almost three between 1896–98 and 1899–1901.[99] Over that period, sales of electricity from public supply undertakings also leapt considerably, by a factor of 4.7, while most provincial tramways were electrified and an increasing number of processing industries started to replace steam engines with electric motors.[100] This was the kind of market stimulus British electrical manufacturers had been waiting for since the early 1880s, providing the incentive to rebuild ailing businesses and establish a competitive product range. Unfortunately, however, in retrospect it would seem that the boom had come at least five years too late, because the market prospects proved to be so alluring that those foreign manufacturers which had built up substantial first-mover advantages in the previous decade used the opportunity to expand their horizons. Furthermore, such was the illiquid state of British firms that they were too weak to withstand the onslaught. The problems were especially acute in those sectors which had been slow to develop domestically, for example in electric traction, where by 1898 ninety-five per cent of the generating equipment came from the USA.[101] Indeed, competition in the generator market proved to be particularly difficult, accentuating the difficulties for firms like S. Z. de Ferranti Ltd which had recently invested in new designs and production plant.

Another problematic feature of the late 1890s boom was the prominent position local authorities achieved as purchasers of electrical equipment, municipal trading having reached the pinnacle of its influence by that time.[102] These bodies were among the most extensive employers of consulting engineers who could advise them on the type of plant required, the detailed specifications to be followed by contractors, and the installation and running of plant. Although consulting engineers were a ubiquitous feature of British engineering markets,[103] as far as electrical manufacturers were concerned up to 1914 this institutional feature of the relationship between customer and supplier prevented the standardisation of designs and resulted in the fabrication of fresh templates almost every time an order was received.[104] This illustrates the high level of technological content which went into the production process, simply increasing costs at a time when competition from much larger firms was beginning to make major inroads into the domestic market. Ferranti pleaded to the Municipal Electrical Association in 1897 to allow greater standardisation in generator design as a means of improving production efficiency and reducing delivery times.[105] However, even when the Electric Plant Manufacturers' Association was formed in 1898 the local

Ferranti switchgear, 1899. (*Museum of Science and Industry at Manchester.*)

authorities were in such a strong position that little came of the negotiations.[106] In Germany and the USA, on the other hand, most manufacturers actually owned substantial shares in domestic electricity supply operations, having played a major role in establishing many undertakings.[107] This not only provided a captive market for their goods, it also allowed firms the opportunity to standardise output across a range of products, reducing their costs and allowing them to invest in substantial production runs. In contrast, for reasons which will become apparent later, the Electric Plant Manufacturers' Association was a dismal failure.

While local authorities were able to impose the whims and fancies of their consulting engineers on contractors, their financial strength also created even further problems. For example, local authorities usually insisted on the inclusion of a retention-money clause in every contract. This system proved especially pernicious, because not only were the usual penalty clauses included in the contracts, manufacturers would also receive only small payments during installation, while up to twenty per cent of the total price was retained for as long as six months, or until the customer was satisfied with its purchase. It was this long wait for full payment which proved especially irksome to S. Z. de Ferranti Ltd, forcing the clerks in Anderson's accounts department at Hollinwood to keep a meticulous record of payments due from customers.[108] It was a system which further exacerbated the illiquidity problems facing the firm during the 1890s, particularly as much of their efforts were committed to the steam-alternator business which was as badly affected as any other by the intensifying competition from American and German firms.

The 'new generation'

While these features of the domestic electrical market were troublesome enough for the Hollinwood venture, by the turn of the century most were beginning to pale into insignificance when compared to the intensification of competition at that time. In particular, having tested out the British market with exports, by 1900 American firms were establishing subsidiaries which in terms of financial and technical resources swamped indigenous plants. Of course, the German firm of Siemens had been operating in the UK since the 1860s, taking a prominent position in the telegraph cable industry especially. By 1899, though, after deciding to expand its electrical engineering activities, around £400,000 was spent on a new factory in Stafford (a facility which was later to become a key component in the interwar combine, English Electric, after its acquisition by the Custodian of Enemy Property during the First World War).[109]

This was a substantial investment for the British electrical industry, most indigenous firms having spent around a quarter of this sum in the previous five years. However, it was paltry when compared to the £3 million spent by the American firm of Westinghouse on an enormous plant at Trafford Park, Manchester, while its rival, General Electric, pumped £700,000 into its subsidiary, British Thomson-Houston, at Rugby. It was also at this time that Hugo Hirst decided to spend £300,000 on new premises at Witton, near Birmingham, to house the heavy departments of the GEC business. Dick, Kerr & Co also raised £800,000 to open a new electrical factory in Preston, employing American engineers to design both the product range and its manufacturing facilities.[110] To give some idea of the enormous differences in scale that this invasion created, in the period 1896–1904 British Westinghouse, British Thomson-Houston and Dick, Kerr & Co. had increased the value of their assets by £5.8 million, while a comparable figure for the four largest electrical manufacturers already established prior to 1896 (Brush, Crompton, Electric Construction and Ferranti) would be less than £1 million. It was a development the latter could well have done without, because the new investments highlighted all their financial and technological shortcomings within a very short period of time.

Steam-alternator problems

For S. Z. de Ferranti Ltd the competition from this new generation of electrical manufacturers was to prove especially troublesome in the engine and alternator departments which had been recently expanded after the move to Hollinwood. The much greater capacity of firms like British Westinghouse, BTH and Dick, Kerr, allied with their access to American technology, put relatively small British firms at a distinct competitive disadvantage. At Ferranti, in particular, because both the steam-alternator design took some time to perfect and the methods of production limited efficiency, the intensification of competition was soon felt. There was a general consensus that the Ferranti steam-alternator was based on solid design principles. For example, a test-run lasting six weeks resulted in the loss of less than a pint of oil,[111] while when in 1911 the City Co. dismantled the 1,500 kW units supplied by Ferranti, such was the joint's perfection that the flywheel shrink rings parted with a noise heard right across the whole neighbourhood.[112] On the other hand, the firm's propensity to deliver late certainly antagonised customers, highlighting the problems associated with the engineering-led strategy which demanded greater attention to technical excellence rather than selling for profit. The City Co. units, for example, although ordered for delivery at the end of 1896, took until 1899 to install. Similarly, the delivery of steam-alternators to Paisley was two years late, Worcester had to wait three years for a 300 kW unit, and in 1900 Cardiff City Council took the firm to court because the penalties for late delivery had exceeded the contract price (£5,000).[113]

The steam-alternator business actually proved to be a substantial burden on Ferranti finances throughout the late 1890s. Although over £33,000 had been spent developing the engine, on the first twenty contracts (worth £60,000) secured between February 1896 and May 1898 a loss of £28,321 was made.[114] Even with a healthy meter department, such a lame duck could not be sustained. This prompted Ferranti to institute a major review of the business in 1899. Interestingly, though, it was the Hollinwood accounts department manager, A. B. Anderson, who was invited to carry out this study, reflecting the new role he had taken on as the founder's closest advisor. As we noted earlier, since his appointment as chief accountant Anderson had exploited the geographical distance between Ferranti and Ince. Indeed, Ince complained in 1899 that he was no longer being sent regular ways-and-means reports from the accounts department,[115] depriving him of the vital information on which to base executive decisions. This was typical of Anderson's opportunism, causing some ill-feeling within the company at a time when Ferranti needed regular advice on running the business.

The Anderson report

While there was some friction over Anderson's increasingly important role in the company, at the same time it is important to emphasise how he had the firm's interests at heart, providing orthodox advice which usually made commercial sense. This can be seen in the central conclusion of Anderson's 1899 report, because apart from a poor works organisation, he noted that the fundamental obstacle to improved performance was 'the want of money'.[116] This point was demonstrated by showing how a shortage of capital had prevented the purchase of much-needed equipment, resulting in punitive half-measures which had merely overstaffed the works, rather than increased its productivity. Anderson also went on to report that the company's poor credit-worthiness had damaged relations with suppliers, leading to the refusal of bulk discounts which would have reduced production costs. This problem was compounded by a failure to coordinate purchasing across the departments, keeping stock levels unrealistically high at a time when efforts should have been made to control cash-flow.

In identifying the 'want of money' as a major problem which Ferranti had to overcome quickly, Anderson had clearly struck at the heart of the founder's desire for independence. Furthermore, when he went on to criticise the manner in which the engine department had been managed, he also highlighted the acute dangers associated with the engineering-led strategy which was at the firm's core. Anderson gave the following reasons for this department's commercial failings:

1. Having put an experimental engine on the market.
2. Entire lack, in the work, of system, organisation, experience, in fact everything that leads to cheap production ... There is no disguising the fact that for two-and-a-half years these works have been entire chaos. There has been no system of works management, no method whatever of governing costs.
3. Bad practice of pushing things out unfinished (for several reasons, principally for want of money) and leaving them to be finished by inexperienced people.
4. Lack of touch between indoor and outdoor work owing to the fact that no one person has ever been in full control.

By going on to say that the first factor had done the most damage, and that a smoother production process would have limited the impact of late-delivery penalties which frequently took away any profit on the contracts, Anderson had unleashed an unequivocal attack on both Ferranti and Sparks. As the former had been responsible for developing the engine, while the latter was in charge of works management, to Anderson neither had performed their functions adequately.

Of course, Ferranti in particular had never been interested in conventional business practices, ignoring the advice meted out by Francis Ince since 1883, when the older partner reprimanded the young engineer for 'constant tinkering' with products (see section 1.10). Above all, the founder was principally concerned with engineering excellence, arguing consistently over the period 1882–99 that as it was his money which was at risk then the firm would continue to operate in this way. In 1899, however, such was the power of the financial and market pressures currently being exerted on the British electrical industry that Ferranti was obliged to heed Anderson's advice, resulting in a considerable reorganisation of the firm's organisational capabilities. Much to Anderson's credit, these aims were also achieved, one contemporary commenting in 1900 that the Crown Works exhibited 'an admirable organisation'. Even in the engine department

> a place is allotted for everything, hence there is no apparent confusion, and there is not seen machines of various sizes and types indiscriminately mixed up. The rough material enters at one end of the shop, and after working round, leaves in the shape of a finished article at the other.[117]

One must be careful not to imply from this description that mass-production methods had suddenly been imported into the Crown Works, because each steam-alternator still had to be modified to the particular requirements of each customer. Nevertheless, the organisation of production had clearly been substantially improved, resulting in a significant improvement in departmental performance. Indeed, in 1900 the engine department made its first profit, of £3,521, by which time contracts were passing through the factory in an average of just under nine months, compared to the previous average of over twenty-three months.[118]

Merger talks and restructuring

Not only had Anderson convinced Ferranti and Sparks that their production techniques were commercially unsound, he also substantiated all the warnings Ince had been making since the late 1880s about the financial implications of remaining a private company. To Anderson, the fundamental problem of 'a want of money' had to be overcome if S. Z. de Ferranti Ltd was to compete with the new generation of electrical manufacturers, advice which prompted Ferranti into a radical solution. Since establishing contact with B. I. Wire in 1891, Ferranti had developed such an excellent relationship with its management that in October 1899 firm proposals for a merger between the two companies had been produced. Merger activity among British manufacturers was in fact rife at that time,[119] many arguing that this strategy was the most effective means of competing against intensifying foreign competition. Certainly, the proposed British Insulated & Ferranti Co. Ltd fitted well into the mood of the era. Unfortunately, though, because the cable company's stockbrokers advised them against issuing the projected £2 million capital, the merger talks were dropped.[120]

This direct link with B. I. Wire was the first time since 1885 that Ferranti had considered sharing control of the business with anyone other than his father-in-law, revealing the extent to which Anderson's report had affected his business thinking. Although the merger never happened, however, it is interesting to note how Ince and Sparks used this opportunity to sever their connections with Ferranti in the early months of 1900. In Ince's case, the influence Anderson now had on the company was the principal factor which persuaded him to fulfil the threat he had often made to resign from the company.[121] Sparks, on the other hand, probably left in disgust, because the Anderson report of 1899 had been a severe critique of his role as general manager at the Crown Works. In fact, the relationship between Sparks and Ferranti had not been too easy since the move to Hollinwood, largely because the latter rejected any claims to a greater share in the business made by his junior partner.[122] The transfer to Hollinwood had also caused family friction, because Mrs Sparks had been reluctant to leave her family and friends in London. After the Anderson report Sparks consequently secured a post as chief engineer to the County of London & Brush Provincial Electric Lighting Co.,[123] bringing to an end the partnership which had sustained Ferranti since 1885.

3.6 New company: new beginning?

Scott Lings and capital reconstruction

Although Ferranti was naturally saddened at the resignation of his two partners, as a result of the Anderson report he was well aware of the need to overhaul the organisation if it was to compete in the same market as British Westinghouse, BTH and Dick, Kerr. In the first place, Ferranti decided to elevate four of his departmental managers – A. B. Anderson (accounts), Charles Day (engines), George del Rivo (meters), and A. E. Hadley (installations) – on to the board of directors.[124] This provided more effective communication between strategic and functional management, reinforcing the structural innovations introduced in 1896. Certainly, as Anderson had already succeeded in forcing through a review of production and stock controls after his report of 1899, the company would appear to have been in better shape to deal with the new competition. Furthermore, as Appendix C illustrates, with profitability improving substantially after the Anderson reorganisation and the reserve account growing significantly, S. Z. de Ferranti Ltd 'gave every appearance of a sound and promising investment'.[125] This encouraged Ferranti to reconstruct the company, when in July 1901 Ferranti Ltd was registered with an increased capital of £400,000, indicating how Ferranti was clearly keen to participate in the expansion upon which other firms were engaged at that time.

Ferranti Ltd's prospects in 1901 looked extremely promising. The orderbook had increased in value by thirty per cent, new polyphase switchgear was coming on stream,[126] consulting engineers were beginning to accept his steam-alternators without insisting on too many additions,[127] and the meter business continued to prosper from increased sales of electricity to a larger number of consumers. However, one must remember that in financial terms Ferranti Ltd was no different from S. Z. de Ferranti Ltd. Of course, the nominal capital was expanded to £400,000, but no less than ninety-six per cent of the 100,000 controlling ordinary shares issued were allocated to Ferranti, while only 120,000 £1 non-voting preference shares were placed on the open market. This demonstrates how, in spite of the previous decade's experiences, he was still unwilling to be pushed around by financiers, a characteristic inherited by both his son (Vincent) and grandson (Sebastian). One must add that 1901 was a bad year for domestic investment, because financiers' attentions were still dominated by the Boer War. On the other hand, many expressed grave reservations about purchasing Ferranti preference shares, limiting the amount of fresh capital which came into the company as a result of the reconstruction.

When assessing the failure of this issue, it is not difficult to discover the principal reasons behind investor caution. In the first place, apart from Anderson, all of the directors were engineers. Furthermore, few knew much about what was a family firm dominated by its founder. Sir Vincent de Ferranti later replied to similar criticisms in the 1950s by arguing that there was nothing a director with City interests could add to the board. In 1901, however, investors were extremely reluctant to invest in firms unless they were known to the financial world. Ferranti was consequently persuaded to change the board's composition, having come to the decision that 'we cannot do better than get on our directorate one or two outstanding businessmen whose names are known to the public, and whose knowledge and experience will be valuable to us in the conduct of our business'.[128] This resulted in Day, Hadley and del Rivo stepping down from the board, Anderson being elevated to the post of assistant managing director (alongside Ferranti), and a prominent Manchester company promoter, Scott Lings, coming in as a director. Lings had recently been heavily involved in the big cotton company mergers of the late 1890s, floating such giant enterprises as the Fine Cotton Spinners & Doublers' Association Ltd on the Manchester stock exchange.[129] This gave him excellent credentials for a relatively unknown firm like Ferranti Ltd, a point confirmed by his success in selling the outstanding 60,000 preference shares in 1902.

The introduction of Scott Lings into Ferranti Ltd had undoubtedly been a clever move by Ferranti and Anderson. In fact, £25,000 of the £60,000 raised from the 1901 sale of preference share had been used to clear the overdraft extended by Parr's Bank, reducing the firm's liability to interest payments. However, the significant expansion of activity at the Crown Works soon absorbed the rest of this money. Such was the popularity of Ferranti electrical equipment that by 1901 the workforce had grown to just over a 1,000, compared to approximately 400 at Charterhouse Square in 1896. At a cost of £35,000, the firm had also recently acquired the neighbouring Windsor Mill, to house the expanding switchgear department. As Appendix C reveals, the general reserve account had consequently dwindled from £50,000 in 1899 to just over £6,000 by 1902. Although a record profit of

£25,000 was recorded in 1901, the fresh injection of another £60,000 was absolutely essential if the company was going to survive in what was an increasingly competitive market.

Competition and prices

Although by 1901 Ferranti Ltd had an extensive product range, and the meter department continued to perform admirably, one must always remember that in view of substantial investment in designs and production facilities, the principal determinant of the company's fortunes at that time was the steam-alternator business. In this context, S. Z. de Ferranti Ltd had actually achieved a fifteen per cent share of the generator market in 1899,[130] by which time Ferranti equipment was being used in twenty-eight of the seventy-nine electricity supply stations operating in Britain.[131] Prestigious orders also continued to come into the Crown Works in 1900–01, for example, for four 2,500 hp steam-alternators for the London County Council, and two 1,100 hp units for the Capetown Corporation in South Africa. Just at that time, though, the new generation of electrical manufacturers started to make deep inroads into the British generator market, completely altering Ferranti Ltd's prospects for continued success.

The *Electrical Review* had warned in December 1900 that prices would tumble once the new factories reached full production.[132] At Dick, Kerr & Co., for example, the board decided in 1902 to tender 'on all inquiries at a sufficiently low price to warrant our quotations being considered'.[133] To make matters worse, after 1900 a sharp recession in Germany prompted AEG to undercut British prices.[134] Anderson consequently reported in 1901 that while in 1899 Ferranti Ltd had received £7 per kW for its steam-alternators, by 1901 this had plummeted to £4 10s. (£4.50p).[135] Furthermore, constraints on local authority expenditure, imposed in the wake of the Boer War, also made it increasingly difficult to exact payment for equipment from municipal customers, accentuating the illiquidity experienced by many firms. Most importantly of all, though, the price collapse was accompanied by an even more precipitous fall in orders placed with Ferranti Ltd. Byatt shows how British Westinghouse, BT-H and Dick, Kerr were able to increase their share of the generator market from six per cent in the period 1893–98 to fifty-two per cent by the period 1904–08, while, respectively, the Ferranti share plummeted from fourteen to just one per cent.[136]

The new generation clearly posed major problems for the Ferranti steam-alternator business, undermining all the efforts made by Anderson to improve the organisation of production in 1899–1900. American-designed machinery was proving especially popular with British central station engineers, given their lead in developing the more powerful type of generators which competed directly with the Ferranti steam-alternator. British contemporaries actually complained of an in-built bias among engineers against British products, especially when American-designed equipment started to fall in price.[137] This badly undermined all the changes made at Ferranti Ltd within the previous three years. Indeed, such was the speed with which the impending crisis overtook the company that profits slumped badly in 1902, to just under £4,000 (see Appendix C), leading to the even more rapid absorption of the money raised by Lings through the sale of preference shares. Ferranti was even forced to resort to the unprecedented measure of requesting Scott Lings to place 41,000 of his ordinary shares with private investors, bringing in additional funds at a time when the sheer force of new competition was threatening the company's very survival as a major force in the British electrical engineering industry.

3.7 Crisis and change in the company

The financial crisis

The sale of equity in Ferranti Ltd is a clear sign of the desperate state reached by the company finances. Much to Ling's credit, however, he was able to persuade several leading cotton manufacturers to buy these securities at a time when there seemed little prospect of a good return.[138] In retrospect, though, Ferranti had moved too late, because by that time the business was saddled with an increasing fixed-interest debt – £102,500 in debentures, £120,000 in preference shares, and an overdraft of almost £38,000 – which accounted for eighty per cent of the capital employed. Of course, the sluggish rate of investment in British electricity supply up to the mid-1890s had limited opportunities for the kind of expansion which American and German electrical manufacturers had been enjoying since the early 1880s, preventing the accumulation of reserves for investment in both production and distribution facilities and in new technology. By the time demand started to increase substantially in the late 1890s, foreign rivals had consequently gained what Chandler calls 'first-mover' advantages which they were able to exploit effectively in world markets.[139] On the other hand, the founder's desire for independence had clearly played a major role in determining the capital structure of Ferranti Ltd, forcing him to accumulate an enormous debt base in his drive to build a business capable of supplying high quality products. Whether British financiers would have been willing to risk their money buying equity interests in such a company remains a moot point, especially after the 1882 mania. The reality, however, was that Ferranti resisted Ince's efforts to introduce professional investors, arguing that the firm was an embodiment of his drive for engineering excellence. It was a position which in the much-changed circumstances of 1900–03 rapidly became untenable, providing an historical precedent for the experiences of his grandson during the 1960s and 1970s.

The appointment of Tait and Whittaker

The crisis-point for Ferranti Ltd occurred in September 1903, when it was calculated that a loss of £57,810 had been made on the previous nine months trading. This forced the debenture-holders' trustees to place Ferranti Ltd in the hands of receivers. One of these trustees was Hector Christie, manager of Parr's Bank in Manchester, whose support had been so crucial over the previous seven years. By 1903, though, there was very little else he could have done to protect the interests of Ferranti Ltd investors and creditors. Also active in this move was Charles Morrison, a London financier who held £4,000 worth of Ferranti debentures. It was Morrison who introduced A. W. Tait to the company as one of two receiver-managers. A chartered accountant, Tait had already built up a reputation as 'a force in industrial

Arthur Whittaker, *c.* 1943 a director of Ferranti Ltd from 1905. (*Museum of Science and Industry at Manchester.*)

finance' by the time of this difficult appointment, having worked for G. A. Touche & Co. in London on company flotations.[140] He was also a director of Bruce Peebles & Co., an Edinburgh firm of engineers which ironically, as we noted at the end of section 3.3, had diversified into electrical engineering after Colonel Peebles had listened in 1894 to Ferranti talking in Edinburgh to the Royal Scottish Society of Arts about the prospects for electrical energy. This gave Tait some knowledge of the electrical business, leading him to play a pivotal role in Ferranti affairs as chairman from 1905 to 1927. He was extensively assisted in this task by Arthur Whittaker, another chartered accountant who was the second receiver-manager appointed in 1903 as a representative of Parr's Bank. Together, these men were responsible for salvaging a much-streamlined business from the wreckage inherited in 1903, revealing how the collapse of 1903 was by no means a disaster when one comes to consider the valuable talent introduced by the creditors.

When the receiver-managers first addressed the task given them by the creditors, it was quickly recognised that most of the business had a viable future. This is a clear reflection of the technical successes achieved by Ferranti and his team since 1896. However, Tait and Whittaker were also convinced that the product range had to be streamlined if Ferranti Ltd was ever going to have a commercial future. In their first report, published by the end of September, they concluded that:

> The deficit shown … arises … from the works not having dealt with a sufficiently large output in proportion to the heavy standing charges, and also from faults of a technical nature in the construction and design of the company's manufactures … [However] the difficulties of manufacture have now, in a large measure, been overcome, and the management of the various departments is in the hands of a highly trained and efficient staff.[141]

This analysis led them to recommend at a later meeting of creditors in November that the steam-alternator business should be terminated, focusing the staff's attention on developing the profitable meter, switchgear, transformer and instrument departments. Of course, while this brought into question the wisdom of S. Z. de Ferranti Ltd's move into steam-alternators in the mid-1890s, only with hindsight could one criticise the attempt to exploit the firm's reputation as manufacturers of the largest generators. It was only competition from a new generation of largely American firms which had undermined this strategy, a development which could not have been anticipated when the Crown Works opened in 1896. One should also note that Ferranti Ltd was by no means unique in experiencing such difficulties after

The inventor's drawing of the Ferranti AC Meter (new type), 1905. *(Museum of Science and Industry at Manchester.)*

1900, because by October 1904 the intense competition had so eroded the market position of older manufacturers like Brush and Electric Construction that they were leaving the heavy electrical business to concentrate on specialised areas.[142] Furthermore, British Westinghouse, BT-H, Siemens, GEC and Dick, Kerr all experienced financial difficulties as a result of the fall in both prices and demand after 1904, indicating how the British electrical market caused problems for even the world's largest manufacturers.[143]

The decision to end steam-alternator production had been an entirely rational response to the intense competition in this market after 1900. Tait and Whittaker would also have been aware of another factor influencing this decision, because it was becoming increasingly obvious that the commercial prospects of reciprocating engine production were by 1903 extremely limited, largely because Charles Parsons had been able to demonstrate that his turbine was much more economical.[144] Ferranti had actually recognised the imminent obsolescence of his steam-alternator rather earlier, as we shall see in the next chapter, leading him to initiate a turbine development project at the Crown

Works in 1902. By 1904, Parsons had also achieved a 21.6 per cent share of the generator market,[145] forcing all the other major manufacturers to introduce their own turbo-alternators. One could not argue that Parsons had contributed extensively to the demise of the steam-alternator business in 1903, however, because he never accounted for more than five per cent of the market until 1904. Nevertheless, many recognised that the future lay with this technology, rather than with reciprocating engines, severely limiting the steam-alternator's shelf life.

Tait's deteriorating relationship with Ferranti

Ironically, the last steam-alternators produced by Ferranti were delivered one month early, to the Capetown Corporation, in the early days of 1904. This brought to an end the long and technologically-fruitful association Ferranti had enjoyed with large generating equipment, a development he accepted as an inevitable corollary of the recent trends in electrical engineering. What Ferranti did not accept too easily, however, was the extensive power exerted by Tait and Whittaker over company strategy. In particular, the firm's founder was extremely annoyed at their decision, made in December 1903, that 'it was considered very desirable in future not to take up new branches of business'.[146] In the first report on Ferranti Ltd written by Tait and Whittaker in September 1903, they had drawn attention to excessive expenditure on new product development, especially in relation to the turbine, as well as electrically-powered textile machinery. Much to the founder's disgust, all this work was brought to an abrupt end by the receiver-managers in December. Furthermore, it rapidly became apparent that Tait was very much against what he later described as 'the curse of individualism', arguing that it had dogged the recent progress of British business by preventing the necessary rationalisation of production and the infusion of more venture capital.[147] This naturally brought him into conflict with Ferranti, substantiating the founder's fears that Tait and Whittaker were about to change the company culture from a desire to contribute to engineering innovation to one which was more concerned with liquidity.

By the early months of 1904, given these fundamental differences of opinion, it had become patently obvious that Ferranti, Tait and Whittaker would never be able to work effectively together. In the past, Ferranti had argued with Francis Ince and A. B. Anderson over both production control and the need for more finance, winning the argument simply because he owned the bulk of the equity. The difference in 1903–04, of course, was that Tait and Whittaker had been granted power by the courts to effect any necessary changes. The creditors had actually petitioned the courts to allow Tait and Whittaker an extended period in which to effect these changes,[148] giving them even greater authority to squeeze Ferranti out of the Crown Works. As a consequence, when Ferranti Ltd was finally reconstructed in February 1905, although it retained his name the company was no longer controlled by the man who had spent the previous twenty years building up its reputation. Ferranti retained a seat on the board, but only as technical advisor to the company, while Tait took the position of executive chairman. The nominal capital was also drastically reduced, from £400,000 to £130,000 (see Appendix C). Crucially, each share was allocated a vote at company meetings, substantially reducing the influence Ferranti could exert on policy. Ferranti was actually allotted the 10,000 £1 deferred shares, in lieu of his previous ordinary shareholding, while the 60,000 £1 preference shares were distributed among the creditors, and the former preference shareholders received the 60,000 £1 ordinary shares.

Ferranti Ltd was consequently a very different kind of company in 1905 from the type of organisation which had prevailed up to 1903. In the first place, not only had a complete divorce between ownership and control been effected by the receiver-managers, the founder was marginalised to such an extent that professional managers dominated senior management. While Anderson remained as chief accountant, the board in 1905 was composed of Tait, Whittaker, S. Z. de Ferranti and J. M. Henderson,[149] indicating how trained accountants were by far the most influential source of policy-making. This was 'managerial capitalism' at work, in contrast to the highly personalised style which had prevailed up to 1903. Indeed, with A. W. Tait at the helm, Ferranti experienced great difficulty in gaining access to those parts of the Crown Works which were after 1905 to be run by professional managers. This would lead to the founder's virtual exile from the Crown Works over the following nine years, giving Tait the opportunity to introduce much more cautious policies aimed at making extensive use of all the most recent accounting and organisational innovations. Of course, Ferranti had not been slow to hire managers once the business started to grow in the mid-1890s, leading to the introduction of departmental reporting procedures to give Ince a clearer view of the financial position. A. B. Anderson had also been given his head in reorganising production and stock control in 1899, indicating how Ferranti was willing to learn from his managers. Nevertheless, the fierce individualism manifested in his outright refusal to sell any equity in the company until the last hour, coupled with a continual desire to develop new products, had meant that engineering priorities were pursued above those advocated by either Ince or Anderson. Only the collapse of 1903 would bring a change in organisational culture, something the family learnt from in the decades ahead.

The hiatus

Ferranti was to feature only fitfully in affairs at Hollinwood over the following nine years. Although, as we shall see in the next chapter, this gave him the freedom to venture into a wide range of interesting projects, it must have been hard for him to leave the business he had built up since 1882 into one of the country's leading names in electrical engineering. He *had* wanted 'works that would be bigger than Palmers at Jarrow', as Francis Ince had complained. He was also committed to building a competitive British electrical industry. Unfortunately, though, slow growth in the market up to the mid-1890s had deprived such companies of the resources to compete with more powerful American and German rivals, while individualism proved to be incompatible with the demands of such a technologically-progressive industry, emphasising once again how a combination of factors contributed to the traumatic experiences of 1903–05.

4

The Independent Engineer

The crisis of 1903 was clearly a traumatic time for Ferranti, having struggled over the previous twenty years to build a successful and innovative business which would support both his employees and expanding family. However, when it became apparent that Tait and Whittaker were taking over the executive management of the company he had founded, Ferranti decided to use this freedom to venture off on his own into a fresh career. He had already been working on several new ideas at the Crown Works prior to the company's collapse, some of which he was able to develop further at other companies' works. In addition, over the following eleven years as a freelance engineer he became involved in a series of other projects, taking out a total of sixty patents covering such diverse fields as turbines, steam valves, textile machinery, rubber tyres and gyroscopes (see Appendix B).

When assessing this period in his life, it is interesting to see how all the frustrations Ferranti had experienced as an electrical engineer were to reappear, in particular with regard to the propensity of his contemporaries to support new ideas and the conducive nature of British demand for high technology products. When invited to give the James Watt Lecture in 1913, Ferranti argued that one of Watt's greatest discoveries had been Matthew Boulton, the 'courageous capitalist' who had financed the production of his condenser steam engine. Ferranti pleaded for more 'Matthew Boultons' to come forward, a plea that came from the heart of an engineer who had spent a lifetime canvassing support for his schemes. It will become apparent that the British scene was uneven in this respect, because although some of his ideas were rewarded with both adequate financial support and considerable commercial success, others were left to flounder in the sands of apathy. The experience proved especially galling to Ferranti when he drew a comparison with the much more supportive American scene, substantiating all his fears concerning the reasons why Britain was falling behind in the development of key new technologies.

Apart from providing a further insight into the British approach towards innovation, a study of this period in his life will also reveal how Ferranti was able to exploit his stature in the electrical industry to achieve significant changes in attitude and organisation. This will indicate how, while no longer directly involved in managing Ferranti Ltd, he was instrumental in creating a more stable trading environment for the firm he had created. Ferranti also assisted by continuing to publicise his dream of an 'All Electric Age', making an impassioned plea for a radical overhaul of electricity supply operations in the presidential address he gave to the IEE in 1910. Indeed, as he had consistently advocated this theme in both his public speeches and major engineering achievements, he was undoubtedly one of the more influential voices in the campaign to rationalise and modernise electricity supply. This would have been enormously important to Ferranti Ltd, with its more limited product range of meters, transformers and instruments. Especially when combined with the ambitious market-led strategy which Tait, Whittaker and Anderson had devised, it helped to effect a solid recovery from the traumas of the period 1896–1903. The whole period was a peculiar episode in the life of Ferranti, illustrating how he remained dedicated to his love of engineering innovation as a freelance operator, sustaining a commitment which had characterised an already distinguished career.

4.1 Textile machinery

In their first assessment of Ferranti Ltd, Tait and Whittaker had drawn the creditors' attentions to: 'Patents, concessions and experimental work [which had] made demands on the resources of the company in excess of its working capital'.[1] This comment referred to two projects Ferranti had recently instigated at the Crown Works, on turbines and electrified textile machinery, leading to some expenditure on non-core activities which in the circumstances was regarded by the receiver-managers as wasteful. In fact, while only £4,728 had been spent on the experiments by the end of 1903,[2] the receiver-managers decided that 'it was considered very desirable in future not to take up new branches of business ... but rather to concentrate on making the existing business of the company more remunerative'.[3] This would naturally have irritated Ferranti, confirming his suspicions that Tait and Whittaker would thwart his efforts to sustain a technology-led strategy. Although he had actually attempted to interest Babcock & Wilcox and J. & P. Coats Ltd in the patents, nothing had come of the negotiations by the time Ferranti Ltd had been placed in voluntary liquidation, leading to the temporary suspension of all work between September 1903 and May 1904.

Albert Hall and the team

Before going on to analyse the progress made in converting the patents into products, however, it is important to emphasise that he was by no means a lone operator. We noted how in building the Deptford station Ferranti had assembled a group of engineers and draughtsmen to provide the necessary expertise in the more routine aspects of construction and installation, leaving him free to develop the basic ideas. By 1903, a similar team had also been formed, building on the small experimental group which had been working on the steam-alternator since the mid-1890s. One of the key members of this team was Albert Hall, an expert on thermodynamics who was to work with Ferranti for almost thirty years. Indeed, Hall would appear to have replaced Sparks as right-hand-man to Ferranti, acting as team-leader on a wide range of projects from the time they left the Crown Works in 1904. Other important members of the team were Albert Tucker, who later made a significant contribution to Ferranti transformer design, and R. H. Parsons, a cousin of the leading turbine engineer of this era, Charles Parsons. Over the period 1904–14, Ferranti and his engineers (never numbering more than six) acted as a professional consultancy firm, venturing into a series of schemes which appeared to be ripe for exploitation. It was an approach which Ferranti was later to instil into the very fabric of his company, after returning to the helm in the crisis year of 1914, laying the basis for a diversification strategy which became a hallmark of its expansion from the 1920s.

The Coats connection

Although the initial negotiations with J. & P. Coats Ltd had been unsuccessful, this prominent cotton-thread manufacturer was clearly interested in the ideas Ferranti had been developing. He had been introduced to the firm by Robert and William Watson, two paper-makers of Linwood, Renfrewshire, who had come to know Ferranti through their work with the British Insulated Wire Co. In fact, the Watsons would appear to have acted as 'Matthew Boulton' to Ferranti in 1904, giving him an interest-free loan of £5,500 with which to purchase all his turbine and textile machinery patents from Ferranti Ltd, as well as providing the initial contact with J. & P. Coats Ltd, their near neighbours in Paisley.[4] J. & P. Coats, first formed in 1826, was actually one of the most powerful companies in the country at that time, with a market value of £42 million and a market share in cotton thread of eighty-five per cent.[5] When Ernest Coats agreed in May 1904 to provide £5,000 to support the spinning and doubling projects which Ferranti had initiated in the Crown Works, progress consequently seemed assured.[6] J. & P. Coats also put up a further £1,000 for work on the Ferranti turbine at that time, on condition that another backer was found for this project. As we shall see in the next section, this led Ferranti into a relationship with the country's leading engineering firm, Vickers, revealing again how Ferranti was frequently able

512 spindle twisting machine, made at Hollinwood, 11 August, 1923. *(Museum of Science and Industry at Manchester.)*

to raise funds from prominent businessmen who possessed the financial independence and engineering skills to take a risk on his ideas. Indeed, with hindsight one can only wonder what would have happened had he brought in more partners to finance the 1890s expansion programme at Hollinwood.

One of the most obvious challenges which must have confronted Ferranti when moving to Hollinwood was to persuade cotton manufacturers to convert from a traditional reliance on steam power to electrification. At that time, 'electric power [was] very little used in Lancashire for driving textile machinery'.[7] As Ferranti also stated in an application to have his basic patents extended, after arriving in the region: 'I had continually under consideration the question of how electricity could be used to improve or speed-up textile processes'.[8] Typically, he believed firmly in his ability to overcome all the engineering and economic obstacles which had confounded other innovators. The north-west was very much the centre of cotton production, with the famous 'Oldham Limiteds' dominating the spinning sector.[9] It is important to note, though, that many have criticised British cotton-textile manufacturers for their reluctance to adapt production processes to the technological opportunities of that period. In many cases, there were sound economic reasons for clinging to traditional ideas, particularly in relation to production, while the small-scale nature of most cotton firms had inhibited a more aggressive attitude towards new ideas. Byatt has calculated that, while in 1911 the average cotton spinning mill had 60,000 spindles, electric drive would only be economical in plants operating over 100,000 spindles, providing a significant obstacle to any attempts at influencing techniques.[10] Notwithstanding these hard facts of life in British cotton-textiles, Ferranti embarked on a most ambitious diversification strategy in 1901, initiating a series of experiments which lasted intermittently for over thirty years.

The first experiments

The very simple, yet technologically complicated, aim of the project was to raise the speed of spinning from the conventional 5,000 rpm up to 30,000 rpm. To achieve this he installed a sixty-spindle Platts spinning frame and a smaller Dobson & Barlow doubling frame in the Crown Works on which to experiment. A master-patent was secured in 1903 (see Appendix B), to be followed over the next three years by a further eight patents on detailed aspects of spinning and doubling. Ironically, though, although achieving a speed of 15,000 rpm with electric motors, he soon replaced this power-source with air-driven turbines as a more effective means of achieving 30,000 rpm. Furthermore, the spinning machine experiments were also dropped at an early stage, largely because the British cotton industry was dependent on the intermittent mule spinner, while his designs were more appropriate to the continuous ring-spinning machine.[11] In this context, it is surprising that Ferranti does not appear to have approached one of the large textile machinery manufacturers in the region, because firms like Platt's of Oldham were among the world's leading exporters of ring-spinners.[12] On the other hand, the interest shown by J. & P. Coats Ltd in his doubling machine would have persuaded Ferranti in 1903 that it would be more sensible to concentrate on that part of the project for which finance was forthcoming.

By focusing attention on doubling, and in particular wet-doubling, Ferranti was inevitably bowing to the pressures imposed by J. & P. Coats, because this was the basic production technology employed throughout their mills in Paisley and Ferguslie. One should also note that he was taking on a much more complicated technology than the spinning process, undermining the project's viability, given his lack of expertise in wet-doubling.[13] As a forward-looking company, J. & P. Coats was nevertheless committed to technological innovation. Ernest Coats, in particular, as director in charge of production, was particularly keen to encourage Ferranti in his attempts at raising productivity. The firm was already famous for the 'Ferguslie System', by which the efficient organisation of the Coats mills was widely known. More

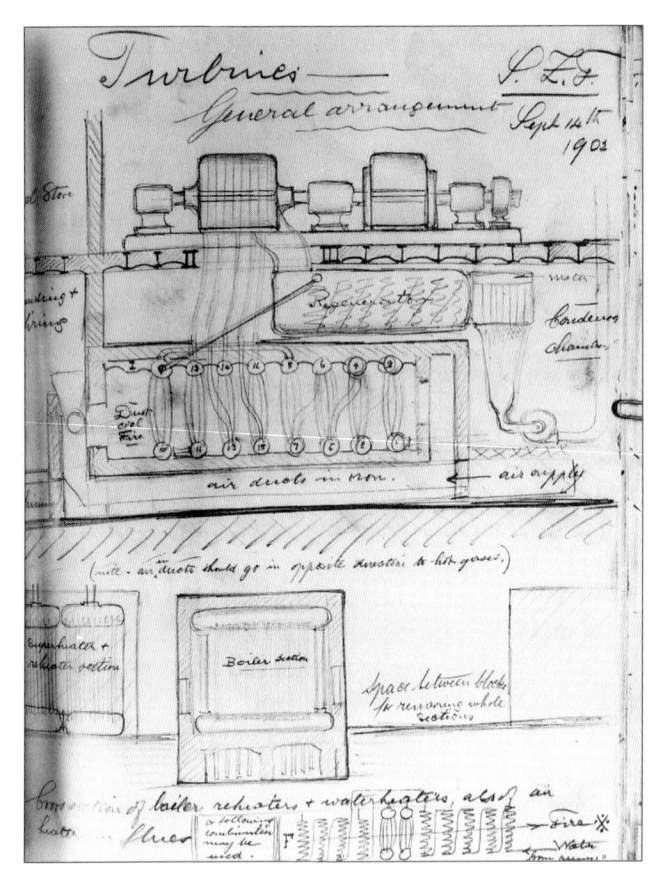

Page from S. Z. de Ferranti's notes showing early ideas for steam turbines, 1902. (Museum of Science and Industry at Manchester.)

importantly, though, with plenty of finance from their profitable business they could afford to take on what must have been high-risk projects like the Ferranti doubling machine.[14]

Having dispensed with electric power by 1903, one of his first tasks was to devise special miniature air turbines which would be capable of providing a continuous drive to the flyers (see Appendix B). The main difficulty, though, was to balance dynamically the tubular flyers as they spun round at the unprecedented speeds of up to 30,000 rpm. Indeed, this proved to be one of the most intractable features of the whole project even though Ferranti was responsible for introducing gas bearings into textile technology for the first recorded time. Imaginative use of chromium and carbon was made in the manufacture of more vulnerable components, while air, rather than oil, bearings were also introduced to reduce the amount of friction involved. However, in spite of spending over £52,000 by 1914, a finished machine was not yet ready.

The failure of these early experiments was a source of great regret to both Ferranti and Ernest Coats. Over the following years, though, further development work was funded, culminating in a major test-run in 1927. Unfortunately, though, Ferranti could only report that more refinements were required. The Coats board later commented of this experiment that: 'It was felt that over the years that as one trouble developed something else was fitted to the unit to counter the trouble, so that ... the whole unit was so complicated that special mechanical attention was necessary'. They calculated, rather unfairly, that a 10,000 spindle machine would require 10,000 machinists to operate it, such was the degree of complexity.[15] More accurately, it was discovered in 1927 that when the Ferranti machines could be coaxed into performing consistently their output per square foot of mill floor was considerably higher than in the conventional wet-doubling process. Any advantage gained here, though, was lost when the former's greater labour costs were included in the equation. In effect, the Ferranti machine produced yarn quickly, but in smaller quantities, increasing its removal and loading costs at a time when great emphasis was placed on improving labour productivity. This finally convinced Ernest Coats and his board that the experiments had been 'an utter failure'. Even though in 1931 a final test-run was carried out, they were forced to write off the total cost of £125,000 as a loss.[16]

A failure?

That the textile machinery experiments never amounted to a breakthrough in wet-doubling may be regarded as an indictment of both the technical skills of Ferranti and Coats's foresight as an expert in this field. Balanced against this harsh judgement might well be the British cotton industry's 'historical tendency ... to be most conservative towards innovation',[17] because had Ferranti been allowed the opportunity to develop his spinning machinery then one might have expected greater success. After all, as his assistant at Paisley argued, while the Ferranti patents were more appropriate to continuous ring-spinning, over eighty per cent of the sixty million spindles in operation at that time were of the intermittent mule variety.[18] There were also few cotton spinning companies in Lancashire with the resources to sponsor such ambitious development projects, forcing Ferranti to adapt his ideas to the wet-doubling demands of J. & P. Coats. He was clearly constrained by the cotton industry's attitude towards technological innovation. Even though one company was willing to sponsor the experiments, this pushed Ferranti into a direction for which he was ill-prepared, undermining the value of his potentially valuable spinning machinery innovations.

4.2 Turbines and valves

Parsons vs. *Ferranti*

Although the relationship with J. & P. Coats Ltd failed to produce positive results, one can hardly say the same about the turbine project, because it brought both direct and indirect benefits to all concerned. By associating himself with this revolutionary form of prime-mover, typically Ferranti was also placing himself at the forefront of steam engineering technology, convinced as he was that it would dramatically improve the competitiveness of electricity in the energy markets.

Ever since Charles Parsons had lodged his momentous patent in 1884 for an impulse-type turbine, this machine had been growing in popularity. By the 1890s, many were beginning to accept its value as a viable replacement for the reciprocating steam engine.[19] One of Parson's most successful early installations was at Portsmouth in 1894, where a small 150 kW turbo-alternator ran next to the steam-alternators supplied by Ferranti (see section 3.3). This had led the latter to predict in his 1894 speech to the Royal Scottish Society of Arts that the former must triumph if the industry was to progress.[20] Although Ferranti also patented an impulse-type gas turbine in 1895 (see Appendix B), the pressure of business prevented further experimentation until 1902, when it became apparent that Parsons turbines were increasing their market share. The successes Parsons achieved in London especially were making engineers sit up and take notice, especially when his firm achieved a thirteen per cent share of the power station generator market in the period 1904–08. By then, other electrical manufacturers were either purchasing licenses to use his patents or introducing foreign designs in order to keep in touch with this technology.[21] It was a challenge Ferranti could not resist, leading him in 1902 to purchase a 2000 kW Parsons turbine on which to experiment.

The initial idea of developing a gas turbine had actually been dropped by 1902, because in a patent of that year (see Appendix B) he produced a steam-powered variant on which he worked for the next twelve years. His basic premise revolved around the concept that the higher the working temperature the greater is the economy to be obtained, especially when a superheater was incorporated into the machine.[22] This device had actually been tried by Parsons as long ago as 1892, when installing three 100 kW turbo-alternators in the Cambridge power station. At that stage, though, the pioneer had soon dispensed with them after discovering problems with their design. Ferranti, on the other hand, confident of his own ability to overcome the mechanical problems of working at high temperatures, was able to steal

Welding blades in the Stator of a 3000kW Ferranti Superheating Steam Turbine, Vickers, Sheffield, 1911. *(Museum of Science and Industry at Manchester.)*

a march on his rivals by radically improving this design. In the Ferranti turbine, steam was superheated to 420°C. before passing through the first stage, after which it was reheated between each successive stage in the cycle, while at the end all the steam was transferred to the feed-water by means of a regenerator to minimise any heat-loss. This economising was further improved in 1906, when the process of re-heating was devised, by which the boiler would have to give less heat to a pound of steam, but the work obtained would not be reduced in anything like the same proportion. Together with the 1902 patent, and fifteen other related patents taken out in this period (see Appendix B), this put Ferranti ahead of the field in terms of ideas. However, even though a 1000 hp turbine was constructed at the Crown Works to his designs, practical success still needed to be demonstrated.

The Vickers experiments

As Babcock & Wilcox had pulled out of the negotiations over the turbine patents in 1903, and J. & P. Coats Ltd were only willing to provide temporary support until a backer was found, Ferranti was obliged to look for another partner. One of the most obvious targets was Vickers Sons and Maxim Ltd (hereafter Vickers), a leading engineering firm which had recently diversified into this field by opening up an electrical division at its large River Don works in Sheffield.[23] Like J. & P. Coats Ltd, Vickers was one of the largest businesses in the country at that time, having a market value of £12 million and a reputation for producing high quality products in the defence and civil markets.[24] As they were diversifying into a range of new product markets as a result of a decline in their staple munitions trade after the Boer War, the opportunity to acquire turbine patents not already covered by Parsons came at an opportune time for Douglas Vickers, the head of their electrical division. The growing popularity of turbo-alternators was naturally an excellent selling-point in 1904. Ferranti, though, was keen to emphasise the distinctive nature of his patents, naively informing Douglas Vickers: 'I think that your risk in the matter would be extremely small. I am satisfied that there is little doubt as to the success of the resuperheating turbine'.[25] While in hindsight one might question the basis for this claim, it was enough to persuade Douglas Vickers to provide £6,000 for a series of experiments at the River Don works, revealing once again how Ferranti had the ability to time his bids to powerful businessmen and convince them of the need to fund his schemes.

In the period up to the First World War, Ferranti clearly spent more time working on his turbine project than on textile machinery, indications of which are the substantial bundle of notes and sketch-books he left for posterity and the large number of patents covering the experiments (see Appendix B).[26] It was also an extremely challenging project, because the adoption of temperatures in excess of 400°C. tested his mechanical skills to

3000kW Ferranti Resuperheating Turbine installed at Vickers, Sheffield, 1912.
(Museum of Science and Industry at Manchester.)

the full. One area in which Ferranti experienced considerable difficulty was manufacturing the blade positioned at the rim of each separate stage, because he discovered that until he was able to devise an automatic electric welding machine many actually fell off during test-runs. He also decided to experiment with the composition of blades, adding to the commonly-used soft steel body an outer coating of nickel which by 1905 had proved extremely effective. This, however, was only one aspect of a highly complicated project which occupied Ferranti and his team at Sheffield for over eight years. Like Ernest Coats, Douglas Vickers proved to be very supportive over that period, sinking by 1912 approximately £50,000 into the project.[27] The River Don works superintendent, George Nelson (later, as Lord Nelson [1887–1962] the head of English Electric), was also obliged to devote some of his technical resources to the Ferranti team. At that juncture, however, Vickers decided to terminate the experiments, even though the mechanical design had by then been perfected and two Ferranti turbines were working at various sites in the company.[28] The main reason given for this decision was a resurgence in demand for munitions, as a result of Britain's intensifying arms race with Germany. Crucially, though, it was also apparent that British power stations were just too small for the Ferranti turbine, forcing Vickers to commit its resources to sectors which were much more lucrative.

The Ferranti contribution

Vickers' decision to drop the turbine seems highly rational, given their preoccupation with armaments production. As Irving has commented of such companies in general, it was only common commercial sense to concentrate on what was a highly profitable staple business.[29] Only in hindsight can one describe the move as extremely short-sighted, given the undoubted long-term importance of the resuperheating turbine to power station practice. By 1913, the Admiralty, Yarrow's and the French engineering company Schneider were all conducting tests on the Ferranti turbine and its blades.[30] The *Engineer* was also claiming that 'a machine built somewhat on the lines of Mr Ferranti's turbine will have its day'.[31] This demonstrates the wide interest aroused by his innovations, a point reinforced at the first World Power Conference in 1924, when Parsons magnanimously admitted that Ferranti had been largely responsible for refining the concept of resuperheating turbines.[32] Unfortunately, however, prior to the First World War not only were British power stations too small for such a machine,[33] but the conventional Parsons turbine was also cheaper. In fact, it was only after 1919 that the resuperheating turbine became accepted practice in Britain, after the firm partly created by Vickers, the Metropolitan-Vickers Electrical

Manufacturing Co. (Metro-Vic's), built a 10,000 kW unit for the North Tees power station of the Newcastle Electricity Supply Co. Although Ferranti received £2,000 in royalties for this order, by that time his main patents had expired, resulting in no further payments for work on the design.

Ferranti had been responsible for a crucial development in turbine design while working with Vickers on the resuperheater, a fact recognised by most of the key authorities in that field. It was perhaps indicative of the progress in British electricity supply by 1914 that such a product was years ahead of its time, and Vickers paid the price (to the tune of £50,000) of backing such an advanced project. Ironically, though, Ferranti received ample compensation for his work, when in 1924 he negotiated a fee of $150,000 (c. £31,000) from the major American company, General Electric, after discovering that they had been using his patents for several years.[34] This would have been further evidence to Ferranti of the enormous contrast in attitudes and environment which he had constantly alluded to when demanding a more encouraging approach towards new ideas in Britain. As we have commented several times in this history already, American companies possessed the significant advantage of a much larger domestic market for advanced technology, while since the 1880s British electrical manufacturers had been held back by a distinctly negative approach towards the new power source. It was a situation individual businessmen could do little to alter, directly affecting innovators like Ferranti at a crucial time for the electrical industry.

The stop-valve

Although in only a technical sense was the turbine project consequently successful for both Ferranti and Vickers prior to 1914, it is important to stress how in resolving one particular problem associated with this work he did manage to achieve some commercial success. Working with such high pressures on the resuperheater, the team discovered that conventional stop-valves were inefficient, prompting Ferranti to set about devising his own solution which involved reducing the size of its orifice in order to convert the pressure of the steam into velocity. While this was nicknamed 'Ferranti's Folly' during tests in 1906,[35] much to the dismay of his team it was discovered that engine capacity could be improved by almost one-third by incorporating Ferranti stop-valves. As a reflection of its significance, *Engineering* claimed that this was a radical departure in valve design and construction.[36] However, at first the leading stop-valve manufacturer, J. Hopkinson & Co. of Huddersfield, was so sceptical that they refused his offer to purchase the patent outright for £2,000. This proved to be an expensive decision, because instead Hopkinsons pursued the less risky policy of paying a 7.5 per cent royalty on all sales, leading to an income for Ferranti between 1906 and 1921 of almost £32,000.[37] It actually took a year before the first major order was secured, from the Sunderland Electricity Supply Co. Thereafter, though, Hopkinsons generated a business worth nearly half a million pounds, confirming their position as market leaders in stop-valves. In addition, agreements with two European companies, Franco Tosi of Milan and Schaffer-Budenburg of Magdeburg, were also signed, earning Ferranti a further £1,500 in royalties, emphasising how the stop-valve contributed significantly to both engineering practices and his family fortunes. By 1930, an estimated 70,000 Hopkinson-Ferranti valves had been installed all over the world,[38] while modified versions were still being produced in the 1970s.

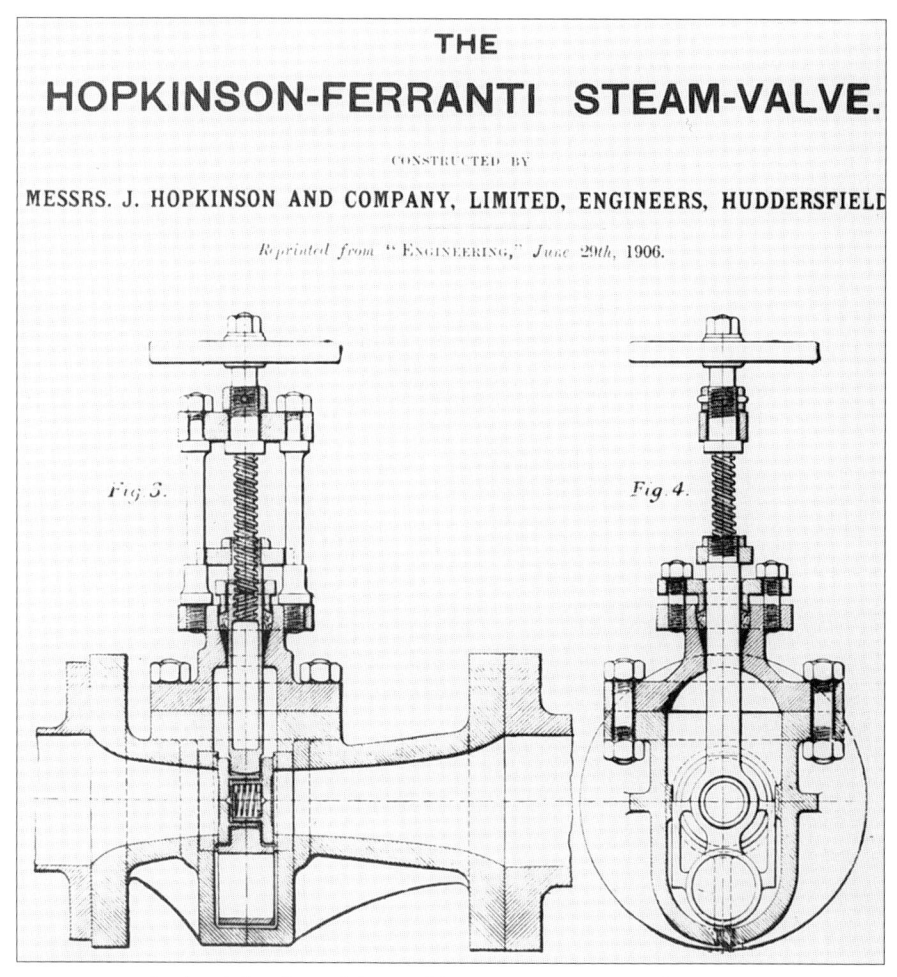

Sectional drawings of the Hopkinson-Ferranti steam valve, 1906.
(Museum of Science and Industry at Manchester.)

4.3 Motor-bikes, automobiles and aeroplanes

Ferranti family affluence

As the annual income from stop-valve sales slowly built up, from just £9 in 1906 to around £3,000 by 1913, the Ferranti family was able to enjoy an unprecedented period of financial prosperity. Although the monthly fees of £100 paid by Vickers and J. & P. Coats Ltd were largely dissipated in salaries for Albert Hall and the engineering team, Ferranti also drew an annual stipend of £500 as a director of Ferranti Ltd, while, as we shall see later, a good income was earned from acting as a consulting engineer and parliamentary advocate for electricity supply companies. This ensured that the financial problems experienced in the 1890s would be banished, providing a much better standard of living for the three sons and four daughters Gertrude had borne by then (see Appendix A). Ferranti later claimed that the Hopkinson royalties paid for the education at Repton between 1907 and 1912 of his two oldest sons, Basil and Vincent. Indeed, such was their new-found affluence that by 1913 a country house had been purchased near Chatsworth, known as Baslow Hall.[39]

Dr and Mrs S. Z. de Ferranti and family at their silver wedding, 1913. Yvonne (b.1913) is sat on her mother's lap, while from the bottom right there is Vera (1898), Denis (1908), Yolanda (1902), Zoe (1889), Basil (1891) and Vincent (1893).
(Museum of Science and Industry at Manchester.)

Life for the Ferranti family during the Edwardian era was consequently extremely comfortable. Gertrude fondly reminisces about 'those rather happy-go-lucky days' when her husband indulged both himself and Basil and Vincent by buying three motor-bikes.[40] This became something of a family craze at that time, and although Gertrude was a little concerned at her husband's growing love of speed, it provided him with a distraction from all his engineering projects. Of course, while the family had by then moved into the country, one should never be deluded into believing that Ferranti was becoming 'gentrified', because his love of engineering kept him just as busy as when he had been developing the zig-zag alternator in 1882. Basil and Vincent might well have received expensive gifts like motor-bikes, but their father also encouraged them to read as much about engineering as possible and apply their knowledge in experimental work. After leaving Repton School, Basil was sent to Sheffield University on a two-year engineering course, following which he spent a further two years at Yarrow's, the Clyde shipbuilding and engineering firm. Vincent was also an extremely bright young man who won many prizes for scholastic achievement. Indeed, had it not been for the First World War, Vincent would have taken up a place at Hertford College, Oxford. However, prior to the War he had joined Basil at Yarrow's, where he learnt much about engineering practice which would be of great use.

Tyre experiments

Motor-cycling was only one of the pastimes distracting Ferranti and his sons at this time, because they were just as interested in that other vital transport innovation of the era, motor-cars. Ferranti first come into contact with the automobile in 1906, at the Paris Motor Show, when his interest was aroused by what was one of the period's major technological innovations. By 1913, he had even purchased his own car, a Ford, driving the family and himself all over the country. One of the major handicaps associated with pre-war driving, however, was the poor state of road surfaces, and as somebody who loved the thrill of speed – one contemporary remembered that 'he never allowed the grass to grow under his car'[41] – Ferranti was frustrated at the large number of punctures he experienced. Immediately after the 1906 Paris Motor Show, recognising the potential in this industry, Ferranti consequently came up with a design for a reinforced tyre which he patented in the same year (see Appendix B). The basic idea was to pour molten rubber on to a backing of woven fabric to produce what he called a 'fibre-on-end', or reinforced, tyre which would be better able to withstand the rough treatment of British roads. It was a breakthrough in design which Ferranti felt would significantly improve the driving experience, leading him in November 1907 to approach the Dunlop Rubber Co., in Birmingham, with a view to testing the tyre. This was yet another example of the assistance provided by the Watson brothers at this time, because they were substantial shareholders in Dunlop and were able to persuade the du Cros family which controlled its management to back the experiments.

Although it was not until March 1909 that Ferranti was able to conduct full field trials with his 'fibre-on-end' tyre, from the limited surviving records it is apparent that they did not prove conclusively any better than the standard solid-rubber Dunlop product.[42] Ferranti complained that Dunlop engineers insisted on comparing his results with the best they had ever achieved with their own tyres, while casting aspersions on the casual manner in which the experimental department was managed. The trials actually lasted for just four months, after which, much to his annoyance, Dunlop refused to invest further in the Ferranti design. Another factor in this equation was the introduction of reinforced tyres by rivals like the British Insulated & Helsby Co., the company formed after British Insulated Wire had acquired the Helsby Tyre Co. in 1902. This proved to be an embarrassment for Ferranti, in that his long-standing position as a director of British Insulated Wire created a conflict of interest. Consequently, before the Dunlop trials started in 1909 he resigned his post on ethical grounds, 'owing to the company having widened its operations so largely as to conflict with his connections private and otherwise'.[43] Perhaps this was a little premature, given the brevity of Dunlop's trials. On the other hand, Ferranti was always so optimistic about his ideas, while his relationship with the Prescot company was no longer as close as in its early years.

Gyroscopic stabilisation

Although the 'fibre-on-end' tyre never went into full production, it is yet another example of his diverse technical interests, a point further reinforced when we consider the work on another novelty of those Edwardian days, the aeroplane. As part of their diversification strategy, Vickers had sent Ferranti and his wife to the Grande Semaine d'Aviation de la Champagne, at Rheims in 1909, hoping to learn from his technical appraisal of aeroplane technology.[44] Although no subsequent report exists, it is apparent that at this stage Vickers were not inspired to venture into this new market. Ferranti, on the other hand, was naturally captivated by the aeroplane, especially in the methods employed to stabilise flight, filling many pages of a sketch-book with ideas which in 1909 eventually resulted in a patent (see Appendix B) for gyrostabilised platforms. In fact, he had not been the first to propose the use of gyroscopes in this way, several American and German engineers having preceded him with equally ingenious applications.[45] However, the Ferranti concept was as advanced as any other, leading to yet another adventure which tells us much about the British approach to innovation.

The most famous of his rivals was the American inventor and entrepreneur, Elmer Sperry, who had been working with the US Navy since 1907 on a method of automatically steadying both ships and aeroplanes. After achieving considerable success by 1909 in developing what is known as the 'active' principle of gyroscopic stabilisation, the US Navy pumped over $200,000 into exhaustive testing which finally resulted in the first successful maritime application of this concept.[46] This 'active' principle involved the use of fully-controllable precession which employed a sensitive pendulum to activate a motor, thereby heading off any rolling in a ship much more effectively than in other stabilisation systems. In 1912, after applying Sperry's ideas to aircraft stabilisation in a US Navy Curtiss hydroplane, at the Aero Club of France trials he was awarded 50,000 francs for improving the safety of flying. A year later the Sperry Gyroscope Co. was established, after a group of Wall St financiers had agreed to provide enough funds for a full development and production programme.

It is interesting to see how Sperry had been able to raise support from both public and private sources between 1907 and 1913 in the USA and France, resulting in the development of what many regarded at that time as the most advanced gyroscopic stabilisation equipment. His achievements were reported at length in the *Engineer*, indicating how British interest had been aroused by Sperry's achievements. However, the *Engineer* article prompted Ferranti to write a fierce critique, in which he explained how his 1909 patent was based along the same principles used by Sperry.[47] Indeed, not only did the Ferranti gyroscopic platform employ the 'active' principle, it also pre-empted the use of gyroscopes in tandem which Sperry adopted at the Bezons trials in 1912. The technical value of this patent has also been verified by more recent investigations, indicating how its use of two contra-rotating gyros provided the necessary resistance and indirect control.[48] Furthermore, on the occasion of Sperry's visit to London in 1911, Ferranti claims to have 'explained to him the importance of the use of two gyroscopes suitably coupled in any airplane stabilising', when the two met over a private dinner at the IEE. This reveals how Ferranti could well have provided the vital clue to successful aeroplane stabilisation, because the 1912 Bezons trial was a great success and led to the establishment of a powerful manufacturing business. Of course, one cannot confirm this picture of events categorically, even though the Ferranti patent and his conversation with Sperry fit neatly into the chronology. Nevertheless, there is every likelihood that Sperry benefited from his trip to London.

Another point which Ferranti made in that letter to the *Engineer* which deserves close attention was the obvious inference that 'in this country one cannot readily find support for new ideas, whereas in the States so far as one can see this does not appear to be very difficult'. Having been a consistent theme of his public utterances since the 1880s, the case of gyroscopic stabilisation provided Ferranti with another excellent example of the contrasting experiences of innovative engineers on either side of the Atlantic. Ferranti had engaged in lengthy correspondence and discussions concerning the 1909 patent, involving prominent authorities in the aviation field like the French military, F. W. Lanchester and A. A. Campbell-Swinton.[49] Prior to Sperry's success in 1912, however, the conservative British view that pilot skill was more important than mechanical devices proved too strong an influence on contemporaries. Finally, in 1914, he was able to persuade the Royal Aircraft Establishment (RAE) at Farnborough to test the equipment. These experiments actually proved to be a technical success, Mervyn O'Gorman of the RAE reporting that the duplex principle of working gyroscopes in pairs possessed some potential. Unfortunately, though, as a new branch of the armed services, aviation budgets had yet to become a major priority in British defence circles, giving O'Gorman little opportunity to experiment further. As he noted in his final report, 'the amount of "working-out" to be done at present would appear to make it impracticable unless very considerable sums of money are to be sunk in experiments on this line alone'.[50] This view was in stark contrast to the attitudes expressed by the US Navy, emphasising in graphic form what Ferranti had claimed in his letter to the *Engineer* a year earlier.

Britain and innovation

In view of his experiences as both an electrical manufacturer and freelance engineer, Ferranti was well qualified to comment on the propensity to support new ideas in Britain. Throughout a career dominated by the growing threat of American and German ascendancy in high technology sectors, he had frequently fallen foul of what might be described as the short-termist British approach to innovation which limited the opportunity to build up industries with a real competitive advantage.[51] Of course, the experiences with gyroscopes and tyres can be contrasted with those associated with J. & P. Coats and Vickers, while Hopkinsons had taken up the stop-valve license, albeit at little risk to themselves. While one might well question the commercial viability of both the textile machinery and turbine experiments, at least these leading businessmen were willing to finance the development of radical new ideas which appeared to possess some potential. Yet even where the technical problems could be overcome, for example in the resuperheating turbine, market conditions failed to encourage further innovation, indicating how the environment for enterprise would not appear to have been as conducive as in the USA.

Indeed, the propensity of British markets to stimulate innovation would appear to have been the key ingredient, forcing businessmen to take a more conservative approach towards research and development. And when one combines the gyroscope, tyre, turbine and textile machinery experiences with the story related in the last two chapters of how the expansion of British electrical engineering was sorely constrained, it is difficult to escape the conclusion that between 1880 and 1914 entrepreneurs were faced with some insurmountable obstacles in establishing the commercial viability of new technology. In asking for more 'Matthew Boultons' to come forward and finance research, Ferranti was providing a partial solution to the real problem. What Britain required was a responsive market for new products, because once this appeared 'Matthew Boultons' would be more likely to support ventures with commercial potential. In the USA, financiers invested significantly in new industries which were expanding rapidly, while Ferranti would continue to struggle in a market which failed to provide the same degree of encouragement. While after the First World War conditions improved for British electrical manufacturers, prior to 1914 British industry was unable to exploit the opportunities provided by the Second Industrial Revolution, giving American and German corporations the chance to gain a competitive advantage in vital advanced technologies which became the high growth sectors of international trade.

4.4 The senior statesman

Regardless of the frustrations he experienced in the first thirty years of his career, one can conclude this review of the period by noting that by the Edwardian era Sebastian Ziani de Ferranti was regarded as a 'senior statesman' of some status. Although the years since 1903 had been very different to his first twenty years in business, the financial embarrassments at Ferranti Ltd had not tarnished his reputation as one of the country's most famous electrical engineers. For example, at a time when power supply companies were seeking authority through private Acts to serve much larger areas than formerly accepted by parliament,[52] Ferranti was hired to give evidence in favour of what had been a common theme of his contributions to electrical engineering. This reputation for advocating large-scale supply systems actually earned him almost £3,000 between 1902 and 1911, when he supported the extension schemes of NESCo., and the Bills seeking to establish the Somerset & District Power Co. and the North Wales Power Co.[53] Electricity supply in Britain was by then beginning to awaken from the lethargy imposed in the 1880s by statutory and commercial restrictions which ignored its full potential, giving Ferranti the opportunity to popularise further his dream of an 'All Electric Age'.

Ferranti and the IEE

The most famous event when Ferranti publicly demanded greater progress in achieving this aim came in 1910, when in giving his presidential address to the IEE he laid out a simple plan for the future. Becoming President of the IEE was yet another indication of his status in the industry at that time, added to which is the important point that he was the first to serve in that capacity for two consecutive terms. The IEE had recently been reassessing its position as electrical engineering's premier professional association, largely because there was a growing feeling that it was losing contact with the practical men of the manufacturing sector.[54] It was also outgrowing the temporary facilities hired from the Institute of Civil Engineers, as a result of which in June 1910 the current premises in Savoy Place, London, became the IEE's permanent home. Ferranti was consequently the first to give his presidential address in Savoy Place, in November 1910. More importantly, he worked vigorously to expand recruitment by introducing an associate membership scheme which allowed people from commercial or managerial backgrounds to join the organisation. This was known as the 'Broader Policy', publicised energetically by the President on a tour of the country which carried over into his second term. One commentator noted how Ferranti had 'aroused the Institution to a realisation of its magnificent possibilities',[55] prompting an increase in membership from 6,200 in 1910 to 7,045 by the time his reforms had taken effect, in 1914. Ferranti also instituted the Industrial Committee of the IEE, reflecting a need to address issues other than the technical matters which had been the organisation's initial rationale.

The 'Broader Policy' of the IEE was, of course, a reflection of the growing interest in co-operation among electrical engineers at that time, a point to which we shall return in the next section when discussing the origins of BEAMA. Ferranti was also equally anxious to use his prominent position to publicise further the concept of an 'All Electric Age', giving a presidential address in 1910 which aroused considerable interest in industrial and political circles. Entitled 'Coal Conservation, Home-Grown Food, and the Better Utilisation of Labour',[56] the speech was a classic expression of the 'Ferranti Dream' in which he prophesied the eventual victory of electricity in the fields of lighting and power. This victory, he argued, could be achieved by constructing one hundred power stations, each with a capacity of 25 MW and located at strategic points close by cheap supplies of fuel, all of which would be linked into a national distribution network to supply the main urban and industrial regions. In effect, he was arguing that the ideas encapsulated in his Deptford station would by then have been commercially-viable, adding further to his wide reputation as a futuristic visionary. Ferranti also extended his theme by explaining how the by-products of the stations, especially the estimated three million tons of sulphate, could also be used as fertiliser for the cheaper production of food, while large supplies of tar and its derivatives would compensate for the inevitable reduction in gas production as the use of electricity expanded.

Unfortunately, few costings were provided to back up the suggestions Ferranti made in 1910, leading many contemporaries to question the economics of the scheme.[57] It is interesting to note, however, that sixteen years after this speech a Central Electricity Board was established with powers to build a system comparable to the Ferranti scheme. In the interim, as we shall see in the next chapter, he also lobbied vigorously in favour of such an integrated approach towards electricity supply as an essential basis for the 'All Electric Age'. Although other prominent British engineers like Charles Merz and W. McLellan were demonstrating the practical advantages of integrated working at their NESCo. station, the Ferranti rhetoric proved to be an equally powerful influence. Electricity consumption had, indeed, been increasing significantly since the turn of the century, from 180 gWh to almost 2,000 gWh by 1913,[58] substantiating the Ferranti claim that electricity was very much the power source of the future. Unfortunately, though, until the First World War parliament refused to accept the need for direct intervention in the organisation of production or distribution, undermining the practical achievements of Merz at NESCo. and the political lobbying of Ferranti.

'The Doctor'

Naturally, as one of the industry's most prominent figures, Ferranti remained undaunted by this unsupportive stance, advocating at every opportunity his belief in an 'All Electric Age'. The prominent positions within the IEE (and BEAMA) were a reflection of this status, giving his public speeches much greater authority. In 1912, the University of Manchester also conferred upon him an honorary doctorate for contributions to the field of electrical engineering. It was a title which revealed a general acceptance of his pioneering role in British electrical engineering, providing public recognition of a lifetime spent pushing forward engineering possibilities. Although he would never have sought out this kind of accreditation, preferring at all times to commit his considerable energy to work on more practical achievements, after 1912 he answered to the title of Dr Ferranti when addressed by employees and fellow-directors or engineers. Hereafter, we shall consequently refer to him as Dr Ferranti, reflecting the stature he had by then attained as one of the most distinguished men in the British electrical industry.

4.4 A market-led strategy for recovery

Competition and prices

Dr Ferranti had clearly made excellent use of the enforced sabbatical he was obliged to take from his company after 1903, rehabilitating the Ferranti family finances by selling his services and patents to a number of firms. At the same time, it is important to stress how some of this work aided Ferranti Ltd's recovery, indicating how the firm was able to effect a significant recovery from its earlier liquidity crisis. This recovery was also achieved in the face of substantial competition provided by the new generation of electrical firms created in the period 1897–1902. In fact, since 1903 trading conditions within the electrical industry had deteriorated to such an extent that both the older manufacturers and those established between 1897 and 1902 were forced to accept even lower prices and profit margins. Contemporaries had started to complain about these trends as early as 1904,[59] while by 1907 the *Electrical Review* was noting that the whole industry was 'in a precarious condition', prices having fallen by up to forty per cent in the previous four years.[60] Three years later, the same commentator could report no better tidings, arguing that:

> a reasonable degree of competition is an excellent stimulus to progress and invention in industrial affairs ... But any good thing in excess becomes an evil, and too much competition tends to bring about the lowering of quality, the sweating of labour, and not infrequently the ruin of the employer.[61]

Ironically, though, the problems were not caused by a depression in demand, because total domestic production of electrical machinery (at 1907 prices) leapt from an annual average of £2.8 million over the period 1902–4 to £3.6 million between 1905 and 1907, reaching £4.6 million in the years 1908–10.[62] The major difficulties would appear to have been a combination of overcapacity after the expansions of 1897–1902, a general reluctance to engage in discussions on prices, and the power vested in local authorities which prevented greater standardisation of production. These issues certainly seemed to create a highly competitive and price-conscious market after 1903, resulting in a story of 'dividends passed, of capital reduction, and of liquidations'. Such were the financial implications of this scenario that between 1900 and 1910 the proportion of unremunerated capital across the industry as a whole varied between 49.2 and 64.4 per cent.[63]

It is important to stress how, in coping with this trading environment, the largest of the new generation, British Westinghouse, would appear to have suffered more than its rivals.[64] As the Trafford Park works of this American subsidiary had been planned on the basis of a much greater level of demand, after a string of poor results it was finally decided in 1905 that the entire senior management should be replaced by American managers from the parent headquarters in Pittsburgh, while half of the equity capital was written off, along with forty per cent of the preference capital. Although no other company experienced quite that level of financial crisis, most which had expanded capacity from the late 1890s struggled to make it pay. Siemens, for example, suffered problems at its new plant in Stafford, accumulating over the period 1906–16 losses of £700,000. Similarly, GEC's Witton works did very badly, Dick, Kerr & Co. at Preston was forced to consolidate their interests, while 'Brush were continually bumping along the ceiling of short-term borrowing'.[65]

Apart from overcapacity in the industry, another factor forcing down prices was the "buyer's market" which had typified relations between producer and customer since the 1880s, particularly with regard to the dominant position gained by local authorities as the principal purchasers of generating plant and electric traction equipment. In the tender columns of trade journals, there are examples of local authorities requesting manufacturers to lower their prices before allocating contracts,[66] creating mutual distrust among manufacturers and accentuating the lack of cohesion which had contributed to the downward pressure on prices. We saw in the last chapter how attempts at forging an alliance among electrical firms, in 1898 and 1902, had amounted to very little, increasing the levels of uncertainty within the industry.[67] Thereafter, while ratepayers benefited from improved access to electric lighting and transport, manufacturers were left to compete aggressively in a market dominated by municipal interests, leaving them with little or no profit for investment into improved products. Furthermore, just as in the 1880s and 1890s, the British electrical industry was deprived of much-needed venture capital. As we noted in sections 3.7–3.8, because financiers were generally only willing to provide debt capital to an industry which had yet to establish a reputation for making decent returns, this accentuated the liquidity problems many faced at a time when profits were hard to generate.[68]

The Ferranti response

Tait, Whittaker and Anderson would clearly have viewed these deteriorating market conditions with increasing alarm, given the parlous state of Ferranti Ltd's finances after 1903. Their response, however, stands out in stark contrast to the technology-led strategy formerly adopted at the firm, providing an interesting exercise in assessing how professional managers approached the difficult task of determining policy. One of their first tasks was to introduce effective reporting procedures which would provide improved monitors of the company's financial health. Of course, ever since 1896 departmental managers had been obliged to report weekly to the board, while as a reflection of his newly-acquired status in 1899 Anderson had succeeded in tightening up the accounts department's grasp of cash-flow. However, under Dr Ferranti this organisation had been ineffectively employed, largely because of his preference for product development strategies which required liberal managerial discipline. After 1905, though, Tait, Whittaker and Anderson imposed much more rigorous central direction on the systems already in place, severely limiting departmental autonomy in the interests of maintaining a healthy cash-flow. This centralised approach was to be an essential

The Ferranti stand at the Electrical Exhibition of 1911 at Olympia. *(Museum of Science and Industry at Manchester.)*

feature of the company's development over the following fifteen years, introducing a more managerial culture into what in the past had always been a highly devolved organisation.

Anderson's meter strategy

The second main task Tait and Whittaker took upon themselves was to streamline the product range, in order to concentrate on the sectors in which they had a competitive advantage. This demonstrates how the new regime was more interested in matching the firm's resources to the prevailing environment, a strategy which again was anathema to the approach previously followed at the company. As we saw in the last chapter, steam-alternator production was the first to suffer from the new approach, terminating production in 1904 after two big units had been exported to South Africa. Instead, the meter business received most of the senior management's attention over the following decade, building on the earlier successes which had already made this department the company's financial backbone. A. B. Anderson was largely responsible for implementing this policy, committing his considerable energy and negotiating skills to the pursuit of a market position which would make the meter trade a model for others to follow after 1911. Indeed, not only did Anderson rise to the post of managing director of Ferranti Ltd in 1908, he also became one of the key figures in the British electrical industry, overcoming many of the prejudices against cooperation in his attempt to forge a permanent alliance among hard-pressed manufacturers. While his personality did not endear him to many people, a natural pushiness allied to a clear vision ensured that this policy would succeed.

One of the first challenges facing Anderson was to settle the various patent disagreements which had disrupted relations between meter manufacturers since the 1890s. This exercise became all the more important when in 1905 Ferranti Ltd lost a four-year-long case against BT-H over a DC meter patent of 1887, resulting in the threat of writs from Chamberlain & Hookham and British Westinghouse.[69] Anderson was able to defuse the situation by arranging a mutual exchange of patents between these firms, assembling together a group of interested parties which by the early months of 1907 had agreed on standard prices for all DC meters. He was not as successful in the AC meter market, largely because British Westinghouse refused to abide by any regulations which would have undermined its competitive advantage in this field. Nevertheless, at least the DC meter business was now guaranteed stable prices over the recovery period. In fact, BT-H actually withdrew from the agreement between 1907 and 1909, but as long as Chamberlain & Hookham stuck to the agreed prices Ferranti Ltd was able to work effectively with what was their main DC meter competitor.[70] Ferranti Ltd had also joined the National Electrical Manufacturers' Association (NEMA) in July 1906, providing Anderson with a forum in which he could voice his ideas on the need for greater stability.

The agency network

Although price stability was important to the company's recovery after 1905, this was only one feature of Anderson's strategy to expand sales and profits. As meter production was such a highly seasonal business, with electricity suppliers placing the bulk of their orders in the autumn, in order to keep the Crown Works busy throughout the year Anderson recognised the need to pursue an aggressive marketing strategy in both home and overseas markets. To date, Ferranti Ltd had built up its reputation on a technology-led strategy which had created an advanced product range. In contrast, its marketing strategies were poorly developed, relying largely on attending exhibitions or having their founder visit potential customers. In the highly competitive environment of the Edwardian era, however, it was essential to be more customer-oriented, resulting in the fashioning of an ambitious market-led strategy which put Ferranti ahead of many of its rivals. As Anderson argued at a board meeting in October 1906, 'the prospect of obtaining the necessary turnover at remunerative prices is such as to necessitate the consideration of some more drastic steps than merely quoting and following tenders'.[71] This new approach was quickly endorsed by Tait and Whittaker, following which an extensive network of salesmen and agents was built up to cover every major town and city in Britain. A London headquarters, in Central House, Kingsway, was also acquired in 1912 to house the newly-created sales department, reforging a link with the capital which had been abandoned fourteen years earlier. This domestic marketing and sales network was then augmented by the establishment of contacts with agents in many overseas markets, Anderson himself embarking on trips to Europe, South Africa and North America to recruit suitably connected houses which might serve Ferranti interests.

The market-led strategy pursued by Anderson and the company after 1906 reinforces the arguments of those who refuse to accept that in this area of management 'the British approach was essentially conservative and individualistic, and at times apathetic and indifferent'.[72] Indeed, many firms in a wide range of industries were investing in both domestic and overseas marketing and sales networks as a vital means of meeting the challenge of foreign competition, economising substantially on the transaction costs associated with the traditional form of selling through intermediaries like merchants and commission agents.[73] Ferranti Ltd was so committed to this strategy that several overseas subsidiaries were established at this time, while agencies were started in all the major European countries, as well as in Japan, South Africa and South America. Some of these agents were also well-connected. For example, in Italy Anderson appointed a man called Pandiani, the father-in-law to the Italian Edison Co.'s chief engineer. More generally, he looked for men with some technical appreciation of the products they were selling, establishing a network of agents which matched that of most other British electrical firms.[74]

The start of Ferranti Canada

Perhaps the most outstanding feature of this market-led strategy was the overseas companies formed in Austria, Germany and Canada. In fact, the first two never proved very successful and Ferranti Ltd sold them to AEG in 1912 at a knock-down price.[75] The Canadian venture, on the other hand, proved to have more substantial foundations, laying the basis for a company which eventually became a major competitor in the North American electrical markets. One must remember, though, that although ostensibly a part of the British Empire, Canada was economically dependent on the USA, posing an enormous challenge to electrical manufacturers which would then have to compete directly with American giants like General Electric and Westinghouse. It was, however, a market with considerable potential, one journal exhorting British firms to send 'the brightest man the company can muster' to assess its prospects.[76] Four years earlier, Anderson had appointed D. A. Mills as agent to Ferranti Ltd in Canada. Although he passed on the agency to the Gas & Electric Power Co. in 1907, this provided an opening for the meter department which sold several hundred in the Ottawa region.[77] Unfortunately, though, the Gas & Electric Power Co. was dissolved in 1908, forcing Anderson to visit Canada personally to secure further contacts. It was on the outward voyage to Canada that he met George Royce, a man who was not only related to Sir Henry Royce, of Rolls Royce, but who also owned and managed the Toronto Suburban Railway Co. By February 1909, Royce had agreed to act as agent to the Ferranti meter in Canada, initiating an enterprise which survived with considerable parent company support for many decades.

Faced with an expanding market, George Royce immediately hired two salesmen, J. Showatter, a qualified engineer, and J. G. Monahan, a man noted for both his forceful selling techniques and ability to celebrate a good sale. The enterprise was largely organised by F. W. Rowntree, who remained with Ferranti Canada until 1952. From the start, sales expanded appreciably, from

FERRANTI ELECTRICAL COMPANY OF CANADA, LTD.

90, Sherbourne Street, TORONTO.

ALTERNATING CURRENT TWO-RATE WATT HOUR METERS.

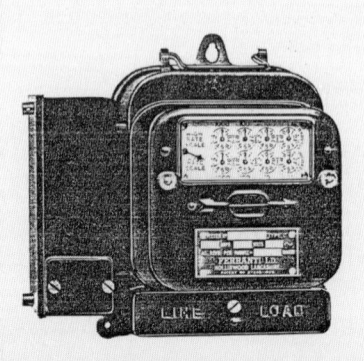

Fig. 1.
Type "C."
Single and Poly-phase Balanced Load.
Sheet Steel Cover.
Supplied with Bottom Terminals only.

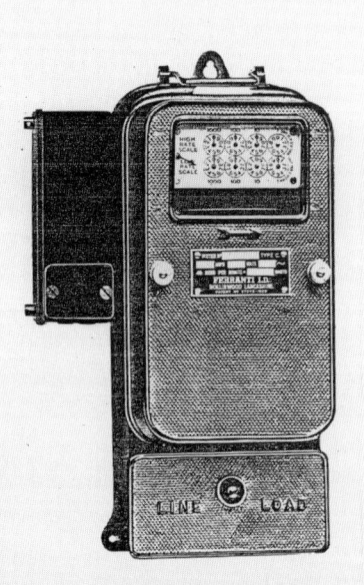

Fig. 2.
Type "CT."
Poly-phase Unbalanced Load.
Supplied with Cast Iron Cover
and Bottom Terminals only.

Issued October, 1913.

THIS LIST CANCELS PRIOR PUBLICATIONS AND
IS SUBJECT TO ALTERATION WITHOUT NOTICE.

List A.C.M. 18.

One of the earliest Ferranti Canada advertisements, issued in 1913. All meters were imported from the Hollinwood factory.

4,655 meters in 1909 to 16,616 in 1913, acting as a solid base for the introduction of other Ferranti products. However, it soon became apparent that a sales agency was ill-equipped to deal with some of the technical problems associated with assembling switchgear or instrumentation, resulting in engineers from the Crown Works moving to Toronto to act as technical advisors to both employees and customers. Although American corporations tried to forestall the entry of this new venture into what they regarded as a captive market, Royce and Anderson worked hard to build up credibility. The Canadian Westinghouse Corporation even issued an injunction against the Ferranti AC meter in 1911, on the grounds that it infringed their patents. All Canadian power suppliers also received a little booklet, *Twenty-Six Knocks against Ferranti Meters*, forcing Anderson to rush over to Canada and negotiate a settlement. It was on that trip that Anderson planned with Royce the formation of the Ferranti Electrical Co. of Canada, an enterprise which began trading in 1912 after the parent company and Royce had invested (Canadian) $175,000 in new offices and assembly facilities.

Marketing successes

Later chapters will describe in greater detail how what was known as Ferranti Canada developed in the twentieth century, because it was to become an important aspect of the firm's marketing strategy in relation to a variety of products. Crucially, while no similar developments occurred in any of the other agencies established at this time, it is clear that Anderson was determined to create a viable marketing and sales network which would substantially aid the company's recovery. Catalogues in several languages were also printed and circulated to the agents, while more direct technical advice would be provided, either by Anderson on his many trips abroad, or from engineers sent to consult agents on specific market requirements. It was an ambitious policy based on Anderson's desire to spread production at the Crown Works over the whole year, rather than continue bearing the costs of having plant lie idle during the spring and summer months when British customers traditionally ordered very little equipment. As the meter was evidently the pivot around which the entire strategy revolved, it is also apparent that the strategy worked, because exports from this department increased from forty-five per cent of its expanding sales in 1908 to almost seventy per cent by 1912. One should note that between those years meter sales consistently accounted for approximately two-thirds of total company output (see Appendix C, Table 3),[78] indicating how the Anderson strategy was essential to any recovery which Tait and Whittaker might have effected in Ferranti fortunes after 1905.

4.5 Products and prices

Instruments and switchgear

While Ferranti achieved considerable success with both its DC and Type B meters, as far as the remainder of Ferranti Ltd's product portfolio was concerned in this recovery phase, one can only describe the story as a struggle to convert high technical prowess into solid commercial results. The engineering staff Ferranti had recruited by 1903 was certainly of a high quality, with each department managed by well-qualified individuals who were widely known for their design skills. For example, Dr C. C. Garrard had become manager of the instrument department by 1903, having arrived at the Crown Works in 1901 after an extensive technical education which included a period at Finsbury Technical College, under the famous specialists Professors Ayrton and Perry, and doctoral training at the University of Gottingen. Although he only stayed with Ferranti Ltd for seven years, leaving in 1908 for a successful career with GEC, in that time a complete range of testing and registering instruments was developed for use in laboratories, switchboards and sub-stations. As with meters, every attempt was also made to standardise production, publishing an extensive range of catalogues through the agency system to support the marketing and sales strategy instigated by Anderson.

While the instrument business was expanding after 1903, in contrast the switchgear department experienced great difficulties. By that time, of course, Ferranti switchgear had established an extensive reputation for its design qualities, leading to the 1902 expansion into a neighbouring factory, Windsor Mill, to cope with the increased orders. Tait and Whittaker decided as early as 1903 to concentrate all production in the Crown Works, leading to the closure of Windsor Mill. Unfortunately, though, this persuaded the switchgear department manager, H. W. Clothier, to leave and find employment with a major rival, A. Reyrolle & Co. This was a serious loss to Ferranti Ltd at a time when competition in this market was intensifying as a result of both the development of specialist manufacturers and the American invasion. Dr Ferranti was well aware of this threat, advising Tait and Whittaker 'to appoint someone knowing US and Continental practice and a good and appreciative designer who can copy what is common property and can appreciate broadly what is wanted in the department to get contracts'.[79] However, not only was this an ambitious job description, it is also unlikely that such a well-qualified commercial-engineer would have joined such a financially stretched company which was closing facilities. Although M. B. Field was elevated from the development team to switchgear department manager, and in the following ten years he was able to extend the

Ferranti reputation in this field by developing a highly competitive product range which sold in increasing quantities, this department continued to struggle commercially.

Switchgear design had advanced considerably since Ferranti had introduced his cellular design at Portsmouth in 1894, most especially as a result of the joint work of Reyrolle with Charles Merz at the Newcastle Electricity Supply Co.[80] The most significant improvement was metalclad, compound-filled, draw-out type switchgear developed by H. W. Clothier, B. Price and Merz by 1905. Within a couple of years, M. B. Field at Ferranti Ltd had also devised a similar range which was regarded as reliable and flexible,[81] leading to many prestigious orders. For example, in 1908 John Brown & Co. ordered Ferranti switchboards for the two Cunard ships *Mauretania* and *Lusitania*.[82] When the management of Ray Mills in Stalybridge decided to electrify their cotton plant, Ferranti was commissioned to install a suitable switchboard, sparking off a run of orders from other mills in Lancashire and Yorkshire.[83] Unfortunately, though, standardisation of production proved impossible in this department, largely because so many of the contracts required individual attention. Even when switchgear sales topped £100,000 in 1912–13, a meagre trading profit of just over £4,500 was recorded. This was an improvement on the losses of almost £13,700 in 1903, when sales were only half the 1913 level. Clearly, though, it was only because of the successful meter department that Ferranti Ltd was able to lever itself out the 1903 crisis, irrespective of the switchgear department's highly prestigious sales successes.

The creation of BEAMA

Another problem affecting the switchgear department's profitability was the intense price competition between both specialist manufacturers and the larger firms created after 1897. Of course, this was a general problem for all electrical manufacturers at that time, as we noted earlier, a point reinforced by the *Electrical Review* observation that 'cut-throat competition prevails in almost all branches of the industry'.[84] At the same time, Anderson and his counterparts at Chamberlain & Hookham had managed to stabilise the DC meter trade by agreeing on technical and pricing measures which ensured that their staple product would prove profitable. Furthermore, at NEMA meetings the Ferranti managing director advocated similar strategies in other markets. Indeed, Anderson was regarded as one of the leading influences in a series of meetings which eventually resulted in the formation of an effective electrical trade association in 1911. The first move was to create in 1910 a joint committee with representatives of NEMA and the IEE to push the idea of an 'Electrical League'.[85] As President of the IEE, Dr Ferranti was also heavily involved in these negotiations, indicating how his ideas concurred with those of Anderson. This committee then published a pamphlet, *The Need of Co-operation in the Electrical Industry*, which was widely circulated, following which the *Electrical Review* was able to attract influential businessmen to a 'Round Table' conference on the subject of price stability.

The *Electrical Review* proved to be a useful vehicle for presenting such ideas, not only through its work on the conference, but also by publishing the views of prominent electrical engineers on combination. Dr Ferranti was naturally one of those lobbied for an opinion, leading to an article in which he argued that the current state of affairs in the industry would destroy any competitive advantage gained as a result of technological innovation. Referring to the recent rash of mergers and consolidations in industries like cotton, brewing and engineering, he also felt that 'the whole tendency of modern business is to avoid excessive competition by some process or other. Combination, reasonably and fairly carried out, seems to be distinctly beneficial in this direction'.[86] Fortunately for the industry, after the work of the *Electrical Review* and advocates like Anderson, many other electrical manufacturers were also beginning to accept the logic in such sentiments. As a consequence, by September 1911 an extremely influential trade association had been created, the British Electrical and Allied Manufacturers' Association (BEAMA). Just to confirm the importance of the roles played by Dr Ferranti and Anderson, one should also note that the former was the first chairman, to be succeeded in 1913 by the latter.

The emergence of BEAMA from the debates of 1910–11 was a major breakthrough for those who had been working actively towards a more united approach on pricing and other market issues. It was actually run by a full-time director, the first of whom, D. N. Dunlop, was largely responsible for widening the membership to incorporate 125 firms by 1914, including the American and German subsidiaries. Ferranti and Anderson also used all their influence as successive BEAMA chairmen to encourage independently-minded businessmen to join the fold, offering the inducement of mutually-agreed prices and even the promise of a guaranteed share of the market. These matters were actually arranged in the fourteen sub-groups within BEAMA which covered the major product areas, the proceedings of which were 'not for general publication'.[87] BEAMA went on to act as a major influence on prices in the industry over the next forty-five years, providing for the smaller firms like Ferranti Ltd an opportunity to plan pricing and marketing strategies in a more stable environment. The alternative strategy of acquiring either Chamberlain & Hookham or Reyrolle, in order to eliminate competitors, was hardly a feasible option for Ferranti at that time, emphasising the logic behind Anderson's moves to combine interests in other ways. Of course, one can debate the welfare implications of such trading practices, because clearly customers were affected by the reduction in price competition. On the other hand, it was rational for the firms to engage in stabilisation policies at a time when market forces were widely regarded as the ultimate arbiter.

Ferranti finances

It is interesting to note that BEAMA's formation came just at the time when demand for electrical products started to rise considerably, with total British electrical output nearly trebling to an average of £12.1 million per annum over the period 1911–13, compared with the previous three year average of £4.7 million.[88] Ferranti Ltd undoubtedly benefited from this boom, with output rising from just over £160,000 in 1910 to almost £300,000 by 1913 (see Appendix C). Even though net profits were never large, given the need to service the fixed-interest capital, at least the bottom line remained in the black from 1907. In fact, the profit and loss account did not begin to register a positive figure until 1910, after having sustained losses of over £106,000 between 1903 and 1906, leading to the adoption by Tait and Whittaker of highly conservative accounting policies based on the aim of restoring the company's financial position by accretions. The company was also saddled with substantial quantities of debt capital, the 1905 reconstruction having failed to bring any fresh equity capital into the company.[89] Even the accumulated overdraft at Parr's Bank was secured by the deposit of £30,000 in second mortgage debentures. This overdraft was finally repaid in 1912, albeit after the issue of yet another fixed-interest mortgage in the form of £50,000 in six per cent Five Year Notes, adding further to the burden of debt which by 1913 exceeded the issued capital by over £20,000 (see Appendix C, Table 1).

The dead-weight of fixed-interest debt repayments was a major financial obstacle to the complete recovery of Ferranti Ltd right up to the First World War. Interest payments actually averaged almost £8,000 per annum over this period, far exceeding the net profits until 1913 and draining away the very life-blood of a company which was struggling to survive in a highly competitive and research-intensive industry. Furthermore, no dividends were paid out to either the ordinary shareholders or the deferred shareholder (Dr Ferranti), reinforcing the contemporary preference for fixed-interest securities when it came to supporting the company. Such was the extent of their liquidity problems that short-term loans were provided by one of the directors, J. M. Henderson. Although these never exceeded £6,000, survival depended on such strategies. Capital expenditure consequently had to be sparing, even in the profitable meter department, where under-investment in essential new capacity forced the management to request high levels of overtime from the workforce.[90]

Only slowly after 1905 did Ferranti cast off the mantle of a bankrupt, the cautious policies of Tait and Whittaker ensuring that financial resources were focused on mainstream activities. For the first time, Ferranti also pursued a policy of depreciating plant, opening a depreciation reserve account which stood at over £53,000 by 1913. Another director was also appointed to the board in 1913, Major R. W. Cooper, bringing extensive experience of City matters which was to be of great use to Ferranti in the fifty years he spent as a director. Although Major Cooper was initially introduced to the firm as a representative of Parr's Bank, until 1963 he offered useful advice on financial matters based on extensive experience as a prominent City gentleman, bolstering the senior management team at an important time for Ferranti.

Domestic appliances

In view of the low level of reserves held by Ferranti, it is surprising that the company should venture into a new market which at that time was only just beginning to expand. The increasing use of electricity from the 1890s had actually prompted some manufacturers to introduce new domestic appliances to British consumers, imitating what had been happening in the USA on a much greater scale. It was at the 1896 Crystal Palace Exhibition that the first electric cookers were marketed in Britain, with companies like GEC diversifying into what was potentially a massive market once electricity prices came down to the levels of gas and coal. Although Dr Ferranti was also keen to see this market expand, as part of his dream of an 'All Electric Age', it was not until 1910 that Ferranti Ltd ventured into this area, buying the heater and cooker patents of their Canadian agent's brother, James Royce. Ranges of irons, stoves and fires were also added to this new department's activities by 1912,[91] in the company's attempt to diversify into the mass market. However, one can only regard domestic appliance production as a minor branch of the business up to 1914. Indeed, sales peaked in 1913, at just £2,527, and only in the inter-war period did domestic appliances begin to catch on with British consumers, leaving Ferranti with a wasted investment prior to the War.

Ferranti and Anderson

Domestic electrical appliances apart, however, it is clear that in the ten years or so prior to the First World War Ferranti Ltd was managed in a highly conservative manner. Even though Dr Ferranti would never have agreed with what he regarded as a parsimonious approach to engineering, the strategies adopted by Tait and Whittaker were essential if the firm was to survive in a highly competitive and cash-conscious environment. Notwithstanding this comment, of far greater importance to the actual recovery process was the role played by A. B. Anderson, not only in developing an extensive marketing and sales network which was capable of exploiting any competitive advantage the company possessed, but also in stabilising prices, initially for meters, and later for other products. Ferranti himself recognised the value of these services, commenting in reply to an inquiry regarding Anderson's employment status at Ferranti Ltd by stating that: 'He is the company'.[92] Vincent de Ferranti always remembered Anderson as an opportunist who was ready to push people out of his way. On the other hand, without Anderson's tireless promotion of the Ferranti name and its products on a whole series of trips to markets at home and abroad, Tait and Whittaker would have been faced with an acute shortage of business. It was Anderson who re-established the credibility of Ferranti Ltd's reputation in the market, and through his work at BEAMA he undoubtedly became one of the more important influences within the pre-war British electrical industry.

5

The Return from Exile

It would be all too easy to view 1914 as a watershed in British, and world, history which divided the Victorian and Edwardian eras of peace and prosperity from the following much-troubled years of war, mass unemployment and political extremism. This approach to history is far too simplistic, ignoring the continuous aspects of life which feature just as prominently as the new developments. It would, perhaps, be better to view the First World War as 'a precipitant of changes already under way',[1] and in particular in the British context as an opportunity to stimulate the extensive adoption of electricity as a major source of energy for use in all aspects of life. Schumpeter has described the early-twentieth century as a long wave of economic development carried in large part by the increasing use of electricity.[2] While one might well push the timing of what in effect he is referring to as a 'Second Industrial Revolution' back into the 1880s, it would certainly be accurate to say that in the industrialised economies such a transformation was well under way by 1914. Even Lenin was ready to accept the new energy source's importance, noting that: 'Communism is Soviet power plus the electrification of society'.

Having been slow to emerge from its 'First Industrial Revolution', Britain had lagged behind many countries in the adoption of electricity, as we have seen in previous chapters. From 1914, however, there appeared to be a much more encouraging environment for electrical manufacturers, especially once the state had created new bodies like the Central Electricity Board and the British Broadcasting Co. The construction of a national grid network, in particular, marked the achievement of a goal for which engineers like Dr Ferranti had been striving for over thirty years. It was consequently fitting that, as we shall see in this chapter, Ferranti Ltd should participate extensively in the design and manufacture of certain aspects of the system, accelerating the process of recovery initiated by Tait, Whittaker and Anderson after the 1903 crisis. Moreover, it is important to emphasise how Dr Ferranti was to play a much more prominent role in the company's affairs after 1914.

The First World War was actually to prove crucial to the British electrical industry as a whole, by creating both a valuable breathing space in which foreign competition was excluded from the market and a significant stimulus to demand. Heavy involvement in munitions production would also provide the funds for future product development programmes, in Ferranti Ltd's case resulting in the creation and expansion of two new lines, large transformers and radio. As Dr Ferranti had always been keen on product development, having returned to Ferranti Ltd in 1914 he was able to re-establish his technology-led strategy as the central driving force within the enterprise. Of course, one must remember that the professional managers continued to supervise the finances and organise marketing and sales, providing greater balance with the engineering ethos established by the founder. The continued importance of these individuals within the organisation also freed Dr Ferranti from the more routine aspects of management in which he had never been interested. In consequence, while achieving a more balanced approach in exploiting its organisational capabilities, the technology-led strategy preferred by Dr Ferranti once more became a major influence on what was after 1914 an expanding company, establishing the foundations of an organisational culture which flourished for several decades.

5.1 The munitions business and Ferranti at war

Anderson's death and policy drift

Although Ferranti Ltd had recovered impressively from its earlier financial troubles, and the professional managers had demonstrated astute financial skills in restoring credibility to the balance sheet, the company was extremely slow to respond to the problems posed by the onset of the First World War in 1914. Even though sales had already started to fall earlier in the summer, after the initial proclamations of war were made in August and orders from foreign customers especially dried up alarmingly, Tait and Whittaker refused to envisage any radical measures.[3] Like most of their contemporaries, they believed that the War would not last very long, preferring instead to cut back on production and wait until custom picked up again, perhaps in three to six months time.[4] It is also important to add that the company was hampered significantly by the untimely death of its managing director, A. B. Anderson, on the return leg of yet another trip to Canada. It was on that fateful journey, on 29 May 1914, while travelling through a bank of fog in the Gulf of St Lawrence, that his ship, the *Empress of Ireland*, struck a Norwegian collier. Of the 1,476 passengers and crew on board, 1,014 were lost. Not only was this the biggest maritime incident since the sinking of the *Titanic* in 1912, it also deprived Ferranti Ltd of its most dynamic executive. Indeed, his absence from the board meetings of late 1914 could well have been decisive in explaining the drift in company policy. Anderson's death, at the age of just forty-four, was also felt throughout the electrical industry, with the BEAMA council meeting of June 1914 passing a resolution which noted 'the untimely death of their late Chairman ... through whose efforts mainly [BEAMA] has reached its present position'.[5]

Dr Ferranti was as affected as anybody else by Anderson's tragic death, having built up an enormous amount of respect for his contribution to the company's recent development. He was also conscious of the vacuum Anderson would leave at Ferranti, especially when it became evident that the policies pursued by Tait and Whittaker lacked any direction. Although Dr Ferranti had attended board meetings sporadically over the previous nine years, in August 1914 he suddenly started paying close attention to the company, instructing the senior sales manager, R. H. Schofield,[6] to submit reports on the market and financial prospects for the immediate future. These reports made poor reading, persuading Dr Ferranti to commit himself full-time to rebuilding Ferranti. While Tait was unhappy about this development, there was little he could do to suppress the founder's renewed interest in the company's management.

It is important to emphasise that Dr Ferranti was by no means a member of the 'Business as Usual' movement which had gripped British society at that time,[7] arguing forcibly that the War should be seen as an opportunity to extinguish German competition. As he stated at a BEAMA council meeting: 'It should be as much a part of our policy to permanently [sic] cripple our enemies in trade as it is to defeat them in war, and all means to that end should be relentlessly pursued'.[8] These were sentiments expressed by many contemporary businessmen, particularly at BEAMA, which had earlier passed a resolution stating 'that it is against the national interest to buy from or sell to German-financed British companies'.[9] R. H. Schofield was consequently instructed to circulate all electricity supply stations 'to see if there is anything [Ferranti Ltd] could make for them here which they will be unable to get from the Continent'.[10] All agents were also alerted to the opportunities afforded by any German retrenchment from foreign markets, indicating how effort was put into recouping some of the business lost as a result of the prevailing political and economic uncertainty.

Munitions contracts

It is clear from Appendix C (Tables 2 and 3), however, that the severe downturn in demand for electrical goods materially affected company profitability, necessitating the adoption of a more radical strategy. One of the most obvious sources of alternative business to Dr Ferranti was shell production, because he was aware of the tremendous strain imposed by the large government contracts placed with companies like Vickers and Armstrong-Whitworth.[11] The board had initially refused him permission to negotiate with his former colleagues at Vickers, having decided instead simply to lay off staff. By January 1915, however, faced with the imminent closure of much of the Crown Works, his fellow-directors relented and a small contract was signed for machining 50,000 shrapnel cases.[12] Although only worth £15,000, this contract opened up the possibility of an extensive munitions business, leading Dr Ferranti into detailed negotiations with War Office officials to convert the Crown Works into a major supplier of shells and fuzes.[13] One might note here that many non-British industrialists, and even American-owned businesses, experienced a jingoistic backlash during the War. In spite of his Italian name and ancestry, though, Dr Ferranti was regarded as a loyal British citizen who was willing to make a substantial contribution to the war effort. In several trade journals he is either depicted waving the Union Jack, or encouraging counterparts to exploit the War as an opportunity to improve the competitiveness of British electrical engineering, reinforcing his reputation as a major component in his country's industrial efforts.

As the War stumbled on into the spring of 1915, it became apparent that companies like Ferranti were going to be used much more extensively as munitions suppliers. The government had initially relied on a combination of the Royal Ordinance and an elite group of major defence contractors to service the needs of its military machine. After the 'Great Shell Scandal' of Spring 1915, however, when front-line troops ran short of ammunition, politicians realised the need for a more rigorous approach towards supplies. The first step taken was the creation of a Ministry of Munitions, following which over 700 engineering firms were 'controlled' for the purposes of coordinating the production of larger quantities of armaments.[14] Although it was September 1915 before Ferranti was 'controlled', as a result of the earlier negotiations with War Office officials contracts had already been secured (for eighteen-pounder shrapnel cases, six–inch shells and No. 100 fuzes) worth £330,000. Just as importantly, the War Office also provided £100,125 as a mortgage on the factory to finance the construction of an extension to the Crown Works (measuring 220 by fifty feet) and the purchase of all the machine tools required to fulfil these orders.

The business worries of late 1914 had by the summer of the following year all been forgotten as Dr Ferranti and his team set about the task of converting the workshops from civil to defence production. As this changeover would naturally require a major reorganisation of factory layout, Dr Ferranti reported to his son Vincent as late as 1917 that: 'It is a very difficult business getting our work changed over onto the new lines'.[15] Shells and fuzes must

Some of the first women employed by Ferranti Ltd, 1916. *(Museum of Science and Industry at Manchester.)*

inevitably be produced in a standardised and interchangeable manner, with the Ministry of Munitions laying down stringent specifications which all contractors had to follow in designing their production lines. Of course, ever since the early days at Charterhouse Square, Ferranti had been mass-producing meters, building up an extensive reputation for its use of these techniques in manufacturing a range of electrical instruments. However, munitions production posed new challenges in terms of accuracy and interchangeability, forcing Dr Ferranti to work long hours at the Crown Works to perfect the new techniques. To assist the production planning process, some American automatic machine tools had already been installed in the Crown Works to deal with the first Vickers contract, bringing new techniques into the company which would prove useful in the future. This experience was matched in much of British industry at that time, indicating how the First World War precipitated a significant move towards mass-production techniques on a scale previously unknown in many sectors.[16]

The executive committee

Another important innovation arising out of this period was the establishment of an executive committee within each defence supplier. Such was the scale of business distributed by the Ministry of Munitions that in 1916 it decided to appoint its own representatives to all 'controlled' companies, insisting that an executive committee should be formed as a means of monitoring progress on all contracts. This new body would also serve the useful internal purpose at Ferranti Ltd of supervising the work of Dr Ferranti, because by 1915 he had once again become the major influence on company policy. As Tait and Whittaker were naturally keen to ensure that all their carefully planned financial and managerial systems would remain in place, the executive committee was to be composed of Dr Ferranti, Arthur Whittaker and the Ministry of Munitions appointee. This provided a combination of engineering and managerial talent, maintaining the balanced approach which had characterised the firm's evolution since 1903. The second of the government appointees, Captain P. D. Thomas, would also appear to have been a useful addition to the management team, because as a result of his war-time contributions in 1918 he was invited to join the board of directors.[17]

With the safeguard of an executive committee in place, the board was consequently willing to allow Dr Ferranti free rein in production matters. In fact, because he actually installed in the Crown Works the small engineering team which had assisted him on the turbine and textile machinery experiments prior to the War, substantial progress was made in raising productivity levels. Although Dr Ferranti patented his own method of forging and manufacturing shells in 1918 (see Appendix B), it was his engineering team which was primarily responsible for the works' achievements. It is also notable that, such was the amount of time Dr Ferranti committed to munitions production that in 1916 and 1917 he did not take out a single patent. More importantly, he managed to increase efficiency levels from the original output of 500 shells per week in September 1915 to 4,500 by December 1918, while over the same period weekly output of eighteen-pounder shells rose from 800 to 6,000.[18]

The successful completion of these large munitions contracts would appear to have allowed Ferranti to emerge from the War in a financially stronger position. Output certainly expanded, from an annual average of under £250,000 in the five trading years from 1910–14 to almost £600,000 per annum in the period 1916–18 (see Appendix C, Table 3).[19] Similarly, the level of profitability improved, with the company recording a gross profit of £347,690 over the period 1916–18. Of course, not all of this profit was available for internal use, because by 1918 a total of £165,212 was owed to His Majesty's government on account of the loans for new plant. Similarly, an excess profits tax was also payable, while Parr's Bank had extended the overdraft considerably (see Appendix C, Table 1). However, the government debts had actually all been settled by 1920, allowing the board to utilise the residue to build up the reserves to £72,000 by 1920 and redeem £11,000 of the debenture stock. At the same time, the Crown Works had been expanded

THE RETURN FROM EXILE 185

Ferranti employees of the 6-inch shell department during the First World War. *(Museum of Science and Industry at Manchester.)*

and re-equipped with the latest American machine tools, revealing how the company's first direct contact with the state as a customer had brought significant financial and organisational benefits which would substantially assist future development.

Basil's death

It is, of course, deeply ironic that a major military conflict should produce such positive rewards for Dr Ferranti and his company, particularly when one considers the colossal loss of human life witnessed in what has mistakenly been called 'The Great War'. The Ferranti family was to suffer as much as any other from this conflict, because while the firm benefited from the large munitions contracts this could never have compensated for the death in action of the eldest son, Basil. Like many of their generation, the two older sons of Dr Ferranti and Gertrude were anxious to join up as soon as War was declared, seeing this as a great adventure.[20] Vincent was commissioned in the Royal Engineers as early as September 1914, when he entered the School of Military Engineering at Chatham. This was followed by a posting with the 67th. Field Co., one of the units badly disrupted by the ill-fated expedition to Gallipoli in July 1915. Basil received his commission a month after his younger brother, joining the 21st. Siege Battery at Bristol. By May 1915, this unit had been sent to Boulogne as part of the Second Army front stretching from Verblondenmolen to the Douve. Basil was actually put in charge of communications, having promised his senior officer that Ferranti Ltd would provide a telephone switchboard 'to connect up his various lines and to make a proper exchange system'.[21]

The experiences of both young men in those dark days of full-scale and bloody war were, of course, far from the romantic images many had cherished when first joining up as patriotic members of Kitchener's forces. The lack of leadership at Gallipoli impressed Vincent very deeply, because the failure to follow up the initial advances had resulted in exceptionally heavy losses which many thought could have been avoided. A little later Basil was involved in the carnage associated with action along the Ypres-Comines canal in 1916, and in the battle for Mount Sorrel. It was in this period that Basil was both awarded a Military Cross for distinguished and gallant service, and sent home for treatment to shrapnel wounds. This was to be the last time he saw his family, because after returning to France in December 1916 with a command of his own, he was to die in the build-up to the Battle of Messines. It was early on the morning of 24 June 1917 that Basil was fatally wounded, when a direct hit from German artillery struck his canvas hut. The two fellow officers sharing the hut with Basil were actually killed outright, while he was sent to the military hospital at Wimereux for treatment to his badly injured legs. In fact, one leg was amputated immediately, such was the damage sustained. This operation was only a partial success, because his condition deteriorated to such an extent that by 12 July he had died.

The loss of their eldest son was naturally a great shock to Dr Ferranti and Gertrude, especially as the War Office had refused them permission to travel to France early in July, on the grounds that Basil's wound was regarded as serious, rather than dangerous. 'It was the first terribly sad thing that had happened to us in our married life', remembered Gertrude. Out of respect for the family, Ferranti Ltd closed the Crown Works for a memorial service at the Church of the Holy Name in Manchester.[22] To Vincent, who had also been wounded in action during 1917, it too meant a dramatic change in his prospects, because as Dr Ferranti informed him: 'You … will have all the more to do to help me, and a hard time when you get back …'.[23] As Vincent had been in Salonika with the 500th. Wessex Field Co. when Basil died, it was actually some time before news of the tragedy reached him, compounding the feelings of sorrow for his brother and friend. As we shall see, Vincent was more than capable of performing all the tasks set him by his father. Like his parents, though, he took some time to come to terms with Basil's death, wondering like many of their contemporaries why all the carnage had been necessary. The family's grief was also further intensified when in January 1919, at the tender age of nineteen, the third daughter, Yolanda (1902–1919), died as a result of acute appendicitis. This sad event was followed shortly in

1920 by the death of Gertrude's father, Francis Ince, the man who had guided the young Ferranti so carefully through his early business career. This brought to an end a tragic period for the Ferranti family, leading all to hope that the new decade would bring better tidings.

5.2 Rationalisation and transformer expansion

Product rationalisation

It was January 1919 before Vincent was freed from his military duties with the Royal Engineers. The company to which Vincent returned, however, was by then very different, not only with respect to its improved financial status, but also in terms of its product range. Munitions production naturally dominated the Crown Works for much of the period from January 1915 until the early months of 1919. Furthermore, the executive committee had also devoted some attention to rationalising the civil side of the business in preparation for a return to normal trading. In many ways, their strategy was severely constrained by an acute shortage of basic raw materials like steel and copper, while poor demand for some products forced them to consider more drastic action.[24] Much of the executive committee's work was consequently focused on how best to use both time and materials in the production of electrical goods. As early as January 1915, Dr Ferranti instructed that: 'Meter parts should be so finished from the tools that they can be put together without any fitting or adjusting ... by passing them along a fixed route and parts being added as they travel along'.[25] This indicates how mass production ideas were infiltrating both the civil and defence sides of the business at this time, building on the earlier success with meter production. Female labour was also introduced into this department for the first time since the company had moved to Hollinwood. This resulted in the recruitment of Miss Forbes (the daughter of Vincent's landlady in Yarrow) as lady supervisor, marking what we shall see in the next chapter was a distinct change in industrial relations policies at Ferranti.[26]

While output figures for the electrical business have not survived for the period 1915–17, it would appear that in the meter department orders stabilised at approximately forty-five per cent of the 1913 level. As the agency network was maintained in an effective state, even at the height of the War in 1917 Ferranti was able to report the receipt of export orders from Europe, India and Australia worth £46,000.[27] In fact, while sixty-two per cent of electrical output was exported in 1917, one must emphasise that meters accounted for almost the whole of this business, indicating how the other departments suffered badly from war-time deprivation.[28] Not surprisingly, greatest difficulty was experienced in the new domestic appliance department, where sales had been hard to boost even in peace-time. The wartime difficulties consequently persuaded the board to sell all their domestic appliance patents and stock to the Jackson Electric Stove Co. (later part of Thorn-EMI) at the end of 1915.[29]

Similarly, while the switchgear business had never been consistently profitable in the pre-War years, raw material shortages, increased labour costs and a dearth of orders forced them to curtail production drastically. Although Whittaker was requested by the board to negotiate a trade-sharing agreement with Reyrolle, little came of the discussions, leaving the board with little choice when considering future strategy.[30] The switchgear department's plight was further worsened in 1916 when its manager was captured by the Germans while on a business trip in Holland. Consequently, by March 1918 all its stock and patents had been sold to Ferguson, Pailin & Co. for just £2,250.[31] Ironically, both Ferguson and Pailin had been trained as switchgear engineers at Ferranti, only leaving the company in 1913 after Tait had warned them that the department would be closed down unless its performance improved. With the Ferranti patents, they managed to develop a successful, if highly specialised, business, surviving as an independent concern for over sixty years.

Growing popularity of electricity

Ferranti emerged from the War with a much streamlined business composed of meters, instruments and transformers. It would, however, be a mistake to believe that no attention was paid to planning for the future, because although two departments were closed the executive committee was persuaded by Dr Ferranti to channel resources into the development of a much-expanded transformer department. Of course, Ferranti had a well-established pedigree in this field, having been responsible for designing and producing the world's first modern transformer as long as ago as 1885.[32] After Deptford, however, the company had concentrated on generating, rather than distribution, equipment, largely because the traditionally small size of British power stations in the 1890s had not encouraged Dr Ferranti to develop the type of large transformer which was in increasing demand by the 1910s. Prior to the War, either German imports or transformers made in the British subsidiaries of American firms had supplied most of the large types ordered by the small number of power supply companies. After 1914, though, British firms were provided with a captive home market. Furthermore, the War years witnessed a rapid extension of electricity usage, sales leaping from 1,964 gWh to 3,569 gWh between 1913 and 1918, while annual investment in new plant reached £23 million.[33] Although most of this new capacity was linked to munitions production, where ninety-five per cent of the new factories were equipped with electric motors,[34] this indicates how a much-expanded and captive market was at last materialising in Britain.

World War One can consequently be regarded as a major fillip to the British electrical industry, in terms of both production and supply, substantially improving the prospects for a more integrated system along the lines advocated by Dr Ferranti in his 1910 IEE presidential address.[35] As we have seen in previous chapters, the electricity supply industry in particular had been handicapped by a combination of the statutory powers vested in municipal hands and a sluggish growth in demand, leading to a proliferation of plants and operations which were technologically antiquated by the late 1890s. Even though the 1898 Cross Committee had supported the establishment of large power companies to serve whole counties, most local authorities opposed any attempts at reducing their control over urban electricity supply.[36] For example, even though LESCo. was still operating along the lines laid down by Dr Ferranti, another seventy power stations competed for the London market. Only NESCo. and a handful of small power companies demonstrated how electricity supply ought to be developed.

The supply network was consequently characterised by a wide diversity of systems, both private and municipal, the vast majority of which operated at such low load factors that the dreams of men like Dr Ferranti who hoped to see an 'All-Electric Age' in their lifetime were being thwarted. Fortunately, though, this outmoded state of affairs was increasingly regarded during the War as a major obstacle to improved economic performance in Britain. Indeed, such was the interest in raising the industry's efficiency that by 1916 a department of electricity power supply had been formed by the Ministry of Munitions to coordinate activity. Extensive discussion was undertaken about such matters as power station interconnections, standardising frequencies and voltages, and expanding the system, while in the debates over post-War reconstruction Charles Merz demanded that the institutional barriers to integration be removed.[37] Even the Municipal Electrical Association pledged its support for legislative reform, leading the Minister for Reconstruction, Charles Addison, to draw up a bill in 1919 which he claimed would, if implemented fully, 'open up possibilities comparable with those of the industrial revolution a century ago'.[38] This move seemed to offer much to the advocates of rationalisation like Merz, McClellan and Ferranti, particularly with its plans for district electricity boards. Sadly, though, those who sought a return to the old non-interventionist principles of pre-War Britain tore the heart out of the proposals, by refusing to grant the new bodies any power to insist on integration and perpetuating all the old features of an industrial structure rooted in municipal power. It was an opportunity missed for the politicians to bring electricity supply up to the standards prevailing in many of Britain's rivals.

Large transformers

In spite of the political failure of 1919, it is important to emphasise how the expanding use of electricity, combined with the virtual absence of foreign competition in the home market, stimulated British manufacturers to make good any technological backwardness which might have been evident in 1914.[39] For Ferranti, the obvious area to exploit was transformer technology, an area in which from 1915 the engineering team invested considerable effort to design and produce much larger units in response to the growing demand from British customers. Transformer production at the Crown Works had actually been a sideline of the instrument department since 1896, where the largest unit produced by 1914 was for a rating of 800 kVA (kilovolt-amperes), ordered by Kilmarnock. By 1915, however, a 1000 kVA unit had been supplied to Manchester Corporation, while in 1918 seven 1250 kVA units had been supplied to Birmingham Corporation. This put Ferranti on an equal technological footing with both the large general electrical manufacturers like British Westinghouse, Dick, Kerr & Co., and BT-H, as well as the specialist transformer manufacturers like Berry's and Fuller, in what was very much a growth sector of the electrical market.[40]

It is important to emphasise that not only was this strategic switch in direction the brainchild of Dr Ferranti, he also took charge of the transformer development programme. Typically, he was anxious to improve their mechanical construction, patenting in 1915 and 1918 (see Appendix B) a series of improvements to the casing, the springs holding the induction coils, and the method of cooling. New ways of impregnating the insulation were also introduced to avoid the damaging accumulation of moisture in the coils, while in 1919 a licence to use the Lulops patents for oil-immersed, water-cooled transformers was acquired to improve further the Ferranti design.[41] This indicates how Ferranti was never afraid to look outside its own confines for ideas, substantially enhancing the team's expertise in designing and manufacturing the largest size of transformer. Most notably, by 1922 the department had won a contract for seven 4000 kVA transformers from the Mangaho power station in the northern island of New Zealand, to be used to step up the voltage from 11,000 V to an unprecedented 110,000V. This was significant because Ferranti was the first to make transformers of this size and capacity in Britain. As one contemporary commented, the firm was 'manufacturing equipment that, as yet, there was no demand for at home, which had created

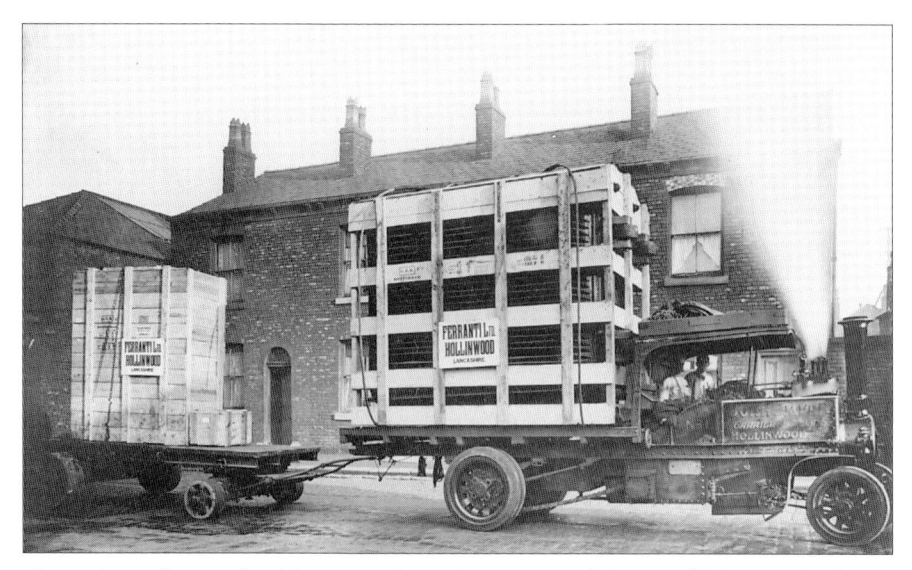

Ferranti transformers for shipment to Rotterdam, c. 1919. *(Museum of Science and Industry at Manchester.)*

the erroneous impression in electrical circles that British manufacturers were incapable of entering this field'.[42] Clearly, the breathing-space afforded by the War had allowed British firms the opportunity to make up for any 'technological lags' which had been evident up to 1914.

Testing transformers and E. T. Norris

Apart from these larger transformers, in 1918 the Crown Works team was also engaged in designing new testing equipment to guarantee the insulation's durability under the most intense pressures. This work was taken over in 1920 by a highly promising electrical engineer, E. T. Norris,[43] who was recruited to lead the development team as they strove to enhance the Ferranti name in this market. Having been trained at Finsbury Technical College, Norris had served an apprenticeship at British Westinghouse, in their famous Trafford Park Works, Manchester. During the war, he joined the Royal Engineers Signals Regiment at the same time as Vincent, providing a strong link with the future manager of the Ferranti transformer department. Once Norris had joined Ferranti in 1920 as a transformer designer, they were able to build a strong partnership which contributed extensively to maintaining the firm's position as a leading player in this market. Although he preferred to work on rotary equipment, A. W. G. Tucker was also persuaded to take charge of the mechanical design of transformers, an area in which he contributed some useful improvements to oil-cooling gear and on-load tap-changers.

With Norris and Tucker devoting all their attention to transformer development, Ferranti was placed in a good position to exploit what was a growing market for these products. Dr Ferranti had by then also been appointed to the post of technical manager to the company, giving him direct responsibility for the supervision of the various development teams established at the end of the War in each department. This demonstrates how team research had become a major feature of the Ferranti style by 1918, indicating how the profits generated from munitions contracts were used to good effect in boosting the company's competitiveness in its chosen fields. Like many of its counterparts,[44] Ferranti was committed to a significant investment in research and development facilities, with Dr Ferranti providing the dynamic leadership required in pursuing this strategy. Even the government was helping to stimulate a wider interest in applied research, having established the Department of Scientific & Industrial Research in 1915, indicating how Britain was beginning to wake up to the possibilities in this approach.

The one million volt arc

As a direct indication of how Ferranti benefited from the development work on transformers, by 1919 transformer output had exceeded £155,000, compared to just £45,000 two years earlier. Dr Ferranti also managed to persuade the board in October 1920 not only to sell £12,000 worth of disused munitions plant,[45] but also to capitalise £73,000 of the general reserve account, to implement a three-stage expansion programme for transformer production. This programme allowed output of transformers to increase markedly, from £155,000 in 1919 to over £230,000 by 1921, as Dr Ferranti, Norris and Tucker brought new designs on to the market. Once again, though, it is interesting to see how the firm was not blinkered to developments outside the company, because by 1924 Ferranti had acquired the rights to use the Dessauer patent covering the connection of transformers in 'cascade'. This form of testing transformer had initially been developed by Haefely, a Swiss firm of electrical manufacturers, leading Dr Ferranti to negotiate a licence for what was generally regarded as a first-class design. The system involved the series connection of the high voltage windings of separate transformers whose insulation levels were suitably graduated. This allowed the high voltage output of the separate units to be added together, by which means the output voltage of the system was increased in steps. By 1925, such had been the rate of progress that E. T. Norris had constructed a one million volt unit in the Crown Works testing area, producing the first arc of that capacity ever seen in Britain.

Ferranti had clearly managed to build up a considerable reputation in this field by the 1920s. Widespread interest was especially shown in the production of a one million volt arc at the Crown Works, with one contemporary noting that it was 'an event of great historical interest', considering the long Ferranti association with high voltage work.[46] Ferranti was also able to convert this curiosity into a growing business, securing such prestigious contracts as a one million volt unit supplied to the National Physical Laboratory in 1925, as well as supplying similar equipment to major electrical and allied manufacturers like Steatite & Porcelain (one million volts), Callenders' Cables (one million volts), GEC (one million volts), Pirelli Cables (667,000 volts), and Reyrolle (650,000 volts).[47] This is further evidence of the growing commitment to research and development within British industry at that time, substantiating Sanderson's claim that the source of new ideas in electrical technology was moving away from the universities into well-organised industrial research departments staffed by trained technicians.[48] At Ferranti, by bringing in E. T. Norris and investing in new development facilities, management ensured that the company would participate fully in this movement, reaffirming the belief in technological progress as an essential means of improving competitiveness.

The first ever million volt arc at Hollinwood, 1925. *(Museum of Science and Industry at Manchester.)*

Ferranti Canada

This competitive advantage in the most sophisticated type of transformers was also exploited further by extending the firm's commitment to its Canadian subsidiary. As we saw in section 4.5, while A. B. Anderson had been responsible in the post-1905 recovery period for building an extensive agency network, the Canadian agency was by far the most significant of these outlets, contributing substantially to the main aim of improving throughput in the British factory. Continually since the creation of the Ferranti Electrical Co. of Canada in 1912, however, the agency had been lobbying for permission to initiate some production of meters and products which would prove even more suitable for its domestic market. However, while during the First World War a meter and a pole-top distribution transformer were developed, the main board at Hollinwood insisted on a conservative strategy of simply selling British-made products. Ball and Vardalas have consequently concluded that the Ferranti board frustrated the development of Ferranti Canada by its 'very conservative, if not colonial, attitude' to the local management's ideas.[49] The influence of British managers over Ferranti Canada was also extended in 1922, when Ferranti bought out its owners for $15,000, a move which seemingly terminated any discussion of Canadian independence.

It is well-known from principal-agent theory that in a world of uncertainty agents can act opportunistically, unless effectively monitored.[50] By acquiring a controlling interest in Ferranti Canada, the British management would consequently be in a better position to ensure that local managers would not jeopardise the central purpose of establishing the agency network, namely, boosting British-based production. Ironically, though, 1922 marks the start of a much more dynamic era in Ferranti Canada's history, because its new general manager, A. B. Cooper, proved to be much more adept in persuading his British owners to invest further in production and development plant.[51] In this context, the crucial change was not so much the purchase of the Canadian company's stock, but the greater levels of trust between Vincent de Ferranti and A. B. Cooper, confirming Casson's claims that trust is an essential ingredient in developing an effective multinational organisation.[52] We shall trace the early career of Vincent de Ferranti in the next section, but it is clear that after he had met Cooper while visiting Canada in 1923, they struck up a close friendship based on mutual technical interests and confidence. Indeed, it was on Vincent's recommendation that the board backed Cooper's bids for funds in 1923 and 1929, while once the second generation Ferranti had succeeded his father as chairman of the firm in 1930 he continued to place considerable faith in the Canadian subsidiary's management. Indeed, from 1931 Ferranti Canada was allowed to develop its own international

A. B. Cooper (left) and R. H. Schofield at the time of Ferranti Canada's launch in 1922.

marketing strategy. Even though the Wall St Crash of 1929 severely dented the fledgling corporation's prospects, both the range of products and its total sales continued to increase after the early 1930s depression.

The conversion of Ferranti Canada from an agency into a production plant is a clear reflection of Nicholas's view on how multinationals evolved from relatively humble origins.[53] This process can also clearly be closely related to Dunning's 'eclectic paradigm',[54] because in terms of satisfying the Canadian market's preference for home-made goods, exploiting the Ferranti name in meters and transformers, and gaining complete control of the agency, all three conditions in the model were fulfilled. On the other hand, while as we shall see later a personal preference emerged in the Ferranti multinational strategy, of far greater significance in the 1920s was the initiative of local management, because not only was Cooper in 1923 able to raise parent company finance for a larger transformer production plant in Toronto, by 1929 the main board had also agreed to his proposal for a further expansion costing $400,000, to build a new factory at Mt. Dennis, on the outskirts of Toronto. This confirms Taylor's view that technology transfers to Canada at that time were largely the result of entreaties from local management, rather

The Mt. Dennis factory of Ferranti Canada, opened in 1929.

than the desire of firms to exploit any of the advantages associated with Dunning's paradigm.[55]

Clearly, Cooper was instrumental in forcing the parent company to alter its approach towards the agency network established since 1907. Ferranti Canada was still heavily dependent on the commercial viability of British-designed products, especially meters, power transformers and (for a brief spell between 1926 and 1932) radio components. However, after moving into the Mt. Dennis factory in 1929 Cooper encouraged his engineers to reduce the reliance on British designs even further. This strategy also seemed to work, because not only did the firm start to develop equipment specifically for Canadian and certain export markets, it also later diversified into new electronics markets which the parent company had yet to enter. In one important respect, the subsidiary even managed to contribute substantially to Ferranti expertise, because after developing small pole-top transformers during the First World War, Ferranti Canada proceeded in the mid-1920s to assist the parent company's engineers in the design of similar equipment for the British market. Unfortunately, though, because of the severe 1930s slump in North America, Ferranti Canada struggled to achieve financial independence from its parent, recording losses of over $350,000 in the period 1932–37 which forced Cooper to call on parent company subsidies to keep the subsidiary afloat.

The financial dependence of Ferranti Canada on its parent company is further testimony to the strong bonds which linked Cooper and Vincent de Ferranti, because at no time in those difficult years did the latter threaten to usurp his local manager's hegemony. Indeed, since 1922 Ferranti had allowed Cooper considerable latitude in managing the Canadian venture, typifying in stark form the general British approach towards the organisation of their multinational subsidiaries. As Buckley and Casson have noted, the management structures adopted by multinationals in general have largely been determined by the entrepreneurial cultures of their domestic economies.[56] In this context, there is little doubt that the loose organisational structures adopted by British businesses after expanding from an initial base was imitated extensively in the development of overseas operations. This is further confirmed by the work of Jones on a sample of major British multinationals, including Glaxo, Vickers and Dunlop, revealing how up to 1939 'many British companies paid only spasmodic attention to their foreign subsidiaries', with most relying on irregular reports and occasional visits by a main board director to distant outposts.[57]

It was a system which reflected the persistent use by family firms of loose holding company forms in the UK, providing a strong clue in explaining the general failure of British multinational manufacturing subsidiaries to fulfil their initiators' expectations. Of course, as far as Ferranti was concerned, a high level of operational autonomy was also one of the hallmarks of the ethos instilled into the company by Sebastian de Ferranti since the 1890s. Crucially, in dealing with the distant Canadian subsidiary Vincent was willing to trust Cooper to run the business as successfully as possible. Certainly, there is very little evidence of extensive board discussion of Ferranti Canada's plans or fortunes, even when a substantial investment decision was required. It was a tradition which was sustained for many years, indicating how the Canadian subsidiary was run just like one of the British departments.

Trust, losses and boltholes

Ferranti Canada was consequently quite typical of British multinational business up to the 1950s, not only in the stages through which it had passed and the structure adopted, but also in terms of its generally poor financial performance. Even though considerable faith was placed in the management skills of its general manager, A. B. Cooper, he was clearly unsuccessful in converting potential into commercial viability. The persistent losses made after the major expansion in 1929 also confirm the difficulties associated with operating in the Canadian market, a point which calls into question the firm's wisdom in competing against much larger American subsidiaries in a market which seemed to be prone to marked vicissitudes. In describing how British multinationals focused much of their attention after 1914 on the developed Empire markets like Canada, Stopford accuses them of taking 'the path of least resistance', by establishing subsidiaries in allegedly 'safe haven' economies which would provide easy pickings for products from the motherland.[58] This argument, however, is hardly credible, because not only has Nicholas demonstrated that such a strategy was highly rational, because 'Empire markets offered host economy advantages in terms of psychic proximty, government, tariffs and nationalism',[59] Jones also shows how the Canadian market was far from easy.[60] The initial justification for opening agencies would appear to have been valid, and Ferranti exports leapt as a consequence, but little credibility can be attached to the investment in Canadian production facilities, and the firm's financial resources were certainly stretched by its subsidiary's poor performance.

In evaluating the reasons why Vincent continued to support Ferranti Canada through the difficult 1930s, once must return to the personal factors to which we alluded earlier, and in particular Vincent's growing belief that it would be wise to diversify his investment away from the United Kingdom.[61] Although personal factors are rarely accorded much credibility in the models proposed by economists like Dunning and Nicholas, there is no doubt that one of the main reasons why Vincent persisted with Ferranti Canada was a feeling that in view of the era's economic and political troubles he could establish a bolthole if matters deteriorated badly. At the same time, of course, economic considerations were never far from this businessman's mind, highlighting again why Ferranti had embarked on an ambitious export strategy in 1907. The big difference by the 1920s and 1930s was that power transformers, rather than meters, had become the main emphasis of the relationship, initiating a relationship which over the following forty years influenced the firm's multinational strategy.

This can be confirmed by noting how not only was Vincent committed to Ferranti Canada, in spite of its poor financial performance, he also took a substantial stake in another Canadian electrical manufacturer, Packard Electric, based at St Catherine's in Ontario.[62] Although connected to the American car firm of Packard, Packard Electric had been an independent transformer and meter manufacturer since its formation in 1894. However, while it possessed considerable technical expertise in its main product areas, like Ferranti Canada it had never been a very successful firm. Vincent de Ferranti, on the other hand, was confident enough in 1936 to acquire one-third of its equity, in the hope that his other subsidiary might benefit from some pooling of resources.

In fact, for over twenty years Ferranti was frustrated in this respect by both Packard management and shareholders, resulting in the two firms remaining entirely separate and competing fiercely for the unprofitable business of the 1930s, a story we shall return to in section 8.2. Clearly, though, the investment in Canada was a bold venture which reflected the desire of Sebastian and Vincent, and later of Sebastian between 1963 and 1982, to extend its influence into other parts of the world, especially where it had a competitive advantage. While little return was earned from this activity, it was again symptomatic of the long-term approach which was becoming a hallmark of the Ferranti way. It was an approach the Canadian management appreciated, because when Sebastian de Ferranti died in 1930 they erected a plaque at the Toronto factory which bore the inscription:

> This factory is dedicated to the memory of Sebastian Ziani de Ferranti, D.Sc., F.R.S., Engineer, Pioneer and Inventor, beloved founder of the company which bears his name.

No better testimony exists to the remarkable achievements of a man loved and respected well away from his native shores.

5.3 A family firm again

Vincent's early career

The Dr Ferranti imprint was, of course, to be found in the elaboration of this strategy. Crucially, though, as we have already seen with regard to Ferranti Canada, by the 1920s another member of his family was beginning to make what eventually became a substantial contribution to the company's fortunes. Indeed, on returning from military duties Vincent threw himself energetically into company activities. One clear indication of his commitment was the decision he took to purchase 1,800 Ferranti ordinary shares, approximating to around ten per cent of the controlling equity. His grandfather, Francis Ince, advised him against making what was still a risky investment. Quite characteristically, though, Vincent replied that now he had an incentive to improve the business's prospects.[63] One must remember that Vincent's formative years had been dominated by his father's exile from the Crown Works, an episode which provided such a harsh business lesson that throughout the following forty years he always insisted on keeping the business solvent and in family hands. In this sense, he differed markedly in approach from Dr Ferranti, because while Vincent appreciated the value of engineering excellence, he also understood the imperative need to make a proper return on capital employed, introducing a more realistic aspect to the engineering-led approach of his father.

It was not until January 1921 that Vincent was given a position of responsibility, however, largely because A. W. Tait remained sceptical of his ability

Vincent de Ferranti by the Ferranti DH Moth, 1930. This plane was used in the firm's first experiments with radar. *(Museum of Science and Industry at Manchester.)*

at the age of 27 to contribute much to the company. After four years of military service, on the other hand, during which he was awarded the Military Cross, Vincent was convinced that he had the managerial skills required to cope with running a department, arguing that if one could operate effectively under fire anything was within one's grasp. Dr Ferranti had also been careful to provide both Basil and Vincent with some technical training after their formal education. On joining Ferranti in 1919, he was immediately seconded to the instrument department's high voltage laboratory, where he would learn much about transformer technology. It was only after some hard lobbying by his father, however, that Tait finally agreed to appoint Vincent as the transformer department's first manager in January 1921.

Financial reconstruction

The chairman's reticence over his appointment would clearly provide Vincent with another incentive to succeed in business. By that time, of course, the company was much stronger than it had ever been, having invested the munitions profits into improved facilities and advanced engineering programmes. No doubt much to Tait's surprise, Arthur Whittaker was also convinced that the improvement in fortunes 'was mainly due to Ferranti'.[64] This contribution was reflected in the remuneration awarded by the board to members of the executive committee at the end of the War, Dr Ferranti receiving £1,500, compared to the £500 payments made to Whittaker and Thomas.[65] Tait was also persuaded to appoint Dr Ferranti to the post of technical manager. However, because Whittaker went on to say that the 'great danger is his known disposition for continual experimentation and alterations of design', the executive committee continued to monitor the technical manager's day-to-day activities at the Crown Works. In this way, Dr Ferranti was able to re-establish himself as a permanent member of the Ferranti management team. Even though he was never to hold anything like the power he had possessed up to 1903, his new position was sufficient to ensure that after 1918 he would continue to act as the main inspiration behind the company's growth.

In fact, the executive committee faded away within a couple of years, indicating how much greater faith was placed in the technical manager by the 1920s. Most importantly, it is also noticeable that the extensive centralisation of financial controls pursued by Tait and Whittaker since 1905 was being modified by the reintroduction of Dr Ferranti as technical manager, facilitating the pursuit of technology-led strategies which the founder had always preferred. One must stress that the rigid departmentalisation of activity prevented Dr Ferranti from interfering directly in the commercial activities of any manager, while Tait and Whittaker continued to monitor financial performance from their offices at the centre. On the other hand, after 1920 especially Dr Ferranti was in a much better position to stimulate innovation within the company, acting in the capacity of an 'ideas man' for the various departments.

Indeed, such was his central position within the company by the early 1920s that Tait could no longer justify refusing to grant Dr Ferranti an opportunity to regain control of Ferranti Ltd. Although a reconstruction package had first been devised in 1921, because of 'the financial stringency in the country' at the beginning of a major economic depression the plans were shelved.[66] In 1923, however, the issued capital was raised from £123,374 to £206,166 by the creation of 40,000 6% £1 cumulative preference shares (to rank with the 60,000 already in existence), 40,000 7% £1 non-cumulative second preference shares (to rank with the 60,000 ordinary shares, which in turn were converted into 7% £1 non-cumulative second preference shares), and 90,000 ordinary shares (to rank with the 10,000 deferred shares, which in turn were to be renamed ordinary shares). It is important to stress that this reconstruction actually brought no new capital into the company, because £82,792 of the general reserve account (see Appendix C, Table 1) was capitalised to purchase all the new shares issued. More significantly, all the deferred shares owned by Dr Ferranti and Vincent were converted into ordinary shares (at the rate of five ordinary shares for every one deferred share held), once more giving the family control of the business which bore their name (see Appendix D).

It is vital to stress once again, though, that Ferranti was a very different type of family company to the one which had collapsed in 1903. In the first place, Tait was still executive chairman and the board was dominated by accountants and financiers.[67] The company's finances had also been substantially improved, because although the 1923 reconstruction represented a nominal change in capitalisation Ferranti was in a better position than ever. As Appendix C (Table 1) reveals, all the debenture capital had been redeemed by 1923, leaving the preference shares as the only fixed-interest securities, on which all the accumulated arrears had also been repaid. The net profits had also been appreciably better in the post-war years, averaging over £31,000 between 1918 and 1923, compared to just under £4,400 in the six pre-War years. Furthermore, the unaudited figures provided in Appendix C (Table 2) for gross profits indicate how there were general improvements in this area. This provided the board with the resources to build a useful general reserve account, from which funds could be directed into enhancing productive facilities at the Crown Works, demonstrating again the renewed strength of a company which prior to 1914 had been largely a meter manufacturer.

5.4 The 1920s electrical industry

Meter department expansion

One must never forget, of course, that in describing how Ferranti extended its presence in the transformer market the firm continued to be a major player in the meter market. Meter output recovered swiftly after the war, with output rising from just over £91,000 in 1918 to almost £365,000 by 1923. This reflected the considerable success achieved with the new type of AC meter, marketed as the FD meter, which sold especially well in the export markets served by Ferranti agents. The man most responsible for this marketing drive was the sales manager, R. H. Schofield, who worked industriously to maintain and improve the agency network established by A. B. Anderson. Consequently, Ferranti exports rose significantly in the immediate post-War years, from £75,058 in 1918 to £234,317 in 1923. Although they fell off in the severe early 1920s depression, by 1923 they still stood at over £206,000. Meters consistently accounted for well over half the company's exports in this period, while as a proportion of total British exports of 'house service meters and instruments' Ferranti provided over forty per cent.[68] This re-emphasises a point made on several earlier occasions, that the meter continued to provide Ferranti with its staple source of income, in both domestic and overseas markets. Dr Ferranti consequently devoted a considerable amount of time in the 1920s (see Appendix B) to improving its design, taking out twelve patents on this subject alone.

Domestic opportunities

The growing strength of Ferranti after the First World War is clearly an important conclusion to draw from this analysis of the period. An additional point to make at this stage, however, would be that the company's performance was not always a reflection of the industry's general development. The pre-War years had been extremely difficult, even for the American subsidiaries established around the turn of the century. Reflecting a subtle change in attitude, Lloyd George's wartime coalition government had set up an influential committee in 1918, composed of several representatives of leading electrical firms (including R. H. Schofield of Ferranti), which was charged with the task of reviewing the post-war opportunities for key industries. After considerable deliberation, this committee concluded that

> it is essential to establish confidence in the future of the electrical manufacturing industry by assuring it the support of the home market, without which the manufacturers practically all agree that it is hopeless to expect any great development of the industry.[69]

This sentiment tied in very closely with the protectionist stance most electrical manufacturers had taken in the Edwardian era, many having supported Joseph Chamberlain's Tariff Reform Campaign of 1903–06 and the consequent Tariff Commission.[70] Prior to 1914, of course, the British electrical market had been totally dominated by either American or German subsidiary plants or cheaper imported equipment, in the face of which indigenous manufacturers like Ferranti had been obliged to develop highly specialised product ranges.[71] During and after the First World War, however, not only was there a substantial reduction in imports, the expansion in demand for electricity stimulated a significant growth of the industry, resulting in average sales of £17 million per annum between 1920 and 1927, compared to just £6.8 million in 1913.[72]

Merger talks

Although electrical manufacturers did not receive the tariff protection for which they had lobbied since 1903, it is clear that they were benefiting from a substantial growth in demand after 1914. This conducive environment also stimulated a series of mergers which drastically altered the industry's structure. The War had further highlighted the benefits of cooperation brought by the formation of BEAMA in 1911. As a consequence, by 1919 two new companies had appeared, English Electric (formed by amalgamating Dick, Kerr & Co. with the Siemens assets acquired from the Custodian of Enemy Property) and Metropolitan-Vickers Electrical Co. (after the merger of British Westinghouse with Vickers' electrical division).[73] During the 1920s, largely as a result of American intervention, English Electric was reorganised, while in 1929 Metro-Vic's was combined with BT-H to create Associated Electric Industries (AEI). GEC had also been heavily involved in this combination movement, absorbing several smaller specialist firms in its bid to compete with the American-owned giants of the industry.

By 1930, GEC, AEI and English Electric consequently controlled sixty per cent of the heavy electrical business in Britain and thirty-five per cent of the total market.[74] Even Ferranti was embroiled in this 'merger-mania', when in 1918 the Berry Electric Transformer Co. approached Tait through the prominent company promoter, F. A. Szarvasy, with an offer to purchase the company outright.[75] The combination of Tait's tight conditions and, one might suspect, objections voiced by Dr Ferranti to such a move, were enough to deflect the predator. However, the proposal was a clear reflection of both the industry's new mood of optimism and the attractiveness of Ferranti as a major player in the transformer market. In retrospect, though, Ferranti were wise to refrain from participating in this merger wave, because not only did many of the new, larger companies perform poorly in the interwar years,[76] the Hollinwood firm was able to grow generically as a result of the successful combination of engineering innovation and effective management.

Price depression

While the creation of large electrical firms would have been a major threat to smaller operations like Ferranti, one of the more potent influences on this industry during the 1920s was the dramatic fall in prices for most goods after the severe cyclical downturn in 1921. In fact, electrical engineering output fell by thirty per cent between 1920 and 1922,[77] dashing the post-war hopes of a long-term expansion in demand for the industry's more advanced products. BEAMA was also unable to control what amounted to the intense price competition which followed on from this slump. Even though only 3.2 per cent of the industry's capital was unremunerated at that time, compared to an average of almost sixty per cent in the period 1909–13,[78] trading conditions were still difficult. Ferranti, for example, discovered that the average price per kVA received for transformers fell from £1.88 between 1919 and 1922 to £0.63 in the following seven years, indicating how even when orders could be secured there was little profit in the business.[79]

This slump in prices was actually to prompt many manufacturers to withdraw from the price agreements which had been negotiated by BEAMA since 1911. Indeed, although Ferranti retained some arrangements with other meter manufacturers, by 1927 most of the electrical price rings had been disbanded. Ferranti had left the transformer association as early as 1922, such was the level of mistrust in this sector, indicating how even a founder-member of BEAMA refused to be tied to practices which had earlier been so popular. Not surprisingly, then, during the mid-1920s profitability slumped alarmingly in the electrical industry. One survey noted that the proportion of net profits to total capital for eleven major manufacturers (including Ferranti) fell from 9.35 per cent to 7.7 per cent between 1925 and 1928.[80] As we shall see later (see Appendix C, Table 2), while Ferranti performed better than this industry average, one is left with the distinct impression of a troubled period at a time when new technological opportunities were beginning to appear.

Export difficulties

Not only were conditions in the domestic market increasingly difficult after 1920, export markets were also more hostile. The export price index (1913=100) for electrical goods actually fell from a peak of 303 in 1920 to 188 by 1929,[81] compounding the problem of having to deal in a currency which was over-valued by at least ten per cent after the decision to return to the pre-War parity of $4.86 to the pound sterling.[82] One must also mention how most developed and developing economies pursued protectionist trading policies. In contrast, although eighty-two per cent of electrical firms were in favour of a similar policy for Britain, the electorate in 1923 rejected Baldwin's proposals for a drift away from the traditional allegiance to Free Trade.[83] Even in the Empire, British exporters no longer had it their own way, with movements like the 'Made in Australia' campaign persuading indigenous consumers to favour their home producers.[84] This combination of protectionism with louder calls for economic independence among Imperial countries forced Ferranti to boost their marketing efforts by extending the agency contacts, giving R. H. Schofield the difficult task of providing the Crown Works with a steady supply of orders.

The difficulties in both home and domestic markets are reflected in the struggle Ferranti experienced in restoring output levels to the record peak of 1920, when a total of almost £800,000 was achieved (see Appendix C, Table 3). Exports actually expanded consistently in the early 1920s, reaching almost £300,000 by 1926 (or one-third of total output), revealing the success attached to Schofield's work. It is important to note, though, that at least seventy-five per cent of all Ferranti exports in the 1920s went to Empire countries, revealing how most attention was paid to the less-developed economies of the world, rather than attempting to compete with the strong American and European companies in their own markets. While this might well be described as a rather defensive policy, at the same time one could also argue that Ferranti pursued the highly rational strategy of selling goods in markets where competition was less intense, compensating considerably for the problems in the domestic market.

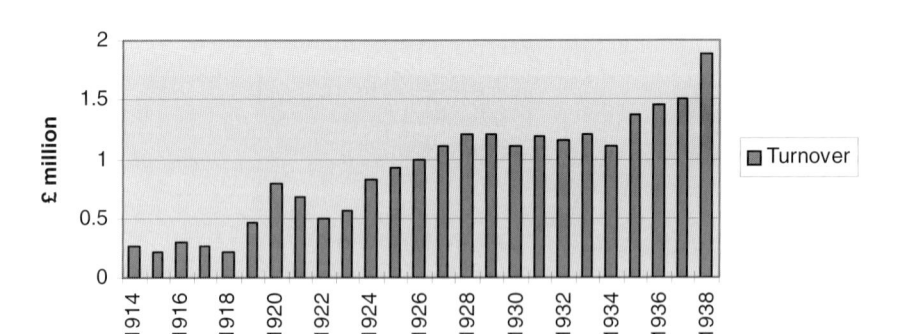

Figure 5.1. *Ferranti Ltd Turnover, 1914–39*

Clearly, the 1920s would have tested the patience of management after the considerable post-War expansion of capacity. As figure 5.1 reveals, turnover fell off badly during the early 1920s and only recovered after 1924. Interestingly, though, profitability at Ferranti continued to improve in spite of these problems, largely as a result of the substantial reduction in fixed-interest security payments arising from Tait's policy of redeeming as much of the debenture capital as possible. This allowed management to build up the reserves for future product and production development. Indeed, it is interesting to note how (see Appendix C, Table 1) by 1929 the general reserve account (£270,000) was larger than the issued capital (£246,166). Ferranti was consequently in a much better position to finance the technology-led strategy fashioned by the owning family, emphasising once again how the combination of Tait's financial skills with the engineering instincts of the Ferranti family was beginning to produce solid rewards.

5.5 The construction of a grid network

One of the major departments to benefit from the availability of more liberal product development funding in the 1920s was transformers, building on the impressive achievements of the War-time years when Ferranti had come to be recognised as one of the leading manufacturers of both testing transformers and large grid-type equipment. We have already noted how Ferranti benefited substantially from the publicity surrounding the manufacture of 4000 kVA transformers for a New Zealand customer, revealing an ability to make goods for which no indigenous demand had yet materialised. This reputation was also further reinforced when the Tata Power Co., in India, ordered twelve 10,000 kVA transformers,[85] while between 1923 and 1930 the Victoria Falls & Transvaal Power Co. was supplied with transformers ranging in size from 500 to 20,000 kVA. Similarly, the 1925 experiments with one million volt arcs placed Ferranti at the very head of this field. The joint research work of Vincent de Ferranti and E. T. Norris on surge absorbers (to protect transformers from lightning strikes or short circuits) also provided much greater security levels at the highest operating voltages. By 1929, after six years of research, they had developed a surge absorber which was capable of reducing the impact of such an occurrence by eighty-five per cent,[86] Dresden University concluding that it 'definitely and appreciably flattens the wave front of an incoming surge'.[87]

The reform of electricity supply

Of course, the most important opportunity of the 1920s for Vincent's transformer department was the government's decision to construct a national grid network. After the political failure of 1919 described earlier, this belated move was seen as an essential means of coordinating activity in the supply industry, a policy which would cheapen the costs of distribution, and potentially the price of electricity.[88] In spite of the post-War reluctance of politicians to galvanise suppliers into a more rationalised structure, electricity sales had continued to rise impressively, from 3,570 gWh in 1918 to 5,817 gWh by 1926.[89] Nevertheless, of the 597 stations under the Electricity Commissioners' jurisdiction in 1926, only fifteen were capable of producing over 100 million kWh, while fifty-six per cent generated a maximum of just 2.5 million kWh.[90] This situation was regarded as wholly unacceptable by most industrialists and knowledgeable commentators, especially when schemes like those advocated by Dr Ferranti in his momentous 1910 presidential address to the IEE lay idly on the drawing board. While the prominent economist Sir Leo Chiozza Money had argued in 1919, such a scheme 'would be fruitful almost beyond imagining',[91] it was only in 1924 that a Conservative government appointed Lord Weir to review the future development of electricity supply.

Lord Weir was an admirable choice for this task, because as a prominent industrialist himself he recognised the need to improve competitiveness by providing extensive access to cheaper sources of power.[92] It was also well known that electricity in Britain was up to four times the price charged in Switzerland, Italy and France,[93] prompting Lord Weir to warn the Prime Minister, Stanley Baldwin, that fundamental structural changes would be required to bring the system into line with best-practice elsewhere. Predictably, the local authorities objected to his suggestion that a central body ought to be established, resurrecting some of the difficulties which had scotched reform in 1919. However, in 1925 there was a stronger political will to succeed in an area where the earlier Lloyd George coalition had failed, resulting in the enactment of the 1926 Electricity (Supply) Act. Problems remained in the system, as we shall see later, leading some contemporaries to complain about excessive state intervention. Nevertheless, there is little doubt that this Act proved to be a significant milestone in the history of electricity supply.

Planning the grid network

The major achievements of the 1926 Act were to appoint electricity commissioners with powers that extended over the entire supply industry, creating a Central Electricity Board as the governing body responsible for operating the national grid network on behalf of the state. This was not nationalisation, because each power station would remain in either private or municipal hands, introducing the concept of the public corporation at a time when greater interest was being shown in the relationship between the state and the economy. The commissioners would divide the country into seven regions, appointing 'selected' stations as the core around which the national grid would be built. Although it had initially been intended that only sixty power stations would be 'selected', this status was rather more liberally bestowed in order to curry favour with supply engineers, resulting in the establishment of a nucleus of 144 stations.[94] This was the kind of idea Dr Ferranti had been advocating in 1910, indicating how he was one of the more powerful voices influencing the 1920s debate about the future of electricity supply. He clearly played no part in the final drafting of Lord Weir's report, because he was not invited to give evidence and engineers like Charles Merz and Sir John Kennedy were more directly involved in the planning process. On the other hand, in constantly pushing forward the idea of an 'All-Electric Age' through practical achievements, speeches and work with the Electrical Development Association, Dr Ferranti had helped to create a favourable climate in which such ideas would be more widely accepted.[95]

Although under the chairmanship of Sir Andrew Duncan it was March 1927 before the CEB began its work, Kennedy and Merz had already set out a basic plan to which the new organisation would work over the following five years. One of the more interesting features of their plan was the decision to use 132 kV as the operating voltage of a national grid network, instantly raising the highest transmission pressures pertaining in Britain by a factor of thirteen. This would naturally pose an interesting challenge to manufacturers unused to producing such advanced forms of equipment, unless, of course, as with Ferranti, they had already been exporting high voltage transformers. Indeed, the construction of a national grid provided Ferranti with an excellent opportunity to demonstrate its competitive advantage in high voltage work. At first, though, Dr Ferranti and Vincent had to lobby vigorously for a change of policy by the CEB.[96] The commissioners had actually decided on the use of single-phase transformers, forcing the Ferranti engineers to point out that three-phase equipment would achieve much more substantial economies of scale. In simple terms, the commissioners' plans would entail the use of three single-phase transformers for the three-phase AC grid voltage, while the Ferranti suggestion would require only a single three-phase transformer, an argument which would eventually win the day.

Grid orders

The decision to use three-phase transformers was clearly a rational move by the commissioners, giving them an excellent opportunity to reap all the potential economies of scale which such a system offered in the distribution of electricity. Although the transformer price ring was annoyed at the wrecking of its plans to tender only for single-phase equipment, Ferranti had actually left this association in 1922. Furthermore, as one of the few firms capable of manufacturing large three-phase transformers, this guaranteed a significant share of the orders. Grid construction did not actually begin until 1929, at which time the transformer contracts were placed. By the end of 1930, though, Ferranti had been awarded thirty-two per cent of the £1.5 million worth of business in 66 kV and 132 kV transformers. This substantial share was a reflection of their position as the leading transformer manufacturer, because their nearest rivals, Berry Electric Transformer, received twenty-seven per cent of the orders, while other major electrical manufacturers like BT-H (fourteen per cent), Metro-Vic's (six per cent), and English Electric (four per cent) were unable to match Ferranti in this field. In total, by 1932 Ferranti had received orders from the CEB and 'selected' stations valued at over £780,000. One of the contracts was for transformers with a rating of 80,000 kVA, the largest of their kind made in Britain to date.[97] This indicates how Vincent de Ferranti and his team were extremely competitive in this market, allowing Dr Ferranti to take great pride in witnessing the substantial contribution his company made to the construction of a grid network for which he had continuously lobbied.

Another aspect of the grid network to which Ferranti contributed was the production of accurate summation metering equipment to monitor consumption across the system. This equipment involved the use of kWh meters which transmitted pulses to summators to indicate the output of alternators, printing out the number of kWh consumed every half-an-hour. However, while the first contracts were placed in 1929, at that time none of the designs had been completed, forcing the instrument department manager, Wilfred Holmes, to assemble a team of engineers for this purpose. Apart from his son Sidney, this team also included a man who would eventually go on to succeed Holmes as instrument department manager and contribute extensively to the Ferranti reputation in this field. This man was Eric Grundy,

One of the 132kV transformers supplied by Ferranti to the British grid network developed between 1929 and 1932.

a young engineer who had first joined Ferranti in 1921, before leaving to take a degree in engineering at the University of Manchester. He had completed the degree just at the time the summation metering equipment contracts were placed in 1929, providing him with an excellent opportunity to demonstrate his recently-acquired skills. The company eventually went on to sell substantial numbers of these meters to the south east and north west regions of the CEB, a success which helped to extend the instrument department's reputation in the booming 1930s.

The grid was consequently a major fillip to both Ferranti and the electrical industry as a whole. It is important to note that a policy decision had been taken at the highest levels of government that the CEB ought to deal only with home-based manufacturers, providing contracts worth £27 million at a time when the international economy was wrecked by the Wall St Crash of 1929. Even in the worst year (1931) of the major depression lasting from 1929 to 1932, electrical output only fell by 3.9 per cent, compared to 6.4 per cent for all British industries.[98] For Hollinwood, this business would have

The Ferranti meter assembly line at Hollinwood in the 1930s, staffed by women and supervised by men.

been vitally important, compensating to a certain extent for the cotton textile industry's continued decline. Indeed, employment at the Crown Works more than doubled over the period 1923–32, rising from 2,056 to 4,663 by 1932, indicating how Ferranti became a refuge from the severe vicissitudes of that era.

5.6 Domestic appliances

Publicising electricity

Not only did Ferranti benefit considerably from the extension of electricity distribution in the interwar years, the firm also diversified into products which would be used by the individual consumer. As he had always been, in the 1920s Dr Ferranti was at the forefront of the campaign to popularise the use of electricity, exclaiming in 1924 that: 'We cannot have too much electricity. We want it everywhere, and we have not anything like enough of it'.[99] Such was his prominence as a leading figure in the industry that in 1926 he was elected president of the Electrical Development Association (EDA), an organisation formed in 1919 by the IEE, BEAMA, the Cable Manufacturers' Association, and the Incorporated Municipal Electrical Association, with the specific aim of advertising the advantages of electricity in the home.[100] It was this organisation which was largely responsible for enhancing electricity's public profile in the 1920s, embarking on campaigns each autumn and winter to convince housewives in particular that this energy source would produce both labour-saving benefits and improve the domestic ambience.

The work of the EDA was also reinforced by the activities of the Electrical Association for Women (EAW), another publicity vehicle for the industry. In this movement not only did Dr Ferranti help arrange visits and chair meetings, Gertrude de Ferranti also formed the North Wales branch of the EAW, acting as president for several years.[101] Publicising the domestic benefits of using electricity was indeed a family affair with the Ferranti household. Gertrude even wrote a lengthy description for the *Electrical Review* of how her homes were fitted out with all the latest gadgetry.[102] This complemented the work of her husband, who not surprisingly worked hard to convince people that electricity could make a difference in the home. When he gave the 1928 Faraday Lecture, Dr Ferranti took as his title 'Electricity in the Service of Man', arguing that:

> We have learnt that electricity is, before all things, the greatest labour-saver, and a little investigation shows that in the application of electricity to the

requirements of the home we have open to us a field almost unimaginably wide.

These were the kind of sentiments he had expressed as a rather naive youngster, when informing his parents in 1878 of the perpetual-motion machine he had invented, indicating how throughout his life Dr Ferranti stood firm to the belief that electricity had a bright future (see section 1.4).

One of the most impressive demonstrations of the Ferranti belief in an 'All-Electric Age' was how between 1921 and 1925 he completely re-equipped Baslow Hall with all the latest electrical appliances, making it one of the earliest 'All-Electric' homes in the country.[103] The principal novelty of his system was to ensure that the generator was always running at full load, because if the power was not being used for either cooking or lighting, it was heating up a 1,000 gallon water tank as a reserve for the storage heaters. While Dr Ferranti had actually designed a system of storage heaters as early as 1904,[104] by the 1920s many leading authorities were advising supply

Baslow Hall, where Dr Ferranti and his family lived, one of the first the 'All Electric Houses' *(Museum of Science and Industry at Manchester.)*

operations to offer this service to customers as a means of spreading the load throughout the day.[105] Other interesting features of the Baslow Hall system were electrical milking apparatus for the estate's cows, as well as heating for the egg incubation sheds and hot-houses. Although some of the hens were unfortunately electrocuted as a result of early teething problems with the imported American incubator, in general the system proved extremely successful. Indeed, no aspect of their lives was left untouched in the attempt to convince sceptics that life could be radically improved by the use of electricity.

One of the greatest sources of annoyance to Dr Ferranti was the relatively low level of domestic connections to a source of electricity. In 1926 only eighteen per cent of British houses were wired to a power station, while in Switzerland it was 96.5 per cent, Canada 62.3 per cent, Japan 73.4 per cent, and Germany 20.4 per cent.[106] It was the aim of the EDA and the EAW to increase this proportion substantially. Naturally, the construction of a national grid network would significantly facilitate this process, given its intended aim of cheapening the price of electricity and spreading the system into hitherto untapped regions. There was also an increasing realisation among supply authorities, and especially those which were municipally owned, that marketing and publicity could be improved. Schemes offering two-part tariffs, deferred payment, hire purchase or instalment trading were introduced at this time, with well-lit showrooms equipped with all the latest devices used to stimulate greater interest in converting from gas or coal to electricity.[107] In this respect, the electricity supply industry was more adventurous than its major rival, gas, indicating how organisations like the EDA and EAW worked effectively to build up the domestic load throughout the inter-war era.

The first Ferranti electric fire

In view of his private work in this field, it would have been surprising had Dr Ferranti not extended his interest in the domestic uses of electricity to the design and production of equipment to serve what he felt would be an expanding market. As we saw in section 4.6, the company had started a small domestic appliance department just before the War, using patents developed by a member of the Royce family. Although this activity had been closed as a result of the strict rationing of raw materials after 1915, in the early 1920s Dr Ferranti decided to produce an electric fire which would ultimately become one of the company's most successful domestic lines. This device actually emerged as a result of his discovery that the most effective means of relieving some rheumatic pain in his shoulder was to sit next to an electric fire. Initially, he had used a small Dutch electric fire, the *Inventum*, for this purpose. However, having realised that he could improve substantially on the design of the parabolic reflector used to focus the element's heat, in 1927 Dr Ferranti produced what was later described as 'the first fire of aesthetic merit'.[108]

The parabolic reflector fire provided an excellent opportunity for Ferranti to re-enter the domestic appliances market. A team of designers was consequently assembled at the Crown Works, including R. J. Hebbert, W. V. Butterfield and R. Weaving, as well as an artistic designer, W. N. Duffy, leading to the development of a range of water-heaters, fires and cookers to complement the electric fire. Sales growth, however, proved difficult, because by 1930 the new department's output had reached just £21,000. The main reason behind this apparent failure to break into what was an expanding market was the intense competition from cheaper and more efficient American products. Moreover, as we shall see in later sections describing Ferranti efforts to break into mass markets, the firm was more interested in producing high quality goods which were well engineered, increasing their price substantially. Even when in 1932 protective duties were imposed on all imported domestic appliances, Ferranti continued to struggle against the specialist manufacturers which dominated this market (see section 7.3). Nevertheless, Ferranti had at least established a presence in the domestic appliance market, reflecting a willingness to diversify its product base as a result of innovative engineering programmes.

5.7 The venture into radio

Market constraints and opportunities

The opportunities for a technologically astute company were clearly broadening in this era of expansion for British electrical engineering. Indeed, Ferranti could well be seen as a microcosm of the post-War electrical industry, in that not only were the traditional sectors expanding, there were also new branches opening up as a result of major technological breakthroughs. The most notable of these developments was the virtual creation in the 1920s of a radio industry. One must emphasise, though, how this was not so much a 'Schumpeterian Leap' as a hop, skip and a jump: the hop being when Marconi brought his 'magic black box' to Britain in 1896;[109] the skip when it was realised how valuable radio telegraphy could be in the field of wartime communications;[110] and the jump coming after the state created the British Broadcasting Company in 1922. These moves would eventually spark the emergence of an electronics industry during the interwar era, considerably augmenting the opportunities for firms which possessed the requisite design and development skills. Although radio was seen very much as a new branch of electrical engineering, the established firms were largely responsible for exploiting the potential in what to contemporaries was a technological marvel which became an essential feature of life in a very short space of time.[111]

The emergence of radio was one of the most important industrial and social phenomena of the inter-war years. After the creation of the British Broadcasting Company (later changed to the British Broadcasting Corporation in 1925) in 1922, demand for this new form of entertainment expanded so rapidly that by 1930 over 3.4 million households had purchased a licence to receive broadcasts. One must emphasise, though, that venturing into this industry was by no means a straightforward matter of designing products and selling them to consumers, because two main features of the market constrained such a strategy. In the first place, radio set manufacture in Britain up to the 1930s was dominated by the Marconi Co., not simply because of its founder's role in developing the first effective means of transmitting and receiving electromagnetic waves, but mainly because since the firm's formation in 1896 it had gained control of the thirteen master patents covering radio components. These patents could consequently only be used by acquiring a Marconi licence, on which a royalty of 62.5 pence was payable per valve-holder in each set manufactured. Inevitably, this severely limited the attractiveness of set production. Compounding this situation was a second major feature of the embryonic industry, namely, the predominance of radio 'hams' as consumers who preferred to build their own sets, forcing new entrants to build up extensive goodwill in a knowledgeable market.[112]

The AF transformer

Any decision to diversify into radio production would clearly have to be worked out very carefully, given these overwhelming characteristics. Typically, though, Dr Ferranti was convinced that he could find a way round the obstacles by developing his own designs. He first took a radio home to dissect in 1923,[113] following which it became apparent that an opening existed in providing some essential improvements to the audio frequency (AF) transformer employed to provide equal amplification over an extensive sound range. Sound reproduction in early radios was notoriously poor, largely because either the speakers or the valves were badly designed. Dr Ferranti, on the other hand, recognised that an improved audio frequency transformer would be capable of covering a much greater sound range than that of the

Marconi device. We saw in section 2.2 how as long ago as 1885 he had assisted G. L. Addenbrook in the correction of some problems with telephonic induction coils, using only florists' wire and a meter coil. In 1923, of course, he had greater resources at his disposal in the form of a development team which was immediately seconded to work on AF transformers. At the head of this team was his right-hand man, Albert Hall, while Wilfred Holmes was moved from the instrument department to apply his design skills to what was an exciting new challenge.[114]

Hall's first task was to conduct some experiments on amplification curves. These experiments were also to bring him wider recognition, because after his method of measuring amplification curves was demonstrated at the Olympia Radio Exhibition of 1926, scientists at the National Physical Laboratory adopted them as standard practice. This indicates how the firm's reputation as innovators in this field was significantly enhanced by their research techniques, providing excellent publicity for later experiments which pushed Ferranti into new technologies. The immediate result of this work, though, was Hall's discovery that 30,000 turns of wire would be required in an AF transformer induction coil in order to provide the necessary amplification levels. Dr Ferranti then set about producing laboratory models with these specifications, laboriously hand-winding the turns on to the tiny coils.[115] As Hall commented at the time, though: 'It is one thing to make a few laboratory transformers, where price and time of construction do not count; how could this laboratory model be converted into a commercial article – this was the problem'.[116] This naturally represented a substantial challenge if the firm was going to produce these devices in bulk at a competitive price.

In dealing with this challenge, it is apparent that over the previous twenty years Dr Ferranti had learned some valuable lessons in the science of mass production. The first stage was to devise a method of making thermoplastically-moulded coils for the transformer. Dr Ferranti then adapted the small air turbine used in the textile machinery experiments to wind automatically the 30,000 turns of 47 gauge wire (one-five-hundredths of an inch) in a matter of minutes. The end result of all this design and development work was the AF2 audio frequency transformer, a product launched on to the radio components market at the end of 1923. Ferranti proclaimed the unique ability of their product to meet an amplification curve of fifty to 5,000 cycles, appealing directly to the intense demand for more sophisticated means of improving the quality of reception. Certainly, the AF2 marked a significant advance on the Marconi variant (which could only produce sound in the range of 250 to 4,000 cycles), providing Ferranti with a successful springboard into what was a highly competitive industry.

The highly successful Ferranti AF3 audio transformer which provided the firm with an entrée into the booming inter-war radio market.

The windings and thermo-plastic innards of a Ferranti AF3 tramsformer.

Within eighteen months of launching the AF2, such was the continued development of these products at Ferranti that the AF3 was announced. This device proved even more successful, because with its ability to operate between fifty and 8,000 cycles there was nothing to match the AF3. Dr Ferranti actually vetoed the radio department sales manager's suggested use of the word 'perfect' in the publicity material. He also persuaded the board to sell the AF3 at a highly competitive price, undercutting the Marconi price of £1 15s. (£1.75p) by ten shillings (50 pence), such was his confidence in the product's ability. As a consequence, what was marketed as the 'Nearly Perfect Transformer' became a major best-seller in the radio components industry.[117] By 1925, monthly sales of 10,000 AF3 transformers had been reached, establishing the Ferranti name firmly in the highly competitive and demanding home constructors' market. Ferranti also built on this goodwil to extend their product range by manufacturing speakers and condensers. In order to gain favour with the 'hams', a regular pamphlet, *True Radio Reproduction*, was also published from the Crown Works as a means of publicising Ferranti components and extending the firm's reputation for quality products.

The Stalybridge factory

By exploiting an in-house capability in designing and manufacturing induction coils, Ferranti had effectively diversified into an expanding sector which was to open up enormous opportunities in the next twenty years. The 1920s radio industry was still based essentially on thermionic technology, using crystals and later valves as the means of converting electromagnetic waves into sound. As we shall see over the next few chapters, though, progress was so rapid that a vast new field opened up which we now describe as the early stirrings of an electronics industry. However, while in technological terms Ferranti was well placed to exploit these developments, by 1926 it was apparent that the small area of the meter department initially assigned for radio component production was limiting the growth potential, forcing the company to think about acquiring new premises. The risky nature of building an extension to the Crown Works was rejected as beyond their financial resources. Instead, in November 1926 a lease was taken from Simon Engineering on their disused works at Stalybridge,[118] marking the firm's first extension of civil production since the switchgear department moved into a neighbouring Hollinwood mill in 1902.

One of the most interesting features of the new facilities at Stalybridge, on which over £25,000 was spent, was the establishment of 'one of the finest laboratories devoted solely to radio work in this country'.[119] Reflecting how Ferranti had already made a substantial commitment to high voltage research in the transformer department, the radio laboratory was further evidence that the technology-led strategy of Dr Ferranti was by the 1920s a hallmark of its general approach towards product development. The radio department also recruited the services of leading academic scientists as consultants to advise on more theoretical aspects of this new and rapidly-developing technology, giving the laboratory direct access to the most recent ideas. As early as December 1925, Dr L. S. Palmer, head of the department of pure and applied physics at the University of Manchester, was hired to provide advice on his specialist field of short-wave radio. By 1927, as we shall see in section 7.2, Professor G. I. Finch of the Imperial College of Science & Technology was also beginning to advise Ferranti engineers on the development of radio valves. This assistance was to prove absolutely essential if Albert Hall and his team of laboratory technicians were to build on the initial success with the AF3, emphasising how the firm was keen to keep abreast of all the most recent advances in a rapidly developing technology.

The investment in new facilities at Stalybridge would certainly prove remunerative, in both short- and long-term senses, as the radio industry expanded significantly after the reorganisation of the BBC in 1925. While radio department output had reached £100,000 by the trading year 1925–26, over the next three years it almost doubled. Significantly, the AF transformer accounted for sixty per cent of these sales, but the range was extended to include condensers, melody coils, chokes and wireless instruments. In 1929, Ferranti also introduced an anode feed system, giving radio reception greater stability by channelling the voltage more carefully to each valve.[120] This was matched by further improvements to the AF3 design, resulting in the production by 1927 of the AF5 which gave a fiftyfold amplification over the entire musical scale.[121] The most important innovation in this field was the introduction in 1929 of a Ferranti push-pull AF transformer, splitting the amplified signal between two output power valves and thereby reducing the 'chatter' caused by overloaded valves.[122] This kept the firm ahead of its main rivals in a specialised niche of the components market, emphasising how much of their early success in radio was dependent upon the company's well-established expertise in the design and production of induction coils.

Marketing difficulties

Another vital point to remember here is that diversification into radio components production was by no means trouble-free. In particular, although considerable effort was put into both product development and marketing, a lack of coordination across these two departments gave management some painful experiences which brought into question the whole venture. Of course, as this was a mass market composed of millions of home constructors and households, it needed a completely different approach to selling when compared to the company's traditional policy of selling to technically-aware customers like power station engineers. A domestic salesforce had been first established by Anderson in 1906, while each department had its own sales manager who would provide feedback to production personnel on the major market trends. On the other hand, given the nature of their product range, Ferranti salesmen were only used to dealing with electricity supply authorities, rather than the mass market, leading to substantial problems when the radio components (and domestic electrical appliances) were first introduced. The company recognised the need to advertise extensively, spending on average over £13,400 per annum in the late 1920s on this activity. Where they really fell down, though, was in catering for the fickle tastes of a mass market, revealing poor levels of communication between marketing and product development.

The first point to note about this new challenge is the highly seasonal nature of radio selling. The season actually lasted from the Olympia Radio Exhibition in September until just after Christmas, providing only a small window in which consumers had to be informed of new products or new components immediately. Failure to coordinate production and sales and marketing could consequently have disastrous results. This point can be substantiated by looking at the case of loudspeakers, because after spending twelve months developing a horn-type and bringing it into production for the start of the 1928 season, Hall discovered that BT-H had acquired rights to use the Rice-Kellog moving-coil speaker from General Electric. As the radio sales manager (C. P. Beardsall) complained:

> We were on a good thing, but we are just twelve months too late. Eight or ten times the number would have been sold at a good price had we entered production twelve months sooner. Fashion has changed and today horn-types can hardly be given away. Radio moves quickly and we have got to move quickly too and produce things that will sell at the same time as we are seeking perfection.[123]

Ignoring the idealism in Beardsall's argument, the example reveals how Ferranti struggled to come to terms with selling in the mass market. In fact, Ferranti later took out a licence for the moving-coil speaker from BT-H, resulting between 1929 and 1931 in the award of the prestigious *Wireless World* prize for speakers.[124] However, by then they were competing against an established product, undermining the department's commercial viability.

There was clearly room for improvement in this aspect of the business.

As A. B. Cooper (general manager at Ferranti Canada) argued, the company's maxim seemed to be: 'After the business opportunity has passed we will try to do something about it'.[125] This was an overly harsh judgement of radio department strategy, ignoring what we shall see in chapter seven were to be some adventurous new ideas emerging from the radio laboratory. Nevertheless, if the substantial success with AF transformers was to be exploited more extensively, Ferranti needed to think more positively about its marketing activities, especially if set manufacture was seen as a logical progression for the new department. Dr Ferranti had actually written as early as September 1926 that 'the thing most wanted is a complete set',[126] indicating how the firm was planning this move four years before it was actually implemented (see section 7.2). It is important to note, though, that while the technological basis for set production was being fashioned in the late 1920s, the harsh lessons learnt with speakers and some of the other components needed to be applied to marketing if Ferranti was ever to establish a commercially viable presence in mass markets. It was a challenge with which Ferranti struggled to come to terms over many decades, indicating how an engineering-led ethos constantly posed difficulties for a firm which was always more interested in the technical, rather than the commercial, opportunities.

5.8 Ferranti by 1930

The period since 1914 had consequently seen a series of new openings for the electrical engineering industry, including highly lucrative munitions contracts during the War, an expansion in the demand for more sophisticated electrical equipment, and diversification into applied technologies which would experience significant growth as the inter-war period progressed. One must also say that Ferranti benefited from these trends, in spite of the substantial concentration of electrical manufacturing which resulted in the establishment of the 'Big Three' (English Electric, GEC and AEI). This contrasts sharply with its experiences in the difficult period leading up to the debacle of 1903, when the formation of a 'new generation' had substantially affected market prospects (see section 3.7), indicating how by the 1920s Ferranti was a much stronger organisation with a sounder financial base. The lucrative munitions contracts had clearly played their part in this process, providing Tait with the funds to redeem much of the debt capital accumulated since the late 1890s. More importantly, though, it was the successful gelling together of the different strategies which had featured prominently over the previous thirty years.

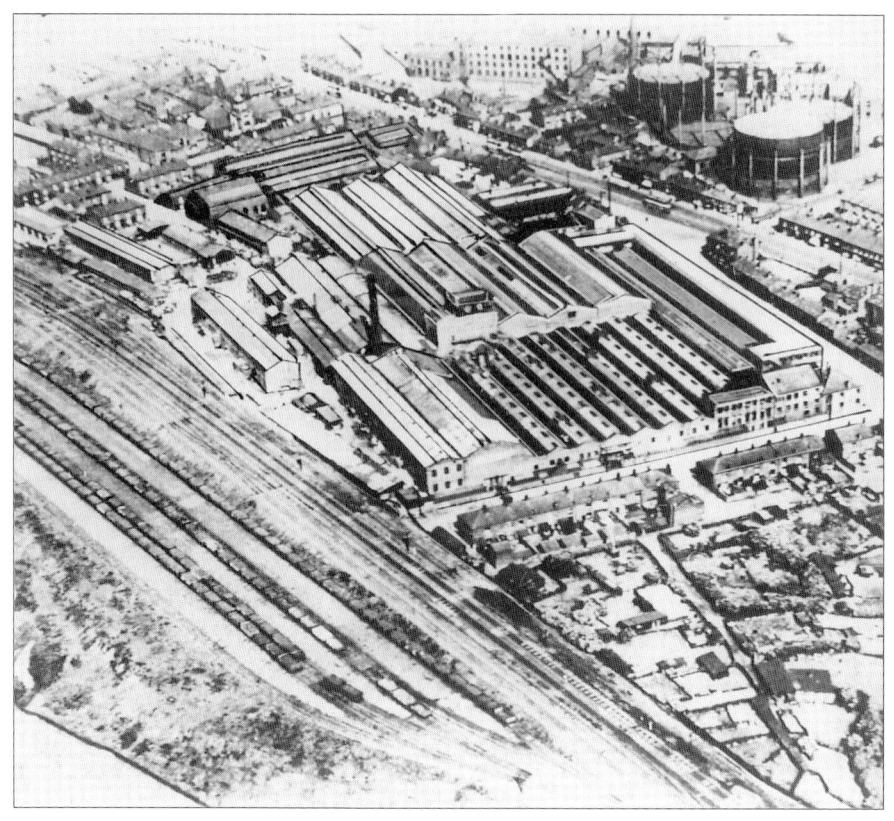

The Ferranti factory at Hollinwood from the air, 1931.
(Museum of Science and Industry at Manchester.)

'The Ferranti Spirit'

Of central importance to this progress, of course, was the technology-led strategy for which Dr Ferranti had always been famous, although one must stress that after the establishment of a specific post of technical manager, the creation of specialised research departments, and the recruitment of both trained engineers and academic scientists, by the 1920s greater sophistication had been applied to this approach. Indeed, a new catch-phrase, the 'Ferranti Spirit', was beginning to creep into the company vocabulary, reflecting the founder's contribution in fashioning a culture which emphasised particularly the belief in technological innovation. At the same time, it would be foolish to forget that the financial disciplines introduced by Tait and Whittaker, allied with the market-led strategies initiated by Anderson, were essential complements to the 'Ferranti Spirit', revealing how the necessary degree of discipline and balance had by the 1920s been built into the organisation.

Financial themes

Achieving a balance between commercial and technical aims has been one of the eternal challenges associated with running an electrical business in the twentieth century. As we shall see in the following chapters, Vincent was also anxious to ensure that such a balance was maintained after he succeeded his father in 1930. At the same time, though, an additional problem at Ferranti was the desire to remain a family-controlled firm, sustaining the reliance on either self-generated capital or fixed-interest securities which had hindered progress up to 1903. Consequently, as we saw in the period up to 1914, the availability of finance was a major constraint upon expansion. Fortunately, though, between 1916 and 1930 profitability had improved to such an extent that all the finance required for the expansion and diversification programmes pursued by the board could be generated internally. Furthermore, as Appendix C (Tables 1 and 2) reveals, not only were the improved returns on capital employed providing real growth in the company, all the debentures had been redeemed by 1923, reducing the drain on profitability which had been so damaging prior to the War. We also noted earlier how by 1929 the general reserve account was greater than the company's issued capital, while in 1923 the company bought over £75,000 worth of 5% War Loan stock, an asset which was sold in 1925 to finance radio components production. In fact, almost £110,000 was spent on new plant at the Crown Works and Stalybridge facilities between 1925 and 1928, at a time when total output rose from almost £750,000 in 1924 to over £1.2 million by 1930 (see Appendix C, Table 3) and Ferranti diversified into new technologies which were about to spark an enormous revolution in so many aspects of life.

Although the rapid expansion of the late 1920s was testimony to the improvements in the company's financial status,[127] it is apparent from Appendix C (Table 1) that towards the end of the decade a worrying feature of past balance sheets was beginning to gain prominence when Ferranti started to borrow more from its bank. In fact, while the board had actually managed to survive without a bank loan since 1922, by 1929 the overdraft had returned to haunt them, forcing the directors to consider a major capital reconstruction. One must emphasise how Ferranti enjoyed a good relationship with its bankers, even though as a result of several mergers Parr's Bank had been absorbed into what had become by 1923 the Westminster Bank.[128] By 1930, however, when the overdraft stood at over £170,000, even this supportive bank was beginning to question the wisdom of financing a family-controlled firm at a time of increasing stringency. Early in 1929 a bonus issue of 40,000 ordinary shares had been distributed among the Ferranti family,[129] but as this raised no fresh capital the board commissioned Skelton & Co., a Manchester legal firm, to prepare a scheme which would 'provide for future requirements'.[130] The timing of this reconstruction would appear to have been a little awry, because not only had the major British boom in share issues peaked towards the end of 1928,[131] the summer of 1929 had also witnessed one of the most calamitous financial disasters of the previous 200 years, the Wall St Crash. Fortunately, though, because the company had chosen Foster & Braithwaite as its stockbrokers, this firm's long tradition as a supporter of electrical engineering provided some assurance that all the 250,000 seven per cent preference shares could be placed.[132]

While raising fresh capital in this way was crucial to the firm's continued expansion, the most important feature of the 1929 reconstruction of Ferranti capital was that it gave the Ferranti family over fifty per cent of the voting stock. In fact, the nominal capital was raised from £300,000 to £900,000, by the creation of 300,000 new preference shares and 600,000 ordinary shares. At the same time, all shares were reduced in value from £1 to ten shillings (50 pence). Only 400,000 of the ordinary shares were issued, however, all of which were given to Dr Ferranti and his eldest son by capitalising £200,000 of the general reserve account (see Appendix C, Table 1). Crucially, while one must remember that since 1905 the preference shareholders were also allowed to vote at annual general meetings, by 1929 the Ferranti family possessed 54.6 per cent of the voting stock (see Appendix D), reconfirming the board's decision of 1923 that ownership should be vested in the hands of those people who were primarily responsible for creating and building such a successful company. By the 1920s, even A. W. Tait was loath to disagree with claims that Ferranti was very much a creature of the family commitment to engineering innovation, agreeing with Whittaker that this culture had provided the dynamic behind the firm's growth since 1914. This substantiates Schein's view on company culture, which emphasises how founders have a major influence on the way in which firms perceive their mission and build structures capable of achieving those aims.[133] By 1929, the family was back in control of a firm which owed much to its drive and foresight.

Dr Ferranti had clearly made a successful return to the company he had left under such a dark cloud in 1904, contributing enormously to the successes achieved in the key areas of munitions, meters, transformers and radio. Of equal importance to Dr Ferranti, however, was the board's decision to make him executive chairman when A. W. Tait retired in 1928. During the early 1920s, Tait had been involved in some dubious East African soda mine investments which badly soured his reputation in the City, particularly after a financial scandal associated with his name broke in 1925. Although he struggled on for another three years, the troubles had also affected his health,[134] forcing him to resign from all his business activities in May 1928.

This left the position open for the man he had excluded from the Crown Works twenty-five years earlier. Unanimously voting Dr Ferranti back into the chairmanship would also have been no idle gesture from experienced businessmen like Arthur Whittaker and R. W. Cooper, because they knew just how dependent the company had always been on his inspiration. Tragically, as we shall see in the next chapter, Dr Ferranti was to enjoy less than two years back at the helm of his company. Nevertheless, he died safe in the knowledge that Ferranti was by then a financially sound enterprise with a management team closely attuned to the challenges of running a business at the forefront of technology.

6

The Elder Statesman

When Dr Ferranti died on 13 January 1930, at the age of sixty-five, the British electrical industry lost one of its most respected figures. Having been at the forefront of electrical engineering virtually since the industry's birth, he had worked consistently and effectively in pursuit of the ideal with which he had become synonymous, the 'All-Electric Age'. As a Royal Society obituary noted,

> in his own view his life's mission was to spread the gospel of the use of electricity for every possible purpose ... It is clear that he exerted great influence on contemporary thought in electrical engineering all over the world.[1]

His passionate belief in this mission certainly inspired him to great efforts over a career spanning almost fifty years, during which he committed considerable foresight, energy and engineering skills to the improvement of electrical technology. While one might criticise the commercial rationale behind some of his work, there always ran the consistent thread of thought through the large number of projects in which he became involved, namely, 'how to shape the project in hand to the economic needs of the future'.[2] His belief that engineering innovation was the prime source of new wealth spurred him on to improve everything with which he came into contact, indicating how he was, above all else, a man of vision.

Of course, one of the main problems hindering the progress of visionaries like Dr Ferranti was the environment in which they operate. Clearly, as we have seen continually throughout the last five chapters, in his case considerable energy was expended in struggling against the governmental and statutory, as well as the market-cum-technological, obstacles placed in the path of greater electrification. While amongst his peers Dr Ferranti was always regarded as an engineer of great achievements, he consequently never attained the great business heights of American contemporaries like Edison and Westinghouse, largely because of this obstructive environment. One might also add that he never developed the kind of commercial instincts that they had demonstrated in exploiting the new opportunities. Indeed, it was no coincidence that only when two chartered accountants were brought into the company after 1903 that Ferranti Ltd started to perform more successfully. At the same time, his technology-led strategy provided the philosophy for an expanding business which has since contributed extensively to electrical and electronic technologies. In this brief resume of his career we shall be principally concerned with highlighting this legacy, because while his broader achievements in the industry will feature prominently in the first section, it was Ferranti Ltd which represents the lasting monument to a life committed to the conversion of engineering concepts into workable solutions. While this legacy was effectively built on by succeeding generations of his family, as we shall see in later chapters, it is important to emphasise at this stage just what Dr Ferranti had achieved in creating this vibrant firm.

6.1 The electrical engineer and electrical publicist

It was apparent from his very early experiments with magnets in 1878 that the young Ferranti had been converted into an arch-advocate of the electrical cause. Over the following fifty-two years he advocated in word and deed the clear philosophy that this new energy source would be the fuel of the future. Central to his hopes for an 'All Electric Age' was the need for more efficient generating and transmitting machinery, leading him constantly to put forward ideas for new types of generators, steam engines, turbines, transformers, switchgear, cables and meters. Indeed, his designs often laid the basis for future work: in the 1880s, the Grosvenor Gallery and Deptford alternators and their transformers were the first to demonstrate the advantages of high-tension AC; in the 1890s, cables capable of carrying these pressures were designed, and his switchgear innovations established new practices in this field; in the 1900s, the resuperheating turbine provided the increased power later required in generating stations; and in the 1920s, Ferranti produced the most advanced transformers for the national grid.

These were just some of his most outstanding contributions to power station technology. In addition, one ought to mention the 1910 IEE presidential address which laid the basis for a wholesale reconstruction of electricity supply in Britain. Perhaps Dr Ferranti never achieved the practical successes accredited to Charles Merz at NESCo. On the other hand, what Hannah describes as his 'futuristic vision of engineering genius' was always to the fore.[3] The grid network was very much the fulfilment of what was called the 'Ferranti Dream', a phrase coined as early as 1890 by the *Electrical Review* to depict his hopes for rationalising electricity supply by concentrating production in large-scale, high-tension, super-power stations built where land was less expensive, water available, and fuel cheaper to transport.[4] Again, one

Portrait of Dr S. Z. de Ferranti in the 1920s. *(Museum of Science and Industry at Manchester.)*

must emphasise how he was not the only advocate of this essential reform. Nevertheless, it was no coincidence that these were the principles eventually implemented in the 1920s, after politicians finally accepted the logic in what Dr Ferranti had been pushing for over forty years. Only in 1932 was the 10,000 V LESCo. cable replaced, appropriately enough by the CEB's 132 kV mains, an event marked by an article headed '*Sic Transit*'.[5]

While it is clear that Dr Ferranti contributed effectively to the development of electrical engineering, one must always remember that, while his name is most frequently associated with certain spectacular projects, in the less publicised field of meter design he had few peers. Deptford, steam alternators and turbines were naturally more glamorous aspects of his career. At the same time, Dr Ferranti developed a meter business which produced both reliable and accurate instruments and a steady flow of profits for other departments. From the mercury-motor meter of 1885 through to the FD meter of the 1920s, Ferranti products consistently dominated the British market. While other electrical manufacturers exploited bulb patents as a means of providing a staple income for their businesses, for Ferranti Ltd it was the meter which ably performed that role, financing the diversification into high-risk areas like steam alternators in the 1890s or radio in the 1920s. This was possible for four main reasons: Dr Ferranti always ensured that the design remained competitive; he introduced mass-production techniques to keep costs down; after 1905, Anderson established an extensive sales network to exploit the firm's competitive advantage in this market; and from 1907 price rings were maintained with other meter manufacturers, guaranteeing the department's profitability. The meter business was perhaps one of the most outstanding technical and commercial achievements of Dr Ferranti, a fact which must never be ignored when assessing his overall contribution to electrical engineering.[6] Ferranti Ltd would certainly have struggled without this department, giving the meter a place of honour in the company history.

Apart from his extensive electrical engineering achievements, one must also stress how in exploiting this reputation for innovation and achievement Dr Ferranti worked hard for the industry as a whole. Perhaps it was his Italian blood which aroused such passion, but Gertrude de Ferranti was correct to claim that his 'enthusiasm was certainly an inspiring force in the electrical world'.[7] His contributions to the activities of the IEE, the EDA and the EAW have all been charted in previous chapters, reflecting a belief that: 'We cannot have too much electricity. We want it everywhere, and we have not anything like enough of it'.[8] As a consequence of this committed proselytising, he was given significant recognition by contemporaries. In the first place, because he had been responsible for pushing through the reform of the IEE, he served the first ever dual term as its President in 1910–11. At the same time, BEAMA's creation was at least partly the result of his lobbying and persuasive skills, resulting in his appointment as the association's first chairman. Even in the USA, where rivals like Edison had criticised his work, Dr Ferranti was held in similarly high esteem, having been made an honorary member of the American IEE in 1911, one of only five such persons at that time. This world-wide reputation was further reflected in the recognition given to his achievements at the first World Power Conference, held in 1924, when many referred to his pioneering work at Deptford, as well as with cables and turbines. The ultimate accolade from fellow-engineers would come in 1927, when the Royal Society made him a Fellow of that august institution, a position regarded by many as a worthy recognition of his prowess. Three years earlier, the IEE had awarded him their highly prestigious Faraday Medal, adding further to the general feeling that here was an engineer who had clearly been one of the most influential of his generation.

6.2 The innovator

The emphasis placed on continuous improvement had always been a strong characteristic of the way in which Dr Ferranti had conducted his business, successfully laying the foundations of what became an engineering-led strategy which was at the heart of the 'Ferranti Spirit'. From his earliest days as a manufacturer until his last days as technical manager, Dr Ferranti continually strived for better designs. He was, indeed, an incorrigible developer, a characteristic which frequently affected his relationships with Francis Ince, A. W. Tait, and J. S. Forbes (at LESCo.). In an industry with such a high rate of technological obsolescence, though, product development is such an essential aspect of any manufacturer's approach to the market that his innovative approach was recognised as crucial. Although we saw in the last chapter how the post of technical manager was created for him in 1918, as early as the 1890s he had established development teams for the main product ranges, developing this further in the 1920s by establishing laboratories and special facilities for these teams. The policy of buying licences for ideas developed outside the company, or of hiring academic scientists to advise on specific products, also ensured that a high level of technical input went into all Ferranti goods.

Of course, while by the 1920s many leading electrical manufacturers had recognised the value of planned research and development programmes,[9] few regarded a technology-led strategy as being so central to their capabilities as Ferranti did. Vincent de Ferranti and his son, Sebastian, were also able to build on this as a strong foundation for further diversification and expansion. It was this encouragement of innovation which induced engineers of some ability to join Ferranti, resulting in the employment of men like Charles Sparks, H. W. Clothier, S. Ferguson, S. Pailin and E. T. Norris. Many others also joined the product development teams as a means of furthering their careers as innovative engineers, providing a strong inducement to those who were interested in furthering knowledge and extending technical possibilities. What better way, therefore, for the IEE to commemorate his contribution to electrical engineering than to establish a Ferranti Research Scholarship for promising young engineers, a scheme he would have heartily encouraged.

Dr Ferranti had been a remarkably inventive individual, taking out a total of 176 patents in a career that spanned forty-nine years. These patents are listed in Appendix B, where the tremendous variety of his thinking comes through clearly. Although electrical engineering obviously dominates the list, the work on reciprocating engines, turbines and production processes reveals a major talent for mechanical engineering. As chapter four illustrated, he was also interested in textile machinery, stop-valves and the gyroscopic stabilisation of flight, while in the 1880s he had even patented rimless spectacles which had been developed to relieve Gertrude's poor eyesight.[10]

Another of his growing fascinations was driving and the automobile. Although Dunlop had not shown much interest in his fibre-on-end tyre in 1908, by the 1920s he was developing another aid to drivers, nail-catchers. Dr Ferranti loved driving his many cars very fast,[11] but contemporary roads were of such poor quality and so many nails from wagons and horses' hooves were to be found that speed could be extremely dangerous. On at least one occasion he almost crashed in North Wales while travelling at top speed, leading him to invent a nail-catcher in 1921 which his company manufactured for every make of car being produced in the 1920s.[12] It was claimed that fitting a Ferranti nail-catcher would add twenty per cent to the life of tyres. While major improvements in both tyres and roads during the 1920s made the product redundant, it typifies his whole approach to life. Nothing was safe from his efforts at improving things-mechanical.

6.3 The paternalist

Although team-work had become a key feature of the Ferranti technology-led strategy, it is clear that Dr Ferranti would have been appalled had anyone interpreted this ethos as an acceptance of industrial democracy. In fact, because of his frequent presence on the shop-floor, he was often referred to affectionately as "The Guv'nor", as a reflection of the close personal terms on which he kept with the workforce. On the other hand, Dr Ferranti retained a strong distaste for trade union interference in management. We saw in section 3.5, for example, how his uncompromising stand in the 1897 engineers' lock-out created a difficult situation in Hollinwood, when he was willing to risk his reputation in the interests of complete managerial hegemony. Indeed, until the First World War Ferranti remained a union-free stronghold, a policy which Tait and Whittaker heartily supported in those cash-conscious days. At the same time, Ferranti was always willing to pay accepted rates for certain types of job, indicating how the anti-unionism only extended to the level of shopfloor control.

It was only during the First World War that the company's attitudes changed, largely as a result of the greater general tolerance of trade unionism at that time. The most positive indication of this new approach was the creation of a works committee in 1917, as a means of improving communications between management and the expanding workforce (see Appendix C). Typically, though, Dr Ferranti complained that it was only an excuse for wasting valuable time. At the end of the war, reflecting his persistent hatred of what he called 'socialism', he also expressed some of the widespread middle class fears when commenting that:

> I look upon the labour position as most serious as if we win the present war we have a worse enemy to fight in the shape of a misled lower class who want to nationalise everything and tax people who have or who are capable of making anything out of existence.[13]

In common with many firms, Ferranti also attempted to exploit the extensive wartime dilution of workshop practices by refusing to replace the unskilled female labour employed since 1915 with skilled engineers. While the Joint Committee of Engineering and Kindred Trades, set up as part of the industrial relations machinery introduced by Whitley in 1918, forced Ferranti to change its policy on manning procedures,[14] the episode was indicative of a firm belief in the right of management to run the company as they saw fit.

Having noted this strong anti-union feeling within Ferranti, it is important to remember that the board, like many of their counterparts in the engineering and other industries, was well aware of the advantages inherent in company welfare policies.[15] Industrial paternalism was, of course, a strong tradition in industrial Lancashire, with a pedigree which stretched back into the eighteenth century. Well into the twentieth century, employers remained aware that by providing certain services, as alternatives to those of trade unions, more effective relations with the workforce might be achieved. Dr Ferranti had always been interested in maintaining a healthy relationship with his workforce, providing 'Bean Feasts' and day-trips as early as the 1890s. Of course, mainly because the firm was never very substantial, he had not indulged in the type of community-building which ambitious paternalists like William Lever or Titus Salt had attempted. On the other hand, he made a conscious effort to build effective relationships with the shop-floor, as a means of motivating staff and instilling sufficient loyalty in paid employees.

Just as in the sphere of industrial relations, it was during the First World War that Ferranti Ltd started to develop a more ambitious approach. For example, over thirty cottages were purchased close by the works to house foremen and other employees.[16] When the large-scale employment of female labour started in 1915, Dr Ferranti also recruited a close friend of the family, Olivia Forbes, as the company's first Lady Supervisor. Miss Forbes was actually the daughter of the lady with whom both Basil and Vincent had boarded while undergoing their training at Yarrow's in 1913–14. She remained with Ferranti for over forty years, contributing extensively to the fashioning of a shopfloor culture which attempted to instil loyalty in the workforce. Arising from her experiences in recruiting and supervising women,

J. W. Davies, c. 1945 the first Ferranti works manager. (*Museum of Science and Industry at Manchester.*)

Miss Forbes also lectured to the Industrial Welfare Workers' Association on the practical aspects of what for many employers had been the neglected art of motivating workers, later earning an MBE for her work in this field.[17]

This greater attention paid to personnel management was largely a reflection of the significant growth in employment at the Crown Works after 1915. Appendix C (Table 3) reveals how the labour force expanded from 1,752 in 1914 to almost 4,800 by 1930, indicating how the firm needed to establish a more systematic approach towards industrial relations. One of the most significant refinements in this respect was the establishment in 1925 of a new post of general works manager, when J. W. Davies was appointed to provide the board with informed insights into shop-floor activities. Davies had already forged strong local links with both trade union leaders and employers' associations, giving him a strong understanding of feelings at that level. This would prove invaluable over the following decades, because the Ferranti family was all too well aware of their inability to comprehend fully the personal aspirations of shop-floor workers. Davies consequently became the essential medium of communication between the different levels within the organisation, facilitating the transmission of decisions and providing invaluable feedback on their practical implications.

It is worth noting that, apart from the 1922 engineering dispute and the General Strike of 1926, Ferranti experienced only minor industrial disputes after 1918, indicating how the new approach towards welfare policies and greater professionalisation of labour management provided stable industrial relations. Of course, one must remember that, as a result of cotton's difficulties, the spectre of unemployment haunted the Hollinwood area throughout the inter-war years, possibly providing a workforce willing to acquiesce in management's policies. On the other hand, one could never accuse Ferranti of exploiting this situation, because by pursuing the welfarist strategies outlined above the board provided a firm basis for effective cooperation between workers and employers. The continued presence of Ferranti family members in senior positions also helped to cement this bond, providing the kind of healthy atmosphere which was essential if the firm was going to exploit effectively any competitive advantage it gained by pursuing product development strategies.

6.4 The 'Ferranti Spirit'

Developing both existing and new products was, of course, the legacy Ferranti inherited from its founder. Inevitably, though, as this strategy of product proliferation forced significant changes to the company's organisational structure, gradually a management hierarchy evolved which reflected the greater need for professionalism and sophistication. The changes did not come instantly, having started as long ago as 1896 when the firm moved to Hollinwood and new reporting procedures were introduced at departmental level. These reforms were further built on by Tait and Whittaker after 1903, providing senior management with a supply of financial information on departmental and overall performance which ensured that they kept their fingers on the company's vital pulse. At the same time, it is vital to emphasise how decision-making at Ferranti, particularly with regard to product development, was highly devolved, allowing departmental managers and their chief engineers considerable latitude when developing new ideas.

The company structure by the 1930s will be examined in greater detail in chapter seven, but it is important to emphasise how the technology-led strategy which Dr Ferranti had established as the corner-stone of company culture provided for a highly organic pattern of relationships. Of course, especially after the capital reconstructions of the 1920s, the Ferranti family would have been principally responsible for fashioning the company's strategic direction. Indeed, as we shall see in the next chapter, the professional functionaries would rarely have been capable of changing Vincent's mind on key aspects of company policy. On the other hand, departmental managers were increasingly given greater authority to institute their own product development policies, providing a balance between centralised control and delegated decision-making. Ferranti could never be described as a multidivisional form of organisation, because all the main functions were centralised at Hollinwood. Nevertheless, in the area of product development departments possessed considerable autonomy.

It was this freedom of action which was at the root of what came to be known as the 'Ferranti Spirit', creating an atmosphere which encouraged entrepreneurship at all levels of management. Inevitably, financial criteria would have to be applied to all decisions. However, as long as departmental managers could justify the commercial rationale behind new ventures, then the family owner-managers would prove supportive. In conjunction with the financial controls developed by Anderson, Tait and Whittaker, later generations of the family were able to persist with this technology-led strategy for at least another forty years. This is the story we shall go on to tell in the following chapters, remembering how much the later generations owed to the company founder. Above all, it was Dr Ferranti who first enunciated the gospel on which so much of this was based. This again supports Schein's claim that a company's culture is often dependent upon the traditions passed down by its founder,[18] because in the case of Ferranti there is little doubt that Dr Ferranti had been the principal architect of its overriding strategy based on engineering innovation and excellence.

6.5 Dr Ferranti

While considerable emphasis has been placed on describing the career of Dr Ferranti, one must never forget that he was a great family man. We saw in chapter one especially how his parents' financial difficulties had spurred him on to success in the 1880s, and until their deaths both Cesar and Juliana were dependent upon their only son. This strong bond was further perpetuated after his marriage to Gertrude in 1888, because their three sons and four daughters (see Appendix A) were incorporated into the broader family, providing a solid base. Gertrude describes how the pre-War family weekends at Baslow Hall were wonderfully idyllic occasions.[19] Naturally, the deaths of Basil and Yolanda, in 1917 and 1919, respectively, naturally affected them very badly, and like so many families they were glad to see the end of that decade. Overall, though, they were a tightly-knit family which enjoyed each other's company, most notably on long driving trips through Europe.[20]

The life of Dr Ferranti had clearly been spent in the dual pursuit of building a successful business and publicising the 'All Electric' ideal. Tragically, though, while by 1930 Ferranti Ltd had become a major component in the British electrical industry, its founder was to die before the national grid came into service. In fact, throughout the 1920s Dr Ferranti had suffered from chronic rheumatism and severe prostate problems. Ironically, however, because he took a dislike to the surgeon who treated him in 1918, he never made use of the technology available which would have prevented such an early death. He was actually taken ill while on holiday in Switzerland, where the cold air aggravated his prostate gland to such an extent that he was rushed to a hospital in Chur, where it was finally removed. Sadly, this operation proved only partially successful, because a day later he died suddenly when a clot of blood found its way to his heart. It is perhaps an abiding memory of the man, though, that even when being wheeled on a stretcher along the railway platform at Chur he insisted on stopping for some time to inspect an electric locomotive and explain its workings to his youngest son, Denis. Not even severe pain could quench his thirst for knowledge, just as other difficulties had never been allowed to thwart his work as an engineer. This indomitable spirit inspired those around him to a fuller realisation of the prospects for electricity, while in the process British power station technology made great strides through the implementation of Ferranti ideas. While one must be wary of eulogising about his achievements, Dr Ferranti was clearly one of Britain's most innovative engineering industrialists who played a leading role in the electrical industry's evolution. His lasting achievement was a firm which epitomised the 'Ferranti Spirit' for another two generations, building solidly on the base forged up to 1930.

Part Two

The Second Generation

7

Electronics and Defence, 1930–1945

The death of the company's founder had naturally come as a great shock to many at Ferranti in those early months of 1930. Such was the deep sense of loss amongst those who had worked for and with him at the Crown Works that for a time it was difficult to focus on the work in hand. After an appropriate period of mourning, though, the second generation of the de Ferranti family soon took on the mantle of leader, sustaining the spirit of enterprise and innovation which had been the firm's driving force since the 1880s. Indeed, the firm under Vincent de Ferranti was fortunate to have a chief executive with the vision to commit a high proportion of its engineering and financial resources to the exploitation of new opportunities in expanding sectors of the economy. This resulted in an extensive diversification of the product range, which as Figure 8.1 (p. 290) reveals even by the 1940s resulted in dramatic changes to the business. Undoubtedly, this transition was partially induced by the general economic problems arising from the Wall Street Crash of 1929 and the completion of all CEB contracts by 1932 (see Figure 5.1 p. 206). The late 1930s rearmament programme also contributed extensively to these changes, offering Vincent new opportunities to establish profitable lines as a substitute for certain ailing departments. On the other hand, diversification was an inevitable consequence of what we can recognise as the 'Ferranti Spirit', a philosophy which encouraged managers and engineers to try new ideas and build on existing strengths.

It will be the purpose of this chapter to examine the combination of these external and internal pressures in the context of what in retrospect would appear to have been a crucial period in the company's development. Indeed, it was in the 1930s and 1940s when Ferranti laid down the foundations of a product range which carried it into the 1970s, establishing under Vincent's diligent supervision a strategy and structure which enabled the company to exploit the era's vast range of opportunities and challenges. Why such a relatively small, family-run firm should be so successful in some of the era's most advanced technologies requires a clear explanation of how Vincent proved capable of harnessing the scarce resources at his disposal in exploiting what were some exciting market opportunities. It is a story of effective leadership which inspired the senior management and engineering teams to take chances, ignoring the conventional in favour of the invigorating because the family was willing to take risks which others might have rejected. Above all, it is a story of family-based capitalism demonstrating its inherent advantages over managerial capitalism.

7.1 New Regime; New Environment

Second Generation Takes Over

Vincent de Ferranti was unanimously elected chairman of the company just thirteen days after his father's death. Of course, this could be regarded as a simple case of the eldest son inheriting the estate, especially as he had made strenuous efforts to acquire a controlling interest in the firm. On the other hand, there was general agreement about his ability to run the firm. Indeed, under Vincent's guidance Ferranti embarked on thirty years of continuous expansion, combining the technology-led strategy of his father with astute business acumen and clear guidance from the centre. One must remember that Vincent's formative years had been dominated by the period (1903–13) in which Dr Ferranti was excluded from the Crown Works, a lesson in the harsh realities of business life which he never forgot. The experience since 1921 as manager of transformer development and production had also equipped him with the technical and business acumen required when running a high technology business. Consequently, over the period 1930–63 Vincent won the admiration of employees, customers and competitors in fashioning a regime which encouraged both high quality technological innovation and studious supervision of costs. He never lost his interest in engineering innovation – as he said in his evidence to the Selsdon committee in 1934, 'I feel that we want to get on and do something'.[1] Nevertheless, at the same time his belief in sound management principles ensured that Ferranti was run as a commercial enterprise. To paraphrase the words of J. M. Keynes,[2] it was the 'Ferranti Spirit wisely-managed' which prevailed over those thirty-three years, providing a balance between the technological and commercial challenges facing Ferranti in a period of extensive opportunity.

In this context, it is important to note that the board's composition changed dramatically over this period. A. W. Tait had departed in 1928, while the death of Dr Ferranti also persuaded Major Thomas to retire (see Appendix E). This left just Arthur Whittaker and R. W. Cooper from the 1920s regime. Vincent decided to strengthen the board by appointing as

Sir Vincent de Ferranti, c. 1945. (*Museum of Science and Industry at Manchester.*)

directors H. W. Kolle in 1930, Denis de Ferranti in 1933, and R. H. Schofield in 1934. Kolle, of course, had worked with Dr Ferranti at Deptford and at Portsmouth, providing a happy link with the past. Since 1895, he had been the London office manager of Babcock & Wilcox, rising in 1927 to a directorship of what was one of the country's major engineering companies. Kolle would consequently bring an extensive experience of the electricity supply industry to board deliberations, an asset which would prove invaluable to Ferranti as it attempted to develop a competitive power transformer business. R. H. Schofield, on the other hand, had been the driving force behind Ferranti sales efforts since 1914, providing a balance between engineering and commercial interests. When Denis de Ferranti joined the board, it was simply regarded as an inevitable extension of family influence. However, as we shall see later, his relationship with Vincent lacked the harmony so essential at senior management levels, leading to a family split which would have damaging consequences.

Management style

It is apparent that in having a board composed of just six directors (see Appendix E) Vincent was anxious not to develop a top-heavy organisation which might have limited flexibility in deciding company policy. It is also vital to note that the other directors were used by Vincent more as a sounding-board, indicating how it would be the chairman's vision and drive which was to provide the dynamism over the following three decades. This reflected Vincent's dominant position in the company by 1930. In fact, one of his first actions after rising to the post of chairman was to purchase 77,500 £1 ordinary shares from his father's estate.[3] This brought his holding of the ten shilling (50 pence) ordinary shares to 600,000, or 54.5 per cent of the total voting stock (see Appendix D). Dr Ferranti had actually left his entire estate to his widow, Gertrude, forcing Vincent to invest more of his personal wealth in the voting stock. However, such was his desire to ensure that he would dominate the company that he took out a large loan from the Westminster Bank to purchase a controlling interest. By 1934, he had also become managing director, preventing any other director (and especially Denis) from challenging his decisions. Strategy formulation was consequently highly centralised at Ferranti, with all employees left in no doubt as to who ran the business. Of course, one must remember that within Ferranti departmental managers since the 1890s had been encouraged to develop new ideas, an organisational characteristic Vincent was keen to see continue. Nevertheless, as the owner of over fifty per cent of the equity Vincent was able to impose his own personal predilections on the company, interfering wherever he saw fit in departmental matters. As he always told senior employees: 'There's no substitute for fifty-one per cent'.

The one aspect of company affairs which Vincent consequently preserved as his own domain was monitoring the company's finances. He often said to his eldest son, Sebastian, that while it was necessary to have chartered accountants to construct annual balance sheets and advise on the legal requirements of being a joint stock company, the crucial information came from internal accounting procedures which told management what was happening on a daily basis. Later in the 1930s, he was also to establish a cost and works accounting department (see section 7.2), to provide a more accurate flow of internal information. This demonstrates how considerable thought was given to controlling an expanding company from the headquarters.

In the meantime, Vincent developed his own monitoring system, by drawing a series of graphs which recorded trends in capital employed, sales and profitability. Although one might describe this as a rather arcane method of monitoring performance, to the chairman it was an essential part of his working life.⁴ Similarly, financial statements from the departmental managers were personally vetted by Vincent himself prior to each board meeting. These managers would also have to report personally to the chairman if either new projects came up, or problems arose in financing their activities. This emphasises how Ferranti operated in much the same personalised manner as most of the other expanding companies of that era.⁵ As Ferranti continued to expand, some modifications were introduced to provide greater autonomy at divisional level, as we shall see in the last section of this chapter. Nevertheless, in the 1930s the firm was a classic family-dominated venture, with the predilections of its owners consequently dominating the formulation of strategy and structure.

Personnel management

Having noted how the family retained absolute control over the company at this time, an important feature of the organisation was how Vincent developed an effective means of recruiting the kind of staff required for managerial posts. Ferranti never developed its own internal management training programmes, preferring instead to rely on the traditional practice of spotting potential talent and nurturing it through a series of junior and middle management posts. On the other hand, as Vincent noted in a circular to senior staff: 'In connection with staff appointments, I have long felt the need of some systematic record and a coordination to enable us, so far as possible, to fill new vacancies as they arise, by the promotion of our own people'.⁶ This memo resulted in the appointment in 1936 of R. J. Hebbert as the first Ferranti staff manager.

Hebbert's main responsibilities involved developing a comprehensive register of all staff, as well as recording their training, experience, qualifications and potential for management. In many ways, Hebbert performed the role of military secretary to the chairman, liaising directly with Vincent on major appointments and establishing a system which worked effectively at a time of considerable expansion for the company. Ferranti even started to recruit a few graduates into the company, principally to act as salesmen. Hebbert was actually one of the first to participate in what came to be known as the university 'Milk Round', during which employers visited institutions to search out suitable employees. This role was later taken over by Hebbert's successor, T. J. Lunt, maintaining an effective link with the graduate labour market as it started to develop after the 1940s especially. In general, though, and reflecting contemporary attitudes, Vincent still believed that 'Managers are born, not made'. More specifically, perhaps, he placed considerable faith in engineers as the major source of managerial talent. Indeed, as we shall see over the next few chapters, it is important to stress how for many years this group influenced most of the key developments within the company, illustrating how the organisation remained engineering-led over the following decades.

As far as the shopfloor workforce was concerned, Vincent left much of the day-to-day industrial relations to his works manager, J. W. Davies, the man appointed to keep the chairman in contact with his workforce (see section 6.3). Under this highly influential individual was Herbert Gardner, who took on the role of personnel manager, instigating cohesive workforce training from apprenticeships through to higher level development. Gardner was, indeed, a very ambitious personnel manager with a clear grasp of what later was regarded as the development of human resources. His apprentice training school was just as ambitious as any other provided by Manchester engineering employers like MetroVick's or Platt Brothers, establishing a tradition at Ferranti which was sustained right through to the end in 1993. At the same time, given the manner in which Vincent ran the business, it was engineering training which remained the uppermost priority in personnel development, whether it be managers or shopfloor workers.

Deteriorating market prospects

The engineering ethos consequently continued to dominate Ferranti in the 1930s. In many ways, though, while Vincent's tight grip over company finances was a reflection of his desire to retain control, such an approach was absolutely essential in the increasingly difficult trading circumstances of the early 1930s (see Figure 5.1 p. 206). The Wall Street Crash of 1929, and consequent 'Great Depression' up to 1933, had dramatically upset both domestic and international trade, creating severe difficulties for most industries. As we saw in chapter 5, constructing the CEB grid network had cushioned electrical manufacturers from the full effects of this slump. However, by 1932 BEAMA was reporting a 'downward sweep of home orders' as the project neared completion.[7] In fact, by 1933 the industry's profit index had fallen to seventy-one, compared to 114 in 1929.[8] The proportion of unremunerated capital also increased from 16.5 to 20.8 per cent over those years, provoking grave predictions about the industry's prospects.[9]

These disturbing trends were even more troublesome in export markets, because with Britain's traditional customers in the Empire so badly affected by the vicious downturn in commodity prices in the 1930s, their purchasing power was severely curtailed. According to the BEAMA index, heavy electrical manufacturers recorded a decline in orders from 228 in 1929 (where 1920=100) to just sixty-nine by 1932. The total value of British electrical exports also fell, from £106.3 million in 1929 to £56.9 million in 1933. There was some recovery over the next two years, with exports by 1935 standing at £70.5 million. Clearly, though, problems persisted well into the decade, prompting new challenges for the industry.[10]

Vincent's first years as chief executive were to prove extremely challenging. This is reflected in a significant reduction in the returns on capital employed at Ferranti (see Appendix C, Table 2), from 10.3 per cent in 1930 to an average of around six per cent in the following eight years. Although the company continued to invest in new facilities throughout this period, in the trading circumstances of the early 1930s it proved difficult to improve overall returns. One must note that investors were reasonably happy with Vincent's management, because the publicly-traded £1 preference share rose in market value from nineteen shillings and six pence in March 1930 to twenty-nine shillings and six pence by November 1934.[11] At the same time, given the government's decision to keep bank rate at two per cent throughout the 1930s, it is important to remember that investors were much keener in the 1930s to acquire industrial shares. In this context, the seven per cent Ferranti preference shares were certainly an attractive proposition. Needless to say, though, the shares would never have been traded so extensively had Vincent and his management team not pursued rational business strategies, indicating how the rise in their value was principally a reflection of the sound trading base they were building at Hollinwood.

Export strategy and price rings

In response to these external trading difficulties, one of the crucial departments which at this time Vincent strengthened and extended was sales. In particular, building on the solid foundations laid by A. B. Anderson and R. H. Schofield, he decided to establish an export sales department. The world-wide agency system had proved to be a considerable success since the pre-War days, confirming the efficacy of Anderson's vision. Even by the 1930s, though, there was no-one in the organisation with the responsibility for taking an overall view of export policy. In view of the difficult trading conditions, Vincent consequently became aware of the need to build an extensive information network to inform managers of customers' requirements, a view which resulted in the appointment of Frank Rostron as the first export sales manager. Rostron had worked his way up through the organisation, having attended evening classes for five years in order to earn a HNC in engineering at the Manchester College of Technology. In addition, he had also taken a two-year evening course in French and German. Over the following twenty years, he effectively used these skills, as well as a natural charm, as a highly successful export sales manager. In 1958, he was also made a director of Ferranti, having by then established a wide network of contacts in export markets which substantially enhanced the company name. As a further indication of his achievements with Ferranti, he was later elected chairman of the Manchester Institute of Exports, he sat on the BEAMA Export Panel, and in 1958 was appointed president of the Manchester Chamber of Commerce. This work earned him a knighthood in 1958, for services to exports, reflecting the esteem in which he was held across the business community.

Ferranti exports had actually declined significantly in the early 1930s, falling from almost £250,000 (or twenty per cent of output) in 1930 to £108,000 (nine per cent) by 1933. Thereafter, though, they rose considerably, reaching £350,000 in 1937 (twenty-four per cent). This recovery, while partly attributable to the easier mid-1930s international trading conditions, was largely an indication of how Rostron succeeded in implementing his chairman's aims, especially in the Empire. While the Empire markets had accounted for approximately seventy per cent of Ferranti exports in the 1920s, as a result of Rostron's aggressive selling this rose to over seventy-five per cent in the 1930s. Clearly, important treaties like the Ottawa Agreement of 1932 helped to reinforce the bond between Britain and her colonies, while the difficult conditions in Europe and the USA limited opportunities in those markets. On the other hand, it was a matter of Ferranti policy to reinforce its traditional relationship with customers in the Empire. For example, Rostron cultivated such contacts as A. E. Hadley, a former manager of the Ferranti steam-alternator department in the 1890s (see section 3.4). By the 1930s, Hadley was chief engineer to the Victoria Falls & Transvaal Power Co., a customer which purchased almost £390,000 worth of Ferranti transformers during the 1930s.[12]

Another activity in which Rostron was heavily involved during the 1930s was negotiating the company's involvement in the large number of international price rings which appeared at that time. Following the termination of Free Trade policies in 1931, the British market was for the first time in almost 100 years heavily protected, providing trade associations with an unprecedented opportunity to reinforce price agreements without the fear of foreign competition. As we saw in section 5.4, the 1920s had in contrast been a difficult decade for British trade associations, resulting in a considerable diminution in their influence when compared to the period since 1911.[13] By 1931, though, R. H. Schofield was reporting that even companies not formerly members of the meter pool were negotiating for entry,[14] while in 1932 the Transformer Makers' Association was reformed after having been moribund for eight years.

As in 1910–11, when BEAMA first appeared (see section 4.5), Ferranti again played an important role in rebuilding the electrical price rings. Indeed, in 1938 Vincent was elected president of BEAMA, the first time a son had taken the position previously held by his father (in 1911). With regard to the domestic market, Vincent was convinced that, as manufacturers were faced with a monopsonist, in the form of the CEB, it was logical that a monopoly supplier should operate through the auspices of BEAMA.[15] He argued that this would benefit the purchaser, because companies would then be obliged to compete on technical, rather than commercial, grounds. At the same time, the remunerative prices would provide not only the funds for intensive research and development of better designs, but also greater financial security for the industry. It was an argument which in the 1950s was to fall on deaf ears (see sections 8.2 and 12.2). However, in the previous twenty-five years all British electrical firms conformed once again to what industrialists regarded as a sound pricing policy. As a consequence, by 1938 the percentage of unremunerated capital in the industry stood at just 3.4, compared to 20.8 in 1933, demonstrating the success with which the work of BEAMA was reflected in improved profitability at this time.[16]

What happened in the domestic context was also paralleled by negotiations on the international front, because with all countries pursuing a protectionist policy the different indigenous industries were beginning to accept the need for market-sharing on a global scale. Much of the activity was conducted in a highly secretive fashion,[17] limiting our knowledge of the policies implemented at that time. Nevertheless, it is known that in 1930

Ferranti staff dinner at the Midland Hotel (Manchester), 1936.

the International Notification & Compensation Agreement had been signed by the major American, German, French and British firms. This was followed in 1934 by the formation of the even more comprehensive International Electrical Association, by which the world's markets were divided up between the oligopolistic conglomerates. In effect, this signalled the end of foreign penetration of domestic markets until the 1950s, providing for British firms much greater security at both home and in the Empire. Rostron strongly recommended that Ferranti should join these international pools, describing them as 'the royal road to increased turnover and profits'.[18] Consequently, the firm signed both the meter and transformer agreements. While this certainly did not provide Ferranti with a route into the much larger American or European markets, in reducing foreign competition at home and in the Empire international cartels were crucial, allowing Schofield and Rostron the opportunity to extend their sales drives secure in the knowledge that price levels could be guaranteed.

7.2 The move into electronics

The greater attention paid to marketing and sales by senior management at Ferranti is a clear indication of the recognition by most British businessmen that this aspect of management deserved some investment in both time and resources. Moreover, in the difficult trading circumstances of the 1930s this was even more apparent. With specific regard to Ferranti, it was also a reflection of the growing commitment to markets which required more attention to such delicate managerial tasks. One can see from Appendix C (Table 2) that at exactly the same time that the early 1930s depression was biting deepest Ferranti was increasing its capital employed, from £741,321 in 1929 to £930,750 in 1932. Some of this expansion can be attributed to the provision of manufacturing facilities for the large CEB transformer contracts which occupied much of the Crown Works. At the same time, another area of the company which was expanding was radio production, prompting management to invest considerably in building up a side of the business which was recognised as an essential springboard for further ventures into a rapidly-moving technology.

Vincent actually announced at the 1933 Ferranti AGM that the main departments were 'turning their attentions to the apparatus required for the distribution, measurement and use of electricity'.[19] It is clear, though, that this strategy had already been implemented several years earlier, not only in building up a larger domestic electrical appliance business (see section 5.6), but also in extending the Ferranti reputation as a major force in the radio industry. Vincent consistently argued that ventures into such areas as radio and television were not only challenging and glamorous, they also kept the Ferranti name very much in the public eye. This working philosophy was to act as one of the main justifications for persisting with these activities for many years. As we shall see later, problems were experienced in exploiting the commercial potential of radio production. Nevertheless, it was a strategy which was eventually to bring rich rewards, especially after Ferranti rejoined the elite ranks of defence suppliers. Indeed, by the 1940s such was its reputation in the field of electronics that the firm was participating in, and leading, some of the UK's most advanced projects.

The first Ferranti radios

In the 1920s, from the premises at Stalybridge, Ferranti had operated simply as a manufacturer of radio components, the audio-frequency transformer helping to establish the firm's reputation as an effective competitor in a rapidly expanding industry (see section 5.7). Dr Ferranti had written in his notes as early as 1926, however, that: 'The thing most wanted is a complete set'.[20] He even approached Marconi in 1928 to negotiate terms on a licence to use its monopolistic patents controlling most aspects of radio design at that time.[21] Marconi, though, was reluctant to relax the tight grip it held over radio technology, imposing a prohibitively high royalty of twelve shillings and sixpence (62.5 pence) per valve-holder on all those who acquired its licence. Consequently, companies like Ferranti were obliged to remain components manufacturers. It was only in 1929, after the Brownie Wireless Co. and the Radio Manufacturers' Association challenged the Marconi monopoly, that conditions started to change.

Although Marconi actually won the legal case on appeal, its management craftily decided to reduce the royalty. The main reason for this magnanimous gesture was that by 1934 all Marconi patents would have expired, persuading the company that it might be able to exact more income from a reduced royalty rate of five shillings (25 pence) per valve-holder, as long as clients signed a five-year contract. Another opportunity emerging by that time was the growing difficulties experienced by home constructors in producing circuits which were sufficiently sensitive to receive the larger number of broadcasts available by the late 1920s. This provided a much larger market for the ready-made set, at a time when the number of radio licences was growing rapidly.[22]

Albert Hall, in the well-equipped radio laboratory at Stalybridge, had actually been receiving American sets from the company's New York agent, G. F. Chellis, since 1926.[23] Not surprisingly, Dr Ferranti had participated in these experiments, examining means by which the Marconi stranglehold could be obviated. The major stumbling block would appear to have been the high tension battery eliminator patent, upon which Hall was never able to improve. Consequently, in 1929, taking advantage of the reduced royalty rate, Ferranti was obliged to take out a licence from Marconi. By the time of the prestigious annual Olympia Radio Exhibition that autumn, they had launched their first set, the Standard Model 21, priced at £16. According to the sales leaflets, it possessed an ability to receive regional programmes up to fifty miles away and long-wave stations at a distance of seventy miles. Such characteristics were essential if Ferranti was going to compete effectively with the host of specialist radio manufacturers emerging at exactly the same time. In fact, the lure of an expanding market, combined with a cheaper Marconi licence, had stimulated considerable enterprise, leading to the emergence of specialist firms like Bush, Ferguson, Decca, Pye, EMI and Cossor.[24] It was, indeed, a highly competitive market, because apart from these specialists Marconi continued to dominate the scene, while all the other major electrical engineering firms had started radio production. Furthermore, even though in 1932 protective duties were imposed on the extremely popular American sets, such was their sensitivity that in this field considerable competition from imports continued to hamper progress.

The superhet circuit

In fact, the first Ferranti venture into set production was not spectacularly successful, leading to the sale of just 1,000 sets (see Table 7.1). As we have just noted, the main focus of competition at this time was the level of sensitivity in radio reception, an area in which Ferranti could not match its rivals. For example, when Ferranti produced their Model 32 in 1930, critics claimed that the firm had compromised on the issue of sensitivity, because even though the set was cheaper than most rivals it could not pick up as many stations.[25] For this reason, in July 1931 Vincent travelled to the USA in order to acquire access to what was then regarded as the most sensitive of circuits, the superheterodyne. When introduced in 1924 by the Westinghouse Corporation, this circuit immediately replaced the traditional form of receiver, the Marconi-Lodge coherer, giving rise to major advances in radio reception.[26]

During the late 1920s, though, the Westinghouse variant was actually surpassed by the Hazeltine Electronics Corporation's superheterodyne circuit,[27] leading Vincent to turn for technical assistance to this firm when attempting to improve the sensitivity of Ferranti radios. Hazeltine was actually an engineering consultancy, rather than a radio manufacturer, giving Vincent the opportunity to acquire a licence to use its technology by paying an annual fee of £300 (plus the cost of models and parts supplied by Hazeltine). This proved to be a wise investment, because as Vincent himself claimed, the Ferranti radio would become 'the best method of achieving the selectivity which is now necessary to secure satisfactory reception of the many powerful broadcasting stations now available'.[28] It is yet another illustration of the company's willingness to exploit external expertise, a strategy which was absolutely necessary if Ferranti was going to make the successful transition from component to set producer in a highly competitive industry.

Academic links and valves

Not only did Ferranti seek outside assistance in the design of sensitive radio circuits, the company also built up a new branch of the radio department principally by recruiting the technical services of several academic scientists. As we saw in section 5.7, Albert Hall had consulted various academics during the 1920s,[29] establishing a precedent for what in the 1930s would become a prominent feature of the firm's technology-led strategy. In fact, in developing an entirely new branch of the radio department, complete reliance was placed on a team from Imperial College, London, as a means of further improving radio sensitivity.

By the 1920s, thermionic emission valves had become the fundamental building block in circuit design, replacing the cumbersome and relatively inefficient crystals and coherers formerly used in the era of radio telegraphy. The origins of this crucial device lay in the work of a British scientist, J. A. Fleming, who in 1904 had combined J. J. Thomson's theoretical work on electrons with Edison's accidental discovery (now known as the 'Edison Effect') that within an incandescent bulb current flows from a cathode to an anode. Fleming's experimental work was to prove extremely successful, because after a few months he had come up with what he described as 'a very simple easily managed detector of electric waves in radio telegraphy'.[30] This diode (two-element) valve was in 1907 substantially improved by an American industrialist, Lee de Forest, who added a third element to produce a triode. Consequently, over the next forty years thermionic emission valves came to be regarded as of central importance to circuit designers.[31] Ferranti, however, possessed no in-house expertise in this vital technology. More importantly, the valve market was already by the 1920s dominated by major companies like Marconi-Osram, EdiSwan, Western Electric and Mullards (a subsidiary of the Dutch firm of Phillips), making entry extremely difficult.

In spite of the mighty competition facing new entrants in the valve market, Vincent was so committed to building up Ferranti expertise in radio technology that by 1929 he had taken the bold, yet necessary, step of establishing a valve development laboratory.[32] It is important to note, though, that although several Ferranti staff were seconded to this new facility, including a promising research engineer in the radio laboratory, M. K. Taylor, much of the expertise would come from outside the firm. Most notable in this respect was Professor G. I. Finch, of the chemical technology department of Imperial College, London, one of the academic consultants used by Ferranti in the 1920s. Not until 1929, however, was his expertise in the area of thermionic devices utilised to the full. It was in that year that two of Finch's staff, R. W. Sutton and M. E. Sions, displayed at the Physical Society's annual exhibition the results of their research into creating 'hard' vacuums inside valves. It was research which Vincent immediately recognised as of great value to his plans for an in-house capability in all aspects of radio design and construction. He negotiated with Professor Finch for the transfer of Sutton and Sions to Stalybridge, as a first step in establishing a valve department. Sutton was actually appointed manager of the new activity, while Sions acted as chief research engineer, assisted by M. K. Taylor. Ferranti was also able to recruit A. L. Chilcot from GEC and T. C. Black from EdiSwan, boosting considerably the resident expertise in valve-making.

By the end of 1929, a development programme had been initiated which was to push the company into new technological territory. Although it was actually 1932 before the first Ferranti valves came on to the market, a complete range of valves for use in AC, DC and battery-powered sets had been

The complete range of Ferranti valves available by the 1940s.

developed by the intimate research team. Sutton also visited the USA to acquire greater expertise in the methods of designing and producing these devices, returning with equipment acquired from the Eisler Corporation which would help to implement these aims. This team was further augmented in the early 1930s by the recruitment of two engineers who would go on to make valuable contributions to developing the Ferranti reputation as electronics experts, Dr James Darbyshire and Dr Norman Searby. Furthermore, contact with Professor Lawrence Bragg of the University of Manchester and Professor L. S. Carpenter of Southampton University was made at this time, extending substantially the source of technical expertise available to circuit design at Stalybridge. Professor Finch later published a book, *Researches in Combustion Catalysis and Structure of Surfaces*, which revealed in great detail the extensive range of experiments conducted both at Stalybridge and in his laboratory at Imperial College. Clearly, Vincent was prepared to invest substantially in building up this side of the business.[33]

It is apparent that the valve department was a first step for Ferranti on the road to becoming one of the country's premier centres of research into the expanding new field of electronics. As we shall also see in section 7.5, by the late 1930s Ferranti had consequently been recruited to assist in the development of some of the most advanced types of equipment for the rearmament drive of that period. Ironically, though, valve production never amounted to a substantial business at this time, total sales reaching a peak of just £13,283 in the year to June 1936. The venture was clearly never intended as an assault on the position established by major suppliers like Ediswan, Osram and Mullard's. Nevertheless, as long as it proved capable of developing the specialist valves which would enhance the sensitivity of Ferranti equipment, it would have justified the investment in design and production facilities. In fact, sixteen types of valve had been developed by 1933, including the first British-produced pentagrid frequency-changer, the VHT4 heptode. This multipurpose tetrode control grid valve was regarded as a satisfactory alternative to the American ZA7, giving a greater degree of selectivity, especially when fitted in a mono-dial set.[34] When combined with Vincent's decision to acquire a Hazeltine licence to incorporate the superhetorodyne circuit into Ferranti sets, it was an essential means of improving on the level of sensitivity required in what had become by the early 1930s a highly competitive radio market.

Commercial performance and market difficulties

By the time in-house valves were being incorporated into Ferranti sets, radio department sales (see Table 7.1) had reached almost £140,000, compared to just over £55,000 two years earlier. The 1932 Ferranti superhet model won the 'Best Value for Money' competition at the Northern National Radio Exhibition, held in Manchester,[35] while the first of these models, released in the 1931 season, was described as having reached 'a high level of perfection'.[36] This was a substantial improvement on the poor publicity received with the earlier models, confirming the efficacy of buying in expertise and advice on circuit and valve design. On the other hand, while Ferranti was benefiting in a long-term sense from the acquisition of new ideas and staff, Stalybridge struggled to generate any surpluses on its trading activity, raising a question mark over its long-term durability. The first signs of major financial difficulties came in the year to June 1934, when the radio department recorded a loss of over £27,000, while in the next five years these deficits escalated, totalling over £310,000 (see Table 7.1). This was especially worrying to the board, because not only had radio production risen to almost one-third of total company output by 1934-35 (see Appendix C, Table 3), this department also benefited from substantial investments in new development and production facilities. Senior management was consequently obliged to insist on radical improvements in departmental performance.

Before going on to analyse these commercial difficulties, it is firstly important to emphasise how the nature of the radio business handicapped manufacturers.[37] Each autumn, it was essential to introduce a new design or model at the Olympia Radio Exhibition which captured all the latest technological and fashion developments. This would inevitably involve substantial design changes each summer, all of which would have to be incorporated into the production runs by altering templates and adapting final assembly to suit the new requirements. To meet the fickle demands of a mass market, firms were also obliged to make and market several different models each year, a pressure which forced Ferranti to increase its range from the one type announced in 1930 to ten by 1933 and twenty-six by 1935. By that time, as Table 7.1 reveals, while Ferranti set sales had increased to over 64,000, compared to 2,500 four years earlier, it is apparent that this proliferation in model types could not be justified commercially.

One of the areas in which Ferranti clearly experienced some difficulty was controlling production costs. The radio department had actually adopted the method of standard costing, by which manufacturing costs were estimated before production began. As an illustration of the problems experienced, though, while the 1932 superheterodyne model was estimated to cost £2.19.10 per set to produce, when Stalybridge started manufacturing this set in May the actual costs exceeded the projections by over £43. Although as production increased over the summer and costs were inevitably reduced, it was November before they had fallen below £3. Albert Hall had actually anticipated an initial loss on this model of almost £20,000, because of the tooling and development costs. However, due to an increase in the price of materials, labour and on-cost charges this had been exceeded by over £16,000,[38] putting a substantial financial strain on the company as a whole. This further highlights the difficulties of having to redesign products each year, in order to keep up with the competition. Clearly, in the Ferranti case, in spite of imitating techniques employed successfully in the meter department and the employment of advanced managerial tools like standard costing, radio production remained commercially difficult.

Table 7.1. *Ferranti radio sales and profits, 1930–1938*

Year to June	No. of sets made	Value of sales £	Departmental Profit/(Loss) £
1930	1,073	NA	NA
1931	2,547	212,434	43,194
1932	9,787	183,254	10,227
1933	6,614	228,762	39,935
1934	29,934	273,169	(27,217)
1935	64,006	443,159	(85,322)
1936	31,553	413,743	(34,316)
1937	38,443	288,651	(63,722)
1938	22,266	175,768	(79,560)

Key: NA signifies that the information is not available

Cost & works accountants and management consultants

As the losses on radio production mounted in the mid-1930s, Vincent was obliged to hire specialist consultants who might be able to improve productivity. One of the more interesting general business developments at that time was the widespread experimentation with what was known as 'scientific management', or 'Taylorism'.[39] Since the 1880s, much of American industry had been adapting the ideas on production control devised by F. W. Taylor, buying increasing quantities of comptometers and other types of accounting machinery developed by firms like Hollerith and Burroughs to give them a clearer idea of their costing structures. While these ideas took some time to travel across the Atlantic, by the interwar era British businessmen were beginning to realise that a more scientific approach towards production might well ease some of the difficulties they had been experiencing in competitive markets. Vincent was well aware of these managerial and technical innovations, advising in 1935 the company secretary, W. Tyldesley, to find a qualified cost accountant who would be capable of introducing Hollerith comptometers into the firm. This resulted in the recruitment of John (Jack) Toothill as the company's first expert in a field which was increasingly being regarded as essential to manufacturing efficiency.

Although Toothill had formerly been cost accountant to the leading furniture manufacturers Harris Lebus, it is important to emphasise how during his period of training, at T. S. Motors Ltd, he had also undertaken an engineering apprenticeship, demonstrating considerable powers of initiative and intelligence. Indeed, such a combination of skills made Toothill a highly suitable person to employ in establishing the firm's first cost accounts department. As we shall also see later, he was to play a central role in the company's development, imposing his unique style of management on a new venture which saw Ferranti establish a new division in Edinburgh (see section 7.6). Of more immediate importance was his role in instilling greater discipline into costing, because in conjunction with the production control department which Vincent also created at exactly the same time this provided senior management with much more accurate data.

In fact, to complement the activities of Toothill and his cost accountants, in the summer of 1936 Vincent commissioned two firms of management consultants to inspect the radio department's facilities and recommend means of raising productivity.[40] The first to visit was Urwick, Orr & Partners, a firm headed by the doyen of British management thinkers, Lyndall Urwick. His consultant recommended greater supervision of labour costs by the employment of time-and-motion study techniques, introducing for the first time new notions of control within the company. A month later, though, British Bedaux also visited the firm, resulting in the establishment of a production control department. British Bedaux was actually the most popular management consultancy of the 1930s, selling the techniques of its founder, Charles Bedaux, to over 250 firms in a wide range of industries. The scheme involved a meticulous examination of production using time-and-motion study techniques which broke each unit of work down into B-units, allowing management to focus on particular problem areas and introduce improvements. Unfortunately, however, because Bedaux insisted on posting daily bonus performances for all workers on public noticeboards, not to mention the much more intense supervision of working routines, worker opposition to this form of scientific management was so virulent that immediately after the consultants' seven month stay in the radio department much of the scheme had to be abandoned. Nevertheless, the production control department remained as a significant organisational innovation, reinforcing the work of Toothill's cost accounts department.

The move to Moston and reorganisation

While costing difficulties had undoubtedly been one of the major reasons why the radio department had struggled to generate any profit in the 1930s, another major problem was the acute lack of space in the Stalybridge factory, especially as the number and range of products increased in 1932–33. Although the manufacture of radio cabinets had already been moved to Hollinwood by 1933, Vincent decided that if the commitment to this venture was going to produce more positive rewards then additional facilities would have to be acquired. It was this combination of pressures which led ultimately to the purchase of a disused wire mill in Moston towards the end of 1934, establishing the long Ferranti connection with this area. The board decided in 1934 to invest over £107,000 in the most advanced production and laboratory facilities for the Moston facility. As Table 7.1 indicates, it was also just at this time that the radio department reached the peak of its set production.

Even though Moston exceeded its capital budget by over £20,000, this was regarded as essential expenditure if the venture was to succeed.[41] It was also at that time that the whole department was substantially rationalised, because as M. K. Taylor remembered: 'It had become clear to management by 1935 that if you want to make a profit on radio you had better buy at least some parts of it from bulk producers who could sell to you at a lower cost than your manufacturing cost'.[42] Given both the considerable success achieved with the components business in the 1920s and the poor results recorded in Table 7.1, one might question the commercial sense in this decision. At the same time, this was a further reflection of Vincent's determination to make radio a viable business.

Of course, Vincent was well aware of the risk he was running with this department.[43] It is also apparent that he was willing to subsidise this activity for some time. This position was based on a firm belief that, in the first place, radio production kept the Ferranti name very much in the limelight, while at the same time equipping various departments with expertise which would otherwise have never been developed at Ferranti. On the other hand, the mounting losses of the late 1930s would have substantially tested his patience, particularly as after 1935 Ferranti also lost its reputation for making one of the most sensitive British sets on the market. Arising out of the fierce competition of that period, Albert Hall decided to reduce costs by cutting down on the number of components used, thus again compromising on the issue of sensitivity. This policy actually resulted in some novel innovations – to compensate for the abandonment of some tuning refinements, Ferranti engineers introduced the magnascopic dial,[44] whereby frequency location was facilitated by the incorporation of a magnifying glass on the dial. Generally, though, the quality of reception declined. It was said of model 837 that: 'It is frankly built to a price'.[45] Ferranti did not even exhibit at Olympia in 1937, the senior radio sales manager, C. P. Beardsall, explaining to Vincent that 'we were more concerned with profits than prestige'.[46]

Sales techniques and the Ferranti engineering ethos

While sales techniques are of prime importance in such consumer-oriented businesses, as we saw in section 5.7 during the 1920s Ferranti had struggled to cope with its inexperience in dealing with a mass market. These teething problems had largely been overcome by the establishment in 1929 of a Radio Conference, which was an annual meeting held each summer of all the senior personnel responsible for production (A. W. Edwards), sales (C. P. Beardsall), research and development (M. K. Taylor), as well as Albert Hall (the radio department manager) and Vincent de Ferranti. This provided a forum for coordinating the activities of each section of the department, by deciding on the coming season's requirements through the interchange of commercial and technical information. It was through such meetings that Vincent was informed of the need either to acquire new patents or build up the production and sales efforts, bringing an important new dimension to the radio department's policy-making process.

Considerable effort was, in fact, invested in boosting the Ferranti name among radio purchasers. For example, Beardsall was instructed in 1934 by the Radio Conference to open showrooms in Manchester, Bristol and London.[47] These facilities, apart from advertising Ferranti products, also acted as regional headquarters for small teams of sales representatives who were hired to travel around their respective regions in the company's first fleet of cars. This coincided with the development of a new policy which resulted in the first Ferranti use of trade-names for their products, radios after 1933 being called *Gloria, Lancastria, Nova, Parva,* or *Arcadia*. Service engineers were also hired to deal rapidly with any faults in Ferranti radios, with ten Austin vans purchased to expedite their activities.[48] In common with all other manufacturers, these sales and after-sales services were complemented by the provision of hire purchase terms for customers, while Beardsall devised a bonus scheme for retailers, offering substantial discounts for bulk purchases and a wide range of publicity material.

Ferranti was clearly concerned about the development, marketing and selling of its radio products, experimenting imaginatively with all the techniques at their disposal. However, Table 7.1 reveals the limited amount of success achieved in either continuing to boost sales or improving the Moston plant's commercial viability. To a certain extent, this failure can be explained by the inherent difficulties associated with competing in this market. Not only were firms expected to bring out constant improvements to their increasing range of models, the declining rate of growth in the market was also accentuating the competitive element. In fact, while from 1929 to 1931 the number of licences issued had leapt by forty-seven per cent, between 1933 and 1935 this rate had fallen to twenty-four per cent, while after 1937 it was just five per cent.[49] One must also emphasise how, because the rate of technological obsolescence slowed significantly after the major advances in circuit design had been introduced by 1932, consumers were less likely to replace their sets on a regular basis. Total British sales of radio sets actually increased from 506,000 in 1930 to just over 1.9 million in 1938. However, one must note that in 1934 over 1.75 million had been sold,[50] indicating how the rate of growth of demand tapered off significantly after the initial major surge. As a consequence, after many firms had entered the industry and expanded their capacity in response to the demand stimulii, by the mid-1930s there were signs of surplus production and rampant price competition. The Radio Manufacturers' Association, created as early as 1924, was actually one of the weakest trade associations of the era, controlling only forty-five per cent of domestic sales at a time when American sets were still selling in substantial numbers.[51]

Of course, in evaluating the company's performance in this field, one must remember that all the other firms had to deal with exactly the same market difficulties, indicating how to a significant extent Ferranti failed to cope with the demands of a mass-consumption business because of its internal characteristics. An obvious point to make about the radio industry was its dominance by a large number of specialist producers like EMI, Phillips, Cossor, Murphy, Bush, Ekco, Pye and Ferguson. Clearly, these were also much more successful than general electrical businesses like Ferranti in dealing with the mass market. The Ferranti response to intensifying competition, of compromising on the issue of sensitivity, was a reflection of this weakness, indicating how there seems little doubt that the firm was poorly equipped in the area of marketing and mass sales. Above all, it was the desire to produce the highest quality engineering product which was the major drawback at Ferranti. Even though a considerable investment in new facilities was made at Moston, as a commercial venture radio department consequently struggled to fulfil Vincent's aim of reducing his firm's traditional reliance on heavy electrical engineering. The firm was much better equipped to design and sell products for technically-aware customers who could make a considered judgement on the quality, rather than the price, of the Ferranti offering. Such an ethos was anathema to the mass-consumption market, indicating why radio and domestic appliance production was never a commercial success at Ferranti.

7.3 Television

Electronics research

Although there would appear to be little doubt that by 1932, after the acquisition of technical assistance from Hazeltine and Professor Finch, Ferranti radios were as advanced as any of their rivals, the combination of intense competition and the inherent characteristics of a mass-consumption market undermined the company's attempts at maintaining this technological advantage. This accounts for the poor commercial performance of a department in which Vincent had invested substantially since the late 1920s. On the other hand, one cannot measure the benefits arising from this initiative purely in terms of balance sheet statistics, because it was more important in converting Ferranti from an electrical engineering concern into one of the new breed of electronics firms. The contact with Hazeltine engineers, collaboration with Professors Bragg, Carpenter and, most importantly, Finch, and the establishment of a valve development laboratory, had all helped to push Ferranti into a new technology which in the following decades was to help fashion a revolution in work patterns and lifestyles. As we shall see later, by the mid-1930s Ferranti was already supplying specialised radio equipment to the War Office. Dr Darbyshire was also encouraged to pursue a wide range of development projects, resulting by 1938 in work on cathode-ray tubes, low-voltage diffraction tubes, X-ray tubes, electron multipliers, and high-voltage tests with condensers.[52]

The diversity of activity in the radio and valve development laboratories at Moston was symptomatic of the way in which Vincent spurred staff on to maximise their technological opportunities in order to provide solid foundations for future businesses. While he was extremely disappointed with the financial performance of this department, at the same time he was aware of the positive benefits accruing from his perseverance with electronics. Nowhere is this commitment to electronics better illustrated than in the decision to venture into another new technology, television, because in the mid-1930s Ferranti was regarded as one of the leading players in this sector. In this context, Vincent pursued the dual strategy of, on the one hand, buying an interest in another television company, and at the same time directing M. K. Taylor to develop a cathode-ray tube capable of providing a picture people would watch for several hours at a time.

Scophony and Selsdon

The decision to take this dual track was forced on Ferranti by the heated controversy surrounding the available technologies. While some advocated an optical-mechanical method, others felt that electronic techniques were more suitable.[53] The latter had been proposed as long ago as 1908, when A. A. Campbell-Swinton postulated that 'distant electric vision' was possible by the 'employment of two beams of cathode rays'.[54] More recently, since 1922 John Logie Baird had been experimenting with the former, using an arrangement which consisted of a Nipkow scanning disc, several mirrors and a selenium photo-electric cell. While his name has since become synonymous with the pioneering days of television, by the 1930s Baird's optical-mechanical system was faced with formidable competition from a joint electronic venture arising from collaboration between Marconi and EMI. It was this combine which introduced the emitron camera developed by V. K. Zworykin of the mighty American firm, RCA.

Initially, though, a government-appointed committee, the Selsdon Television Committee of 1934, was unable to chose between the two. Even though all agreed that Baird's experimental transmissions on 30-lines were a failure, it was decided that both should be given alternate weeks to transmit broadcasts through the BBC's Alexandra Palace station. It was during these trials, started in 1936, that the Marconi-EMI equipment established its superiority, offering a high definition service on 405-lines, compared to the distinctly hazy 240-lines provided by Baird. The electronic system was also more mobile than Baird's, which had to be bolted to the floor. Consequently, by 1937 the BBC had committed itself to Marconi-EMI as the transmitting method for the world's first public television service.[55]

While the debate was still raging as to the merits of the two systems, Vincent de Ferranti was beginning to express some interest in the possibilities of television as another branch of the expanding radio department. He was actually approached in 1933 by the Scophony Co., a firm which since 1929 had been developing an optical-mechanical system. Ferranti seized the opportunity to acquire some expertise in this area by purchasing 3,000 of its £1 ordinary shares.[56] Scophony was the brainchild of G. W. Walton, an engineer who had designed a television transmitter which, unlike Baird's variant, dispensed with the cumbersome Nipkow scanning disc and substituted the principle of split-focus, providing a very large, high definition picture. Walton was convinced that 'if television is to be one day a universal reality, the pictures must approximate to the home cinema in size, definition and brightness'. As a reflection of the interest sparked by this system, representatives of the film industry (including the Gaumont Film Corporation) sat alongside Arthur Whittaker of Ferranti on his board of directors.[57]

As Scophony would appear to have been principally an engineering consultancy firm, Ferranti was brought in to manufacture the receivers, as well as assist Walton in the further development of transmitter technology.

M. K. Taylor was consequently seconded to Scophony's laboratory, where by 1935 he had so improved the initial patent that they were able to offer a 240-line system to the Selsdon Committee.[58] Unfortunately, though, mainly because of the large screen, few regarded Scophony as appropriate to the entertainment requirements of that era, leading Selsdon to reject its bid for equal treatment with Baird and Marconi-EMI. By this time, while Ferranti had loaned a further £2,505 to Scophony, development costs were beginning to spiral out of control, forcing Vincent to reject any further Walton entreaties for help.[59] In fact, Vincent had also instructed M. K. Taylor to start work on an electronic television receiver using a cathode-ray tube, exploiting the work of Professor Finch's team at Imperial College to produce a novel device which gave Moston yet another useful branch. This reflects the growing importance of M. K. Taylor as a key development engineer at Ferranti. Although he would never have been suitable as a departmental manager, Taylor's originality and flair ensured a constant flow of exciting new ideas into several areas of the business. With regard to cathode-ray tube development, it is interesting to see that his devices were actually ready by the time the BBC conducted its first trials in 1936. The Ferranti 'televisor' (as televisions were known in the 1930s) was launched at that year's Olympia Exhibition, provoking favourable comparisons with those produced by other pioneers like Marconiphone, Baird, Halcyon and Phillips.[60]

Commercial difficulties

Although a large market for television failed to materialise during the 1930s, Vincent had clearly ensured that his company would not miss out on this new technology. In fact, by the 1950s Ferranti had become a major television manufacturer. In the first few years, though, little success was achieved with their televisors. Market research by Ferranti sales staff discovered that the major dealers would not push the product, largely because broadcasts could only be received in London, while few saw in television a major breakthrough in home entertainment.[61] In this respect, it is interesting to quote the views of M. K. Taylor, who argued:

> [I] cannot believe that anyone will be content to watch the end of a small cathode-ray tube at home at any rate for long and that one of the essential features of being entertained is to get out and go somewhere, to a theatre or cinema ... At home television will not compare with radio broadcasting, however perfect.[62]

Taylor was simply reflecting the general scepticism surrounding television, providing an interesting perspective on contemporary attitudes towards what was to become by the 1950s a major industry in its own right. It was a perspective, moreover, which in the 1930s was generally accepted, undermining the attempts of firms like Ferranti to build up a substantial business in receivers. Indeed, a grand total of forty-one sets were sold by Ferranti in the late 1930s, in spite of Taylor's decision to use 'lavish and costly cabinets' as a means of persuading wealthier people that here was the latest upper class status symbol.[63]

As with some of the other ventures described so far in this chapter, the Ferranti coffers were not filled with profits from the television business. On the other hand, as we noted with regard to radio and valves, and reflecting Vincent's genuine commitment to following exciting new ideas, the venture extended the company's expertise in this new technology, opening up various civil and defence markets over the following decades. Taylor's work on cathode-ray tubes was so innovative that even the Hazeltine Corporation purchased a licence to use these patents in 1938.[64] Similarly, Dr Darbyshire in the valve development laboratory was continuing to improve on these designs as a result of the company's drive to extend its expertise in electronics technologies. As we have already noticed, the short-term commercial rewards for all this activity were in the 1930s slight. In time, though, Vincent's faith in the potential of electronics was to bring more positive results, especially once Ferranti had joined the expanding ranks of defence equipment suppliers in 1935. This again reinforces the point, that the de Ferranti family were in business for the long-term, taking risks on a range of exciting new technologies as a means of building for the future.

7.4 Finances and fuzes

The radio department's commercial failure, especially after 1933, combined with the heavy commitment to electronics research and development, was in fact part of a much broader financial scenario at Ferranti. As we saw earlier, after 1930 returns on capital employed fell significantly compared to the typical levels of the 1920s (see Appendix C, Table 2), limiting substantially the access to investment funds which were required if this family firm was to exploit new opportunities or build on existing strengths. In spite of this, however, almost £400,000 in capital expenditure (including the Moston expansion) was sanctioned by the board between 1931 and 1935, stimulating the steady rate of turnover development at this time (see Figure 5.1, p. 206). Apart from indicating how Vincent was prepared to plough back the bulk of the company's profits directly into the business, this contradicts Chandler's claims that British family firms were only interested in high dividend payouts.[65] Unfortunately, though, the departments benefiting most from this investment (radio, transformers and domestic appliances) were generating little profit, leaving meter department to perform its traditional role as company financier. In fact, in the period 1931–38, an annual average departmental profit of almost £110,000 was produced by meters, demonstrating the crucial importance of what had been since the mid-1880s the company's major source of investment funds.[66]

Domestic appliances

The meter success story certainly continued well into the twentieth century, a theme to which we shall return in section 8.2. However, even such a steady performer could not compensate for the financial problems experienced in other parts of the business. Radio department's difficulties have already been recounted, while the collapse in orders for transformers after the grid's completion in 1932 can account for the deteriorating performance of this department. On the other hand, it is not yet clear why domestic appliances should have struggled so badly. By 1934, transformer department had actually recorded its first loss, having made £130,000 in the previous two trading years. Over the following five years, it also struggled to reach the levels achieved while the CEB contracts had been passing through the Hollinwood works.[67] At the same time, demand for domestic appliances was continuing to increase during the 1930s – the number of houses connected up to the grid network grew from 3.5 million in 1931 to 8.7 million by 1938 – and given the protection of a twenty per cent tariff imposed on (especially American) imports in 1932 one might have expected a better performance.[68]

Ever since Dr Ferranti had introduced his parabolic reflector fire in 1927, the Ferranti range of domestic appliances had been considerably extended over the following five years to include water-heaters, clocks and new fires. This business was assisted not only by the considerable increase in electricity consumers over this period, but the establishment of a standard frequency of 50 cycles per second on the national grid, obviating the need to adapt devices to the peculiar requirements of each region or even town. The electric clock industry was one which benefited especially from this innovation, leading to the secondment of Wilf Holmes in the instrument department to develop a synchronous electric motor capable of serving the growing demand for this type of product. After taking out nine patents on synchronous motors and timing mechanisms between 1931 and 1934, Holmes had produced an electric clock which was regarded as 'safe, neat and simple'.[69] The firm's industrial artist, W. N. Duffy, also designed attractive cases for these instruments, making imaginative use of Wedgwood china, ebonite and wood. As a result, in 1935 two Ferranti clocks were chosen by the Royal Academy to be included in its exhibition of 'British Art in Industry'.[70] Perhaps most crucially, though, Ferranti arranged a price-fixing arrangement with their major competitor, Smiths, forming the Clock-Makers' Association to formalise the agreement.

The story of the electric clock is typical of the whole domestic appliance business, because while some inroads into the market were made, and Ferranti received widespread recognition for the design of its goods, this department failed to live up to initial expectations. After having been created in 1927, and experiencing only sluggish growth up to 1931–32, thereafter over the next five years sales increased five-fold, jumping from almost £21,500 to nearly £108,000. Unfortunately, though, only in two years (1934–36) did this department record a profit (of £15,000 in total), while the accumulated losses of the period 1928–39 amounted to £128,116.[71] This was not on the same scale as the deficits appearing in the radio department accounts (see Table 7.1). However, not only was the scale of operations considerably smaller, when added to the problems in other parts of the company they must have created some concern at board level. In simple terms, Vincent realised that he needed another secure source of profits to supplement the meter department's sterling service. As a result, when the defence programme started to escalate in the mid-1930s, Ferranti soon realised that here was a possible complement to its existing businesses.

The move into defence

Diversification into defence production was not, of course, new to the firm, because during the First World War Ferranti had contributed as a munitions producer (see section 5.1). On the other hand, this had been a relatively risk-free venture, given the enormous demand for shells and fuzes at that time, while even in the highly unstable political situation of the 1930s there was no guarantee that business would prove secure. In peace-time, as a monopsonist, the government wields enormous market power,[72] while J. H. Whibley (chief meter engineer) warned Vincent: 'Inspection is extremely severe, all parts having to conform to limits as specified, material being selected and sent for inspection before manufacture begins'.[73] In spite of these potential difficulties, Vincent was nevertheless confident that the company's long history in manufacturing intricate mechanisms would stand them in good stead, demonstrating his confidence in the senior engineers Ferranti had assembled as a result of its encouraging approach towards innovation. Of particular importance would be the instrument department development team, because Vincent decided very early on that all defence orders would be directed to this part of the business, in order not to deflect the attentions of meter and transformer engineers. This was an important policy decision by Vincent, giving instrument department the role of a sump, from which many new businesses originated as a result of its ability to develop successful ideas.

Although the re-entry of Ferranti into the defence business was clearly a rational decision, as a result of severe difficulties with the first contract Vincent's attitude soon changed, particularly with respect to the financing of government contracts. This first experience involved production of what was known as fuze No. 206, the development of which had been baffling engineers at both Vickers-Armstrong and the Admiralty since 1933.[74] One of the civil servants working on this project was T. W. Midmer, deputy chief superintendent of armaments supplies at the Admiralty, whose son, Ken Midmer, had recently acquired an apprenticeship with the Ferranti meter department through a friend of the family, J. H. Whibley (chief meter engineer). The Midmers had apparently discussed their mutual occupations in the course of 1933, resulting in Midmer Senior arranging to meet Whibley at the Ferranti London office to discuss possible terms on a production development contract. This was actually typical of the 'industrial diplomacy' conducted by Whitehall officials at this time, government by the 1930s having realised the need to develop a closer relationship with industry, especially where strategic interests were at stake.[75] Vincent was also convinced by this time that war with Germany was inevitable, encouraging Whibley to bring Midmer Senior and his team to Hollinwood as a means of persuading the Admiralty that Ferranti could contribute effectively to the rearmament programme. While negotiations dragged on into 1934, by August Ferranti had been given a contract to produce 10,500 No. 206 fuzes, drawing the firm back into the elite ranks of defence equipment suppliers at a crucial time in British history.

Although both patriotic and financial reasons were at the heart of Vincent's thinking in restarting fuze production at Hollinwood, the new business was at first a commercial disaster. In the first place, because of the contract's small size, Ferranti was obliged to provide all the manufacturing facilities, at least until bulk production could be achieved. This resulted in the erection of a 7,000 square feet extension next to the instrument department, on land purchased from the Lancashire & Yorkshire Railway Co.[76] More importantly, instrument department struggled to devise a suitably efficient production technique for the fuze. Even as late as the summer of 1937, three of the eighty-seven separate parts were still awaiting attention.[77] This forced Vincent to depart temporarily from his policy of focusing all defence business in the instrument department, because such were the pressures from the Admiralty that expert advice on the highly intricate timing mechanism was required from the meter department engineers. In the meantime, the Admiralty had placed a further contract for 100,000 No. 206 fuzes, such was their need for munitions after Hitler had remilitarised the Rhineland at the end of 1935, indicating how technical and political pressures were being put on Ferranti to complete the development stage.

Vincent's Defence Business strategy

After the first friendly exchanges between Ferranti engineers and Admiralty civil servants, by 1936–37 the relationship had deteriorated seriously. Indeed, Sir Reginald Henderson, Third Sea Lord and Controller of the Admiralty, even threatened to cancel the contracts in March 1937.[78] The meter department engineers also had to deal with an antagonistic inspector who disliked the idea of dispersing fuze production away from the established centres in London.[79] Another major bone of contention was Vincent's hard bargaining over how the government contracts were to be financed, because having suffered severe losses on the first fuze contract he insisted that the sponsoring ministry ought to bear any risk involved at both the development and production stages. It was a policy which he pursued consistently throughout his period as chairman, establishing a tradition at Ferranti which was sustained into the 1980s. Moreover, by sticking firmly to his principles he was able to exact generous financial support for future contracts.

Initially, of course, the Admiralty was unhappy about Vincent's stance. A top-level conference involving Vincent and two of his closest advisors (Arthur Whittaker and W. G. Bass) and senior civil servants was called to discuss the details. Although it was not an easy meeting, as a result of some hard bargaining the Admiralty agreed to pay for all the production and testing plant, while Ferranti provided the buildings and services. The latter took the form of Fuze Factory No. 1, an extension to the Moston factory covering over 85,000 square feet, while between June 1937 and June 1938 the Admiralty provided £120,000 as its part of the bargain. By 1937, then, instrument department and the new fuze department had been permanently relocated at Moston, establishing a base for operations which lasted for over fifty years. Ferranti also purchased the Hollinwood Tram Depot in 1937 as part of its plans for fuze production. However, once the Admiralty had agreed to help finance Fuze Factory No. 1, later it was adapted for development use by some of the electronics engineers.

By the end of 1937, after the meter engineers had managed to overcome the production problems earlier experienced by instrument department, the new facility at Moston was ready for bulk production of the 100,000 fuzes ordered in 1936. The War Office was also showing interest in this new factory by the beginning of 1937, this time as a source for its No. 199 fuze. Consequently, by the summer a major contract was placed which, until production was curtailed in 1943, amounted to sales worth £1.65 million.[80] Ferranti had clearly established a business which was destined to grow rapidly during the 1930s and 1940s. Indeed, by 1938–39 government contracts had become the largest contributor to company output, accounting for 35.5 per cent of sales (compared to 27.4 per cent for meters). Initially, though, in spite of Vincent's hard bargaining over financial support, fuze department remained unprofitable, producing losses of over £20,500 on the first No. 206 contracts.[81] The investment of £245,000 in new facilities during 1936 and 1937 also stretched company resources, a point clearly substantiated by Appendix C (Table 1), which reveals how in 1936 a bank overdraft appeared in the balance sheet for the first time in five years. It was this development which prompted Vincent to call an extraordinary general meeting in 1937, in order to raise the directors' borrowing powers to £800,000. This demonstrated how Vincent was able to convince the local manager of Westminster Bank in Manchester (see section 8.4) that his business was based on solid foundations, leading to the provision of sufficient liquidity for the company's late 1930s diversification programme.

As a commercial venture, fuze production was consequently yet another source of concern to Vincent and his board, adding to the mounting problems with radio production and domestic appliances. This demonstrates how the organisational innovations described earlier were absolutely vital to the firm's development, in particular the establishment of departments to supervise cost accounts and production control. Vincent was always careful to ensure that he would be provided with accurate financial information on departmental performance, indicating again how his managerial style rested very much on the ability to read the trends reflected in his charts (see section 7.1). In addition, he also negotiated further with government departments, after realising in 1937 the financial implications of taking on even more fuze contracts. As a result, Ferranti succeeded in securing an agreement from both the Admiralty and the War Office that they would pay a guaranteed profit margin of seven per cent on top of all development and manufacturing costs. When combined with the provision of government funds for all production and testing plant, this cost-plus style of contract would substantially improve the fuze department's profitability, especially when more contracts were placed by both the Admiralty and the War Office early in 1939. In fact, because the War Office order was for a new type of fuze, No. 207, the civil servants agreed to provide over £213,000 for plant which would go into a second extension at Moston.[82]

After the initial difficulties, Ferranti clearly benefited substantially from its enterprise in moving back into a market which had showed some potential. By 1939, not only had the company added two new factories to its Moston facility, both equipped by government departments, sales of fuzes had exceeded £0.5 million. One should also remember that the domestic economy suffered one of its periodic slumps in 1937, while in the unsettled political climate of 1938–39 international trade was badly upset, creating severe difficulties for the civil side of the Ferranti business. At the same time, it was in 1939 that the return on capital employed reached 14.2 per cent for the company as a whole, more than double the average for the previous eight years (see Appendix C, Table 2), demonstrating how the fuze department rescued Ferranti from major trading difficulties. Furthermore, by becoming a government contractor, Ferranti now had an entree into major Whitehall departments, providing contacts which had significant long-term implications for many parts of the business.

7.5 The venture into radar

Reflecting the general late 1930s difficulties in civil markets, Ferranti was clearly willing to commit its resources extensively to the defence business. Indeed, a government contracts department was established by the London office manager, W. G. Bass, as a means of cultivating contacts in Whitehall. Bass was very much at home with senior civil servants and military personnel, having been an ADC in the army before joining Ferranti, as well as mixing with many of these people at his club, the Atheneum. Consequently, he soon struck up an effective relationship with those departments which were significantly increasing their expenditure at that time. Vincent was also keen to learn more about this type of business. He even consulted Wing Commander (later Air Commodore) Leedham on the best policy to adopt. This meeting led Vincent to instruct all his managers to quote on all enquiries on the basis that they would be for substantial quantities, even if initially orders would only be relatively small.[83] This served to convince officials that Ferranti was serious about developing the wide range of products required by the Services in the late 1930s rearmament drive, leading to a significant expansion in the defence order-book from fuzes to electronic equipment.

Defence electronics

When the rearmament drive is considered in historical perspective, it is clear that one of its most important benefits was the considerable stimulus given to electronics research and development. In this context, not only were several government research stations working on new ideas in this field,[84] many firms were also brought in to assist them in the production of working models and final versions. As C. P. Snow noted: 'The lesson to the military was that you cannot run wars on gusts of emotion. You have to think scientifically about your own operations'.[85] Crucial to this success was what Burns and Stalker describe as the highly 'organic' nature of radar development, because civil servants, RAF officers, government scientists, and industrial engineers worked together in such a highly participatory and cooperative manner that a swift exchange of information was effected between all levels.[86] One of the most influential advocates of this new approach was Sir Henry Tizard, head of the Air Ministry's Committee for the Scientific Survey of Air Defence (or Tizard Committee). In spite of constant criticisms of his priorities from influential government advisors like Lindeman, Tizard pushed ahead with the perfection of a system of air defence using radar. Although both the Americans and Germans were working along similar lines, Tizard's perseverance ensured that by the late 1930s British radar technology was the most advanced, making what became the Home Chain the first effective radar defence system.[87]

The radar development programme had actually started in 1933, when Robert Watson-Watt, head of the National Physical Laboratory's radio department, submitted a plan to the Tizard Committee for the detection of aircraft by transmitting pulses of ultra-short radio waves.[88] Although much of the development work was carried out at the Department of Scientific & Industrial Research's (DSIR) Bawdsey research station, following Tizard's directives on this issue by 1938 several large electrical firms had been brought in to build the transmitters and receivers, linking the two sectors inextricably. Ferranti had actually been supplying radio sets for fighters since 1936,[89] establishing a good relationship with the Air Ministry. When the radar production contracts were being distributed in 1938, the firm was consequently asked to cooperate with Metro-Vics on a project to produce what were known as 'sound locators'.[90] This device, more commonly known as IFF (identification friend or foe), created an opportunity to participate in what was one of the most advanced projects of that era, establishing the Ferranti name as a major supplier of radar equipment. Interestingly, the IFF equipment had been developed at Bawdsey by Dr F.C. Williams, establishing another contact which in the 1940s (see section 9.2) was to prove extremely useful to Ferranti, particularly with regard to computer technology.

The Galletti experiments

The invitation to join Metro-Vics in developing IFF was a reflection of the reputation Ferranti had gained as an innovator in the field of electronic technology by the mid-1930s. Ferranti had actually been experimenting with ultra-short wave radio telegraphy several years before Watson-Watt had made his first proposals to the Tizard Committee. In fact, as early as 1927 Vincent's father-in-law, R. P. Wilson,[91] had informed Dr Ferranti that an Italian inventor, R. Galletti, had patented a system of directional wireless telegraphy which would allegedly assist aircraft navigation. Dr Ferranti soon established contact with Galletti, who at that time was living in Lyon, and after some detailed negotiations a development project was initiated. The Galletti patent was actually similar to an idea developed by one of Marconi's assistants, H. T. Round, who during the First World War had been working on a device capable of detecting aircraft. Fortunately for Galletti, though, the system had been neglected after 1918 because of Marconi's greater interest in the development of what was known as the 'beam' wireless system eventually employed in the Imperial Chain of Communications.[92] Although the major American radio firm Western Electric had turned down Galletti's application for funding,[93] Dr Ferranti decided to back a series of experiments on the navigational system.

The Galletti experiments did not, in fact, start in Hollinwood until 1928, largely because considerable preparatory work was required in order to test the patent. As the system actually involved the fitting of receivers to an aircraft which would be capable of picking up the beams transmitted from airports, in order to test it out Ferranti was obliged to purchase a de Havilland *Gypsy Moth* two-seater bi-plane, as well as construct a metal-free tower to act as the transmitter. The latter was actually located over part of the works formerly used by the Crown Works' previous occupants to test boilers, a construction which thereafter was known as the Beam Tower. Personal assistants also had to be seconded to Galletti, one of whom, G. Hoyle, worked permanently in Lyon. Furthermore, Professor L. S. Palmer was asked to provide advice on these experiments, given his position as one of the leading academic experts on short-wave wireless telegraphy. All this resulted in the expenditure of over £3,100 by August 1928,[94] at which point one of Galletti's assistants, S. Atkinson, was sent to operate a transmitter from the Toronto offices of the Ferranti Canadian subsidiary, while Hoyle and Galletti worked from Hollinwood. There then followed three years of largely unsuccessful experimentation. Although the *Manchester Evening Chronicle* saw in the Galletti system 'vast possibilities',[95] and the Royal Aircraft Establishment (RAE) at Farnborough also tested the equipment,[96] nothing concrete ever emerged from the project.

In retrospect, as Atkinson later reported to Vincent, it is clear that Galletti's proposed use of wavelengths as short as three metres was flying in the face of established theoretical principles which stated that the ionosphere does not bend them back towards the earth.[97] Professor Palmer had from the start been sceptical about the whole scheme,[98] persuading Vincent in the summer of 1931 that the project ought to be terminated. Galletti had simply been over-ambitious in his use of short wave telegraphy. In fact, had he adapted the knowledge gained from experiments, which revealed that when the beam struck obstacles intervening between plane and transmitter they were deflected back to the Beam Tower,[99] then he would have been working along the same lines as Watson-Watt. As it was, although in fairness few recognised the advantages to be gained from this knowledge at that time, Galletti, the RAE and the Ferranti engineers missed what was to become the basis of radar. By 1938, however, once Watson-Watt and his team had established the viability of radar, as one of the few firms which had worked with ultra-short wave telegraphy Ferranti was an obvious choice to assist in its development.

The first avionics contracts

The cooperative venture with Metro-Vic's was, in fact, a major stepping-stone in the history of Ferranti, because it laid the basis of an avionics business which from the 1940s became one of the company's most successful product lines. It started in relatively humble circumstances, because in 1938 only M. K. Taylor (from the radio laboratory) and Hubert Wood (an Oxford science graduate) were working on the development stage, largely in association with F. C. Williams at Bawdsey. Wood and Williams were also responsible for developing what was known as a 'Woodascope', providing a means of testing IFF sets through the use of cathode-ray tubes.[100] In time, the project was passed on to the Telecommunications Research Establishment (TRE) and Dr B. V. Bowden took over from Williams as head government scientist on IFF development,[101] laying the basis for a major leap forward in the production of on-board radar equipment. There is little doubt that the project assisted the RAF's efforts substantially in securing accurate identification of aircraft, and in the Battle of Britain especially radar proved invaluable. For Ferranti it also secured access to a major business, because as a result of its participation in these projects the firm was well placed to benefit from the substantial increase (from £5.5 million to £123.6 million between 1939 and 1944) in armed services expenditure on radio and radar.[102] The company also joined the Admiralty Signals Establishment (ASE) Supporters' Club, whose aim was to coordinate the development activities of major radar producers like Metro-Vic's, Cossor and the Gramophone Co., providing an entree into another major branch of the expanding radar business.[103]

One of the key contracts on which the ASE Supporters' Club was engaged at that time was a project aimed at increasing the accuracy of gun-laying.[104] As the standard optical range-finder used up to the late 1930s was only capable of making a series of spot measurements which were then fed into a predictor, the Ministry of Aircraft Production (MAP) was keen to increase the accuracy of gun-laying. This led to a development project which resulted in the design of trailer-mounted radar capable of substantially improving aircraft detection. Although it was 1941 before production by Ferranti of what was known as GL (gunlaying) Mark I started at Moston, this provided yet another branch to the company's expanding radar business. Further improvements were also made to this equipment during the War, as experience with its design increased. Tragically, though, it was while working on the Mark II version, developed in association with the Gramophone Co., that in 1942 Albert Hall died in a car accident while on his way to inspect the latest experiments. Apart from leaving the radio department without a manager at a crucial time in the War, this brought to a sad end Hall's distinguished career with Ferranti. He had indeed played a major role in developing the technology-led strategy of his boss, Dr Ferranti, working intimately with the founder on a range of projects, from the turbine and textile machinery experiments right up to the production of new electronic equipment in the 1930s and 1940s. Vincent was the first to recognise how in developing so many new ideas he had symbolised and perpetuated the 'Ferranti Spirit', establishing traditions which by the 1940s were well-entrenched features of the firm's organisational culture.

The 'Centimetric Revolution'

Apart from the development and production of GL devices, another crucial consequence of joining the ASE Supporters' Club was the introduction of Ferranti engineers to what was called the 'Centrimetric Revolution'.[105] Fundamental to the success of radar during the War was the development of high-powered, low frequency valves which were able to transmit miniscule pulses of electromagnetic waves capable of discriminating between objects. Initially, the research on this valve conducted by a team led by Professor Oliphant at Birmingham University produced poor results, largely because of a reliance on the American variant known as a klystron which proved incapable of generating sufficiently powerful short-wave pulses. However, as a result of experiments on a hybrid variant conducted at TRE by two other members of the team, Dr J. T. Randall and H. A. H. Boot, they devised what came to be called a magnetron valve. In effect, the mass introduction of magnetrons allowed radar engineers to improve the accuracy of on-board and ground-based equipment, instigating what is now known as the 'Centrimetric Revolution'.

One of the first practical applications of the magnetron devised by the TRE centrimetric valve development group was to design a bombing aid (for the *Sunderland* aircraft) known as ASV (aircraft to surface vessel).[106] Ferranti was actually invited to assist D. W. Fry of the TRE in the production of a prototype version, leading to the creation of a team headed by Dr Norman Searby. However, before TRE gave permission to go into full production, a team headed by EMI came up with the H2S bombing aid which significantly improved on the TRE design. Consequently, Dr Searby was obliged to drop his ideas. The EMI product, codenamed the 'Magic Eye', in giving an aircraft its height and a map of the area below by translating radar echoes into picture form on a cathode-ray tube, significantly improved the accuracy of bombing, especially at night and in bad weather. Ferranti actually manufactured the modulator T64, which provided the pulse power to a magnetron transmitter, keeping the company in touch with what were some of the most notable contemporary advances in electronics. Indeed, by 1943 Ferranti had instigated its own centrimetric valve development programme, sending M. K. Taylor to the USA in order to learn more about their manufacture. In 1944, the firm also hired Dr I. H. Motz of Sheffield University as a consultant, reflecting again a general willingness to utilise academic experts as means of forging ahead in these areas.[107]

The acquisition of Gem Mill

As a result of these new contracts, not surprisingly the Moston valve department actually expanded enormously over this period. However, it is important to note that had Vincent been granted his wish to serve in the armed forces Ferranti could well have missed out on some of the main technological developments in this crucial area of the electronics industry. In fact, typifying his desire to serve the country in times of crisis, as soon as war with Germany was declared in 1939 Vincent offered his services to the War Office. This resulted in a commission to command the 242nd. Field Co., Royal Engineers, with which by October he was once again in France on active duty. It was in his absence that, having suspended radio and television production in 1939, the board (headed by Arthur Whittaker as deputy-chairman) also took what in retrospect would appear to have been a short-sighted decision to close down the valve activities.[108] This move was quickly rescinded, however, when after the 1940 debacle at Dunkirk the

Director General of Munitions Production requested that Vincent should return to Hollinwood. Fortunately for the Ferranti electronics strategy, it was consequently as chairman of Ferranti that Vincent contributed to the War effort. Not surprisingly, his first task was to reopen the valve department, cognisant as he was of its intrinsic value as a major source of expertise in circuit design. Contracts were also secured, after the Ministry of Supply (MOS) was persuaded that dispersing valve production away from its traditional base in the Home Counties would provide greater security from bombing raids.

Vincent was so successful in winning valve contracts that by the end of 1941 he was asking MAP for permission to requisition a factory to expand production and leave Moston free to concentrate on fuzes and instrumentation. As a result of this move, Ferranti first occupied the Gem Mill factory at Chadderton, in which over the following fifty years the firm focused its electronics activities. More importantly, it also gave valve development engineers their own dedicated premises for the first time, providing the facilities to launch ambitious research programmes. In addition, as a result of MOS contracts, Gem Mill soon started to expand production. MOS policy was to assign a set of five valves to each firm, the production of which would be facilitated by the provision of second-hand American machinery. MAP also later placed production contracts for a twelve inch cathode-ray tube, further expanding capacity. Indeed, by 1945 annual production at Gem Mill was worth over £406,507,[109] compared to valve department's peak of only around £13,500 in the 1930s.

Although much of Gem Mill's attention during the War was focused on the production of standardised products designed outside the company, new ideas were also developed which eventually resulted in some significant advances. One of these initiatives was work on a cold cathode tube conducted by A. L. Chilcot, Ferranti having received a development contract in 1939 from MOS to examine a German prototype. Vincent was particularly interested in Chilcot's work, assigning him facilities in what had previously been the Hollinwood Tram Depot acquired by Ferranti in 1937. Chilcot was also provided with an assistant, Sydney Jackson, from the fuze department toolroom.[110] While Jackson's manager, Oliver Cowpe, was reluctant to allow this promising young engineer to leave, one day Vincent actually marched into the toolroom and personally escorted Jackson to Chilcot's laboratory, typifying the chairman's form of control. Working closely to Chilcot's designs, Jackson went on to develop a technique of producing the small cold cathode tubes, by making the bulb in two halves and sealing it automatically. This was the first of his substantial contributions to Ferranti production technology, indicating how over thirty years electronics department came to rely significantly on Jackson's ability to devise efficient and technically-ingenious means of mass-producing a wide range of products. Chilcot had also contributed significantly to cold cathode technology, leading the GPO's chief research engineer, Dr W. G. Bradley, to describe the Ferranti product as smaller and more accurate than the American products.[111] Substantial contracts from the Admiralty and MOS were consequently placed with Ferranti, while in 1943 Chilcot was awarded the MBE for his work in this field.

Ferranti had clearly made substantial progress as a radar and electronics manufacturer between the late 1920s and mid-1940s, advancing from the early stumbling experiments with Galletti's primitive short-wave transmission system through to the development and production of highly sophisticated valves and equipment. Not only did this provide a regular and increasing flow of orders for what in the 1930s had been a relatively small branch of the company, it also equipped the firm with much-enhanced facilities and a team of engineers capable of continuing the success story. Senior development personnel like Drs Searby and Darbyshire, as well as M. K. Taylor, A. L. Chilcot and Hubert Wood, were to go on to make significant contributions to the Ferranti product range over the following decades, establishing the nucleus of a team which expanded enormously after 1945. At the first post-War exhibition organised by the north west branch of the Institute of Electronics, held at the Manchester College of Technology, Ferranti demonstrated a wide range of radar equipment which was to provide a solid basis for their activities as a major post-War radar and electronics firm. Vincent's decision to cooperate with the late 1930s rearmament drive had consequently paid handsome dividends, placing Ferranti at the forefront of technologies which in the 1920s had only been the stuff of scientific dreaming.

7.6 Off to Edinburgh

The significant diversification of Ferranti electronics activities had been one of the major benefits arising from participation in Britain's rearmament drive since the late 1930s, giving the company an opportunity to emerge from the War as one of the leading manufacturers in this field. This reputation would result in invitations to join some of the major late 1940s pioneering work on computing and guided weaponry, a point we shall examine further in chapters nine and ten. Of more immediate importance to the company's expansion and development during the War, though, was how the radar business provided contacts with government research establishments which resulted in a further permanent widening of the product range. The instrument department benefited most from this relationship, especially when in the early 1940s it acquired development and production contracts for several gyro-based products which evolved into one of the most important new technologies for improving the combat effectiveness of British aircraft.

Gyro gun-sights

Gyrostabilisation of flight had, of course, been around since before World War One. As we saw in section 4.3, Dr Ferranti had been one of the pioneering engineers working on this technology, devising similar ideas to those which eventually gave Elmer Sperry and the Americans an early lead in this field. Although the RAE's reluctance to spend much money on the Ferranti patents had limited development at that time, by the 1930s a wider range of applications had been devised for gyros by British government scientists, leading to a substantial investment in their development and production. Indeed, by 1943 Ferranti was producing three of the resulting instruments: an AB (air-blast) gyro, used to steer torpedoes; the gyro rate unit, which measured the relative rate of turning of a ship and/or a target, transmitting the data to remote fire-control apparatus; and the GGS (gyro gun-sight), a radical innovation in the automatic sighting of aircraft gunnery.[112] The expanding business in these instruments forced Eric Grundy, manager of the instrument department, to seek additional capacity, largely because the big increase in fuze production created major problems at Moston. MAP was consequently asked to find instrument department some new premises, resulting in the acquisition of a former Cooperative Wholesale Society factory in Bury during 1942. Later, more capacity was taken in Hyde, Ardwick and Newton Heath, such was the scale of activity, while over 100 sub-contractors were employed to supply machined parts for the increasing number of instrument contracts.

By far the most important of the gyro contracts was the GGS, because by 1943 such was the demand for this sighting mechanism that Ferranti was for the first time obliged to move outside Greater Manchester for factory space. The GGS was born out of growing recognition at RAE that an automatic sight was required for aircraft which by the late 1930s flew much faster than their predecessors. However, although extensive development work was carried out at Farnborough, it was not until mid-1942 that a suitable version was ready to be tested in a *Spitfire*,[113] when MAP invited the Ferranti instrument department to assist Elliot Bros. in perfecting the design. This was a task Eric Grundy regarded as an interesting and potentially fruitful challenge, leading him to set up a small team at Bury under S. W. (Sydney) Holmes.

Such was the pressure of business at the Bury site, though, that Grundy was obliged to look elsewhere for a suitable GGS base. It was just then that he was negotiating with MAP to establish an instrument factory in a disused power station near Edinburgh, where a plentiful supply of female labour could be secured. This actually failed to live up to Grundy's expectations, forcing him to look at other sites, including a former roller-skating rink, a wellington boot factory, and an ex-printing works. At the same time, Holmes was convinced that a purpose-built facility was required for the efficient production of what was a highly intricate instrument.

Crewe Toll and Toothill's appointment

As these deliberations dragged on into early 1943, MAP finally agreed to finance half of a new factory's construction costs, after W. G. Bass at the London office had been brought in by Eric Grundy to negotiate with the civil servants. This resulted in the choice of a greenfield site on Ferry Rd., Edinburgh, where what came to be known as the Crewe Toll factory quickly took shape. McCallum records that while Vincent had originally objected to this decision, MAP had already agreed to the construction before the chairman was consulted, indicating how Crewe Toll started off in what was to become the independent fashion for which it was always noted.[114] It was also early in 1943 that Vincent decided to appoint a manager of this new venture, Sydney Holmes having been charged only with engineering development. Reflecting the trust placed in him by the chairman by that time, the head of cost accounting, Jack Toothill, was asked to take on this tricky mission.

1943 was consequently an important milestone in the company's history as it moved out of Manchester and into a business which would prove extremely successful. The factory was actually completed by June 1943, MAP having contributed £134,537 to the cost of erecting and equipping Crewe Toll, and Ferranti £167,764.[115] At the same time, Toothill recruited the nucleus of a team, from fuze department at Moston and instrument department in Bury, which was to make the Edinburgh operation so effective over the following twenty years. A total of twenty actually made this move, including Sydney Holmes as chief engineer and Tom Neal as works manager, the majority of whom stayed at Crewe Toll for many years. While their first task was to develop suitable techniques for mass-producing GGS, this venture proved to be capable of generating a life of its own, indicating how under Toothill's leadership Crewe Toll was to become a major component in the Ferranti portfolio.

Having devised a GGS production process which involved complete jigging and automatic tooling, the Crewe Toll team was faced with the equally difficult job of training the mostly female manufacturing operatives. In fact, during the first few months Tom Neal and his men were only able to produce GGS at the end of the normal working day, setting to at 5.30 p.m. after the women had left. It was consequently December 1943 before the first squadron was equipped with GGS, when such was their concern with security that Toothill, Neal and Holmes delivered them personally.[116] Another problem which arose at that time was RAE's decision to switch priority from the bomber to the fighter variant, forcing Holmes to make some changes to the production process. It was also discovered that the 'radio-metal' supplied by Hall Telephones, a major subcontractor, required special machining techniques which they had yet to develop. These teething problems prevented Crewe Toll from achieving their target of 1,000 units per month until March 1945. By that time, though, Ferranti employed almost 1,000 people in Edinburgh, establishing the business as a major component of the local scene.

By August 1945, Crewe Toll had eventually produced a total of 9,594 GGS for the RAF, contributing substantially to the effectiveness of British aircraft in the later years of the War. It is important to note that while the American firm of Sperry had also been working along similar lines during the early 1940s, by 1944 their design had been rejected by the RAF in favour of the Ferranti GGS, given the latter's ability to calculate more effectively the lead angles and range continuously during an attack by automatically varying the position of the aiming mark.[117] Tests proved that the Ferranti GGS increased the number of 'kills' from twenty-six to fifty per cent, substantiating MAP's claim that this had been 'the most outstanding instrument development of the War'.[118] Ferranti had consequently contributed to a significant success story, allowing Crewe Toll the opportunity to build on this reputation as a producer of highly sophisticated instrumentation capable of substantially improving aircraft performance. Some problems were experienced in the late 1940s, when purchases of GGS plummeted. However, as we shall see in the next chapter, Jack Toothill committed much of his team's energies to the development of new types of avionic equipment, resulting in successful lines which generated substantial profits. It is also important to emphasise how after 1945 Toothill was allowed to develop Crewe Toll because of the freedom given to departmental managers by Vincent's managerial style. Naturally, geography dictated that Crewe Toll would always be isolated from the rest of the company in Manchester. On the other hand, because the Ferranti structure allowed departmental managers the freedom to pursue their own product development strategies, Toothill exploited this free-booting relationship to the full in building a highly successful avionics business in a relatively short space of time.

7.8 War and Ferranti

Financial challenge

Ferranti emerged from the Second World War a very different enterprise from the one Vincent had inherited in 1930. By 1945, from an initial base of meters, transformers, electrical instrumentation, domestic appliances and radio, as a direct consequence of its participation in the rearmament drive of the late 1930s and early 1940s the firm had moved into electronics, avionics, electro-mechanical instrumentation and fuzes. While output during the 1930s had never exceeded £1.9 million, peaking in 1938 (see Figure 7.1), by 1944–45 it had risen to over £5.6 million. Even taking into consideration the mild War-time inflation, substantial progress had clearly been made in expanding turnover. One should note that fuze production accounted for almost one-third of company output throughout the War.[119] At the same time, domestic appliance, radio and television production was completely suspended, while meter and transformer output fell to only fifty per cent of pre-War levels. This reveals the growing importance of the new departments established since 1936, a development which in the post-War era provided Ferranti with solid foundation for further diversification into the expanding fields of electronics and avionics.

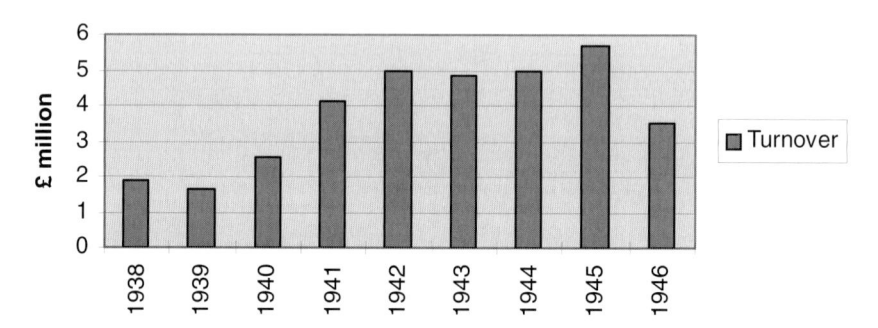

Figure 7.1. *Wartime Turnover at Ferranti Ltd, 1938–46*

An inevitable corollary of this expansion, though, would be the traditional problem for family firms of finance. Capital employed in 1945 stood at almost £4.3 million (see Appendix C, Table 2), compared to just over £1.2 million in 1939. Although by 1945 MAP and MOS had contributed a total of £1.5 million towards construction and equipment costs, Ferranti was still left to find a substantial amount of capital itself. In this context, a major source would have been the improvement in profitability, because as annual average gross profits rose from £65,400 between 1930 and 1939 to over £540,000 in the following seven years this gave Vincent the opportunity to build up reserves of nearly £360,000 by the end of the War (see Appendix C, Table 1). On the other hand, another obvious feature of Ferranti finances over this period was the substantial rise in bank borrowing, the overdraft reaching almost £2.4 million in 1945. This made it imperative that Vincent should maintain a healthy relationship with his bankers. A meeting with Sir Charles Lidbury, chief general manager of the Westminster Bank, was arranged in 1939 to assure him that Ferranti was worth backing. In 1943, Vincent also brought his brother-in-law, W. C. Pycroft, on to the board, to act as a valuable link with the City. Pycroft was a chartered accountant (and director of Nestle's Milk Products). Although he was rarely to be seen in the factories, he provided Vincent with useful advice on company finances over the following fifteen years, adding valuable experience to board discussions at a time when all other directors were in-grown.

Organisational adaptation

Although the Westminster Bank would have been impressed with the company's expanding order-book, in considering extensions to the Ferranti overdraft Sir Charles Lidbury was above all assured by Vincent's firm grasp of his business. The graphs compiled to show trends in capital employed, sales and profitability provided all the information the chief executive required to monitor the vital pulse of the company. At the same time, a system of flexible budgetary control was introduced by the cost accounts department which focused managers' attentions on the key production costs of direct labour, materials and overheads. This imposed a more rigorous system of effective book-keeping on departments. Furthermore, when Toothill moved to Edinburgh in 1943 he was replaced as chief cost accountant by E. F. Brown, who along with his assistant, Harry Kirkham, introduced further improvements to the system which MoS and MAP officials later copied. Ferranti also sent clerks to the Manchester College of Technology for a period of basic training in that institution's famous department of industrial administration, ensuring a steady supply of talented individuals capable of implementing these controls.[120] By the end of the War, over 200 staff worked in cost accounts, confirming the chairman's strong belief in maintaining a careful eye on cashflow.

Apart from expanding cost accounts, Vincent also recognised that the company's administrative structure needed to adapt to the dual pressures of rapid expansion and geographical dispersion. After all, by 1943 Ferranti had moved into five new factories in Manchester and one in Edinburgh. Of course, those occupied by instrument department in Bury, Hyde, Ardwick and Newton Heath were both temporary and much smaller than the original premises at Hollinwood and Moston. Nevertheless, they still had to be managed. We noted earlier how Vincent had always been willing to encourage individual initiative amongst his departmental managers, allowing them latitude as long as their activities remained commercially viable. At the same time, functional departments like sales, marketing, purchasing, personnel, costing and transport were all centralised at Hollinwood, providing such services to the operating departments as a cost to the whole company.[121] This arrangement was further consolidated in 1943 by the establishment of Central Services, coordinating the activities of all functional departments in order to streamline activities.

Figure 7.2 illustrates how the structure would have appeared in 1945. However, it is always important to remember that form must never be mistaken for reality. In the first place, one must never forget the absolute power vested in Vincent's position as chief executive and majority shareholder. On the other hand, to see this as the key to his company's development would be extremely misleading. Indeed, while much of the strategic and functional management may well have been centralised at Hollinwood, departmental managers were vital influences on company development, reflecting the degree of devolution instilled into the organisation by the Ferranti family. Although all departmental managers reported to the chairman and managing director, Ferranti prided itself on the informal manner in which this system operated. Right up to the 1970s, the family refused to introduce rigorous centralised monitoring, on the grounds that regimentation would stifle innovation and devolved decision-making. This informal system was seen as crucial to the company's *modus operandi*. While Figure 7.2 provides some indication of how information travelled within the company, one must not be misled into believing that a hierarchical structure had been constructed to reinforce the family's control.

A vital feature of the Ferranti organisation which emerged at this time was the elevation of senior managers on to the board, often as a reward for long service with the company. This tradition started in 1942, when the company secretary and chief accountant, W. Tyldesley, was made a director. Unfortunately, though, his period on the board was cut short by ill-health and he was forced to retire in 1943. The general works manager, J. W. Davies, was also made a director in 1942, bringing to the board a vast experience of industrial relations matters at a time when employment at Ferranti expanded from 5,800 in June 1939 to over 11,200 in 1945. Other directorial appointments at this time were W. G. Bass from government contracts and C. W. Bridgen from sales, increasing the board size to eight (see Appendix D).[122] It is above

Figure 7.2. *The Ferranti Structure in 1945*

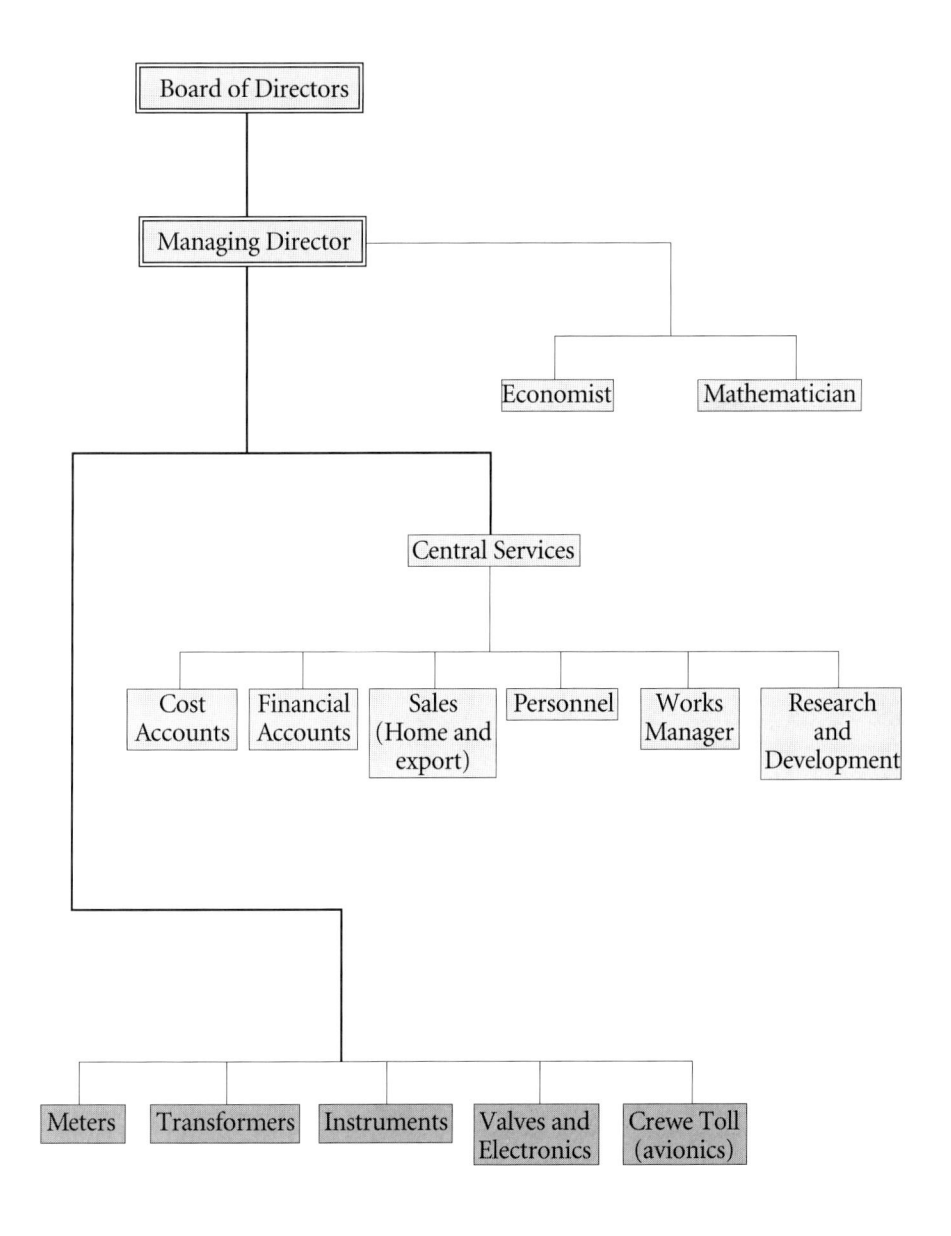

```
Board of Directors
        |
Managing Director ─────────────┐
        |                       |
        |              Economist   Mathematician
        |
Central Services
  ├── Cost Accounts
  ├── Financial Accounts
  ├── Sales (Home and export)
  ├── Personnel
  ├── Works Manager
  └── Research and Development

  ├── Meters
  ├── Transformers
  ├── Instruments
  ├── Valves and Electronics
  └── Crewe Toll (avionics)
```

all important to stress, though, that apart from W. C. Pycroft (who, in any case, was the chairman's brother-in-law) they were all internal appointments, emphasising how Vincent was reluctant to bring outsiders into the company. Of course, this was typical of that era,[123] when ownership and control were intimately connected. At Ferranti, though, it helped to motivate senior management by providing a long-term career aim for individuals who could just as well have moved to another company.

Another interesting organisational innovation of this period was Vincent's decision to create a single central research department out of the three previously separate chemical, physical and production control laboratories. This move was prompted by warnings from the chief research engineer, J. L. Miller, that as a result of the substantial increase in work at the beginning of the War: 'The importance of scientific and long-term development work for the future success of the company tended to be obscured by the immediate requirements'.[124] Vincent had been surprised to hear from senior staff that few knew what other departments were developing, prompting him to publish a monthly pamphlet, the *Ferranti Journal*, which would overcome this problem. Consequently, F. W. Taylor was invited by the chairman to create a small team, including T. J. Lunt as mathematician and statistician and Brian Edwards as the mechanical engineer, which was responsible for monitoring progress in the various departments and producing regular reports which were circulated through the newly-established *Ferranti Journal*. After 1945 the *Ferranti Journal* continued to provide an essential means of communicating new ideas around the company. Taylor was also instructed to provide quarterly reports on the work of his staff for distribution among all senior managers and engineers, spreading the benefits of any new ideas further than would have been the case in the 1930s.

This period had consequently seen the establishment of both an organisational structure and the nucleus of a product range which carried Ferranti through the following forty years. One could never argue that the company's contribution to the War effort had been unusual, British industry in general having committed the bulk of its resources to arming the Allied services. Notwithstanding this point, Vincent ensured that effective use was made of Ferranti expertise in designing and producing a wide range of products. He would have preferred to have served his country in the Royal Engineers. This, however, was never going to be allowed after 1940, forcing him to channel his considerable energy and talent into managing an expanding business. It was consequently as a reward for his company's services to the War effort that in the 1948 New Year's honours list Vincent was awarded the title of Knight Bachelor, indicating how highly he, and Ferranti, was regarded. Sir Vincent was also ready for the post-War challenge of reconstruction, devising a strategy which would build on the solid technical and financial foundations laid between 1930 and 1945.

8

Post-war Reconstruction

Having committed over ninety per cent of its resources to the War effort, Ferranti was faced in 1945 with the enormous dual challenge of rebuilding its civil businesses and coping with an ever-changing, and often challenging, environment. The defence contracts secured over the period 1936–45 had proved extremely important in compensating for the trading difficulties experienced by radio and domestic appliances, allowing Ferranti the opportunity to emerge from the War in a strong financial position. At the same time, in the immediate post-War years Sir Vincent felt that his company would be in a more secure position if it could achieve a balance between the civil and military businesses. He also realised that after six hard years of war there would be a suppliers' market for both capital equipment and consumer goods, providing a conducive environment for his beloved transformer and radio departments. With hindsight one might question the validity of such a judgement, because from 1950 especially defence spending remained a major priority of all governments, Conservative and Labour. On the other hand, contemporaries were well aware of the fickle nature of this business, indicating how hindsight views which criticise Sir Vincent's stance are simply untenable, given the contemporary's difficulty in predicting accurately how the markets would develop.

In spite of the chairman's commitment to achieving a balance between civil and defence businesses, it is interesting to see that Ferranti never fulfilled this aim. Sir Vincent was willing to persist once again with radio and television production, investing in new facilities and production runs. However, this commitment was never rewarded with commercial success, leaving the meter and transformer departments to generate much of the civil-based profits. Conversely, the Moston and Crewe Toll ventures into military aircraft instrumentation (or avionics) were extremely profitable, especially once significant contracts from both home and overseas airforces could be secured in the 1950s. Even when new civil technologies were developed out of work on defence projects, we shall see how managers experienced great difficulties in selling equipment to conservative British customers. This chapter will consequently demonstrate how once again Ferranti could be regarded as a study of the electrical industry in microcosm, because it will become apparent that, like so many of its counterparts, the company struggled to compete in the mass-consumption markets, yet in the capital equipment and defence markets it was able to develop good businesses. The establishment of an expanding and increasingly profitable business at Crewe Toll in Edinburgh was especially symptomatic of the post-War history of Ferranti, emphasising how the 'Ferranti Spirit' was much more successful when applied to capital equipment and defence businesses, while in mass-consumption markets there was little commercial achievement.

8.1 The third generation and new appointments

Sebastian and Basil join the firm

Before going on to describe the main departmental stories, it is first of all necessary to examine various aspects of the Ferranti organisation, and especially the means by which Sir Vincent ensured a steady progression at the highest managerial levels. Failure to provide for succession can severely constrain a firm's development. It is vital to note, though, that Sir Vincent put no pressure on his two sons, Sebastian (born 1928) and Basil (1930), to join the business or train as engineers. After attending Gilling Preparatory School, both boys were asked whether they would like to go to either a Catholic boarding school, Ampleforth, or to Eton. Reflecting a family preference for a more practical form of education, they both chose the former. Sebastian remembers how the whole process was by no means deliberate, but because engineering and business was 'sweeping all around us' they became absorbed and fascinated by the culture which the firm epitomised.[1] Basil was actually later to go to Eton, from where he went on to study engineering at Cambridge. Like his elder brother, though, he was never an academic high-flyer. Sebastian certainly did not enjoy academic work, leaving school in 1947 to join the 47th Royal Dragoon Guards, in which he enjoyed some challenging assignments, including a spell in the much-troubled Palestine region. It was while he was in the Guards that Sebastian decided to commit himself more fully to business. Consequently, when his four-year commission expired he asked his father to arrange for a series of placements at Brown Boveri in Switzerland and Alsthom in France, in order to learn more about electrical engineering.

The training which the natural heir to the firm received was consequently of a very traditional kind.[2] Above all, though, it was very much Sebastian's decision to join his father, emphasising how the whole succession issue was treated cautiously. Crucially, though, given his experiences with Denis (to be related in the next section), Sir Vincent was very much against sharing

Spanning three generations. Sebastian de Ferranti with a Ferranti-Thomson Alternator made in 1883, 23 February 1966. *(Museum of Science and Industry at Manchester.)*

power between the two brothers, leading him to encourage the younger son, Basil, to embark on a different career. Although for a while Basil worked in the domestic appliances department (see section 8.3), it was to be in politics where he made his most effective contributions. Sebastian, on the other hand, followed his father's path into the company, joining the transformer department in 1950 where he worked with Murray Robson in sales. His time in sales was divided between the high voltage and distribution transformer activities, resulting (see section 8.2) in an initiative which led to the establishment of a distribution transformer department. By 1954, Sebastian had also been made a director of Ferranti Ltd, after Sir Vincent had transferred 153,535 ordinary shares to each of his sons, making him a major figure in the firm at the relatively tender age of twenty-six.[3]

Strategy and structure

By providing in this most subtle of ways for both his succession and continued family control, Sir Vincent was following a much-trodden path so

290 FERRANTI: A HISTORY

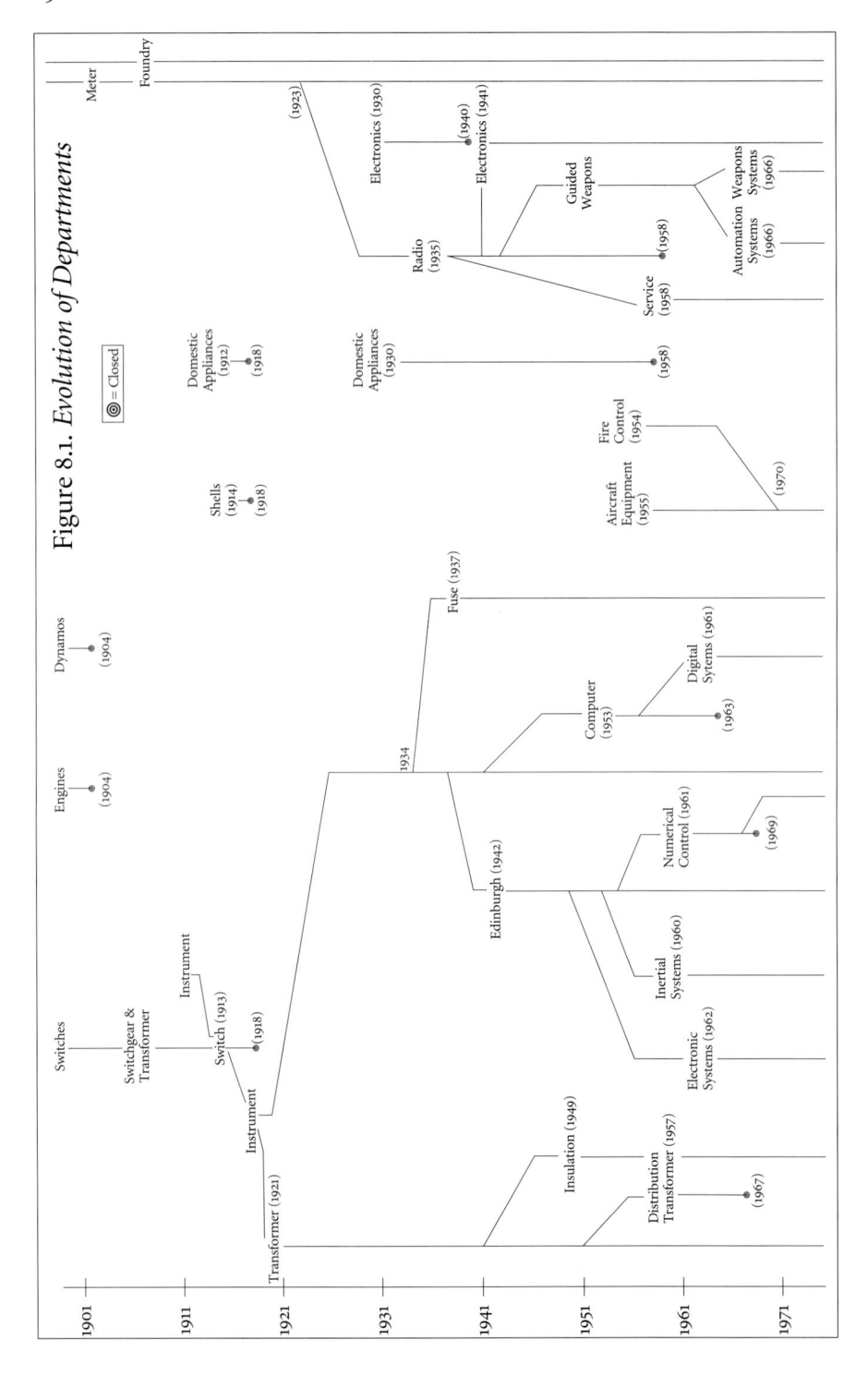

Figure 8.1. *Evolution of Departments*

typical of British business over the previous 200 years. By the 1950s, of course, far fewer firms were continuing family traditions in this way,[4] as an extensive transfer of ownership and control took place in most large businesses. To Ferranti, however, family control and ownership was regarded as fundamental to its whole approach, because it allowed for a longer-term approach to product development which was essential in exciting new technologies. Of course, strong centralised supervision of the expanding empire remained paramount in the chairman's eyes, reflecting his commitment to maintaining solvency. At the same time, as Figure 8.1 demonstrates, fresh organisational challenges were emerging as a host of new departments emerged out of internal development work. Furthermore, with turnover continuing to expand into the 1960s (see Figure 8.2) the family was continually faced with the need for increased liquidity.

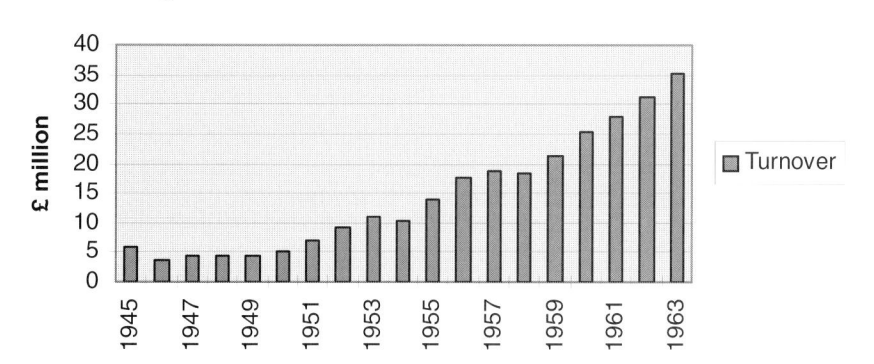

Figure 8.2. *Turnover Growth at Ferranti Ltd, 1945–63*

In reviewing the organisational response to this process, one must always remember that financial management remained Sir Vincent's personal domain. He certainly continued to draw up his graphs (see section 7.1) charting such crucial indicators as capital employed, profitability and turnover. As we noted at the end of the last chapter, considerable attention was paid to cost accounting control systems, building effectively on the innovations introduced first by Toothill and later by Brown and Kirkham. This provided Ferranti with an effective balance between centralised control and the delegation of authority, allowing the chairman to empower managers, yet monitor their performance in fine detail. As we shall see in section 8.5, Crewe Toll's case demonstrates how this balance created a conducive environment in which engineers and managers could flourish. Clearly, then, by effecting centralised financial control over the departments, Sir Vincent was able to perpetuate the 'Ferranti Spirit' at a time of considerable growth.

One must hesitate to describe Ferranti as a multidivisional form of organisation, because of Sir Vincent's strong role at the centre and the retention of most functions (sales, purchasing, transport, accounting) by the headquarters. Nevertheless, in spirit the firm encouraged devolution and responsibility at the departmental level, leaving Sir Vincent with the task of devising overall strategic policies.

Apart from extending the range of financial controls, another post-War innovation was the appointment of two new key personnel in the form of a mathematician and an economist (see Figure 7.1, p. 282). As company mathematician, Sir Vincent brought in T. J. (Tom) Lunt, a mathematics graduate of Liverpool University who had worked for Ferranti during the War, firstly in the Moston radio laboratory and later as a mathematician in the research department.[5] At the end of the War, Lunt had actually decided to embark on a teaching career, taking up a post at the Royal Technical College in Salford (now Salford University). Within a year, though, he had decided to return to Ferranti, a decision he never regretted. His title was company mathematician and Denis de Ferranti invited him to develop new statistical methods for the manufacturing departments, especially where mass production techniques were employed. As a member of the central research department, he consequently came into contact with all of the departmental managers, giving him an extensive insight into how the organisation worked. Moreover, from 1948 Lunt was working directly with Sir Vincent, presenting corporate

From the British Electrical Power Convention, a photograph of Sir Vincent de Ferranti (centre) in evening dress posed in a formal group.
(Museum of Science and Industry at Manchester.)

information in a much more sophisticated manner. After talking further with the chairman, this would eventually lead him to become R. J. Hebbert's natural successor as staff manager, given the intimate knowledge he had accumulated about the Ferranti structure and its modus operandi.

The success with which statistical techniques had been introduced after 1948 also induced Sir Vincent to hire an economist. In fact, he asked T. J. Lunt to find his own replacement, leading to the appointment of Lester George from instrument department as company economist, whose principal task was providing an overall view of both company performance and the general scene. Although George had actually started his working life as an engineering apprentice at Napier's, after winning a scholarship to enter Oxford University through extra-mural studies at Ruskin College and at Liverpool University, he became an economist with a special interest in financial control.[6] Lester George was to prove especially helpful to Sir Vincent during the 1950s, because not only was the company beginning to grow at a considerable pace, the chairman also found himself engaged in an increasing range of external activities. This extra-company work was, of course, a reflection of Sir Vincent's reputation as one of the electrical industry's leading figures. At the same time, it was no doubt a major distraction from the personal mission of making a success of Ferranti. In the first place, he had been on the Council of the IEE since 1933, while in 1946 he became the first son to follow his father as President of the industry's premier organisation. In 1950, Sir Vincent was also elected chairman of the International Executive of the World Power (later Energy) Conference, while from 1946 he was a vice-president of BEAMA and in 1957 and 1959 its president. These duties were further overlapped with work for such bodies as the International Commission on Large Dams, the International Electrotechnical Commission, and the Conferénce Internationale des Grands Résaux Electrique á Haute Tension. It was a fiercesome workload involving considerable travel around the world, clearly indicating the need for assistants like George and Lunt to lighten the burden.[7]

8.2 Meters and transformers

Meter expansion

Having described the main post-War organisational and personnel changes, we can now go on to examine how the operating departments fared. In particular, bearing in mind his strategy of rebuilding the civil businesses, it is important to assess the success with which Sir Vincent invested heavily in the meter and transformer departments. Another factor of importance influencing this decision was the direction of macro-economic policy in the 1940s, because in view of the fear of both inflation and balance of payments difficulties the new Labour government decided to suppress consumption of relative luxury items like radios and domestic appliances.[8] Meter production, which had always been a major source of income for Ferranti, was consequently regarded as an obvious area for development, especially after struggling throughout the War to maintain even a nominal production run. Sales of electricity actually increased significantly in the mid-1940s, from 31,363 gWh in 1945 to 38,821 gWh in 1948.[9] However, this growth was largely a function of industry's greater use of this energy source, rather than increased domestic use, putting a tremendous emphasis upon success in export markets if meter department was going to expand output.

Frank Rostron (export sales manager) was charged with the task of swiftly reconstructing the overseas agency network, while an updated version of the FL meter was launched. Of course, with reconstruction going on all over Europe and developing economies ordering equipment which for six years had been in short supply, overseas demand was extremely buoyant. This provided such a conducive environment for meter department that by 1946–47 the value of output had exceeded £1 million for the first time (amounting to 330,000 meters), while by 1951–52 the department was producing half a million meters a year. Meter exports actually accounted for sixty-five per cent of the department's increased sales totals, indicating how the FL meter was able to build on the solid reputation it had gained during the 1930s. As we shall see later, Rostron and the board of directors also invested considerable effort in marketing and sales efforts in the post-War era, boosting substantially the meter department's drive to increase sales and contribute to Britain's much-needed export drive.

Although the FL meter was a success in the late 1940s, it is important to note how this fooled the meter department manager, J. Prince, into believing that there was little need to introduce the new ideas on meter design which were growing in popularity at that time. The Electricity Supply (Meters) Act of 1936 had stipulated that meters should be accurate at one-twentieth of full load, imposing a high technical specification on British meter manufacturers, particularly as most of the Empire countries also adopted this regulation in the late 1930s.[10] As the FL meter met the 1936 specification, this gave it a significant competitive advantage over its European and American rivals which were based on the less stringent technical specifications adopted in their domestic economies. Ferranti and its British counterparts (Smith's, Aron and GEC) consequently enjoyed a market which was protected in a technical sense from foreign competition, further encouraging investment in meter production at the Crown Works.

A Ferranti
Pre-Payment Meter,
1968. *(Museum of
Science and Industry at
Manchester.)*

While meter department successfully exploited its technical superiority in the immediate post-war years, by 1950 there is evidence that problems were emerging on the design side. While the Ferranti meter employed the well-established technology based on pivot and jewel suspension, American and German manufacturers were introducing the new technology of magnetic suspension. Although the chief meter engineer, M. Whitehead, was at that time designing a new meter, the FM, and he advocated strongly the transfer to magnetic suspension technology, Prince refused to accept this advice, on the grounds that the old design met all statutory requirements. One must add that Whitehead and Prince never enjoyed a friendly relationship. More importantly, though, Prince was so strongly attached to the FL design that he forced Whitehead to incorporate the old technology into the FM mechanism. This was to be a mistake, because not only was customer pressure moving in favour of magnetic suspension, plenty of new products were already on the market. Consequently, just before the FM meter went into production, Whitehead was instructed by his manager to squeeze the new ideas into the existing design.[11] The FM meter eventually proved to be a great success, one contemporary describing it as 'a considerable advance over the older type FL'.[12] However, Prince's caution had done some damage to the business, at a time when house building was becoming a major priority of British governments.

Denis de Ferranti

Another source of difficulty in the 1950s meter market was Denis de Ferranti. Ever since his elevation on to the board of directors in 1933, and even though he was meter department manager in the 1930s, Denis had been complaining that he was never given the responsibility commensurate with his position as a major shareholder.[13] This situation had festered throughout the 1940s, causing much consternation at senior management levels. Such was the antagonism, indeed, that Sir Vincent decided to remove his brother from the board. R. W. Cooper felt that this would simply create greater antagonism, especially if either the younger brother refused to resign, or he fulfilled

D. Z. de Ferranti, Sir Vincent's younger brother. *(Museum of Science and Industry at Manchester.)*

his threat of creating a rival firm. Finally, though, Denis decided that 'owing to the hostile attitude of the majority of the board towards me', it was better to leave.[14]

Clearly, most of the directors had backed Sir Vincent's style of management. At the same time, Cooper would be proven correct, because Denis went on to make a real nuisance of himself. His first move was to buy the Pearson Electrical Co., one of the smaller meter manufacturers. After changing its name to the Denis Ferranti Meter Co., he pursued a policy of undercutting the prices set by the long-standing Meter Manufacturers' Association. He was eventually accepted into the Association in 1956, but only after he had forced them to agree to his right to quote lower prices to established customers. Sir Vincent was also concerned about the potential confusion caused by two meter producers having similar names, unsuccessfully going to court to try and force Denis to alter his firm's title. Generally, the whole situation proved most embarrassing to both the family and Ferranti,[15] especially when Denis went around criticising his brother and claiming that he was too old and cautious to run a high technology company. We shall also see in section 11.8 how in the late 1960s Sir Vincent's two sons were obliged to borrow heavily, in order to prevent Denis from taking control of Ferranti, further exacerbating the financial problems of that era.

In spite of Denis and the initial problems with the FM design, however, the meter department was able to rebuild its former dominant position by the well-established route which combined technological innovation with effective price-fixing. As in the past, Ferranti ensured that the Meter Manufacturers' Association continued to operate in much the same way as it had done since the 1930s. Although some of the smaller manufacturers (Measurements Ltd, Smiths and Venner) refused to be tied to this price agreement, the market was reasonably stable throughout this period. Sir Vincent also attempted to strengthen his company's position in the meter market by acquiring in 1949 one of its competitors, BICC Meters. In the 1960s, further acquisitions were made as a means of eliminating competition.[16] Indeed, once the FM went into full production in 1952, and the FL was phased out, the meter department established a strong trading position, contributing extensively to company profits in the 1950s.

In fact, the return on capital employed in this department amounted to thirty per cent over the period 1946–60, contributing almost £2.75 million to company funds. As we shall see in section 12.1, however, although this helped to finance the struggling new ventures, it is also clear that little investment was made in meter development after the FM went into production. This situation did not cause any problems while the market was booming in the 1950s. Circumstances changed in the 1960s, though, especially once electricity consumption levels stabilised and the price rings were dismantled by statutory intervention. The neglect of the 1950s consequently resulted in some acute trading difficulties, at a time when many other demands were being placed on Ferranti finances. Notwithstanding these later developments, the significant net contribution meter department made to company funds up to the early 1960s was one of the main reasons why Sir Vincent was able to take risks on some of the exciting new technologies emerging after the War.

Transformers and the Avenue Works

The other major civil business on which Sir Vincent lavished some attention after 1945 was transformers, particularly after the manager, A. W. G. Tucker, had estimated that this market would grow by at least five per cent per annum.[17] Although the grid network constructed in the early 1930s had been augmented during the War, by 1945 the CEB was projecting that new capacity of 4,619 MW would be required over the following four years, such was the optimism in the supply industry at that time.[18] Tucker consequently suggested that Ferranti ought to be capable of producing at least £1 million worth of transformers per annum to satisfy this demand, prompting Sir Vincent in 1947 to agree funding for a new factory. While it was Tucker's successor, J. E. L. Robinson, who oversaw this expansion programme, it was a gesture of faith in the transformer department which reflected Sir Vincent's keen interest in this market. The site chosen was across the railway from the Crown Works, on land known as Bower Clough, where the foundry had been based since 1930, substantiating the initial decision made by Dr Ferranti to choose Hollinwood as a base for an expanding business. The new factory, known as the Avenue Works, was to be a major commitment over the following thirty years, emphasising how Sir Vincent was anxious that his old department should be given every opportunity to re-establish the position it had held in the interwar years as one of the world's leading large transformer producers.

The first stage of this expansion programme would cost Ferranti £259,000, including the land, providing 176,000 square feet of factory space, or three-times the amount of production capacity available to transformer department prior to 1939.[19] In the six years after 1945 Ferranti also spent almost £800,000 re-equipping and extending the Avenue Works, creating one of the best transformer factories in Europe. This confidence was also well substantiated by the number of orders transformer department was able to generate: by 1947, twenty-seven transformers of over 40,000 kVA were being made, including a 60,000 kVA unit for the CEB and four 65,000 kVA units for export to Finland. Although some concern was expressed about the low

An indication of the transport problems associated with shipping Ferranti transformers. This 241 MVA 3 Phase Transformer was for New South Wales (Electricity Commission), Australia. *(Museum of Science and Industry at Manchester)*

profit margins on which this business was secured, export orders were particularly buoyant, with deliveries by 1949 being made to almost thirty countries all over the world.[20]

In a technical respect, Ferranti also recorded other notable achievements in transformer design and construction, when in 1950 they produced the first 230 kV units, for Finland. Even larger units of 71,000 kVA were supplied to the Aluminium Co. of Canada over the following few years, while in 1957 Ferranti received from the Kariba hydro-electric project the largest transformer order received by a British firm to date, worth £1,341,000 for two 120 MVA and eleven 60 MVA units. It is important to note that the Kariba contract was for the first 330 kV power transformers ever manufactured in the UK, reaffirming the company's role as a pioneer in developing such highly advanced equipment. The nationalisation of electricity supply in 1948 also provided a significant boost to demand at home, with the newly-constituted British Electricity Authority (BEA) predicting that its sales would increase at the compound rate of seven per cent per annum. This encouraged manufacturers to undertake a considerable investment programme, with both home and export markets booming.[21] By 1950–51, Ferranti transformer sales had consequently grown to almost £2.3 million, compared to under £600,000 in 1945–46, confirming the faith Sir Vincent had expressed in his old department's future.

310,000 kVA, 306,500 volt Ferranti Transformer – the largest transformer ever supplied to the CEGB for Blyth Power Station, Northumberland.
(Museum of Science and Industry at Manchester.)

Export successes

Although the expansion of electricity supply at home was a major boon to this department, because Britain emerged from the War with an acute balance of payments problem governments were particularly keen to encourage exports, especially in high-growth sectors like electrical engineering.[22] Sir Vincent paid tribute in 1945 to the 'helpful attitude adopted by the Department of Overseas Trade and the Board of Trade' in assisting the company's export efforts,[23] emphasising how the government was at that time contributing effectively in this respect. However, it was left mostly to companies themselves to go out and sell the goods, indicating how Frank Rostron's work in rebuilding the export sales department was crucial in the late 1940s. Much of his time was spent reestablishing links with the overseas agencies, while along with members of the board he travelled extensively to rekindle contacts which had proved useful in the past. Initially, though, selling abroad proved difficult, largely because of the severe dislocation arising from a World War. By 1947, it was also apparent that another factor had emerged, namely, 'the growth of manufacturers' capacities and the development of secondary industries in export markets where British products formerly sold on prestige'.[24]

Although some initial difficulties were experienced in selling overseas, when in 1949 the pound sterling was devalued by thirty per cent, from $4.03 to $2.80, British firms were provided with a competitive edge over some of their rivals. While most of the other European economies also devalued at the same time, the Americans were able to maintain their exchange rate, giving Rostron the idea that Ferranti might well exploit what was the largest and most affluent market in the world. Sir Vincent was rather more cautious when Rostron first presented him with this idea, largely because American firms controlled the international price rings established in the 1930s. Furthermore, any encroachment on their home market could well provoke severe price retaliation from powerful corporations like Westinghouse or General Electric.[25] On the other hand, because Britain needed to earn dollars, in order to pay for its increasing import bill, Sir Vincent was persuaded to back Rostron's plan for a major assault on the American market. There then followed a flurry of letters from Rostron requesting an interview with all chief engineers running American power stations. In anticipation of a positive answer, he also flew out to the USA to make direct contact with the largest potential customers.

The American market had always been difficult to penetrate, largely because of the protection afforded all industries since the late-nineteenth century. This protectionism had been further reinforced by the 'Buy American' Acts of the 1930s, when restrictive conditions were imposed on public utility purchasing policies. Another feature of the American electrical market was the close relationship between supply companies and equipment manufacturers, the two interests often having interlinking ownership and management structures. These difficulties ensured that Ferranti was never able to sell any transformers to private supply companies. Although Rostron records that he was always well received by American power station staff, this cordiality was never converted into actual orders. Even when Ferranti underbid their American competitors, they stood little chance of winning contracts.

The difficulties of securing American orders is best demonstrated by the 1949 case, when Ferranti undercut General Electric and Westinghouse by almost $200,000 in tendering for six transformers required by the Seattle Power Co.[26] Ostensibly, the Seattle chief engineer rejected the Ferranti bid on the grounds that noise levels in their transformers did not meet his requirements. Although a revised tender was submitted to deal with this problem, General Electric was still given the contract. The *New York Times* concluded of the Seattle incident that Britain 'had seen the first glimmer of economic chauvinism',[27] while the *Seattle Post* reported that the town's taxpayers were 'dismayed at the prospect of paying $200,000 for American transformers'.[28] Sir Vincent also explained in a letter to the power company how Britain was trying to earn its dollars, rather than having to ask for handouts.[29] Such arguments, however, would appear to have fallen on deaf ears.

In spite of the 'economic chauvinism' of private business interests in the USA, it is also important to remember that the American government had always taken a dim view of monopolistic trading practices. Indeed, arising out of general concern about incidents like that in Seattle, a measure was introduced which stipulated that foreign-made equipment should be considered if a saving could be made through its purchase.[30] Although this regulation was not imposed rigidly on private companies, in the public sector great care was taken to prevent any undue bias against non-American tenders, encouraging British firms to bid for such business. In this context, Rostron seized the opportunity to tender for the transformer contracts placed by the major rural electrification scheme, the Garrison Dam Project in North Dakota, managed by the US Army Corps. Again, Ferranti undercut the American prices, this time by sixteen per cent, leading in 1952 to a major contract worth $887,000 for nine 33,333 kVA transformers. This was followed up a year later with a further order for six 56,000 kVA units, this time for the McNary Dam Project, while in 1956–57 the Tennessee Valley Authority purchased eighteen transformers ranging in size from 12,000 kVA to 33,333 kVA. In total, Ferranti transformer exports to the USA were worth over £3.7 million in the 1950s, accounting for a third of that department's overseas sales. It was valuable business secured in the teeth of fierce competition, emphasising how British firms were able to compete in the most protected of markets. Although Sir Vincent had been sceptical of Rostron's plans, they worked extremely well once the initial breakthrough had been made.

The late 1940s investments in improved transformer production facilities had clearly proved to be a major success, repaying Sir Vincent's faith handsomely as annual sales rose to over £5 million by 1959–60. The transformer department actually reported a cumulative profit of over £5.6 million between 1945 and 1960, contributing effectively to the company's overall performance. This record was also further improved by the standard practice at this time of customers, both overseas and British, providing large progress payments during production, reducing substantially the cash-flow difficulties of a company which carried high stocks and employed an increasing labour force. Sir Vincent often expressed concern at this reliance on prepayments, offering the prophetic view that if they should stop then Ferranti would no longer be able to afford to remain in such a business.[31] As we shall see in section 12.1, this prediction slowly unfolded in the late 1960s and 1970s, at a time when in both meter and transformer markets severe price competition had emerged as a result of both statutory intervention over price-fixing and intensifying foreign competition, compounded by a stagnating market for electricity. Nevertheless, in the fifteen years after the Second World War Ferranti was able to flourish in a market which continued to expand, enhancing its reputation as designers and producers of the most advanced and largest transformers. Avenue Works was a flourishing hive of activity throughout this period, providing a solid foundation for the diversifications of this era.

Distribution transformers

Not only was Ferranti enjoying considerable success in the production of large transformers, the firm was also able to exploit new opportunities in the development of the smaller distribution transformer. In fact, Ferranti had learnt how to design and manufacture these products from its Canadian subsidiary, after it had started a small business in pole-top distribution transformers during the First World War. When Sebastian de Ferranti joined the transformer department after spells in several major European firms, he

Ferranti Canada's Mt. Dennis factory by the 1950s.

realised that with the standardisation of frequencies made possible by nationalisation of electricity supply in 1948 they were then able to produce the same distribution transformer for all parts of the country.[32] This led him to persuade his father that it would be a viable idea to establish a new department which would be solely dedicated to this business. Although the new distribution transformer business was clearly a relatively small affair, after expanding from its initial base in the Crown Works to new premises in West Gorton in 1956 Sebastian was able to introduce mass-production techniques which helped to establish a successful department. It was yet another example of the company's expertise in this market, further strengthening the Ferranti reputation in the electricity supply industry.

Ferranti in Canada

Mention of the role played by the Canadian subsidiary in stimulating the creation of a distribution transformer business provides an opportunity to emphasise how the Ferranti transformer strategy was very much global in nature. Indeed, not only did the firm invest in North American facilities, through which it could exploit further its competitive advantage in this field, by 1960 Sir Vincent was also building up other links which would assist in achieving this aim. As we saw in section 5.2, while the Canadian subsidiary had provided a major boost to Ferranti meter and transformer exports up to 1922, especially after the young Vincent in that year had encouraged the Ferranti board to begin production in that country, its commercial performance had been poor. In spite of this, Vincent had also invested in another Canadian venture, buying one-third of the Packard Electric Co. in 1936, in the hope that by merging the two corporations greater inroads into the transformer market could be achieved. We noted in section 5.2 that while commercial considerations had been prominent in the assessment of the Canadian subsidiary's development, one of the main reasons behind the investment was Sir Vincent's conviction that this would provide a bolt-hole if matters deteriorated sufficiently in the UK to warrant emigration. Of course, even in the depths of the 1930s and 1940s difficulties, he never seriously considered moving to Canada, such was his patriotism. Nevertheless, the investment emphasised how personal factors were just as important in motivating the development of Ferranti as a multinational, an explanation which helps to understand why the company was willing to accept the substantial losses made by Ferranti Canada right up to the 1940s.

By 1945, reflecting the chairman's long-term approach towards departmental viability, Ferranti had invested just over £140,000 in its Canadian operations.[33] In the immediate post-war years, as part of the strategy aimed at reviving the civil businesses, Ferranti Canada was expected to play a role in boosting the firm's presence in what was regarded as its strongest civil market, transformers. This strategy would also appear to have succeeded, because not only did the much-expanded British plant in Chadderton come to be recognised as one of the world's major centres of transformer technology, both Ferranti Canada and Packard Electric took significant shares of their expanding domestic market. Ferranti Canada even started generating reasonable returns over the period 1945–54, when it produced a total profit of $1.2 million.[34] Little of this money was ever repatriated to benefit the UK operations, because Ferranti Canada required investment capital to expand and modernise its own facilities. Nevertheless, the improved returns did prompt the Ferranti board in 1948 to invest £470,000 in new plant.

Over the period 1948–56, Ferranti Canada actually increased its issued capital from $500,000 to $6 million for expansion purposes, with the parent company pumping £1.56 million into the business. Furthermore, from its profits Ferranti Canada was also encouraged to purchase as many Packard Electric shares as possible. By 1956, its holding was valued at almost £1.1 million, bringing the group's Canadian investments to £2.66 million. One must remember that the issued capital of the Ferranti group was only £3 million at that time, indicating just how far Sir Vincent was willing to extend his commitment to Ferranti Canada. Furthermore, in view of the improved returns, this investment seemed at last to be paying off.

While power transformers were clearly central to the overseas strategy pursued by Vincent since the 1930s, one should also add that Ferranti Canada had started to diversify away from its traditional reliance on heavy electrical engineering. In the first place, the production of X-ray equipment had been started, after the acquisition of the Solus X-Ray Co. in 1936.[35] This venture was reasonably successful, but of far greater significance was the late 1940s move to establish an electronics division within Ferranti Canada. This decision confirms what Nicholas identifies as a major reason for foreign direct investment by firms, local government encouragement.[36] In fact, it was directly as a result of a meeting between Sir Vincent and the head of Canada's Defence Research Board (Dr O. Solandt) in October 1948 that Cooper was encouraged to effect this diversification. Although Dr Solandt was only able to offer limited support, as Cooper concluded 'it might be in our general interest not to ignore Solandt's suggestion of unpaid cooperation'. This persuaded Sir Vincent to transfer to Canada several key staff from the British divisions, including two highly innovative engineers, M. K. Taylor and Dr Arthur Porter. Some development funds were also forthcoming from the military, resulting in the development of a system known as DATAR which combined digital computing and displays to produce better communication for the navy.

Unfortunately, DATAR never went into commercial production, because of various political and financial constraints. Nevertheless, it laid the basis for a new activity at Ferranti Canada which later produced good rewards. Among its more successful products were mail and cheque sorting systems, digital computers and tape-readers, while the airline reservation equipment (RESERVEC) developed for Trans-Canada Airlines was well ahead of either its American or British rivals.

Apart from diversifying away from the highly volatile heavy electrical market, the electronics division demonstrated above all that the Canadian subsidiary was capable of designing and producing equipment without relying excessively on parent company support. This success was also an excellent manifestation of the management philosophy enacted by Sir Vincent throughout the company, encouraging managerial independence and responsibility at the highest levels. Cooper at Ferranti Canada demonstrated this culture at work just as much as those managers who ran the expanding avionics operations at Edinburgh or the digital systems venture at Bracknell. We shall also see in section 9.10 that in the 1960s the Canadian subsidiary was a pioneer in the development of high-speed mainframe computers, while its product range expanded considerably from the mail and cheque sorting systems developed in the 1950s into superconductivity, fuel cells and numerical readout systems for machine tools. Perhaps its most significant achievement was M. K. Taylor's flip-disc display system, in which the firm built up a flourishing international business once the Montreal Stock Exchange had placed a highly prestigious order in 1961. In fact, by 1977 it had claimed one-half of the world market for display systems in commodity and stock markets, while in world markets for highway traffic signalling it was equally strong.[37] While the electronics division never contributed much to the Canadian operation's profitability, largely because of an excessive commitment to a technology-led strategy, once again this reflected the long-term commitment at Ferranti to building businesses with a viable technological base.

Ferranti-Packard

While Ferranti was substantially increasing its commitments in Canada, with major new factories coming on stream at Toronto and St Catherines, in the mid-1950s Sir Vincent was made aware of new obstacles which would seriously jeopardise these investments.[38] In the first place, not only had Canadian manufacturers been affected by a substantial increase in imports, in 1954 demand for electrical equipment collapsed and failed to revive for the rest of the decade. These market difficulties also coincided with two cases (1956 and 1960) which severely restricted the ability of electrical manufacturers to collude on prices, following the tightening up in 1950 of Canadian restrictive practices legislation. Of course, Ferranti Canada had experienced difficult times before, especially in the 1930s. However, while Sir Vincent had trusted A. B. Cooper to deal effectively with market problems, this was no longer possible in the 1950s since the Canadian general manager had retired in 1947. In these circumstances, Sir Vincent was even keener to implement the broader vision which had been at the heart of his 1930s acquisition of a substantial holding in Packard Electric, because not only would a merger between the two companies strengthen their position in a challenging market, it would also ensure that Ferranti Canada would once again possess a manager who could be trusted.

Although the loss of A. B. Cooper would hardly have been felt in the booming post-war years, as the 1950s unfolded Sir Vincent realised that firm management was required if Ferranti Canada was going to sustain this position. This point was particularly well substantiated when in May 1956, just three months after the firm's expensive new plant had been officially opened, workers' frustration over new working practices boiled over, precipitating a strike which lasted 135 days. By that time, after ten years of profitable performance between 1945 and 1954, Ferranti Canada was once again reporting substantial losses, amounting to an annual average of over $550,000 in the period 1955–59.[39] Packard Electric was also suffering badly from the depression, emphasising the need for a merger if both operations were going to survive.

Once again, Sir Vincent was thwarted in his strategy by intransigent Packard shareholders, who dragged out the equity purchase for four years. Finally, though, by 1958 Ferranti Canada held 100 per cent of Packard Electric shares, bringing the Ferranti investment in that country to a total of almost £4.6 million. It was in that year that Ferranti-Packard Electric Ltd was formed as the single corporation which would combine the two operations. It is vital to note, however, that by far the most important part of this package as far as Sir Vincent was concerned was the acquisition of the management skills of Packard Electric's president and general manager since 1951, Tom Edmondson. In fact, because Sir Vincent was so impressed with Edmondson's business acumen, Ferranti Canada had made several approaches to Edmondson since Cooper's retirement in 1947. Edmondson had resisted these entreaties largely because of his reluctance to move from St Catherines to Toronto. Once the merger had been effected, he was consequently given the opportunity to rebuild the organisation around his beloved St Catherines factory.

The creation of Ferranti-Packard and the installation of Edmondson as president and chief executive officer was the culmination of a plan which

Sir Vincent had been hatching for over twenty years. It also indicates how while Ferranti played only a peripheral role in the routine management of the Canadian operations (see section 5.2), its chairman did have a long-term vision of how they ought to develop. In particular, because he was anxious to recruit senior management whom he could trust, Cooper and Edmondson were given the resources to develop a firm which while never matching the giants like Canadian Westinghouse or General Electric, was capable of competing effectively in its chosen niche markets. More importantly for Sir Vincent, the Canadian venture was an effective vehicle for extending his firm's competitive advantage in power transformer technology into the North American market, particularly after Edmondson decided that if the expensive new capacity constructed in the mid-1950s was going to be used efficiently the firm had to embark on the ambitious strategy of breaking into the US market. After all, as we have just seen, the parent company had sold over £3.7 million worth of power transformers to American customers between 1952 and 1960, persuading Edmondson that this reputation could be exploited to boost Ferranti-Packard sales.[40]

A growing network

In fact, the recovery process was fitful. Even though Ferranti-Packard recorded some progress in breaking into the American market, much of this business was taken at cut-throat prices, resulting in a cumulative net loss of almost $2.8 million during the firm's first seven trading years up to 1965. Thereafter, however, while the firm's electronics division continued to record losses up to the early 1970s, Ferranti-Packard was able to exploit the North American growth in demand for power transformers, contributing $6.7 million in net profits over the following ten years.[41] Once again, not only did the parent company receive very little financial benefit from this improved performance, in 1968 the board also agreed to invest a further £825,000 in another expansion of capacity. Nevertheless, Ferranti-Packard's success reinforced the reputation of the group as a whole in the power transformer market, fulfilling at least one of the main aims of the initial strategy formulated when Ferranti first decided to build an overseas production plant. The strategy was also complemented during the 1960s, when Ferranti purchased substantial holdings in two other transformer manufacturers, the Wilson Electric Transformer Co., in Australia, and Industrie Elettriche di Legnano (IEL), in Italy, extending the Ferranti name into other expanding markets. The Australian investment, amounting to almost £62,000 for twenty-three per cent of the Wilson Co., was aimed at boosting the firm's position in the southern Pacific region, while the purchase of forty-five per cent of IEL's equity (for almost £417,000) reflected what was a major switch of emphasis from Commonwealth markets to Europe which typified much British multinational activity at that time.[42]

Ferranti was clearly willing to go to some expense in creating a network of affiliated companies which would help boost its power transformer business. The Canadian subsidiary remained by far the largest single investment up to the 1970s, where Tom Edmondson was encouraged to build up an established position throughout North America. On the other hand, as Britain's political and economic links with the Commonwealth were disintegrating, and Europe was beginning to loom large on the agenda, the link with IEL would be seen as a springboard for the future. Unfortunately, though, these plans for the power transformer division never reached fruition, because as we shall see in section 12.1 as a direct result of the collapse in domestic demand the British factory started reporting substantial losses, precipitating major liquidity problems for the group as a whole.

Notwithstanding this point, it is also clear that Ferranti never exacted much financial benefit from its overseas operations, either reinvesting what profits were ever made into expanded facilities, or subsidising the many years of losses. Perhaps one explanation for this was the lax management structure employed by Sir Vincent in the development of these businesses. On the other hand, anything more intrusive would have been anathema to the Ferranti ethos, indicating how Cooper and Edmondson were left very much to their own resorts, in spite of long periods of losses and commercial difficulties. Notwithstanding these losses, because Sir Vincent was convinced that the successes achieved by both Ferranti Canada and the Packard Co. during the late 1940s and early 1950s contributed extensively to the growing impression that Ferranti was a major player in the power transformer business, this was sufficient justification for continuing to support their managements.

8.3 Consumer goods

Radio

With such a flourishing staple business in meters and transformers, Sir Vincent was in a good position to develop other civil departments, especially radio and television. Although we saw in the last chapter how little commercial success had been achieved in these markets during the 1930s, Sir Vincent was again keen to encourage radio and television development as major components in the company's civil product portfolio, particularly as consumers had been deprived of such products for so long. When questioned about this diversion of resources into such markets, Sir Vincent responded by noting that radio and television gave Ferranti excellent visibility in British markets, bringing the company's name to the attention of people who would not necessarily have heard of its achievements in other technologies. This again emphasises how Sir Vincent often took a broad perspective when assessing company strategy, speculating substantial sums on high-risk areas like consumer appliances, even though in the past the firm had never achieved much success in these markets.

Ferranti was actually quick to restart radio production at Moston in 1945, and a new laboratory was built in 1946, where forty-five staff worked under the chief radio engineer, Dr Norman Searby. Sir Vincent also hired a former Murphy salesman, L. Hall, to develop the direct-dealer side of the business, given the company's earlier failure to 'nurse the trade'.[43] At the same time, a cabinet designer was also brought in to improve the appeal of Ferranti radios. Unfortunately, though, these positive moves to overcome some of the earlier problems with radio production (see section 7.2) were largely unsuccessful. Although some of the obstacles to increasing radio sales were beyond the company's control, major difficulties were experienced in making this department commercially viable.

One of the major post-War difficulties Ferranti faced in this market was the degree of government interference with consumer goods consumption. In the first place, purchase tax on radios fluctuated between one-third and two-thirds, severely depressing demand at various times,[44] while the government also imposed production quotas on all firms which were based on pre-War output levels. Ferranti had actually stopped producing radios in 1938, such was its commitment to the rearmament programme, and as a consequence it was initially given a market quota of just 0.89 per cent. This was eventually raised to 2.5 per cent, after extensive lobbying by Sir Vincent, but over the three years from 1946–47 Ferranti radio production still fell, from 53,548 to 13,379, even though domestic consumers' expenditure in this market rose, respectively, from £3.5 million to almost £21 million.[45]

In considering how the radio department could improve its performance, F. C. Aitken (its manager) estimated that the company would have to be prepared to spend £500,000 to expand production. Sir Vincent, on the other hand, regarded this as far too risky, forcing Aitken to keep output at approximately 20,000 sets per year up to 1954. One area in which Ferranti had anticipated substantial demand was the export trade, but although forty per cent of total sales went abroad in 1945–46 substantial losses were made on this business. The main reason for this was a contract for 25,000 sets placed by the Indian government. Not only had special features to be added to the circuits, in order to accommodate for the special climatic conditions, the number ordered was later reduced to 13,500. These difficulties severely limited the economies of scale which could have been exploited in such a contract, resulting in a net loss of almost £35,000. Furthermore, because the contract had been signed in secret, Ferranti was associated with what the *Radio Times of India* regarded as an outrage, because the order had come 'from a Government which could not see its way to arrange for imports of food grain to relieve the primary need of hungry millions'.[46]

Television

In the immediate post-War years, radio department consequently failed to improve on its poor financial performance of the 1930s (see section 7.2), even though under Dr Searby considerable effort was made to develop improved circuitry. At the same time, it is important to remember that one of the reasons why Sir Vincent refused to allow Aitken the funds to increase his department's market share was the preference shown to television development over this period. Nationally, television sales had taken off at a rate which surprised many people, given the limited successes of the late 1930s trials, especially once the decision had been taken by the BBC in 1946 to remain with the 405-line system. While in 1945 there had only been 46,000 licence-holders, mostly in London, by 1952 the number had grown to 1.9 million nationally, rising even further by 1956 to over 5.7 million. In terms of consumers' expenditure, television sales increased from just £460,000 in 1946 to almost £11.5 million by 1949.[47] Ferranti, however, was slow to market a new television, even though over £40,000 was spent developing a new design in the Moston radio laboratory. Furthermore, when it did appear the price of £62.50p was over £14 greater than the market leaders, EMI and Pye.[48] The price differential was eventually reduced to just a few pounds, though, leading to an increase in sales from just under £40,000 in 1947–48 to almost £500,000 in 1951–52. Profitability remained poor, however, forcing Sir Vincent to take a deep look at this department.

In 1954, two years after Aitken had been succeeded as head of radio and television by Hubert Wood, Sir Vincent was finally persuaded to make a major bid to improve the department's fortunes. Of course, consumer demand was substantially boosted in 1954 by the Chancellor, R. A. Butler, as part of a pre-election boom, providing a highly conducive environment for investment in new facilities. Sir Vincent consequently agreed to back Wood's plans to acquire new premises, at Derby St in Oldham, while Ferranti House was opened in London as a new marketing headquarters for the consumer goods businesses.[49] Initially, it also seemed as if the strategy was working, because the sale of radio sets leapt from 16,173 in 1953–54 to 36,857 in 1954–55, while, respectively, televisions sales expanded from 21,874 to 55,546. Unfortunately, however, consumer spending was severely curtailed at the end of 1955, because in over-expanding the economy Butler had precipitated a balance of payments crisis, leading to the introduction of deflationary measures like the imposition of credit controls and hire purchase restrictions.[50] This forced Wood to cut back on radio and television production 'to line up with conditions arising from the credit squeeze and to permit the stock of receivers held at the end of the season to be at an economic level'.[51] Tragically, not only did Ferranti have to deal with such market vagaries, the firm also lost its radio department manager in October 1955, when Hubert Wood died prematurely. As it could be argued that Wood was one of the very few people within Ferranti who posessed the ability to make the radio department a commercial success, this indicates how factors beyond the company's control could severely affect investment programmes.

What happened to the Ferranti radio and television businesses in 1954–55 was a classic manifestation of the problems facing consumer goods producers at this time. In effect, the 'stop-go' economy arising from the government's preference for bolstering sterling, instead of boosting industrial activity, created such severe fluctuations in demand that firms were often unable to recoup sufficient returns on their investments.[52] Of course, one cannot put all the blame on government policy, because Ferranti had clearly yet to overcome all the challenges associated with mass-production and mass-selling. Nevertheless, problems like the 'stop-go' cycle simply compounded the traditional Ferranti struggle to make this business commercially viable. In effect, Ferranti was never able to sell enough sets to recoup its development and production costs,[53] emphasising once again its difficulties experienced in mass-consumption markets. Losses on radio and television production in the period 1945–58 amounted to almost £2 million, sixty-three per cent of which was attributable to the latter. When combined with Hubert Wood's premature death in 1955, this forced Ferranti to take some hard decisions. Sir Vincent's persistence with what he regarded as the popular front to his general electronics business had consequently proved extremely costly, placing a considerable burden on the profitable departments at a time when many demands were being placed on increasingly scarce funds.

Valves and cathode-ray tubes

The radio and television department's fortunes would also impact very much on those of valve and cathode-ray tube production at Gem Mill. In the 1930s, Sir Vincent had been keen to develop both the components and end-product sides of the radio industry, a policy which had contributed enormously to the company's extensive diversification into electronics during the 1930s (see section 7.2). During the War, a team with considerable expertise in these fields had consequently been built up which was capable of designing a wide range of devices for use in radio, radar and testing equipment. For reasons which remain vague, however, it is important to note that initially the electronics department was slow to recover from the termination of many defence-related contracts. Indeed, the lease on the Gem Mill factory was not renewed in 1945, leading to the relocation of electronics at the much-underused Moston plant. In fact, the owners of Gem Mill (Kaputine Ltd) had invited Ferranti to buy the facility, but Sir Vincent felt that their price was excessive. By 1952, however, when Wood was planning his major assault on the television market, Kaputine had actually been liquidated, giving Ferranti the opportunity to acquire Gem Mill at a much-reduced price for the bulk production of cathode-ray tubes.[54] This provided electronics department with a permanent base, where over the following thirty-five years Ferranti developed a highly innovative business which eventually established a world-wide reputation.

During the 1940s, Ferranti had actually fallen well behind the major cathode-ray tube producers, largely because at Moston they still used the second-hand American machinery supplied in 1942, while firms like Mullard, GEC and Mazda had invested in much-improved production facilities.[55] The industry was also heavily cartelised, with giants like Mullard, BT-H, EMI, GEC, Marconi, Philips, E. K. Cole and Ferguson accounting for most of the market allocations. Nevertheless, Sir Vincent was willing to back the electronics department manager, Peter Hall, in his plan to automate production of cathode-ray tubes. Two engineers were consequently sent to the USA in order to learn about flow-line production techniques.[56] These engineers were the chief designer, George Turner, and a man who had developed the first Ferranti cathode-ray tube production process, Sydney Jackson. By 1954, they had devised plant capable of making 150,000 units annually, ranging in size from twelve to twenty-four inches. Sadly, though, Gem Mill never made a profit on this business, because cathode-ray tube prices were dictated by the larger producers who were able to operate on much tighter margins because of their larger throughput. It is also important to remember that by the time Turner and Jackson had completed the new production line Hubert Wood decided to switch from using Ferranti cathode-ray tubes to the Mullard variant, because they were cheaper and more effective. This forced Peter Hall to negotiate with Mullard's for a licence to manufacture its cathode-ray tubes. Such was his weak bargaining position, however, that although he secured a contract to supply 15,000 tubes at £4.50 each, Gem Mill was only able to produce each unit for £6.47. Ferranti did manage to increase its cathode-ray tube sales, from £180,000 in 1951–52 to over £560,000 by 1958–59. However, losses of £320,000 were made over this period, while since 1945 valve production had also recorded a deficit of over £280,000.[57]

The poor performance of Gem Mill's electronics department reaffirms our earlier conclusion about the Ferranti ventures into mass-consumption businesses. Notwithstanding this gloomy story, as we shall see in sections 11.2 and 11.3, at exactly the same time that Gem Mill engineers were struggling to compete in the valve and cathode-ray tube businesses Peter Hall was also directing a team which was responsible for developing what became the second generation of electronic components, semiconductors. Indeed, the electronics department was showing great promise in this area by the mid-1950s, leading to the creation at Gem Mill of one of the principal European centres of innovation in this new technology. Indeed, semiconductor production provided a solution to the real commercial problems experienced by the old electronic components business at Gem Mill, leading Peter Hall's department into an exciting new world which expanded rapidly after 1954.

Domestic appliances

The final episode in this story of civil department development is the attempt to rebuild domestic appliances as another important branch of the Ferranti civil business. Once again, though, we can see how all the same problems which affected radio and television production were mirrored exactly in this department. Although contemporaries anticipated a major boom in this sector,[58] and Ferranti was able to sell £250,000 worth of electric fires and water heaters in 1946–47, the late 1940s restrictions on consumer spending severely limited prospects for several years. The main problem with Ferranti products, however, would appear to have been their price, because while they were always a first class piece of engineering this simply made them more expensive than their rivals. National sales of domestic appliances actually increased significantly in the 1950s, rising from £67 million in 1950 to £232 million by 1959.[59] Ferranti sales, on the other hand, failed to match expectations, peaking at only £252,154 in 1956–57. In effect, the firm just could not compete with the large-scale manufacturers like Hoover, Belling or GEC, largely because the designers were more interested in engineering and aesthetic qualities, rather than mass-producing for a highly price-sensitive market. Of course, the increases in purchase tax and tighter credit controls imposed in 1951 and 1955–56 did not help the trade. On the other hand, restrictions of this kind affected all firms, indicating how the failure of the domestic appliance department can largely be blamed on internal factors.

The fridge-heater developed by Basil de Ferranti and produced by the firm in the 1950s. *(Museum of Science and Industry at Manchester.)*

Of course, this lack of commercial success did not prevent Ferranti engineers from developing plenty of new ideas. One of the more interesting 1950s innovations was the introduction of a novel form of heat pump, or fridge-heater. This device was actually developed by Sir Vincent's youngest son, Basil, who joined the firm specifically with the intention of commercialising the concept. He claimed that this device was capable of reducing the cost of domestic water-heating by two-thirds, because it worked by using freon to extract heat from a larder, after which the energy was then transferred to a house's hot water system.[60] By 1954, he had risen to the post of domestic appliance department manager, in preparation for his later elevation to more senior managerial posts. Unfortunately, though, he was only taking on a major loss-maker, because over the period 1945–58 domestic appliances produced a total deficit of £415,263, or twenty-seven per cent of total sales. Although industrial heaters and pumps were produced well into the 1960s, in 1959 the electric fire business had actually been sold to E. K. Cole Ltd (Ekco) for £26,000, while rationalisation of all the other lines was being considered. As with radio and television, Ferranti simply could not compete on commercial terms with the larger or more specialised firms which dominated these mass-consumption markets, forcing Sir Vincent to think seriously about their future role within the Ferranti portfolio.

8.4 Rationalisation

Overdraft pressures

This brief survey of the meter, transformer and consumer goods departments reveals how Sir Vincent was faced with a difficult act if he was to achieve any balance between civil and defence businesses. As we shall see in both the next two sections and chapter ten, the latter was expanding so dramatically by the mid-1950s that Ferranti was being forced to decide on its priorities, especially as problems in the former were prompting the Westminster Bank to request positive action. Indeed, a factor of increasing concern after the relatively cash-rich 1940s was a growing reliance on bank borrowing, with the overdraft (see Appendix C, Table 1) once again starting to reach significant proportions in the 1950s. It is important to remember how ever since the rearmament era of the late 1930s the Westminster Bank had been extremely supportive of the company, cementing a relationship which was crucial to the post-War expansion. In fact, while by 1949 the overdraft had been reduced significantly from its 1945 peak of almost £2.4 million, during the Korean War expansion (1950–53) and the mid-1950s it rose considerably, reaching a peak of £4.4 million in 1956. In this context, it is interesting to see how in 1953, instead of the old system of producing a balance sheet for the year to June, Ferranti decided to run its accounting year from April to March. This change was introduced because it provided certain taxation advantages, while because of the highly seasonal nature of consumer goods and meter production, stocks were always at their lowest in March, making this item look particularly impressive in the balance sheet. At the same time, the Bank was not fooled into believing that this accounting reform had much impact on the company's cash requirements.

Reliance on bank borrowing was clearly a major problem during the 1950s. Moreover, as a representative of Denis de Ferranti complained in 1956: 'If [the Westminster Bank] get tired of being electrical manufacturers the company is going to be in the soup'.[61] It is also pertinent to point out that all the 1950s capitalisations (see section 8.7 and Appendix C, Table 1) did not bring a single penny into the company. Sir Vincent consoled himself with the thought that the Bank would never have lent so much money had it not been confident that Ferranti was a sound business with an effective organisation. Furthermore, as returns on capital employed were generally acceptable throughout the 1950s, this calmed any fears about a liquidity crisis (see Appendix C, Table 2).[62] Nevertheless, given the problems associated with the loss-making consumer goods departments and the need to find space for expanding defence businesses, it was increasingly necessary to deal with the situation, especially as the Bank was beginning to voice some reservations about the overdraft. The major opportunity facing Ferranti at that time was a big contract to produce the *Bloodhound* guided weapon (see section 10.4), but this would involve taking some hard decisions about radio and television production, where losses were continuing to mount.

Sell-offs

The major meeting between Sir Vincent and the Bank took place in October 1956,[63] when it became apparent that further extensions of the overdraft were dependent upon the financiers' view that radio and television production should be terminated. In fact, even though Moston's divisional manager, Eric Grundy, had already offered these businesses to Thorn for £1 million, nothing had come of this approach, leaving Sir Vincent to discuss the possibilities with a close friend, Eric Cole of E. K. Cole & Co. (Ekco). The talks evidently went well, because after Ekco's works manager (F. S. Allen) visited Moston in November 1956 a deal was struck giving Ferranti £300,000 for their ailing radio and television businesses.[64] This provided both a financial solution to Sir Vincent's problems, as well as space at Moston in which the guided weapons department could locate production. There is no doubt that the chairman was saddened by this move, given his long association with radio and its attendant technologies. In the circumstances, however, it was inevitable that some rationalisation of activity had to be introduced.

Of course, the sale of radio and television (and later domestic appliances, to the same firm) could be regarded as a sign of weakness at Ferranti, because clearly the firm had struggled to compete in what was an expanding market. On the other hand, this rationalisation programme must not be seen in isolation, because many British electrical firms were obliged to focus activity more intensely as a result of competitive pressures,[65] indicating how this decision was a rational response to the firm's environment. Similarly, one must remember another crucial factor influencing the decisions of electronics firms, namely, the technological obsolescence of valve, or first generation, technology, a trend we shall be examining over the next three chapters (see especially section 11.2). To have coped with this fundamental change would have involved Ferranti in a considerable investment in new designs, at a time when the radio and television department was not generating any surpluses.

Even though Peter Hall was directing a team in the electronics department which was working on the new devices, it would have been commercially prohibitive for the Ferranti radio and television department to redesign all their models. Indeed, if Hall was going to find space for producing the new semiconductor devices, there would also have to be substantial changes at Gem Mill.

As we noted at the end of section 8.3, Ferranti had also been struggling to keep pace with the major cathode-ray tube producers, forcing Gem Mill to act as a subcontractor to Mullard's. Once these contracts had been completed, though, it was decided that Gem Mill would be converted into a base for the new semiconductor venture.[66] The specialised cathode-ray tube business was retained, and as we shall see in section 10.8 considerable progress was made in developing screens for highly advanced research work. However, after the general business was closed in 1958 electronic components radically changed direction, embarking on an even more adventurous strategy which will be analysed in section 11.2.

Ferranti had clearly taken some hard decisions during the mid-1950s, expanding significant new ventures at the expense of loss-makers which were still using outdated technology. Furthermore, these transformations at Gem Mill and Moston made the achievement of Sir Vincent's intended balance between civil and defence businesses impossible. Nevertheless, while attempts had been made to build viable consumer goods departments, the heavy losses made up to 1957 were an investment of retained earnings in Sir Vincent's vision of a firm dedicated to both markets. The failure to achieve the balance can be ascribed to an inherent naivety in the firm's approach towards mass markets and their fluctuations. Clearly, though, another factor was a much greater interest in the exciting new technologies which advanced rapidly after 1945. That certain government agencies and ministries supported them was obviously an added attraction. More importantly, Sir Vincent felt that his company could develop and exploit these exciting new technologies, emphasising how he was always prepared to risk internal funds on such ventures. It was an approach which over the 1940s and 1950s led Ferranti into a host of high profile activities, further strengthening the chairman's vision of creating a firm capable of contributing to the advancement of knowledge.

8.5 Avionics at Moston and Bracknell

One of the areas in which Ferranti was especially successful was avionics. Not only was this an expanding market, it also provided for the Moston group considerable relief from the financial difficulties experienced by the consumer goods departments. Initially, though, while the civil businesses in Moston experienced a period of expansion after 1945, in contrast the other departments and sites suffered a period of severe retrenchment as government contracts declined in size and Sir Vincent decided to implement a policy of rationalising capacity and streamlining overhead costs. At the same time, engineers at Moston especially were examining a range of avionics developments which might provide some compensation for the decline in defence business after 1944. Since the late 1930s, Ferranti had been closely associated with some of the major avionics innovations like radar and on-board instrumentation (see sections 7.5 and 7.6). Similarly, by the 1950s both Moston and Crewe Toll had established world-wide reputations as designers and producers of high quality products which were purchased by both civil and defence customers. Indeed, by the late 1950s Crewe Toll was contributing more funds to the company coffers than the meter department, indicating how a distinct watershed can be detected in the balance of Ferranti finances, a point to which we shall return in the last section of this chapter.

Moston strategy

Although the radio, television and domestic appliance departments had been expanded considerably from the late 1940s, it was several years before the Moston site recovered from the severe downturn in government orders for fuzes and instruments. For this reason, Eric Grundy (instrument department manager) was given the role of general manager of the Moston group of businesses, with all departmental managers responsible to him 'until we got it right and in a stable state'.[67] He was also instructed by Sir Vincent to rebuild his business along civil lines, and especially to continue to act in the capacity of product development centre, just as he had done during the 1930s rearmament drive. This dual role was actually to pull Grundy in different directions, because while the radio, television and domestic appliance businesses were expanded, the instrument department was actually more interested in defence contracts. Some of these projects (guided weaponry and computers) will be discussed in later chapters, but the crucial developments to which we shall refer here were in the avionics field, sustaining the contacts established over the previous twelve years.

During the War, instrument department had extended its traditional base of recording and measuring instruments into the technologically-demanding fields of gyroscopic stabilisation and fire control. The latter was actually to be expanded into a separate department, after the Admiralty in 1947 placed a development contract worth £32,000 per annum with Moston for an electrical flyplane predictor and associated regenerative tracker. This was a significant development for Moston, because what would eventually become the fire control department was able to produce a piece of electronic equipment which predicted the course and range of a target, information on which was automatically relayed to the anti-aircraft guns. As the Admiralty regarded this as an essential improvement to its armoury, by the time the fire control department was eventually established in 1955, and Humphrey Nelson was recruited from the Admiralty as its manager, annual sales had expanded to over £900,000. More significantly, the Admiralty provided large progress payments which covered a high proportion of departmental stocks and work-in-progress, reducing significantly the capital employed in this department.[68] The contract price was also based on departmental turnover, with a guaranteed profit of seven per cent added to this figure, ensuring a steady flow of funds from the mounting orders.

Of course, the manner in which government contracts were negotiated and funded is a matter of some concern, forcing us to return to a more detailed analysis of its inherent weaknesses when the *Bloodhound* project is described in chapter ten. As far as we are concerned at this stage, though, one must emphasise the attractive nature of this business, given the generous progress payments and guaranteed profit. Indeed, it is not surprising that several Ferranti departments focused their attention on serving the needs of Britain's Armed Forces, rather than compete in the more demanding civil sectors. This would have been especially attractive to Eric Grundy when faced with the task of rebuilding the Moston departments devastated by a collapse in government contracts. He was especially keen to build on the expertise acquired over the previous decade in designing and producing avionics equipment. One of the first moves was to offer to redesign all the gyroscopic navigational instruments used by the RAF and convert them from air to electric drive.[69] Although this offer was not accepted at the time, Grundy persisted with his strategy, eventually securing from the Ministry of Supply (MOS) a development contract for artificial horizons – an instrument which indicates the attitude of an aircraft in relation to the real horizon – which laid the basis for a highly successful business.

Artificial horizons

The first artificial horizon produced by Ferranti came off the production line in 1948. It was a four-and-half inch diameter, hermetically-sealed instrument which met all the specifications laid down by the Air Ministry.[70] At this time, while the Americans had devised a more compact instrument of three-and-a-quarter inch diameter, they were already thinking about replacing this device with remote-controlled, gyro-stabilised platforms, causing some debate in Britain. The Air Ministry eventually decided that even if such platforms were superior, it was still vital to have a self-contained artificial horizon, otherwise an electrical failure would render the pilot helpless without any means of gauging the aircraft's attitude. On the other hand, they liked the miniaturised version produced by the Americans, initiating a design competition amongst British suppliers which Ferranti won with its FH7 model. This put Ferranti in a strong position, especially after the Air Registration Board ruled that the installation of a stand-by artificial horizon should be compulsory on all aircraft using a stabilised platform. Indeed, not only did the RAF and Fleet Air Arm accept the FH7 as standard equipment, civil aircraft like the *Comet*, the BOAC Boeing 707, the *Vanguard* and the *Argosy* also placed substantial orders. This success was later followed in the American market, because no indigenous firms had developed a rival instrument to cope with the introduction of a Federal law which stipulated that artificial horizons should be incorporated into both civil and military aircraft.

The artificial horizon was certainly one of the instrument department's post-War successes. By 1954, when the aircraft equipment department was formed at Moston as a means of coordinating the business, development contracts from the Ministry of Aircraft Production (MAP) and the Admiralty had by then reached £350,000 per annum. Furthermore, in order to sustain the initial progress made with the FH7 in 1955 a new development centre was planned, a move regarded as essential if Ferranti was going to reinforce its market position. However, one of the main constraints Ferranti faced in pursuing this strategy was persuading talented engineers and graduates to move to Moston, as opposed to the relatively more salubrious locations of rival firms in the Home Counties. Furthermore, the major government research centres were mostly situated in those areas, isolating Moston from the focus of activity. These factors finally persuaded Eric Grundy to look for a more conducive laboratory site in the south of England, a decision which eventually led to the acquisition of a large country house called Westwick, just outside Bracknell, providing ready access to the department's main customers. It was at Westwick that a three-and-a-quarter inch artificial horizon was developed, as well as a series of alternative products which would allow the department to diversify away from its dangerous reliance on a single market.

Inertial platforms

In spite of these attempts at diversification, involving a transformer-rectifier for the Vickers *Vanguard* and the Vickers VC10, as well as a standby directional gyro, artificial horizon production continued to provide the bulk of aircraft equipment's business throughout the 1950s. At the same time, it is also important to emphasise how the expertise in designing and manufacturing gyro-based equipment led to further contracts, none of which were more significant than the 1959 Ministry of Airways (MoA) order to develop what would eventually become the Type 100 inertial platform for the supersonic aircraft of the 1960s. More will be said in section 11.5 about this project, but it is important to note how the Type 100 put Ferranti right at the forefront of gyro technology, providing access to the most advanced work of several American firms. The special feature of the Type 100 was the large azimuth gyro which gave accurate heading information without the need for an external monitor. It carried three force-feed back accelerometers developed by the American firm Kearfott, while stabilisation was effected by a large Kearfott gyro and two smaller gyros produced by another American pioneer, Honeywell. Ferranti actually purchased a licence to manufacture the Kearfott gyros in March 1959, at a cost of $100,000 plus five per cent of the selling price,[71] while the Honeywell gyros were actually made in Britain by English Electric. This substantially extended the range of expertise in directional gyroscopic stabilisation available to the aircraft equipment designers, laying the foundations for later work at the Crewe Toll factory, where engineers availed themselves of this expertise when they started to develop their own inertial platforms.

8.6 The Crewe Toll Adventure

The Moston aircraft equipment department had undoubtedly done well to build up a successful business from the limited base of 1945. However, this pales into insignificance when compared to the Crewe Toll story, because from an even less promising start the Edinburgh factory had by the 1960s established a world-renowned business in avionics and precision engineering. As we saw in the last chapter, Crewe Toll had been successfully built up by Jack Toothill and his team to manufacture gyro-gunsights. The prospects in 1945 must have seemed bleak, however, because demand for this device plummeted. Undaunted by this situation, the Crewe Toll Foremen's Conference voted unanimously to stay in Edinburgh, rather than return to Moston. Similarly, Toothill and his works manager, Tom Neal, were willing to commit their considerable energies and talent to expanding the business.[72] Some have quipped that it was Toothill's love of Scottish golfcourses which influenced these decisions, while the prospects of moving from the relative comfort of Edinburgh back to Moston might also have played a part in convincing them that Crewe Toll was their future. Sir Vincent, on the other hand, was characteristically blunt, warning Toothill that while the company was willing to encourage entrepreneurship it was vital that departments should pay their own way. This provides a classic opportunity to witness the Ferranti philosophy in action, because Toothill was continually faced with the imminent threat of closure throughout the late 1940s, creating a massive incentive to succeed.

The late 1940s was indeed a testing time for the Crewe Toll team. Not only did the workforce fall from almost 1,000 in 1945 to less than 400 by 1949, the capital employed also fell by a half to just over £350,000. In fact, according to the financial accounts Crewe Toll made a loss in 1946–47 of almost £10,000, although the management accounts kept in Edinburgh actually record a tiny profit for each year between 1945 and 1950.[73] Whatever the true position, the factory survived largely because sales of gyro-gunsights remained buoyant, especially in export markets (for example, to Switzerland when the *Meteor* and *Vampire* aircraft were exported there).[74] Even though alternative businesses were tried, it proved difficult to break into new markets. For example, a joint project with Weston Engineering of Colne was initiated to develop breakage indicators for pirn winders. However, Crewe Toll lost £62,000 on this project when its partner went into liquidation. Other schemes which came to nothing included the development of sensitive magnetic amplifiers for the atomic energy industry,[75] while the electronic instrumentation controlling steam catapults for aircraft carriers (made in association with Brown Bros. of Edinburgh) resulted in just one order, for HMS *Perseus*.

The Toothill strategy

Of much greater significance to Crewe Toll than these timorous ventures was Toothill's more adventurous idea of creating four new laboratories – radar, instruments, vacuum physics, and applications – which were to be staffed by a newly-recruited team of talented engineers and designers. Toothill's overriding strategy was to build up a business which combined precision engineering and electronics, with the four laboratories acting as the media through which new products exploiting these dual technologies would emerge. He also spent some time travelling around the main government research establishments quite simply asking them for development contracts, resulting in the acquisition of small contracts for measuring instruments and an electrical flyplane predictor.[76] These contracts (worth in total approximately £160,000 per annum) created the rationale for establishing the four laboratories, a strategy which was enormously boosted when Toothill managed to convince M. K. Taylor to move from the Moston radio development team

324   FERRANTI: A HISTORY

to head the Crewe Toll applications laboratory. Arthur Chilcot was also persuaded to leave valve development at Gem Mill for a place as chief of vacuum physics, while from outside the company Toothill recruited Mal Powley from RAE, D. M. McCallum from the Admiralty, and several other interesting people like J. Stewart, J. B. Smith and D. T. N. Williamson. McCallum recalls how, after consulting his former tutor at Heriot-Watt College, Professor Say, on the prospects of working with M. K. Taylor, he was told that: 'I would find it very interesting as he was a good, old-fashioned, Victorian inventor'.[77] Indeed, McCallum's memoirs provide a fascinating account of those early days at Crewe Toll, indicating how Toothill was developing an ethos based on innovation and entrepreneurship as the guiding philosophy within the new laboratories.[78]

A clear indication of the hit-and-miss nature of work at that time was M. K. Taylor's applications laboratory, where a wide variety of projects were initiated, some of which 'were almost bizarre'.[79] For example, J. B. Smith worked on an electric pencil, while McCallum was asked to develop an autopilot for the yacht owned by Denis de Ferranti, as well as a supersonic

The Duke of Edinburgh being introduced to the Nimrod Digital Computer c. 1968.
(*Museum of Science and Industry at Manchester.*)

airspeed indicator. Although the latter was funded by the RAE, early trials produced such inconclusive results that support was withdrawn. Indeed, Crewe Toll succeeded not because of the applications laboratory work, but because of the development of a successful radar business under the leadership of J. Stewart (formerly of the TRE). Toothill had been especially keen to build up this side of the business in 1945, having negotiated the transfer of all the remaining IFF contracts from Moston as a means of initiating a radar equipment production line. Furthermore, he also took the extravagant step of hiring as a consultant Sir Robert Watson-Watt, the British pioneer of radar,[80] as well as the engineer most responsible for designing the IFF equipment, F. C. Williams (see section 7.5). This proved to be a major step forward in providing Crewe Toll with a viable alternative to the gyro-gunsight business. Although it was several years before substantial orders were secured, Toothill had ensured the survival of his department by focusing on one of the major post-War growth areas for avionics.

The first scheme developed by the radar team was to design and produce what Sir Robert Watson-Watt regarded as the next major project, distance measuring equipment (DME). This system, working at what was then the unexplored frequency of 1,000 megacycles, provided pilots with accurate and continuous visual information on distance measurements from selected ground beacons. Early tests on the de Havilland *Comet*'s flights between London, Rome and Cairo also produced good results,[81] leading Watson-Watt to suggest the use of DME at the International Civil Aviation Organisation's 1946 conference. Ferranti was consequently given a contract by the TRE to develop DME equipment for use on the Comet, confirming the efficacy of employing Watson-Watt as a consultant. However, in 1948 the British scheme ran into the powerful opposition of Boeing and Lockheed, the two American corporations which were advocating the use of an alternative radar system, VOR (very high frequency omnidirectional range).[82] Given their position as the world's leading aircraft manufacturers, Boeing and Lockheed were able to eliminate DME from the scene. This was not the first time, nor would it be the last, that Ferranti had come up against the overwhelming might of American competition. In this case, while a strong team of engineers and designers had been assembled in the various laboratories, it ensured that Crewe Toll would continue to struggle.

Ironically, the major breakthrough for Crewe Toll at that time was not in-house work but the Korean War, because from its start in June 1950 government establishments rushed to support projects which might have military applications. By 1952–53, Crewe Toll had secured government development contracts worth almost £830,000, compared to just under £100,000 in 1947–48, substantially boosting activity in the various laboratories. One of the largest projects was *Blue Study*, a blind bombing system for the *Canberra* which had been commissioned by the RAF, while McCallum was appointed head of development for a new military aircraft radar. The first big production contract, however, did not arrive until 1953, when the American firm, Hazeltine, sub-contracted Crewe Toll to manufacture the latest variant of IFF, the Mark X. This equipment had been designed as a result of NATO's (the North Atlantic Treaty Organisation) insistence that all IFF systems ought to be standardised, while because at that time the American government was anxious to support British military production several companies were given substantial contracts to produce Mark X.[83] In the Ferranti case, because this business was worth over £1.4 million, it allowed Crewe Toll engineers an opportunity to develop invaluable experience in mass-producing sophisticated radar equipment. Just as crucially, the contracts provided an essential breathing space while some of the in-house projects initiated in the late 1940s came to fruition.

Monopulse Radar and AI23

By far the most important of these in-house projects was that headed by Donald McCallum.[84] Working closely with scientists at the RAE, in 1954 the Crewe Toll team was beginning to investigate some of the new fields opening up in the design of radar equipment. Toothill, Powley and Stewart also travelled to the USA, in order to inspect the original work of the Hughes Aircraft Co. in this field, only to discover that the RAE and MoS refused to pay the $3 million demanded for a licence. Hughes had actually been working in the new field of monopulse radar, a technology which was to sweep away all the old ideas. Monopulse worked by dispensing with the traditional method of mechanical scanning, introducing the idea that by transmitting pulses in two slightly different directions, and by simultaneously comparing the two slightly different signals received, as well as comparing the magnitude of the two lobes and adjusting for the directions of transmission, it was possible to detect when the echo was symmetrically disposed and thus find the range.[85] This inspired Dr Wilson at the RAE to commission Crewe Toll to work on what was known as *Radar Range* IV, the first British monopulse radar. One can only speculate at the possibility that had it not been for the exorbitant price Hughes wanted to charge for a licence this project would never have been started. At the same time, it is also important to remember that this commitment to monopulse conflicted with the plans of TRE (Telecommunications Research Establishment) and RRE (Radar Research Establishment) to re-engineer the wartime radar equipments. Consequently, as we shall see later, Ferranti and RAE were frequently faced with opposition

The AIRPASS radar being loaded into the nose of a Canberra at Turnhouse Airport, Edinburgh, for flight testing. *(Museum of Science and Industry at Manchester.)*

from such quarters when introducing their novel concepts. Furthermore, TRE and RRE preferred to conduct most of the development in-house, while RAE was more interested in subcontracting this to industry, creating a major conflict over both the technology and modus operandi.[86]

At the same time that Ferranti started work on *Radar Range* IV, English Electric was beginning to develop for the RAF what was to be a revolutionary concept in strike fighters, the *Lightning*. While the onboard radar for this aircraft was being designed by TRE in association with Ekco, because it made use of spiral scanning techniques which were notoriously difficult to follow in a single-seater aircraft, it became increasingly apparent that this system would be most unsuitable for the *Lightning*. Toothill was made aware of this problem when attending a cocktail party at Regent's Park House in London, indicating how he was able to keep in close contact with RAF 'gossip' through the use of such informal channels.[87] This information prompted him to invite the Air Staff to inspect the work of McCallum's team at Crewe Toll, a move which led to the choice of Ferranti as prime contractor for the new aircraft's onboard radar. Apart from the innovative use of monopulse, which allowed a single pilot to operate the radar with ease, *Radar Range* IV's other major advantage was the replacement of brass waveguides with an aluminium block which 'produced a very much more compact, efficient and lighter form of microwave circuitry and ... it gave us a big technical advantage over any of the competitors, either American or British'.[88] Although the Air Staff's decision further exacerbated the conflict between RRE and RAE, because the latter came out very much on top Crewe Toll was able to establish a strong position in the airborne radar market at a crucial early stage.

It is important to emphasise that many of the refinements to this radar, now renamed AI23 or *Airpass*, were only developed once the main contract was placed by the RAF, at times working with the Moston aircraft equipment department.[89] A major role in this development process was also played by Crewe Toll's trials and installation division at Turnhouse, near Edinburgh.[90] The flight trials actually started as early as 1955, providing invaluable information to the team in revealing any flaws in the design. The code-name *Airpass* denoted the system's dual functions as an airborne radar and pilot attack system, incorporating a computer to calculate the course and present information in the sight. Using this system, the pilot was consequently able to 'lock-on' to a target by manipulating the radar beam, tracking it automatically and making a 'blind' attack if necessary. This fulfilled all the planners' earlier expectations for the *Lightning*'s ability to find and destroy its target while travelling at supersonic speed, making this aircraft one of the most effective interceptors of its day. Even the Americans were unable to match this level of sophistication, especially once the RAE scientists introduced several improvements in 1959, resulting in the development of what came to be known as AI23B. Contemporary authorities were also extremely impressed with *Airpass* (AI23), *Aeronautics* describing it as 'one of the most advanced and versatile airborne radar systems in the world'.[91] As a consequence, Ferranti had sold over £13.5 million worth of *Airpass* by 1965-66, fulfilling both the technical and commercial potential in a project which RAE had backed heavily in the mid-1950s.[92]

While working on AI23, and at the same time beginning to dominate the RAF market for on-board radar equipment, it is also interesting to note that Crewe Toll was commissioned in 1956 to work on a similar design for the Royal Navy, for incorporation into the *Buccaneer*.[93] This caused some conflict within the radar teams, because Toothill asked Stewart to head the team, while contrary to Powley's wishes McCallum continued to work on AI23, as well as another system known as *Blue Parrot*, cutting down on any potential duplication of design and production effort. In fact, the system eventually developed was very different from AI23, partly because the RRE technicians from Malvern insisted on several notable design changes with which Ferranti engineers disagreed. These modifications were later to be dropped from the end-product, illustrating the difficulties of working with this particular research establishment. When *Blue Parrot* was later combined with what was known as 'Strike Sight', this also provided the *Buccaneer* with an effective system which was still in service until the 1990s. More importantly, this Royal Navy contract emphasised the growing dominance Ferranti was beginning to achieve in the interception and strike radar market, especially as English Electric was able to export the *Lightning* to Saudi Arabia and Kuwait. The Indian Air Force had also purchased the *Blue Study* blind-bombing system in 1956, at a cost of £2.6 million, for incorporation in their *Canberra* aircraft, serving to reinforce further the Ferranti name in domestic and export markets.

Terrain-Following Radar

Having achieved this dominant position in the airborne radar business, it was vital that Ferranti did not rest on its laurels and allow the competition time to catch up on the use of monopulse. In fact, chance intervened to ensure that Ferranti would stay ahead, because the next major development in airborne radar arose out of an unplanned meeting between Donald McCallum and Mal Powley from Ferranti and an English Electric engineer, A. Simmons.[94] On a visit to English Electric's aerodrome at Warton, near Preston, to meet engineers from de Havilland, Simmons took the opportunity of a delay in the latter's flight to explain to the Ferranti men his ideas on terrain-following radar. The Simmons system involved the use of very high frequency radar, an altimeter and a tape-recorder. Powley, however, immediately responded by describing this as highly primitive, suggesting instead the use of monopulse radar. Although nothing immediately came of this chance meeting, when in 1959 the Air Ministry started discussing a new project which eventually became the ill-fated *TSR–2*, Powley and McCallum were invited to the initial planning meetings in London largely on the recommendation of English Electric. While the RRE was actually more interested in buying a terrain-following scanning radar from an American source, the Ferranti angle tracking system was finally given the go-ahead by the Ministry, further antagonising RAE's main rival. Once again, having proved the RRE technicians wrong, Ferranti had succeeded in making another important breakthrough in airborne radar systems. This terrain-following radar, or forward-looking radar (FLR) as it was known during the development stage, provided Crewe Toll with its next major programme.[95]

Inertial navigation

The *TSR–2* story belongs to chapter 11, but it is interesting to note that the FLR was capable of flying an aircraft at a pre-selected height of between 200 and 1,000 feet consistently over any type of surface, whether it be the hills of Cumbria or a flat terrain with buildings or other man-made obstacles. This was a crucial feature of what would have been a major stride forward in military aircraft technology, especially when combined with another important component supplied by Ferranti, the inertial navigation platform. As Crewe Toll had been built around its ability to manufacture gyroscopically-controlled equipment, under Mal Powley the instrument and fire control department had embarked on an ambitious development programme during the mid-1950s which investigated the possibilities in inertial quality gyroscopes. At that time, RAE was working on the *Blue Streak* guided weapon, for which Ferranti developed a stand-by integrating accelerometer.[96] *Blue Streak*, of course, was eventually cancelled, along with many of its counterparts at that time (see sections 10.5 and 10.6). However, Ferranti had by then assembled a team which Powley wanted to employ in producing an inertial navigation platform. RAE was also interested in employing this highly sophisticated equipment as the guidance system for what would become the *Blue Steel* programme to produce a British long-range nuclear guided weapon. Although the Massachussetts Institute of Technology (MIT) had been building on the expertise acquired through recruiting the German V2 rocket team (see section 10.1), the RAE was keen to establish a British capability in what was increasingly seen as a vital technology. This resulted in Ferranti receiving £150,000 from the RAE to construct a 'clean-room' production plant at Crewe Toll, providing the facilities for another major development project.

Just to illustrate the difficulties encountered by Powley and his team in developing an effective inertial navigation system, it is important to note that its workings are based on an application of Newton's second law of motion, whereby matter resists change in its motion, that is, it possesses inertia.[97] The Ferranti inertial platform involved the arrangement of three single-axis gyroscopes mounted with their sensitive axes mutually at right angles and coinciding with their reference axes, all mounted on a system of gimbals with each gyroscope fitted with a pick-off or signal generator which produced a signal proportional to the angle through which the gyroscope was rotated. Provided the platform was fed with the position of departure, it would maintain stability throughout its flight, and being completely self-contained it required no external reference sources. The most difficult problem, however, was the production of such intricate mechanisms, providing an enormous challenge to the engineering team, led by K. Brown and J. Drury, and ably assisted by the works manager Tom Neal. As with the Moston activity, Powley's inertial systems department was obliged to acquire licences from the American firm Kearfott for high quality gyroscopes. Visits to MIT were also made in order to assess what was regarded as state-of-the-art technology. This was followed by the construction of new production facilities at Silverknowes, in Edinburgh, using RAE funds for the production of what was code-named BAINS (the British advanced inertial navigation system). So sensitive were the testing facilities at Silverknowes that movements of the tide over three-quarters of a mile away in the Firth of Forth could be detected in what was described as 'the cleanest rooms in Europe'.[98]

Another remarkable feature of this project was its funding, because while the RAE provided £150,000 for 'clean-room' production facilities, in 1959 Powley was given a further £200,000 from central company funds to initiate the development programme. As we saw in the last chapter, while Sir Vincent had always been reluctant to use company funds on military development contracts, in this exceptional case his instinctive backing of Powley's team produced startling results. In fact, within eighteen months of receiving the go-ahead, Brown and Drury had completed the design work on what was to become a minitiaurised inertial navigation platform which weighed only twenty pounds, compared to the MIT's first effort of one ton. Of course, they had not only been assisted by the acquisition of Kearfott's latest gyro, the Type 2519, Moston's aircraft equipment department also provided accelerometers during the early stages of development. Nevertheless, for such an outcome the time-span was remarkable. As Drury noted, 'a tight budget is one of the most powerful disciplines one can apply to a development team',[99] emphasising how as Ferranti was providing approximately sixty per cent of the funds the engineers were made constantly aware of the financial constraints. Unfortunately, though, while flight trials were started in 1961, it was 1965 before any firm orders were given by the MoA for this platform, largely because the *TSR-2* was not planned to go into production until that time and no other project had yet come off the drawing-board. This was a source of great disappointment to the inertial systems department, especially as the two American rivals, Lytton and Sperry, were provided with several years in which to catch up on Ferranti, resulting in a fierce competition for the big orders of the late 1960s.[100]

Financial performance and expansion

These struggles we shall return to in chapter 11, but once again it is clear that the Crewe Toll engineers were breaking new ground in a highly advanced technology which would eventually produce solid financial rewards. Indeed, after the difficult early years, the inertial platform was in production continuously until the early 1990s, helping to reinforce Crewe Toll's position as one of the major contractors to British and other air forces. By recruiting such a high calibre team of engineers, Toothill was able to fulfil his aim of maintaining a presence in Edinburgh, not to mention establish a major activity capable of integrating electronics and high quality precision engineering. Of course, Sir Vincent's warning that the site would be closed if losses started to appear in the books was an ever-present threat in Crewe Toll's whole approach from the late 1940s. Nevertheless, the successes with AI23, AI23B and *Blue Parrot* ensured that the ambitious risk associated with opening four development laboratories would prove remunerative. Indeed, by the mid-1950s Crewe Toll's early financial worries were over, while by 1958–59 (on a turnover of £5.6 million) Toothill was able to report his first £1 million profit. Moreover, because government development work had also increased remarkably, from £643,000 in 1949–50 to almost £4.6 million by 1958–59, large progress payments significantly reduced the level of capital employed, indicating how Crewe Toll had become a substantial net contributor to company funds.

This review of Crewe Toll's history (and that of Moston's avionics business) over the post-War decades has revealed how more success was achieved in the defence business, compared to the civil side. In this context, though, Burns and Stalker have criticised Toothill for pursuing 'the more friendly path of military aircraft and instruments, rather than the more treacherous domestic market related to industrial processes'.[101] However, one must question the logic behind this statement, and in particular ask whether Crewe Toll could have succeeded in the latter. After all, while various civil ventures were started in the late 1940s, none proved sufficiently profitable to sustain the presence in Edinburgh. We shall also see in the next section how the attempt to develop numerical control failed to raise much interest among British engineering companies, emphasising again how Toothill pursued the rational strategy of exploiting the talents and contacts at his disposal in the more promising defence sectors. Furthermore, one could never describe the defence business as either risk-free or a safe-haven from the harsh competitive winds blowing in the 1950s. In particular, the long gestation periods between development contracts and actual orders increased the uncertainty attached to this market. The struggles with RRE also illustrate the difficulties inherent in this sector, because had RAE not been able to convince the Air Ministry of the merits of Ferranti equipment much would have been lost. Of course, prepayments and guaranteed profits provided some compensation for this uncertainty. On the other hand, in the struggles for orders there was always a premium on technological excellence. Fortunately for Crewe Toll, Ferranti engineers were able to win out over both RRE and firms like Ekco and Cossor. The defence business was, indeed, highly competitive, and only those firms capable of developing the most successful products found Burns & Stalker's 'friendly path'.

Toothill and the Scottish economy

Any criticism of Toothill's work at Crewe Toll is also undermined when one considers his attempt to establish an electronics industry in Scotland. The Scottish economy had for many decades been heavily dependent upon textiles, coal and heavy engineering, sectors which by the 1940s had for a generation been in decline. To arrest this collapse in traditional forms of industrial employment, the Scottish Council for Development and Industry had been formed in 1931. Although it had by the 1940s achieved little in this respect, after the War greater effort was put into devising a long-term strategy based on diversification. One of the most obvious problems facing the Council in its attempts at stimulating some diversification of the Scottish economy was an acute shortage of suitably skilled workers for the new industries, largely caused by a failure of the education system to adapt to new requirements. Although a Crewe Toll apprentice school had been established by 1945, to provide the factory with electronic and mechanical engineers, this was actually the only one in the Edinburgh area. Largely to correct this imbalance, in 1949 Toothill was invited to join the Scottish Council as a member of the executive committee. In this capacity, in 1951 he proposed that the Crewe Toll apprentice school should become the examination centre for the ONC in engineering, coordinating the training provided by twenty-five firms in the area. The MoS accepted these plans, providing £513,000 to build a new laboratory block opposite Crewe Toll on Ferry Rd. Furthermore, the standards adopted by Ferranti were accepted for both mechanical and electrical engineering ONC's in Scotland, giving Ferranti a central place in the expansion of Scottish technical education.[102] When HRH the Duke of Edinburgh opened the new laboratory in 1954, Ferranti had created the largest facility of its type in Scotland.

Unfortunately, though, the hopes espoused for this plan in 1951 were never really fulfilled. It had been hoped that not only would engineers from the twenty-five firms be trained at the laboratory, any government contracts earned as a result of projects initiated there would also be distributed within the group. Although a good plan on paper, in practice little of substance emerged during the 1950s, largely because the firms were reluctant to collaborate at anything other than the training level. Ironically, only when later in the decade a host of American subsidiaries established production facilities in Scotland did the electronics industry start to grow. These new firms were attracted to Scotland by the generous grants offered by government regional development programmes, accentuating the skill shortages and resulting in poaching and other dubious practices. Indeed, the Hewlett-Packard factory at South Queensferry was staffed largely with former Ferranti employees, while others left Crewe Toll to work at IBM and Honeywell plants. On the other hand, the American firms certainly stimulated a significant diversification of the Scottish economy, offsetting the decline in employment opportunities in traditional industries. Toothill was again instrumental in furthering this process, by writing a report in 1959 which the Conservative government used as a basis for encouraging the expansion of science-based industries.

Toothill and Crewe Toll clearly had more to offer the Scottish economy than a single source of employment. Indeed, it was widely recognised that Ferranti had created a base for considerable expansion in the post-War period. The Scottish Council chairman, Sir Steven Bilsland, commended Toothill to Sir Vincent de Ferranti, noting how 'this Council is indebted to your company's general manager in Edinburgh for the able and effective assistance he is giving in dealing with Scottish problems'.[103] Of course, Toothill had much to gain in working with the Council, because Crewe Toll needed skilled workers and contacts with government agencies. Notwithstanding this direct benefit, by the late 1940s he was so committed to the Scottish cause that one cannot simply attribute his work to selfish motives. Apart from his work with the Scottish Council, he also represented Scottish interests at the National Economic Development Council, created in 1962 by the Conservative Government as a means of planning economic growth and industrial expansion. This was followed in 1964 by a knighthood for services to Scottish industry, indicating how because Sir John Toothill was widely recognised as a major force in the country's economy the decision to remain in Edinburgh proved so successful in many different ways.

8.7 Maintaining the balance

It is interesting to contrast the successes achieved by both Moston and Crewe Toll in the military avionics market with the dismal failure noted earlier in exploiting the substantial growth in demand for products like radio, television and domestic appliances. Of course, while Ferranti maintained a strong reputation in the meter and transformer businesses, herein lies the rub, because these civil markets both at home and abroad were dominated by a single, technically-oriented customer, in the form of national electricity supply authorities, with which Ferranti found it much easier to deal, when compared with the mass markets for their other civil products. In simple terms, Ferranti was always more effective when developing and selling products with a high technological input which could be adapted to a customer's special requirements. Furthermore, as we noted earlier, this was typical of most British electrical manufacturers, because in the wake of extensive foreign competition by the 1960s many were pulling out of domestic appliances and concentrating on the capital equipment and defence markets.[104] Indeed, only Hoover seemed capable of competing effectively in the mass markets against larger American and European firms. In the Ferranti case, and possibly more generally, this was clearly a rational move, given the prevailing conditions in these two sectors, making it increasingly difficult for Sir Vincent to achieve the balance he had intended to create between the civil and military businesses.

Crewe Toll is an excellent illustration of this dilemma, because while Toothill's team eventually achieved great success with ventures into airborne radar and inertial platforms their civil enterprises struggled to break even, in spite of several significant technological innovations. A. L. Chilcot's vacuum physics laboratory, for example, was working on TR (transmitter/ responder) cells and a specialised range of thermionic valves, magnetrons and gas-discharge tubes. By 1954, this department was renamed special components and relocated in Dundee, after MoS had agreed to provide £153,000 towards the cost of plant and machinery. On the whole, though, much of its work went into supporting the defence businesses at Crewe Toll.[105] Similarly, after transferring the small transformer department from Moston to Crewe Toll, this venture also concentrated on the production of equipment for radars, even though in 1948 the National Deaf Aid Association adopted these devices for use in their equipment. This further reinforces the image of a defence-oriented business at Crewe Toll. Even though Toothill agreed with Sir Vincent that balance was important, it is clear that the civil departments were never given the same opportunities as the others.

Numerical control

One exception to this general rule was numerical control, or put more simply the use of electronics and computerisation in precision engineering. The American pioneer in this technology was MIT, which had been experimenting in this field during the early 1950s. After hearing about this during yet another cocktail party, Toothill and his engineering development chief, D. T. N. Williamson, travelled to the USA to inspect what they soon realised was a vision of the future for production engineers.[106] As we shall see in the next chapter, while Moston had recently started developing and producing computers, Toothill was confident that independently Crewe Toll could open up its own advanced programme and apply it to radar production. Indeed, Williamson was principally concerned in the early stages with in-house requirements. The initial challenge was coping with the problems associated with producing small numbers of precision instruments, demand for which fluctuated sharply, causing severe manning problems at a time when there was an acute shortage of skilled machinists.[107] Later, machining the waveguides for the AI23 radar also became a major problem, because as we noted earlier one of the unique features of this equipment was the replacement of brass with two blocks of aluminium which were mirror images of each other, imposing high levels of accuracy on the fabrication process.

There is little doubt that the development of numerical control was a major reason why AI23 proved to be such a successful business for Crewe Toll.[108] While traditional milling techniques had taken almost 300 hours to produce a single wave-guide from a block of aluminium, numerical control could perform the task in a couple of hours. To achieve this level of accuracy, Williamson decided against using the conventional lead screw of the machine tool and placed his faith in digital, rather than analogue, computer control.[109] Much of the computer technology had actually to be developed in-house, rather than copied from Moston, because little progress had been made in this area at that time. The use of digital techniques also required a new short-range position measuring device, for which purpose the moiré fringe technique was adopted in order to provide a light output capable of conversion into electrical signals. In this area they received much help from the National Physical Laboratory, where Dr L. Sayce was experimenting with large gratings for infra-red spectroscopy, resulting in considerable improvements to the moiré fringe equipment.[110]

Although a complete diffraction grating measuring system was first produced in May 1954, it was followed by an improved version which was patented in the following year, while in 1956 the Mark III version was ready for the annual Olympia Machine Tool Exhibition. It was at that first public demonstration of Ferranti numerical control (NC) equipment that machine tool makers and users started to realise what impact this equipment could have on production engineering. One forward-looking company, Fairey Aviation, even proposed a collaborative venture to design and produce the first integrated numerical control machine tool. This venture was not only instrumental in persuading Ferranti to move from electrical to hydraulic servos and transistorising the circuits, it also resulted in the development of Europe's first machine tool which was specifically designed for numerical control.[111]

Unfortunately for Ferranti, however, the collaboration with Fairey was unique. Although the two companies utilised this Mark IV version extensively in their own factories, in the case of Crewe Toll for the production of AI23 and AI23B, few British engineering firms were ready to follow suit. This was in stark contrast to what was happening in the USA, where as early as 1949 the

Ferranti Mk. IV numerical control machine supplied to Sud Aviation in France. *(Museum of Science and Industry at Manchester.)*

US Airforce had sponsored the development work at MIT, while in 1956 the US government placed an order for $30 million worth of numerical control equipment with Bendix, General Electric, Bunker-Ramo and the Cincinnati Milling Machine Co., as part of its policy of creating a stock of advanced machine tool capacity. Hamilton argues that NC firms like Ferranti ought to have made more of an effort to encourage machine tool manufacturers to adopt NC. At the same time, such was the degree of conservatism in this sector that NC was only developed by one firm, Alfred Herbert's.[112] Although R. H. Davies at Ferranti Electric Inc., the New York agency, attempted to persuade American government officials that his company possessed what was generally regarded as the best NC technology in the world, they were not interested in sponsoring a British company.[113]

Ferranti did eventually establish a joint venture with the Bendix Aviation Co. in 1960, after having been rejected by several other potential partners.[114] By that time, however, the American firms had caught up technologically as a result of the market stimulii provided by their government. As we shall see in later chapters, not only was this a recurring theme of the post-War period, when we come back to the Burns and Stalker criticisms of Toothill's defence-oriented strategy it is also clear that the domestic civil market simply was both so small and conservative that it did not provide a sufficient incentive to pursue advanced projects. The MoS in 1958 sponsored the development of what was Europe's first hydrostatic slideway machine tool, made jointly by Ferranti and Fairey. However, the late 1950s recession in aircraft production severely curtailed demand for equipment which was as sophisticated as anything being produced in the USA. It was also at that point that Fairey pulled out of the project, leaving Ferranti with the task of stimulating interest in NC. By 1960–61, while NC sales had risen to £460,000, a loss of £167,000 was made on this business and development costs since the mid-1950s had exceeded £530,000. Of course, Crewe Toll had benefited internally from the introduction of this machinery, but only in the production of military radar, demonstrating graphically the difficulties Ferranti experienced in maintaining a balance between civil and defence businesses.

Profits and capitalisation

In retrospect, as we noted at the start of this chapter, in the fifteen years after 1945 achieving a balance between civil and defence businesses proved to be impossible at Ferranti. While meters and transformers flourished, the consumer goods departments floundered in the face of severe demand fluctuations and a failure to match the price and quality standards set by their rivals. On the other hand, when innovative ideas like NC were introduced into the civil markets, demand failed to materialise, forcing Ferranti to withstand heavy losses before sales started to grow, in this case after 1963. At the same time, after 1950 especially defence development and production contracts were acquired in increasing numbers, compensating substantially for the problems experienced elsewhere. Figures 8.1 and 8.2 (pp. 290–1) also demonstrate how the firm was expanding rapidly up to the early 1960s. Although detailed figures are hard to find, for the period 1948–56 it is clear that the gross profits on defence contracts accounted for approximately two-thirds of the total.[115] Furthermore, there is no reason to believe that this proportion fell over the next decade as consumer goods sales struggled to make any return and Crewe Toll improved its performance. Most importantly, though, while this trend undermined Sir Vincent's broad aim of maintaining a balance between the two sectors, and in spite of the periodic slumps experienced at that time, Ferranti substantially improved its financial performance over this period, recording an annual average return on capital employed during the 1950s of 12.8 per cent (see Appendix C, Table 2).

The company's post-War financial record was certainly more impressive than in the 1930s, particularly after the difficulties experienced by the mass-consumption departments at Moston had been eradicated by the rationalisation programme (see section 8.4). Of course, it is important to remember that Ferranti had emerged from the War in a strengthened financial state, having accumulated reserves of £300,000 (see Appendix C, Table 1). As Sir Vincent was committed to a technology-led strategy, these funds proved useful in developing or expanding product ranges. Furthermore, as in the 1930s, a rigorous policy of retaining most of the profits was pursued throughout this period, as a means of funding this programme. Of course, it is important to point out that the late 1940s Labour government imposed restrictions on dividend distributions. On the other hand, even when profits were rising in the 1950s Sir Vincent refused to pay more than six per cent on the ordinary capital, allowing the general reserve to reach £4.85 million by 1960. This reflects the chairman's consistent desire to prevent the recurrence of his father's experience in 1903, when illiquidity had resulted in a change of management, a message passed on to the third generation as a cherished piece of advice in running the firm.

In fact, while low dividends were paid up to the late 1960s, the Ferranti family did benefit from this improved performance, because a series of capitalisation schemes was effected which created additional income-earning shares. In 1949, for example, by the capitalisation of £700,000 from the general reserve account, 500,000 five per cent second redeemable cumulative preference shares of £1 and 400,000 ordinary shares of ten shillings (50p) were created, all of which were distributed to existing shareholders. Similarly, in 1953 500,000 three-and-a-half per cent third cumulative preference shares of £1 and one million ordinary shares of ten shillings were created by the capitalisation of £1 million. In 1958, a further 500,000 three-and-a-half per cent third cumulative preference shares of £1 and two million ordinary shares of ten shillings were also created, by the capitalisation of £1.5 million. In both cases the only beneficiaries were existing shareholders (see Appendix C, Table 1), while the equity-holders' voting powers rose from sixty-seven to eight-nine per cent. Although Denis de Ferranti could challenge the family from outside the boardroom, he held just seventeen per cent of the equity, compared to the family directors' sixty-three per cent. Of course, as we noted in section 8.3, the Bank had influenced events in the mid-1950s, reminding Sir Vincent of the need to maintain a reasonable level of liquidity. Nevertheless, when it came to making major decisions the family board members were still very much in charge.

'First into the Future'

Having noted this crucial feature of the Ferranti organisation, it is vitally important to remember that Sir Vincent had built a highly devolved structure which encouraged managers to venture into new fields. Figure 8.1 demonstrates how this philosophy, or the 'Ferranti Spirit', provided the driving force behind the company's considerable diversification from the 1930s. Jack Toothill at Crewe Toll perhaps epitomised the whole story, but Eric Grundy at Moston was just as entrepreneurial, while other divisional managers (see chapters nine and ten) were to exploit this freedom in creating and expanding their activities. Catchphrases like 'First into the Future' were also coined to publicise this philosophy, attracting many engineers and managers because of this freebooting culture. In the next two chapters we shall examine some more manifestations of this culture in action, illustrating how in the fields of computerisation and guided weaponry Ferranti was in the vanguard of crucial technological developments which were cementing further its relationship with government defence programmes. This analysis will also reveal further evidence of another crucial post-War trend, the rise of foreign competition. When combined with the highly conservative domestic market for advanced technology goods, this factor ensured that Ferranti would continue to concentrate even more on markets it could control more successfully.

9

The Computer Story[1]

It is apparent from the previous two chapters that by the mid-1950s maintaining an intended balance between civil and defence businesses had clearly been difficult for Sir Vincent and his managers. Although the entrepreneurial approach instilled into departmental managers had resulted in the development of some exciting new technologies (see Figure 8.1), it was defence-related businesses which proved to be more successful. It will be the purpose of this chapter to examine how these features of post-War Ferranti were manifested in the development of a wholly new product line, data processing computers. At the same time, we can also begin to examine three of the main post-War themes which characterised the experiences of British high technology firms, namely, intensifying American competition, the limited scale of demand in Britain for advanced technology equipment, and the attitude of successive governments to improving this situation. With specific regard to data processing computers, the former became a major problem in the 1960s, when IBM especially started encroaching significantly on what was a relatively small British market. Moreover, governmental responses failed to provide a sufficiently conducive environment in which the indigenous industry could flourish. For Ferranti this combination of intense foreign competition, small markets and unhelpful government policies certainly exacerbated the problems associated with pursuing a technology-led strategy in a family firm.

As we have already noted several times, Sir Vincent had a clear strategic vision for his firm, as well as a commitment to building a commercially viable business. However, because this position did not always tally very closely with the aims espoused by interested government agencies, we shall see throughout this chapter that the nature of public support acted as a distinct obstacle in the development of a competitive computer industry. The specific issue here was the nature of government funding, because after his experiences with late 1930s fuze contracts (see section 7.4) Sir Vincent maintained the consistent position that if the state wanted a product then public money ought to be provided for both its development and production. With specific regard to computers, though, we shall see that the efforts of the government agency responsible for sponsoring activity, and especially its head, Lord Halsbury, took a line which just did not provide the kind of support necessary which would have created a competitive industry. This view does not tally with the criticisms of Ferranti by both its contemporaries in the 1950s and later commentators,[2] many pointing to the 1963 sale of mainframe civil computer business as evidence of the firm's preference for allegedly safer defence markets. On the other hand, it is important to ask whether internal or external constraints precipitated such a sudden departure from a major civil technology in which Ferranti led the world in 1951. Crucially, this exercise also provides a fascinating insight into the excitement and challenge associated with running a high technology business.

9.1 The emergence of computing

Pre-history

Although up to the 1930s a 'computer' was regarded as an operator of mechanical calculators, after the extensive wartime experiments in code-breaking and ballistics calculations a new meaning was applied to what is now a ubiquitous word. Few contemporaries in the 1940s felt confident that what they called 'the electronic brain', or 'electronic calculator', would ever develop into anything more than an aid to scientists or mathematicians.[3] By 1945, however, scientists were beginning to talk about the 'universal automatic computer', a concept developed in a paper published in 1936 by one of the brightest mathematicians of the twentieth century, Dr Alan Turing.[4] Although in 1945 this 'universal' machine was only known inside top-secret government research establishments,[5] it could be used to solve a wide range of problems, as long as a 'program' had been fed in to dictate its actions.[6]

The 'universal' machine was later described as a 'stored program computer', the two principal characteristics of which were an internal store for both instructions and data which can be selectively altered, and an ability to vary its functions according to inputted instructions.[7] In fact, as long ago as the 1830s a pioneering mathematician, Charles Babbage (1792–1871), had devised what he called 'engines', the 'analytical' variant of which came close to realising the later achievements in building a stored-program computer.[8] Sadly, however, even though Babbage actually built (with a lot of government money) parts of these 'engines', his proposals and theories never amounted to much. Evans has argued that the main reason for this failure was the era's primitive technology. However, it is apparent from Lingren's research that it was Babbage's own bad management which hindered progress, revealing

Described as a 'roomfull of racks linked by a dangerous-looking network of wire', this was the prototype for the first Manchester-developed computer which took shape in 1948–49

substantial flaws in the character of what in many other respects was a genius.[9]

Although the pioneering work on computers has often been associated with American and British experiments during the early 1940s, a major advance was achieved by the German engineer, Konrad Zuse, who between 1936 and 1941 built a working computer with automatic control. This machine, known as the Z3, while not having an internally stored program, has been recognised by most authorities as an important stepping-stone in the evolution of computer technology.[10] However, although an improved version, the Z4, had been developed by 1942, largely for use in designing aircraft at the Henschel works, further refinements were abandoned because of wartime constraints. It was consequently the American and British teams which after 1945 were able to build more effectively on their previous five years' work. It is important to emphasise, though, that while there was a considerable difference in the budgets provided by their respective governments, the former spending at least twice as much as the latter, little difference in technological progress can be discerned at this stage. Indeed, given the progress made by Alan Turing on the code-cracking machines known as *Colossus*, erected at the one of the government's research bases at Bletchley Park,[11] and the work of F. C. Williams on cathode ray storage tubes,[12] one might even say that the British had an edge over their Transatlantic rivals. Nevertheless, by the spring of 1947 three American engineers working at the Moore School of Engineering, in Pennsylvania, J. P. Eckert, J. Mauchly and J. Von Neumann, had come up with a proposal which is generally recognised as the world's first attempt at building a stored program computer, the EDVAC (electronic discrete variable automatic calculator).[13]

Competition between American and British scientists was consequently extremely acute during the 1940s as they struggled to convert theory into practical achievement. While the British scene suffered from severe post-War budgetary constraints, several government agencies were willing to sponsor what appeared to be promising work. In 1945–46, for example, Alan Turing was financed by the new mathematics division of the National Physical Laboratory to design a 'universal' computer. Although in October 1948 he left to join the University of Manchester mathematics department, his theoretical work eventually resulted in the ACE (automatic computing engine) computer later manufactured by English Electric.[14] At the Telecommunications Research Establishment (TRE), even though two of their brightest stars (F. C. Williams and Tom Kilburn) had left in 1946, A. M. Uttley was working on what became the TREAC (TRE automatic computer), using Williams storage tubes.[15] Another promising line of development was at Cambridge University, where a team built up by Maurice Wilkes recruited in several scientists who had formerly worked at government research establishments like TRE and ASE on similar projects. This team was heavily influenced by an American design, known as the EDVAC computer, resulting in work on the similarly-named EDSAC (electronic delay storage automatic calculator). So successful was Wilkes and his team that the machine went into service before the Americans had completed their design. A more interesting aspect of this project was the financial support given by the catering company of J. Lyons & Co.[16] Indeed, by 1954 Leo Computers had been established to produce the Cambridge-designed machines, illustrating how (as with English Electric and the ACE) fruitful partnerships often evolved out of the late 1940s experiments.

University of Manchester Team

In this context, the most interesting partnership which emerged at this time was between the University of Manchester and Ferranti Ltd. The University was certainly blessed with considerable resources in the fields of computing and programming, because not only had Alan Turing moved there in 1948, he was also working with Professor M. H. A. (Max) Newman, the mathematician who had earlier designed the functional aspects of *Colossus*, the wartime code-cracking machine at Bletchley Park. Newman was so enthusiastic about building a stored-program computer that by the end of 1946 he had recruited F. C. Williams as Professor of Electrical Engineering, having recognised in his work at TRE an innovative and practical means of storing digital data on the screen of a cathode-ray tube.[17] Of course, as we have noted in section 7.5, Williams had been principally responsible for overseeing the technical development of IFF equipment during the early 1940s, familiarising him with key aspects of, and characters at, Ferranti. In particular, he had worked with one of the most outstanding members of the Ferranti radio laboratory, Hubert Wood, to produce a 'Woodascope', a device which was capable of giving visual observations of IFF set performance. It was while still employed by TRE that Williams discovered what is known as the 'anticipation pulse' effect, whereby long-term storage of data on a cathode-ray tube screen could be achieved, laying the technical foundation for the hardware required for the first Manchester computer.

The TRE team headed by Williams was in 1946 actually investigating the possibilities of building a stored-program computer. He was assisted by a mathematician called Tom Kilburn, who because TRE was keen to continue sponsoring this work was seconded to the University, where they formed the nucleus of a team which over the following years contributed extensively to computer technology. Their initial aim in 1946 was to design and build what is now known as the 'baby' computer, using a Williams storage tube, which had the capacity to store thirty-two words and perform 3,500,000 calculations in just fifty-two minutes. Lavington claims that the 'baby' was the world's first stored-program computer to operate, because after a first successful run on 21 June 1948 this had beaten the American EDVAC and its rivals by several months.[18] The Williams tube was also far in advance of

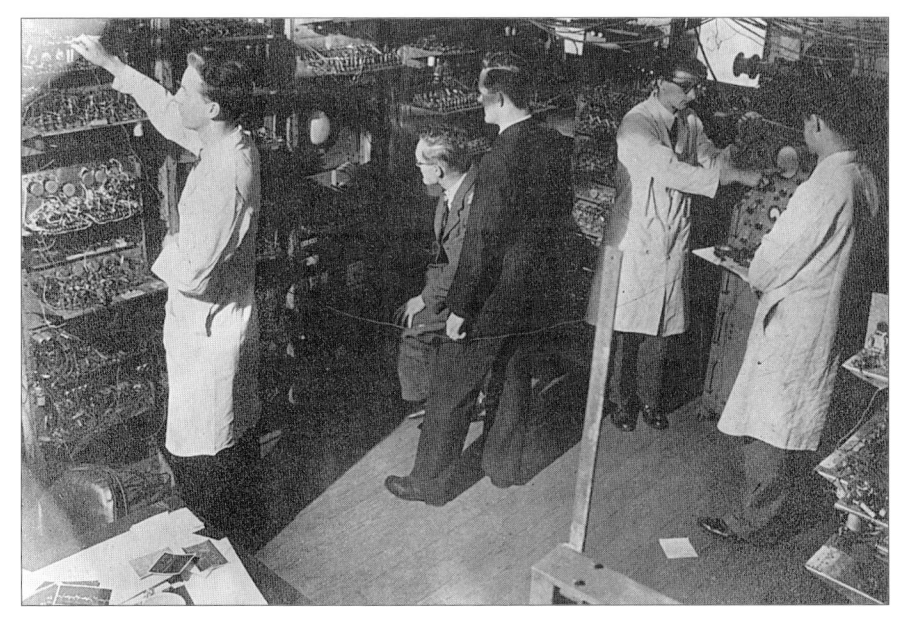

Professor F. C. Williams (bending, centre) and his Manchester Mark I development team working on MADM (Manchester Automatic Digital Machine) in 1949.

other storage devices because it allowed random access, compared to the sequential access offered by the delay-line methods used in both Cambridge and the USA. This is why in 1949 the American firm IBM purchased the rights to use the Williams patents, marking the first predatory step of a firm which would later pose a major obstacle to the development of a British computer industry.[19]

9.2 Ferranti and the first computer trials

Moston's strategy

In refining their ideas on computer design and operation, Williams and Kilburn, ably assisted by Newman and Turing in the mathematics department, had clearly made substantial progress by the summer of 1948. It was soon realised, however, that not only would additional finance be required to build improved versions, a larger store was needed to back up the Williams tubes. These pressures combined to create an opening for an electronics firm to participate in the experiments. It is vital to stress that in the late 1940s influential and far-seeing scientists like Professor P. M. S. (later Lord) Blackett were convinced that academic research should be better utilised by British industry not only in defence-related sectors, but also as a means of boosting its international competitiveness.[20] An excellent example of this policy at work came in October 1948, when Blackett arranged for the MoS's chief scientific advisor, Sir Ben Lockspeiser, to witness a demonstration of the Manchester 'baby' computer. It was this event which sparked off the search for a suitable private collaborator. Just at that time, Ferranti engineers in both the radio and instrument departments had either been, respectively, working informally with Williams or discussing the possibility of using computers for control purposes. This provided the basis for an arrangement, because after the Moston divisional manager, Eric Grundy, met Lockspeiser and the Williams team,[21] a venture was initiated which provides an object lesson in how to handle university-industry relations.

As Hubert Wood had by then become manager of the radio department, it is not surprising that Professor Williams should revive the wartime links with his former IFF collaborator. Indeed, Ferranti had already supplied a range of components for the 'baby' computer well before Grundy met Lockspeiser. On the other hand, it is not clear why Eric Grundy's instrument department should have ventured into this field, because as we saw in the last chapter Sir Vincent had instructed him to rationalise the activities of his Moston Group after the War. The chairman also turned down Grundy's request for £20,000 to pump-prime a computer project. Regardless of this rebuttal, however, after listening to a talk by Dr Arthur Porter (of the Military College of Science) on electronically controlling industrial processes, Grundy set up a study team to investigate this new technology.[22] In fact, Grundy had worked with Dr Porter during the War, the latter having been one of the government's wartime defence contract monitors. Realising the Ferranti interest in computers, Dr Porter recommended Dr Dietrich Prinz as a suitable head of any investigations Moston might conduct. While Hendry argues that Grundy was more interested in military applications of Dr Porter's ideas,[23] there is no evidence that at this stage such a use had a higher priority than civil applications. In fact, as we shall see, the latter dominated activity at Moston (and later West Gorton) until the business's sale in 1963.

In spite of being interned on the Isle of Man during the early years of the War (because of his German background), the lively and rather extrovert Dr Prinz had later performed valuable service on the top-secret MoS panel working on servo mechanisms. As the early computer development team leader at Ferranti, he was also to produce similarly impressive results. His first task was to visit the USA and inspect progress at Harvard and in Pennsylvania. On his return, though, Dr Prinz informed Grundy that Williams and Kilburn at Manchester were far ahead of anything the Americans had achieved with stored-program computers.[24] It was just at this juncture that Lockspeiser approached Sir Vincent about forging a formal link with the University of Manchester's computer team, forcing the chairman to decide between the instrument and radio departments as the natural base for this activity.

Although Hendry describes the debate as 'a strange battle within Ferranti', this ignores the organic way in which decisions were made at Ferranti, with managers vying personally for the chairman's support.[25] A complicating factor in these deliberations was finance, because as we have noted several times before Sir Vincent had always insisted that departmental managers should fund their own development programmes. In the late 1940s, though, as we saw in the last chapter, neither of these departments could afford the potentially huge development costs. This matter was eventually settled by Lockspeiser, who in October 1948 agreed to provide approximately £35,000 per annum for five years, a development we shall discuss later. Nevertheless, this still left the issue of which department would run the project. In this context, while it is most likely that Williams would have preferred to work with his old friends in the radio department, especially Hubert Wood and Dr Norman Searby, Sir Vincent had other tasks for this team, as we shall see in the next chapter.[26] This left the field free for Grundy. Unfortunately, though, personnel problems in the instrument department also hampered progress, because within a few months his first two appointees as head of computer development (Jim Carter and G. I. Thomas) had moved to other jobs, Carter in meter department (of which he later became manager) and Thomas as a development engineer at Crewe Toll. Only by the end of 1949 did the organisation settle down, when Brian Pollard was given the job.[27]

The Lockspeiser Letter and the NRDC

There were clearly some initial organisational problems at Ferranti when the firm started working with the University. However, once they had been overcome substantial progress was made in converting the scientists' designs into a working model. Before describing this work, though, it is important to examine the nature of the government support for this project, because while Lockspeiser had promised to provide an annual sum of £35,000 for five years, it is clear that as Hendry states the formal agreement signed in February 1949 'broke many of the rules of government contracting. There was no proper specification and no competitive tender. There was no vesting clause giving the Ministry of Supply patent rights ...'.[28] The October 1948 letter to Eric Grundy had simply stated:

> I am glad we were able to meet with Professor Williams as I believe that the making of electronic calculating machines will become a matter of great value and importance.
>
> You may take this letter as authority to proceed on the lines we discussed, namely, to construct an electronic calculating machine to the instructions of Professor F. C. Williams.
>
> If you have any trouble, please let me know.[29]

Lockspeiser later justified this promise on the grounds that it was vital to have a domestic supplier of what increasingly was regarded as a crucial technology in both military and civil fields. One must also note that at this time he was given considerable latitude in forging links between the academic and business worlds, a point which will be further substantiated in section 10.1 when we shall consider how he coordinated activity within the electronics and aircraft industries.[30] Nevertheless, Hendry is correct to indicate the problems with this arrangement, because the latitude afforded to Lockspeiser by his superiors was both unusual and contravened standard practice.

Much of this latitude was, however, lost when in 1948 the National Research Development Corporation (NRDC) was established under the powers granted by that year's Development of Inventions Act.[31] This organisation was charged with the crucial task of developing the fruits of research conducted in the public domain (at universities and research establishments), as well as controlling the patent rights arising from this research. Reflecting Treasury concern over potential financial profligacy, the NRDC was given a budget of just £5 million, in the form of an interest-bearing loan which had to be repaid within five years. A board representing industry, science and the civil service was also created to supervise the operations of the NRDC's executive managing director. For many in the industry, though, it was a matter of considerable regret that not only had the funding process been bureaucratised, but also that Lockspeiser had been replaced as the key agent of change.

Although Hendry claims that the NRDC's first executive, Lord Halsbury, was regarded as an excellent choice, because of his combination of practical experience (as a former research manager at Decca), scientific ability and solid social credentials, his role over the following decade has come in for some harsh treatment. One should remember that his duties were severely circumscribed by the 1948 Act, inevitably ending the informal work conducted by Blackett and Lockspeiser. Equally, though, his strategy for the computer industry left much to be desired from the vantage point of the leading figures like Sir Vincent. Indeed, we shall see later that Ferranti often experienced severe difficulties when negotiating with this body, largely because as Hendry demonstrates there was an inevitable 'conflict between the firm's self-interest and the NRDC's fairness and desire to disseminate information throughout British industry'.[32] It was the NRDC's strategy, however, which was to cause such severe difficulties, because while Ferranti was actually to receive a substantial share of the NRDC's computer budget over the following fifteen years, this does not necessarily imply that there was harmony in its relations with the organisation. While Halsbury described the NRDC's task as 'Pushing Mules Uphill',[33] in dividing up the paltry budget between the interested parties, in the hope of controlling the industry's development, he simply antagonised firms like Ferranti which were anxious to see much greater focus in the strategy. It is above all clear that Sir Vincent was keen to safeguard Ferranti interests, bringing him into conflict with the NRDC on several occasions. We shall also see how the relationship between firms and sponsoring government agencies was to play a key role in determining the level of success enjoyed, not just by Ferranti, but by the whole British computer industry.

9.3 The Mark I, Mark I* and Relations with the NRDC

Cooperation between Grundy's instrument department and the University of Manchester computer team had actually started well before Lockspeiser agreed to finance the next stage of development. As early as August 1948 Tom Kilburn had instituted a series of lectures on computing at Moston, while

Ferranti Mark 1* Computer at Fort Halstead MOS. *(Museum of Science and Industry at Manchester.)*

G. C. Toothill (another former TRE scientist who had moved with Williams to Manchester) was seconded to work with what by December amounted to a development team of twenty engineers.[34] The actual construction work on what was named the MADM (Manchester automatic digital machine) took place between June 1948 and October 1949, when what has been described as a 'roomful of racks linked by a dangerous-looking network of wire' took shape at the University.[35] By August 1950, after forty-two computer patents had been taken out as a result of improvements to the original design, the Mark I was announced. This machine not only possessed an ability to perform the work of an average comptometer (600 ten-digit multiplications in eight hours) in just three seconds, it was also fitted with a magnetic drum store capable of holding 150,000 words, indicating how the Ferranti-Williams link had made a significant breakthrough.[36] While the approach was based largely on 'inventing things as the need arose', clearly the Mark I was a momentous achievement for the team.[37]

When in February 1951 Ferranti completed and installed the Mark I in the University's machine computing laboratory, the firm could claim to have been the first to make a commercial delivery, preceding the Eckert-Mauchly UNIVAC I by four months.[38] The formal commissioning of the Mark I computer took place on 9 July 1951, an event witnessed by over 150 people from industry, scientific laboratories and government departments. A four-day conference was also held that week, at which both the Mark I's technology was discussed, as well as new ideas like those of Maurice Wilkes on micro-programming.[39] This marked the real beginning of modern computing in Britain, giving Ferranti an excellent opportunity to exploit the technological and commercial possibilities of being associated with the Mark I. At the same time, of course, the production of the Mark I was also a reflection of the environment at Ferranti, in that its technology-led strategy matched very well the atmosphere in an academic department. While this might have provided the basis for an effective design team, over the following twelve years it became increasingly apparent that other skills and resources were required if the 1951 opportunity was going to be converted into real commercial rewards, posing a major challenge to a family firm like Ferranti.

More NRDC negotiations

Although Ferranti had clearly established a substantial lead over its rivals by 1951, it was also faced with two major and complementary problems: how to exploit, and then sustain, this advantage in the market. One of the most obvious problems faced by the pioneers was the attitude of potential British customers, because most were extremely wary of something few understood, especially as the costs of buying, installing and maintaining computers were regarded as prohibitively high.[40] More important as an immediate problem to Ferranti was the rising development charges involved in continuing the progress made with the Mark I, especially as the University team was considering further improvements which would have plunged Pollard's team into a major financial crisis. Fortunately, though, although he had moved to the Department of Scientific & Industrial Research (DSIR), because Sir Ben Lockspeiser had retained an interest in the Manchester project he persuaded the MoS to provide another contract, based on the same terms as its predecessor, in order to keep the team together.[41] It was also at this time that the NRDC first started talking to Ferranti about computer production, initiating negotiations which proved crucial to the future of Pollard's embryonic computer department.

Before describing the early Ferranti-NRDC negotiations, one must remember that two years earlier Lord Halsbury had failed to raise any support for a joint computer development project from either the punched-card office machinery firms (BTM and Powers-Samas) or major electrical firms like

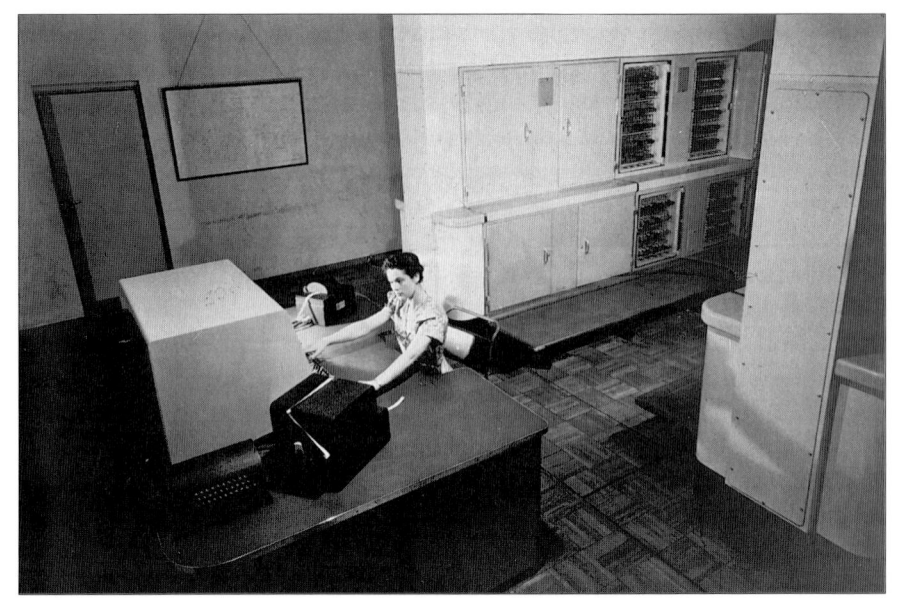

The Ferranti Mark I as supplied to customers. Note how the racks had been enclosed and a more user-friendly style was presented. *(Museum of Science and Industry at Manchester.)*

GEC, AEI and EMI. Although an advisory panel on electronic computers was formed by the NRDC in December 1949, on which sat representatives of most electrical firms, because of a widespread suspicion of both computers and backdoor government intervention, Halsbury was unable to persuade any to initiate a joint venture. More importantly, while the idea of building partnerships was typical of Halsbury's general strategy, we have already noted how it met with little approval from the industry, where greater interest was expressed in a more focused approach. By the time the Mark I had been commissioned, and further MoS finance had been negotiated for another development stage, Halsbury was consequently in a weak bargaining position when he approached Ferranti about a production contract.[42] This position was also further undermined by the NRDC board's refusal to back Halsbury's suggestion that it should finance computer production.

When in March 1951 Sir Vincent was offered an interest-bearing loan of £50,000, to cover development costs only, this was flatly rejected on the grounds that a bank loan was cheaper.[43] Typifying Sir Vincent's general stance when dealing with government agencies, an approach which stemmed from his late 1930s experiences with fuze contracts (see section 7.4), Ferranti wanted the NRDC to underwrite production, thereby minimising any risk involved in making computers for as yet unknown customers. However, in view of the established government contracting conventions which prevented the NRDC from giving special preference to one firm, the NRDC was still unwilling to back such a proposal. Only when in November 1951 Halsbury finally managed to convince his board that the most effective way forward was to finance production of an updated Mark I did the NRDC agree to Sir Vincent's terms. This indicates how at an early stage in the Ferranti-NRDC relationship there was a fundamental conflict between Sir Vincent's business mind and the bureaucratic attitude of Halsbury. Over the following pages, we shall see how this conflict frequently hindered progress at crucial stages, emphasising how British post-War corporatist tendencies were inherently destabilising.

In spite of these more general defects in the British institutional scene, two key points arise from the negotiations between Ferranti and the NRDC: that Halsbury was ready to stimulate private enterprise in computer development and production; and that Sir Vincent was always going to succeed in extracting favourable terms because of the hand dealt to Halsbury. Again, one must remember that little interest had been raised in 1949 from even the largest electrical firms, while Ferranti and the University of Manchester had made such remarkable progress that it had to be sustained if Britain was to establish a position of strength in the world computer industry. Vivian Bowden, the first Ferranti computer salesman, was also confident that the business would grow, recommending to his chairman that: 'I feel … that Ferranti's stake in this new enterprise is a very large one and that the possibilities are almost unlimited'.[44]

It is important to stress how while NRDC was able to secure complete control of all patents emanating from the Ferranti-Manchester work, this was only a secondary consideration to the firm, because there is no doubt that Sir Vincent was highly satisfied with the final agreement. In fact, the NRDC agreed to purchase four of the new computers arising out of the development work on the Mark I, paying Ferranti all the development and production costs plus 7.5 per cent profit. Furthermore, a five per cent commission was payable to Ferranti on the final selling price in 'using their best endeavours to find customers'.[45] This was quite a coup for Sir Vincent, because all the short-term risks attendant on participating in the project had now been transferred to the NRDC, while at the same time the agreement provided further finance, strengthening the firm's position as Britain's leading computer producer. Of course, NRDC would have the computers, while Ferranti carried the longer-term risks associated with keeping its team together and maintaining a factory. Nevertheless, Sir Vincent had secured the deal he had initially wanted, giving Pollard the funds to go ahead with the production of an improved computer.

The Mark I* and the next stage

Having made this negotiating breakthrough with the NRDC, Ferranti went on to produce the Mark I* computer. One must note that the University of Manchester team did not provide much assistance with this product, because they were already beginning to think about what was later known as the Mark II, or MEG (megacycle engine), a computer which by 1957 Ferranti was producing and marketing as the *Mercury*. Such had been the rate at which Ferranti engineers had mastered computer technology by 1951, though, that the Mark I* represented a substantial improvement in reliability on the Mark I exhibited in 1951, with much greater storage capacity and enhanced speed of calculation.[46] In the meantime, not only was Ferranti preoccupied with selling the Mark I*, Pollard and his sales team were also drawing up ambitious plans for additional facilities and development programmes which would further sustain their lead in the market. The sales effort we shall describe later, but inevitably further development work would involve negotiations with either the NRDC or the DSIR, emphasising how the clash between commercial and functional aims was a constant feature of this department's activities.

When Pollard first approached the DSIR in September 1953 with a proposal for a three-year development programme costing £435,000, only £75,000 of which would come from Ferranti funds, he was greeted with some hostility from an organisation which had already become suspicious of the firm's use of public money.[47] In fact, all computer work at the DSIR was handled by the Brunt Committee, formally the DSIR Advisory Committee on High Speed Calculating Machines, established by Sir Ben Lockspeiser in 1949 and chaired by Sir David Brunt. While Lord Halsbury and F. C. Williams sat on this committee, it still expressed considerable concern at the lack of control over how its 1951 grants had been spent by Ferranti. Although no proof can be found to support the claim, the de Ferranti family was convinced that, because they wanted more support for their *Deuce* computer, executives at English Electric were mounting an anti-Ferranti campaign in government circles. Whatever the case, and even though no formal investigation was ever conducted, sentiment at DSIR was hostile towards Pollard's proposal, forcing Ferranti to turn once again to the NRDC. In fact, because the University of Manchester had already approached this body for funding of its Mark II programme, there was some logic in this move. On the other hand, as the 1951 negotiations had been so protratced and tortuous, Pollard was wary of making another bid to the NRDC, especially as the DSIR had proved so hostile.

Pegasus emerges

The preliminary negotiations with the NRDC over this next project actually took until March 1954 to arrange. It is also important to note that at exactly the same time Ferranti was negotiating another development and production contract on what would eventually become the *Pegasus* computer,[48] events we shall examine in the next section. Unfortunately, though, the NRDC could never be persuaded to support the Ferranti proposal (involving an NRDC purchase of ten Mark II computers at a cost of £500,000), resulting in a rejection of the Mark II development programme. This was extremely frustrating for all concerned, especially as Ferranti went on to develop the Mark II computer from its own funds and sold eighteen of what were marketed as the *Mercury*. One can only conclude that the NRDC had missed an opportunity to participate in another successful project, indicating how Halsbury was poor at picking potential winners.

In view of its previous actions, the NRDC refusal to finance a Mark II project stands out as a rather odd position to take, particularly as two months earlier (see section 9.4) funds for what became the *Pegasus* computer had been agreed. In retrospect, though, the hard negotiating stance adopted

The Ferranti Pegasus Digital Computer at the London Computing Centre, 13 April 1957.
(Museum of Science and Industry at Manchester.)

by Sir Vincent at a meeting with the NRDC in March 1954 could well have been the key factor. Lord Halsbury jotted down some notes after that meeting, providing an interesting insight into his perception of Sir Vincent's negotiating position. He wrote that:

> The Ferranti family own the whole of the equity capital in Ferranti Ltd; [they] have all the money they need for personal purposes and money is not an object of interest to them; they are in business for fun and will therefore under no circumstances agree to any proposition whatever that is from their point of view not so funny; in particular they will not open one crack, cranny or crevice whereby any third party could gain a permanent toehold inside the Ferranti group of enterprises; if Sir Vincent were looking for a new enterprise to invest Ferranti money in, he would not himself pick computers. He has, however, no objection to a Government agency picking computers for him provided that he is fully compensated for the use of Ferranti facilities. [49]

This is clearly a rather jaundiced view of both Sir Vincent and his business, because the firm was much more than a hobby. Crucially, as we saw in chapter seven, one of Sir Vincent's main aims had always been to keep his firm in the vanguard of electronics developments, while at the same time ensuring that expensive development contracts would never lead to serious illiquidity problems. Furthermore, even though the NRDC negotiations proved fruitless, Ferranti did develop the University of Manchester's Mark II design into the *Mercury* computer, revealing how Sir Vincent was interested in computers, whether 'funny' or not. One might also ask whether the last sentence in Halsbury's notes represents a highly logical and rational stance for a commercial enterprise. Certainly as far as Sir Vincent was concerned, this would have been extremely useful for his computer department. The very fact that Ferranti went on to produce *Mercury* indicates that Sir Vincent was simply attempting to secure the best terms for his firm, a position Lord Halsbury clearly misinterpreted, creating the false impression that Ferranti was simply the plaything of its owners. Moreover, in highlighting the generally unhelpful nature of Halsbury's interventions and his desire to control the industry by splitting up the limited funding between teams of firms, one must question whether the NRDC could ever have achieved much.

9.4 Pegasus and progress

While Ferranti struggled to extract further development funding for the Mark I* successor, it is important to emphasise that the NRDC was actually supporting a contemporaneous project which was to have even greater implications for general computer technology. One should remember, though, that this machine (later marketed as *Pegasus*) had originally been an Elliott Bros. project, and only because of personnel problems at that firm's Borehamwood research division did Ferranti succeed in acquiring a new approach towards computer circuitry. Although Elliott Bros. had been in existence since 1801 as a producer of scientific apparatus, after participating in the wartime development of gunnery control equipment it had diversified into digital electronics at Borehamwood.[50] Support from the Admiralty for this equipment, codenamed MRS5, was actually withdrawn in 1949, because of budgetary constraints. A year later, however, the NRDC agreed to support the work of Elliott Bros.'s computing division chief, confusingly named W. S. (Bill) Elliott. By 1952, the prototype for what became the Elliott 401 computer was being built, again (after much deliberation) financed by the NRDC. Unfortunately, though, the decision by Elliott Bros. management to move the Borehamwood chief (John Coales) back to the London headquarters had already precipitated a confidence crisis in the development team, resulting in the resignations of Bill Elliott and several others by November 1952.[51]

Bill Elliott and Pegasus

Elliott Bros.'s loss was certainly a considerable gain to Ferranti, because not only had Bill Elliott joined the latter by September 1953, he also brought with him a team of engineers – Peter Dorey (later to become a key figure in the Ferranti defence computer business), C. Owen, C. H. Devonald, and G. Felton – which was to play a major role in developing the southern Ferranti computer activities. In addition, and of much greater immediate importance, Elliott was principally responsible for developing new circuit technology which was to have such a significant impact on the computer world that as a result Ferranti was able to expand its business considerably. Although the NRDC had been reluctant to see the 401 project move from its original home, the Cambridge mathematician Christopher Strachey was able to persuade its computer sub-committee that Ferranti should benefit from the advances made at Borehamwood.[52] Consequently, by early 1954 NRDC funds had been provided for what came to be known as the FPC1 (Ferranti packaged computer).[53]

Some delays in implementing this agreement were caused by a major difference of opinion between Bill Elliott and Strachey on the prototype's design. By May, though, a compromise proposal had been tendered by Ferranti which allowed work to start.[54] The contract was also reminiscent of the first agreement in 1951, because it included a promise by the NRDC to

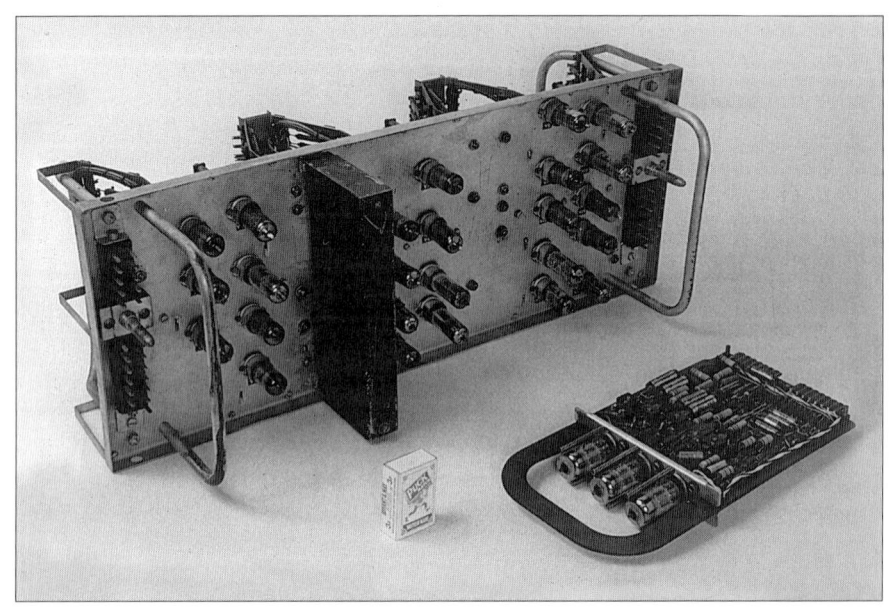

The Ferranti Pegasus modular plug-in unit (foreground) compared to an English Electric rival and a matchbox. *(Museum of Science and Industry at Manchester.)*

purchase at cost plus 7.5 per cent ten FPC1 computers, up to a maximum of £200,000. However, because Ferranti was at that time experiencing some difficulties in its negotiations over NRDC funding for work on Manchester's Mark II project, Sir Vincent proved unwilling to accept all the conditions attached to the first FPC1 agreement. In fact, while Sir Vincent had not been personally involved in negotiating the latter, when he discovered that the NRDC would be given a veto over all design changes, as well as property rights to all patents arising from the development, Pollard was instructed to demand concessions.[55]

The FPC1 contract is yet another example of the uneasy relationship between Ferranti and the NRDC. Once again, though, the latter was forced to submit to Sir Vincent's stance, waiving the veto over design changes, compromising over property rights, and agreeing to raise its liability for the first ten machines to £250,000. While this was a significant victory for Ferranti, however, this weak approach was to create grave difficulties when the development stage fell behind schedule. In fact, by May 1956 not only had costs exceeded by twenty-five per cent the initial budget of £250,000, Ferranti had also sold nine of the computers at prices based on the old estimates. So incensed was the NRDC at this predicament that by November 1956 legal proceedings were being threatened against the company. While little came of this in the next fourteen months, it was important for Sir Vincent to defuse the situation. In fact, typifying his personalised approach to such negotiations, in February 1958 he took Sir William Black out to lunch at the Savoy Hotel, when Sir Vincent agreed to make an *ex gratia* payment of £75,000 'in recognition of the help the NRDC has given us in getting into the industry'.[56] Of course, because the FPC1 contract had not included any veto over the many design changes which were introduced in the following two years, Ferranti refused to accept in law that they were liable to repay anything to the NRDC. On the other hand, as a gesture of good faith £75,000 helped to ease the losses of over £210,000 made by the NRDC on this contract. It also opened up the possibility that Ferranti might participate in what was at that time being described as Britain's 'Fast Computer' project, an episode we shall be examining later. Most notably, though, it is clear that the NRDC's inconsistent negotiating stance had created severe problems in the FPC1 development stage, a situation which had only been defused by the chairman's diplomatic skills.

Computer Department politics

When examining why the FPC1 proved to be so much more expensive than its initial estimates, it is first of all important to understand what was happening in the Ferranti computer department at that time. Of course, as we shall see later, there were technical difficulties associated with the FPC1 technology. More importantly, the conflict between Brian Pollard and Bill Elliott was holding up progress at a crucial stage. Bowden had already warned Sir Vincent that Pollard 'lacks the maturity to comprehend and to discharge staff',[57] a point well confirmed by his dealings with Elliott. It should be noted that because Elliott had once refused his new manager a job at Elliott Bros., he was reluctant to accept Pollard's authority.[58] As Elliott Bros. had also discovered to their cost, Elliott was a highly independent engineer who would brook few superiors. Of immediate significance was his refusal to move out of London to join Pollard's computer department at Gem Mill. As Grundy was reluctant to lose Elliott's undoubted design skills, not to mention his access to NRDC funds, new premises in the capital were consequently found to house the FPC1 team. Interestingly, these premises were at 18 Manchester St, just around the corner from a house formerly occupied by Charles Babbage, the nineteenth century computer designer. More significantly, geographical dispersion of this kind was only going to accentuate the communication difficulties arising from Elliott's relationship with Pollard, because it created a dual structure, whereby Elliott was responsible for a team in London, while Pollard ran production at Gem Mill.

By 1956, the Ferranti computer effort had consequently evolved into two distinct 'empires'. As sales had increased from £126,666 in 1952–53 to £336,015 by 1955–56, Pollard's team was rapidly outgrowing the cramped facilities at Gem Mill. This led him in February 1956 to move into a disused textile machinery factory in West Gorton, where he established what became the largest computer production plant in Europe. Similarly, not only did the London sales effort take on a much greater role at this time, Elliott also reinforced his independence from the northern activities by planning to establish a new laboratory in Bracknell. This friction was further intensified when Pollard decided to focus more on the Manchester Mark II project, while Elliott was left to work on the FPC1, contributing significantly to the latter's cost overruns. A good example of these difficulties was the confusion over the FPC1 prototype, because while by January 1956 Pollard claimed that it lacked a main drum store, this had been installed in the new Ferranti sales centre in London because Elliott was convinced that his machine was ready to start work as a demonstration model.[59]

Of course, it is easy to exaggerate the degree of conflict between Pollard and Elliott, because eventually, as we shall see in the next section, sales of both *Mercury* and *Pegasus* were reasonably successful. Problems often arise when extremely bright people work together, especially in a pioneering phase of development when standardised designs had yet to appear. In fact, when at the end of 1956 the London development team eventually moved into its Bracknell facilities, at Lily Hill House, Sir Vincent instructed the staff manager, T. J. Lunt, to ask Elliott to resign. Clearly, as the chairman was not prepared to see two of his managers arguing over crucial decisions, he felt it was vital that either Elliott should show total loyalty to his boss or leave the firm. Elliott was actually given a generous £3,000 redundancy payment by Ferranti, in recognition of what Sir Vincent described as 'your major contribution to the creation of our London computer laboratories and to the design of the outstandingly successful Pegasus computer'.[60] Indeed, he had fulfilled all the expctations raised at the time of his appointment, especially in developing the package technology, building up a development team and securing government contracts. Clearly, though, it was essential to harmonise activities in order to exploit effectively the lead gained by that time. On the other hand, it was unfortunate that not only did Elliott leave to establish the UK research centre of the major American computer firm of IBM (at Winchester), he also took with him several key members of the Ferranti team in London. The whole story was an object lesson in organisational dynamics, contributing significantly to the problems Ferranti experienced in both the completion of its FPC1 development contract and handling the NRDC's complaints. Indeed, leadership of the Ferranti computer efforts had been a consistent problem, a point to which we shall return later.

Apart from these personnel problems, of course, one must remember that technologically the FPC1, or *Pegasus*, project marked a significant breakthrough in the development of computer circuitry, providing a major influence on later Ferranti and ICL machines. The key to this new technology was Elliott's concept of fabricating standard, interchangeable circuit modules, or 'packages', building on the wartime successes in designing radar sets achieved by his former boss at Elliott Bros., John Coales. This 'package' was a piece of electronic equipment which could be plugged into a larger assembly, obviating any maintenance and repair difficulties which often arose in the older designs. *Pegasus* also used ultrasonic delay lines as a short-term memory. Although this was similar to the way in which EDSAC had operated, the Ferranti delay lines took the form of a long wire arranged in a spiral and mounted on a printed circuit card, rather than mercury-filled tanks. Fears were expressed about the possibility that varying delays and amplitudes might be created by the different pulses generated within each unit, posing a major challenge to Elliott and his team. Nevertheless, after Elliott had overcome these difficulties by conservative design work,[61] when the first machines were produced just six standard packages were used for eighty-five per cent of the construction work on twenty different assemblies. While *Pegasus* was certainly more expensive than some of its rivals, at approximately £50,000,[62] it was also much easier to use, had a larger store, and operated reliably. Indeed, it was described as 'a trusty workhorse, well-suited to a large number of programs, inexpensive to maintain and through long-service even inspiring affection in its users'.[63] This allowed Ferranti the opportunity to generate significantly more sales (see Table 9.1, p. 368) than with the older machines, especially as the NRDC had underwritten the initial production programme. At the same time, as we shall now go on to consider, in spite of this consistent technological lead the firm discovered that marketing computers and convincing customers to place firm orders remained difficult.

9.5 Marketing, sales and innovation

Designing and producing computers had been difficult enough for a firm suitably equipped to handle advanced electronics projects, but as a commercial venture Ferranti also had to sell these machines, bringing the firm face to face with another of the industry's problems, a highly cautious market. As we have seen in earlier chapters, Ferranti had never been successful in fields like radio, television and domestic appliances, largely because of marketing inadequacies. With regard to computers, similar problems also seemed to have been apparent. Commentators like Tweedale have been highly critical of the firm's efforts, questioning especially its commitment to the civil computer business.[64] However, before accepting such a judgement one must assess a variety of factors, in particular the market difficulties experienced by the pioneering British computer firms.

Of course, when assessing such difficulties it is hard to avoid a comparison with the American scene, where firms like IBM, Burroughs and CDC succeeded in establishing major computer businesses. This also brings up similar issues to those examined in chapter 3, where we saw how around the turn of the century American electrical engineering firms had been able to swamp British producers as a result of the significant competitive advantage gained from exploiting their enormous domestic market. With regard to computers, the situation was different, in that British firms were as technologically advanced as their American rivals, brooking no rivals in the development of advanced machines. On the other hand, the British market was innately conservative and small, forcing Ferranti to work hard to overcome these characteristics by expanding sales facilities and developing computers which appealed to a wider range of customers. At the same time, while one cannot question the firm's commitment to computer technology, it is important to recognise significant weaknesses in the way Ferranti approached the market, especially with regard to product planning and marketing.

In criticising the Ferranti marketing effort, one of Tweedale's more important arguments is based on the position of computer development and production within the firm. He claims that as a highly diversified family-run enterprise insufficient attention was paid to specific product needs.[65] This is a rather curious point, not simply because he ignores the substantial successes in areas like meters, transformers and at Crewe Toll, but mainly because he does not take into account the highly devolved structure which gave departmental managers the responsibility to build their own businesses. Moreover, having a range of allied businesses in the same company must prove useful to a new department, for example, in giving Ferranti computer engineers access to a range of engineering skills which substantially boosted their development work. Of course, most of the leading American computer firms were specialists in the field, allowing them the opportunity to focus their activities more effectively. Nevertheless, most had a commercial and technological background well suited to computers, in stark contrast to the British firms in this field.

When assessing early computer developments in Britain, it is also interesting to repeat the point that rivals like GEC, AEI and EMI (which were also highly diversified firms, yet run by professional managers for thousands of shareholders) had in 1949 rejected Lord Halsbury's request to join a collaborative venture.[66] Most significantly, as owner of over fifty per cent of the equity Sir Vincent was able to take a detached view of new projects without having to consider the feelings of professional investors who were not always interested in risky investments. One should also remember that the freedom given to departmental managers to develop new businesses, as long as they did not precipitate severe liquidity problems, was a vital feature of the Ferranti effort, providing a company culture which must be seen as the essential internal context in which the Ferranti computer department operated. Halsbury complained that he was not sure with whom he should negotiate, Pollard, Grundy or Sir Vincent.[67] However, this reflected more the NRDC's own failings, because it was always the chairman who took the key decisions, leading all the negotiations at their crucial stages.

Market characteristics and early sales efforts

Having reiterated these essential features of the Ferranti culture, one must also stress how the technology-led strategy could well have adversely affected the firm's ability to develop an effective marketing position, especially in view of the domestic market's limitations. In particular, it is vital to note that one of the first problems Ferranti had to overcome in developing a successful computer business was the attitude of contemporaries towards these very powerful, yet seemingly unfathomable, machines. We have already noted that while initially they were mostly referred to as 'electronic calculating machines',[68] the speed at which they worked was regarded by many as beyond the realms of possibility. One must also note that such was their power that some of the most distinguished scientists of the period felt that few would be required to deal with the calculating requirements of the whole country.[69] For example, when giving evidence to the Brunt Committee in 1949, D. R. Hartree claimed that: 'We have a computer in Cambridge, there is one in Manchester and one at the NPL. I suppose there ought to be one in Scotland, but that's about all'.[70] One must remember that Hartree was a pioneering designer of calculating machines, as well as Professor of Mathematics at Cambridge University. If he could not be persuaded that computers ought to come into common use, then producers were faced with potentially insurmountable obstacles.

Notwithstanding these blinkered perceptions, and bearing in mind the risk-free position it had established on the Mark I* by negotiating a production deal with the NRDC, Ferranti was by no means reluctant to embark on an energetic sales strategy. Indeed, before the Mark I's successful launch in July 1951, Vivian (later Lord) Bowden had been seconded from his job as an electronics development engineer to act as head of sales.[71] During the War, Bowden had actually worked with both Peter Blackett at the Cavendish Laboratory in Cambridge and F. C. Williams at TRE, providing strong links with the tight-knit scientific community of those immediate post-War years. It was through these avenues that Ferranti made its first sale, to Toronto University, when Professor Watson placed an order for a Mark I to help him contribute to the calculations being made on the St Lawrence Seaway project. As we shall see later, while this machine (known as FERUT) experienced severe teething problems, it was regarded as a major challenge to the American computer experts. As far as Ferranti Electric (the Canadian subsidiary) was concerned, it also laid the basis for more successful work in this field (see section 9.10).[72] To build on the initial success, at the official launch of the Mark I in July 1951, Bowden commissioned a publicity pamphlet to commemorate the occasion,[73] distributing this extensively in order to exploit any euphoria. This was followed in 1953 by a book, Bowden having decided that a popular introduction to the subject was required. In editing *Faster than Thought*, Bowden was the first to break down the jargon developing in the computer industry and explain exactly what such a machine entailed.

While it is easy to dismiss Bowden's work as amateurish and unsystematic, Ferranti was clearly making some efforts to exploit its initial lead in computer technology. Furthermore, by 1951 B. B. Swann (a former statistician at the Board of Trade) had been recruited as the sales manager to help coordinate Bowden's highly idiosyncratic approach. However, although Tweedale claims that a 'coherent computer sales policy ... was slow to emerge',[74] it is not clear what exactly this would have entailed, given the market's initial perception of computers. Of course, while Bowden's highly personal approach might well be regarded as uncoordinated, this would appear to have been the only rational means of breaking down prejudices, while Swann was soon brought in to provide greater cohesion. As Swann himself noted, and Tweedale also quotes, selling in the early 1950s was 'interesting and often exciting, but unrewarding. Time and again we could only report that, after customer visits, that they were showing a keen interest, but no order'.[75] Nevertheless, once production of the Mark I* increased in 1953 – in fact Swann and Bowden were able to sell seven of these machines (see Table 9.1), compared to the initial NRDC plan to make four – on the latter's recommendation the computer department was expanded and moved from Moston to Gem Mill.[76] More significantly in marketing terms, as a means of providing a hands-on facility for potential customers, Swann also lobbied both the board and Lord Halsbury for funds to establish a computing centre in London, revealing how positive thought was being given to this crucial aspect of the business.

London Computing Centre

Swann's idea of creating a London Computing Centre was certainly a major marketing innovation, especially once an Adams period house at 21 Portland Place had been adapted for this purpose.[77] The plan had actually been accepted by Sir Vincent in June 1952,[78] when some cramped quarters in Great Ormond St were acquired. Soon after, however, they moved into Portland Place, spending £25,000 on revamped facilities.[79] Some of the development team also worked at Ferranti House, the sales centre in London, where the top floor was used as a computer laboratory, emphasising how the southern team expanded significantly at that time.[80] The main problem, though, was Swann's failure to secure a computer for this Centre, because the NRDC had rejected his early approach for a Mark I* on the grounds that it was supporting enough of the Ferranti work.[81] At the same time, because Halsbury recognised the need for such a sales strategy, when the NRDC agreed to finance the FPC1 project Swann was able to persuade them to provide one of the ten machines to be made under this contract for his Centre. Given the difficulties inherent in handling the Mark I*, acquiring what became the extremely user-friendly *Pegasus* machine was also a crucial step. When it was first installed at the beginning of 1956, Swann and his team were consequently able to pursue a much more rigorous sales approach. This team actually totalled eighteen by 1956, seventeen of whom were graduates, while a further eleven graduates worked in the programming research unit under Stan Gill.[82]

The whole aim of Swann's strategy was to bring potential customers into the Centre, both to experiment on the *Pegasus* and to solve their own problems. This was clearly a success, because within a year eighty groups had visited Portland Place.[83] Indeed, so successful was the Centre that larger premises in Newman St were later acquired. Furthermore, the problems solved on the *Pegasus*, using programmes generated by Gill's team, were widely disseminated through the publication of what came to be known as the CS Lists.[84] One might argue that forcing potential customers to come into the Centre was hardly a pro-active approach towards marketing and selling. On the other hand, given the embryonic nature of computer technology and the current size and complexity of these machines, it would have been impossible for a team of salesmen to travel around the country performing similar work. Table 9.1 also reveals how sales of *Pegasus* in both of its forms far exceeded the initial NRDC projection of ten, providing the West Gorton production facility with an opportunity to exploit substantial economies of scale in executing the orders. Indeed, it is clear that the Ferranti computer sales effort was 'vigorous',[85] both under Bowden in the early

1950s and at the Centre after 1956. What would now be referred to as the user-friendly nature of *Pegasus* undoubtedly facilitated Swann's work, especially once Elliott had been sacked and the design specifications were finalised. Notwithstanding this asset, even so the machines still needed selling to highly cautious domestic customers.

Export efforts

Another criticism of Swann's approach might well be that it was oriented largely towards the British market. In fact, just over twenty per cent of total Ferranti computer sales were exported (see Table 9.1), reflecting a strong bias in sales activity. For example, while the Mark I (known as FERUT) sold to Toronto University in 1951 was regarded by the Americans as a major threat, and even though Sir Vincent and Vivian Bowden both visited the USA in the early 1950s, no further orders were secured in North America. Of course, one could point to the early operating difficulties experienced by FERUT, a problem partly caused by Toronto University's insistence on early delivery and the machine's construction at Ferranti Electric, where little expertise in this area existed. Similarly, the input/output facilities on the early machines were far from satisfactory. Another obstacle to sales outside, and later within, the UK was the terms (rental and deferred payments) American and British punched-card machinery firms were willing to offer, posing major challenges to relatively cash-poor firms like Ferranti. Ultimately, though, as we noted when examining Frank Rostron's attempt to sell large transformers in the USA (see section 8.2), American customers were inherently nationalistic when considering the purchase of high technology equipment, leaving foreign firms frustrated by the wall of silence after making an initial contact.

The North American computer market was consequently impossible to penetrate after 1951, cutting British firms off from the world's largest source of demand for this product. By 1960, while 240 computers had been installed in the UK, when one compares this with the 5,400 purchased by American customers it is clear that the two markets were very much different in size.[86] To take a more objective measurement, in 1965 there were 105 computers per million inhabitants in the USA, while in the UK there were just twenty-one.[87] By that time, 1,582 computers had been installed in the UK, compared to 24,700 across the Atlantic, revealing how American firms were provided with an extremely conducive environment which encouraged the expansion of development programmes and production facilities. As Lord Halsbury conceded as early as 1953, 'the enthusiasm of the American user was a big factor in determining the rate at which progress can be made by a manufacturing and development centre. In England potential users are not enthusiastic'.[88] In this context, one can only wonder at how one firm like Ferranti could have stimulated more interest in computers, because as far as the UK was concerned there seems to have been a general reluctance to buy such advanced equipment, when compared to the prevailing American attitude. Table 9.1 provides further evidence of the difficulties experienced by Ferranti in selling to commercial customers (other than to defence-minded aircraft companies), because it reveals that while forty-eight orders of this type were received, none had materialised prior to 1959, while ten of these sales were to Ferranti divisions.[89]

Government and domestic sales

Apart from the enormous difference in sales, another source of contrast between the UK and USA was the nature of government support for the computer industry. We noted earlier how not only did the NRDC need to be self-financing, its budget initially amounted to an interest-bearing loan of just £5 million, a sum which had to be repaid to the Treasury within five years. An Act in 1954 extended the time limit to ten years, while another in 1958 increased it further to twenty years and raised the loan to £10 million.[90] However, when compared to the sums provided by American government agencies like the US Air Force, atomic energy and weapons research establishments, and later NASA, the British effort looks paltry. IBM probably benefited most from this support during the 1950s, receiving government grants worth approximately $500 million (£175 million), largely for the SAGE defence system,[91] which accounted for nearly sixty per cent of its development effort.[92] This firm's encroachment into the British market will be examined in a later section, but clearly with such generous grants (as opposed to the loans distributed by the NRDC) it is no surprise that its transistorised 1401 series launched in 1959 should prove so successful. One should also note that not only did American firms like IBM receive generous development funds and pump-priming prices at the beginning of the product cycle, their government added nine per cent to the budget in order to 'maintain the art', encouraging development in an upward spiral. The relatively low level of British government support, divided up by Halsbury in a most manipulative manner, stands out in stark contrast to what was happening in the USA (and later Japan). Quite simply, it was this enormous American budget which provided the base from which firms like IBM, Burroughs and CDC came to dominate the world computer industry after 1960, while Ferranti and its British counterparts struggled to raise the necessary funds for what were path-breaking computer concepts.

Table 9.1. *The Number of Ferranti computer sales from the West Gorton computer department, 1951–63*

Type and period of production	Scientific organisations	Aircraft Co.s	Other commercial	Total sold	Exports
Mark I (1951–52)	2	—	—	2	1
Mark I * (1953–57)	4	1	2	7	2
Pegasus I † (1956–61)	10	5	11	26	3
Pegasus II † (1959–62)	2	2	8	12	1
Mercury (1957–61)	14	—	5	19	6
Perseus (1959)	—	—	—	2	2
Orion (1963–65)	—	—	10	10	1
Sirius (1960–63)	4	—	12	16	6
Atlas (1963–64)	3	—	—	3	—
TOTAL	39	8	48	97	22

* This category includes universities, government research establishments (domestic and overseas), and atomic energy authorities.

† Hendry (1989, pp. 183–5) claims that sales of twenty-five *Pegasus* I and thirteen *Pegasus* II computers were made, but no evidence is produced to say why Swann is incorrect.

Source: Swann (1975).

9.6 Commercial computers and punched-cards

Although substantial qualifications can be made to any critical assessment of the Ferranti computer marketing effort, particularly in view of the relatively feeble level of both demand and government support in the 1950s, it is still not entirely clear why Ferranti experienced such grave difficulties converting its technological advantage into extensive commercial success. In this context, one must consequently examine the central direction of both product development and the company's sales effort, emphasising in particular the failure to focus more intently on the commercial market. Bearing in mind our earlier point that the commercial computer market grew very slowly, one might conclude that the policy of developing machines for, and selling principally to, the scientific market was the only rational strategy for Pollard and Swann. Indeed, a significant investment of both technical and sales resources was made in building up this market, giving Ferranti a strong position as the leading firm in this field. At the same time, as it was hoped that *Pegasus* would prove more attractive to business users, Table 9.1 reveals that nineteen of the thirty-five machines sold in this range went to 'Other Commercial' customers. This was extremely important for the department's image, demonstrating how the Computing Centre in London was successful in overcoming some of the fears expressed by potential customers. On the other hand, Swann was aware that even *Pegasus* was unsuitable for perhaps the largest potential computer market, data processing, where attempts at designing a machine attuned to this area were started in late 1956.[93] It is also important to emphasise that in criticising the alleged lack of effort Ferranti invested in the civil business, all of the other major sources on British computing history have ignored this project completely.[94]

Perseus

A crucial point to remember about this data processing computer project, or *Perseus* as it was eventually marketed, was the role played in its commercial development by Harry Johnson, a former mathematician at the Ministry of Civil Aviation who had been recruited into Swann's London Computing Centre. Although by no means the leading influence on computer sales at that time, and other members of the London centre like Alan Bagshaw (its manager), Dr Chris Wilson (later a managing director of ICL), Hugh McGregor Ross, Peter Hunt and John (later Sir John) Fairclough represented the dynamic edge to Ferranti marketing, Johnson contributed some useful ideas at various points in the story. In particular, we shall see later that Johnson was to produce a sales blueprint which later became the basis for a major generation of computers produced by ICL, the computer firm created to act as the British flagship in what had become by the 1960s a highly competitive market.[95] His first major task, though, was to develop the commercial side of the *Perseus* project, working with the company's insurers, Royal Insurance, to produce a report which laid the basis for what in effect was a variant of *Pegasus*. *Perseus* was actually just a larger version of *Pegasus*, employing longer delay lines in which the ultrasonic pulses were transmitted as torsional waves, as opposed to compression waves, in order to reduce the distortion effects. It was just at that time, however, that Bill Elliott was sacked, hampering progress at a crucial time. Although one of Elliott's assistants, C. H. (Hugh) Devonald, eventually took responsibility for the project, it was 1959 before *Perseus* was launched.

The development of *Perseus* could well be used as evidence to demonstrate that Ferranti was capable of assessing gaps in the market. Indeed, by utilising the design innovations of the FPC1 project Devonald produced a computer which possessed an unmatched capacity to store and handle vast quantities of data. On the other hand, it is vital to stress that this machine, being three times the size of a *Pegasus*, was inordinately expensive to develop and produce, leading to significant delays in delivery. In fact, because it took almost three years to perfect, by which time new circuit designs using the more efficient and less costly transistor technology were coming on the market, Swann was obliged to drop the sales campaign.[96] As Table 9.1 also reveals, not a single British insurance company (including Royal Insurance) showed any interest in purchasing the machine, resulting in only two sales to insurance companies in Stockholm and Cape Town.[97] Although this might well reflect further on the unresponsive nature of a small domestic market, it is also important to stress that what amounted to the sales department's fixation with a machine for the specialist field of insurance indicated how attention could be distracted away from the general data processing market. In simple terms, *Perseus* was both too expensive for most potential customers and technologically outdated. Moreover, while it confirmed the company's reputation for producing large machines, it ignored the potential in the mass data processing (office machinery) market which others were beginning to exploit more effectively.

Powers-Samas & BTM

This conclusion should perhaps come as no great surprise to anyone who has read the previous chapters, because the Ferranti history is littered with examples of how the firm excelled in taking the most difficult technological paths, leaving the mass markets for relatively straightforward products to more commercially-minded rivals. At the same time, it is important in the computer context to stress that another major obstacle prevented Ferranti from developing the office machinery market, namely, a partnership which had been negotiated with one of the two leading office machinery producers, Powers-Samas. This partnership possessed considerable potential, especially in the development of suitable input-output peripherals and providing access to a mass market for office computers. Pollard reported in 1958 that the failure to produce adequate punched-card machinery was preventing *Pegasus* from making an even bigger impact on the market, enabling companies like Elliotts and English Electric to make inroads into what had formerly been regarded as Ferranti territory.[98] On the other hand, disagreements between Ferranti and Powers-Samas over crucial issues created intense friction, leading ultimately to severe difficulties in harmonising needs and results.[99]

When Ferranti first started working on computer technology, engineers soon realised that while they had the expertise in circuit design and production, they knew little about the necessary input-output equipment which would be needed to communicate with the machine. The Mark I computer, for example, had used a line printer supplied by the Bull Co., of France. While later tape readers were developed to take 8-hole tape, at first Ferranti engineers were obliged to rely on 5-hole tape. In 1950, Lord Halsbury at the NRDC was consequently encouraging the two leading British office machinery producers, British Tabulating Machine Co. (BTM) and Powers-Samas, to participate in a computer development project.[100] These two firms dominated the British and Commonwealth office machinery market, having originally been established to perform exactly that function as subsidiaries of powerful American firms, respectively, Hollerith (later IBM) in 1904 and Powers in 1915 (known as Acc & Tab, and from 1929 Powers-Samas).[101] In 1949, however, BTM had freed itself from what was a highly constraining agreement with its parent company, by then IBM, while Powers-Samas had been acquired by Vickers. Campbell-Kelly describes how thereafter they expanded rapidly in the following decade by exploiting the considerable post-War expansion in sales of office machinery.[102] In this period of growth, they also developed electronic machinery, with BTM especially exploiting its old links with IBM to introduce a new range of calculators which incorporated significant advances. Clearly, the substantial customer base built up by BTM and Powers-Samas, in addition to their extensive marketing and sales facilities, provided a big attraction to firms like Ferranti which were struggling to increase their order book.

When Halsbury first approached the office machinery firms in 1950, in the hope that one could be persuaded to collaborate with Ferranti, it did not take him long to settle on BTM as the most promising firm. The main reason for this decision was his view that Powers-Samas was 'an almost completely fossilised organisation'.[103] In fact, both firms were managed along highly traditional lines, creating severe problems later when they acquired most of the computer producers.[104] More importantly, though, BTM's Hollerith equipment was also regarded as potentially more effective, given its use of electrical, rather than mechanical, sensing, leading to discussions about a joint venture with Ferranti.[105] As we have already noted, while such a partnership possessed considerable potential and BTM was certainly interested in computer technology, its insistence that Ferranti would have no role to play in marketing proved to be an insurmountable obstacle. Swann, as head of the Ferranti sales team, in particular was very much against this plan, because both he and Sir Vincent were strongly antipathetic towards introducing the kind of aggressive, commission-based selling activity so typical of the punched-card firms. The Ferranti sales effort was highly traditional and 'gentlemanly' in character, staff even taking around different attire to wear, depending upon which customers they were approaching. Of even greater significance to Sir Vincent, though, was his fear that any arrangement would have relegated Ferranti to the position of subcontractor to BTM, a role he would never accept for a department which had already made significant technological progress.

When the two companies initially started talking, Halsbury had hoped that they would cooperate on the production of a computer for the 1951 Festival of Britain. However, although some work was done on this project, and Sir Vincent was involved in the BTM negotiations, nothing ever came of this machine.[106] Although some BTM punched card input-output machinery was installed on the first Mark I* machines, this was all that ever came out of the negotiations. BTM, on the other hand, was keen to acquire access to the new technology, sponsoring the work on small computers by a Birkbeck College scientist, A. D. Booth.[107] This machine was first known as HEC (Hollerith electronic computer), a prototype of which was first exhibited at the 1953 Business Efficiency Exhibition. Its chief asset was the economical design employed in the logic circuits, added to which was a multiplier unit which was twice as fast as its rivals. When in 1954 they changed its name to the BTM 1200, the firm established a highly successful business in small office computers. Indeed, although only five 1200's were sold, the improved version introduced in 1956, the BTM 1201, outsold every other British computer over the following five years, with seventy orders.[108] This indicates how because these firms could exploit their extensive customer base to provide a solid base for computer innovation, it was unfortunate that the Ferranti sales team was unwilling to accede to BTM's demands in the early negotiations.

Pluto

The 1950 negotiations with BTM had consequently proved doubly frustrating, because not only could little help be secured in developing efficient input-output machinery from the experts, the BTM 1201 also proved to be a cheap alternative to purchasing one of the large, expensive mainframe computers made by Ferranti. Again, this encapsulates the Ferranti problem, because West Gorton was focusing on big machines which were only in limited demand, while the punched-card firms were exploiting their substantial customer base with cheap models. Halsbury's judgement of Powers-Samas had also been typically poor, because by 1954 this firm had produced its PCC range of electronic calculators which although not a computer was marketed and classified as being capable of performing similar functions.[109] This success also prompted the Powers-Samas board to venture further into computing, leading to further negotiations with Ferranti in September 1954, after the parent board at Vickers decided that it would be useful to seek assistance from an established computer firm. This provided yet another opportunity for the West Gorton team to acquire access to both expertise in office machinery and an extensive sales network. Once again, though, problems arose in reconciling the marketing efforts, emphasising how such arrangements were fraught with difficulty.

Although the Powers-Samas agreement certainly promised much, in retrospect it would appear to have been a disaster, largely because, as in the earlier negotiations with BTM, Powers-Samas refused to give Swann and his team any access to their sales network. Indeed, because of their lack of commitment to the new machines, Swann described the Powers-Samas computer sales effort as 'more than pathetic'.[110] On the other hand, like BTM, they were able to build successfully on their extensive customer base to establish a strong position in the office machinery market, revealing once again the differences between Ferranti and punched-card machine producers. The agreement actually gave Powers-Samas the right to deal exclusively with their established customers, compounding the problems Ferranti had already experienced dealing with a cautious market because its partner preferred to sell its own equipment to what had always been a captive market.[111] The delays associated with bringing *Pegasus* to the market further compounded the difficulties, resulting in the belated announcement of a Ferranti-Powers machine as late as 1958, when *Pluto* was first marketed. *Pluto* actually made a good impression when first announced at the 1958 Computer Exhibition, because it used transistors and printed circuit boards,[112] providing the basis for a more concerted attack on the market. However, after so much time in the development stage only Ferranti showed much interest, making it difficult to coax potential customers into placing an order. In fact, while a *Pluto* was almost sold to the London & Manchester Assurance Co., typically Powers-Samas was so annoyed that Ferranti had approached one of its customers that the order had to be cancelled.[113]

Merger talks

Clearly, one might conclude that Ferranti was considerably frustrated in its attempts at breaking into the commercial market by the reluctance of the two office machinery firms to allow any access to their customers. The difficulties with the Powers-Samas agreement not only affected sales of *Pluto*, it could also help to explain why *Perseus* never sold in the British market. Sir Vincent later quipped that the only benefit he gained from the Powers-Samas agreement was a nutcracker given to him as a Christmas present.[114] On the other hand, as Campbell-Kelly argues, Ferranti was just as much to blame for the failure of these agreements, because of its preference for developing the large machine market.[115] Certainly, neither *Pluto* nor *Perseus* received as much attention as *Pegasus* or *Mercury*, while Swann's traditional approach to selling would never accommodate the Powers-Samas style. Ferranti had still to realise that the low-volume market for large, scientific computers would never provide the returns necessary to cover its rising development costs. This left the punched-card firms free to build on their established customer base, having developed a successful range of small office machines with which Ferranti could not compete.

This situation was also further compounded by the July 1958 decision of Powers-Samas and BTM to merge, creating a much larger rival called International Computers & Tabulators Ltd (ICT).[116] While on the one hand it seemed to be a reflection of the growing awareness of the need to concentrate British computer activity, for Ferranti it simply meant that its former reluctant partners had now combined to compete for the scarce custom. The main reason behind this merger was a shared fear about the growing threat from American competitors, and especially from IBM. Moreover, by 1957 Powers-Samas was beginning to experience severe financial difficulties, largely because after a considerable expansion of capacity in the mid-1950s demand had collapsed to such an extent that it was difficult to cover the increased overheads.[117] Of course, Powers-Samas's financial troubles would only have exacerbated the difficulties experienced in forcing the pace with *Pluto* and *Perseus*, forcing them to pull out of the agreement with Ferranti. This left the latter with both no partner in its commercial computer business, as well as a new competitor which was committed to expanding the old BTM range of machines. It was also in October 1959 that IBM announced its 1401 transistorised computer,[118] shaking the British computer industry to its very foundations. In this new environment Ferranti was faced with the stark choice of continuing its work on commercial computers or focusing more on the scientific market.

9.7 Scientific computers

While one can understand why the office machinery firms had pursued the rational strategy of wringing the last drop of profit out of their traditional businesses, it is clear that their refusal to allow Ferranti access to what was an extensive customer base had been the main reason why these arrangements (with BTM in 1950–51, and with Powers-Samas between 1954 and 1959) had proved commercially unsuccessful. This is confirmed by the point made at the beginning of the last section, when it was noted that Ferranti only sold thirty-eight computers to commercial customers (other than to Ferranti divisions and aircraft firms), compared to thirty-nine to scientific bodies. In view of these figures, it is not surprising that in the late 1950s Ferranti put more effort into developing machines for their largest market. In fact, while even the scientific computer market had been slow to develop,[119] until the IBM 1401 persuaded a wider range of customers to use these machines it was universities and research establishments which accounted for most of the sales.

Ferranti had also committed most of its marketing energy to this sector. This can be confirmed by examining *Pegasus* sales, because while Swann had hoped that the range would help to increase interest in the commercial markets, as Table 9.1 reveals twelve of the thirty-eight sales went to 'Scientific Bodies', as well as seven to aircraft companies involved in original research. In view of the limitations in other markets, this strategy would appear to have been highly rational. Indeed, because developing scientific computers resulted in continued cooperation with the University of Manchester, Ferranti was able to sustain its reputation as a pioneer in the large computer market. At the same time, the reliance on academics created a technology-led department which was reluctant to break away from this niche position, leading Ferranti into a series of highly prestigious, yet unprofitable, projects.

Mercury

After the early successes with both the Mark I and Mark I*, the next major project in this area was Tom Kilburn's Mark II machine. Even though, as we noted earlier, the NRDC had refused to provide funds for this concept, Ferranti nevertheless agreed to finance the construction of what was actually known as MEG (megacycle engine). Swann was highly sceptical about the commercial prospects for what eventually became the *Mercury* computer, partly because its projected price of £80,000 was twice that of the English Electric *Deuce*, while the operating efficiency of early prototypes did not instil much confidence in its marketability. In fact, Swann predicted that no more than four of these machines could be sold.[120] However, largely as a result of

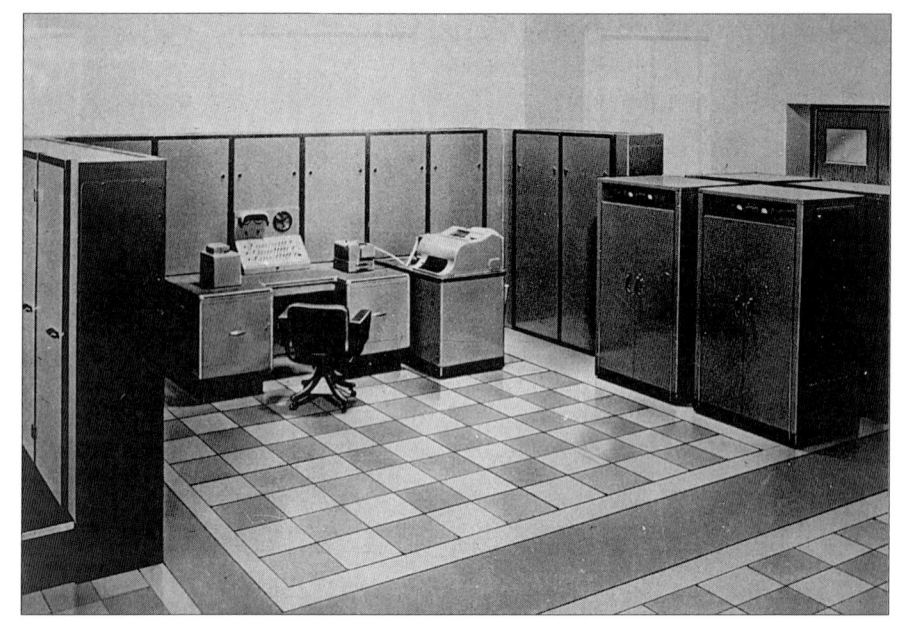

The Ferranti Mercury computer (1957), formerly known by its Manchester University designers as MEG (megacycle machine). *(Museum of Science and Industry at Manchester.)*

the dramatic improvement in reliability by the time it went into production in 1957, *Mercury* sales totalled nineteen, six of which went abroad (see Table 9.1). Indeed, *Mercury* was a major technological and commercial success story, pioneering the use of floating-point arithmetic and incorporating a new ferrite core store (developed by Plessey) which provided immediate access to almost sixty per cent extra storage space. *Mercury* was actually twenty times faster than the first Mark I machines,[121] attracting the interest of several research establishments in both the UK and Europe, especially those working in the complicated fields of atomic energy research.[122] Although five were sold to commercial companies, largely for research and development purposes, as Table 9.1 reveals almost three-quarters were taken by scientific establishments, reaffirming the Ferranti lead in what was regarded as the most sophisticated aspect of computing.

Swann had clearly been wrong when assessing *Mercury*'s commercial potential, because apart from its technological significance the machine also proved to be extremely profitable over the six years (1957–62) of production. We shall be examining the computer department's financial performance in the final section, but one should remember that profitability was often difficult to achieve after the early 1950s, especially as both *Perseus* and *Pluto* were making losses. *Mercury*'s success also encouraged Pollard to continue working with Tom Kilburn on even more advanced government-sponsored projects, especially as he was well aware that as early as 1956 Britain was in danger of falling behind in the race to produce computers with both faster speeds and greater memories.[123] Another crucial technological development at that time was the replacement of valves by transistors, a story which will feature more prominently in the next chapters (see sections 11.2 and 11.3). It is important to emphasise at this stage, though, that first generation valve technology was rapidly becoming outdated as American engineers especially experimented with second generation semiconductor materials.[124]

At that time, both IBM and a French company, Bull, were engaged separately in the development of what were to be known as 'High Speed' machines using transistor technology. British computer scientists were also left in no doubt about the importance of this work. At Ferranti, Maurice Gribble was in the mid-1950s building computer circuits with audio frequency junction transistors, while the University of Manchester engineers were experimenting with these revolutionary new devices. Progress in the UK, however, was extremely limited, largely because of the costs involved in developing reliable devices. As the IBM version, known as 'STRETCH', commissioned by an American government laboratory in 1956, was part of a corporate research and development budget worth $28 million per annum, Pollard was right to express concern about his firm's ability to compete.[125] In fact, Sebastian de Ferranti noted that 'STRETCH might have been renamed TWANG',[126] because IBM engineers took some time to deal with the project's basic requirements. At the same time, and largely for the first time, Lord Halsbury was ready to listen to proposals for a similar scheme, conscious as he was of the imperative need to keep British technology in line with this new work. Ferranti, of course, was keen to join such a project when in 1958 funds were made available. However, it will become clear that embarking on the development and production of a high-speed machine determined the ultimate destiny of its computer department, because as a result of the commercial implications inherent within this programme the firm was obliged to take some hard decisions just five years later.

Atlas

In the autumn of 1956 Tom Kilburn's team at the University of Manchester had already started preliminary investigations into the whole concept of high-speed computers, code-naming their Mark III project MUSE (microsecond). As early as November 1953 they had also built an experimental transistor computer, which Lavington claims was the world's first of its type to work successfully.[127] Utilising this expertise, by autumn 1956 further experiments had been started. Although encouragement from the atomic energy authority was certainly forthcoming,[128] neither they nor the University could afford to finance all the development, leading inevitably once again to NRDC involvement. In fact, because at that time the IBM 704 computer was regarded as more powerful than even the *Mercury*, under pressure from both the Atomic Weapons Research Establishment (AWRE) at Aldermaston and the UK Atomic Energy Authority (UKAEA) at Harwell, Lord Halsbury started to consider the possibility of an advanced British machine which would outpace anything the Americans could offer.[129]

Once again, however, even though the IBM STRETCH, as well as the Univac LARC, were threatening Britain's position as a technological innovator, the negotiations dragged on because of disagreements about who should finance the project and exactly what should be its main aims. Consequently, it was April 1959 before the NRDC had decided to back any scheme. An added complication was EMI's 2400 project, because some within the NRDC (especially Chistopher Strachey, the Cambridge mathematician who had designed its basic features and later devised the seminal *Pegasus* programme) preferred this project to the Manchester-Ferranti design. This forced Halsbury to divide the funds between EMI and Ferranti, rather than take a more focused approach, perpetuating the divisive strategy

The world's largest computer, Atlas, under construction in the West Gorton factory site, December 1962. *(Museum of Science and Industry at Manchester.)*

he had pursued since the late 1940s. Ferranti was actually given £300,000 for work on MUSE, while EMI was given £250,000. In the three years it had taken the NRDC to decide on its policy, however, several rivals had built machines which were to undermine the commercial viability of anything the two teams could produce.

In recounting the reasons why the British advanced computer efforts stalled, not only had vacillation clearly prevented the two teams from making progress on concepts which had tremendous technological significance, dividing the funds was yet another example of how Halsbury was trying to control the industry, rather than build a competitive series of products. As Hendry comments, 'the saga of the British fast computer does not seem to reflect well on the NRDC'.[130] The EMI project, later changed to the 3400, had actually been dropped by July 1962, when that firm's computer department was absorbed into ICT. Only three of the machines were ever sold.[131] There were also changes at Ferranti, when in December 1959 after much debate the new managing director, Sebastian de Ferranti (see section 11.1), decided to replace Pollard as manager of the computer department with Peter Hall. By 1959, as we shall see in the next section, the department's fortunes had deteriorated so drastically that Peter Hall was transferred from his job as electronics department manager to bring greater synergy to the West Gorton-Bracknell operations. This provided much better leadership at a crucial time, not least because of Hall's extensive experience of semiconductor design work (see section 11.2). On the other hand, while from 1960 progress on MUSE was much faster, this effected little change to the general direction taken with regard to computer strategy.

As a result of the royalties raised from sales of the Mark I, Tom Kilburn had been working on MUSE since 1956. When Ferranti finally managed to start work on what was marketed as *Atlas*, technologically the project had already started to chart new territory. While its peripherals might well have been poorer than those built into the American machines,[132] on its inauguration in December 1962 *Atlas* was described as the most powerful and flexible computer in the world. The most notable advantages associated with *Atlas*, apart from the extensive use of transistor technology, was the pioneering work on virtual storage and paging which contemporaries regarded as being years ahead of developments in the USA.[133] Just to indicate some of the speeds available on *Atlas*, the access time to the main store was just 2 microseconds, and to the fast store 0.3 microseconds, while time-sharing (or, multi-programming) was controlled by supervisory routines in the fixed store to prevent interference from other users.[134] By the end of 1963 an *Atlas* II had also been developed in association with the Cambridge University Mathematical Laboratory, partly because the latter would not accept a design originating in Manchester. Whatever the variant, though, *Atlas* was generally regarded as 'the world's fastest computer'.[135] In effect, it was said to have out-stretched STRETCH, allowing Ferranti to boast about its achievements in collaborating on the development and production of yet another significant milestone in computer history.

In a technological sense one might consequently argue that the NRDC's vacillation had not hindered work in Manchester. On the other hand, as we hinted earlier, such had been the length of time involved in *Atlas*'s development that several American firms had launched rivals at highly competitive prices, severely undermining its commercial prospects. The main competition came from the IBM STRETCH and Univac LARC launched in 1960, while CDC copied some of the *Atlas* technology to produce in 1962 the 6600.[136] A crucial point of importance here is that, while the NRDC provided £300,000 in development funds, by February 1959 Ferranti had already spent £375,000 on the first prototype, while by October 1962 expenditure amounted to £930,000.[137] This forced Ferranti to price *Atlas* at £2 million. Not surprisingly, then, as the American firms preferred to rent their machines on a monthly basis – IBM charged $2,500 for its 1401, Univac charged $135,000 for the LARC, and CDC $85,000 for the 6600 [138] – sales were difficult to achieve. One should also note that American peripherals were much more advanced than those installed on *Atlas*, emphasising how they had paid much closer attention to the needs of customers when designing what were still regarded in the early 1960s as sources of great mystery. In fact, as Table 9.1 reveals, apart from the University of Manchester order, only two *Atlas* computers had been sold by 1963, to London University [139] and to the UKAEA. While two more were made in the mid-1960s, by then Ferranti no longer had an interest in this business. In the summer of 1962, Ferranti even made a major effort to market *Atlas* in the USA, sending one of their leading programmers, Dr S. Gill, to accompany Dr D. G. White (a former Plessey engineer) on visits to potential customers like government departments, atomic energy establishments and aircraft companies. Unfortunately, though, little interest was shown in this British product, partly because of nationalistic attitudes in the USA, but mainly because Ferranti could not promise early delivery of a computer which was still being perfected.[140]

9.8 Completing the range: Sirius and Orion

While the NRDC had succeeded in its initial aim of encouraging one or more firms to build a high-speed computer, it is clear that the failure to sell *Atlas* on a commercial scale was linked to the delays created by those interminable negotiations between 1956 and 1959. Tweedale has argued that the main reason for this failure was 'amateurish marketing techniques [at Ferranti] ... inappropriate sales strategies and poor coordination between R & D and marketing'.[141] On the other hand, as the same source accepts, by the early 1960s competition in the high-speed computer market was extremely intense, both at home and abroad. It is also true to say that American and British computer firms experienced great difficulty in developing a profitable business at this end of the market. Ultimately, though, in contrast to the vacillation and skewed thinking at the NRDC, it was the sheer scale of American government support which created an incentive for firms like IBM, CDC and Burroughs to expand their efforts, a factor which ultimately determined the fate of British projects like *Atlas*. Campbell-Kelly has also argued that while a merger between Ferranti and ICT in 1959 would have boosted competitiveness considerably,[142] in view of the difficulties experienced in negotiations between these companies during the previous decade this hardly seemed likely at that time. As we shall also see in the next section, it was another

The incongruous sight of a Ferranti Sirius Computer being despatched to Turin. (*Museum of Science and Industry at Manchester.*)

four long, unprofitable years before anything positive was done about concentrating computer efforts in order to match the American industry.

The sales and marketing problems Ferranti experienced in this business were certainly difficult enough. However, another factor one might consider when assessing the commercial viability of computer production was the firm's costing procedures and their failure to provide accurate control over what was a dramatic escalation in development during the 1950s. Halsbury had complained as early as 1953 that: 'Ferranti base their quotations on a notional cost price without any proper attempt to cost out. It became clear that they had no proper notion of costs and did not very much care ...'.[143] Ferranti defended their practices by noting that it was essential to spend heavily on what was pioneering work, an argument which explains why the FPC1 development costs spiralled, from the initial price of £250,000 for ten machines in 1954, to over £500,000 by February 1958 (see section 9.4). In addition, one should remember that within Ferranti there were two teams working on computers at that time, in London and at West Gorton. NRDC had also been foolish in agreeing to drop its original demand for a veto over any design changes, giving Ferranti *carte blanche* to use public money on extensive development work. On the other hand, Pollard was regarded as culpable in failing to provide the NRDC with vital, up-dated information, forcing Sir Vincent to make the *ex gratia* payment of £75,000 as a gesture of good faith.[144] Clearly, there were problems with the computer department's costing procedures, and even when Elliott was sacked at the end of 1957 there was still a division of activities between Bracknell and West Gorton which was not harmonised. Even though the appointment in 1959 of Peter Hall as computer department manager brought greater coordination of activity, by then development costs were spiralling on *Atlas* and it is clear that difficulties remained in the early 1960s.

Sirius

Apart from the substantial increase in computer development costs, probably the most important factor determining the firm's attitude towards this business was the rapid rate of technological advance. It is important to note in this context that not only was Ferranti engaged in collaborative ventures with Manchester academics and on NRDC-funded projects, a series of in-house development programmes (other than *Perseus* and *Pluto*) was initiated in order to keep pace with the competition. As we noted in the last section, one of the crucial technological advances in the 1950s was the replacement of valves by transistors, or a move from first to second generation electronic components. While Tom Kilburn's team in 1953 had started to build transistorised computers, Ferranti was not privy to this work, forcing Pollard to initiate his own programme. Gordon Scarrott was asked to take on this project in 1953, developing up to 1960 a transistorised circuit code-named 'neuron'. The basic idea to which he worked was to employ packages similar to those developed for *Pegasus* to produce on a single card a self-contained multi-function logical element which made use of transistors and magnetic cores in combination. Although the concept seemed viable, unfortunately Scarrott struggled to convert theory into practice, largely because the neuron was a serial element which proved unsuitable to the large parallel machines currently under development. In fact, it was 1957 before he had incorporated neuron circuits into a test-bed computer code-named NEWT. This machine actually worked very well, 'amazing everyone' in the development team.[145] However, while a further three years of development work was invested in the neuron concept, it was finally dropped in 1960 in favour of a circuit developed by Maurice Gribble for the guided weapons department.[146]

Although Scarrott had failed to develop an effective transistorised circuit, Ferranti did eventually produce a computer based on the NEWT prototype. The circuits developed by Maurice Gribble were based on high-frequency germanium transistors and diodes, operating at a frequency of 500 kilo-Hertz. They had been developed for what would later become the *Argus* process control computer (see section 10.8), giving the computer department a major boost. NEWT had in fact evolved by that time into *Sirius*, a serial decimal, transistorised computer with ultrasonic delay-line memory which was designed to compete with the Elliott 803 and the ICT 1301 in the market for small, general-purpose machines. In fact, *Sirius* was not technologically-superior to its rivals, but at £20,000 and just five hundredweight it was advertised as 'the smallest and most economically priced computer in Europe'.[147] The use of a *Sirius* to predict the 1959 general election result also provided excellent publicity,[148] resulting in sixteen sales between 1960 and 1963 (see Table 9.1). In fact, two of the sixteen *Sirius* computers were used at the company's Newman St Computer Centre, as well as one in a Ferranti sales agency in Melbourne, Australia,[149] giving the machine excellent publicity. This demonstrates how Ferranti was at last beginning to wake up to the possibilities in the commercial market, utilising its renowned expertise in second generation technology to exploit markets other than the scientific and military.

Orion

The apparent success with *Sirius* clearly contradicts claims that Ferranti lacked a broad computer strategy.[150] At the same time, a broader perspective is required before critical views are completely dispelled. In particular, one must stress how *Sirius* was aimed more at scientific uses in the commercial market, rather than at the high-volume data processing market. This emphasises once again how the Ferranti marketing and sales effort always had a limited horizon, especially when compared to the strategies devised at ICT and IBM. To substantiate this point further, it is important to remember that in 1960 yet another computer was launched, as a result of experiments with second generation technology. Development of this machine, *Orion*, actually started in September 1958, but because of the problems with Scarrott's neurons, as well as substantial difficulties manufacturing the final design, it was 1963 before the product was available. In spite of these delays, though, Ferranti (and later ICT) sold thirteen *Orion* computers, all to commercial customers (see Table 9.1). The main reasons why these customers were willing to wait for Hall to overcome the production difficulties were the advanced time-sharing facilities developed by G. E. Felton, a Ferranti mathematician, while P. Hunt wrote a highly advanced computer language called NEBULA (natural electronic business language) which was as good as anything the Americans had designed.[151] One might criticise Ferranti for writing its own computer language, instead of using the widely accepted COBOL version. On the other hand, it typified their approach in pioneering computer technology which they hoped would catch on universally. Nevertheless, it is difficult to accept the Ferranti claim that by the early 1960s they had built up 'a range of computers in size, speed and application comparable to anyone, anywhere',[152] because even *Orion* and *Sirius* were for niche markets and they still had no rivals to those produced by ICT and IBM for the high-volume, data processing market. In effect, Ferranti was focusing even further on the specialist research-type computer, an approach which would have serious consequences for the department as the 1960s progressed.

9.9 The Bracknell story

Apollo and Poseidon

Before examining the financial repercussions of producing a range of mainframe computers which catered for the scientific requirements of large, medium and small users, it is first of all important to examine other aspects of the computer department's activities, particularly at Bracknell. Of course, although the Bracknell development team had played its part in perfecting the packaged techniques which had gone into *Pegasus*, the *Sirius, Orion* and *Atlas* machines were Manchester projects, leaving the southern team with freedom to venture off on their own after Bill Elliott's departure in 1956. In fact, even before moving to Bracknell, the London computer laboratory had already started to work on a range of new projects, prompted by Bill Elliott's belief that computers could be adapted to a wide range of purposes. Aware that Sir Vincent was unwilling to provide venture-capital for departmental projects, Elliott decided to approach government departments for funding, resulting in contracts from RAE and RRE to examine the possibility of developing computerised digital data links. Pollard was also optimistic about the possibilities in this technology, requesting permission from Sir Vincent in May 1957 for more development staff, especially as a contract from the ASRE was five months behind schedule.[153] One of the most interesting study contracts secured at this time came from MoS, to apply computer techniques to air traffic control. This project was code-named *Apollo*, responsibility for which was given to Harry Johnson, the former Ministry of Civil Aviation employee who was working in Swann's London Computing Centre.

Johnson, of course, was not just a salesman, having been trained as a mathematician. Using a combination of his mathematical skills and the experience acquired as a result of designing the *Perseus* computer, he came up with a specification entitled Automated Flight Information Store (AFIS) for *Apollo*.[154] This was yet another adaptation of the FPC1 packaged techniques, using the logic circuits designed by Maurice Gribble for the *Argus* process control computer (see section 10.8). When presented to the MoS, it was accepted as a viable means of improving air traffic control systems. Unfortunately, though, after consulting Johnson's former employers, the Ministry of Civil Aviation, the civil servants decided to advertise for competitive tenders, thinking that AFIS was in some way connected to his previous work there. The Bracknell team was inevitably horrified at this development, and it took several weeks to convince MoS that AFIS was a Ferranti project. In the meantime, Johnson and his team at Bracknell decided to change the specification by substituting transistors for valves. Although this naturally created some confusion among the civil servants, they finally agreed that Ferranti ought to be given a contract to build *Apollo* using second generation components. Its main task was to provide up-to-the-minute information on traffic conditions and print out flight progress slips, using displays designed by RRE.[155] Such was the Ferranti achievement that when the first machine was produced in the spring of 1961, although only intended for experimental use, the Ministry decided that it should be immediately installed in the Oceanic Area Control Centre at Ringway, Manchester, where it performed sterling service until 1982.

The *Apollo* project was not only important because the machine worked successfully in a crucial role, it also established computers as an effective vehicle for operational control in real-time situations. Moreover, it provided a new market for the Bracknell team on which they were keen to build. In fact, while only one *Apollo* was ever sold, it provided the basic specification for a successful range of computers for the Royal Navy. As early as 1955 the Admiralty Surface Weapons Establishment (ASWE) had approached Bill Elliott about the possibility of coordinating radar displays with a computer.[156] By 1962, a system known as Action Data Automation (ADA) had been developed to provide better air defence for aircraft carriers and later the *County* class of guided missile destroyers. This system was actually incorporated into a computer called *Poseidon*, the first order (worth £1 million) for which was placed in 1962 by the Admiralty for HMS *Eagle*,[157] an aircraft carrier. This initiated a long and intimate relationship between Bracknell and the Royal Navy which lasted almost thirty years.

Digital Systems Department

The development of *Apollo* and *Poseidon* demonstrated how Bracknell was beginning to move in different directions to the West Gorton team, the former working on real-time applications, while the latter concentrated on mainframe computers for data processing purposes. Of course, as Bracknell was still controlled by the northern operation, by the early 1960s a strong case for devolution was being made by the southern team, given the growth in output from just £52,000 in 1955–56 to over £300,000 by 1960–61. Since Bill Elliott's departure at the end of 1956, Bracknell had actually been run by a triumvirate of engineers, the most outstanding of whom was Peter Dorey, one of the team which had moved to Ferranti from Elliott's in 1954. It was this man Peter Hall chose to set up what was to be called the digital systems department at Bracknell, providing the kind of dynamic leadership required for an expanding business.[158]

Certainly, Dorey was put in charge of a booming department, because when *Poseidon* went into production sales suddenly leapt to over £950,000. Indeed, such was the success of *Poseidon* that the Royal Navy decided to equip all its latest ships with ADA, providing Dorey with a regular source of custom. In fact, in the first six years sales grew at a compound rate of fifty per cent per annum, reaching £4.6 million by 1967–68, making digital systems one of the more profitable parts of the Ferranti organisation. This growth in sales also prompted digital systems to acquire additional manufacturing facilities, at Cairo Mill in Oldham, while by 1963 larger premises in Bracknell, on Western Rd., were purchased to cope with the increased development work. By 1970, the Western Rd. laboratory (also housing the aircraft equipment department development team) employed over 800 graduates and qualified

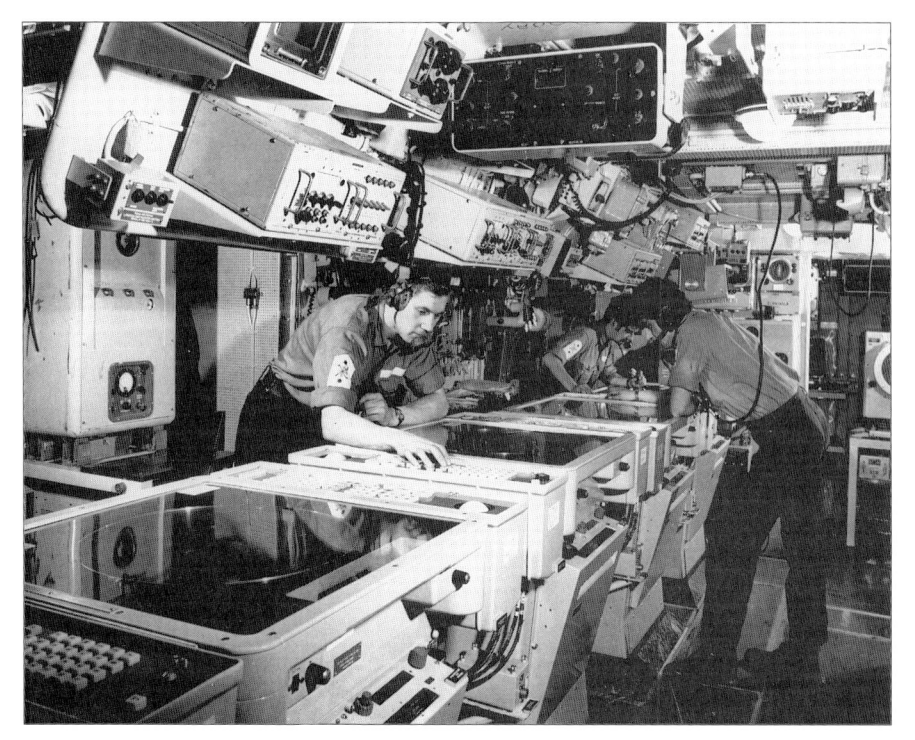

First Ferranti Computer Assisted Action Information System that went to sea in HMS Torquay, 1972, made at Bracknell division. *(Museum of Science and Industry at Manchester.)*

engineers in 100,000 square feet of space. As we shall also see in section 11.7, digital systems department under Peter Dorey proved to be an excellent illustration of how the Ferranti culture instilled an entrepreneurial approach into its managers.

9.10 Computer finances and computer mergers

Financial performance

Digital systems was a real computer success story for Ferranti, providing over thirty years of success in home and export markets (see section 11.7). However, because its product base and sales portfolio was essentially defence-oriented, by examining the events of the early 1960s we shall see once again how Ferranti was unable to sustain a balance between this and its civil business. In particular, it is important to stress how by the early 1960s West Gorton was becoming a major financial embarrassment for the company. Of growing concern was the escalating cost of computer development, because while since 1950 the NRDC and MoS had funded various projects, especially the Mark I, *Pegasus* and *Atlas*, this had by no means covered all the expenditure in this category. Furthermore, reflecting the parsimonious British approach to government funding, the NRDC money came in the form of loans which had to be repaid from sales, rather than from any profits, indicating how the state was not sharing in the risk associated with developing these machines. Indeed, Ferranti regarded the NRDC's role as distinctly unhelpful, especially when combined with its attempt at partnering off the main firms.

With specific regard to NRDC aid, the £300,000 provided by the NRDC for *Atlas*, for example, had been repaid by Ferranti in March 1963, severely affecting the department's financial viability. As Table 9.2 also reveals, while government development funds certainly increased between 1954–55 and 1960–61, internal commitments were much greater in every single year except 1956. Furthermore, when the former stopped once the *Atlas* contract had finished, the latter leapt even more dramatically, reaching almost £1 million in 1962–63. We noted in section 9.8 how while the NRDC had complained about the manner in which Ferranti controlled development expenditure, it is clear from Table 9.2 how from the mid-1950s Pollard and then Hall were in charge of what would appear to have been a rolling snowball. Although information on the first few years of operations is difficult to find, by October 1953 a profit of almost £52,000 had been made on a total turnover of over £501,000,[159] indicating how performance deteriorated badly thereafter. Sales did increase, especially after 1956–57, but as the final column reveals, after 1953–54 there was a substantial cash outflow from the computer department in every year except for 1959–60. In total, the net losses between 1951–52 and 1962–63 amounted to almost £3.5 million.

It is clear from Table 9.2 that the computer department's financial performance was miserable, especially if one takes into consideration the technological lead established by Ferranti with the Mark I and sustained through *Pegasus, Mercury, Sirius, Orion* and *Atlas*. Characteristically, because Ferranti was in at the start of computer development, expenditure on new ideas had to increase, otherwise rivals (especially from the USA) would soon have overtaken West Gorton. While Sebastian de Ferranti said in an interview with the *Sunday Times*: 'We go for the difficult things, where we can build up a technical edge',[160] it is clear that his firm paid a high price for working on the frontiers of computer technology. Ultimately, of course, the huge rise in development expenditure must also contradict any claim that the company was not committed to this business, even if the pioneering instinct failed to provide the basis for a profitable business.

Table 9.2. *The financial performance of the computer department, 1952–1964 (£)*

Year to March	Sales	Government Development Expenditure	In-house Development Expenditure	Profit (Loss)
1952	150,027	NA	NA	27,704
1953	121,445	NA	NA	5,221
1954	315,037	NA	NA	16,707
1955	267,881	33,194	37,018	(18,808)
1956	336,015	51,632	NA	(82,668)
1957	564,279	90,877	122,327	(374,704)
1958	1,077,001	95,718	138,628	(122,936)
1959	1,399,036	142,911	184,741	(163,075)
1960	2,004,007	203,570	274,473	165,162
1961	2,644,779	306,031	541,150	(233,283)
1962	1,976,240	—	597,146	(889,181)
1963	2,412,803	—	987,336	(1,804,241)
1964	5,586,262	—	415,743	766,917

Key: NA: Not available

Source: Ferranti Management Accounts, 1950–63.

In this context, one must note that while the Mark I, Mark I* and *Pegasus* projects were profitable, partly because government support was forthcoming for both their development and production, Ferranti only made a profit on one of its in-house projects, *Mercury*. In contrast, losses on *Perseus, Sirius* and *Orion* by 1962–63 amounted to over £920,000, three-quarters of which was attributable to the latter's production difficulties.[161] Furthermore, losses of nearly £385,000 were made on the NRDC's high-speed computer project, *Atlas*, because while £300,000 of public money was provided for this project, Ferranti actually invested £820,000 and the public money had to be repaid by 1963. Government development funding had also dried up by 1962, leaving the firm to provide all the capital required for new projects. Ferranti was clearly fully committed to the development of civil computers which had only a limited commercial appeal, but the heavy financial commitments created such difficulties that by the early 1960s drastic actions were being considered.

Competition

In addition to these pressing financial problems, another feature of the computer market worried Sir Vincent, namely, the intensifying competition and his company's falling share of British orders. Contemporaries had expressed concern for some years about the highly atomistic British computer industry,[162] because even after the ICT merger in 1958 there were still ten independent firms, as well as three American offshoots and a French subsidiary, competing for what was relatively scarce business. As Table 9.3 reveals, the British firms (apart from Ferranti) were Elliotts, EMI, GEC, ICT, English Electric, Leo, Marconi, STC and AEI, four of which accounted for most of the sales.

Table 9.3. *The share of computer sales in the UK, 1950–59*

	% of total sales
Elliott Brothers	32.4
Ferranti	26.4
Leo Computers	16.5
English Electric	15.5
ICT	7.1
IBM	2.0

Source: Campbell-Kelly (1989), p. 215.

A more detailed analysis of UK computer sales is provided by Hendry,[163] demonstrating that by 1960 no less than twenty-three different types of computer were on sale in Britain. The most popular British ranges were the Ferranti *Pegasus* (with thirty sales), the Elliott 405 (twenty-eight sales) and 803 (twenty-six sales), the ICT 1201 (fifty-one sales), the English Electric *Deuce* (twenty-eight sales), and the STC *Stantec Zebra* (thirty-seven sales). The IBM 650 (ten sales) was the only major foreign competition at that time, indicating how in general the British market was largely self-sufficient.

Although the atomistic structure was clearly causing severe problems by the late 1950s, these were relatively minor when compared to what happened in the early 1960s, when after the launch of several new second generation models the situation changed dramatically. This development would appear to have taken Ferranti by surprise, because having leased one of the four central display areas at the 1961 Computer Exhibition, Peter Hall was embarrassed to see competitors' second generation computers on their stands, while his company's designs still languished either on the drawing board or in the development laboratory.[164] Of crucial importance was foreign competition, because while American manufacturers had sold only a few computers in the UK by 1959, four years later IBM had installed 138 of its 1401 range (only launched in 1959) and a further thirty-three other machines. In total, by 1963 forty-five per cent of the British market had been captured by the Americans.[165] To compound this problem, as we noted earlier, in 1958 the two British office machinery manufacturers, BTM and Powers-Samas, had merged and created ICT, while by 1962 this firm had acquired the computer interests of both GEC and Elliotts,[166] concentrating a considerable proportion of the industry's domestic capacity. Even though Ferranti had developed a range of computers to cater for certain types of mainframe users, Hall realised that it would be increasingly difficult to recoup the substantial development expenditure from increased sales. In fact, by 1963 Ferranti could probably claim no more than ten per cent of annual UK computer sales, most of which (see Table 9.2) was taken at unprofitable prices. Indeed, both the Elliott range and ICT's new 1301 and 1500 computers were achieving sales of at least thirty per year by 1963, compared to a handful of Ferranti machines like *Atlas, Orion* and *Sirius* (see Table 9.1),[167] forcing a radical solution to the top of the agenda.

Merger talks

Ultimately, of course, it was the financial situation which would determine the attitude of Sir Vincent and Sebastian de Ferranti towards computers, because with competition intensifying, losses mounting each year (see Table 9.2), and development costs seemingly out of control, there seemed little chance of building a profitable business. A rational solution to these problems was to follow the GEC/Elliotts example and sell the business to ICT. Indeed, the possibility of a merger between Ferranti and ICT had been discussed several times since the late 1950s. Peter Hall had actually been the main advocate of this solution, having realised that the computer department's product range would not provide the necessary throughput which would recoup the mounting development costs. Late in 1959 he consequently persuaded Sir Vincent to enter into some negotiations with ICT over a possible sale of the West Gorton business, involving Sebastian de Ferranti, who was by then managing director of the firm (see section 11.1). It is vital to note, though, that in protecting his family's significant investment in the West Gorton activity, Sebastian was not going to give in easily to ICT's demands.

The position taken by the de Ferranti family in these negotiations was based on the premise that while ICT had undoubted marketing strengths, their firm's technology was far superior to anything ICT had developed. At the same time, while trying to secure the best price possible for the highly prestigious computer technology, they were also keen to ensure continuity of employment for all West Gorton employees. While Hall was disappointed that Sebastian did not take a more amenable line in the discussions, he was not risking his own money in this affair. Indeed, at the meeting Sebastian was most scathing about the ICT technological base. It was a clash of cultures, between the technology-led Ferranti team and the market-led ICT board, leading to serious disagreements over the way forward. While the ICT directors were also still reticent about giving the Ferranti operation complete access to the ICT marketing and sales base, ultimately this conflict over the relative position of technological prowess brought the discussions to an end, indicating how a merger would have been impossible to negotiate at that time.

Had the Ferranti-ICT meeting been more successful in 1959, then Campbell-Kelly might be correct in claiming that 'the history of the British computer industry would ... have been very different'.[168] Certainly, it would have been a powerful alliance bringing together the best technology in Europe and an extensive commercial network. At the same time, ICT did not provide the kind of safeguards Sebastian had insisted upon as part of the deal. In fact, it was 1961 before a possible merger was discussed again, when a committee composed of Harry Johnson and Frank Keay from Ferranti and P. Ellis and K. Lightstone of ICT actually proposed a rationalisation scheme. The main stumbling block to a merger in 1961, though, was Bernard Swann's advice to the board, because he felt that a more logical move would be to combine the computer department with another electronics firm, rather than allow the office machinery sector to swallow the industry whole.[169] This view was an excellent manifestation of Swann's disdainful attitude towards the ICT sales and marketing organisation (see section 9.6), demonstrating the huge gulf which still existed between the traditional approach taken by Ferranti and the commission-based techniques employed by the aggressive punched-card machinery salesmen. By 1962–63, however, faced with a staggering computer department loss of over £1.8 million (see Table 9.2), Ferranti could no longer delay what in retrospect would appear to have been the inevitable sale to ICT.

Peter Hall has claimed that the merger with ICT arose out of a realisation at Ferranti that 'success in the computer business depended on a marketing operation and a base of data-processing users that Ferranti did not have and ICT did'.[170] Clearly, with regard to the need for a customer base, contemporaries agreed that the company 'lacks the sales organisation to break into the mass market'.[171] Tweedale has also argued that, when compared to the American giant IBM, the Ferranti marketing effort was weak. At IBM, its founder, Thomas Watson, 'endowed marketing with an almost spiritual significance',[172] an approach which had rubbed off on its British counterparts, BTM and Powers-Samas. Of course, one might regard such a comparison as extremely misleading, because IBM, BTM and Powers-Samas were slow to enter the computer market, leaving the development of appropriate circuits and software to other firms. Another point to make, as we have noted earlier, is to ask what else Ferranti could have done to boost its marketing drive in the pioneering period up to 1960. The London Computing Centre was a significant innovation which many of the firm's rivals copied as a means of familiarising customers with the mysterious computer, while Swann and his team of salesmen and programmers worked effectively to help improve the user-friendly nature of the new technology. Notwithstanding these points, above all one must stress the concentration on large, expensive machines which characterised the Ferranti computer effort throughout this period. The whole venture was essentially technology-led, typifying the approach Ferranti adopted in most markets. Moreover, in failing to develop effective product planning for the mass market, the company was saddled with a department which was based on low-volume sales. This was the main reason why Peter Hall encouraged Sebastian de Ferranti to sell West Gorton to ICT, a debate he finally won in 1963 when the new chairman (see section 11.1) decided that serious negotiations should be initiated.

The merger

Having made the decision to sell the computer department, much to Sebastian's annoyance ICT initially proved reluctant to accept the offer. One of the reasons why ICT was actually not too keen on a merger when first approached was board worries over their share price, which at that time was at a very low level after the announcement of a rationalisation programme in the office machinery departments. This had created some concern at board level that they could have paid an inflated price for the Ferranti business, consequently further depressing their share price.[173] In addition, ICT felt that the Ferranti range did not fit neatly into what ICT was building with the 1301, 1500 and Elliott 803. Indeed, even as late as May 1963 ICT was playing down the possibility of a merger, stressing instead how cooperation with Ferranti had increased over the previous few years.[174] This smokescreen hid from prying eyes what was really going on, because behind the scenes Sebastian de Farranti was encouraging Hall to work strenuously to convince ICT of the substantial advantages to be gained from acquiring Ferranti hardware and software technology, not to mention Europe's largest production facility at West Gorton. At the same time, Sebastian de Ferranti was extensively advised on the merger negotiations by the prominent accountant from Cooper Bros., Henry (later Lord) Benson, a factor which proved crucial in persuading ICT to buy the Ferranti mainframe computer department. There was another factor which also convinced ICT of the substantial fillip the acquisition would give to their emerging ranges, a point to which we shall return later. Finally, though, in July 1963 it was announced that West Gorton and its team was being purchased for £8.4 million.[175] The *Economist* described the move as 'a welcome further rationalisation of the still irrational computer industry',[176] reflecting the widespread feeling that such acquisitions should take place if the competition from IBM was to be withstood.

In reviewing this rationalisation exercise, it is vital to emphasise that not for one minute did Ferranti consider selling digital systems at Bracknell. Of course, this could easily be interpreted as Ferranti refusing to allow a highly profitable defence business to fall into the hands of a competitor. On the other hand, Sebastian de Ferranti and Peter Hall deliberately kept Bracknell out of the merger negotiations, because the central strategy was to create a market-led mainframe computer firm which would be more likely to compete with IBM and its counterparts. It was also Hall's particular view that the dominance of engineering interests within digital systems would have 'corrupted' ICT's development.[177] More importantly for Ferranti, though, by offloading the mainframe business for what was generally regarded as a generous price for a loss-making department, Sebastian achieved a significant coup. At the same time, another aim was achieved, because as part of the deal ICT agreed to employ Basil de Ferranti as joint managing director (with specific responsibility for R & D), in order to preserve a Ferranti link with the West Gorton facility. Apart from the logic of this move, it would also have reduced the possibility of fraternal rivalry, because as we shall see later (see section 11.1) by 1963 Sir Vincent had passed the reins of management on to his eldest son, Sebastian, and pushing Basil off to ICT would prevent the possibility of a situation similar to the earlier problems with Denis de Ferranti (see section 8.1).

The FP6000

The ICT deal was undoubtedly a good move for Ferranti in offloading a major loss-maker. In addition, reflecting the family's general approach towards rationalisation (see section 12.1), it also ensured that their employees at West Gorton would have a secure future. For ICT it also brought real benefits, because apart from the advantages stressed by Hall in the negotiations it is important to stress that the purchasers were also attracted by another asset which seemed to promise much for the future. At the time when Hall abandoned Scarrott's neuron device and decided to develop *Sirius*, Bernard Swann was keen to persist with his belief that Ferranti needed a computer which would succeed *Pegasus*. Moreover, he wanted to take more account of the needs of potential customers. West Gorton consequently continued on its path of building up a range of second generation mainframe computers, while Swann commissioned Harry Johnson to draw up a specification which would fulfil his aims.

Once again, though, the north-south conflict within the Ferranti computer department was renewed, because Hall rejected Johnson's proposals, initially code-named *Harriac*, in favour of the commercially disastrous *Sirius* and *Orion* projects. Hall was actually faced with little choice at that time, because his team was already overloaded with existing development work, while Johnson's design simply amounted to a sales specification which would have required considerable development before appearing on the market. At the same time, because Ferranti-Packard (the Canadian subsidiary) was looking for an easy route into the computer industry, its management decided to develop the *Harriac*. It is also important to stress that the Canadian team incorporated the *Argus* logic circuits (see section 10.5) into this blueprint, giving what turned out to be the FP6000 a highly novel architecture. It was launched at the American Spring Joint Computer Conference in July 1963, provoking widespread interest in its possibilities on both sides of the Atlantic.[178] ICT had also been made aware of the FP6000, because Hall took several of its board members to that launch. As a consequence, they insisted that a condition of the West Gorton purchase was the inclusion of rights to develop and produce what was felt to be an excellent specification for small and medium sized computers.

In fact, the acquisition by ICT of the FP6000 technology proved to be even more important than just assisting its work on small computers, because it provided the basis for what was ICT's most successful range of computers, the 1900. The importance of the 1900 range will be examined in section 11.4, when we shall make an overall assessment of Britain's ability to compete in the more advanced areas of the electronics industry. There is no doubt, though, that it was essential in bolstering ICT's struggle to compete with IBM.[179] One of the most momentous computer events of the 1960s was IBM's announcement of its System/360 computers, because having shocked the computing world with its 1401 this new range was seen as a major threat to the British industry's ability to survive. It was this threat which prompted even more mergers among mainframe computer producers, as a result of which by 1968 (see Figure 9.1) there remained only one firm in this field, International Computers Ltd (ICL). Although the creation and fortunes of this enterprise are beyond the brief of this study,[180] it is important to emphasise the ways in which British high technology industries were obliged to respond to the pressures imposed by American competition, in this case resulting in the concentration of all civil mainframe activity in one firm.

Figure 9.1: *Mergers in the British computer industry, 1959–68*

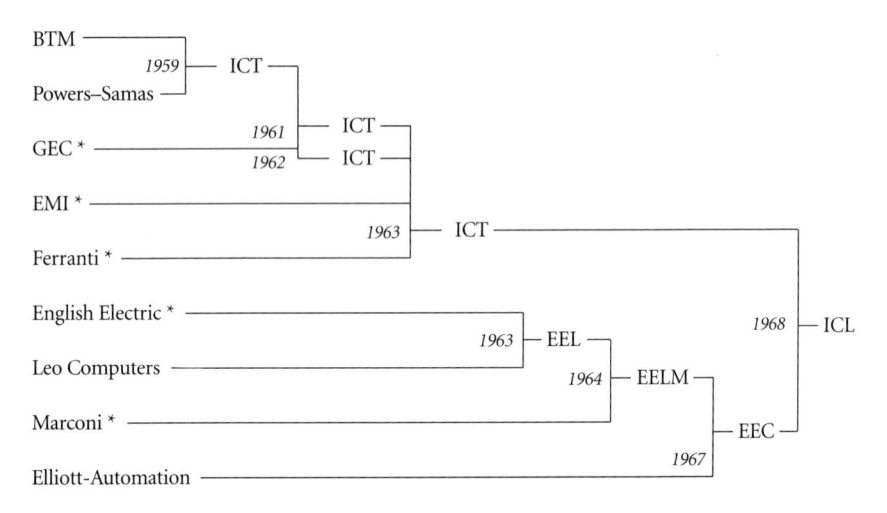

[Diagram showing mergers:
- BTM and Powers-Samas → ICT (1959)
- GEC* joins ICT (1961)
- EMI* joins ICT (1962)
- Ferranti* joins ICT (1963)
- English Electric* and Leo Computers → EEL (1963)
- EEL and Marconi* → EELM (1964)
- EELM and Elliott-Automation → EEC (1967)
- ICT and EEC → ICL (1968)]

Key: * indicates that only the data processing computer departments in these firms were involved in the mergers.

EEL – English Electric Leo
EELM – English Electric-Leo-Marconi
EEC – English Electric Computers

Source: Campbell-Kelly (1989), p. 217.

9.11 Conclusion

Of course, American competition was by no means the only reason why Ferranti had been forced out of the mainframe computer business. The key factors revolved around a combination of internal pressures peculiar to Ferranti, and an external environment which simply did not provide the incentives for firms willing to risk substantial sums on ambitious development programmes. A significant feature of the latter was Halsbury's strategy for the computer industry and the NRDC's paltry level of funding, neither of which failed to deal effectively with the problems associated with building a competitive range of products, especially when contrasted to the American government's efforts in this field. A related point is the high rate of technological obsolescence which characterises computer development, forcing firms to commit substantial financial and personnel resources to research and development. As Ferranti was unable to sell enough computers to cover these costs, as well as those relating to production and selling, this forced senior management to think about selling the business. Compounding the governmental and financial pressures was the highly conservative British market, because even though Bowden and Swann built up imaginative marketing campaigns, using what was a unique computing centre, customers were slow to appear in significant numbers. On the other hand, as we have continually emphasised, one must also stress how the emphasis on large, scientific computers, and a neglect of the high-volume data processing market, prevented Ferranti from building up a business which would recoup the rising development costs. This approach was one of the main reasons why most of the sales went to either scientific bodies or aircraft companies engaged in the production of military aircraft (see Table 9.1). While designs like *Orion* and *Atlas* might well have brought Ferranti great prestige, they were distinctly unprofitable.

The computer department is consequently an excellent example of the Ferranti technology-led strategy in action, because the firm focused on work which was exciting and prestigious, yet commercially disastrous. Of course, as Lavington has observed, 'the "computerised society" did not get under way in Britain until about 1966',[181] emphasising how Ferranti was in at the industry's very beginning when demand was slow to emerge. On the other hand, as early as 1954 the market for computers in the USA was described as 'tremendous',[182] providing a substantial incentive for American computer firms and giving them a distinct competitive advantage when demand started to grow in the UK. It is interesting to see that, as a result of this competitive advantage, by 1967 IBM had installed in the UK almost 300 of its 1401 computers and over 400 of the System/360, while Honeywell, Digital and Burroughs were also selling in significant numbers.[183] This is in stark contrast to the level of demand pertaining up to 1960 in Britain, when Ferranti was trying to stimulate interest in its range of scientific computers. Clearly, such crucial comparisons determined the West Gorton department's fortunes. Crucially, though, unlike both ICT in the UK and IBM across the Atlantic, Ferranti did not possess an established customer base of data-processing users, and it is perhaps no coincidence that the more profitable computer producers of the 1960s were those which were able to convert this base to the new technology.

The computer story as a whole reveals the innate possibilities within the Ferranti structure, because from a tiny base Eric Grundy had been able to establish the foundations of a business which within ten years had become one of the company's flagships. In this context, one must stress that Tweedale is incorrect in claiming 'that Ferranti got the computer business it wanted – a profitable niche in the defence market'.[184] As Table 9.2 illustrates, a considerable amount of capital was invested in the development of civil computers right up to the sale of West Gorton to ICT. Similarly, while Halsbury might well have described the NRDC's relationship with Ferranti as 'Pushing Mules Uphill', Hendry also admits that Sir Vincent was right to protect his firm's interests.[185] In any case, while a commercial company usually has a better perspective on what type of products ought to be developed, Ferranti financial contributions to computer development far exceeded those of the NRDC and MoS. Clearly, Ferranti persevered with the computer business for as long as commercially possible, reflecting the firm's commitment to advancing the frontiers of technology. While it ended up with a defence computer business, this was certainly not the original aim in the late 1940s, nor an aim during the 1950s. Ultimately, it was the market which determined the fortunes of the Ferranti mainframe computer business. Clearly, while several internal problems hindered progress at various junctures, the very fact that all but ICT had pulled out of computer production by 1968 demonstrates that the external environment was far more significant.

10

Bloodhound and Wythenshawe

Although the mainframe computer business had been sold off by 1963, it is important to remember that the West Gorton and Bracknell businesses were not the only instances of how Ferranti ventured into designing and producing computers. In fact, as a result of a guided weapon development contract, another department had by 1960 become a pioneer in this field, developing one of the earliest and most successful British 'minicomputers' which further enhanced the Ferranti reputation in this sector.[1] Indeed, as a result of close cooperation with the Bristol Airplane Co. and several defence research establishments, Ferranti was also associated with the period's most successful guided weapons project. This was significant in itself, reinforcing the firm's position as one of the UK's most reliable defence contractors. At the same time, some of the guided weapons engineers exploited their expertise in automation equipment to diversify into the production of process control computers, or 'minicomputers'. Moreover, this adventure resulted in exactly the opposite outcome to the computer department: while the loss-making West Gorton facility was sold off to ICT and the profitable Bracknell defence business was retained, in this chapter we shall see how the guided weapons department was wound down, while by the 1960s process control computers had become a major spin-off.

The Ferranti guided weapon story is one of the most outstanding British examples of a civil product originating from a defence project. However, before any clear conclusions can be drawn about the firm's ability to make this kind of move, one must remember that, after an alleged excess profit had been discovered, a major political scandal forced Ferranti out of the guided weapons market. In this context, it is important to emphasise certain key points about the whole story which provide greater balance to the analysis. Firstly, Ferranti and the Bristol Airplane Co. developed and produced a guided weapon which was not only delivered on time at the contract price, but also one which remained in service for over thirty years. It was the contracting system itself which was widely regarded to have been at fault, as many contemporaries accepted. Crucially, it was later revealed that Ferranti had never done anything improper.[2] Secondly, one must remember that ever since the late 1930s, when Ferranti had been obliged to take a heavy loss on an Admiralty fuze contract (see section 7.4), Sir Vincent had always insisted that the state should provide most of the funds for developing and making the products it required, an attitude his son continued to pursue when he became chairman in 1963. Thirdly, while with the benefit of hindsight some have argued that the firm ought to have negotiated a deal with the Ministry before the politicians and journalists were able to exploit the discovery of an alleged excess profit, the extensive soundings taken by Sebastian de Ferranti from some of the country's finest legal minds confirmed the young chairman's view that the state had no legal redress on a contract negotiated according to conventional standards. Indeed, as the family was convinced that a contract could only be interpreted according to strict legal criteria, Sebastian was encouraged by his legal advisors to fight on against politicians and civil servants who seemed to be changing the rules midway through the game.

Of course, the family discovered that as soon as politicians entered the debate this position became untenable, leading to some highly dubious attacks on the firm. In the build-up to a forthcoming General Election, Ferranti also fell victim to a revived Labour Party which saw the revelations as another stick with which to beat the struggling Conservative government. Above all, though, one must remember that Ferranti exceeded the contractors' initial hopes, while in establishing the foundations of another computer business the firm initiated a venture in Wythenshawe which was to flourish long after the political debate had been forgotten.

10.1 The first guided weapons contract

Although there had been some work on guided weapons prior to World War II, it was only in the 1940s that governments and engineers turned their attentions to what thereafter became one of the major foci of military (and later, space) activity. The most important work, of course, was in Germany, where a team led by Wernher von Braun developed the infamous V2 rocket as part of Hitler's forlorn attempt at panicking British citizens into defeat.[3] Allied efforts in this field were still halfhearted during the early 1940s. While in 1944 Cossors was commissioned by Anti-Aircraft Command to start work on what was codenamed *Brakemine*, little came of this project. The main reason for this apathetic approach was the attitude of Lord Cherwell, Winston Churchill's wartime scientific advisor, whose belief that guided weapons would never provide a reliable defence prevented the government research establishments from committing more resources to what the Germans felt was a potentially fruitful field of scientific endeavour. Cherwell's opposition to guided weapons also explains why in 1945 Britain did not object to the

Russians and Americans recruiting von Braun and the German team for their work on guided weapons. Although the German engineers did actually visit Britain in 1946, they soon returned to the USA after realising that little support was forthcoming for their projects. Another problem was the RAF, because this service had initiated work on the V-bomber projects – the Vickers *Valiant*, the Avro *Vulcan*, and the Handley-Page *Victor* – leaving little money for the expensive ideas of von Braun.

The British approach towards guided weaponry up to the mid-1940s has been described as 'a failure of imagination',[4] giving the Americans and Russians the opportunity to take the best talent. In fact, the only agency willing to commit some effort to this field was the Royal Aircraft Establishment (RAE), at Farnborough, where Morien Morgan fought for two years between 1945 and 1947 to establish a team of guided weapons scientists and engineers.[5] At the same time, in spite of the RAF's antipathy, by 1948 the Army and Navy were beginning to show some interest, resulting in commissions for, respectively, English Electric to work on *Red Heathen*, while a syndicate composed of Armstrong-Whitworth, GEC and Sperry had started *Seaslug*. Armstrong-Whitworth had actually asked Ferranti to join the project before recruiting GEC. However, after some preliminary discussions Sir Vincent was informed by his chief radio engineer, Dr Norman Searby, that the two companies were unlikely to work together in complete harmony.[6] At the same time, Dr Searby was keen to enter this field, encouraging his chairman to maintain contact with the firms and government establishments which were beginning to spend more money on guided weapons.

Lockspeiser and Job No. 2220

In spite of this commitment to the new technology, there was some concern at Ferranti by the beginning of 1948 that after the early negotiations with Armstrong-Whitworth the firm was being ignored. Sir Vincent responded to this possibility in the spring of 1948 by pursuing a much more pro-active strategy of developing contacts with people and agencies working in this potentially fruitful technology. This activity took him to a conference organised by the RAE, where he met Sir Reginald Verdon-Smith, chairman of another firm ready to begin guided weapon development, the Bristol Airplane Co. It is also important to note at this stage that, as with developments in computing (see sections 9.1 and 9.2), senior MoS officials like Sir Ben Lockspeiser were anxious to disseminate the fruits of research in agencies like the RAE to firms willing to act as partners in the production of new, high-technology goods. In this context, it was George Gardner of MoS who acted as intermediary in the following discussions between Ferranti and

Bristol. This consequently brought together two firms who over the following seventeen years were responsible for the most successful guided weapon project of its era.

Having met at the RAE conference in the spring of 1948, Ferranti and Bristol spent several months in what can only be described as a period of courtship, during which Sir Vincent and Sir Reginald attempted to discover whether they could trust each other.[7] It is important to stress how, like Ferranti, Bristol was also a family firm, Sir Reginald being the great-nephew of George White, the man who had established the enterprise in 1910. This provided a degree of commonality which encouraged the two chairman to trust each other. The preliminary meeting took the form of a dinner in Manchester, at which the two firms 'circled suspiciously around each other and each came somewhat reluctantly to the conclusion that the other was perhaps fairly all right – with a few reservations'.[8] Unfortunately, though, because funds were difficult to raise, it was March 1949 before George Gardner was able to place a formal contract with Ferranti, when he approached W. G. Bass in the company's London office with an offer 'to investigate the guidance and control problems associated with [an RAE] project'.[9]

In fact, Bristol would be the prime contractor for Job No. 2220, codenamed *Red Duster*, as well as designer of an airframe and propulsion system for the supersonic missile, while Ferranti was asked to work under contract to the MoS on what were called 'robot-systems for guiding anti-aircraft rockets'.[10] The nature of this contract will be examined in section 10.6, but it is important to stress that development funding was based on cost-plus, and the original estimate for this stage was £1.5 million. As we shall see later, though, both of these features were to change dramatically by the time production was being considered.

The Ferranti team

Guided weaponry is yet another example of how in the late 1940s Sir Ben Lockspeiser (chief scientist at MoS) was able to develop effective partnerships between science and industry (see section 9.2). The contract negotiated in March 1949 actually stipulated that a team of Ferranti engineers would spend six months travelling around various government research establishments investigating the progress made on new guidance systems, indicating how the firm was to benefit enormously from Lockspeiser's strategy. In effect, this provided access to the most advanced theoretical and experimental work in the country, especially in relation to the centimetric technology developed during the war. Fundamental to the success of radar over the previous decade had been the development of high-powered, high frequency valves which

Denis Best, the man responsible for the technical success of Bloodhound, with another of his prodigies, the Argus 200 (production model). *(Museum of Science and Industry at Manchester.)*

were able to transmit pulses of electromagnetic waves capable of discriminating between objects. This had led to what was known as the 'Centimetric Revolution' (see section 7.5), providing the basic technology for the guided weapon experiments of the late 1940s.[11]

As Dr Searby had been involved in both of the major Ferranti contributions to this programme, after a succession of interviews he finally convinced Sir Vincent in March 1949 that he would make an effective head of guided weapon development. Furthermore, because the Ferranti radio department was struggling to lever itself out of the late 1940s difficulties (see section 8.2), Dr Searby as chief radio engineer was virtually redundant. Even though in 1948 his manager, F. C. Aitken, had been reluctant to let him work any closer on the University of Manchester computer project (see section 9.2), by the spring of 1949 Sir Vincent had intervened to appoint him as guided weapons team leader. One should also mention in this context Denis Best, because while Dr Searby headed the team, it was Best who was brought in to supervise much of the technical development, providing decisive leadership at crucial stages of the project.

Dr N. H. Searby (right) and R. C. Grove (centre), two of the men principally responsible for the *Bloodhound* success, with D. Roth (left), in the Wythenshawe workshops. *(Museum of Science and Industry at Manchester.)*

Dr Searby and Denis Best started work in May 1949. Their first task was to recruit R. Evans (gyroscopes) and H. Nelson (fire control) for their specific expertise, after which they all set off on a three week tour of the RAE and RRE facilities. Their principal aim was to investigate the work of, respectively, Morien Morgan and R. Lees,[12] who had been instructed by MoS to give Ferranti free access to their research. Dr Searby was even briefed by G. L. Hutchinson, the team leader at RAE working with English Electric on *Red Heathen*. At the same time, Bristol had also gathered together a guided weapons team, the head of which was David Farrar, a man described by his Cambridge University tutor as one of the most brilliant engineers of his generation.[13] This team has passed into that company's folklore as 'The Fortyniners', commemorating the year in which they came together. Given the novelty of their responsibilities in an aircraft manufacturer, they were able to develop a 'pioneering fervour [and a] swashbuckling approach' which provided dynamic leadership to Job No. 2220.[14]

Working closely with Dr Searby and Denis Best, by November 1949 the

Bristol-Ferranti syndicate had drafted a proposal to design and produce a guided weapon which MoS accepted within a matter of weeks. One must remember that the stirrings of what became the Cold War created a strong sense of urgency in government thinking at that time. As Adams also reports, once the Korean War had started in June 1950: 'The Ministry [of Supply] never stopped reminding their contractors that they had to build up their organisations very fast, so that the R & D programmes could be speeded up, and the projects got into production at the very earliest possible date'.[15] As Job No. 2220 was a specification for a surface-to-air supersonic missile, the Bristol-Ferranti partnership was under constant pressure to improve the Army's anti-aircraft facilities.

10.2 Early progress and trials

Work on *Red Duster* started as soon as MoS had agreed to fund the Ferranti-Bristol proposal. Before progress could be made, however, it was necessary to settle on a single design, forcing the two teams to coordinate activity very closely, resulting in the creation of a joint working party which deliberated on this challenge for almost exactly a year.[16] They finally decided to build what David Farrar described (in engineers' speak) as a 'ram-jet engined, semi-active pulse [radar] homing-all-the-way, twist-and-steer missile with moving monoplane wings'.[17] In simple terms, this means that *Red Duster* was based on the semi-active homing principle, by which a target is located by long-range radar, information on which is fed by a computer to another radar set which projects a beam towards the target and at the same time controls the bearing of the missile launcher. In flight, signals relfected from the target are received by the missile, which senses their direction and homes itself on the target. However, what in theory sounded in 1949 like a sound idea had yet to be converted into practical results, providing a challenge which the engineering teams took up with relish.

While the ram-jet engine was developed by Bristol, largely using expertise provided by the American aircraft manufacturer Boeing, all the other features of the system had to be designed and tested using what either of the companies possessed. Initially, this resulted in excessive duplication of effort, especially of the guidance systems for use in the testing process. Only once Denis Best had visited Bristol, to demand that such work should be immediately terminated, did this problem begin to diminish. This reflected the quiet authority Best imposed on the two teams, creating at an early stage in the project a harmonious relationship which would be crucial to its success. Even though his Bristol counterpart, Don Rowley, felt that 'there were stresses and strains at some level or another practically all the time', generally he concluded that the 'Bristol-Ferranti interface worked very well', largely as a result of Best's clear thinking.[18]

Early testing

Early testing of *Red Duster* was actually one of the main bones of contention between the two firms, because while Bristol started work on guidance systems Ferranti had also employed its own aerodynamicist to help design their own vehicles. In fact, Bristol had been slow to develop their own test vehicle, the JTV, produced in association with Boeing. Consequently, Denis Best decided to use an RAE prototype, the CCTV–4, measuring just five feet in length. Although this angered his southern partners considerably, by making this breakthrough he was able to conduct preliminary testing on the guidance and control systems as early as March 1950. Most importantly, such was the success of Denis Best's work on this equipment that considerable early progress was made in developing the twist-and-steer system for which *Red Duster* became famous.[19]

This 'twist-and-steer' system might more accurately be referred to as 'roll-and-pitch', because the missile rolled by tilting its wings in opposite directions, and pitched by tilting them in the same direction. Some of the RAE staff had been sceptical about the use of 'twist-and-steer', especially when at first substantial problems were experienced at the interception point, when misses of up to forty feet were frequently reported. Nevertheless, through meticulous experimentation the cynics were proven wrong and *Red Duster* became a great success. The solution developed by Best's team was produced after a three-dimensional simulator was constructed to test out the missile's geometry. This work resulted in the installation of a large capacitor to slow the pitch demand rate, allowing the missile to complete a roll manoeuvre before it started pitching. In testing, of the fifty-nine rounds fired, eighty per cent passed within forty feet of the target's centre of gravity, convincing the RAE experts that Ferranti was close to solving the problem.

It is interesting to note that much of this testing was conducted at the RAE's Aberrporth range. In charge of the Ferranti team was R. (Bob) Grove, a former Royal Navy chief petty officer whose organisational skills provided the necessary leadership at a crucial time in the project. Aberrporth, however, provided only limited facilities for the *Red Duster* trials, partly because it was difficult to photograph the missile's flight over Cardigan Bay, and partly because it was impossible to retrieve anything after a test. These problems forced the team to look for an alternative site, especially as by 1957, as we shall see later, two types of missile were being tested. It was consequently fortunate to acquire the Woomera testing facilities owned by the Weapons Research Establishment 300 miles from Adelaide, Australia, where by 1958 all of the Ferranti test engineers had been moved. By that time, Alan Bell had been made chief engineer (trials), after Bob Grove was asked to take charge of production at Moston. Among those who first worked for Ferranti on this job were Albert Dodd, who under the tutelage of Denis Best and Alan Bell developed into a highly effective engineer who would later become a leading member of the senior management team. Dodd's role was to inform Denis Best about any problems the missile experienced in flight, having been instructed by his boss that he did not want to hear from the Bristol team about any Ferranti weaknesses.

Electronic componentry

While the testing procedures provided a major challenge to Denis Best and his team, another crucial feature arising out of the early 1950s trials was the development of more effective electronic components. Ferranti started working on second generation electronic components like transistors and diodes as a separate development project in the electronics department, as we shall see in section 11.2. It was these devices which would later provide the basis for some pioneering achievements with the Mark II version of *Red Duster*. In the first Mark, however, because first generation valves were employed, the initial task was to replace the standard miniature valves with a more effective variant. It was soon discovered that in flight high acceleration and vibration forces distorted the fine wire grids within miniature valves, thereby changing their characteristics and preventing the guidance and control systems from operating effectively. Dr Searby consequently presented this problem to one of the leading valve producers, Mullards.[20] Unfortunately, though, once the newly-designed valves went into production a problem known as 'linting' occurred, in which fibrous, carbonised dust particles picked up from the manufacturing process bridged the inter-grid spacings of just a few thousandths of an inch. Mullards eventually overcame this difficulty, though, producing lint-free, reliable sub-miniature valves which proved vital to the success of *Red Duster* when fitted into specially developed Ferranti circuit boards

While this work was progressing on what eventually resulted in a Mark I version of *Red Duster*, it is important to emphasise how at exactly the same time Ferranti engineers had started certain experiments, the results of which would later be incorporated into a Mark II. One of the more notable aspects of this work was the development of continuous-wave transmitters, the perfection of which was dependent on the support provided by R. Lees of

RRE. *Red Duster* Mark I actually used pulse radar guidance, which at that time was regarded as adequate for contemporary anti-aircraft requirements. However, as continuous-wave radar provided a much more sophisticated means of tracking the supersonic aircraft which were being produced by the mid-1950s, MoS was keen to encourage Ferranti to cooperate with Lees on his ideas as early as 1951.[21] Furthermore, because D. W. Fry at the TRE was working on a linear magnetron which would overcome the limitations of more conventional transmitters, and Dr Searby had worked with this scientist on the ASV project during the war (see section 7.5), Ferranti were able to secure access to expertise on the crucial aspects of this system.[22]

To expedite work on the linear magnetron, Dr Searby invited Peter Hall to set up a development team at Moston. Hall was not only a talented electronics engineer, he had also previously worked on government development projects, giving him a good insight into how best to coordinate the Ferranti and TRE teams.[23] Hall was also responsible for recruiting as his assistant John Pickin, a Cambridge physics graduate who was then employed in the BT-H valve department. Unfortunately, though, while these two men contributed extensively to various Ferranti activities over the following decades, they could not persuade Fry's magnetron to generate enough power for the continuous-wave radar. Instead, Hall turned his attentions to a klystron valve which was being developed at GEC's central laboratory in Wembley. This work was clearly successful, because by April 1952 the Royal Navy Scientific Service was promising further support for klystron and magnetron development, their agent having reported that he was 'particularly impressed by [the Ferranti] team working on microwave amplifiers'.[24] By 1959, indeed, such had been the progress in this field that even American corporations were buying licences to use Ferranti technology.[25] This indicates how the *Red Duster* contract was responsible for initiating and supporting several important electronics projects, putting Ferranti in the vanguard of an exciting new technology.

10.3 The move to Wythenshawe

Ferranti had consequently acquired an interest in what was a major growth area for electronics manufacturers in the 1950s, particularly as MoS was anxious to push forward the development programmes so essential to successful production. At the same time, Dr Searby wasted no time in building up a series of interdependent teams, adapting part of the underused Moston factory to house the laboratories. By the summer of 1950, sixty-two people were working on *Red Duster* development, as well as a further forty-seven

The Ferranti Wythenshawe facility. The laboratories are on the right and the production operations were carried out in the buildings on the left.
(Museum of Science and Industry at Manchester.)

in an adjoining workshop and eighteen in a dedicated drawing-office. Moston, however, proved to be a poor base for this project, partly because the factory did not possess the right facilities, and partly because scientists and graduates were reluctant to move into an environment which compared badly to other parts of the country.[26] Of course, until the 1940s, the second factor had not stopped Ferranti building up a business based on advanced technology. In the post-War years of full employment, though, it was increasingly necessary to offer employees an attractive environment in which to work, especially those highly qualified people who were in great demand at laboratories in the south of England. It was a problem which had also certainly affected the computer department (see section 9.4), forcing Sir Vincent to accept Dr Searby's pleas for a new location.

When faced with these problems, it is important to note that Dr Searby was actually reluctant to move away from Manchester just to serve this purpose. In lobbying MoS for funds to build a new facility, Sir Vincent was consequently advised to relocate guided weapons development to a thirty-six acre plot in Wythenshawe, to the south of Manchester. Wythenshawe was one of the newly-planned 'garden cities' of the 1950s, designed to provide people with an attractive alternative to the grimy environment nearer the centre. An added feature of this area was immediate access to Ringway (now Manchester International) airport, facilitating transport to the research establishments in the south at a time when motorways and faster, more reliable cars were not yet available. These advantages convinced Sir Vincent that Wythenshawe had much to offer as a base for high-technology industries, resulting in a bid for £310,000 to build a showpiece facility there.[27] It was just at that time, arising out of Britain's commitment to fight in the Korean War, that MoS was encouraging Bristol to spend more money on GW development.[28] By 1952, the MoS had also informed Ferranti that the government had given aircraft and GW projects 'Super Priority'.[29] This encouraged Sir Vincent to increase his bid for funds to almost £1.3 million, a request which was accepted in its entirety.

Building design

While the move to Wythenshawe is interesting in itself, another vital point to make about the building work was how the architects, Cruikshank & Seward, were given clear instructions about the layout to be followed. Work on designing the Wythenshawe factory started in October 1950, when the architects were informed by Dr Searby that complete functional efficiency in the laboratories should be their first priority.[30] In the first place, a central workshop was built, in order that the engineers could have all their models and prototypes produced by a local team of skilled workers. More importantly, each wing of the six laboratory blocks was to be composed of six sections, each of which would have adequate space for five engineers. These sections were allocated their own laboratory and office facilities, but a common coffee room would also be located on each wing as a means of providing an opportunity for engineers to discuss mutual problems. The wings of each building were controlled by group leaders, who in turn reported on progress to the chief engineer (Denis Best) at monthly progress meetings, giving senior management the opportunity to monitor and direct activity across the organisation. It was a layout which also proved to be a great success, both in encouraging small group work and effective communication through informal and formal channels.

It was symptomatic of the much higher priority given to GW by the early 1950s that almost £1.3 million was spent on building and equipping the Wythenshawe laboratories. As W. H. Wheeler (director of GW research and development at MoS) said just before the official opening: 'Nobody has been able to forecast whether the Ministry's first reaction will be shock at our extravagance, or gratification at the vision and foresight of the department'.[31] Certainly, one can say that by 1954 Ferranti possessed one of the most advanced laboratories in Europe. Even though one might argue that the facility had been built as a showpiece to impress the Americans, it also served to convince potential customers that Britain was serious about GW. By that time, Ferranti employed 165 laboratory workers, as well as forty-four in the drawing office and another 275 engineers in the workshop. With specific regard to the workshop, it is interesting to note that Dr Searby had recognised the potential difficulties of persuading all the Moston staff to move across the city, especially in a period of full employment. Consequently, an apprentice school was established at Wythenshawe, giving his team a steady supply of skilled workers. When Duncan Sandys, the Minister of Supply, officially opened the laboratories in June 1954, Ferranti was ready to escalate GW activity.

10.4 Into production of Mark I

From Red Duster to Bloodhound

There seems little doubt that, in contrast to wartime conservatism, by the early 1950s Britain had developed a much more professional approach towards GW. In spite of the considerable expenditure, though, there was still little to demonstrate that the projects had been worthwhile. For example, while Wythenshawe was a first-class acquisition for Ferranti, it had been built at a cost of £1.3 million. Furthermore, by 1954 MoS had paid out a further £1.62 million on *Red Duster* development at Moston.[32] This scale of expenditure is a clear reflection of MoS's commitment to GW in the early 1950s. At the same time, it was politically necessary for them to demonstrate some practical results, especially as the potential customer had changed. Although *Red Duster* had initially been seen as an anti-aircraft weapon, responsibility for this role passed from the Army to the RAF in 1954, forcing MoS to redirect its selling efforts for what had by then been renamed *Bloodhound* at a crucial time in the project's history.

The main problem with this transfer of authority for anti-aircraft operations was that, as we noted in section 10.1, since 1945 the RAF had been more interested in manned-flight, spending most of its budget on a series of bomber projects. Certainly, by the mid-1950s GW was regarded more favourably. However, the RAF was more demanding as a customer and the Bristol-Ferranti syndicate had to tread carefully if they were to win any production contracts. There was some debate within the firms over whether to delay submitting a tender until the more advanced work had been completed. On the other hand, there was an urgent need to impress the RAF with evidence that public money was being used effectively. Consequently, a Mark I version of *Bloodhound* was proposed. The RAF was evidently satisfied with this tender, because by the Spring of 1955 a firm order had been placed, substantiating the faith placed in the two development teams by their respective senior managers.[33]

While the financial details of the Mark I contracts will feature prominently in section 10.6, one might note that as a result of increased worries over the spiralling costs of guided weapon development the MoA insisted on a fixed price, while both parties agreed to delay estimating costs until production had begun. More importantly, there is no doubt that for Dr Searby and Denis Best this order was a further vote of confidence in Wythenshawe's progress as a high technology development centre. Production, however, posed a fresh set of problems, especially as Wythenshawe did not have the capacity to undertake this function. Dr Searby was consequently obliged to consider alternative premises. In fact, he actually rejected as unsuitable the West Gorton factory eventually chosen for mainframe computer production (see section 9.4). Instead, he was persuaded by Eric Grundy's claims that the spare capacity at Moston would prove suitable. As we saw in section 8.4, arising out of the commercial difficulties experienced in the consumer goods departments like radio, television and domestic appliances, Moston experienced a period of severe retrenchment during the mid-1950s. Unfortunately, though, the transition was not effected immediately, partly because it was difficult to find purchasers for the consumer goods departments at a time

Final Assembly Test on the Bloodhound radar system Wythenshawe.
(*Museum of Science and Industry at Manchester.*)

when the government had implemented a series of severe deflationary measures. At the same time, because they were still unsure about the potential in these weapons, the RAF had only placed a small order for Mark I, giving Grundy little incentive to clear Moston quickly. Indeed, it was early 1957 before radio and television production was terminated,[34] at which time even larger *Bloodhound* contracts were being promised by MoS after exhaustive trials had proved a great success.

Production contracts

1957 was a momentous year for both Ferranti and the RAF. In the latter's case, the 1957 Defence White Paper placed a much higher priority on GW, forcing them to concentrate attention on projects like *Bloodhound*.[35] In the case of Ferranti, it marked the complete rationalisation of its Moston businesses (see section 8.4). The flight trials of *Bloodhound* at Aberporth and at Woomera had been so well organised that the RAF found it difficult to resist ordering the weapon, especially as the Ministry of Aviation was beginning to think about ending manned flight. There had been the odd mishap during these trials, for example when one missile executed an inverted loop and returned to Aberporth, instead of travelling out to sea.[36] However, in general *Bloodhound* worked extremely well in these tests, flying as high as 53,000 feet without any loss of homing accuracy. This achievement prompted MoS to place an even bigger order on behalf of the RAF on 14 September 1956, for 576 missiles and associated equipment.[37] The first *Bloodhound* Mark I was actually installed in October 1958, at the North Coates RAF station, following which over the next three years all the remaining missiles were delivered on time. Prior to this successful completion, though, Ferranti had been forced to think more seriously about production and its organisational and financial implications, precipitating a major rationalisation of activity at Moston.

Of particular importance to the future development of the GW business in the mid-1950s was the firm's ability to finance production, because at that time Ferranti was beginning to be pressured by the Westminster Bank to take some hard decisions about its increasing overdraft. These discussions are reviewed in section 8.4, where it was revealed that as a direct result of the overdraft's rise to almost £4.4 million by 1956, a series of meetings between Sir Vincent and senior Bank officials were convened. Although discussions with the Bank about expanding the GW department had actually started in May 1955,[38] by that time no substantial orders had been placed by MoS, providing little hope that Ferranti would be able to cut its losses on the ailing Moston departments.

The main bone of contention, of course, was the need to close down the struggling consumer goods departments at Moston, but as we noted in section 8.4 this had been dragged out, because Ferranti had not been able to find firms who would purchase the businesses. It is also important to remember that while MoS had paid for the GW development programme, Ferranti had made a return of just four per cent on the total output of this business, at a time when the capital employed at Wythenshawe had grown to over £1 million and interest rates were rising to over five per cent.[39] By September 1956, however, not only had satisfactory arrangements been made to reduce activity drastically in consumer goods production, substantial MoS orders for *Bloodhound* had been placed, calming fears about the increasing overdraft. Indeed, when Sir Vincent met the Bank's officials in October 1956 he took along MoS representatives,[40] following which Ferranti was given access to all the short-term funds it required to effect the change-over.

It was consequently in 1957 that Ferranti concentrated its activities almost exclusively on capital equipment goods and electronic components, having closed the radio and television departments at Moston and sold its patents and stock to a series of rivals. Ferranti could even be described as the electronics industry in microcosm, because by 1957 production of first generation electronic components had finished at Gem Mill and second generation products were taking their place. This further confirms our earlier point about the importance of 1957 in Ferranti history. A year later, the third generation Ferranti had also taken over as the firm's managing director, when after Sir Vincent retired from the post his fellow-directors appointed Sebastian to this onerous position. These were truly momentous times for an expanding company. Moreover, in acquiring the *Bloodhound* contracts Ferranti was provided with the opportunity to improve its prospects, financially and technically, at a time when in other parts of the electronics industry firms were beginning to feel the cold chill of foreign competition sweeping through their markets.

10.5 Progress to Bloodhound Mark II

Completing Mark I

Acquiring the Moston production base was a major move for Dr Searby's expanding department, providing all the space necessary for what was by September 1957 a major contract to complete the Mark I stage. As Bob Grove was placed in charge of assembling these highly advanced missiles, such was the pace at which he managed to keep the department working that delivery times were markedly reduced. Indeed, *Bloodhound* Mark I was unique among

British guided missiles of that era, because it was produced to budget and delivered on time. This contrasted sharply with its counterparts, the English Electric *Thunderbird* and De Havilland *Firestreak*. It was also an achievement which said much for both the design and engineering work of Denis Best's team, as well as the drive and organisational skills of Bob Grove. Furthermore, in spite of intense competition from the American *Hawk* (produced by Raytheon), export orders for *Bloodhound* worth almost £2.6 million had been achieved by the Bristol-Ferranti syndicate by 1962. It is interesting to stress how the countries which bought this missile system, Sweden, Australia and Switzerland, had the political independence and technical ability to evaluate the different merits of the two products. In choosing *Bloodhound* they confirmed the syndicate's engineering achievement, because as Dr Searby rightly claimed, *Bloodhound* was far superior to the *Hawk*.[41] To substantiate this, *Flight* noticed how the overseas governments still bought British, even though Bristol-Ferranti did not 'offer weapons on the "give-away" terms offered by the Americans'.[42]

Obsolescence and challenge

As Adams has noted of GW, though, 'what is, is obsolete'.[43] Although substantial contracts had been secured for the Mark I, both Bristol and Ferranti were anxious that the preliminary development work already done on a possible Mark II should not be wasted. In the mid-1950s, MoS had also been considering the paths to be followed by the two main teams at English Electric and Bristol-Ferranti, in the hope that missiles could be developed with a longer range, greater altitude and better performance. Consequently, in a scheme known as the 'Vulgar Fractions' project, English Electric was asked to take on Stage 1.5 of the *Thunderbird* programme, while Bristol-Ferranti was charged with the task of producing a Stage 1.75, known as *Blue Envoy*. Unfortunately, though, in that year's defence spending review, *Blue Envoy* was cancelled, while it was 1967 before the English Electric product was commissioned. The Bristol-Ferranti syndicate was not, however, deterred by this decision, particularly as Maurice Gribble at Wythenshawe had developed some highly effective transistorised digital circuits for *Blue Envoy* which were later to form the basis of the next generation of control computers. Dr Searby, in particular, negotiated vigorously with MoS to finance what by that time had been code-named *Bloodhound* Mark II. This new project had allegedly been 'invented in a taxi outside Ferranti, by David Farrar, Taffy Higginson, and Don Rowley', all of Bristol. However, it was Dr Searby who argued the case before MoS officials, presenting such a powerful case that another development contract was secured.[44]

Full-scale trials of the Mark II missile did not start until the end of 1960. By October 1961, however, not only had production orders been placed, for delivery between Autumn 1962 and Spring 1963, export orders to Sweden and Switzerland had also been achieved. These successes reflected the superiority of *Bloodhound* Mark II over both its domestic rivals and the American competition, helping to suppress any talk at that time of the British government buying such advanced equipment from abroad. In fact, fulfilling the MoS's initial expectations, the Mark II provided four times the range of its earlier version, a thirty-five per cent increase in speed, and much greater operational altitudes.[45] Mark II was also a mobile weapon system, as opposed to the static nature of Mark I, giving it a competitive edge particularly in export markets. Furthermore, the Wythenshawe engineers were assisted by other parts of Ferranti, because the new homing head and guidance receiver, code-named *Indigo Corkscrew*, was developed by Crewe Toll's J. Stewart from the earlier continuous wave radar work of R. Lees at RRE. The remainder, though, was developed at Wythenshawe, and there was little doubt at either the RAF or MoS that this provided a significant advantage over the old system.

The progress made in developing more powerful radars was among the most impressive aspects of the Ferranti contribution to *Bloodhound* Mark II. Nevertheless, it is crucial to remember that in another important respect, circuitry, a major breakthrough was achieved. As we saw in section 10.2, Dr Searby had been responsible for improving the reliability of Mark I circuits by replacing the miniature valves traditionally used with sub-miniature variants developed by Mullard. At exactly the same time, however, MoS was encouraging Ferranti to experiment with the new semiconductor technology emanating from Bell Telephone Lab's, in the USA, instigating a major development programme which put the firm right at the forefront of a trend which was beginning to shake the whole electronics industry to its very foundations. We noted in the last chapter how the first generation electronic components like valves were giving way to their second generation equivalents made out of semiconductor material. Using both MoS finance and internal funds Ferranti was provided with an excellent opportunity to build up a team which would over the next thirty years establish a reputation for innovation and high-quality design (see sections 11.2–11.3). The work of Maurice Gribble at Wythenshawe was particularly important in this respect, designing circuits which in the 1960s influenced the architecture of several Ferranti computers. This is yet further evidence of how *Bloodhound* was strengthening the firm's position as a major player in the electronics industry. Although venturing into second generation electronic components involved substantial financial costs, as we shall see in section 11.2, it was vital for Ferranti that it should commit resources to what many regarded as a crucial area.

10.6 The *Bloodhound* revelations

Bloodhound, especially the Mark II version, was undoubtedly the most successful British guided weapon of its era. This can be confirmed firstly by its survival as an intrinsic feature of Britain's defences until the 1990s, as well as its purchase by several independent overseas governments. More importantly to the immediate story, and especially when compared to its contemporaries, it was delivered to specification on time, without overruning the budget. Of course, the price had risen from the original 1950 estimate of £1.5 million to £32 million by 1960. In contrast, problems aplenty dogged other projects. For example, while it was still regarded as clumsy and vulnerable to countermeasures, spending on the English Electric *Thunderbird* had amounted by 1960 to approximately £40 million. Even though the Royal Navy was experiencing difficulties finding a suitable ship on which to install the equipment, the Armstrong-Whitworth *Seaslug* had cost a similar amount. Over £53 million had been provided for the De Havilland *Firestreak*, but its heavy booster rockets caused such excessive drag that it came into service very late.[46]

In total, the *Electronics Weekly* estimated that by 1965 around £700 million had been wasted on cancelled missile development programmes,[47] reflecting badly on the firms, government ministries and agencies involved in this work. Looking at some of the biggest disasters, one might also note that this figure could well have been a conservative estimate: *Blue Steel* had cost £60 million by 1960, as opposed to its projected estimate in 1955 of £12.5 million; and the respective figures for *Blue Streak* were £310 million and £50 million.[48] It was for this reason that in the mid-1950s the MoA insisted on negotiating a fixed-price contract with Bristol and Ferranti, placing considerable emphasis on efficiency when *Bloodhound* moved into production. In fact, while by 1961 *Bloodhound* Mark I had cost £44.5 million, in sharp contrast to the experiences of other systems its effectiveness had resulted in substantial domestic and export orders. Of course, it was soon replaced by the Mark II and a further £35.5 million was spent on this enhanced system.[49] Nevertheless, at least the RAF was by then equipped with one of the most advanced guided weapons in the world which went on to provide long and valuable service.

MoA discoveries

These achievements say much for the Bristol-Ferranti syndicate. However, because of what has passed into political history as 'The *Bloodhound* Incident', most of this has been forgotten. Moreover, for Ferranti the financial consequences of this development created a host of difficulties in the late 1960s, as we shall explain in the course of the next two chapters. It is also important to emphasise that the furore of 1964 provided an extremely testing introduction for Sebastian to the responsibilities of running Ferranti, his father having retired as chairman in January 1963 (see section 11.1). While some internal commentators have in retrospect claimed that Sebastian's relative inexperience as chairman compounded the situation, one should remember that leading figures in the legal world like Jim Thompson (of Allen & Overy) and Henry Benson advised him throughout the negotiations with the MoA. In any case, not only had he been working for Ferranti since 1950 (see section 8.1) and been managing director since 1957, the constant interaction with his father also kept him fully conversant with the driving forces behind the firm's engineering and commercial strategies. Throughout the debate over guided weapon profits, Sebastian was also insisting that his actions were heavily influenced by the need to keep his firm at the frontiers of exciting new technologies, not to mention maintain employment for over 20,000 people.

Most crucially, the traditional Ferranti position on government contracts (see section 7.4), that sponsoring ministries should provide adequate financial cover for all projects, remained uppermost in Sebastian's mind throughout the incident. Indeed, he constantly noted in forthright terms at successive press conferences that Ferranti had done nothing improper, a point confirmed by all informed and balanced contemporary commentators. Some of his colleagues have since argued that he ought to have defused the criticisms several months before the debate started, by agreeing to reduce the profits claimed on *Bloodhound*. On the other hand, he claims that no such situation was ever available to him, the MoA having agreed the price in October 1960 and paid up at the time of delivery completions in 1962. In any case, once the politicians entered the debate over alleged excess profits on *Bloodhound* Mark I, there was little Sebastian could do but deal with the publicity as best he could.

The first stirrings of any trouble with the *Bloodhound* contracts came in October 1963, when the newly-appointed Permanent Secretary at MoA, Sir Richard Way, informed Sebastian that government auditors had discovered serious discrepancies in the prices calculated for Mark I direct labour costs.[50] The public accounts committee's figures can be found in Table 10.1, demonstrating how on a contract worth £11.77 million, while Ferranti had been given an allowance of £770,000, the actual profit had been £4.9 million. One should remember that this report also noted that De Havilland was allegedly guilty of making an excess profit of £1.36 million in the production of the *Firestreak* guided missile. However, as De Havilland had made fewer missiles than planned at the time the technical cost estimates were made, thereby increasing its overheads, perversely the firm was absolved of any blame for the eventual outturn. This reveals in stark form how Ferranti were to be pilloried for achieving such high levels of efficiency. Had it failed to meet the technical cost estimates, there would have been no debate.

The central problem revealed in Table 10.1 had clearly been the failure to gauge labour costs accurately, an error which had been magnified by the overhead charge of 558 per cent. Sebastian immediately invited Henry (later, Lord) Benson of Cooper Bros. to investigate the MoA's claims, while as a director of Ferranti since 1958, J. H. (Jim) Thomson, of Allen & Overy, was also asked to look at the problem. This typified how the chairman would always ensure that, when Ferranti faced a significant problem, the best possible talent was consulted. In this case, it laid the basis for a friendship between Henry Benson and the de Ferranti family which endured for several years. Sadly for the firm, though, Benson confirmed the MoA's claims, that Ferranti had been applying the 558 per cent overhead charge to both the Moston labour savings and certain subcontracted production costs.[51] This forced them to elaborate a defence strategy which might obviate the need to repay any of the profits recorded in Table 10.1.

Table 10.1. *The actual and agreed costs of the Bloodhound Mark I production contract up to 31 March 1961*

	Actual Costs £	Agreed Costs £
Labour	574,000	1,170,000
Overheads	3,077,000	6,633,000
Materials*	3,197,000	3,197,000
Profit allowance	—	770,000
Actual profit	4,922,000	
TOTAL	11,770,000	11,770,000

Key: * Includes subcontracting and tooling.

Source: Public Accounts Committee, Second Report, 1963–64.

Although the letter from Sir Richard Way would clearly have come as a shock to Sebastian, it is important to emphasise how for at least the previous two years senior members of the accounts department like Harry Kirkham and Alf Lawton had been advising Sir Vincent and Sebastian that the GW contracts were generating unusually good profits (see Table 10.2).[52] As many have observed, while Bob Grove certainly achieved excellent returns during the production run, it is not clear why this should have resulted in an average profit of over twenty-five per cent on sales between 1959–60 and 1962–63.

Appendix C (Table 1) also reveals how the company's overdraft fell dramatically between 1959 and 1961. Of course, some of this fall could be attributed to the closure of several loss-making departments at Moston. More accurately, though, the bulk of it was related to the substantial inflow of funds from the MoA in progress payments for *Bloodhound* Mark I production.

As Sebastian was constantly at pains to explain, though, it is vital to remember that on the MoA's insistence the contracts had been based on a fixed price, giving the contractor an incentive to reduce production costs as far as possible, either by good internal practice or by subcontracting manufacture of those components which could be made more cheaply in specialist firms. This point was actually accepted by Sir Richard Way when giving evidence to the Lang Inquiry in 1964,[53] substantiating Sebastian's claim that his firm was simply abiding by the game's rules. Similarly, one must remember that until 1957 Ferranti had earned a return of just four per cent on the cost-plus GW development contracts, at a time when illiquidity in other departments was creating some concern about the firm's ability to continue with this project. It was also another three years before profitability improved significantly at Wythenshawe. Nevertheless, the first two rows in Table 10.1 were still difficult to explain, provoking a wide-ranging debate on several fronts.

Table 10.2. *Financial performance of the Wythenshawe Division, 1959–1963*

Year to March	Col. 1 sales £	Col. 2 profits £	Col. 2 as percentage of Col. 1 %
1957	1,842,434	87,175	4.7
1958	1,852,663	88,741	4.8
1959	2,974,919	179,863	6.1
1960	5,533,408	1,099,601	19.9
1961	6,063,502	2,021,938	33.3
1962	5,515,197	1,637,209	29.7
1963	5,738,407	1,069,147	18.6

Source: Ferranti Management Accounts, 1959–63

In retrospect, one might argue that in view of the firm's dependence on defence contracts Sebastian could have sought an instant settlement with MoA, just as his father had paid the NRDC £75,000 in 1958 as a means of defusing any potential conflict with the NRDC over *Pegasus* development and production costs (see section 9.4). On the other hand, and irrespective of the legal advice provided by Henry Benson and Jim Thomson, any payment for profit overruns on *Bloodhound* would obviously have been far greater than £75,000. Even though in October 1963 Ferranti received a bankers' draft for £1.5 million, as a result of the computer department's sale to ICT,[54] Sebastian had already planned the investment programme for the next few years on the basis of known profit projections. It was the chairman's considered view that his prime objective was to maximise the profit opportunities available to the firm. Moreover, remembering the difficulties Sir Vincent had experienced with unprofitable fuze contracts in the late 1930s (see section 7.4), Sebastian felt that the ministry had simply embarked on a project which had worked out in the supplier's favour.

In replying to Sir Richard Way, Sebastian's main argument revolved around the claims that not only had the MoA no legal redress against the company, given that the contract was agreed on a mutually acceptable basis, Ferranti had also spent a total of £7.134 million on R & D out of its own funds over the previous six years.[55] Indeed, the GW profits revealed in Table 10.2 had not been frittered away on executive perks or higher dividends, but reinvested in new facilities and projects, making it essential that Sebastian should fend off any demands for a repayment. Furthermore, Eric Grundy commented on the uncertainty attached to GW development, even in the late 1950s, given the technical challenges involved and the failure of other firms to develop successful businesses in this field.[56] GW was clearly a high-risk business. Another crucial point was a major rationalisation of the British aircraft and missile industry, after the merger of English Electric, Vickers and Bristol into a new company, the British Aircraft Co. in 1960, reducing the likelihood of Ferranti being included in any further GW projects.[57]

Sebastian's refusal to settle with Sir Richard Way in October 1963 was clearly only an opening shot in a debate which would rage for several months. Given the legal advice just outlined, however, the firm was committed to denying any charges of improper practice. In retrospect, one might also emphasise at this stage that Sir Richard's recent arrival in the MoA, from his previous post of Permanent Under-Secretary in the War Office, was most unfortunate, because in the four months since his appointment he had been unable to develop a sufficiently intimate relationship with Sebastian.[58] Sir Richard consequently found it difficult to urge the Ferranti chairman to settle the matter before all the information became public knowledge, particularly as Ferranti was being advised by a prominent figure like Henry Benson. In fact, the advice coming from Benson was so heavily based on the contractual and accounting facts that the inevitable political consequences were largely ignored when Sebastian first met with Sir Richard Way. The highly formal relationship which existed between the senior civil servant and the contractor also meant that it was difficult to find any even ground in the discussions. There were threats of a judicial inquiry if Sebastian refused to settle with the MoA, which Benson likened to 'an undressing in public', revealing how at this stage an agreement had yet to emerge which would limit the ensuing political posturing.

Lang appointed

Of course, even if Sir Richard had succeeded in persuading Sebastian to negotiate a settlement in October 1963, the matter was largely out of their hands. All government contracts are in principle subject to investigation by the office of the comptroller and auditor-general (hereafter C. & A. G.), and when its report for 1962–63 was published on 24 January 1964 this heralded the beginning of a major public debate about both business ethics and the ineffectiveness of government costing practices.[59] On that day, the chancellor of the exchequer (Reginald Maudling) also announced the establishment of an independent inquiry chaired by Sir John Lang (a senior civil servant at the Admiralty). He would be charged with two tasks:

> To investigate the circumstances in which the prices agreed by the Ministry of Aviation may have allowed an excessive profit to the firm concerned; and to recommend whether any changes in organisation or procedure are necessary to ensure better assessment of prices for similar contracts in future.[60]

This reflects an awareness at official levels of problems with both a specific contract, as well as the manner in which government departments conducted their costings. In the ensuing debate, however, Opposition critics were quick to seize on the latter as a sign of weakness in a Conservative regime which had been in power since 1951. In other words, politics was very much to the fore in 1964, especially as there was a General Election looming. The thrusting new Labour party leader, Harold Wilson, was particularly eager to exploit such events as the Profumo and *Bloodhound* incidents, in order to score points over the allegedly corrupt incumbents of Downing St.[61] The Opposition was especially critical of the government's delay in revealing the extent of the problem, given that Julian Amery, the minister for aviation, had known of the issues for several months prior to the publication of the C. & A. G.'s report.

Of course, political point-scoring was not the only reason why the incident took on such proportions, because popular indignation was quite rightly aroused by the C. & A. G.'s revelations, even if 'the firm concerned' was never shown to have broken the rules. In fact, Ferranti were not mentioned by either the C. & A. G. or the chancellor on 24 January. Nevertheless, after consulting his legal advisors (Jim Thomson and Henry Benson), Sebastian chose to issue a statement welcoming the opportunity to explain why Ferranti had made such a handsome profit. At the same time, the Labour Opposition tabled a motion censoring the government 'for their laxity in permitting excessive profits to be made at the taxpayers' expense on private contracts',[62] sparking off a debate which fluctuated in tone from simple soap-box electioneering to serious accusations about both Ferranti and the MoA.

The de Ferranti family would also bear the brunt of this assault, not only because of their firm's direct involvement in the contract, but also because by February 1962 Basil de Ferranti had become Parliamentary Secretary of the Ministry of Aviation. Naturally, being one of the three major shareholders in a leading defence contractor, his position would have created a potential conflict of interests in the eyes of critics, leading him to attempt to divest himself of this stock in order to facilitate what could have been a flourishing political career. Unfortunately, though, the provisions of a family trust prevented this, forcing him to resign from his junior ministerial post at the MoA in October 1962. However, critics were quick to seize on any possible links between *Bloodhound* and Basil's post, ignoring the crucial point that he had only been appointed in February 1962, the year the contract had been completed.

The political debate clearly contained a particularly nasty flavour, providing extremely bad publicity for Ferranti. The embarrassment was further extended when in answering a Labour parliamentary question, the minister for aviation, Julian Amery, mistakenly claimed that the MoA had never been given access to figures providing the final outturn on any government contract. This was bad enough for the government system, but the situation was compounded when he also made the mistaken calculation that Ferranti should only have made a profit of £400,000, rather than almost £4.5 million.[63] Sebastian was consequently obliged to hold yet another press conference in the London offices, now housed just 200 hundred yards from the Houses of Parliament in Millbank Tower. This provided an opportunity to explain how the Minister had provided extremely misleading statistics which ignored the fixed-price nature of this contract. In simple terms, Sebastian stated that all the risk of keeping on the Moston and Wythenshawe labour forces, as well as undergoing the steep learning curves in production, had been placed squarely on the firm's shoulders.[64] Furthermore, Sebastian also explained how the Treasury had earned a levy of over £1 million from the *Bloodhound* exports, concluding that:

> Had we failed to deliver the goods on time, failed to export, or had the country not got a proper defence system, there would have been no fuss.

But, because we made a tremendous success – technically, commercially, and export-wise – we are in trouble.

Of course, in view of our earlier point that *Bloodhound*'s counterparts had been a financial and technical disaster, such an argument had considerable force. On the other hand, this still left the startling facts revealed in Table 10.1, forcing Ferranti to reveal as much information as possible in order to quell the political storm.

10.7 Lang and its consequences

The first major parliamentary debate about *Bloodhound* was to come after the all-party House of Commons public accounts committee produced its findings on 16 April. This confirmed how Ferranti had made a profit of £4.92 million, compared to the projected allowance of £770,000 (see Table 10.1).[65] Sebastian had actually been interrogated by this committee, publicly accepting for the first time all figures presented, with the exception of an item for materials, sub-contracting and tooling on which £372,000 had been spent in excess of the MoA allowance. While this discrepancy actually reduced the Ferranti profit from seventy-two per cent of the total estimated cost (£6,848,000) to sixty-three per cent, clearly few regarded such a difference as significant.[66] A more important revelation arising from this report was the dates on which the prices had been settled, because for the first time the focus of attention was moving away from disgust over the profit to dismay about the way in which government contracts were costed.

Costing procedures

In reviewing these procedures, it is first of all important to remember that the Mark I production contracts covered the period from November 1955 until March 1961. However, the MoA technical cost officers had not started their investigations until Autumn 1958, Ferranti had only submitted its quotations in July 1960 (when half of the weapons had been delivered), and the final prices were only agreed in October 1960.[67] Although MoA accepted Sebastian's claim that Ferranti would not have been able to estimate the final outturn in July 1960, even when this information was available by the end of 1960 there was no convention which dictated that the cost officers should be informed. Indeed, in no previous case had any contractor done this. It is also apparent that, when MoA agreed to the Ferranti prices, all the information about labour costs and overheads was contained in their records. As

Sebastian emphasised, the profits came to light *because* MoA accountants had the relevant figures. However, to many people's surprise, it was not then the custom in civil service circles to compare the technical cost officers' estimates with those taken by their own accountants from a contractor's books. The officers' inexperience in this area would also have been a factor here, especially their failure to make any attempt to ascertain anything other than projected, as opposed to actual, cost figures. As a consequence, any discrepancy was magnified directly by the rate allowed for overheads (in this case, by 558 per cent).

As the Lang Enquiry later discovered, while in 1959 Ferranti had submitted labour cost figures which overestimated the ideal basic times for direct labour, at no time did the technical cost officers assess the actual costs incurred at Moston. Furthermore, some costs amounting to £500,000 had been verified by a low ranking (Grade One) technical cost officer, without checking the data already collected by MoA accountants.[68] The auditor-general had noticed this point, reporting:

> The Ministry negotiated prices on the basis of prime cost estimates provided by their technical cost officers with the addition of overheads based on the accountants' recommendations. I observed however that the sum total of the amounts included for direct labour and overheads in the agreed prices ... exceeded by seventy per cent, or £2.7 million, the total direct labour and overhead costs for that period as furnished by the Ministry's accountants, although the accountants' figures had been available when the prices were fixed.[69]

MoA argued that this catalogue of errors could have been avoided had Ferranti informed them of the outcome. Once again, though, it is vital to remember that the civil service accountants had been given all the information on both labour costs and overheads, giving the guided weapons division management the impression that the MoA was entirely satisfied with the profit being earned. Similarly, it was the MoA which had insisted on a fixed-price contract, leaving an incentive for the contractor to complete the job efficiently. In any case, returning to the legal position clarified by Henry Benson, Ferranti would have had no redress had losses been made on the contract, undermining any MoA claim that the firm had contravened the spirit of what they falsely regarded as a partnership.

In a detailed academic analysis of the whole affair, Flower is critical of Benson's political naivety. On the other hand, he agrees with the company's general position, that the estimating system employed by the MoA had been the main cause of the problem, confirming Sebastian's view that Ferranti had not at any stage indulged in any illegal activities.[70] The Flower report came out two years after the main debates, however, while in the prevailing political climate of 1964 these points would in any case have been largely ignored.

Although the case presented by Ferranti was legally and morally watertight, this naturally would not have prevented another full-scale public debate after the public accounts committee's report was published in April 1964. To illustrate how far the Opposition sunk in its attempt to exploit every ounce of public approbation from the incident, one Labour MP, George Wigg, using the legal protection afforded by parliamentary privilege, accused the Ferranti family of profiteering from the Second World War 'while others went out and served'.[71] Such an accusation was, of course, entirely false, prompting Basil to give a spirited reply explaining how he and Sebastian had joined up as soon as possible (see section 8.1). As we have also seen, Sir Vincent had served in both World Wars, returning from the First with the Military Cross, while his brother Basil had been killed in action (see section 5.1). On a more positive note, the minister for aviation, Julian Amery, announced that Ferranti had agreed to open its books to the Lang Inquiry. It is also clear from the archives that Dr Searby, Sir John Toothill and Sebastian provided all the help requested during the investigations.[72] Of course, there was no new information to find, MoA accountants having made the essential searches three years earlier. Nevertheless, the firm's openness did much to mollify the criticism until Lang had produced his report.

It is clear from this survey of events that Ferranti, and particularly Sebastian, was being squeezed into a corner from which it was increasingly difficult to extricate themselves without making some payment to MoA. Publicly, Sebastian continued to assure commentators and critics alike that his firm had simply played the contracting 'game' by its own rather peculiar rules. In particular, on Benson's advice, he argued that a contract was legally binding on both parties, rather than something which was open to interpretation if the circumstances changed for one side.[73] Privately, though, while Henry Benson continued to stress the need to fight on, Sebastian was being advised by senior managers like Sir John Toothill, Dr Searby and Alf Lawton (chief accountant) that the incident was doing tremendous damage to Ferranti.[74] In particular, the relationship with its major customer had deteriorated drastically since 1963, pressuring Sebastian into a much more conciliatory position.

The settlement

It was widely accepted by the summer of 1964 that faults had been revealed in government costing procedures, a point confirmed in Lang's report (published on 15 July) which expressed grave reservations about both the quality of the MoA's technical cost officers and the failure of its Contracts Directorate to compare their figures with those collected earlier by its own accountants.[75] On the other hand, Lang also revealed indiscrepancies in the way direct labour costs had been calculated, Ferranti having subcontracted certain jobs which the technical cost officers had assumed would be performed at Moston.[76] Again, one must stress how Bob Grove (production manager at Moston) was simply attempting to expedite assembly, rather than conduct illicit operations. Nevertheless, Lang identified the failure to estimate labour costs accurately (see Table 10.1) as the main reason for the inflated profit. Even though Dr Searby noted in his evidence to the Lang Inquiry that there had been several modifications to the Mark I during production, and MoA technical cost officers had allowed the firm to build in some margins for contingencies,[77] Lang still concluded that if essentially political criteria were applied to the contract then the firm had submitted costs which were not 'fair and reasonable'.[78] Of course, while the MoA could have produced the same conclusion in 1961, government contracts were not costed out in this way, as a result of which the overhead rate of 558 per cent magnified the error and produced a profit of almost £5 million.

On balance, given the labour cost revelations and senior management's advice that Ferranti could not afford to alienate its major customer, Sebastian was under increasing strain to think about a solution which would alleviate the political pressure mounting on his firm. This forced him to accept the necessity of a financial settlement, just as his father had agreed to pay £75,000 to the NRDC in 1958. Consequently, on the day Lang published his report, Julian Amery announced that Ferranti had 'offered to refund a total of £4.25 million', or eighty-six per cent of the final surplus on Mark I production contracts.[79] Sebastian always maintains that this was an *ex gratia* payment, rather than a 'refund' or admission of guilt. Whatever the case, there is little doubt that Ferranti had no choice but to accept publicly that MoA should be compensated. The Chancellor of the Exchequer, Reginald Maudling, also left Sebastian in little doubt that a payment would have to be made, threatening him not with a judicial inquiry, but with the simple statement: 'We will ruin you!'.[80] Furthermore, as early as March 1964 Crewe Toll was beginning to experience some difficulties in its negotiations with RRE and RAE over certain avionics contracts (see section 11.5). Peter Dorey in digital systems had also come up against some animosity in the Admiralty (see section 11.7),[81] illustrating in graphic form just why Sebastian agreed to make this payment.

While Ferranti clearly had no choice but to settle with its major customer, for a company already beginning to experience severe liquidity problems in the mid-1960s the financial implications of having to make such a substantial payment would evidently have been of great importance. Indeed, we shall see in the next chapters how Sebastian and his senior managers struggled with this burden.[82] A more immediate problem was financing production of *Bloodhound* Mark II, because this contract was still passing through the Moston factory and MoA accountants were paying particularly close attention to costs. Although the first orders for Mark II had been placed in October 1961, it was 1965 before they had been completed. Moreover, on a business worth over £8.25 million Ferranti was only allowed a profit of 5.23 per cent, or £431,183. This was one of the main reasons why Dr Searby decided to pull out of GW once Mark II was commissioned. Another factor to consider was MoA's deliberations concerning a possible *Bloodhound* Mark III, for use as an intercontinental ballistic missile (ICBM). In this context one should note that paradoxically Dr Searby was a pacifist, leading him to argue that while as an anti-aircraft defence measure *Bloodhound* was acceptable, ICBM's were more concerned with offence. Above all, though, it was unlikely that Ferranti would ever be considered for the Mark III stage, providing a huge incentive to find alternative employment for the staff and facilities at Wythenshawe.[83]

Second Lang Inquiry

As a final epilogue to this story, it is important to note that a second Lang Inquiry was conducted, this time specifically into how government contracts were costed.[84] Although it was 1967 before its main findings were published, in the interim ministries were much keener to monitor the financial aspects of outside business, particularly at Ferranti.[85] This did not stop similar revelations to those of the *Bloodhound* Mark I contracts, because in 1967 Bristol-Siddeley Engines was shown to have made an excess profit of £3.96 million making the *Viper* and *Sapphire* engines for the RAF.[86] However, by then politicians were no longer interested in such scandals, having expended all their angst on Ferranti. In any case, by that time Lang and the MoD were tidying up the system.

The 1967 Lang report actually espoused the principle of 'equality of information'. While one might argue that both contractors and civil servants had always possessed all the necessary data, thereafter it was necessary to compare information more scrupulously. Furthermore, fixed-price contracts were completely abandoned in favour of the cost-plus system, ensuring no repeat of the *Bloodhound* profit. Of course, as the *Financial Times* commented, cost-plus gives a guaranteed profit (usually of seven per cent), discouraging efficiency and enterprise in the execution of government contracts. Indeed, this would only serve to increase the cost to taxpayers.[87] On the other hand, such was the political concern over alleged profiteering that this change was inevitable, emphasising how, as we shall see in sections 11.5 and 11.7 the *Bloodhound* incident had wider implications for the whole defence industry.

10.8 Automation systems

The July 1964 announcement that Ferranti was to make a payment to MoA was an unfortunate end to what had until the public revelations earlier that year been a significant success story. Dr Searby, Denis Best and the Wythenshawe team had designed and developed a first-class product which sold successfully in both domestic and overseas markets, in spite of intense competition from other British, and even more acutely from American, rivals. Furthermore, the survival of *Bloodhound* as an integral part of Britain's defences for over thirty years is glowing testimony to their achievement. At the same time, especially once the Mark II contracts had been secured in October 1961, they were faced with the most obvious question: 'What next?'. Certainly, in view of the financial revelations, the Wythenshawe team was unlikely to participate further in this programme. During the early 1960s, however, largely as a result of Denis Best's initiative and the support provided by Sebastian de Ferranti, Wythenshawe had already diversified its product portfolio. This move was one of the era's most celebrated adaptations of a military technology to civilian use, because in converting the computer employed in the *Bloodhound* launch control post into a machine capable of controlling real-time processes Best established the basis of a business which expanded rapidly over the following twenty years.

Argus development

The modern guided weapon is a highly sophisticated combination of computing and radar technology, providing opportunities to develop circuitry which could have far-reaching applications in a range of related fields. Much of the guided weapon work at both Bristol and Ferranti was focused on controlling the missile's supersonic flight, providing considerable challenges for both teams. At the same time, it is also important to remember that the Wythenshawe engineers were concerned with controlling performance on the ground through what was known as a launch control post. This control function was effected through a digital computer which had been developed during the *Blue Envoy* experiments in 1956–57. In fact, while the machine was based on the expertise gained designing the *Pegasus* machine (see section 9.4), in using high frequency germanium transistors and a ferrite core memory it proved to be much faster and more adaptable.[88] By this time, as we shall see in section 11.2, Ferranti was very much the British pioneer of second generation electronic components. The team headed by Maurice Gribble at Wythenshawe was also successfully adapting the earlier work of Peter Hall and Alan Shepherd in the semiconductor development team to produce highly efficient circuits for the launch control post. Such was that team's success, indeed, as we saw in section 9.8, that Peter Hall was using these circuits in the *Sirius* and *Orion* ranges of mainframe computer, providing a new market for Wythenshawe at a time when Denis Best was considering the production of a computer for very different purposes.

In utilising second generation electronic components and benefiting from experience with packaged technology, the Mark II launch control post computer had provided Ferranti engineers with exciting new opportunities. By November 1958, Maurice Gribble was also advocating the application of this technology to industrial processes, producing what was known as the PCTP (process control transistor computer) for a symposium on 'Instrumentation and Computation in Process Development and Plant Design'.[89] Although a working model had yet to be built, Gribble had also been discussing with Babcock & Wilcox how best to adapt this machine to the control of boilers during start-up and shut-down. This contact with a potential end-user led to further development work, the end-result of which was shown at the 1959 Computer Exhibition. It was there that Alan Thompson of ICI's instrument department showed such interest in the possibilities of applying PCTP to chemical processes that a firm contract was secured to install a machine at the firm's large soda ash plant just outside Fleetwood. The Wythenshawe management, and in particular Denis Best, consequently realised that a new team was required to manage Gribble's innovation. They also decided to market the PCTP as the *Argus* computer, continuing the Ferranti tradition of naming their machines after Greek gods. Although it was 1962 before the ICI *Argus 200* was commissioned, in the meantime Babcock & Wilcox also ordered one for use in controlling the boiler-house of the CEGB's 200 MW West Thurrock power station, forcing Best into action on the organsiational side.

Maurice Gribble had consequently provided the Wythenshawe team with an excellent opportunity to apply pioneering technology to what was still a new field for British industry. The *Argus* computer was particularly noticeable for both its rugged memory capacity and the extensive use of transistorised technology. The logic circuitry developed by Gribble was later to be employed in a series of other computers, including those made at Bracknell and by ICL, indicating just how far ahead of their competitors Ferranti was beginning to move at that stage.[90] In the early 1960s, though, just as the Edinburgh operation had suffered with its numerical control innovations (see section 8.7),

Circuits designed by Maurice Gribble for the Argus 400, 1966 Wythenshawe.
(Museum of Science and Industry at Manchester.)

The Central Electricity Generating Board National Grid Control, using two ARGUS 500 Computers

Wythenshawe would experience some difficulties breaking into an essentially conservative domestic market for new production ideas. Indeed, what by 1962 had become the automation systems department had a difficult first few trading years. Typically, Sebastian had been willing to back Wythenshawe's diversification programme, using the GW profits to support the exciting technological innovations. However, even though by the mid-1960s Ferranti was regarded as one of the leading firms in this field, this was proving to be an expensive move for a firm which had just been obliged to pay the government £4.25 million. The venture typifies Sebastian's willingness to sponsor exciting new technologies, in spite of financial worries which would have inhibited other chairmen in publicly-owned companies.

Data on the early performance of automation systems are difficult to acquire, largely because it was absorbed into the general affairs at Wythenshawe. Nevertheless, it is clear that until the creation in 1965 of a separate trading department heavy losses were made. By 1962–63, some sales figures were being produced, revealing that while over the following five years annual output averaged £490,000, no profit was generated on these sales. This

Argus computers were used to control the University of Manchester's Jodrell Bank Radio Telescopes. *(Museum of Science and Industry at Manchester.)*

represented a source of severe embarrassment to the automation systems department, especially when in addition almost £600,000 had been spent on *Argus* development. By that time, though, after the announcement of the 400 and 500 ranges of *Argus,* incorporating new circuits developed by Maurice Gribble, automation systems had received some prestigious orders which could be exploited extensively for their publicity value. For example, the University of Manchester bought an *Argus* 100 to control its 125 foot radio telescope at Jodrell Bank, while an *Argus* 300 was ordered by the Medical Research Council for its work on molecular biology. Another major contract, for a seat reservation system, was awarded in 1967 by BOAC, using thirty-nine *Argus* 400 computers and 700 displays in what came to be known as *BOEDICEA* (British Overseas Airways Digital Information Computer for Electronic Automation). The *BOEDICEA* contract was particularly successful, because it not only provided an entrée into what was the rapidly expanding market for airport management systems, Wythenshawe engineers also adapted the basic system to develop command-and-control systems for a range of other uses.

Argus 500 consul system at Esso Petroleum Company's Milford Haven Oil Refinery supplied by automation systems, Wythenshawe 1969.
(Museum of Science and Industry at Manchester.)

Electronic displays

The 400 and 500 ranges of *Argus* computers provided Wythenshawe with an excellent opportunity to move away from its former dependence upon defence contracts. In fact, by 1967 two separate business had been established, weapons systems, headed by H. H. (Tommy) Thompson, and Denis Best's automation systems activities. It is also important to note that as part of the process control equipment business a significant demand for new types of displays emerged. Wythenshawe was consequently obliged to take this on as part of its basic development programme, especially as the *BOEDICEA* contract required 700 monitors. While the first displays utilised alpha-numeric technology, by the late 1960s highly sophisticated graphical systems were being produced, providing Ferranti with a highly successful product which was generally regarded as the most suitable for command-and-control situations. This also led in 1967 to the establishment of a separate division at Wythenshawe, electronic displays, with Tommy Thompson moving from

BOAC Consoles Keyboard, 28 December 1967, part of the BOEDICEA system installed at Manchester Airport by the Wythenshawe automation systems and electronic displays departments. *(Museum of Science and Industry at Manchester.)*

weapons systems to manage this business. Sales by then had reached almost £650,000, providing a solid base for the infant venture. Moreover, by 1971–72 sales of over £5.4 million had been achieved as both military and civil customers started to accept the Ferranti product as standard equipment. Eventually, electronic displays moved out of Wythenshawe into adapted premises in Cheadle Heath, providing the foundations for what in the following twenty years became a flourishing business which diversified further into products like sonar systems and simulators.[91]

Market constraints

While the work on second generation electronic components and advanced displays had undoubtedly given automation systems a strong position in what was now known generally as the minicomputer market, it is clear that this would not by itself generate more business. In particular, there was the usual British problem of conservative customers, many of whom were

Sea King Helicopter Simulator made by Electronic Displays, Wythenshawe, 1970. *(Museum of Science and Industry at Manchester.)*

reluctant to imitate ICI and Babcock & Wilcox and invest in new equipment until it had been accepted by the majority of firms. It is also interesting to note that by 1964, while Ferranti had supplied twenty-two *Argus* systems, all the major American firms had sold at least fifty, while Bunker-Ramo had installed 107.[92] Hamilton has accused British minicomputer producers like Ferranti of pursuing a conservative strategy of focusing on niche positions, while in contrast the dominant American firm of DEC attempted to widen the market.[93] As an example he notes that annual *Argus* sales rarely exceeded fifteen up to the early 1970s, compared to DEC's record of well over twenty systems. However, just as with IBM and mainframe computers, such was the competitive advantage derived from DEC's substantial home market sales that Ferranti and British counterparts like GEC, CTL and Digico were obliged to adopt more cautious policies.

During the late 1960s, government support was provided through MinTech and the NRDC for the minicomputer industry. However, as we saw with mainframe computer policies (see sections 9.3 and 9.4), the main limitation associated with these funds was the threat posed to a firm's independence, because the NRDC insisted on partnership schemes through which a limited amount of money would be channelled. In consequence, management often chose to develop their own strategies, rather than be guided by civil servants. This was an entirely rational approach for Ferranti in particular, given the previously unhappy experience with the NRDC and Lord Halsbury (see section 9.4). Furthermore, just as with Halsbury's mainframe computer strategy, government funding was often divided between pairs of companies, resulting in two firms going for the same (small) market. Hamilton is critical of British firms for refusing to follow government initiatives, accusing them of a blinkered approach which led to the conservative marketing strategies associated with specialised product ranges. On the other hand, in view of the unhelpful nature of these policies, not to mention the domestic market's small size, Ferranti and its counterparts could hardly have justified a more aggressive stance.

Apart from the problems associated with developing a strategy which was appropriate to British conditions, Denis Best also realised that his department was dealing with customers who demanded high levels of service and maintenance. This would have further exacerbated the difficulty of building a profitable business, especially at a time of rising development costs. Customers were particularly wary of breakdowns and lengthy repair periods, because considerable maintenance was often required after an *Argus* machine had been installed. To calm such sentiments, automation systems created new facilities which could deal rapidly with any eventuality. Wythenshawe was obviously used as the base for UK maintenance operations, while in Europe

Argus computers at work controlling the BP North Sea oilfield, Aberdeen.
(Museum of Science and Industry at Manchester.)

the firm's agent in France, CERAM, was given authority to recruit computer staff. Similarly, there were also new arrangements with Industrie Elettriche di Legnano and GRA, in Italy and West Germany, respectively. Of course, this activity was expensive, leading to the establishment of a separate firm for this purpose. At the same time, it was invaluable experience which assisted automation systems engineers in the development of appropriate systems.

As we shall see over the following chapters, in time automation systems became one of the more profitable parts of the Ferranti organisation, selling over 200 *Argus* computers until the department's closure in 1990. This substantiated the decision by Sebastian de Ferranti to encourage Denis Best to venture away from GW into a civil market, even if in the early stages both sales were difficult to generate and development costs impossible to cover. Although Ferranti might well have been guilty of dealing only with niche markets, in view of the domestic pressures there was little alternative until British industry awoke to the possibilities in minicomputers. Electronic displays also became a major business in its own right, and its survival into the 1990s as Ferranti-Thomson Sonar Systems reflects well on the strategy pursued at Wythenshawe. Nevertheless, while these businesses certainly provided a suitable replacement for GW at Wythenshawe, it did nothing to relieve the firm's mid-1960s financial pressures, illustrating in graphic form the kind of problems facing senior management at that time.

10.9 Conclusion

The establishment and rapid growth of Wythenshawe was a major feature of the firm's post-War development. Apart from the prestige associated with designing and producing *Bloodhound* on time and to budget, in second generation electronic components, *Argus* computers and advanced displays Ferranti had added three significant new branches to its expanding electronics effort. Of course, given the publicity associated with the *Bloodhound* revelations, and the financial penalty imposed as a result of the enforced agreement to make a substantial *ex gratia* payment to MoA, one might wonder whether venturing into this field had been worthwhile. On the other hand, guided weapons had been a technological success story which actually put Ferranti in the very vanguard of Britain's attempt to create a competitive electronics industry capable of matching its mighty American rival. The challenge of the 1960s was to deal with this threat and prevent American firms from dominating the domestic market. For Sebastian de Ferranti, unfortunately, this challenge came at a time when not only had the *Bloodhound* repayments started to siphon off valuable resources, the new departments arising out of this contract were not generating any profit. Sebastian had clearly been appointed chairman of Ferranti at an extremely challenging moment, and finding a solution to these organisational and financial dilemmas would clearly be vital to the firm's future as a family affair.

MK1 Bristol/Ferranti Bloodhound Missiles at RAF Marham, 1962.

11

The Ferranti Dilemma

The last four chapters have detailed how under Sir Vincent's management Ferranti continued to be an extension of the ideals laid down by his father. Above all, the technology-led strategy and highly devolved structure which allowed managers to exploit the period's opportunities in electronics and electrical engineering provided a cultural context in which the firm expanded significantly over the period 1930–63 (see Figure 8.1). It was a culture of which the de Ferranti family was justifiably proud, resulting in the creation of a host of exciting and adventurous new departments. Even though some of the ventures had been commercially unsuccessful, particularly in domestic appliances and mainframe computers, on balance Sir Vincent had effectively ensured that enough departments with a viable future were established, providing the cashflow for new activities which might in time generate profits. It was a long-term strategy which the family felt justified in pursuing because they had no outside shareholders prompting them to distribute more of the surpluses in dividends. At the same time, they recognised that the firm had a responsibility to provide continuous employment for the expanding workforce, a philosophy which influenced decisions on departmental closures or rationalisations. Notwithstanding this point, Sir Vincent and his eldest son, Sebastian, were always careful to manage Ferranti as a going concern, watching over the cashflow with eternal vigilance.

Running Ferranti, then, was not what Lord Halsbury disdainfully noted was a matter of having 'fun', especially in view of the firm's substantial growth and diversification over that period. With specific regard to the extremely demanding nature of being both chairman and managing director, however, after over three decades in these roles Sir Vincent decided in the summer of 1962 to pass on the reins to his eldest son, Sebastian. This chapter will consequently be concerned with the transfer of power, assessing in particular the style of management adopted by the new chairman, the problems he faced in the 1960s, and the various solutions devised to alleviate what became a pressing financial position.

In addressing these issues, it is vital to emphasise initially that one should not view the 1960s in entirely negative terms. Indeed, many parts of the business continued to expand and innovate, bringing new products on to

Sir Vincent de Ferranti at his retirement in 1963, as painted by Annigoni.
(Museum of Science and Industry at Manchester.)

the market which were well-accepted. On the other hand, having conducted a planning exercise which presumed that all the *Bloodhound* profits could be invested in new projects, financial worries dominated the years after 1963. Moreover, because major cashflow problems arose in some of both the older and new departments, Sebastian was faced with some difficult decisions which directly affected the way in which the organisation as a whole operated. In commercial terms, the main problems affecting Ferranti by the 1960s were a combination of the failure of a domestic market for advanced electrical and electronics goods to materialise, the collapse in demand experienced by certain staple departments, and greater uncertainty in the defence businesses. The whole story can be expressed as a classic manifestation of the 'Ferranti Dilemma' – how to continue operating on the frontiers of knowledge as a family firm with such a weak financial base. It was also a 'Dilemma' which was compounded by the challenges laid down by a host of American subsidiaries, further highlighting the dangers associated with remaining a family firm.

11.1 Sebastian and his team

Sir Vincent had clearly presided over thirty-three successful years at Ferranti. While the ventures into consumer goods had been problematic, in other civil and defence markets – meters, transformers, data processing, process control equipment, numerical control, semiconductor components, and avionics – Ferranti had often been the British, or even European, technical leader. Even though one might question the commercial viability of some of these ventures, by exploiting a variety of technological openings the firm had developed into one of the country's major electronic equipment and component producers. It is also notable that by 1963 the capital employed at Ferranti had reached £22 million, compared to £800,000 in 1930, while, respectively, output of a much-augmented product range had expanded from £600,000 to over £12 million (see Appendix C, Tables 2 and 3). The turnover data is recorded in Figure 11.1, which reveals how under Sir Vincent the firm had embarked on a period of significant growth after the mid-1940s slump in defence orders. The constant data is especially indicative of real expansion, with the 1950s standing out as decades of impressive improvements in output.

Figure 8.1 charts these changes in dramatic detail, illustrating how the scope of Ferranti activities had spread from the limited base of the 1920s into the post-War era's most challenging electronic and avionic technologies. Figure 11.2 also reveals how geographical dispersion had featured prominently in the way Ferranti had evolved since the 1930s, posing a series of fresh challenges for senior management. Although the Westminster Bank had played a key role in funding liquidity requirements at crucial times, it was a process of expansion and diversification which had also been achieved as a family firm. In effect, Sir Vincent had developed his own strategy and

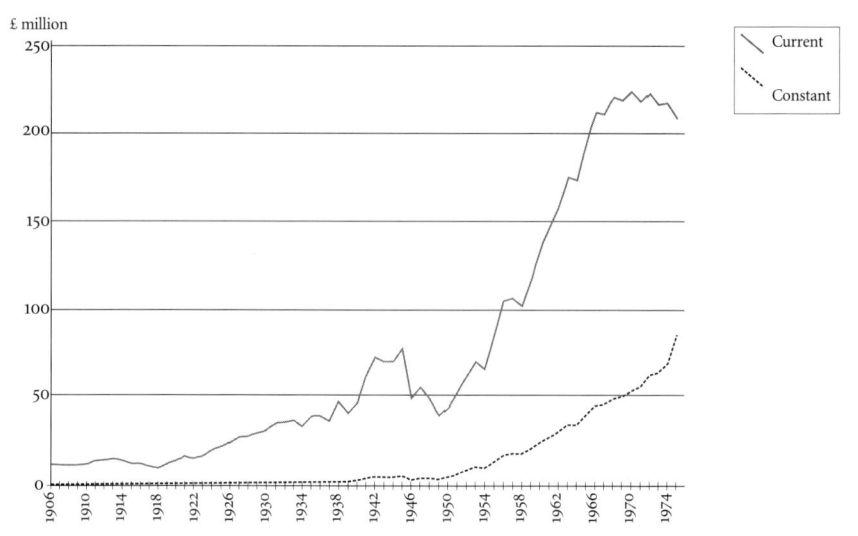

Figure 11.1. *Ferranti Turnover in Constant and Current Prices, 1906–75 (1980=100)*

structure free from the pressures often imposed by outside shareholders. This freedom was crucial to the firm's culture, because when considering the era's technological opportunities Sir Vincent and his managers had been able to take a long-term perspective which was determined not by orthodox commercial criteria, but by considerations like the challenge posed or the openings they offered a firm committed to extending the frontiers of knowledge. 'There is no substitute for fifty-one per cent' is a phrase Sir Vincent never tired of repeating to anyone who questioned the commercial viability of his approach, indicating how it is vital to remember that this commanding position allowed him the opportunity to take what he always referred to as 'sporting swipes' at the new ideas generated by his engineers.

Organisational challenge

While one can all too easily romanticise the achievements of Sir Vincent's era as chairman, it is vital to remember all the hard work he put into monitoring the financial situation by keeping up the graphs started in 1930 (see section 7.1). Similarly, departmental managers are fond of recalling how he would personally remind them of their responsibility to break even on new projects, especially when after reviewing their weekly reports he observed dangerous trends like a significant rise in capital employed matched by stagnant or falling profitability. As he often said to his eldest son, Sir Vincent felt compelled

Figure 11.2. *Main Ferranti locations in the UK by 1975*

1. Hollinwood, Greater Manchester (meter).
2. Chadderton, Greater Manchester (power transformers and testing equipment).
3. Moston, Greater Manchester (instruments, aircraft equipment and fuzes).
4. Gem Mill, Chadderton, Greater Manchester (semiconductors and opto-electronics).
5. Poynton, Cheshire (microwave division)
6. Wythenshawe, Greater Manchester (process control computers).
7. Cheadle Heath, Greater Manchester (simulator, sonar and civil computer systems).
8. Gatley, Greater Manchester (computer systems and later the company HQ).
9. Oldham (Barry St, Cairo Mill and Waterhead), Greater Manchester (naval and civil computer systems and fuzes).
10. Bracknell, Berkshire (digital systems and aircraft equipment design).
11. Crewe Toll, Edinburgh (military electronic systems).
12. Silverknowes, Edinburgh (inertial systems and cockpit displays).
13. Robertson Avenue, Edinburgh (eletro-optic systems).
14. South Gyle, Edinburgh (product support).
15. Dalkeith (measurement and inspection equipment).
16. Dundee (components and laser systems).
17. Cwmbran, Gwent (software development, naval and civil computer systems).
18. Barrow-in-Furness, Lancashire (semiconductors).

'to put the fear of God into my managers', stressing above all a financial imperative which was central to his managerial philosophy.[1] On the other hand, even though Sir Vincent could be described as an autocrat, he was just as keen to encourage a free-booting, entrepreneurial approach at all levels, creating a culture which had attracted a team of high quality engineers into the firm and providing the basis for a period of rapid expansion.

The problem, however, as Murray Robson (the sales manager by the 1950s) observed, was that by the 1960s Ferranti was like a musical instrument which had been designed specifically for Sir Vincent to play. This posed a major challenge in handing over to a third generation, because little thought had gone into how the organisation depicted in Figure 1 (p. 11) could be adapted to changing circumstances. The delicate balancing act performed by Sir Vincent in maintaining financial solvency, yet at the same time stimulating entrepreneurial activity at departmental level, was a task which required absolute mastery of the business. By the 1960s, however, this was becoming increasingly difficult after three decades of expansion and diversification (see Figure 8.1 p. 290). In addition, as we have already hinted, the firm's finances were coming under considerable pressure from the mid-1960s, leaving

Presentation of the Long Service Award to Sir Vincent de Ferranti, by his eldest son, Sebastian, 18 December, 1958. *(Museum of Science and Industry at Manchester.)*

Sebastian with an enormous challenge if he was to sustain the essential features of what had been crucial to his father's success.

In view of these circumstances, it is perhaps not surprising that one of the recurring issues of Sebastian's period as chairman of Ferranti was reform of the firm's organisation (see Figure 1, p. 11). It is consequently vital first of all to examine some of the myths and misunderstandings which have grown up around this subject. One should remember that British business was at that time undergoing a fundamental transformation, largely as a result of intense merger and acquisition activity, leading to the disappearance of the traditionally personal (or family-run) traditions and the rise of a managerial system in which control and ownership was often vested in the hands of professionals.[2] At the same time, because the post-War years also witnessed some dramatic changes in business organisation, by the 1960s especially many firms were beginning to imitate American patterns of organisation, in particular the multidivisional form (or, M-form) which was regarded as the most effective means of controlling these large-scale firms. These changes were by no means as rigorous or as far-reaching as they ought to have been, leading many contemporaries to complain about the inherent weaknesses in 'professional' British management and business organisation. Nevertheless, in this context as a family firm Ferranti was often referred to as an anachronism, given its approach towards decision-making and finance, indicating how there was something distinct about the organisational ethos prevailing at that time. Notwithstanding this contrast, Sebastian was convinced that the organisation was an adequate vehicle for implementing the broad features of his company's strategy, calming the fears of those who might have anticipated changes from the new regime.

Continuity under Sebastian

As the transitionary period clearly had to be handled with great care by Sebastian, it is important to emphasise how in making this move from second to third generation management he was enormously assisted by his father's decision to remove himself completely from the scene. Sir Vincent's contemporaries have often likened this to an actor leaving the stage,[3] because while his retirement actually came as a great surprise to many at Ferranti he refused to take on even an advisory post, leaving nobody in any doubt that as of 23 January 1963 Sebastian was chairman and managing director. Of course, by this time Sebastian and Basil owned over fifty per cent of the Ferranti voting stock,[4] Sir Vincent having transferred much of his holding to them during the mid-1950s. The recent capitalisations had also reinforced the family's position, a point illustrated in Appendix E. While, as we shall see later, Denis de Ferranti still remained a problem, in essence Sebastian was able to rely on his brother and family trusts to maintain control over all key decisions, at least over the following twelve years.

At the outset, when reviewing the new chairman's style of management, it is first of all crucial to emphasise how Sebastian was committed to decentralised decision-making. As he said in an interview with the *Manchester Evening Chronicle*, this 'avoid[ed] an enormous, clumsy central organisation, and put more people in responsible jobs'.[5] In other words, his approach was based on ensuring continuity in the way departmental and divisional managers operated, sustaining the commitment to autonomy and a technology-led strategy which had since 1882 been the hallmark of Ferranti enterprises. As he also said in an interview with the *New Scientist*:

> If you go right back to the early history of Ferranti you will see that we have always chosen to operate on the frontiers of engineering science. It's frightfully risky, but it's what happens to interest us. Our policy remains to invest everything we've got to work on the frontiers of knowledge so that we can really make a contribution to mankind.[6]

This statement reflects similar sentiments to those expressed in a review of his grandfather's 1894 speech to the Royal Scottish Society of Arts (quoted at the end of section 3.3), when reference was made to ploughing back 'the cash earned by some earlier manufacture' into new ideas which would have provided wider benefits. The *New Scientist* article also went on to note how Sebastian had inherited a characteristic which the previous two generations of his family had shown in abundance, namely, 'the questioning instinct to strike out boldly on a promising new line'. As chief executive who represented over fifty-one per cent of the equity, he was also able to sustain that commitment to technological innovation, working industriously to perpetuate the family traditions. While some within the firm argued in favour of a more bureaucratic system of coordination and decision-making, Sebastian felt that such an institutionalised approach would inhibit the technology-led strategy for which Ferranti had become famous, emphasising how he was reluctant to change the structure fashioned by his father.

There is, indeed, little doubt that Sebastian was committed to retaining all the key features of his company's traditional organisation and culture. Certainly, he firmly resisted the pressures imposed by both his advisors and certain external agencies to make any fundamental changes. The most common criticism of Ferranti by the 1960s was that it possessed 'a financial structure fit for a nineteenth century ironmaster',[7] reflecting the contemporary view that the firm's decentralised structure lacked the necessary degree of coordination. Figure 1 (p. 11) provides a reasonable approximation to the structure employed by Ferranti at that time, indicating how the managing director was the pivot around which the entire system revolved. Most importantly, while no formal system of financial monitoring was used at Ferranti, Sebastian was always provided with regular and detailed reports on divisional performance, especially by the cost and management accounts department run by Harry Kirkham. These reports he could use to monitor what was happening anywhere in the company, belying the general perception that Ferranti had failed to develop an internal monitoring system. Lester George, the company economist, was especially keen to see a financial controller appointed who would be able to introduce a more coordinated pattern of decision-making. On the other hand, Sebastian argued that this would simply create an institutionalised and bureaucratic structure which was anathema to the organisation's free-booting spirit, committing Ferranti wholeheartedly to the highly devolved structure which was at the core of his family's approach to business.[8]

The reluctance to bureaucratise decision-making at Ferranti was typical of Sebastian's overall approach towards his duties as chairman, reiterating our earlier point that as owners of the controlling interest the family felt that an institutionalised system of decision-making would stifle initiative. It was an approach which must not be mistaken for incompetence or idleness, because the chairman was both aware of the risks involved and worked hard to channel effectively the efforts of his divisional managers by discussing on an informal and regular basis how the product range should develop. During the late 1950s, Sir Vincent had also been persuaded by Lester George, the company economist, to introduce a system of forecasting financial trends. While Sir Vincent had been sceptical about this idea, preferring to deal with the reality depicted by his graphs, George's system certainly enhanced senior management's grasp of the financial position after it was introduced in 1958.[9] This confirms Sebastian's view that the Ferranti structure was decisively not the problem; if things went wrong it was the quality of the decisions taken by managers at every level in the organisation, a philosophy by which the family stood resolutely throughout the period up to 1975.

The 'barons'

Having noted how the financial reporting system operated and evolved in the 1950s and 1960s, it is also vital to understand the internal dynamics of an organisation which was expanding in scale. In particular, it became apparent especially from the late 1940s that the main divisional managers – Eric Grundy at Moston, Jack Toothill at Crewe Toll, R. M. Hobill at the Avenue Works, Jack Prince at the Crown Works, and Dr Searby at Wythenshawe (including

Gem Mill) – were extremely powerful individuals. Not only did they run their own factories, each would also take responsibility for a series of smaller departments in their geographical area (see Figure 11.2), consulting with the managing director only when major decisions on new products were about to be made. As a result, terms like 'divisional barons' came into common parlance within the organisation, reflecting to some extent how the balance of power was perceived by the 1950s.

Sebastian was also keen to utilise the expertise of these 'barons', bringing them into even more senior positions as the transitionary phase took shape. Sir Vincent had formerly regarded the other directors as a sounding-board for his thoughts and decisions, keeping the board small and compact (see Appendix E). From the late 1950s, however, this level of management took on a more positive role in the organisation. In fact, certain appointments were forced on the company, because by 1960 several of the older board members had either retired (J. W. Davies in 1957 and W. G. Bass in 1960) or died (W. C. Pycroft in 1958).[10] Major R. W. Cooper also decided to retire when Sir Vincent left in 1963, bringing to an end fifty years of service as a director, in which time he had provided valuable advice on financial matters and assisted in the negotiations with the bank over extensions to the overdraft. In his place, Sebastian persuaded F. W. Hardstone (deputy chief general manager of the Westminster Bank) to join the Ferranti board, cementing further the relationship with an organisation which as we saw in section 8.4 had proved vital to the firm's recent expansion.

As we saw in chapter 10, Sir Vincent had also brought the prominent lawyer J. H. (Jim) Thomson (of Allen & Overy) on to the board in 1958, largely to provide a reliable source of legal advice at a time when the company's contractual negotiations were increasingly complicated by defence and international matters. However, Hardstone and Thomson were the only external appointments, because between 1958 and 1963, of the ten people elevated on to the board, nine were from other parts of the company (see Appendix D). Among the first of these new directors (in 1958) was Frank Rostron, the export sales manager, providing both an extensive grasp of the firm's overseas business, as well as good contacts with organisations like the Manchester Chamber of Commerce.[11] The sales manager, O. M. (Murray) Robson, was also made a director a year later, while over the following four years they were joined by each of the leading divisional managers, Jack Toothill (1958), Eric Grundy (1959), Jack Prince (1959), R. M. Hobill (1961), and Dr Searby (1962).[12]

While Sebastian felt that it was important to retain the cooperation of Sir Vincent's generation, there were some within the firm who were sceptical of the benefits this elevation of the 'barons' might bring. In particular, Tom

Lunt (the personnel manager) noted that while these directors were first-rate managers in their own right, as well as being extremely well-versed in their own technologies, it could be difficult for them when discussing policy at board level to reconcile their own interests against those of either other divisions or the company as a whole.[13] As we shall see later, one might also argue that the board lacked the courage to tell Sebastian what to do in certain circumstances, preferring to hold back from making harsh criticisms for fear of losing favour, and their jobs. This reveals yet another source of conflict within a family firm, because with Sebastian in such a commanding position he was always capable of changing any aspect of both strategy and structure. The 'barons', on the other hand, as we shall see in later sections, were much more concerned with their own territories, limiting the range of advice Sebastian might be given when deciding on strategic direction.

In spite of these problematic characteristics of a family firm, it is easy to see how organisationally and culturally Sebastian had retained all the features of his father's regime. Furthermore, even though financial pressures mounted throughout the 1960s, Sebastian rejected organisational change as a solution. It is a moot point, however, whether or not reforms would have solved all of the problems experienced by Ferranti between 1960 and 1975. Although the central problem of Sebastian's era as executive chairman was the financial implications of working in advanced technologies, it was exacerbated by several other features of those years, most notably intense American competition and difficulties in certain defence and civil markets. These features we can now go on to examine in greater detail by looking at the fortunes of four major product areas, semiconductors, avionics, numerical control and digital systems. While each have their own peculiar characteristics, the common denominator is how they demonstrate practical manifestations of the 'Ferranti Dilemma' in action, revealing the nature of the problems with which Sebastian and his team wrestled in those challenging years.

11.2 Semiconductor experiments and products

While other departments (transformers, meters and numerical control) suffered far worse from the changing conditions of the 1960s and 1970s (see section 12.1), the one division which epitomises the dilemma facing Ferranti at that time was the high-risk field of electronic components. Most especially, in committing the firm to an adventurous strategy of matching powerful American corporations like Western Electric (or its subsidiary, Bell Labs.), Texas Instruments and Fairchild, Sebastian was making a bold move which provided the most visible manifestation of his belief in pushing forward 'the

The furnace used by Dr A. A. Shepherd to 'pull' the first Ferranti silicon crystals for use in developing silicon semiconductors. *(Museum of Science and Industry at Manchester.)*

frontiers of engineering knowledge'.[14] With specific regard to electronic components, and especially the transition from first to second and third generation devices, Ferranti realised that the industry was changing rapidly, forcing firms to invest considerable resources if they were to remain a major player in the market. Furthermore, given the vital importance of having expertise in the design and production of components, microelectronics was the crucial battleground on which British firms stood out against the threat posed by American corporations. Unfortunately for Ferranti, though, the venture into a sector which required high levels of expenditure on both R & D and production facilities highlighted graphically the firm's financial shortcomings. Indeed, one might well question whether or not such a strategy should have been pursued.[15] Of course, contemporaries also criticised the level and nature of British government support for an industry which across the Atlantic (and later in Japan) was receiving substantial public assistance.[16] Nevertheless, it was the role of private enterprise which remained crucial if Britain was to retain a presence in this field, especially at firms like Ferranti which possessed substantial technical prowess.

Early experiments

In tracing the establishment of a semiconductor development team at Ferranti, it is vital to stress how a combination of Sir Vincent's instinctive prescience and MoS support pushed the firm into a series of experiments which provided the basis for a major initiative in this field. In the first place, after one of his many trips to the USA, Sir Vincent became aware of American work on new electronic components which many were predicting would replace the thermionic emission valve.[17] Consequently, in March 1952 he encouraged the electronics department manager, Peter Hall, to investigate the potential in this new technology. MoS's inter-services committee for the coordination of valve development, or CVD for short, headed by Dr J. Thomson, was also keen to see British progress on semiconductors. This led to Ferranti being encouraged to take advantage of the new ideas emanating from the USA,[18] and especially from Bell Telephone Laboratories (hereafter Bell Labs).

One should remember that much of the pure research on semiconductor technology had been done in the UK, by A. H. Wilson at Cambridge University, and both GEC and BT-H had worked on various development programmes.[19] However, once Wilson's research had been published in 1945, it was a team at the prominent American firm of Bell Labs (headed by John Bardeen and Walter Brattain) which took the lead by announcing the successful fabrication in 1948 of the world's first semiconductor component, the point contact transistor. The research at Bell Labs had been stimulated by its parent company, Western Electric, a major communications equipment manufacturer which urgently required a more efficient electronic switch to overcome what was widely regarded as the 'tyranny of numbers' associated with circuits using massed banks of thermionic valves. When the breakthrough made by Bardeen and Brattain was quickly followed up by the announcement by another engineer at Bell Labs, William Shockley, that he had developed the junction transistor, many anticipated the end of this 'tyranny' and the dawn of new era.

Although it was at least five years before electronics firms were designing circuits which used only semiconductor components, as opposed to valves,[20] there was considerable interest in the work at Bell Labs. When Western Electric organised a Transistor Symposium in March 1952, thirty-five organisations sent representatives, including ten from outside the USA. This

Symposium was an opportunity not only to hear how Bell Labs had made the initial discoveries, but also to take out a license from Western Electric to use this new technology. Dr Thomson at MoS's CVD group immediately sought Treasury permission to send a British delegation.[21] S. S. C. Mitchell (director of guided weapons development at MoS) had already discussed with Ferranti the possibility of incorporating transistors into guided weapon circuits, resulting in four of the company's senior staff – a director, W. G. Bass, R. H. Davies of Ferranti Electric Inc, and two engineers, Bill Gibbons and John Duckworth – being given funds to attend the Symposium.[22] Progress would appear to have been slow in negotiating a licence with Western Electric, while Bill Gibbons (formerly of STC) continued to work on the development of sub-miniature valves. However, after CVD had agreed to pay the fee, by September 1953 a license had been acquired, at what must be regarded as a relatively paltry sum of £9,000 per annum, leading to the formation of the firm's first semiconductor development team.[23]

Although this development team was to be a part of the Gem Mill electronics department, it was actually based at Wythenshawe, where Ferranti collected together a highly talented and innovative group of engineers. Peter Hall had just been transferred from his role as head of klystron development (see section 10.2) to become electronics department manager. He was soon joined by several engineers recruited from academia, after Eric Grundy had used his extensive contacts in this field to ascertain the names of those whom he thought might be capable of converting their experience of academic research into applied product development.[24] Although this combination of experimental and innovative skills is often difficult to find, Hall was fortunate to secure the services of Dr A. A. (Alan) Shepherd, Dr D. Mason and M. Wallbank. The latter had been working with Hall on klystrons, and his experience of guided weapons requirements proved extremely useful when the product development work started. Dr Mason, on the other hand, was brought in from Birmingham University, where he had been assisting Professor Garlick's investigations into semiconductor materials. Of even greater long-term importance to Ferranti, though, was Dr Shepherd, a physicist trained at the University of Manchester who was intrinsically interested in practical applications of his work. On hearing of the Wythenshawe opportunity, Dr Shepherd immediately left his teaching post at the North Staffordshire University College to join Peter Hall.[25] It was to be Dr Shepherd who provided the technical lead in Ferranti semiconductor development over the following fifteen years, while from the early 1970s he had taken over the management of Gem Mill's electronics operations, creating a dynamic business out of what to date had been a financial disaster.

Having assembled this team at Wythenshawe, one should note that CVD support extended only to paying for the Western Electric licence and no more than one-half of semiconductor development costs.[26] Figures on CVD financial subventions for this specific project are difficult to secure, because the internal accounts give only the total for all electronic component support, including klystrons, magnetrons and sub-miniature valves. However, it is clear that while CVD's financial support and encouragement was partially responsible for precipitating the firm's early entry into semiconductor development, it was internal funds which supported most of Hall's first two years of work. Hall even had to secure permission from MoS to use some of the facilities at Wythenshawe. In fact, only 1,600 square feet was allocated for this purpose, emphasising the low priority attached to the work by its initial sponsor. Sir Vincent eventually agreed to a two year development programme, with an annual budget of £35,000. Naturally, while this would have seemed paltry besides the sums invested by Bell Labs in the USA and Philips in Holland, it still represented a risk, given both the level of competition and the technology's embryonic nature.[27] It is consequently very much to the team's credit that with relatively meagre resources they were able to achieve such remarkable progress, establishing Ferranti as the most innovative European semiconductor firm over the following decades.

Silicon vs. *Germanium*

One of the most important points to remember about the early development work at Wythenshawe was Hall's decision to use silicon as the semiconductor material on which the team would focus, predating the general move to this material by at least five years. This might appear surprising, because not only had Bell Labs and its rivals concentrated on using germanium, silicon was also a much more difficult material to manipulate and process. The leading chemical firms at that time also proved to be incapable of producing crystals of sufficient purity from which reliable devices could be made.[28] On the other hand, given the extensive competition from both American and European firms in the germanium semiconductor market, Hall recognised that repeating the frustrating experience with cathode-ray tubes (see sections 8.3 and 8.4) would undermine the commercial viability of his Wythenshawe development team. An additional stimulus was the possibility of incorporating semiconductor devices into guided weapons, because silicon was more reliable and worked at temperatures of up to 150°C, twice that of germanium. More importantly, though, moving straight to silicon was mostly motivated by the need to secure a niche market which would not be subject to the same kind of competitive pressures undermining other parts of the Gem Mill activities.[29]

Size reductions across the 'generations' at Ferranti Electronics. From the left, a germanium semiconductor diode of the 1950s, a thermionic diode of the 1940s and a silicon semiconductor diode of the 1970s. *(Museum of Science and Industry at Manchester.)*

This insight into Hall's decision to use silicon emphasises how any retrospective view which gives Ferranti credit for adopting silicon at a much earlier stage than its rivals must be heavily qualified by referring to the commercial environment in which the team operated. Another point to make about this decision is the enormous strain it imposed on the development process, because in view of the paucity of knowledge on silicon semiconductors Ferranti was obliged to spend more time than its rivals experimenting with the material.[30] Initially, Mason and Wallbank were sent across to investigate the processing and working techniques employed at Bell Labs. However, early efforts at drawing silicon crystals from a furnace located in the Wythenshawe laboratory resulted merely in the creation of polycrystalline lumps. The main problem revolved around the constancy of furnace heating, and because silicon is highly reactive at its melting point (of 1420°C) it was absolutely essential that a constant temperature should be maintained while the crystal was being drawn from the molten material. Bell Labs even sent across their authority on silicon, G. Pearson. Although this proved helpful, it was only after considerable further experimentation that a suitable process was developed, employing a radio frequency heater in the furnace to achieve a constancy within 0.5°C. It was consequently the end of 1954 before suitable silicon crystals were being produced for Dr Shepherd's experiments on product development. Sir Vincent was naturally concerned to hear that by February 1955 Hall had already gone £2,000 over his £47,000 budget. The chairman was nevertheless mollified by the news that a product was almost ready for the market by that time, providing the rationale for even further support.[31]

The product Hall promised Sir Vincent was a silicon alloy junction diode. It was the first of its type developed and produced in Europe, giving Ferranti the opportunity to exploit a niche market which was just then beginning to expand rapidly.[32] Indeed, considerable interest was aroused by the diode's announcement. Dr Thomson at CVD purchased 100 for testing purposes,[33] while by 1956–57 annual output had reached £100,000. Of course, while it would have been technically easier to produce germanium transistors, as the cathode-ray tube department at Gem Mill had discovered competing directly against such powerful firms as Mullards seemed dangerous, especially as many of the firm's rivals, both at home and in the USA, were spending much larger sums on semiconductor research and development. This confirms the efficacy of Hall's decision to focus on niche markets, a point confirmed by the firm's ability to charge remunerative prices (of c. £3 per diode), because Ferranti remained the only British producer of silicon devices until the early 1960s. At the same time, it was initially difficult to cover all costs, because even though output had risen to almost £100,000 by 1956–57, development costs of over £53,000 per annum ate up all the surplus, forcing Hall to lobby Sir Vincent for further funds to expand and diversify output.[34]

Gem Mill expansion

Hall, of course, was in a strong bargaining position when negotiating the expansion of his embryonic semiconductor department: not only had considerable interest been shown in the first products,[35] the old electronics department at Gem Mill was slowly being wound down at exactly the same time. Semiconductor production had actually been located at Gem Mill in 1955, £40,000 having been spent on new plant to fabricate these highly sophisticated devices.[36] As we saw in section 8.4, the cathode-ray tube and valve businesses were also by then grinding to a halt after a dismal decade of financial losses and poor market performance. Nevertheless, even though this created an obvious gap at Gem Mill for Hall's team, it was still important to convince the chairman that unless semiconductor production was fully automated and new development facilities were built, American competition would soon eliminate Ferranti from what was a crucial new sector of the electronics industry. In this context, it is vital to stress the role played by

Sydney Jackson, Gem Mill's chief plant engineer, because in developing efficient production equipment for the semiconductor team he strengthened Hall's case when it was presented to Sir Vincent.[37] The board consequently decided in January 1957 that while the last cathode-ray tube contracts were being completed every effort should be made to convert Gem Mill into a base for silicon diode production.[38] Hall also succeeded in persuading ICI to start producing silicon crystals, selling them the rights to use the Wythenshawe-developed refining process (devised by Dr Vincent Magee) for £10,000 in August 1957.[39] This reinforces a point made in several previous passages (see Sections 8.4 and 10.4), that 1957 was a crucial year for Ferranti, especially in forcing through the transition from first to second generation electronic components.

The transformation at Gem Mill was naturally not effected overnight, largely because the Mullard cathode-ray tube contract was negotiated to last two years. By 1960, though, after fifteen months of development work, completely new production methods had been developed by Sydney Jackson and installed by Hall's team. This investment gave Ferranti the capacity to produce 43,000 diodes per week, prompting a twenty per cent reduction in prices between 1958 and 1960.[40] At exactly the same time, however, and reflecting the challenges associated with this rapidly-advancing technology, Ferranti was also working on a new means of producing semiconductor components, having been introduced to the 'diffusion' process at the 1956 Bell Labs Transistor Symposium.[41] This momentous innovation, as we shall see in the next section, was creating the technological foundations for yet another leap forward in electronic componentry, especially when combined with other advances like the 'planar' process (developed by Fairchild in 1958–59) and the 'epitaxy' process (Bell Labs in 1960).[42] In simple terms, 'diffusion' allowed the much cheaper production of components which were more reliable than the old pulled-crystal devices, giving firms like Ferranti the opportunity to expand their range of products. By 1960, using the diffusion process, Ferranti had consequently produced its first transistor, the ZT 20 *Mesa*, a specialised device for both military and commercial requirements which was capable of working at up to 100 megahertz.[43]

It is clear from what we have seen of the 1950s experiments that Ferranti clearly deserved its widely-held reputation as 'the foremost British semiconductor company',[44] having established an unchallenged position as the leading silicon component producer through the rapid adaptation of American ideas. Most importantly, with sales rising steadily, Gem Mill had also been converted into a profitable concern, recording an average annual surplus of almost £150,000 between 1957–58 and 1960–61. This contrasted sharply with the consistent losses reported over the previous twelve years on cathode-ray tubes and valves.[45] On the other hand, undermining any claim that Gem Mill could be regarded as financially self-sufficient, by 1960–61 the capital employed at Gem Mill stood at almost £980,000, compared to £421,000 six years earlier, while a total of £823,000 had been spent on semiconductor development at the Wythenshawe laboratories. Indeed, as the pace of technological progress quickened ever faster in the 1960s, both Sir Vincent and Sebastian were constantly lobbied for additional support from Peter Hall and his successors.[46] This pressure was accentuated by the full force of American competition, resulting in frequent and insistent calls for more funding. It also posed fresh questions about the firm's ability to survive in such a market, especially when the decision to move on to third generation devices was being discussed just at the time when Sebastian was facing up to the dilemma of considering the long-term development of Ferranti.

11.3 Starting up in microelectronics

Ferranti had clearly made a successful entrance into the semiconductor industry during the 1950s. By the time the *Mesa* transistor had been introduced in 1960, the revamped electronics department at Gem Mill was generally regarded as one of the most innovative in Europe.[47] However, by

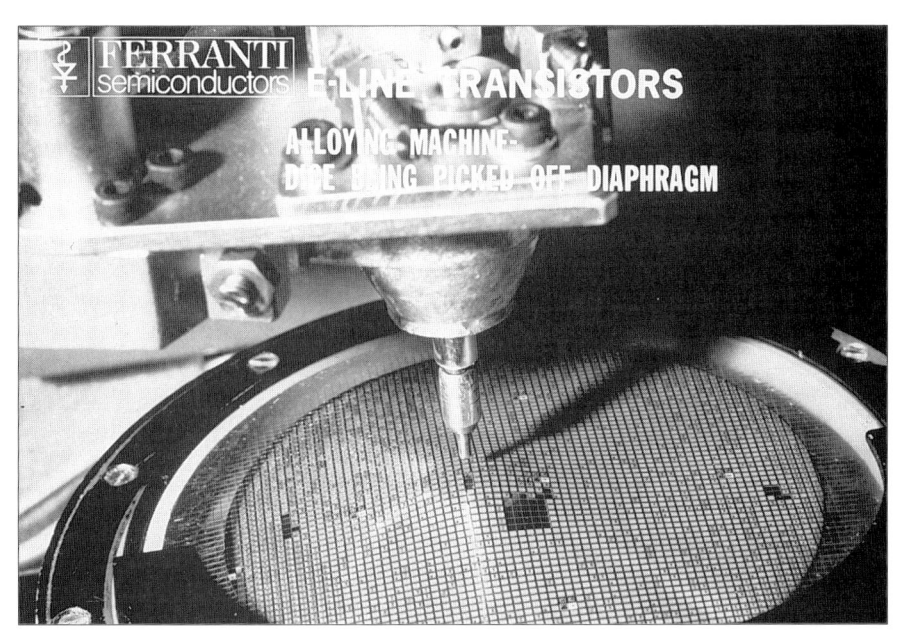

The production equipment developed on the transistor line.
(Museum of Science and Industry at Manchester.)

combining the diffusion, planar and epitaxial processes mentioned earlier, semiconductor production technology was at that time about to make a giant leap forward, precipitating the emergence of what has come to be known as the integrated circuit, or 'chip'. In fact, as early as 1952 G. W. A. Dummer at RRE had suggested the combination of several discrete components on a single 'chip' of semiconductor material.[48] However, even though he produced some working models, it was left to the American pioneers at Bell Labs to make the decisive commercial breakthrough when in 1956 they announced the diffusion production process. Of course, it was only after Fairchild had developed the planar process, and Bell Labs had added further improvements in the form of an epitaxy process, that integrated circuits became a full-scale commercial possibility. Nevertheless, when within six months in 1961 Fairchild and Texas Instruments started mass-production of these advanced components, one can say that the third generation device had arrived on the scene.

Micronor I and II

Building on their success with the *Mesa*, Dr Shepherd and the highly innovative Maurice Gribble (of automation systems) were naturally keen to exploit further the new ideas emanating from American electronics laboratories. They were also encouraged to experiment with improved designs by two other parts of the Ferranti organisation: Denis Best in the automation systems department at Wythenshawe was anxious to improve the reliability of his *Argus* range of computers (see section 10.8); and aircraft equipment department at Moston wanted to miniaturise its equipment. By 1962, the electronics department was consequently able to exhibit its first integrated circuit, variously known as either *Micronor I* (for use in *Argus*) or *Microlin* (aircraft equipment).[49] In fact, although as small as an old-style transistor (because it was produced using selective diffusion and deposition), *Micronor I* was actually a multi-chip circuit which used two 'chips' of silicon interconnected by bonded golden wires to carry two transistors and six resistors.[50] Nevertheless, this demonstrated yet again how Ferranti engineers led the field in Europe, because no other firm outside the USA had succeeded in utilising the new technology commercially.

While demand for integrated circuits had yet to take off in the UK, and Gem Mill relied to a significant extent on sales to other divisions in Ferranti, Dr Shepherd and Maurice Gribble were rapidly establishing a strong position in this nascent technology. In fact, just 2,000 integrated circuits were made and sold between 1962 and 1965.[51] At the same time, development work continued on improved versions of *Micronor I*, largely motivated by internal

Ferranti Micronor II integrated circuit, in this case used for street lighting control.
(Museum of Science and Industry at Manchester.)

requirements, in particular by Denis Best's desire to develop new ranges of the *Argus* computer.[52] As Table 11.1 also reveals, integrated circuit developmentexpenditure was consequently mounting rapidly after the initial breakthrough. Although some CVD support was forthcoming for this work, Ferranti was clearly providing an increasing share of the budget after 1961. The story changes in the mid-1960s, when as we shall see later an interventionist Labour government contributed more extensively in this field. However, when Dr Shepherd was developing the improved version of *Micronor I* it was internal funds which provided the bulk of his budget. This again demonstrates how Sebastian was willing to back this work as fully as possible, given both his confidence in the Gem Mill team, as well as his belief that expertise in this crucial area was vital for the firm's future competitiveness.[53]

Throughout the early 1960s it was Fairchild with its DTL (diode-transistor-logic) integrated circuit which dominated the microelectronics market.[54] However, when in 1965 Ferranti announced *Micronor II* many were impressed with its much greater speed and superior loading capability. Contemporaries were especially impressed with the relatively short period in which the device had been developed, because three years was regarded as unprecedented, in view of the two-month cycle required for each circuit test.[55] It is important to note that in *Micronor II* Dr Shepherd and Maurice Gribble (now assisted by P. J. Bagnall) had developed a single-chip integrated circuit, repaying the faith placed in them by senior management. Indeed, such was *Micronor II*'s potential that Marconi purchased a license to produce this integrated circuit, in the hope that it would stave off the increasingly fierce American competition.[56] Most importantly, because this market was expected to rise in value to £20 million annually, Ferranti invested over £1.2 million in new production plant, giving Gem Mill the capacity to produce 40,000 integrated circuits per week. This once again reaffirmed the Ferranti commitment to electronic components.[57] It was consequently vital that Ferranti should be able to secure a substantial foothold in this sector, having spent so much on both development and production. However, once again a familiar combination of factors conspired to undermine this strategy. Even though its main products were undoubtedly as innovative and progressive as many of its rivals, Gem Mill was to experience great difficulty in matching the mighty American corporations.

Table 11.1. *Ferranti integrated circuit sales and R & D expenditure, 1961–71 (£000)*

Year to March	Integrated circuit sales	Total integrated circuit R & D	Total Semiconductor R & D Expenditure	Government-sponsored R & D (Integrated circuits)
1961	—	32	168	16
1962	—	58	168	27
1963	1	78	172	21
1964	40	135	212	32
1965	85	200	272	58
1966	194	234	266	70
1967	497	308	388	83
1968	688	404	NA	89
1969	756	461	NA	111
1970	1,351	461	NA	92
1971	1,680	570	NA	103

Key: NA signifies not available.

Source: Ferranti Management Accounts, 1960–72.

Testing equipment developed for integrated circuits at the Gem Mill factory.
(Museum of Science and Industry at Manchester.)

The struggle with American ascendancy

As we noted in the case of data processing computers (see Section 9.10), Ferranti sold out to ICT because of an inability to finance the high level of development and production expenditure required in such a rapidly-advancing industry. Although Ferranti technology might well have been as highly regarded as any other firm's, by the early 1960s insufficient demand at home had prevented it from exploiting this lead. Even when UK sales started to increase, powerful American corporations like IBM were able to use the competitive advantage acquired as a result of substantial home sales to eliminate most British companies from the industry. This was a scenario both Sebastian and the Gem Mill team were determined not to see repeated with integrated circuits, even though in many ways the circumstances seemed to be conspiring in a similar way. In the first place, after a considerable programme of investment in both development and production facilities, cash-flow at Gem Mill had been distinctly negative since the mid-1950s, in spite of the profits made on silicon diode production between 1955 and 1961. The discrete components (diodes and transistors) business actually remained

The Ferranti F100-L microcircuit passing through the eye of a sewing needle. (*Museum of Science and Industry at Manchester.*)

profitable throughout the 1960s, and great care was taken to ensure that the healthy position established in this market was maintained while new products were developed. Unfortunately, though, it was these new products, and in particular integrated circuits, which created all the problems, especially when in 1966 Texas Instruments announced its TTL (transistor-transistor-logic) integrated circuit as a direct rival to *Micronor II*.[58]

There is little doubt that up to the 1970s American electronics corporations enjoyed an enormous advantage over any of their rivals. The main reason for this superiority was a market for components and equipment unmatched in size and character anywhere in the world. In the first place, even as late as 1968 the USA accounted for sixty-two per cent of the total world market for all semiconductor devices, as well as eighty per cent of all integrated circuit sales.[59] The main American customers, of course, were the space and defence agencies which at that time were committing enormous budgets to the advancement of electronic technology, offering what are described as 'pump-priming' prices at the beginning of product cycles which would encourage corporations to harness dynamic economies of scale in establishing extensive development and production facilities.[60] For example, the *Minuteman* guided weapon and *Apollo* space programme provided not only the initial development funds for the integrated circuits announced by Texas Instruments and Fairchild in 1961, they also offered the first substantial high-priced market, encouraging these firms to establish major plants. At a later stage, between 1967 and 1969, Texas Instruments alone received $229 million (approximately £96 million) in government funds for its integrated circuit development programme, accentuating its lead over both American and European rivals.[61] In the late 1960s, then, it is not surprising that firms like Texas Instruments, Motorola and Fairchild became so dominant, because the American government and its agencies actually accounted for over fifty per cent of all electronic component sales in the USA, which in turn represented sixty-two per cent of world sales.[62]

The central role played by large-scale government sponsorship and procurement was undoubtedly the crucial theme of the American scene. As Table 11.1 demonstrates with regard to Ferranti integrated circuit development, however, the situation was very different in Britain. The most obvious worry was securing markets for *Micronor II*, because even though the *Argus* 400 range provided a steady source of demand, this could never hope to reach the American levels (see section 10.8). The Gem Mill team was also frustrated in this respect by ICT's decision to use the Texas Instruments TTL integrated circuit in its 1906 range of computers,[63] a development which created much ill-feeling between the two British companies. In fact, ICT managers like Peter Hall, who had formerly been intimately involved with Ferranti electronics efforts, had wanted to buy from Ferranti. However, he found that not only was little effort put into selling *Micronor II*, Ferranti refused to set up a second source of supply.[64] Military customers were also reluctant to place large orders with Gem Mill because the firm only possessed a single production facility.

This handicap was overcome by February 1967, when a new factory was built at Ormsgill, near Barrow-in-Furness.[65] Ferranti consequently made some effort to raise more interest in its advanced products, publicising their intention by 1970 to create the capacity, at Gem Mill and Ormsgill, to produce annually up to fifteen million semiconductor devices. Although the total capital expenditure figures are not available, between 1963–64 and 1969–70 the electronics department capital employed leapt from £1.4 million to £3.4 million, while the Gem Mill labour force rose in size over the same period from 876 to 1788. It was a significant effort which reflected the firm's wholehearted commitment to microelectronics. Once again, though, the commercial viability of such an endeavour was called into question, even after the incumbent Labour government started to provide greater financial support.

11.4 Looking for state support

Sebastian's strategy

By the mid-1960s, it is apparent that as a direct result of the growing American threat British electronics firms were beginning to develop a siege mentality. Sebastian de Ferranti likened the situation to a 'war', explaining in typically forthright terms how powerful American corporations were undermining the domestic industry.[66] This was actually a recurring theme of his public speeches in the 1960s, when on several occasions he invited successive British governments to adopt a much more partisan approach towards vital high technology industries.[67] In particular, using the sharply contrasting stimulus provided by American space and defence spending, Sebastian argued that the outbreak of the electronic components 'war' had gone largely unnoticed by the British authorities. It was also a 'war' which British firms were losing, leading, he argued, to the possibility that the UK would no longer be able to satisfy its own needs.

In fact, while by 1967 only 53.4 per cent of all integrated circuits sold (valued at £5.8 million) in the UK were produced domestically, by 1969 this position had deteriorated to such an extent that the proportion had fallen to 45.8 per cent.[68] Furthermore, an increasing proportion of domestic output was coming from the plants established in the south of England and Central Scotland by American firms,[69] substantiating the claims of those like Sebastian de Ferranti that Britain was losing control of the industry. Although Ferranti enjoyed some successes, securing in 1969 an order from ICL for 700,000 of its integrated circuits, to be delivered over the following three years.[70] On the other hand, while Texas Instruments had already captured one-quarter of the UK market by that stage and a variety of other American and European subsidiaries held a further fifty per cent, Ferranti could only claim eleven per cent of total semiconductor sales and just six per cent of the domestic integrated circuit market.[71]

The crucial point to note at this stage concerning the competitiveness of Gem Mill was its productivity levels, because when one considers the simple fact that Ferranti could only produce an integrated circuit for 12.5 pence, Texas Instruments was selling them at five pence.[72] It was consequently vital to improve the yields on each of the twenty-seven different stages involved in the production of a single integrated circuit, to such an extent indeed that ninety-five per cent yields were required at each stage in order to achieve an overall yield of twenty-five per cent on the total batch.[73] As we noted earlier, American corporations achieved such results because of the pump-priming policies adopted by their customers, a practice which facilitated the harnessing of dynamic economies of scale at the beginning of each product cycle. They were also well-supported by their indigenous financial institutions, many of which were willing to take long-term positions on their investments. British producers, on the other hand, were unable to adopt similar strategies when faced with a lower level of demand, given the inherently short-termist approach of British financial institutions. This inevitably put even greater emphasis on the role government might play in creating the opportunity to exploit technological openings. Sebastian certainly felt that the state ought to play a much more positive role, just as it did in the USA and in Japan at that time.[74] As a consequence, considerable effort was spent in lobbying various ministries for more assistance in the struggle to maintain a presence in this vital sector.

MinTech and the NRDC

Given the difficulties experienced in defence markets during the mid-1960s, a point we shall illustrate graphically over the next few sections, lobbying for support in these areas proved extremely difficult at that time. Notwithstanding this state of affairs, it is important to remember how in 1964 a new Labour government had been elected with a promise to place Britain in 'the white heat of the technological revolution'.[75] We shall question the genuine nature of this commitment in Section 11.5, when the *TSR–2* story will feature prominently. As far as electronic components was concerned, it was clear that the new Ministry of Technology created by Labour, headed firstly by Frank Cousins and later by Anthony Wedgwood Benn, would prove supportive. There were problems with this support, and certainly it was different in scale and nature to the kind of schemes developed across the Atlantic. Nevertheless, in spite of the *Bloodhound* problem, at least Ferranti found favour in civil-oriented areas of Whitehall at a time when other ministries were less interested in what the company had to offer.

Although it was 1966 before anything positive was done, one of the more interesting schemes launched by the newly-created Ministry of Technology (MinTech) was known as the Advanced Computer Techniques Project (ACTP), to be coordinated by the NRDC. In fact, while components producers were encouraged to apply for financial assistance where their ideas might be appropriate, ACTP was mainly concerned with assisting ICT in its drive for improved performance.[76] One must also stress how any funds released by MinTech came in the form of loans, rather than grants, which had to be repaid by a levy on sales, rather than on profits. Similarly, there was no guarantee of orders for the resulting product, demonstrating how the nature of British public support was very different to that offered in the

USA. Furthermore, when compared to the sums provided by NASA or the USAF, ACTP's £1.5 million budget paled into insignificance. Nevertheless, given the huge cost of developing an electronic components business, Ferranti was glad of any assistance. The first loan was actually provided in 1966, totalling £186,000. This was boosted in February 1969, when the NRDC agreed to provide a further £1.205 million for production development work at Gem Mill, bolstering what was a financially-precarious business. After all, as Table 11.1 reveals, integrated circuit development costs were rising inexorably during the late 1960s, at a time when this business had made losses of almost £1.3 million between 1966–67 and 1969–70.[77]

After having moved out of the NRDC's main area of interest when selling the data processing computer department to ICT in 1963, Ferranti had consequently reforged its relationship with an agency which had been of considerable assistance in the development of mainframe computers. Of course, there had been some problems with the Ferranti-NRDC relationship during the 1950s, especially with the *Pegasus* development contracts (see section 9.4). By the 1960s, though, both civil servants and industrialists had learnt from these experiences, leading to the establishment of quarterly meetings, during which both financial and technical progress was monitored.[78] This close degree of liaison between company and sponsoring body was very similar to the American practice, ensuring the productive use of scarce resources at a time of considerable urgency. The second tranche of support actually provided thirty-seven per cent of Gem Mill's negative cash-flow over its duration (1969–71). While the loan had to be repaid by a three per cent levy on integrated circuit sales, Dr Shepherd is in no doubt that it was crucial to his department's survival.

1970 Hiatus, MESS and the CDI process

The Labour government's support after 1966 had consequently proved extremely effective in bolstering Gem Mill's pioneering work with integrated circuits. Unfortunately, however, when a Conservative government was elected in 1970 it abolished MinTech and cancelled programmes like the ACTP, jeopardising the future viability of a vital British high technology industry. The government was headed by Mr Edward Heath, who at that time believed staunchly in reducing what he regarded as the State's damaging influence on the economy.[79] Of course, this not only ignored what was happening in countries like the USA, France and Japan, where government support had proved fundamental to the success of high technology industries, it also coincided with the onset of a major international depression, forcing Heath to execute his infamous U-Turn on economic policy. Having advocated a complete withdrawal of government from industry, by 1972 the old Board of Trade, or what was by then called the Department of Trade & Industry (DoTI), headed by John Davies, was implementing legislation which provided wide-ranging powers for the State in many areas of micro-economic development. Most importantly for Gem Mill, in 1973 the Micro-Electronics Support Scheme (MESS) had been initiated, reinstituting and bolstering the late 1960s programmes. In fact, MESS provided fifty per cent of the costs of approved development programmes. More significantly, the State became a partner in the projects because loan repayments were to be made out of the profits generated from future sales, rather than from the sales themselves. On the other hand, though, there had been a damaging hiatus between the end of the ACTP scheme (1971) and DoTI's reawakening in 1973, badly hindering the progress being made at Gem Mill during a crucial period for the business.

The years between 1966 and 1973 were a make-or-break period for the British microelectronics industry, particularly as while sales of integrated circuits were rising the proportion made in the UK fell drastically.[80] In this context, it was vital to develop a viable strategy for the electronics department, especially as the well-funded American corporations were threatening to eliminate firms like Ferranti from the marketplace. The choices ranged from either leaving the integrated circuit business altogether, competing head on with firms like Texas Instruments in the standard integrated circuit market, or exploiting any niches which might have existed. As we shall see later in section 11.8, Sebastian was advised very strongly by several of his directors to take the first option.[81] The chairman, however, remained just as committed to Gem Mill as his father had been, arguing that closure was anathema to the company philosophy. This support was naturally good news to John Pickin, the man who had succeeded Peter Hall as head of Gem Mill in 1959. On the other hand, it still left the tricky decision about which particular market to assault, especially in view of the growing level of American domination. It is also important to note that Dr Alan Shepherd had left Gem Mill in 1967, having decided to extend his experience by taking on the post of instrument department manager in the Moston group. In his place as head of the design team John Pickin had appointed the highly talented David Grundy, providing tremendous continuity in the development of advanced technologies which would improve Gem Mill's competitiveness.

Dr Shepherd's strategy

Having moved to the Moston group in 1967, though, Dr Shepherd was to find himself back at Gem Mill within two years. In fact, John Pickin suffered a heart attack in 1969, forcing him to stand down from the high pressure role as Gem Mill manager. The chairman responded speedily to this crisis, by bringing Dr Shepherd back from instrument department and initiating over fifteen years of continuity for the electronic components department. Over the following decade, in particular, Dr Shepherd was especially concerned with the operational performance of Gem Mill, focusing the team's energies on raising productivity. He was well aware of the highly cyclical nature of components sales, with some years recording up to twenty-five per cent growth, and others providing a stagnant market. His working philosophy was based on the idea that successful companies in the semiconductor business produced annual sales which were approximately twice the capital employed. In growth years, therefore, to fund internally the twenty-five per cent increase in capital, a profit after dividends, interest and tax of 12.5 per cent of sales had to be produced. It was also well known that while most American semiconductor corporations had failed to pay any dividends during the 1960s and 1970s, a gross operating profit of twenty-five per cent on sales had to be achieved if Gem Mill was going to contribute to corporate

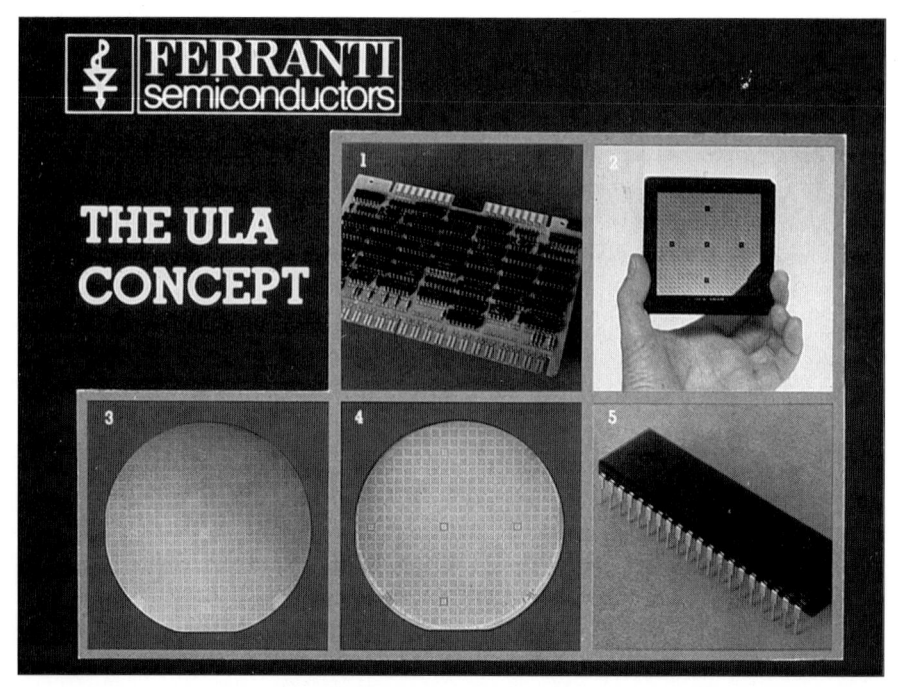

How the ULA concept was marketed by Ferranti in the 1970s. Extensive efforts were made by the sales team to present the concept to the large numbers of potential customers.
(Museum of Science and Industry at Manchester.)

dividends, interest and tax, imposing an enormous burden on Dr Shepherd's team. American corporations were able to survive in this kind of environment because of the support provided by Wall Street financiers and venture capitalists, even though only rarely were any dividends forthcoming from enterprises like Fairchild, Motorola and Intel.

Faced with these financial facts of life, Dr Shepherd decided that Gem Mill would never be capable of competing against the American firms in the market for standard integrated circuits. By 1970, even though the MinTech funds had boosted efforts to raise productivity, foreign-made integrated circuits were still at least fifty per cent cheaper than Gem Mill products.[82] In the late 1960s, however, both Western Electric and Fairchild announced the discovery of yet another new production technology, collector diffusion isolation (CDI). David Grundy was instructed by Dr Shepherd to examine its potential as a means of further improving productivity at Gem Mill, even though neither of the American firms actually used CDI until well into the 1970s. This led to some dramatic developments at Gem Mill, because in successfully adapting CDI to the production of integrated circuits David Grundy and his team were able to claim considerable success in producing the most complex bipolar microcircuits. Indeed, the Ferranti chip was more advanced than its rivals, providing the firm with a substantial technical competitive advantage.[83]

ULA and niche markets

Although Ferranti was later obliged to compensate Fairchild for the use of its CDI patents, paying £150,000 in five yearly instalments,[84] the new process was a major coup for Gem Mill in allowing the much greater large-scale integration of functions on a chip of semiconductor material. Unfortunately, though, it was also in 1971 that ACTP funding was abruptly terminated by the Heath government, while a depression in the USA intensified competition in the expanding British market. It was in these circumstances that Dr Shepherd decided to refocus Grundy's activities on to the utilisation of CDI for the production of non-standard microcircuits, rather than the standard chip. There was, indeed, a growing demand from equipment manufacturers for an integrated circuit which exactly matched their own requirements, as designers started to incorporate chips into their circuits. This led Ferranti to develop what eventually came to be marketed as the Uncommitted Logic Array (ULA), or quite simply a customised bipolar microcircuit. It will also become clear that the decision to focus on a niche market, just as with the production of a silicon diode in 1955, marked a decisive turnround in Gem Mill's fortunes, substantiating Dr Shepherd's decision to launch the ULA.

While academics like Sciberras have argued that Dr Shepherd had taken a highly defensive decision in deciding to concentrate on a niche market, leaving the much larger standard microcircuit market to the Americans,[85] in the circumstances it is difficult to see how else Gem Mill could have survived. In the early 1970s, Ferranti could still only claim six per cent of the integrated circuit market, while losses on this business continued to mount. The electronics department as a whole actually generated a surplus in almost every year between 1956–57 and 1972–73,[86] largely because of profitable discrete components (transistors, etc.) sales. At the same time, not only did the losses on microcircuit sales average almost £300,000 up to the end of this period, Gem Mill's negative cash flow over the previous five years exceeded £2.5 million.[87] In short, Sebastian's decision to back Gem Mill was by the mid-1970s beginning to take on the shape of a major financial millstone. In his first years as manager, Dr Shepherd instigated a major rationalisation programme, cutting the labour force back by twenty per cent as a means of wrestling with the cost problem. It is also important to note that some of the larger British electronics firms were even more badly affected by the early 1970s environment. Even the much larger firm of GEC was obliged to pull out of the integrated circuit business, closing its two factories at Witham and Glenrothes in 1972. Furthermore, American domination of the semiconductor market continued to increase, with eighty-five per cent of all UK sales coming from foreign-owned multinationals by 1977.[88] This was the vital context in which Dr Shepherd and his team were obliged to operate, exacerbated by inconsistent government support which rarely matched the level of funding granted in the USA or Japan.

The siege mentality prevailing in the British electronics industry which was referred to at the beginning of this section was clearly well played-out at Gem Mill. While some support for microcircuit yield-improvement programmes had been forthcoming from a Labour government allegedly committed to advancing technological frontiers, it was clearly insufficient as a bulwark against the overwhelming onslaught from American (and some European) corporations. The American firms had been provided with a much more supportive environment in which they could exploit what was an exciting and highly expensive new technology, forcing even the most innovative European firms either to leave the semiconductor market altogether, or to concentrate on niche markets. For Ferranti, in spite of successfully developing the Western Electric and Fairchild innovations, and building up a wide reputation for introducing and producing promising new products, the only rational strategy was to move out of the mass market and specialise on the ULA concept. It had been a bold move by Sebastian to back the Gem Mill team, especially as by the early 1980s Gem Mill became one of the world's most profitable electronic components producers. Moreover, other Ferranti divisions were able to benefit substantially from having access to such in-house expertise. In view of the problems besetting other parts of the company after the mid-1960s, it is nevertheless possible to question this commitment, particularly as the traditionally profitable defence departments were also struggling to deal with the political machinations of a very different period.

11.5 Edinburgh and the TSR–2

The problems affecting Gem Mill's viability were clearly of substantial proportions, especially given the scale and intensity of foreign competition. Other parts of Ferranti, however, were faced with pressures imposed domestically, especially after 1964. In that year, of course, a new Labour government had been elected on a dual promise to boost Britain's high technology sectors and improve the general competitiveness of business across a wide spectrum. Unfortunately, though, the combination of a highly damaging legacy inherited from thirteen years of Conservative government, along with economic mismanagement over the following three years, placed in jeopardy any hope that the 'white heat of the technological revolution' would ever affect more than a handful of firms.[89] In the first place, Harold Wilson had to deal with enormous balance of payments difficulties in 1964, a situation which was compounded over the period up to 1967 by speculation against the pound sterling on foreign exchange markets. In view of the Treasury's dogged belief in correcting these problems by deflating the domestic economy, this ensured that funds for MinTech and other departments were often squeezed in successive budgets. Indeed, until at least 1968 British economic activity was strangled by the manner in which Labour coped with these macro-economic problems, creating an inhospitable environment for firms dependent to a significant extent on government spending in areas like defence and high technology. This would have been bad enough for Ferranti, but when as a result of the *Bloodhound* revelations new contract conditions were also introduced by defence departments, this created severe difficulties for several divisions which were almost wholly dependent on government business.

Crewe Toll structure

In this context it is vital to examine what had been the post-War Ferranti success story at Crewe Toll in Edinburgh, where as Sections 8.6 and 8.7 demonstrated a flourishing and profitable avionics business had been established by Sir John Toothill and his team. Although Sir Vincent had always referred to Crewe Toll as Sir John's 'toy', in view of its financial performance the chairman was reluctant to interfere too much in the decision-making process. Indeed, because by the late 1950s Edinburgh had become the most profitable part of the far-flung Ferranti empire, while other divisions struggled to generate any positive cash-flow, it was vital to bolster the Scottish branch as far as possible. One means of achieving this aim was to refine the Crewe Toll organisation, particularly after Sir John returned from a business trip to California in November 1958 with jaundice and gall bladder problems. This precipitated a decision to departmentalise the various activities on a more formalised level.[90] Of course, a series of identifiable groups had been in existence at Crewe Toll since 1945, when Sir John first devised his diversification strategy (see Section 8.6). However, using the divisional model emerging in the Hollinwood and Moston groups, it was possible to give departmental managers much greater financial and strategic direction of their activities and reduce the burden on Toothill as the Crewe Toll supremo.[91]

The four new trading departments created in 1959 were applied electronics (run by John Stewart), inertial systems (Jim Drury), electronic systems (Donald McCallum), and numerical control (D. T. N. Williamson).[92] An evident problem with this reform, however, was the managers themselves, in that they were all engineers by training and instinct. In the early years of this system's operation, then, considerable assistance from Sir John and his staff was required in setting financial targets and achieving the necessary control over projects. In this respect, it is important to stress how central coordination of the organisation was effected by a monthly management meeting chaired by Sir John. Of even greater importance was this meeting's secretary, J. B. Smith, because he had the crucial role of interpreting the different requirements of the engineers and accountants. J. B. Smith was particularly successful in instilling a watchful brief into the managers' attitude towards cash-flow, leading McCallum to argue that Ferranti was consequently well in advance of many British companies in monitoring this crucial indicator of a business's health.[93] Smith also developed improved methods of presenting financial information, reforms which proved to have been an invaluable feature of Crewe Toll's development as a viable business during the difficult market conditions of the mid-1960s.

The TSR–2 Story

As well as improving the organisation, having achieved considerable success with the AI23 and AI23B on-board radars senior Crewe Toll figures were also keen to expand the avionics business further. As we saw in Section 8.6, Crewe Toll had by 1960 already started work on both the forward-looking radar (FLR) and inertial navigation platform for the *TSR–2* military aircraft, on which the division's future success depended heavily. For the British military aircraft industry as a whole, *TSR–2* was also vital, particularly as in 1960 the Conservative government had manoeuvred the three main companies (English Electric, Vickers and Bristol) into a merger with the promise of funds to develop what many regarded as the world's most advanced fighter.[94] The resulting company, British Aircraft Co. (BAC), worked hard over the following years to build *TSR–2*, resulting in an aircraft which in 1964 seemed 'bright with promise'.[95] The Ferranti equipments have been described as 'the core around which the entire weapon was created', giving Crewe Toll a central role in the whole project. As BAC itself noted:

> Reliability, safety and ease of maintenance have been designed into this radar from the very beginning – a philosophy backed by nearly twenty years of experience by Ferranti Ltd in the design, flight-testing and production of aircraft fire control stations.[96]

Donald McCallum describes how after a considerable amount of testing around Linlithgow, using *Buccaneer* and *Dakota* aircraft, his department had produced an FLR which provided the *TSR–2* with a distinct advantage over its rivals, both British and American (see Section 8.6). Although the Vickers project manager, George Henson, had been trying for some years to replace the Ferranti radar with equipment made by Texas Instruments – this was known at Crewe Toll as 'the Texas Ranger' – nobody would accept his argument that the Americans had anything better to offer, giving Crewe Toll the clear impression that orders would be forthcoming.[97]

In retrospect, of course, it is clear that by 1964 the *TSR–2* project was doomed. It was just at the initial test flight stage that the new Labour government started to grapple with the implications of major balance of payments problems. As the cost of *TSR–2* had risen dramatically, from an estimated £90 million in 1959 to £200 million by 1963, there was every possibility that the project would be scrapped.[98] Some have argued that Labour had actually decided to scrap *TSR–2* while still in Opposition. However, little evidence exists to confirm this view, especially as even as late as February 1965 Harold Wilson was still in favour of sustaining his pre-Election commitment to the aircraft.[99] Although the Labour Party leader had diplomatically noted in the run-up to the 1964 General Election that his position on *TSR–2* was 'exactly the same as the government's',[100] clearly other pressures were to play a much greater part in the unfolding scenario.

The prospects for firm *TSR–2* orders certainly seemed bleak towards the latter end of 1964, particularly after the new Labour government had cancelled two major aircraft projects, the Hawker Siddeley 681 (a jet transport with a short field capacity) and the Hawker P1154 (a supersonic vertical take-off jet). It is important to note, however, that in the prevailing economic crisis not only was the Treasury keen to see deep public expenditure cuts, there were influential voices in the military and scientific establishments which argued for varying reasons that Britain ought to buy from the USA those equipments which would be prohibitively expensive to develop and produce at home. Among the most prominent of those arguing against *TSR–2* were Lord Mountbatten, at that time chief of the defence staff. It is important to note, though, that his case was built on fears that if the aircraft was ordered for the RAF his beloved Royal Navy would suffer financially. At the same time, Mountbatten's chief scientific advisor, Lord Zuckerman, was more concerned about the implications for spending on other areas of scientific research. Furthermore, even the RAF hierarchy showed less inclination to support *TSR–2*, because by the mid-1960s they were more interested in buying what could have been a superior American aircraft, the *F–111*.[101] Ideologically, the Labour government was also committed to reducing Britain's expenditure on military activity. Indeed, the defence secretary, Denis Healey, took as one of his briefs a reduction in defence budgets from over seven per cent of UK gross domestic output to around five per cent. This target took the initial form of a £400 million (or sixteen per cent) cut in his department's spending, which when combined with the Mountbatten-Zuckerman lobby seemed to imply that by the end of 1964 *TSR–2* would never reach the production stage.[102]

Cancellation implications

Of course, BAC and its suppliers did not act passively while the Treasury and defence staff conspired to kill off their major project, aggressively lobbying both Harold Wilson and Denis Healey at a succession of meetings between October 1964 and April 1965.[103] As Sir John Toothill argued in February 1965, the industrial case was based on the notion that: 'We are not seeking benevolence from the government; what we are seeking is their support where our equipments are better value for money'.[104] Unfortunately, though, *TSR–2*'s perceived superiority over its American rivals created other political pressures, because when as an inevitable consequence of balance of payments difficulties the pound sterling came under intense speculative pressure and the government was forced to seek American support, Hastings claims that this created an opportunity for the presiding President (Lyndon B. Johnson) to insist on the project's cancellation as a condition of bolstering the ailing British currency.[105] Although this particular factor does not feature in either of the Healey or Wilson versions of the cancellation,[106] if true it is yet another manifestation of how American industrial supremacy was supported by indigenous government support. Furthermore, much to the chagrin of every British aircraft and avionics firm, when the *TSR–2* was finally cancelled (in April 1965) the Chancellor announced that American *F–111*'s would be purchased as the next generation of RAF fighter aircraft. In fact, the *F–111* order had also been cancelled by 1968, because the Americans ran into serious design problems, forcing the RAF to take 300 *Phantom* aircraft made by the American firm of McDonnell. Clearly, though, while these *Phantoms* were to be fitted with Rolls Royce Spey engines and some British-made avionics, cancelling *TSR–2* was a devastating blow to many British aircraft and electronics firms.[107] This also substantiated the claims of an increasingly vocal group that in high technology sectors Britain was rapidly becoming, in the words of W. D. Gregson at Crewe Toll, 'the industrial serfs of another nation'.[108]

Although there are many aspects of the *TSR–2* story which have not been related here,[109] the main implications for the future development of divisions like Crewe Toll were all too clear by April 1965 when Sir John Toothill and his managers were obliged to appraise the new situation. It was announced in July 1965 that an order worth £6 million had been secured for the on-board radar which was to be fitted to the RAF's new *Phantoms*.[110] However, this was only a small fraction of the potential business Crewe Toll would have secured from the *TSR–2*'s FLR and inertial navigation systems. In any case, partly because the *Phantom* radars had to be so extensively modified, while in addition McDonnell provided little design and engineering assistance to Crewe Toll,[111] the division made heavy losses on this contract because of the delays attendant on the design and production changes. This demonstrated graphically the problems Ferranti and its British counterparts would now face in dealing with the new military aircraft market, prompting rapid reassessments of future product development strategies.

The situation was also not eased any by the main recommendations of the Plowden Committee, established in 1965 by the Ministry of Defence to consider the British aircraft industry's future, because it argued that government support ought to be cut back to the levels pertaining in other 'comparable' British industries. Of course, apart from struggling with the identification of 'comparable' industries, many critics argued that this conclusion ignored the enormous subsidies given to American and French aircraft firms.[112] More importantly, though, Plowden demonstrated to contemporary observers that the Labour government was looking for ways in which public expenditure in this area could be drastically reduced.

The Plowden Report has been described as 'almost entirely negative and defeatist',[113] given its intention to reduce the scale of British military aircraft production. Clearly, it was difficult to see how advanced British aircraft and avionics projects would ever again receive the kind of support handed out since the early 1950s. On the other hand, in recommending the development of European projects, Plowden accelerated a trend towards cooperation which has since the mid-1960s been the basis of the British aircraft industry's success. Of course, this trend has rarely led to any significant savings in development costs, given the practice of duplicating work done in other countries. On the other hand, joint projects have been vital in creating markets of an appropriate size and complexity to justify the continued existence of this high technology industry in Europe. The first of these was the commercially ill-fated *Concorde* project, which brought together from 1962 British and French aircraft designers in an attempt to compete with the mighty American civil aircraft producers like Boeing and McDonnell-Douglas. After Plowden, though, a more concerted effort was made to coordinate activity across Europe, involving the French, West Germans and Italians in major military ventures.

Concorde taking off from Heathrow, 14 September 1970. Ferranti supplied a range of avionics for this revolutionary aeroplane. *(Museum of Science and Industry at Manchester.)*

European projects and Bloodhound implications

The move towards greater European integration has been one of the major political and economic trends of the post-War era. Certainly, for British firms it seemed to offer a more realistic opportunity both to compete with American rivals and withstand the political machinations of the domestic scene. At the same time, it is also important to stress how there were serious problems in the early stages of this move towards creating a European industry. In particular, the French proved at times to be reluctant partners, largely because they feared British domination of any possible syndicate.[114] Crewe Toll, for example, had initially been given a contract to develop the inertial navigation platform for *Concorde*, signing a cross-licensing agreement with SAGEM (Societe d'Applications Generales d'Electricitie Mecanique) in June 1965 as a means of cementing the relationship with their French partners. Although this further confirmed Crewe Toll's preeminence in the inertial navigation field, in a rather curious twist the prime French contractor, Sud Aviation, decided on a completely different (French) system towards the end of 1966, leaving Ferranti without a customer for what was generally regarded as the most advanced inertial navigation platform in Europe.[115]

Beneficial cooperation with European partners clearly seemed problematical in the mid-1960s, a point further substantiated by Crewe Toll's experiences with what became the *Jaguar* ground attack aircraft. Although the agreement between the French and British defence authorities to start developing *Jaguar* was signed in May 1965, it was March 1967 before Crewe Toll had secured an order for its inertial navigation and attack system. However, this only added to the considerable overload on development which was later to cause such problems with other programmes like the *Harrier*.[116] In fact, as Table 11.2 reveals, after 1963 the return on capital employed (column D) had fallen drastically at Crewe Toll. Even though government development work (column E) continued to provide a steady source of business up to 1968, profitable lines were clearly not emerging in the same way that they had been during the 1950s. While the returns on capital employed had been so healthy up to 1963 because of the large progress payments made by government customers, the new contract conditions introduced by the Lang Inquiry (arising out of the *Bloodhound* revelations) were designed to curb this funding arrangement, making even the 1967 *Jaguar* orders much riskier than their earlier counterparts.

The Lang Inquiries (of 1964 and 1967) had actually created considerable uncertainty in the British defence market. Moreover, for Ferranti there were even greater worries that defence-related ministries might never trust the firm again. In view of the last thirty years' experiences, it is clear that these worries never proved well-founded, because Ferranti continued to receive considerable orders from the services. Notwithstanding this hindsight view, in the mid-1960s executives at Crewe Toll felt some antipathy from MoA civil servants who had been embarrassed by the first Lang Inquiry's revelations. Another factor of significance at that time was Crewe Toll's dominant position in the airborne radar field, because it was government policy never to rely on a sole supplier for any equipment at the development stage. This situation provided an opportunity for Elliott Brothers to establish a position as a major competitor to Ferranti, particularly when RRE decided to focus its development work on continuous wave radar. Donald McCallum actually predicted that the RRE's continuous wave system would never work, exacerbating the difficulties Crewe Toll had frequently experienced in its relationship with this government agency (see section 8.6). When this prediction actually came to pass, the RRE responded by inviting Elliott Brothers to become a second British supplier of airborne radar, providing competition Crewe Toll could well have done without in the difficult political climate of the mid-1960s.[117]

To compound this situation further, it was also at this time that Elliotts ventured into the inertial systems business, offering equipment utilising digital computing techniques, as opposed to the analogue variant employed by Ferranti. Although this again created some concern at Crewe Toll, when quoting for the contract to develop and install the inertial navigation attack system for the only major military aircraft project left by 1965, the *Harrier* jump-jet, Mal Powley was able to convince the RAF that his department's FE541 system was superior to the British and American competition. In fact, this contract was not a commercial success, largely because the cost overruns experienced when converting from development to production were not covered by the price negotiated with the MoD in its post-Lang mode. Similarly, even though the *Jaguar* contracts followed on soon thereafter, the MoD became so concerned at the delays attendant on the FE541's development that the contract was withdrawn and Elliotts were given the job. This further reinforced the growing concern at Crewe Toll about the military avionics market, providing senior management with a difficult task in rebuilding both relations with MoD and the division's fortunes. The situation was not helped when at a meeting with the MoD Controller (Guided Weapons & Electronics), Morian Morgan, Sir John Toothill briefed Sebastian to be as awkward as possible. Indeed, the chairman even told the civil servants to 'buzz off and leave us alone', on the grounds that as a commercial enterprise Ferranti knew more than civil servants about production.[118] Although Sebastian was no doubt correct in his judgement, in view of his company's difficulties the negotiations could have been handled more delicately by Toothill, because the eventual loss of this contract further compounded the difficulties experienced by Crewe Toll.

Table 11.2. *The financial performance of Crewe Toll, 1960–70*

Year to March	A Sales £m	B Capital employed £m	C Profit £m	D C as a % of B %	E Government Development Work £m
1960	5.9	2.2	0.93	41.5	2.5
1961	6.9	2.5	0.77	31.0	3.0
1962	9.8	3.6	0.81	22.4	3.9
1963	9.9	4.3	1.1	25.6	3.2
1964	9.7	5.5	0.87	15.7	3.1
1965	12.1	6.6	0.83	12.6	3.4
1966	13.1	7.6	0.73	9.6	3.3
1967	13.8	6.9	0.45	6.8	5.0
1968	16.2	7.6	0.70	9.2	4.1
1969	17.0	7.1	0.27	3.4	2.6
1970	18.4	7.1	1.1	15.4	2.3

The mid-1960s was clearly a worrying time for Sir John Toothill and his team at Crewe Toll. Even though engineers like Ken Brown ensured that Ferranti continued to retain its competitive advantage over rivals like Elliotts, the *Harrier* and *TSR–2* scenarios demonstrated in graphic form the acute dangers of relying on a single market for the bulk of a business's profits and positive cash-flow. We shall be returning in Section 12.2 to a more detailed analysis of how Crewe Toll fared after 1968, when Sir John Toothill retired and Donald McCallum took over. Clearly, though, developing highly advanced products which outperformed any European, and many American, rivals was no guarantee of success in the much-changed circumstances of the mid-1960s. Senior staff look back to the 1950s as a 'Golden Age', when the British authorities seemed anxious to stimulate indigenous industries by providing sufficient development and production contracts to encourage firms like Ferranti to devote considerable managerial and engineering resources to this area. After 1964, however, military avionics became much more competitive. By the mid-1960s, not only did British firms have to contend with American influence over major RAF and Royal Navy purchases, the poor prospects for substantial new orders had forced them into European projects which were often difficult to negotiate and over which they had less influence. In spite of these factors, however, Sir John Toothill refused to change direction, forcing Crewe Toll to remain a predominantly defence-oriented division which competed in what had become an international marketplace for increasingly scarce orders.

11.6 Numerical control

Returning to a debate discussed in Section 8.6, in view of the changing market conditions of the 1960s one might well argue that Sir John ought to have diversified the product portfolio at Crewe Toll in order to provide greater security from the impact of government decision-making.[119] On the other hand, as we also noted in Section 8.7, not only did Sir Vincent and Sebastian back Sir John's work in building up the defence businesses at Crewe Toll, the attempts at developing numerical control equipment demonstrated how civil markets for high technology products were even riskier. The Ferranti lines were actually as advanced as anything in the USA, largely because D. T. N. Williamson and his team had succeeded in developing a continuous path control system, the Mark IV (see section 8.7). On the other hand, because in the relatively easy trading conditions of the 1950s most British machine tool makers and users clung to traditional equipment, only a small market for numerical control (NC) emerged, limiting the opportunity to generate much profit from the business. One of the biggest sources of business by 1961, providing up to £175,000 worth of orders, was actually the licensing agreement Ferranti had signed a year earlier with Bendix, indicating again how the American market was much more conducive to expansion.[120] By the early 1960s, however, prospects at home would appear to have improved, particularly as in 1959 Williamson had diversified the product range by developing inspection and measuring machines, as well as a coordinate positioning system, which offered customers much greater efficiency levels.[121] Sales still failed to increase significantly, though, leading to serious disagreements between Sir John and Williamson over future strategy.[122]

Market-led strategy

In fact, largely as a result of these disagreements, by 1961 Williamson had left Ferranti, for a position as chief engineer to the Molins Machine Co.[123] In his place H. G. Hinckley was appointed with the specific brief to build up the department's expertise in marketing and customer services. Hinckley was also assisted by the acquisition of customised premises for the NC department, when in 1961 the Board of Trade provided a £600,000 loan from its Development Area programme to build a new factory in Dalkeith.[124] This created much greater capacity to produce up to 200 NC systems each year, at least one-half of which would go to the USA. To facilitate this strategy, further agreements were negotiated with American machine tool firms, in the hope that USA sales might rise in value to approximately £500,000. By 1963, the Sheffield Corporation, of Dayton, Ohio, had consequently agreed to act as a sales agency for Ferranti.[125] Europe was also targeted, leading in 1968 to a collaborative agreement with Grundig, a major West German competitor with twelve sales and service centres dotted around the Continent. This strategy was further reinforced by the announcement of new Ferranti products like the drawing measuring machine (1964) and extensive improvements to the existing range of NC and inspection equipment, emphasising how Dalkeith represented a considerable commitment of resources to a civil technology.

The acid test of this strategy, of course, would be the improved financial performance of Hinckley's department. However, while the approach was

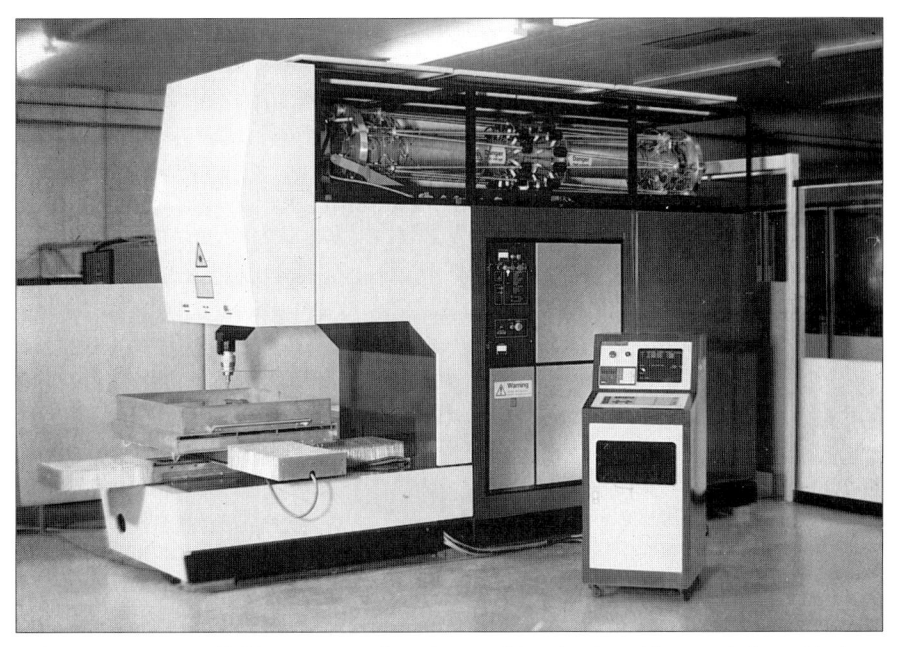

A computer-controlled laser-powered cutting machine developed in association with the Ferranti team in Dundee, where work on lasers was as advanced as any in Europe.
(Museum of Science and Industry at Manchester.)

much more customer-oriented after 1961, it was still difficult to overcome some of the innate difficulties associated with this business. In the first place, sixty per cent of Dalkeith's sales went to established machine tool firms dealing mostly with the aircraft industry. As this meant Ferranti engineers were obliged to modify the control system to each customer's specific requirements, costs inevitably mounted.[126] This actually resulted in no less than 160 separate modifications to Ferranti equipment between 1961 and 1968. In addition, cash-flow was also adversely affected by the need to conduct this work at the customer's works, and as this could take between three weeks and four months remuneration took some time to feed back into Dalkeith.

The Dalkeith engineers responded to this challenge by developing what was marketed as the *Digiturn* system, cutting down significantly on the amount of time required to adjust machine tools.[127] Nevertheless, it was difficult to persuade potential customers that the change-over could be speedily effected. Furthermore, NC development costs had risen from an annual average of just under £107,000 between 1956–57 and 1960–61 to almost £220,000 by the mid-1960s, indicating how the engineering ethos instilled by Williamson had by no means been marginalised. Hinckley actually estimated in 1968 that Dalkeith would have to generate an annual growth rate of at least twenty per cent just to maintain its current level of development.[128] However, in view of the continued difficulties associated with selling such advanced equipment in a highly conservative domestic market, this seemed to be a highly ambitious target, forcing Ferranti to take some hard decisions about Dalkeith's future.

It is interesting to see how, as a result of the marketing innovations introduced by Hinckley in 1961 and product diversification at Dalkeith, NC sales actually increased at the respectable rate of twenty-four per cent per annum over the following seven years. Although the uncertainty associated with government aircraft cancellations had adversely affected the main market for NC, by 1967–68 NC sales had reached £2.4 million, compared to just £111,000 seven years earlier. Inevitably, though, this also meant capital employed was rising significantly at Dalkeith, from approximately £650,000 in 1960–61 to almost £2 million by 1967–68. When the big rise in development expenditure is combined with these cash-flow problems, it is clear that Hinckley was faced with a major challenge if he was to make the department profitable. In fact, as a result of these financial problems, in the five years prior to 1967–68 Dalkeith required a cash-flow infusion from central funds of almost £1.25 million.[129] While Hinckley argued at the end of this period that his department's dependency was being reduced, it was clear that the board could not continue to support such a business.

Market difficulties and IRC intervention

One of the factors to which Hinckley could naturally point when attempting to explain Dalkeith's problems was the domestic market's failure to provide sufficient business to recoup all their costs. Even in 1969 only 2,250 NC machines were operating in British factories, compared to 17,000 in the USA, a situation not helped by the mid-1960s hiatus in military aircraft production.[130] MinTech had attempted to stimulate wider interest in NC by purchasing eleven drawing measuring machines from Ferranti and distributing them to selected companies.[131] However, this had singularly failed to generate additional business, leaving both the NC industry and government with a major problem if this sector was to expand further. In this context, it is also important to note that the Labour government elected in 1964 was not only interested in supporting high technology sectors through MinTech, it also wanted to influence the structure of British industry, establishing the Industrial Reorganisation Corporation (IRC) in 1965 as a means of building bigger firms which would be more likely to compete effectively against the threats posed by giant American corporations.[132] Although much of the IRC's time was taken up either creating or boosting the efforts of firms like British Leyland (motor vehicle production), GEC (electrical engineering) and ICL (mainframe computers), in 1969 attention was focused on NC as an area requiring action,[133] leading Ferranti into some serious discussions which radically affected the Dalkeith operation.

Although many industrialists refused to believe that a government agency like the IRC could positively influence business performance,[134] in many respects the concentration of activity was absolutely essential if high technology firms were going to survive in a marketplace dominated by substantially larger American corporations. To achieve this aim, the IRC's strategy was usually to choose one firm as the natural focus for a much larger business, supporting its bid to acquire competitors with both advice and loan capital where required. In the case of NC, by 1969 it was working closely with MinTech to examine the prospects for a merger. This naturally caused some consternation at Dalkeith, because given its pioneering role as the first British firm to develop NC equipment, not to mention the highly competitive range built up during the 1960s, Ferranti had some claim to be the industry leader.[135] At the same time, as a private company with a relatively weak financial base, the IRC did not view Ferranti as a viable base for a competitive NC industry.

The major threat to Dalkeith was Plessey, because by October 1969, having acquired the NC division of Racal Electronics, this firm accounted for over one-half of all domestic sales, while its financial resources were much greater than anything Ferranti could raise.[136] Donald McCallum nevertheless argued that the NC business required strong technical leadership, something Plessey could not offer at that stage, because it was simply producing equipment designed by the American firm of Bunker-Ramo. Ferranti consequently asked the IRC for £3 million to boost Dalkeith's operations. However, because the IRC refused to sanction the provision of funds for a family firm, this request was rejected. The resources issue was also clearly crucial, because given the substantial losses made at Dalkeith over the previous fifteen years Sebastian and his advisors were reluctant to engage the IRC in a major debate over which company should be backed. Nevertheless, in view of Plessey's technical lag, McCallum and the Dalkeith team were generally disgusted at this turn of events, arguing privately that transferring NC development and production in this way was 'like giving a Ming vase to a child'.[137]

The negotiations between Plessey and Ferranti were actually conducted with great alacrity, because just three weeks after the former had absorbed the Racal NC department the IRC announced that it had brought the two major firms together for talks, while by the middle of November a deal had been finalised. To facilitate matters, the IRC had actually provided Plessey with a £2 million loan, allowing them the opportunity to offer £2.2 million for the Dalkeith NC business, a deal the Ferranti board accepted on 13 November.[138] Although this provided a welcome cash infusion into the firm as a whole, a point to which we shall return in the final section of this chapter, it is also important to emphasise how Plessey only purchased the business relating to machine tool control, leaving the inspection and drawing equipment departments for Dalkeith to develop. This is crucial because after Ferranti acquired in 1971 BAC's interests in these areas Dalkeith was able to establish such a strong position that a highly profitable business flourished there.[139] In the main, though, as with mainframe computers and standard integrated circuits, Ferranti had once again been forced out of an advanced technology sector because of its failure to generate sufficient profit. Much more will be said about this predicament in the final section, but it further highlights one of the main themes of this chapter, namely, the financial problems of the 1960s. With regard to another theme, government involvement, NC reveals a rather different picture, because while military aircraft cancellations undoubtedly reduced the number of possible orders Ferranti could have anticipated early in the 1960s, at the same time IRC intervention provided a financial bolthole which would have been difficult to find in ordinary circumstances.

11.7 Digital systems

The high technology markets of the 1960s were clearly creating severe financial challenges for senior management at Ferranti, especially when one combines this general problem with the downturn in defence expenditure, providing Sebastian with a highly challenging first few years as chairman of his family's company. Of course, ever since the 1880s Ferranti had been coping with the vagaries of a domestic market which had never been as encouraging as that of the USA. At the same time, the defence market worries directly affected what were by the 1960s the company's most profitable divisions, stemming the flow of profits into central coffers. In this context, as Crewe Toll had discovered with airborne attack systems, it is also important to remember the defence establishment's traditional reluctance to rely on sole suppliers at the development stage of a new project, forcing the company to share business with its rivals. Furthermore, after the *Bloodhound* revelations and the two Lang Inquiries, not only were contract conditions tightened up considerably, some MoA officials treated Ferranti with some suspicion, albeit for only a short period.

Again, these changes would have affected several parts of Ferranti, especially at Crewe Toll. However, a division which was to experience particular difficulties in developing an effective product strategy was the digital systems department at Bracknell. Section 9.9 described how, while its initial work was linked directly to the highly successful *Pegasus* computer, since the mid-1950s the London branch of Moston's mainframe computer department had developed a distinct character, especially after receiving a development contract in 1956 from the Royal Navy to produce data handling equipment for the next generation of cruisers.[140] It was also in 1956 that this branch first moved to the Lily Hill House premises in Bracknell. Such was its growth, though, that by 1961 dedicated premises had been found in that town, at Western Rd., where a dynamic young engineer, Peter Dorey, established what came to be known as digital systems department. Under Dorey's leadership Bracknell boasted an annual compound increase in sales of twenty-five per cent over the following seven years. While the Royal Navy and Ministry of Aviation (MoA) accounted for well over half of this business, attempts were also made to break into civil markets by developing training and simulation equipment for air-traffic control, as well as high-speed digital data links for universities.

Emergence of FM1600 and Bloodhound implications

Although Bracknell certainly achieved some successes in diversifying away from the military market, on the whole its fortunes in the 1960s depended largely on maintaining a healthy relationship with its traditional customers, the Royal Navy and the MoA. This emphasises once again the vital importance of military purchasing policy to a Ferranti division. Furthermore, while up to 1966 Bracknell experienced few difficulties in this respect, the situation changed dramatically when the Ministry of Defence (MoD) introduced a policy of standardising computer requirements across the services. During the early 1960s, Bracknell had succeeded in developing a dominant position in the military market for digital systems, because after the initial successes with the Action Data Automation (ADA) system employed in the *Poseidon* computer (see Section 9.9) a standardised design had been produced which was marketed as the F1600. While *Poseidon* had already been installed in new ships like HMS Fife and HMS Eagle by the mid-1960s, the F1600 offered much greater advantages by completely automating the handling not only of picture compilation and tactical displays of air data on radar screens, it was also capable of displaying and analysing sonar-derived data and ballistic calculations.

Notable in a minor way because it was the first Ferranti computer not to be given a name, more importantly when it was launched in 1964 the F1600 marked a decisive breakthrough in this field, giving Ferranti a significant advantage over its main rivals, Plessey and Elliotts.[141] The MoA immediately accepted F1600 for the West Drayton air-traffic control centre, while the Royal Navy wanted to employ the system as Stage I in the development of a combined tactical trainer. However, it was just at that point that the Bracknell engineers were introduced to the integrated circuits developed at Wythenshawe (see Section 11.3), forcing Peter Dorey to inform the Royal Navy that the F1600 was being withdrawn while a new system was designed to incorporate *Micronor II*. Although the Royal Navy was naturally taken aback by this decision, after careful negotiations Dorey managed to convince his customer that it would have been folly to install the outdated F1600. Funds were eventually sanctioned by the Admiralty to assist in the development of a new system, giving Bracknell engineers the opportunity to work on a radical redesign, using integrated circuits and multi-layer printed circuit boards. When the FM1600 was produced in 1966, they were consequently able to offer a computer which was twice as fast as, yet a quarter the size and less expensive than, the F1600. Royal Navy approval quickly followed the FM1600's announcement, leading by September 1966 to five of these systems having been ordered by the Admiralty Surface Weapons Establishment (ASWE) at a cost of over £1 million.[142]

Having reinforced its dominant position in the naval data handling market, Bracknell was anxious to secure further orders for the FM1600. Unfortunately, though, this aim was substantially thwarted for several years by the ongoing struggle within the services over standardisation. Although the MoD had been arguing for several years in favour of adopting a single system for all three services, in view of the defence spending cuts initiated by the Labour government after 1964 (see Section 11.5) more stringent regulations were introduced to cut down on design proliferation. Again, one must also remember that reliance on sole suppliers was never accepted at the development stage of a new project. Furthermore, particularly in view of the MoA's embarrassment over *Bloodhound*, it was clear that even though Ferranti had a technical lead over its rivals this expertise would have to be pooled.[143] At that time, Ferranti, Elliotts and Plessey were all manoeuvring for prime position on what was known as the CAAIS (computer-assisted action information system) project. Consequently, even though the Royal Navy had initially accepted Bracknell's superior FM1600 system, it was apparent that the MoA was going to veto this move. In fact, Ferranti was given a role in CAAIS, but only as part of a consortium involving Elliotts and Decca (a subsidiary of Plessey since 1964), forcing the Bracknell engineers to share data-handling information which nobody else had yet acquired.

Peter Dorey and his team were naturally disenchanted with this situation, particularly as Elliotts was increasingly regarded by the MoA as the prime contractor, even though much of the expertise was derived from Bracknell and the FM1600. Fortunately, though, in a classic example of inter-service rivalry, the Royal Navy was reluctant to see the FM1600 system modified by Elliotts and the MoA, a situation Peter Dorey cleverly exploited at the end of 1967 by withdrawing from the CAAIS consortium and submitting a separate tender based on what was code-named the FM1600B. This new system had been produced for situations requiring less power, which the Royal Navy realised could be employed effectively in the planned new classes of guided missile destroyers (Types 42 and 82) because it was just one-fifth the size of an FM1600 computer, yet capable of providing one-half of the computing capacity. Inevitably, much consternation was aroused at both the MoD and Elliotts at this development. By September 1968, however, the Royal Navy had won the argument over which system to choose, because the FM1600B had been accepted as the basis of CAAIS.[144] In fact, Decca was still to produce the CAAIS displays, but much of the first £1 million order went not to Elliotts but to Ferranti. Furthermore, as FM1600B was designed to NATO specifications, there seemed every prospect of more domestic and export orders.

Table 11.3. *Performance of the Digital Systems Department, 1961–70*

Year to March	A Sales £m	B Capital employed £m	C Profit £m	D C as a percentage of B %	E Government Development Work £m
1962	0.95	0.68	0.07	8.9	0.45
1963	1.50	0.82	0.17	21.2	0.82
1964	1.93	0.86	0.12	13.5	0.85
1965	2.16	1.13	0.21	18.4	0.89
1966	2.69	1.77	0.21	11.8	1.14
1967	3.43	2.18	0.13	5.9	1.14
1968	4.60	2.35	0.22	9.5	1.63
1969	3.80	1.99	0.11	5.7	1.76
1970	4.73	2.10	0.22	10.5	1.90

Sources: Ferranti Management Accounts, 1961–70.

Expansion and profitability

Defeating the MoA on the CAAIS issue was clearly a major step forward for Bracknell. By the end of 1968, FM1600B had not only been accepted by the Royal Navy for its Type 42 frigates, there was also the prospect of orders for the new generation of *Valiant* submarines. Indeed, the FM1600B was to be utilised as the command base for weapons systems like *Sea Cat, Ikara*, the *Bofors 375*, and *Exocet*, demonstrating how Bracknell had managed to reasssert its dominant position in the military naval market after the mid-1960s uncertainties. Furthermore, building on the early successes with *Apollo* (see Section 9.9), efforts were made to expand the business in air-traffic control systems, both for training and operational purposes. This was important in reducing the dependency on defence orders, leading to sales of air-traffic control equipment to airports at home like Prestwick, Hurn and the London training centre. Bracknell also enjoyed some export successes in Holland, Denmark and Italy. Data link equipment was another potentially useful market, in which both home and overseas orders were secured: the RAF and the Army ordered Ferranti systems to control *Bloodhound, Thunderbird* and the *Linesman* guided weapons; and one of the more significant export orders was placed in 1965 by the Swiss air defence authorities for their *Florida* system. Above all, though, it was military naval business which most interested

Bracknell, leading the sales team to devote most of its time negotiating with the Royal Navy, especially during the mid-1960s debates.

From what we have seen with regard to the CAAIS scenario, the time devoted to strengthening relations with the Royal Navy was clearly well spent, even though by the late 1960s contract conditions had changed because of the Lang Inquiries. One of the more attractive features of securing orders from the Royal Navy up to 1964 had been its provision of generous progress payments, allowing contractors to minimise expenditure on stocks and work-in-progress. Thereafter, however, as a result of Lang, this system was abandoned in favour of a much more commercial approach towards contract financing. As Table 11.3 reveals, Bracknell consequently suffered a significant reduction in its returns on capital employed. It is also worth noting that between 1961–62 and 1965–66 government production contracts had earned an annual average return of 13.3 per cent, while over the following four years the return was just 3.75 per cent. Even though sales and government-sponsored development expenditure both continued to rise after 1965, Peter Dorey was consequently extremely concerned about the liquidity position, especially as in the five years prior to March 1968 digital systems had a negative cash-flow of £811,000.[145] This indicates how while it was an expanding business the costs of developing new products and improving the Bracknell facilities led to growing demands for central support, especially once government contract conditions changed after 1965. Although the financial situation started to improve after 1970, and over the following five years digital systems earned much better returns on capital employed, as Crewe Toll discovered the late 1960s had clearly been a difficult period for defence contractors.

11.8 Prospects and proposals

The impact of Bloodhound and Denis

The considerable mid-1960s uncertainty in the defence market had evidently affected the fortunes of two of the most profitable divisions in Ferranti, undermining performance overall at a most critical time for the firm. The downturn in performance at Crewe Toll in particular had an extremely damaging impact on total profitability, because Ferranti was unable to generate a substantial flow of internal resources for cash-hungry divisions like electronic components at Gem Mill. As we shall see in the next chapter, financial worries were even affecting those older divisions at Hollinwood which had been generating significant profits for decades, forcing Sebastian and the board to turn to the firm's traditional bolthole in such circumstances, the Westminster Bank. As Figure 12.1 (p. 523) illustrates, after the loss-making domestic appliance departments had been closed in the mid-1950s and the *Bloodhound* contracts started generating substantial profits, the overdraft had fallen substantially between 1956 and 1961. Although this was actually a period of relatively high liquidity for Ferranti, this did not last long, because after 1963 the overdraft started to mount once again. Many of the senior management felt that Sebastian was placing too much faith in the bank, leading some to predict a tragic end to this relationship. Indeed, when the overdraft reached almost £12 million in the late 1960s advisors were starting to demand decisive action to deal with this situation.[146] Appendix C (Table 2) also reveals how the return on capital employed was falling at exactly the same time, substantiating the calls of those who demanded fundamental change in the organisation to effect greater coordination over cash-flow.

Of course, while performance at the divisional levels was the crucial reason why the Ferranti finances were deteriorating during the 1960s, it is important to remember a series of other influences which had a material impact on the balance sheet. In particular, because Sebastian was forced to make an *ex gratia* payment to the MoA in settlement of the *Bloodhound* contract, Ferranti was left with a debt of £2,048,708. Although the gross repayment had initially been estimated at £4.5 million (see section 10.6), after a deduction of taxation already paid by Ferranti this was reduced to £2,048,708. Furthermore, as a result of extensive negotiations the MoA agreed to accept payment in five annual instalments of £410,000.[147] The first payment was made in June 1965, when provision was made in the general reserve account (see Appendix C, Table 1) for this sum. Over the following four years, however, the chief cost and management accountant, Harry Kirkham, was charged with the task of ensuring that the rest could be met from the overdraft. This consequently created a delicate balancing act for the accounts department, because while the payments of £410,000 were clearly not enormously burdensome, when compared to the average gross profits of the mid-1960s (see Appendix C, Table 2) the problem would have intensified as returns fell after 1967.

Although one cannot credibly argue that in isolation the *Bloodhound* payment was a major problem for Ferranti, the vital point was the context in which it was made: not only were profits falling (see Appendix C, Table 2) both in aggregate terms and as a proportion of capital employed, Sebastian had also conducted a planning exercise which assumed that all this money would be available for internal development purposes. This demonstrates how vital the *Bloodhound* payment proved to be, substantially affecting the forward vision Sebastian had elaborated for Ferranti. It is also worth noting that at exactly the same time the family decided to double the dividend paid out on the ordinary shares. This could be interpreted as an extremely dangerous decision, because even in the years of rapid post-War expansion Sir Vincent had insisted on paying just six per cent on the equity capital. Raising this to twelve per cent just at the time when company funds were coming under unprecedented pressure would simply have exacerbated the situation. However, it is important to remember how the two brothers, Sebastian and Basil, were engaged in a struggle to keep Ferranti a family firm, a struggle they saw as vital if the commitment to advanced technological innovation was to be maintained.

This situation arose because Sir Vincent's young brother, Denis, at first started to challenge Sebastian's right to run the company. After tiring of this debate, he decided in 1967 to sell his twenty-three per cent stake in Ferranti. It is important to remember, of course, that while Sebastian and Basil (together with various trusts) held fifty-eight per cent of the voting stock (see Appendix E), a predator could acquire sufficient ordinary and preference shares to challenge their position. Even the government was concerned at this development, because there was a fear that an American interest would be secured in a major British defence supplier. The minister at the DoTI, Anthony Wedgwood Benn, consequently encouraged Sebastian to prevent a foreign take-over.[148] Denis eventually sold most of his holding to Charter Consolidated, the South African gold mining and dealing firm,[149] putting a substantial quantity of Ferranti stock on the open market. Over the following six years Sebastian and Basil were consequently obliged to keep a watchful eye on Ferranti share dealings, running up large personal overdrafts as a result of their substantial purchases of vote-holding preference shares. This was why Sebastian decided to increase the dividend payments, as a means of funding the defence strategy he initiated.

Asset sales and Gleneagles

The range of financial pressures experienced by Ferranti and its principal owners clearly showed no signs of dissipating as the 1960s progressed. In view of the firm's continued illiquidity, it also became increasingly difficult to justify supporting such a wide range of businesses. Of course, the extensive rationalisation of activities at Moston in the mid-1950s (see Section 8.4) demonstrated how senior management could effect the necessary changes in this respect when circumstances dictated. Throughout the 1960s, similar developments occurred. In 1963, for example, the data processing computer business at West Gorton had suffered the consequences of failing to generate adequate returns (see Section 9.10). The shares Ferranti acquired in ICT as a result of this sale provided the necessary collateral to support extensions of the overdraft.[150] By 1968, after the IRC had forced through a merger of ICT with the computer interests of Plessey and English Electric, a new company was formed, International Computers Ltd (ICL).[151] This provided Ferranti with an excellent opportunity to exploit the euphoria associated with this move, by selling off all its stock of 1.45 million shares at 43s. 6d. (£2.20) each. This sale brought in almost £3.2 million at a crucial time for Ferranti. Furthermore, when in the next year Plessey agreed to pay £2.2 million for the Dalkeith numerical control business (see Section 11.6) additional funds were raised from what had been another major loss-making department.

Although one might argue that these sales were a rational move which would have given senior management the funds to focus on the company's strengths, Harry Kirkham was also right to point out that 'the generation of cash by the liquidation of assets is not the long-term solution to a cash-flow problem for any company determined to maintain its competitive standing'.[152] Of course, while some of the large conglomerates emerging at that time often made substantial profits from trading in company assets, this asset-stripping approach was anathema to what the de Ferranti family stood for in business. Sebastian consequently listened carefully to the advice proffered by one of his senior managers. Kirkham's warning was actually presented in 1968 at a senior Ferranti management conference, held at the Gleneagles Hotel in Scotland. It came amid a flurry of similar critical comments about the firm's financial position.

The Gleneagles conference was actually the second of its type, the first having been held at the same venue in 1965. At both events Sebastian was left in no doubt that some senior managers felt that decisive action had to be taken if Ferranti was to survive in the long-term as a family firm.[153] Of course, both conferences were also extremely sociable occasions, giving Sebastian the opportunity to demonstrate his considerable social skills in forging an atmosphere which was conducive to free discussion. Indeed, the managers exploited to the full all the amenities offered by that prestigious institution, indicating how the conferences proved extremely useful as means of reinforcing the spirit of togetherness at Ferranti. More importantly, though, by examining the principal conference debates and how they were received by Sebastian, it is possible to gain a clear understanding of how strategy and structure were formulated at this crucial time.

One of the more decisive contributions to the first Gleneagles conference was made by Lester George, the company economist, when he targeted three parts of the company where clear action was required before they upset the company's delicately-balanced finances. The first of these departments was

A pencil sketch of Sebastian de Ferranti by Annigoni. *(Museum of Science and Industry at Manchester.)*

data processing computers, which Sebastian had sold off before the conference. The second, numerical control, met with a similar fate (reluctantly) four years later (see section 11.5), indicating how in some respects Ferranti did respond to the economic realities. At the same time, in refusing to act on George's recommendation with regard to a third department, electronic components at Gem Mill, Sebastian showed his true feelings. In fact, selling off Gem Mill was a consistent theme of the advice meted out at both Gleneagles conferences. On both occasions, though, Sebastian bullishly rejected all the advice on the grounds that this division was regarded as central to the general strategy of maintaining the firm's position as one of the leading European electronics innovators.[154] One might suggest that Sebastian was also playing a political game here, in demonstrating to government how his company was committed to an industry which was under severe pressure from American competition at a time when he was publicly demanding more support for this technology. At the same time, Sebastian was also in no mood to see Gem Mill disappear from the firm's portfolio of activities, given the significant progress made by Dr Shepherd and David

Grundy in areas like discrete components and integrated circuits (see Sections 11.1 and 11.2).

While Sebastian's stubbornness over the Gem Mill issue might well have frustrated some of his senior advisors and managers, one should emphasise the clarity in his thinking. This approach will also be apparent when in Section 12.1 the transformer division is discussed, because while in 1965 and 1968 Gem Mill was the focus of attention, at the second conference especially increasing concern was expressed about the prospects for what had traditionally been one of the more profitable parts of the Hollinwood activities. In fact, the transformer division manager in 1968, R. W. (Bill) Nash, argued quite simply that the business should be terminated, advice which Sebastian rejected as wholly inappropriate.[155] As we shall see in the next chapter, this committed the company to several painful years in the business, leading to Nash's resignation. It is consequently clear that the Gleneagles conferences committed Ferranti to two heavy loss-making departments, transformers and electronic components, leading to seven years of acute illiquidity and ultimately to a major crisis.

Debate over structure

In reviewing the debates at these Gleneagles conferences, it is apparent that not only was Sebastian provided with all the information on both company and divisional finances, he was also committed to sustaining the traditional ethos of encouraging technological innovation through an autonomous trading structure. In particular, he argued that any substantial modifications would spoil the free-booting culture which had been the hallmark of the firm since 1882. This returns us to our earlier analysis in section 11.1 of Lester George's suggestion that a financial controller should be appointed, in order to effect the necessary degree of coordination over an increasingly disparate organisation. It was a suggestion which was greeted with open hostility by Sebastian, in the first place because the chairman felt that the advice and information emanating from both Lester George himself (as company economist) and Harry Kirkham (head of the cost and management accounts department) ensured that all in senior positions were appraised of the general situation.[156] Sebastian also argued that: 'If we had a financial director vetting applications for cash, he'd mess the thing up in five minutes'.[157] This reveals again the fear he always had of bureaucratising the organisation; of creating a power structure which both paralleled that of his own and could prove capable of altering the company's innate culture. In simple terms, the big worry was that a bureaucraticised accounting system would prevent the company from having 'sporting swipes' at new technologies, because as owner-controllers the family remained committed to this high-risk, long-term strategy.

While it was consequently clear by 1968 that Lester George was never going to win his argument with Sebastian over organisational reform, at the same time one must also stress how there seemed to be little support amongst the divisional managers for changes of this kind. After all, the direct consequence of George's scheme would be much greater central interference with traditional divisional autonomy, something which would have been difficult for Sir John Toothill, Peter Dorey and Dr Searby to have accepted. The divisional managers were in any case able to fight their corners as directors on the main board, indicating how in protecting their vested interests they implicitly encouraged Sebastian to resist organisational reform.[158] Of course, both the Crewe Toll and digital systems management were resentful of their profits being used to support loss-making ventures like Gem Mill. Nevertheless, their interest in organisational reform would have extended only to persuading Sebastian to close such operations, not to extending central interference. In other words, there is little evidence that the divisional managers were acting in anything other than their own interests. Most importantly, though, Sebastian was strongly against reform. Even though financial pressures mounted throughout the 1960s, Ferranti remained organisationally almost exactly the same as in the 1950s because the chairman felt change was inappropriate to the company culture.

To demonstrate further the resistance to change, it is important to examine the brief experiment conducted at Hollinwood after the 1968 Gleneagles conference.[159] As we noted in Section 11.5, Sir John Toothill had introduced the practice of holding monthly management meetings at Crewe Toll, as a means of coordinating activity across the division as a whole. So impressed was Sebastian with this scheme that in 1968 he introduced a similar structure for the Manchester divisions. J. B. Smith was even temporarily brought down from Edinburgh to advise on how the meetings should be run and what information to present. In fact, substantiating Sebastian's consistent claims, Smith soon realised that there was ample information available in reports presented by Harry Kirkham and Lester George. All Sebastian needed was an effective means of coordinating and assessing this data. Nevertheless, the Manchester management meetings were only held for a few months after the second Gleneagles conference, largely because Sebastian soon realised that he was running what he regarded as an unnecessary encumbrance. Although Crewe Toll continued to operate in this fashion, the company as a whole did not follow the model. This again demonstrates how Sebastian was ideologically opposed to regimentation and orthodox business techniques, persisting with the traditional structure in the face of ever-increasing pressures to change as an expression of complete faith in traditional Ferranti management techniques.

This brief review of the 1960s debates is an essential prelude to what we shall be examining in the next chapter, because it highlights the key feature of the era, namely, consistent thinking on management structure and growing financial worries. Although selling assets had by 1969 forestalled the onset of a major liquidity crisis, as we shall now go on to see this policy proved to be only a short-term palliative, while some of the harder decisions facing Sebastian were either put off or taken incorrectly. Lester George had warned Sebastian in 1965 that unless substantial organisational modifications were introduced: 'It is ... inevitable that in the near future we shall run into serious financial difficulties and it could well mean that the price which we have to pay for an influx of new money is loss of family control'.[160] This prophesy would not come to pass for some years, partly because of the late 1960s asset sales. Nevertheless, it was a clear warning to Sebastian of the dire consequences attendant upon the 'Ferranti Dilemma'. The Ferranti family philosophy on which a thriving and vibrant company had been built had always been to take 'sporting swipes' at ventures, without having either speculative shareholders or financial controllers constantly monitoring activities.[161] However, as we shall now go on to see, as the 1970s progressed this aim became increasingly difficult to fulfil.

12

The End of Family Control

The first seven years as chairman of Ferranti had clearly provided substantial challenges for Sebastian and his team, reflecting both a constantly changing market environment and the emergence of new problems for some of the principal products. In retrospect, one can understand how in the context of rapidly rising expenditure levels on R & D, increasingly competitive markets and changing defence contract conditions, the company found it difficult to generate the funds required to sustain an acceptable level of liquidity. In spite of these difficulties, though, under Sebastian the Ferranti group continued to expand, from a business with sales in 1963 of £35 million to one which by 1975 had a turnover of over £86 million (see Appendix C, Table 3, and Figure 2, p. 15). Similarly, the firm continued to introduce exciting new ideas across a range of technologies. There were many who advised the chairman to overhaul the firm's organisation and introduce specialist personnel in the financial area, indicating how well the problems were reported in the internal accounting system. Nevertheless, Sebastian remained committed to the free-booting structure inherited from Sir Vincent's days as chairman, stressing the need both to give engineers and managers complete responsibility for the destiny of their products and to limit the degree of institutionalised decision-making. Above all, as Sebastian wanted to retain the family's style of control and ownership, all the challenges were accepted as simply part of running a business which aspired to great engineering heights. In the 1970s, however, while one should never ignore the quality of decison-making in this unfolding scenario, not only did the external problems persist, they were also compounded by a series of major macro-economic shocks and other difficulties, exacerbating the illiquidity experienced since the *Bloodhound* payments were made.

The early 1970s was clearly a traumatic period for all concerned. In this concluding chapter, without going in to tremendous detail concerning the macro-economic events of 1974–75, we shall outline the main features of a scenario which ultimately resulted in the termination of family control at Ferranti. One of the most interesting features of the early 1970s story is its striking resemblance to the problems of 1903 (see section 3.9). History seldom repeats itself exactly, but in many ways the events and conditions of both

The official opening of the High Voltage Laboratory, Avenue Works, in 1965.
(*Museum of Science and Industry at Manchester.*)

crises were remarkably similar: the market for one of the company's major products collapsed; the bank played a big role in the unfolding scenario; and ultimately the company's financial problems resulted in major changes at the head of the organisation. There are obvious differences, most notably in the way that the state intervened in the 1970s, as well as the severe macro-economic problems which struck the world economy at that time. For the family members, though, it seemed as if destiny was conspiring against the aim of retaining control over what had been a central part of their lives for three generations.

Ultimately, of course, the story revolved largely around what we have previously referred to as 'The Ferranti Dilemma', because Sebastian was wrestling with the dual challenge of maintaining a commitment to technological innovation, while at the same time relying on dwindling internal financial resources which looked paltry when compared to those of his rivals. Of course, Sebastian was well aware of these problems, having read all the detailed reports presented by his advisors and discussed at length the issues involved. Moreover, he could do little about the macro-economic problems besetting Britain (and the entire industrialised world) at that time, indicating how to a certain extent matters were beyond his control. Similarly, the

THE END OF FAMILY CONTROL

National Westminster Bank's attitude to the Ferranti overdraft was determined by events in the banking and property worlds. On the other hand, Sebastian's refusal either to alter the organisational dynamics of his firm or close major loss-makers contributed enormously to the problems Ferranti experienced during the 1970s, indicating how decision-making played a central role in the unfolding scenario.

12.1 Meters and transformers

It is clear from chapter 11 that during the late 1960s several divisions (Edinburgh, Bracknell and Gem Mill) were experiencing a significant downturn in their profitability. Traditionally, Ferranti had been able to cope with such situations by either transferring funds from the more profitable departments, at least in the short- to medium-term, or seek extensions to a bank overdraft which rose steadily over this period (see Figure 12.1). At the same time, one must remember the difficulties associated with untangling the different divisions from the central core of the company, given the manner in which Sir Vincent and Sebastian had tied the overall success of the company to the performance of the operating departments. While fluidity was regarded as essential, successive chairmen attempted to integrate the entire organisation through a loose form of financial management which imposed a strong

The Avenue Works complex by the 1970s. In the left background is the Hollinwood meter factory. Together, by the 1970s these premises represented a major financial liability.
(Museum of Science and Industry at Manchester.)

sense of responsibility on all managers for both departmental and corporate survival.

One of the major sources of the internal subsidies, of course, had been the company's staple products of meters and transformers. In particular, the former had since the mid-1880s provided a steady supply of funds for the riskier activities initiated by Ferranti engineers. As we saw in section 8.2, after some initial difficulties both had also generated excellent returns during the period 1945–60, competing successfully in home and export markets for a substantial share of the expanding demand for electricity supply equipment. Indeed, the Avenue Works transformer plant and Hollinwood meter production facility were major hives of activity well into the 1960s, providing some balance to the defence orientation of other Ferranti activities at that time, as well as good returns on capital employed. It is consequently surprising to note that by the early 1970s both of these departments were struggling to survive, as they struggled to compete in markets which, for political and economic reasons, had changed radically.

Market background

There are several reasons why in such a short space of time sales of the company's two staple product ranges slumped so alarmingly. As we shall emphasise later, while management decisions played a major role in the scenario, essentially the common denominator linking the explanations is the dramatic change in domestic market conditions. One of the most important of these changes was the manner in which successive post-War governments tackled the price-fixing activities of most electrical engineering firms, leading ultimately to the compulsory termination of all electrical price rings in 1961.[1] Ferranti, of course, had been extensively involved in price-fixing, having instituted discussions with meter producers as early as 1906 and later playing a leading role in the creation of BEAMA in 1911 (see section 4.5). Although BEAMA's fortunes had fluctuated in the following twenty years, after the introduction of protectionist duties in 1931 British electrical engineering, like much of British industry, had been heavily cartelised.

The main rationale behind cartelisation had been to ensure a reasonable level of profitability in both large and small firms, even if the consumer was obliged to pay artificially high prices.[2] After 1945, however, greater concern with public welfare, allied to a belief that cartels were inherently inefficient, prompted both Labour and Conservative governments to introduce legislation which would substantially undermine trade association activity. In particular, when in 1957 the Monopolies & Restrictive Practices Commission (MRPC) presented its report to the Restrictive Trade Practices Court on the supply and export of electrical and allied machinery and plant, it became clear that the industry would no longer be allowed to control prices.

Naturally, BEAMA lobbied the MRPC aggressively while the 1957 report was being prepared, arguing that because of the minimum prices set by the various sub-committees firms were obliged to compete on technical grounds, a state which consequently improved substantially the quality of equipment offered to the electricity supply authorities. In any case, BEAMA argued, many firms only loosely followed the cartel's pricing guidelines, manipulating customer loyalty through the use of some dubious practices.[3] Remunerative prices were also advocated as the most important source of funds for ambitious development programmes, while at the same time ensuring that sufficient productive capacity was kept in existence to meet the increasing post-War demand for electricity. The alternative to price-fixing, BEAMA claimed, was rampant competition which would simply undermine the British industry and reduce its ability to compete technically with the major European and American electrical firms which had done so much damage earlier in the century (see section 3.7). The Ferranti family also believed firmly in the doctrine that the logical consequence of a monopsonist (the CEB and its successors) was a monopoly supplier. Furthermore, along with many of the other leading electrical engineering firms, they felt that the price rings were an essential defence against such a tendency, in that the security they afforded kept the smaller operations in business.[4] The restrictive practices court, on the other hand, was given the simple brief of eliminating price-fixing, unless it was in the public interest. Inevitably, BEAMA failed to demonstrate that its activities were of such general utility, leading to the decision in 1961 to end the price rings.

Mergers in electrical engineering

There is little doubt that while support for the price rings had never achieved complete unanimity among firms, after 1961 British electrical engineering was for the first time in over thirty years experiencing the chill wind of price competition. In the transformer market alone, by 1967 prices had fallen by between twenty-three and fifty per cent.[5] Paradoxically, the MRPC's intervention also encouraged firms to indulge in an unprecedented surge in merger activity, undermining significantly the aims of anti-monopoly legislation and confirming Sebastian's claim that monopsonists create monopolists.[6] Of course, there were other reasons why mergers featured so prominently in the strategies of most industrialists throughout the 1960s and early 1970s, most notably the influence of City financiers. However, for firms like Ferranti, which because of its family shareholdings was never touched by such influences, the concentration of industrial activity significantly compounded the situation, by creating larger domestic rivals which were capable of exacerbating the price competition.

Another reason for the concentration of production in the industry was the role played by government policies. By far the most important political intervention was the 1965 creation by Harold Wilson's Labour government (1964–70) of the Industrial Reorganisation Corporation (IRC). The specific aim of this body was to encourage mergers in key exporting sectors, resulting in some dramatic moves to concentrate activity in electrical engineering. In fact, while the IRC was involved in a series of mergers which affected Ferranti (see section 11.6), the most momentous was the role it played in backing GEC's successful bids for AEI (1967) and English Electric (1968).[7] Although both AEI and English Electric were regarded as technically competitive, the IRC's chief (Ronald Grierson) supported GEC because of its allegedly superior management. There were also rumours that GEC had gained Grierson's support by offering him a board position, indicating how his strategy had been so unpopular in some quarters that attempts were made to undermine his credibility.

By that time, of course, GEC was run by Arnold Weinstock, who to many observers was regarded as an effective organiser capable of substantially boosting the industry's competitiveness at a time when foreign competition was intensifying in both domestic and export markets. One must reserve judgement on whether this aim has ever been achieved,[8] noting that while the company never gained a high reputation for its technological achievements, Weinstock remained chief executive of GEC until 1996. On the more specific point relating to its impact on smaller firms like Ferranti, though, the merger served to create a larger domestic competitor, further exacerbating the difficulties of coping with the post-MRPC environment. As we have already noted, the expansion of GEC also seemed to confirm the Ferranti family's fears that the existence of a monopsonist would result in excessive concentration in electrical engineering. In fact, as we shall see later, Ferranti did embark on a limited acquisition strategy during the 1960s, initiating discussions with several firms on the possibility of forging joint ventures. Overall, though, these efforts proved to be weak palliatives at a time when more ruthless decisions were required.

CEGB errors

The 1960s was consequently a much-changed scene, when compared to the previous thirty years of limited price competition and dispersed industrial concentration. However, not only did this decade see the creation of much larger rivals at both home and abroad, crucially it also witnessed a significant reassessment of demand prospects as the rise in electricity consumption started to level off after twenty years of unprecedented growth.[9] Over the ten years between the nationalisation of electricity supply in 1947 and the creation of the Central Electricity Generating Board (CEGB) in 1957, sales of electricity had risen by 206 per cent, reaching 67,514 GWh. This expansive environment led the CEGB not only to predict further increases in sales of eight per cent per annum up to 1970, it also encouraged electrical firms to expand capacity. Unfortunately, though, while in the early 1960s sales did actually grow annually by 8.7 per cent, between 1965 and 1970 this fell to 5.3 per cent per annum, while in the early 1970s only 3.14 per cent was recorded.

Hannah is especially critical of the CEGB's failure to anticipate and limit the competition emanating from a revitalised gas industry, while managerial shortcomings and technical mistakes in the commissioning of plant compounded the industry's difficulties.[10] Furthermore, one of the periodic slumps in house-building severely affected demand for generating and distribution equipment from the late 1960s, resulting in significant overcapacity in electricity supply and severely curtailing demand for plant and equipment. There was perhaps some naivety in the way firms had planned to cope with the inevitable fluctuations in demand. On the other hand, most had been responding to entreaties from the CEGB, precipitating major problems when the other competitive pressures emerged in the 1960s.

Meter prospects

The meter department had throughout the twentieth century been capable of withstanding competition from domestic and foreign rivals, contributing substantially to the firm's cash-flow since the 1890s. Even as late as 1967, Ferranti still accounted for twenty-three per cent of British meter output, the largest single share alongside Sangamo.[11] This competitive advantage had been built on a series of radical and innovatory designs, backed up by the development of efficient mass-production techniques at the old Crown Works (see section 8.2), as well as long-standing price and market-sharing agreements with its British rivals. Ferranti also played its part in reducing competition within the meter industry, by acquiring Aron Meters in 1962 (for £440,000) and Smith Meters (for £300,000) in 1968. This helped to boost sales from just over £1.7 million in 1960–61 to £3.1 million a decade later. The meter department manager, however, having recently inherited a business which was beginning to suffer from the market problems described earlier, was by 1968 arguing that the meter department was 'dying on its feet'. This stimulated a debate with the chairman, who reluctantly felt that to invest further in what by then was a stagnant business would only have exacerbated the general liquidity problems felt throughout the company.

Ferranti meter sales actually hit their peak in 1965–66, when they were valued at £3.2 million. Two years later, J. D. Carter took over as manager, at a time when the company was faced with a major investment programme if this department was going to survive as a going concern. His predecessor, Jack Prince, had generated substantial sales from the standard FM meter. By the late 1960s, though, this design was almost twenty years old, using few of the new materials and technologies which were incorporated into most of its European rivals. The big debate at that time was whether to move from the old Ferraris-type meter to a mechanism built around solid-state components, a situation compounded by the uncertainty about which way customers would jump when considering new ideas. In fact, this transition has still to be completed in the 1990s, substantiating the Ferranti decision not to change over in the late 1960s. Nevertheless, this still left the firm with an old design which was increasingly difficult to sell in the restrictive market conditions of the late 1960s.

In a similar vein, because of its aged and crumbling structure the Crown Works was not only expensive to maintain, it lacked the capacity to take modern production machinery. Alternatively, a replacement facility would have been expensive to build, reintroducing amortisation into a department which had long ago written off its capital investments. Meter department also continued to run its own toolroom, pushing up the overhead element on a price which was under increasing pressure. Crown Works was still generating a positive cash-flow, amounting to over £910,000 in the five years up to 1967–68. In the following five years, though, this was predicted to fall to just £71,000, reflecting a long-term trend which had started in the 1950s. At the same time, as a result of the overcapacity noted earlier, not only had the Area Electricity Boards cut back their purchases to a level which made new investment a risky venture, they were also refurbishing old meters, providing very little incentive to invest in new products and facilities.

In reviewing the company's attitude towards the meter department, one might conclude that Sebastian was 'killing off the goose that had lain the golden egg'. Clearly, though, in a strictly business sense it was hard to justify a major investment programme in a department which seemed incapable of producing similar rewards over the following decade. Indeed, by the early 1970s meter department had started to record trading losses, amounting to almost £340,000 between 1970–71 and 1974–75, at a time when sales growth was stagnant.[12] One must also note in this context how the meter designers at Ferranti had failed to come up with a viable alternative which might have boosted their competitive advantage. Indeed, there is little evidence that Carter

The complete range of Ferranti meters produced by the 1970s.
(Museum of Science and Industry at Manchester.)

had any decisive plans for the future of his department. Sebastian was consequently unable to sanction new investment expenditure in this area. It was a difficult decision for the chairman especially, given both his grandfather's substantial contribution to meter design and development and the department's consistent contribution to company funds since the 1880s. Ferranti was consequently obliged to allow Crown Works to struggle on in the hope that demand would recover, indicating how in the traditional departments rapidly-changing market prospects were having a highly damaging impact on cash-flow. In fact, during the late 1970s meter department was only saved from outright closure by a merger with the leading German firm of Siemens, indicating how radical solutions were by then required if these ailing ventures were going to survive.

Transformers

The meter department's much-changed fortunes was one of the most significant developments affecting Ferranti after 1965. Tragically, though, it was by no means the only staple business to experience difficulties at that time. Indeed, when compared to the experiences of transformer department the Crown Works looked almost commercially successful. Avenue Works had actually been just as much a symbol of the company's post-War expansion as the ventures into computers and avionics. The addition in 1965 of a high voltage testing laboratory to what was already a major facility opposite the Crown Works testified to the considerable technological and commercial successes achieved in designing and producing transformers. The new testing facilities were required because of the CEGB's 1963 decision to raise the maximum operating voltage employed on the grid from 275 kV to 400 kV, further extending the technical challenges associated with making distribution equipment. The CEGB was also encouraging firms to create additional capacity, in order to cope with the anticipated eight per cent annual growth

Final tests for two Ferranti 3-phase Auto-Transformers for the CEGB, 18 October 1966 at the High Voltage Laboratory at Avenue Works, Chadderton.
(Museum of Science and Industry at Manchester.)

in electricity consumption. This stimulus was combined with a buoyant level of demand in export markets, creating the prospect of a bright future for a department which had grown substantially since 1945 (see section 8.2).

There is little doubt that during the 1960s, under the guidance of its chief transformer engineer Lindley Preston, Ferranti remained one of Britain's premier transformer designers and producers, maintaining a long and distinguished tradition which stretched back to 1885. In 1961, for example, Avenue Works was responsible for making the country's largest transformer to date, a 225 MVA three-phase unit for the CEGB station at High Marnham. This was followed in 1965 by the production of two 230 MVA three-phase units for the Cruachan pumped-storage power station at Loch Awe in Argyllshire. The company had also pioneeed the development of generator-transformers, after the CEGB commissioned in 1961 what would be the world's largest such unit, a 570 MVA three-phase generator-transformer for the West Burton station. By the late 1960s, 750 MVA generator-transformers were coming out of Avenue Works. Some of these units weighed between 250 and 300 tons, posing both novel transport problems and not a little traffic congestion. They also served to keep the Ferranti name very much in the limelight as the country's infrastructure investment programme took shape. The main product line was also augmented by the design of more advanced testing equipment. When in 1968 the Series 200 impulse generator was launched, contemporaries noted how this represented 'a completely rethought approach to the production of high-voltage impulses for use in testing'.[13]

Avenue Works was consequently capable of maintaining its reputation in transformer design and production well into the post-War period. This expansion meant that by 1965 the department's occupied manufacturing area increased to over 383,000 square feet and its labour force to over 1,500. The factory was also kept very busy for much of the 1960s, with sales nearly doubling between 1960–61 (£4.7 million) and 1966–67 (£8.1 million) and capital employed rising to almost £7.3 million. Some critics commented on the low level of labour productivity achieved at the Avenue Works, because it was not only between fifty and seventy-five per cent of its British competitors, when compared to the larger European and American firms it was even worse.[14] On the other hand, as Sebastian argued at the time, it is vital to remember that labour productivity was only a very small proportion of total costs in transformer production, while the very nature of the large contracts dictated that firms designed and produced units virtually from scratch.

Irrespective of these concerns, the major worry in the 1960s was the level of transformer prices, leading to a fall in returns on capital employed from just over eleven per cent between 1960–61 and 1964–65 to just two per cent

The High Voltage Laboratory at the Chadderton transformer factory.
(Museum of Science and Industry at Manchester.)

in the following five years. Furthermore, in the five years up to 1967–68 a negative cash-flow of £1.1 million was recorded.[15] The financial problems were especially highlighted in 1969–70, when transformer department recorded a substantial trading loss of almost £1 million. Coming just eighteen months after Sebastian had been told at the second Gleneagles management conference that this division ought to be sold off, this prompted serious discussions about the future of Avenue Works.[16]

We shall assess the subjectivity of this advice later, because there are important issues here which reveal some of the problems associated with an organisation which was composed of so many competing interests. Significantly, though, it is vital to remember that Sebastian was well aware of these difficulties, having been kept informed of the financial situation by the internal reporting system. Of prime concern at the start of the 1960s was the aniticipated price competition, once the decision to disband all electrical price rings had been taken in 1961. Clearly, with six major domestic competitors – English Electric, AEI, GEC, Hawker-Siddeley, Parsons, and Bruce Peebles – there was little ground for optimism, especially when allied with predictions of the collapse in demand arising from the CEGB's failure to anticipate electricity consumption trends accurately.[17] In fact, the *Electrical Times* claimed as early as 1966 that the transformer market was 'becoming more and more difficult'.[18] As we noted earlier, by 1967 prices had already fallen by up to fifty per cent, a situation which was to deteriorate even further after the GEC acquisitions of AEI and English Electric. R. W. (Bill) Nash, the Ferranti transformer department manager, also predicted in 1968 that by 1970-71 CEGB large transformer orders would have fallen in value to just £19.6 million, compared to almost £38 million five years earlier, reinforcing the view of many within the company that drastic action was required if serious losses were not to undermine general liquidity.

One of the Ferranti responses to this situation was aggressive lobbying of the CEGB in favour of more generous prices. As president of BEAMA in 1968, Sebastian commissioned an Oxford academic, G. B. Richardson, to produce an extensive analysis of the electrical engineering industry's fortunes since the 1961 dissolution of all price rings.[19] Not surprisingly, this report reinforced the claim that, as a result of price instability, serious difficulties were being experienced in the heavier sectors, while the downward trend in CEGB ordering was compounding the situation. BEAMA was distinctly

Series 200 5.2 MV 390 KJ Mobile Impulse Generator supplied to CERC, Leatherhead, August 1972. *(Museum of Science and Industry at Manchester.)*

unsuccessful, however, in changing minds at both CEGB and political levels, the Richardson report having been rejected as a piece of selfish lobbying. Certainly, the political climate prevented any return to the old practices, with governments stressing a combination of alternative solutions to the difficulties, in particular merger activity.

Of course, as we noted earlier, Ferranti remained largely aloof from the big mergers affecting the electrical industry during the 1960s. Even though Sebastian was at times tempted by the irregular but frequent enquiries which were received from British, European and American companies, he felt confident that his firm could survive as an independent concern in a series of chosen niche markets. At the same time, where commercial pressures forced management's hand, Sebastian was willing to listen to realistic offers. For example, with respect to the distribution transformer department which he had been responsible for creating in 1954 (see section 8.1), a major reorganisation was instituted in 1966. This business was also experiencing some problems in the 1960s, with a total of twenty-eight domestic rivals competing in a contracting market. By the mid-1960s, indeed, annual losses of almost £200,000 were being made. Bill Nash was consequently instructed to negotiate with Bruce Peebles and English Electric on a possible deal, a move which resulted in the formation of Distribution Transformers Ltd (or DTL, as it was more commonly known) in 1966. Unfortunately, however, even this proved unsuccessful, forcing Ferranti to pull out of the syndicate in 1969, after selling its interest in DTL for £60,000 to Reyrolle Parsons.[20]

Merger talks and exports

This episode with distribution transformers was an important influence on Sebastian, because it seemed to indicate that merger strategies failed to cope with the increasingly difficult market environment. However, it is vital to stress that when confronted by advice to sell or close the Avenue Works, Sebastian's principal reposte was based on a gut feeling that in view of the historical trend in electricity consumption CEGB capital expenditure programmes would revive, allowing transformer department to return to profitability.[21] With regard to a possible sell-off, he also worried partly about the prospect of continued employment for the 1,500 Avenue Works employees, as well as the fear of relinquishing control of a business which his grandfather had established and which his father had managed successfully in the 1920s. Such was the central position of transformer department to the Ferranti business that Sebastian himself had also come up through the Avenue Works, giving him first-hand knowledge of many of the staff and its work practices. In the many discussions which followed, it was this combination of market expectations and strong personal feelings about the transformer department which always remained to the fore, creating insuperable obstacles to those who attempted to influence his actions.

While a merger was never realistically considered by Ferranti, considerable emphasis was placed on building up the order-book, especially by selling more overseas. It was also at this time that Bill Nash decided to leave the company, largely because he felt that the problems facing Avenue Works would eventually lead to its closure.[22] In Nash's place the former head of transformer sales, Peter McGregor, was appointed, with the simple brief of improving profitability and keeping the Avenue Works busy. Inevitably, though, with the domestic market so depressed, McGregor was obliged to look abroad for additional business, where profitable orders were notoriously difficult to secure. In the first place, since the CEGB had occupied much of the Avenue Works' attention since the late 1950s, Ferranti had not followed up on the major export successes recorded in the post-War years, when selling significant numbers of large transformers to American customers (see section 8.2). Apart from building up the Canadian subsidiary, Ferranti-Packard, substantial holdings in an Australian (the Wilson Electric Transformer Co.) and an Italian (Industrie Elettriche di Legnano) firm had been acquired in 1960–61, in order to boost the company's presence in those markets. However, until the mid-1960s exports still remained on average only ten per cent of Avenue Works sales. More importantly, though, by that time not only were American and European firms firmly entrenched in world trade, the Japanese were also beginning to make deep inroads into market share. Peter McGregor was consequently obliged to boost export sales by taking on both competitively-priced contracts, as well as orders which were technologically the most challenging.

There is little doubt that between 1968 and 1975 Ferranti was able to win some significant foreign orders, including the largest units exported from Britain, two 635 MVA generator-transformers for the Detroit Edison Co., which were completed in 1971. A computer-based marketing system was developed to enhance this activity, after the company purchased an ICT 1903 mainframe computer to run detailed investigations of market and price trends, as well as customers' development plans. In view of the highly competitive market conditions, however, Ferranti was at times obliged to take on contracts for which they were ill-equipped. The most obvious case illustrating this approach was the order for two 400 MVA units placed by the Cordoba station of the Tennessee Valley Authority (TVA). There was actually considerable disagreement within the senior transformer department staff over this contract, with McGregor insisting on the initial tender price, while Lindley Preston (chief transformer engineer) felt that the TVA would slacken the technical specifications if Ferranti reduced its price. This disagreement was never resolved, resulting in the acquisition of a contract which posed an enormous challenge to the Avenue Works staff. It is important to stress that the Swedish firm ASEA also struggled to match the technical specifications demanded by the TVA, most notably its demand that the windings should be placed in an unusually small tank.

After two years, Ferranti was finally obliged to give up the TVA contract, resulting in the accumulation of substantial unremunerated costs. Avenue Works consequently lost almost £3.3 million in 1970–71 and 1971–72, largely because of the Cordoba contract and the tight prices negotiated on most of the other export orders. As one Avenue Works employee later stated: 'In recounting the history of Ferranti transformers, the name "Cordoba" will be engraved on the hearts and minds of many former employees'.[23] Sebastian also remembers vividly the day this unit failed its impulse test, because the event coincided with American allegations that in tendering for the contract Ferranti could be accused of 'dumping'. Ferranti were actually obliged to compensate the TVA as a result of this case, further increasing the losses. It was an engineering and commercial disaster Avenue Works could well have done without.

To be fair to those who actually signed the Cordoba contract, it is clear that too much emphasis can be placed on its impact, because even after Ferranti had discharged its responsibilities to the TVA the department continued to make heavy losses. Indeed, while in December 1973 the order book exceeded £10 million for the first time, prices remained so unremunerative that over the period 1970–71 to 1974–75 transformer department made losses totalling almost £9.6 million.[24] By that time, with the Avenue Works labourforce falling from its peak of over 1,500 to under 1,300, domestic orders for large transformers were also beginning to register losses, further compounding the acute difficulties experienced with the export contracts. Sebastian responded in 1973 by replacing Peter McGregor as manager with Bruce Calveley, in the hope that an injection of new ideas might ward off the impending sense of crisis which pervaded the Hollinwood parts of the business.

Solutions

With both meter and transformer departments struggling to survive in the wake of severe competition and bleak market prospects, Sebastian was once again being bombarded with advice from all sides on the issue of 'lancing the boils' which were badly affecting all parts of the company. In fact, only two years after rejecting Bill Nash's advice on selling the Avenue Works,

Sebastian was investigating the possibility of a joint venture in large transformers with Sir Arnold Hall of Hawker-Siddeley. By this time, Sebastian was being closely advised by a team collected together specifically to deal with the Avenue Works crisis, including Dr Searby from Wythenshawe division, the chief cost & management accountant Harry Kirkham, and later John Pickin, who after his heart attack in 1969 had returned to the company as a technical advisor to the board.[25] All were keen to push Sebastian into ridding the company of 'the transformer problem', possibly by negotiating a deal with Hawker-Siddeley. Clearly, though, this was too radical for the chairman, especially as Sir Arnold Hall insisted on taking sole charge of any joint venture they might have created. Ferranti consequently withdrew from the talks. Although Sir Harold Mullins of Reyrolle Parsons was also contacted at this time, Sebastian rejected his offer to buy Avenue Works for £0.5 million on the grounds that the facility was worth much more.

The Hawker-Siddeley/Reyrolle Parsons negotiations were not the only talks Sebastian had with interested parties in the early 1970s, as GEC and ASEA also entered into the discussions at that time. It is interesting to note, though, that all failed for exactly the same reasons, namely, the chairman's concern for the Avenue Works people and his genuine belief that as transformer sales would soon revive the plant was a valuable asset. In the case of ASEA, its management only agreed to take the business for free, while GEC demanded a £1 million subsidy from Ferranti. Clearly, neither were willing to give any guarantees about the workforce, forcing Sebastian to terminate all the negotiations. Whether or not a sale or merger would have solved the firm's problems remains a hypothetical scenario, especially as other divisions were at that time contributing to the mounting illiquidity (see section 12.2). Nevertheless, it is clear that the Avenue Works' losses had serious knock-on effects throughout the company, at a time when as we saw at the end of chapter 11 Ferranti was already struggling with a serious financial dilemma. Detailed financial calculations were conducted by Sebastian's team to see just how much the chairman's refusal to close the division would cost the company, emphasising again how the cost and management accountants provided all the information necessary for an objective assessment of the situation. Regardless of this work, however, Sebastian stood firmly by the Avenue Works, resisting advice which would have resulted in even more severe economies. We must now go on to place this analysis of the Hollinwood divisions into a broader context, evaluating both the company's financial state and the various solutions proposed and attempted by Sebastian and his team. Particular emphasis must be placed on how they matched the company's resources and values to an increasingly difficult economic environment, posing serious questions about the decisions made by the chairman.

12.2 Finances and organisation in the early 1970s

A detailed analysis of the company's late 1960s financial plight has already been conducted in section 11.8, where we noted how its prospects were dimmed by the growing shortage of ready cash. Apart from transformers, of course, the electronic components department at Gem Mill was also the cause of some concern. Sebastian, nevertheless, resisted all efforts either to close or sell these major loss-makers. Some of his arguments contained elements of sentimentality, for example with regard to the Avenue Works employees. On the other hand, very much to the fore were strategic issues like transformer market expectations and the wish to remain in the vanguard of electronics innovation.

We shall now go on to assess whether these views possessed any commercial sense, especially in the light of both his senior managers' lack of support and Sebastian's continued refusal to appoint a financial controller. As the representative of over fifty-one per cent of the equity, of course, Sebastian was in a position to reject any advice which undermined the technology-led

Members of the Board, 1973, seated from left: Dr N. H. Searby, Basil de Ferranti, Sebastian de Ferranti, Tom Edmondson, Sir John Toothill, back row from left: Archie Gray, Lester George, Peter Dorey, John Pickin, R. H. Davies, Donald McCallum, J. J. Ratcliffe. (*Museum of Science and Industry at Manchester.*)

ethos on which his family had built the firm, arguing that what he felt lay at the heart of the company's successes ought not to be changed. He was also sure that an outsider could not have done a better job, while the reporting system which had evolved over the previous forty years continued to provide him with all the information necesary. At the same time, while senior figures like Eric Grundy, Sir John Toothill and Donald McCallum continued to pressure him into closing the loss-making departments,[26] in retrospect one might argue that not only were the divisional managers simply looking out for their own interests, as we shall see in later sections they would have resented the reduction in powers which would have accompanied the appointment of a central financial controller. Consequently, even though the financial situation deteriorated as the 1970s progressed, it is remarkable how little the Ferranti structure and strategy changed, a development which reflects attitudes at different levels within the organisation.

Cashflow

In reviewing the early 1970s scene, it would be all too easy to blame Sebastian for failing to take decisive action on the transformer and electronic components departments. The debate over the latter actually remains unclear, because the move into customised circuits was to provide Gem Mill with a highly competitive position as the 1970s unfolded. Viewed in strictly commercial terms, on the other hand, it is clear that as early as 1970 Sebastian ought to have either closed the Avenue Works or negotiated a deal with Hawker-Siddeley, because the massive negative cash-flow of this department was the single most important factor accounting for the company's financial woes over the following five years. At the same time, a range of other factors can be adduced to explain this mounting crisis, most notably the overhead structure of a company heavily dependent upon defence contracts secured in a cost-plus environment, as well as the difficulties inherent in competing against much larger firms in high technology markets.

One of the crucial conclusions reached in section 11.8 was that the defence market changed radically after the mid-1960s. The first of these restructuring measures came as a consequence of the post-*Bloodhound* debates and the second Lang Inquiry, whereby contracts would thereafter be placed on a cost-plus basis and both progress payments and prices were substantially reduced. Secondly, defence spending cuts and the cancellation of major projects like the *TSR–2* led to overcapacity in an industry which had been booming since the Korean War. As the post-1945 expansion of Ferranti had largely been based upon the profits and capital assistance grants derived from defence work, these changes posed major challenges for Ferranti management. Furthermore, as this expansion had been accompanied by the establishment of an expensive overhead structure – mainly engineering staff, as well as accountants and some sales staff – the late 1960s changes placed in great peril those parts of the business which were unable to maintain a steady throughput of orders. It is important to stress that the substantial spending on overheads did not extend to the company's headquarters, where Sebastian and his small team occupied almost 'Bohemian' offices in Hollinwood and expenditure was kept to a bare minimum. While Sebastian liked to travel in his own helicopter, in order to expedite trips around the dispersed divisions, even this activity was converted into a subsidiary to serve the booming executive market. Similarly, salaries at the firm were never amongst the largest in Britain's expanding corporate sector. Nevertheless, the pursuit of a technology-led strategy meant that Ferranti possessed an engineering staff which was expensive to maintain, especially as progress payments from defence customers had been dwindling since the mid-1960s.

Across the company as a whole overheads had become a major issue by 1970, with both the avionics activities in Edinburgh (see section 11.5) and digital systems department (section 11.7) clearly struggling to cope with the changed environment. Of course, over the following decade these divisions managed to secure adequate order cover for their fixed costs, contributing significantly to company funds. Up to the mid-1970s, however, they struggled. The smaller aircraft equipment and fuze departments at Moston were also badly affected by the trends in defence spending. In fact, in the five years leading up to 1967–68 the negative cash-flow from fuze and aircraft equipment departments amounted to almost £1.6 million, while in the following five years few were willing to forecast a better performance. Moreover, anticipating improved returns from the civil businesses like automation systems, numerical control or electronic components to compensate for these difficulties would also have been foolish, emphasising how financial problems were deeply endemic in these high technology sectors.

In essence, the fundamental problem affecting Ferranti from the late 1960s was a combination of its failure to generate adequate sales to cover an expensive overhead structure, added to which were the changes in defence contract conditions and the financial penalties imposed as a result of making the substantial *Bloodhound* payment. While one might point to the transformer division as the single most important drain on company funds, it was simply the worst feature of a poor financial situation. Eric Grundy talked occasionally about the possibility of recapitalising the company, by raising some much-needed fixed capital on the stock exchange. Not surprisingly, though, no such proposals were ever brought to the board, because he knew that this was never going to be an acceptable option to Sebastian. Instead of a recapitalisation, as we saw in section 11.8, what had become the traditional Ferranti ruses of selling assets (numerical control and the ICL shares) and bank borrowing provided much of the necessary liquidity at a time when profits proved inadequate.

Table 12.1. *Cash inflow and cash outflow, 1961–75*
(£ million)

INFLOW		OUTFLOW	
Gross profits	46.9	Capital expenditure	59.2
Sales of businesses & investments	8.4	Investments in associated co.s	0.7
Miscellaneous income	2.1	Taxation	9.1
		Interest	11.4
		Ordinary dividends	2.6
TOTALS	57.4		83.0

Source: Harry Kirkham's report to SZF, 1975.

The financial position is starkly revealed in Table 12.1, where the particularly high interest payments are especially noticeable. This confirms the view that bank borrowing was keeping Ferranti afloat at a time when the firm failed to generate enough profits to pay for an increasing cash outflow. Although a considerable infusion of capital had been derived from the sale of businesses and investments, the near £26 million difference between cash inflow and outflow reveals the acute nature of the company's financial problems. Indeed, there seemed to be fundamental financial weaknesses in a family firm operating on the frontiers of knowledge across such a wide range of technologies. When Ferranti recorded a loss of £826,590 in 1970–71, it was consequently apparent that more radical solutions were required, an issue we shall return to in section 12.3. As Appendix C (Table 2) reveals, though, the financial results remained poor throughout the early 1970s, putting Sebastian under increasing pressure to take decisive action on a range of problems which were undermining the whole business.

Scotland's role

One of the people who was to play a prominent role in both the events and deliberations of the early 1970s was Donald McCallum, who as general manager of the Scottish activities was particularly well placed to make suggestions. McCallum had been appointed by Sebastian as the head of Ferranti

Sebastian de Ferranti standing by the new helicopter purchased in 1968 to ferry the chairman around the country. *(Museum of Science and Industry at Manchester.)*

Scotland in 1968, at a time when as sections 11.5 and 11.6 reveal Crewe Toll and its satellites had been badly affected by a combination of the 1960s defence market changes and a couple of failed contracts. By the early 1970s, however, most of these problems had been solved, with the Scottish division was once again making returns on capital employed which averaged over twenty per cent as a result of securing major development and production orders for a range of avionics products. The relative importance of Crewe Toll to Ferranti finances can be seen clearly in Table 12.2, where it is revealed that in the three years leading up to 1973–74 the Scottish activities kept the company liquid. Although the transformer division was clearly a major drain on Ferranti funds, and from the estimated figures for 1974–75 it would appear that the rest of the UK divisions were anticipating improved returns, it was still Crewe Toll which made the largest contribution. As John Pickin jokingly told the Crewe Toll management at a dinner held in 1973 to celebrate *Ferranti Inventors*: 'Keep sending down the million pounds'.

While this speech was taken in good heart on the night, not unnaturally

Donald McCallum and his team in Scotland felt that much better use could have been made of their profits. In partcular, they argued strongly that if the full benefits of Crewe Toll's successes were to be harnessed productively, senior management would have to take decisive action on the loss-making divisions. It was advice Sebastian was obliged to listen to carefully, in view of Crewe Toll's contribution to company profits, giving McCallum a special place in company discussions. On the other hand, it is important to remember that the Scottish division was largely concerned about its own viability, rather than that of the company as a whole. It had also failed to deal decisively with such substantial loss-makers as numerical control, selling it off to Plessey only after a decade of heavy losses (section 11.6). Sebastian consequently remained suspicious of any self-serving advice coming from the Scottish executives, realising that they had always regarded themselves as separate from the Manchester-based activities.

Reorganisation and cost-cutting

The Scottish division was actually well placed to lobby Sebastian in the early 1970s, because apart from Sir John Toothill, who retained his position on the board after retiring as general manager at Crewe Toll in 1968, Donald McCallum was also made a director in 1970. In fact, as a result of retirements between 1968 and 1973 Sebastian was faced with making several changes to the board. While this should be seen more as a natural continuum in the organisation, rather than a major reconstruction of senior management, it did bring in some fresh blood at a crucial time (see Appendix E). In 1971, for example, Eric Grundy left after forty years service, the bulk of which had seen his dynamic influence at the head of the Moston group of departments. His elevation to the board had come at the same time as Jack Prince (meter department manager), R. M. Hobill (transformer department), Sir Frank Rostron (export sales), and O. M. Robson (sales). As Appendix D reveals, though, all of them had either retired or died by 1971. These were highly experienced directors who well understood both the Ferranti culture and its financial implications. Times had changed so dramatically, however, that Sebastian felt the need for a younger generation of advisors which might well have a stronger grasp of the new realities. This resulted in the general works manager, Archie Gray, and the former head of Ferranti Electric Inc., R. H. Davies, joining the board. John Pickin was also made a director in 1972, with special responsibility for engineering matters. A year later, Peter Dorey (digital systems) joined the board, while to replace F. W. Hardstone as the National Westminster Bank's appointee J. J. Ratcliffe was invited to become a director.

Table 12.2. *The financial performance of Ferranti Ltd compared with its major divisions, 1971–72 to 1974–75 (£ million)*

	Average for the three years 1971–72 to 1973–74	Estimated for financial year 1974–75
Output		
Scotland	21.2	25.5
Transformers	5.6	6.3
Rest of UK Co.	33.7	43.5
TOTAL	60.5	75.3
Trading Profit/(Loss)		
Scotland	2.1	1.8
Transformers	(1.5)	(1.4)
Rest of UK Co.	0.9	1.5
TOTAL	1.5	1.9

Source: Information provided by D. McCallum.

Although by 1973 the Ferranti board was both smaller than its 1960s counterpart, as well as possessing a younger age profile, it is clear that its composition was little different. The key point to remember is how strong divisional interests were still represented on the board. Furthermore, as a result of some organisational innovations carried out in 1973–74, the operating divisions actually increased their power-base during this period. These changes, which involved the decentralisation of such functions as sales, purchasing and industrial relations down to the divisions, were an essential part of the firm's evolution since the 1890s, a process which had seen managers accept much greater responsibility for their own destiny. They were also the inevitable result of the firm's growth, because Sebastian was accepting the need to delegate responsibility to the managers who were both responsible for individual product ranges and much more knowledgable than the centre about the associated challenges of remaining competitive in these markets.

Notwithstanding these changes, in financial terms very little was altered, because the accounting system remained highly centralised and no attempt was made to divide capital employed amongst the divisions. This reluctance to convert Ferranti into a full-blown multidivisional form of organisation was a clear reflection of Sebastian's desire to remain in complete control of investment strategy, forcing divisional managers to seek his permission for any significant measures. In other words, the organisational character of Ferranti retained the informal nature which had traditionally been its hallmark. It is also relevant to note that, while all affected were found jobs, the excercise involved the transfer of over 200 staff from the head office in Hollinwood, adding to the general unease about job prospects at what had traditionally been the company's heart.

Having noted how the divisions still remained at the mercy of central decision-making, one must remember that in dealing with the period's financial problems Sebastian and his team of advisors were also attempting to impose greater discipline and supervision over the internal flow of funds. The chief cost and management accountant, Harry Kirkham, was charged with the task of imposing a uniform system of budgetting on all divisions, substantially improving the flow of information to the centre at a time when cash-flow had to be monitored in the minutest detail. At that time, only the Scottish division ran its own accounts, while all other parts of the firm were controlled financially from the centre, providing Sebastian with the opportunity to impose cost-reductions on the managers. A series of what were called 'cash-management exercises' was also launched, encouraging divisional managers and their accountants to cut costs on a wide range of services which might be deemed 'wasteful'. These, of course, were little more than cost-cutting exercises, paring expenses as far as they would go. Inevitably, they also had the adverse effect of antagonising further staff in those divisions which were generating surpluses, reinforcing the feelings of many employees at all levels that they were simply subsidising the losses of other divisions.[27] In the troubled divisions, on the other hand, the economy drive simply exacerbated worries over redundancies and closure. Most crucially, however, as we have noted when previously reviewing the internal financial reporting system at Ferranti (see section 11.1), it is apparent that Sebastian was availed of all the information necessary by an extensive team of accountants and advisors, reflecting the highly centralised nature of the firm's financial management structure at a time when other functions like sales and industrial relations were being passed down to the divisions.

The instigation of 'cash-management exercises', alongside Sebastian's decision to decentralise various functional departments, were clear indicators that he realised the need to effect some savings in response to the illiquidity apparent in the balance sheet. Of course, as with most of the business community, Ferranti finances were not helped by the series of macro-economic and industrial relations problems which beset Britain during the early 1970s, in particular the rising levels of inflation affecting pricing strategy and the short-time working introduced as a result of a miners' strike in 1973 and an energy crisis in 1974.[28] These external influences were a major feature of the business scene at that time, adversely affecting attempts at coping with the severe disruption to international trade arising out of the OPEC decison to treble oil prices in 1973. More importantly for Ferranti, the banking system was rocked by both a crisis in the secondary banking sector and adverse trends in the property market.[29] NatWest were particularly badly affected by both of these crises, as a consequence of which much of the talk within Ferranti about long-term and immediate solutions was brought abruptly to a head by the bank's own problems. Of course, it is always easy to hide behind these general features of the environment and ascribe the Ferranti difficulties to factors beyond its management's control. Ultimately, though, the firm's central problem was the mounting size of its overdraft, focusing attention on the quality of Sebastian's decision-making, rather than an external environment which was affecting every other firm.

12.3 Negotiations with the bank and government involvement

The overdraft

The growing size of the Ferranti overdraft was a trend nobody could afford to ignore during the early 1970s, particularly as the company's issued capital remained at the figure set in 1959, £4.5 million (see Appendix C, Table 1). Figure 12.1 charts the overdraft's history since 1945, indicating how while there had been some serious increases during the mid-1950s (see section 8.4), since 1964 Ferranti had been increasingly dependent upon this short-term form of lending. It is important to emphasise that while the overdraft appears to have fallen after 1970–71, when paradoxically Ferranti actually made a gross loss (of almost £830,000), the figures reported in Figure 12.1 ought to be augmented by the eurodollar loan of £4 million (eurodollar $9,562,800) negotiated with Westminster Foreign Bank Ltd in July 1970 (see Appendix C, Table 1). However, although this loan would naturally have staved off an immediate liquidity crisis at Ferranti, as interest at eleven per cent was charged by the lender it would clearly have imposed further pressures on the balance sheet. This is why Ferranti decided to repay the eurodollar loan in 1972, preferring instead to rely on a standard overdraft, as well as the slightly improved profits of the next two financial years (see Appendix C, Table 2). By 1973–74, though, the liquidity position had deteriorated once again. With gross profits of just £53,880, bank borrowing consequently soared to over £9.6 million, forcing Sebastian into measures which five years earlier would have been highly unlikely.

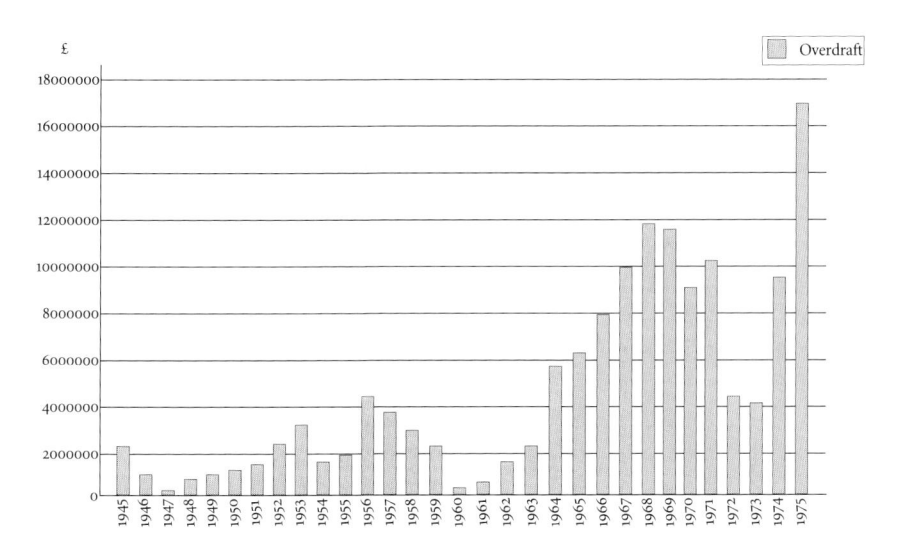

Figure 12.1. *The Ferranti Overdraft, 1945–75*

In reviewing these events, it is important to note that Sebastian did not wait until the crisis had unfolded before considering radical solutions. Apart from the 'cash-management exercises' and decentralisation of various functional departments described earlier, as early as 1970 several possibilities were discussed with the merchant banking house of N. M. Rothschild & Sons. However, such was the manner in which this firm conducted its investigations that Sebastian dispensed with their services before any recommendations could be made. Three years later, NatWest encouraged Ferranti to work with its subsidiary merchant banking arm, the County Bank Ltd, as a possible prelude to the issue of new capital. Once again, though, Sebastian preferred to take a more independent approach to the firm's problems. One could speculate that a Ferranti share issue might well have been a major flop, in view of both the company's parlous state and a gloomy economic scene exacerbated by oil price rises of 200 per cent in 1973. Sebastian also had little confidence in the County Bank's ability to solve his firm's problems.

Whatever the case, it is clear that the main obstacle to change was Sebastian's instinctive belief that family control was crucial to maintaining the Ferranti culture. In retrospect, one might argue that instead of thinking about a flotation, NatWest and Ferranti ought to have negotiated the conversion of all the overdraft into a fixed-term loan, covenanting the latter into pursuing certain objectives as a condition of the deal.[30] This conversion would have made Ferranti less vulnerable to a short-term change of mind by the Bank, while at the same time forcing Sebastian into a rationalisation programme which might have prevented what became in 1974 a full-blown crisis. Unfortunately for both parties, though, neither considered such a move at that time, precipitating a major change at Ferranti as matters deteriorated further.

NatWest difficulties

Apart from an unwavering commitment to the philosophy of family management, another decisive influence on Sebastian throughout his tenure as chief executive at Ferranti was the belief that NatWest would always support the company in its greatest hours of need.[31] One might describe this faith in banking as naive, particularly in view of what happened to Ferranti in 1974–75. On the other hand, a frequently-quoted comment on the banking world in general is the claim that an institution's loyalty to customers varies in direct proportion to the debts incurred: the greater the debt, the greater the loyalty. It was certainly a belief to which Sebastian remained firmly committed throughout the early 1970s, arguing that, in view of the large corporate and personal overdrafts accumulated over the previous ten years,[32] NatWest was 'locked in' to both the company and its two main owners. Furthermore, a representative of the Bank sat on the board, giving him access to all the financial information generated by Sebastian's accountants. This faith in the bank was also seemingly confirmed at the beginning of 1974, when NatWest agreed to another extension of the overdraft (to £12 million). It was a decision some senior figures like McCallum in Scotland and Dorey in Bracknell regarded as most unfortunate,[33] because they simply wanted the big loss-makers to be closed, in order that their own profits could be diverted back into internal development programmes. Events were soon to demonstrate, however, that there is nothing certain about the business world, dashing all Sebastian's hopes of continued bank support.

In some respects, one might argue that in his 1974 dealings with NatWest Sebastian was unlucky, because as the liquidity crisis worsened at Ferranti and the need for additional overdraft facilities became apparent, the banking world was rocked by a series of difficulties which materially affected liquidity. Just to accentuate the problems, this was also a time when the British economy was reeling from unprecedented inflationary and industrial relations worries. One of the more substantial problems of spring 1974 was the slump in property prices, an event which coincided with NatWest suffering heavy losses (arising from its dealings with major debtors like Cunard and Court Line). This was already forcing its senior executives to examine all outstanding accounts much more rigorously, a situation compounded by the secondary banking crisis of the summer of 1974 which led NatWest to look closely at its lending policies.

It is probable that as the Ferranti overdraft was so large, especially in relation to its profits, that in 1974 NatWest would have in any case refused to lend more when in July Sebastian once more approached NatWest to extend the overdraft by another £5 million. This is a hypothetical issue, though, ignoring the degree to which NatWest was under pressure to revise its strategy. What is certain is that the local Manchester office was obliged to refer Sebastian's July 1974 request to head office in London. Representing Ferranti at this meeting were the two brothers, Sebastian and Basil, as well as Donald McCallum and Harry Kirkham (chief cost and management accountant). All realised that the initial refusal of funds was a warning sign the company could ill-afford to ignore. Their fears were also soon confirmed, when just a couple of days later NatWest head office refused to extend the overdraft limit without an independent accountant's investigation of Ferranti, bringing to an abrupt end the cosy relationship between lender and client.

While one might argue that luck was hardly on the company's side, in timing its liquidity crisis to coincide with both NatWest's property and secondary banking problems and the economy's difficulties, on the other hand Ferranti had precipitated its own financial difficulties by failing to act decisively with regard especially to the transformer division. It is fair to point out that NatWest had dealt badly with the earlier pleas for overdraft extensions, because no conditions had been attached to providing the additional funds. Similarly, the option of converting the overdraft into a fixed-term loan should have been considered. Notwithstanding these arguments, as both section 12.1 and Table 12.2 indicate, the crucial issue was how to stem the tide of funds ebbing out of the company through the major loss-making divisions. Whatever his personal reasons for resisting internal demands to close the Avenue Works, on this issue Sebastian alone was culpable.

The Nicholson Report

The accounting firm chosen in August 1974 to undertake NatWest's detailed investigation was Peat, Marwick, Mitchell & Co. One of its senior partners, Rupert Nicholson, was given the task of assessing the Ferranti case, having risen to prominence after deftly securing the survival of Rolls Royce during its 1970–71 crisis. While the three-week investigations were undertaken, in the meantime Sebastian was advised that it would be politic to inform the company's major customer about the situation, leading to a meeting with representatives from the defence and industry ministries. The civil servants were naturally cautious about the situation, particularly in view of the estimated £15 million in government aid the company felt was necessary if NatWest withdrew its support. The political situation also remained uncertain – the incumbent minority Labour government had called a general election for 10 October – consequently preventing the civil servants from taking any decisions on the level of support until they knew both what Peat, Marwick, Mitchell had suggested and which party was in power. Although NatWest also consulted the DoTI at the end of August,[34] in effect little could be done until the accountants had completed their report.

It was early in September 1974 that Nicholson presented his findings to NatWest, precipitating a rapid series of events. In fact, one might argue that by the autumn of 1974 this report was incidental, because during the summer NatWest had already decided to limit its support for Ferranti. Nevertheless, it is important to note that Nicholson was extremely critical of the loose lending practices pursued by NatWest up to January 1974, admonishing its senior managers for extending the Ferranti overdraft without insisting on certain economy or rationalisation programmes. At the same time, while complimenting Ferranti on its thorough reporting system, as well as commenting on the sound nature of the business overall, Nicholson also concluded by pointing to a fundamental weakness: 'This is a good business, but it must be properly run, and while it has been well led, it has been badly managed'. In effect, this focused attention principally on Sebastian's role, indicating how while in leadership terms he was outstanding, as a manager he lacked vision and decisiveness. Of course, Nicholson was applying conventional business thinking to the situation, ignoring the family's willingness as majority stakeholders to take a long-term position on departmental finances. On the other hand, if as a consequence of this strategy Ferranti over-borrowed, then the firm's survival was being threatened, forcing NatWest to refuse any further extensions to the overdraft unless government guarantees were forthcoming.

Ministry and political machinations

The bank's decision was conveyed immediately to Sebastian and several of his directors, coincidentally while they were attending a major sales event, the Farnborough Air Show. In effect, this gave the company's largest customer a decisive influence on subsequent events. However, in view of the year's economic and political circumstances, considerable uncertainty still prevailed. The DoTI had clearly been considering its options since discussing the Ferranti crisis with NatWest in August, while the politicians electioneered hard during the autumn. A preliminary meeting was held with Richard Bullock, one of the under-secretaries, when much to the company's surprise not only was a derisory offer made for all the equity, at the same time the civil servant insisted that a receiver would be appointed unless it was accepted within hours.[35]

This development came as something of a surprise to the Ferranti brothers, in response to which they immediately sought the advice of Arnold Weinstock, chief executive of GEC. Some of the senior Ferranti directors like Donald McCallum and John Pickin regarded this as a dangerous move, given what was a near-paranoia about coming under the GEC wing. However, it is important to remember that Sebastian had actually been a close friend of Arnold Weinstock since the early 1960s, persuading the Ferranti chairman to seek out what was the most respected figure in the British electrical industry. It was also largely as a result of this meeting that the DoTI's threat to appoint a receiver was withdrawn, after the GEC chief executive personally rang up the civil servant concerned. This gave Ferranti valuable breathing space in which to negotiate a rescue package. In the meantime, the brothers also followed another piece of advice given by Weinstock, when he said: 'It's not an accountant you need, it's a lawyer'. Weinstock actually recommended securing the services of the eminent lawyer, Lord Goodman. Again, while the Ferranti board resented the manner in which the brothers relied largely for advice on an outsider, it is clear that Lord Goodman proved to be a most valuable ally in the negotiations to come.

The situation as it developed in August-September was clearly most unsatisfactory, with no guarantee of support coming from the DTI and mounting concern amongst senior management that a creditor could well call in the receivers. Greater certainty was only to emerge when the new industry minister, Anthony Wedgwood Benn, decided to pay closer attention to the Ferranti case. Benn was partly motivated by his ardent belief in state control of the means of production, and partly because of genuine fears that substantial job losses would result from the closure of certain departments. His first move, in the week beginning 9 September, was to provide informal assurances to NatWest that the overdraft would be guaranteed by government. However, as this had to be ratified by Cabinet, he was obliged to pass all the papers to Downing St on 13 September,[36] during which process information was leaked to a reporter from *The Sunday Times*, who ran a major story publicising the Ferranti crisis. This brought to a head what had been intimate discussions involving only the most senior people in banking, company and political circles. It was a most unfortunate development, instilling panic at every level of the company and bringing closer the possibility of a creditor appointing receivers to wind up the Ferranti business. The latter was forestalled by Cabinet's agreement on 17 September to support Benn's rescue package. Even so, it was not until after Labour had won the October general election that a permanent arrangement was negotiated, extending the uncertainty for another month.

By the middle of September, it was consequently clear that the future of Ferranti was no longer to be determined internally, Benn's intervention having instigated a period in which government was going to usurp family hegemony. In fact, even though firm action had to await the general election result, detailed discussions between the two parties proceeded throughout the following four weeks. Over this period, the company management spent many long hours hammering out the details of an equitable settlement which many executives regarded as better than anticipated. Indeed, after the initial concern over the DoTI offer made earlier in the month, it was clear that the civil servants had been instructed to deal more equitably with Ferranti. Benn was particularly impressed by the extensive support Ferranti enjoyed amongst its workforce, having called together all the company's shop stewards to discuss the situation. This was a reflection of the degree of cohesion which the family had engendered within the organisation, indicating how Ferranti possessed an inner strength which would see the firm through a difficult few years.

Once Labour established a working majority at the October general election, the negotiations then moved on to provide the basis of a more permanent relationship. Reflecting the ideological leanings of that government, it is important to note that the meetings were tripartite, bringing together management, politicians and trade unionists to discuss all aspects of the company's strategy and finances. Of course, since the First World War the company's industrial relations structure had revolved around negotiations between the works manager and shop stewards, creating a confrontational atmosphere which at times was regarded by some divisional managers as unhelpful. By the early 1970s, though, some divisions (Moston and Gem Mill, for example) had established liaison committees composed of union and management representatives, as means of introducing a more participatory culture. Benn was clearly impressed with these committees, apart from which the loyalty instilled into the workforce by the Ferranti family and senior management reflected well on the company culture, an asset the minister felt was worth preserving. At the same time, though, mindful of what Nicholson had said about Sebastian's management skills, the DoTI was anxious to make one major change which was to have decisive consequences for the company as a whole. Indeed, within a year it had been agreed that the Ferranti brothers should be removed from executive positions and new personnel recruited in their place.

12.4 Conclusions

When in 1963 Sebastian de Ferranti succeeded his father as chairman of the family firm, much was made of the continuity evident in this move (see section 11.1). Indeed, Sebastian was steeped in the Ferranti traditions, having been heavily influenced by Sir Vincent throughout his life. To engender loyalty at the highest levels of management, he also elevated on to the board all the divisional managers. Just as significantly, Sebastian resisted the pressure to appoint a financial controller, on the grounds that not only would such a move destroy the freebooting atmosphere his father had instilled into the firm, he also felt that the firm's departmental reporting procedures provided all the information required by the board when assessing general performance (see section 11.1). On the other hand, it is also evident that by raising divisional managers to board status Sebastian had ensured that strong vested interests were able to voice resistance to further interference in their affairs. In fact, during the early 1970s Ferranti moved even closer to a highly devolved multidivisional form of organisation, passing responsibility for most functional activities – sales, marketing, purchasing, transport, and accounting – down to the divisions, thereby reinforcing their autonomy (see section 12.2).

Of course, the firm's organisational development after 1963 is a subject of central importance to an analysis of its general performance. However, in view of the mid-1970s financial crisis much greater significance could well be attached to the quality of decision-making and the commercial viability of remaining a family firm. The major problems affecting Ferranti from the late 1960s revolved largely around a single issue, namely, the firm's ability to compete in a wide range of markets against much more financially powerful rivals. As Figure 8.1 reveals, the 1960s was just as marked as the three previous decades by the continued diversification of Ferranti activities, especially in the areas of avionics, microelectronics and computer systems, where new products were emerging regularly. Although this reflected the continued strength of the Ferranti ethos, at the same time it was a process which frequently stretched the firm's finances to breaking point, forcing Sebastian to seek extensions to the overdraft provided by the (National) Westminster Bank. In addition, Sebastian was also obliged to make an *ex gratia* payment of almost £3 million to the MoA, as a result of an alleged excess profit on the production of the highly successful *Bloodhound* guided missile, upsetting significantly the forward projections on cashflow and undermining liquidity at a vital time (see sections 10.7–10.9).

While after 1965 the Ferranti finances certainly appear to have deteriorated, in seeking an insight into the major reasons behind this trend it is important to stress that organisational continuity would only have played a minor part in the unfolding scenario. Much greater stress ought to be placed on a series of coincidental developments. In the first place, the cash-flow situation was affected adversely by the *Bloodhound* payment. At the same time, not only did the defence ministries effect substantial changes to contract conditions and payment mechanisms, the presiding Labour government instituted a series of drastic cuts in defence expenditure which badly affected what had been the major market for Ferranti products. The division worst affected by these developments had been one of the financial mainstays of Ferranti since the mid-1950s, the avionics group at Crewe Toll, Edinburgh, while other departments like digital systems at Bracknell were also suffering (see sections 11.5–11.7). In addition, major cash-flow difficulties were experienced in two other divisions, electronics and transformers, leading to the substantial deterioration in returns on capital employed after 1965 (see Appendix C, Table 2) and prompting Sebastian to consider some drastic measures (see section 12.2).

Although the mounting financial pressures of the late 1960s and early 1970s were clearly well-understood within Ferranti, in dealing with them Sebastian was faced with a major challenge to the basic tenets of his company's traditions. We have already noted that he rejected the advice to appoint a financial controller, a decision his divisional managers generally supported, principally because they feared greater central interference in their activities. On the other hand, the board encouraged Sebastian to deal decisively with the problem divisions, largely on the grounds that the losses were siphoning off their dwindling profits and undermining general viability. It was on this issue that there was widespread disagreement.

One must remember that Sebastian was willing to sell off divisions when he felt that their futures were guaranteed under new ownership, for example with regard to mainframe computers (section 9.10) and numerical control systems (section 11.6). However, no such clear-cut solutions were offered with regard to the electronic components and transformer departments. In the first place, Sebastian argued conclusively that Ferranti should continue to secure an in-house capability in electronic components which would allow engineers across the firm to take advantage of the latest developments in this key area. He also felt that the transformer division's long-term prospects were much better than anticipated, arguing that electricity consumption would recover quickly from the depths plumbed in the early 1970s. Sadly, though, this recovery came too late to save what had been part of the firm since 1885. In the meantime, this division's losses precipitated wider troubles within the company, leading to dramatic changes in the ownership and management of Ferranti.

It is clear from the earlier sections of this chapter that Sebastian's refusal to close the transformer division was the most important reason why in the mid-1970s his firm experienced a major liquidity crisis. Ferranti was also badly affected by the problems besetting the National Westminster Bank, where as a result of poor investment decisions mounting illiquidity placed severe constraints on its lending policies by the summer of 1974. In addition, the cashflow implications of operating in the crisis-torn years of 1972–74 substantially affected Ferranti, indicating how external factors also played a decisive part in the unfolding scenario. While Sebastian argued as late as the summer of 1974 that the bank was 'locked in' to the firm, given the growing overdraft, this naive position was soon dashed, leading ultimately to extensive government intervention in Ferranti finances and management. Indeed, as we noted in the introduction, the major difference between the crises of 1903 and 1975 was the role played by government, because in the latter's case an interventionist Labour government stepped in to rescue Ferranti, providing an infusion worth £15 million on condition that the firm would come under its wing. At the same time, the crises resulted in exactly the same change, because as the state by then owned 62.5 per cent of the equity (see Appendix D) the family was ousted from its position at the head of Ferranti and a professional manager was hired as managing director. It was a traumatic time for all concerned, and for Sebastian in particular the government-induced changes were hard to accept. Although he was allowed to continue as chairman, the spectre of 1903 had returned to haunt the family, this time in the form of state ownership and a new managing director, Derek Alun-Jones.

13

The Ferranti Traditions: A Test of Durability

It would be all too easy to see 1975 as a decisive watershed in Ferranti history, because thereafter family ownership and control was abandoned in favour of more conventional patterns of business organisation. On the other hand, while some of the changes could have altered the way in which Ferranti operated, one must not fall into the obvious trap of arguing that the organisational ethos had been fundamentally affected. In the first place, Derek Alun-Jones, as managing director in the late 1970s, successfully formalised many of the arrangements which up to 1975 had been conducted informally by either Sir Vincent (1930–63) or Sebastian (1963–75). On the other hand, one must stress how in an organisational sense little changed at Ferranti during the late 1970s, with decentralised decision-making remaining a key component of the company culture. Similarly, as far as the product range was concerned only the transformer division was closed. Even here, though, it was 1979 before the final decision was made, while all the other divisions (including electronic components) actually started to generate better returns. This reflected the fundamental viability of what Ferranti had been building since the 1930s, because the successes in avionics and computer systems especially allowed both output and returns on capital employed to rise impressively up to the late 1980s.

Another crucial point to make about the post-1975 regime is its continued belief in encouraging the innovation culture which had been such a central feature of the 'Ferranti Spirit'. Although the creation of an executive committee in 1975 as the central coordinating body might well have been a useful new mechanism to bring together divisional managers and the key directors, autonomous decision-making remained the hallmark of Ferranti organisational development throughout this period. This again emphasises the degree of continuity in terms of corporate ethos. While Derek Alun-Jones coined phrases like 'Creating Real Wealth from New Technology' to represent the allegedly distinctive characteristic of his regime, it is difficult to see how this differed much from what the Ferranti family had achieved. Furthermore, Sir Vincent and Sebastian especially had been able to pursue highly risky product development strategies free of the burdens imposed by financial institutions, ploughing back the bulk of their profits to facilitate this process. Of course, the liquidity crises of 1903 and 1975 reflect the weaknesses inherent in family firms committed to expensive high technology projects. On the other hand, the family felt that it was worth running the risk of encountering such difficulties as long as the business was engaged in challenging areas which would bring long-term benefits. After 1979 especially, when the state sold off its controlling interest in the firm and senior management was obliged to be ever-watchful of City expectations, one might argue that this led to a much more generous dividend policy which deprived divisions of much-needed financial resources.

The greater concern with City pressures was by far the most obvious difference between the regime which took over after 1975 and that which had been dominated by the de Ferranti family. Nevertheless, the long-term nature of the Ferranti ethos was clearly its most enduring feature, and well into the 1980s this approach remained an essential basis for the firm's development. This philosophy created an environment in which engineers and managers could follow their instincts, giving rise to a widespread belief among employees that Ferranti was a 'fun place' in which to work. It was also a philosophy which led to the extensive diversification reflected in Figure 8.1. While critics questioned the commercial viability of pursuing risky strategies in a weakly-financed firm, the Ferranti family argued that such an arrangement was crucial. It was a philosophy which continued to prevail even after the family had been ousted from control in 1975, indicating how their instincts had permeated an organisation which was destined to play a prominent role in the continued development of British high technology.

Another issue which must be raised when assessing the mid-1970s changes is how with great flair and aplomb the brothers extracted themselves from what appeared to be serious personal financial crises. Of course, much of the credit for this manoevre should go to Lord Goodman, the prominent lawyer whom Arnold Weinstock had advised Sebastian and Basil to see. It was Lord Goodman who negotiated a deal with Lord Ryder during the detailed negotiations of 1975, when it was agreed that if Ferranti achieved a stock exchange quotation in excess of £1.50p. per share by 30 September 1978, the government would transfer 12.5 per cent of the equity back to the family. This demonstrates how Goodman had substantially restored the family's wealth, even if he was unable to prevent Lord Ryder from replacing Sebastian with a new managing director.

The full story of these negotiations must await another volume, which will describe how Ferranti fared under the regime introduced by Lord Ryder in 1975. While we leave the story at a fascinating juncture, above all one must remember that such was the durability of the traditions and practices established by the three key people in this story, Dr Ferranti, Sir Vincent de Ferranti and his son, Sebastian, that the new regime found it very difficult to improve on the general nature of corporate life within the firm. This is a testament to the validity of the 'Ferranti Spirit', an ethos which continued to thrive and prosper until the traumatic events of the late 1980s.

Notes

Notes to Introduction

1. For a discussion of these issues, see Thompson (1993), pp. 8–23.
2. Chandler (1990), pp. 235–9.
3. For a review of the Chandler debate, see Wilson (1995), pp. 3–10.
4. Schein (1985), p. 6.
5. See Wilson (1995), pp. 50–6.
6. The University of Manchester conferred an honorary doctorate on him in 1912, in recognition of his contribution to electrical engineering. See section 4.4.
7. Vincent de Ferranti was knighted in 1948, in recognition of both his firm's wartime work and export successes.
8. For a discussion of these types of organisation, see Burns & Stalker (1961).
9. See Wilson (1995), pp. 190–4.
10. Jeremy (1990).

Notes to Chapter 1

1. This section is based on Negri (1903).
2. He is described as an 'eminent captain' in an elegant epitaph inscribed on his tombstone. Negri (1903).
3. I am indebted to the research of Peter Townley for this reference.
4. Bone (1954), p. 115.
5. Quoted in Bone (1954), p. 115. There is now a website (http://www.ga-usa.com/mba-zoti/800/e_zanide.htm) dedicated to this distinguished guitarist.
6. William Scott File.
7. Scott Family Scrapbook.
8. de Ferranti & Ince (1934), p. 24.
9. Bone (1954), p. 323.
10. Scott Family Scrapbook.
11. William Scott Letters.
12. Bone (1954), p. 323.
13. Diaries of JZF for the 1870s.
14. JZF to Emily Scott, June 1858.
15. Scott Family Scrapbook.
16. Cesar de Ferranti File. Clients included the Bishop of Shrewsbury and Harmood Banner, a prominent Victorian philanthropist.
17. This patent, 'Improvements in the Artistic Treatment of Photographic Portraits' (3069), was taken out jointly with E. J. Turner.

18. Ince & de Ferranti (1934), p. 148.
19. Ferranti Sketch-Books.
20. SZF Letter Book.
21. IEE Commemorative Proceedings (1922).
22. SZF to Vanda, 27 Jan. 1878.
23. IEE Commemorative Proceedings (1922).
24. SZF to CZF, 24 June 1874.
25. CZF to SZF, 30 Sept. 1875.
26. JZF to SZF, 26 March 1878.
27. CZF to SZF, 3 May 1878.
28. Hughes (1971), pp. 12–13.
29. Clark (1977), p. 9.
30. SZF to Vanda, 3 Dec. 1878.
31. Wiener (1981), p. 11.
32. St Augustine's School Magazine, 1930.
33. SZF to CZF, 25 May 1879.
34. SZF to JZF, 26 March 1876.
35. See later, section 4.2.
36. SZF to CZF, 17 Nov. 1877.
37. Scholey (1897), p. 35.
38. SZF to CZF, 27 Dec. 1878.
39. CZF to SZF, 5 Feb. 1878; SZF to CZF, 6 Feb. 1878.
40. SZF to CZF, 25 May 1878.
41. Ince & de Ferranti (1934), p. 21.
42. SZF to Vanda, 2 Feb. 1879.
43. IEE Commemorative Proceedings (1922).
44. SZF to CZF, 11 Feb. 1879.
45. SZF to JZF, 2 March 1879.
46. SZF to JZF, 11 Nov. 1879.
47. SZF to CZF, 18 Jan. 1880.
48. *Electrician*, 3 (1879), July 12, p. 87, and 4 (1880), March 27, p. 223.
49. The Jarman Electrical Co. was later acquired by the Electrical Locomotive & Power Co. in 1885. *Electrician*, 15 (1885), Oct. 30, p. 478.
50. SZF to JZF, 2 March 1879.
51. SZF to CZF, 8 Feb. 1880.
52. For a survey of the industry's evolution, see Byatt (1979) and Hannah (1979).
53. Speech by O. Lodge, IEE Commemorative Proceedings (1922).
54. Henry Wilde, FRS (1833–1919), a Birmingham engineer, had been working on an electrical generator since the 1860s, patenting machines in 1861 and 1863 which were used in the electroplating industry. His paper to the Royal Society in 1866 was especially influential in stimulating other engineers to develop the principle of self-excitation, in particular Samuel A. Varley (1832–1921). Mackechnie-Jarvis (1966), pp. 121–3.
55. Crompton (1928), p. 12.
56. SZF to JZF, 12 Jan. 1879.
57. JZF Diary, 6 Oct. 1880.
58. JZF to Juliet, 13 Oct. 1880.
59. £105,000 had just been spent on the new laboratories. *Electrician*, 5 (1880), July 3, p. 73.
60. Sanderson (1972), p. 110.

61. Lodge lectured on mechanics, but he was also a well-known advocate of electricity, speaking publicly on 'The Power of the Future'. *Electrician*, 4 (1882), Jan. 28, p. 172.
62. IEE Commemorative Proceedings (1922).
63. During the early 1880s Sebastian sent his father a total of £596 for the repayment of debts, and from 1886 gave him a monthly allowance of £6. For further work on this topic, see Cox and Cooper (1988), pp. 8–22.
64. Juliana's Diary is the best record of this episode.
65. SZF to CZF, 15 April 1882.
66. Juliana's Diary for 1880–1882.
67. Zenobie T Gramme (1826–1901) was a Belgian who worked mainly in Paris, where in 1870 he produced his first generator based on the Pacinotti armature which was widely regarded as the most efficient of its day. Pacinotti was an Italian physicist who in 1865 patented this improved type of armature. Mackechnie-Jarvis (1966), p. 123.
68. IEE Commemorative Proceedings (1922).
69. Scott (1958), Ch 7.
70. Ince & de Ferranti (1934), p. 48.
71. JZF to Juliet, 14 July 1881.
72. Scott (1958), p. 148.
73. SZF to JZF, 12 July 1881.
74. SZF Sketch Book No 4.
75. *Electrician*, 6 (1881), March 19, p. 219.
76. This section is based on Ince & de Ferranti (1934), pp. 50–52.
77. A. Thompson to SZF, 10 May 1882.
78. *The Times*, 12 July 1882 and 15 July 1882.
79. I am indebted to Mr R. J. Thurman (of Edwards, Geldard & Shepherd, of Cardiff) for this information on Francis Ince.
80. Whyte (1930), pp. 10–11.
81. Clapham (1951), p. 131.
82. Clapham (1951), pp. 131–3.
83. *Electrician*, 5 (1880), May 22, p. 18.
84. *Electrician*, 1 (1878), July 20, p. 124.
85. 1 (1878), Oct. 19, p. 258.
86. Parsons (1939), p. 12. Although Siemens claim that an installation at Godalming was the first, this was soon terminated and replaced by gas lighting. Edison never actually visited the Holborn Viaduct station, leaving the installation work to his London agent.
87. 6 (1881), Jan. 8, p. 90.
88. Byatt (1979), p. 17.
89. Crompton (1928), pp. 96ff.
90. Kennedy (1987), pp. 134–7.
91. 9 (1882), May 20, p. 560.
92. Cottrell (1980), p. 189. Hannah (1979), pp. 5–6, claims that the total raised was only £1.5 million, but this would appear to have been a conservative estimate.
93. Juliana's Diary, 14 Sept. 1882.
94. *Statist*, 9 (1882), May 6, p. 507.
95. *Electrician*, 10 (1883), May 12, p. 618.
96. Byatt (1979), p. 141.
97. 10 (1882), Sept. 23.
98. Sept. 18, 1882.

99. Mackechnie-Jarvis (1966), p. 125.
100. *Electrician*, 10 (1883), Feb. 3, p. 273.
101. 54 (1882), Dec. 1, p. 415.
102. *Electrician*, 10 (1882), Dec. 2, p. 68.
103. JZF to Emily, 21 Aug. 1882.
104. Thompson (1910), p. 103.
105. The nominal capital of £240,000 was composed of 12,000 A shares and 36,000 B shares, both of £5 each, and by the end of 1882 all had been sold. Hammond owned 1,875 of the A shares. *Electrician*, 11 (1883), May 12, p. 618.
106. 10 (1883), Feb. 3, p. 273.
107. *The Times*, 16 Sept. 1882.
108. *The Times*, 18 Sept. 1882.
109. Sept. 29, p. 219.
110. 54 (1882), Dec. 1, p. 415.
111. Kennedy (1987), pp. 134–139 & 156–157.
112. *Electrician*, 12 (1884), Jan. 5, p. 182.
113. For reviews of the legal scene, see Hannah (1979), pp. 5–8.
114. Foreman-Peck & Millward (1994), pp. 165–7.
115. Wilson (1991), Ch 7.
116. Speech to the IEE Commemorative Proceedings (1922).
117. See Hannah (1979), p. 6.
118. Quoted in Musson (1959), p. 212.
119. *Engineer*, 57 (1884), May 9, p. 342. The two Brush subsidiaries with which Hammond was still connected were also brought into this new venture, bringing the total capital to £330,000.
120. Hughes (1962), p. 79.
121. *Electrician*, 10 (1883), Feb. 3, p. 273, quotes one authority, Sylvanus Thompson, as saying that 'AC machines are quite out of the question'.
122. *Electrician*, 12 (1884), Jan. 5, p. 182.
123. 55 (1883), Jan. 5, p. 13.
124. Hammond company annual meeting. *Electrician*, 14 (1884), Feb. 14, p. 295.
125. Sanderson (1972).
126. *Electrician*, 11 (1883), May 12, p. 619.
127. *Electrician*, 14 (1884), April 19, p. 550.
128. 56 (1883), Nov. 2, p. 341.
129. Sir William Thomson to SZF, Sept. 1883.
130. *Electrician*, 17 (1885), June 19, p. 108.
131. F. Ince to SZF, 13 April 1883.
132. *Electrician*, 17 (1885), June 19, p. 108.
133. *Electrician*, 15 (1884), April 19, p. 550.
134. Byatt (1979), pp. 139–143.
135. Charles P. Sparks had been a pupil at the Hammond Electrical Engineering College, and we shall see over the next two chapters how he was made responsible for converting the ideas of his senior partner into workable machines.

Notes to Chapter 2

1. Parsons (1939), p. 32.
2. Hughes (1983), p. 137.
3. Hughes (1963), p. 79.
4. Hughes (1962).
5. See Hannah (1979), pp. 1–35.
6. Wilson (1995), pp. 113–19.
7. This is recorded in an article written by Ferranti in 1886 which was never published.
8. This story is related in a speech SZF gave to the Royal Scottish Society of Arts in 1895 (hereafter referred to as RSSA speech), 'The Ferranti Electricity Meter and its Evolution'.
9. Ferranti Meter Catalogue, July 1885.
10. RSSA speech.
11. H. W. Kolle to VZF, 9 July 1931.
12. 29 (1892), Aug. 26, p. 445.
13. Sketch Book No. 13.
14. Sketch Book No. 13.
15. Parsons (1939), p. 21.
16. This section is taken from Surtees (1993), pp. 142–3.
17. Surtees (1993), pp. 9–10.
18. Appleyard (1939), pp. 11–12.
19. Surtees (1993), pp. 170–85.
20. Parsons (1939), p. 22.
21. Fleming (1900), pp. 68–74.
22. *Electrical World*, 1 Nov. 1930. See also Strange (1977).
23. Fleming (1900), pp. 80–1.
24. Fleming (1900), p. 82.
25. Strange (1977).
26. Dr John Hopkinson, FRS, also acted as consultant to the English Edison Co. and later worked closely with Mather & Platt, who purchased the license to make Edison generators. Mackechnie-Jarvis (1966), p. 125.
27. CPS to SZF, June 1888.
28. Surtees (1993), p. 172.
29. Addenbrook (1930), pp. 4–5.
30. For the work of Zipernowski and his team, see Fleming (1930), pp. 80–100.
31. Addenbrook (1930), p. 6.
32. Fleming (1930), p. 103.
33. Juliana's Diary, 30 Dec. 1885.
34. See Parsons (1939), p. 190, and Hannah (1979), p. 7.
35. Hughes (1962), p. 40. See Passer (1953) for a detailed history of American electrical engineering at this time.
36. Hughes (1962), p. 39.
37. Byatt (1979), pp. 141–2.
38. Letter of reference from H. E. Harrison (Principal of the Hammond Electrical Engineering College), July 1885.
39. This was reflected in the profit-sharing agreement, which gave Ferranti thirteen-twentieths, Ince five-twentieths, and Sparks two-twentieths.
40. Progress Report to SZF, July 1888.

41. The barren years were 1886, 1889, 1914, 1916, 1917 and 1922. It is noticeable that half were years in which he was heavily involved in munitions work, as we shall see in chapter 4.
42. Juliana's Diary.
43. Sketch Book No. 14.
44. Sketch Book No. 15.
45. *Electrician*, 28 (1892), April 18, p. 628.
46. Parsons (1939), p. 24.
47. *Electrician*, 21 (1888), Nov. 9, p. 10.
48. Reported in *Industries*, 16 Nov. 1888.
49. Juliana's Diary, 17 Nov. and 9 Dec. 1886.
50. Sketch Book No. 17.
51. This section is based on LESCo. publicity pamphlets for 1887 and 1888.
52. Parsons (1939), pp. 21–41.
53. Hughes (1983), pp. 135–9.
54. Everard (1949), p. 237.
55. Engineer's Report to LESCo. for 1891.
56. *Electrical Engineer*, 1 (1888), Oct. 26, p. 134.
57. Parsons (1939), pp. 1–25.
58. This section is taken from Surtees (1993), pp. 80–89 & 176–78.
59. The other directors were Sir Coutts Lindsay, Francis Ince, Joseph Pyke (a wealthy Bond St jeweller), and Arthur F. Wade (who had been involved in the original venture as a resident of Bond St).
60. Hennessey (1971), p. 164.
61. This story is best told in de Ferranti & Ince (1934), pp. 71–88.
62. de Ferranti & Ince (1934), pp. 92–4.
63. de Ferranti & Ince (1934), p. 94.
64. This section is based on Strange (1977).
65. SZF to CPS, 12 Feb. 1886.
66. Reported in *The Times*, 10 July 1888.
67. *Electrician*, 21 (1888), July 13, p. 308.
68. Strange (1977).
69. Hannah (1979), p. 8.
70. This section is based on Crompton (1888).
71. 55 (1883), Jan. 5, p. 13.
72. Quoted by Appleyard (1939), p. 126.
73. Reported in the *Daily News*, 26 Sept. 1889.
74. S. Z. Ferranti and F. Ince, *The Dangers of Electric Lighting*, 1889.
75. *Financial News*, 24 Oct. 1888.
76. For an insight into this issue, see Barker & Robbins (1963).
77. *Electrician*, 24 (1889), April 5, p. 498.
78. *Electrician*, 24 (1889), April 12, p. 643.
79. March 13, 1891.
80. LESCo. Extraordinary General Meeting, 15 July 1889.
81. Originally, the Stowage Wharf at Deptford had been the home of Sir John Evelyn, known as Sayes Court, and it was this house which Czar Peter ('the Great') of Russia wrecked when staying there in 1698.
82. *Electrician*, 20 (1888), Oct. 26, p. 980.
83. The information on Deptford is taken from a series of articles published in October

1888, after the first public exhibition of progress at the station, all faithfully collected by Juliana de Ferranti and stored in a scrapbook. The articles come from *Electrician, Electrical Review, Engineer, Engineering, Electrical Engineer,* and *Iron.*

84. The Central Electricity Generating Board only started using this multi-flue system in 1966, when the 2,000 MW Eggborough power station was built. Electricity Council (1982).
85. *Electrical Engineer,* 24 Oct. 1888.
86. H. Inglis (secretary to Hick, Hargreaves) to SZF, 5 March 1888.
87. Sketch Book No. 15.
88. Parsons (1939), p. 32.
89. Addenbrook (1930), p. 11.
90. Sir William Thomson to SZF, 30 March 1886.
91. This section is based on Addenbrook (1930), pp. 9–12.
92. *Electrical Review,* 25 (1889), Nov. 29, p. 613.
93. Hunter & Hazell (1956), p. 65.
94. *Electrician,* 20 (1888), April 20, p. 652.
95. Black (1972), p. 28.
96. Quoted in Hunter & Hazell (1956), p. 72.
97. Engineer's Report to LESCo. for 1890.
98. LESCo. Annual Report for 1889.
99. Third Annual General Meeting of LESCo., March 1891.
100. Parsons (1939), p. 32.
101. These figures are for total expenditure by the end of 1891. *Electrician,* 24 (1892), July 8, p. 252.
102. Parsons (1939), pp. 27–8.
103. Engineer's Report to LESCo. for 1891.
104. Appleyard (1939), p. 117.
105. Engineer's Report to LESCo. for 1892.
106. Engineer's Report to LESCo. for 1891.
107. Fourth Annual General Meeting of LESCo., March 1891.
108. 27 (1891), Aug. 21, p. 429.
109. de Ferranti & Ince (1934), p. 108.
110. Report by P. W. d'Alton, the next chief engineer at Deptford, in his first and only report to LESCo. before G. W. Partridge began his forty-seven year career with the station.
111. Quoted in Parsons (1939), p. 41.
112. Report by J. A. Fleming and Dr J. Hopkinson on Deptford station, 1891.
113. Parsons (1939), p. 38.
114. Parsons (1939), p. 32.
115. Hughes (1963), p. 79.
116. Hughes (1983), p. 135.
117. Hannah (1979), p. 12.
118. Byatt (1979), p. 104.
119. Byatt (1979), p. 103.
120. Hannah (1979), pp. 9–10.
121. Hughes (1962).
122. Chandler (1990), p. 276.
123. Hughes (1963).
124. Reported in the *Electrical Review,* 30 (1892), May 20, p. 646.

Notes to Chapter 3

1. *Echo*, 9 Dec. 1891.
2. Chandler (1990), pp. 276–7 & 285.
3. *Ibid.*, pp. 291–4.
4. See Passer (1953), pp. 282–95 for a review of this project from an American perspective.
5. See Sketch Books 12 and 13. He planned to use the inward-flow 'Victor' water turbine manufactured by Frederick Nell, of London, with a power rating of 10,000 hp.
6. Evershed was a civil engineer employed on the Erie Canal, and the Cataract Construction Co. was partly financed by J. P. Morgan, one of the most influential American bankers of the era. Passer (1953), pp. 282–95.
7. *Ibid.* See also SZF to GZF, 26 Feb. 1890.
8. Quoted in *Engineering*, 22 Dec. 1893.
9. Although Westinghouse was eventually awarded the contract for the first three generators, which transmitted at 20,000 V and were connected to 5,000 hp turbines, General Electric was also to receive orders for generators, switchgear and transformers, illustrating how the two major American manufacturers benefited from this contract. Furthermore, the supply system employed was polyphase AC, the most advanced form of electricity distribution available, a technology in which the Americans gained a distinct competitive advantage as a result of such contracts. A total of $10 million was spent on the Niagara Falls project between 1893 and 1900. See Passer (1953), pp. 282–95.
10. This section on Laufenberg is based on Somers (1975).
11. Felten & Guillaume was associated with a British cable company which acquired the Ferranti patents for high-voltage mains.
12. See Sketch-Books 14–15.
13. Gertrude took an instant dislike to Patin, largely because he monopolised her husband's time while they were in Paris. de Ferranti & Ince (1934), pp. 92–3.
14. The capital of this company was set at 75,000 francs, of which two-thirds was provided by 'S Z de Ferranti'.
15. Agreements File.
16. For a review of this debate, see Wilson (1995), pp. 87–98.
17. These machines, as a condition of the contract, were actually manufactured at the Cail works in Genelle. In Paris, where they conducted an equivalent to the 1888 Marindin Inquiry into London electricity supply, Patin gained the concession to light the Left Bank sector, supplying three alternators to the Les Halles power station. *Electrician*, 23 (1889), 16 Aug., p. 375.
18. *Electrician*, 26 (1891), 13 Feb., p. 447.
19. Patin proved extremely difficult during the winding-up proceedings of Ferranti, Patin et Cie., and it was only after taking him to the Tribunal de Commerce in Paris that he agreed to return the investment made in 1889. *Electrician*, 27 (1891), 29 April, p. 694.
20. Financial information culled from early balance sheets of S.Z. de Ferranti Ltd.
21. F. Ince to SZF, 22 Dec. 1899.
22. SZF to GZF, 19 March 1890.
23. Wilson (1995), pp. 113–30.
24. F. Ince to SZF, 22 Dec. 1899.
25. These 'begging errands' are reported in SZF to GZF, 27 March 1890.
26. For another view of the financial problems, see de Ferranti & Ince (1934), p. 116.
27. *Ibid.*

28. Payne (1967), p. 520.
29. Ferranti also received 1,058 preference shares, and Ince 685. To fulfil the legal requirement of having a minimum of seven shareholders, four senior employees (F. W. Hunter, G. B. Ince, A. Wright, and H. W. Kolle) were each given a single preference share.
30. See Wilson (1995), pp. 98–106.
31. Payne (1967), p. 520.
32. On the cable industry, see Byatt (1979), pp. 152–4 & 174–5, as well as Hunter & Hazell (1956) and Black (1972).
33. *Electrical Review*, 1890, found in Juliana's Scrap-Book.
34. Ferranti received 475 preference shares, 475 A ordinary shares, 3050 B ordinary shares, and 19 founders' shares, all of £5 nominal value.
35. *Electrician*, 28 (1892), 11 March, p. 505.
36. *Electrical Review*, 46 (1900), 9 March, p. 412.
37. Felten & Guillaume were also represented on the B. I. Wire board.
38. SZF to GZF, 27 March 1890.
39. For a while this also benefited Atherton, until he was accused of fraudulently drawing up the company accounts and B. I. Wire dispensed with his services.
40. *Electrician*, 28 (1892), 1 Jan., p. 232.
41. Byatt (1979), p. 138.
42. *Electrician*, 33 (1893), 28 July, p. 85.
43. Byatt (1962), p. 337.
44. Passer (1953), pp. 296–305 & 237–255.
45. Reported in *Electrician*, 34 (1894), 4 Jan., p. 272.
46. Byatt (1962), p. 352.
47. See Hannah (1979), pp. 9–14 & 22–5, for the backward state of British electricity supply technology in the 1890s.
48. Agreements File.
49. *Electrician*, 25 (1890), 16 May, p. 32.
50. *Electrical Review*, 28 (1891), 20 March, p. 338.
51. Sketch-Book No. 15.
52. See Byatt (1979), pp. 154–6, and Jones & Marriott (1972), pp. 1–6.
53. Accurate statistics on generating capacity and electricity sales are not available for this period, but Hannah (1979), pp. 10–22, and Byatt (1979), pp. 98–111, illustrate how progress was beginning to gather some momentum after the late 1880s.
54. The information on Portsmouth is derived from de Ferranti & Ince (1934), pp. 126–31.
55. *Electrician*, 34 (1895), 8 March, p. 578.
56. Byatt (1979), p. 130.
57. This section is based on Warrilow (1901), p. 639.
58. *Electrician*, 39 (1897), 16 July, p. 374.
59. *Electrician*, 33 (1894), 18 May, p. 88.
60. Clothier (1933), p. ii.
61. See Appendix B for the patent they took out together in 1902.
62. Warrilow (1900).
63. *Hampshire Telegraph & Sussex Chronicle*, 9 June 1894. Ferranti had only supplied two alternators to the Portsmouth station at this time, the third unit being a Parson turbo-alternator which was to be used for the low day-time load. Parsons was only just beginning to make an impact on the industry at that time, but we shall see later how by 1900 many had recognised the superiority of his turbine over the reciprocating engine.

64. These were at Hammersmith, Hampstead, Islington, Bolton, Cardiff, Edinburgh, Hanley, Leeds, Huddersfield, Portsmouth, Prescot, Sheffield, South Shields, Harrogate and Deptford. *Electrician*, 37 (1897), 1 Jan., p. 299.
65. Byatt (1979), p. 138. The figures are calculated by measuring the total capacity in kW of the generators installed.
66. Hannah (1979), p. 432, has calculated that the aggregate installed capacity of British power stations increased from 44 MW in 1891 to 102 MW by 1896, while by 1903 it stood at 575 MW.
67. Clothier (1933), p. x.
68. This description is taken from an article published by *Electrical Engineer* in May 1900 which reviewed the company's product range, and was thereafter used as a publicity handout.
69. de Ferranti & Ince (1934), pp. 131–5.
70. de Ferranti & Ince (1934), p. 140. Ferranti was not the only member of his family to suffer from appendicitis, because in 1919 his third daughter, Yolanda, was taken seriously ill with this complaint and tragically died as a result of a failed operation.
71. General Notes, Vol. I.
72. Sparks' Report to Partners, 1896.
73. Saul (1970), pp. 158–64.
74. *Echo*, 9 Dec. 1891.
75. Letter from E. J. Wheeler to VZF, 1 Oct. 1953.
76. Wigham (1972), p. 29.
77. Zeitlin (1983), pp. 25–38.
78. Melling (1980), pp. 72–5.
79. Zeitlin (1983), pp. 33–4.
80. Substantial parts of this speech are duplicated in Wigham (1972), pp. 282–4.
81. F. Ince to C. Sparks, 23 Aug. 1897.
82. de Ferranti & Ince (1934), pp. 141–5.
83. Ferranti Ltd Prospectus, 1901.
84. Report from A. B. Anderson to Partners, 1900.
85. Sparks Report, May 1898.
86. S. Nicol to C. Sparks, 24 Jan. 1898.
87. Collins (1991), pp. 37–41.
88. Chandler (1990), pp. 83, 291, & 543.
89. *Ibid.*, pp. 291–4.
90. Byatt (1979), pp. 166–70.
91. SZF to GZF, 23 Aug. 1898.
92. F. Ince to C. Sparks, 14 Dec. 1897.
93. F. Ince to SZF, 14 Dec. 1897.
94. S.Z. de Ferranti Ltd, balance sheets, 1898–99.
95. Byatt (1979), pp. 158–9.
96. Kennedy (1987), p. 136. Crompton's experienced severe financial and managerial developments throughout the 1890s, so much so that the founder was eventually squeezed out of the company.
97. Byatt (1979), pp. 161–6.
98. Kennedy (1987), pp. 135–7 & 148–63.
99. Electrical machinery purchases rose from £903,000 per annum between 1896–8 to over £2.5 million per annum by 1899–1901. Byatt (1979), p. 140.

100. Electricity sales rose from 38 Gigawatt-hour (hereafter, Gwh, indicating one million kilowatt-hours) in 1895 to just over 180 Gwh by 1900. Hannah (1979), pp. 8–12 & 427.
101. Byatt (1979), p. 144.
102. Foreman-Peck & Millward (1994), pp. 162–89.
103. For the 'baleful influence' of the consulting engineer, see Saul (1970), pp. 168–9.
104. *Electrical Engineer*, 46 (1900) 16 Feb., p. 287.
105. Reported in *Electrician*, 39 (1897), 9 July, p. 330.
106. Byatt (1979), p. 172.
107. For an example of Westinghouse's policy in the USA, see Passer (1953), pp. 140–1.
108. Accounts Department Files, 1896–1903.
109. The data on investments can be found in Byatt (1979), pp. 146–51.
110. For Dick, Kerr & Co., see Wilson (1985).
111. Recorded in the *Electrical Engineer* report mentioned in footnote 68.
112. Bailey (1931), p. 22.
113. This court case resulted in S.Z. de Ferranti Ltd having to pay £2,000 to Cardiff City Council, while receiving no payment for the steam-alternator. *Electrical Review*, 46 (1900), 26 Jan., p. 136.
114. Report by A. B. Anderson, 1899 (hereafter Anderson Report).
115. F. Ince to C. Sparks, 13 June 1899.
116. Anderson Report.
117. *Electrical Engineer* reprint used as company publicity.
118. Engine Dept. Reports, 1900–03.
119. Hannah (1983), pp. 21–3.
120. Agreements File.
121. de Ferranti & Ince (1934), pp. 140–55.
122. Instead, in 1896 Sparks had been given a salary of £500 and a 7.5% share of annual profits. Sparks Correspondence File.
123. Sparks went on to enjoy a highly successful career, becoming President of the IEE in 1915 and 1916, only the second man (after Ferranti) to have this honour bestowed upon him.
124. Ferranti Ltd, Prospectus, 1901.
125. *Electrician*, 47 (1901), 19 July, p. 471.
126. *Electrical Review*, 49 (1901), 13 Dec., p. 1006.
127. *Electrical Engineer* reprint retained by SZF.
128. Ferranti Ltd, AGM, 1902.
129. Lings had also recently published a book entitled *Trade Combination*, in which he argued that owner-managers should hold at least one-third of the equity in any new flotation.
130. Byatt (1962), p. 396.
131. *Electrician*, 47 (1901), 19 July, p. 471.
132. *Electrical Review*, 47 (1900), 28 Dec., p. 1016.
133. Quoted in Wilson (1985), p. 36.
134. Byatt (1962), p. 376.
135. Accounts Dept Report, 1901. See the *Electrician*, 53 (1904), 15 July, p. 505, for a scathing review of the price-war which it complained was 'affecting not only the less stable and robust manufacturing concerns, but also those which possess solid foundations and world-wide reputations.
136. Byatt (1979), p. 139.
137. *Electrical Review*, 47 (1900), 28 Sept., p. 489.

138. Among the principal purchasers were W. H. Houldsworth, A. H. Dixon, and A. L. Rivett. Ferranti Share Registers.
139. Chandler (1990), pp. 276–7.
140. Davenport-Hines (1986), pp. 429–33.
141. Report of Receiver-Managers on Ferranti Ltd, 1903.
142. These firms had also expanded, Brush into new works in Loughborough, and Electric Construction built a larger factory in Wolverhampton, but neither proved successful in increasing their market share. Byatt (1979), pp. 138–48.
143. See Jones & Marriott (1972), pp. 39–69, Wilson (1985), and Byatt (1979), pp. 151–2.
144. For the rise of the turbine, see Parson (1939), pp. 170–83.
145. Byatt (1979), p. 138.
146. Ferranti Ltd, Board Minutes (hereafter FBM), Dec. 1904.
147. Quoted by Davenport-Hines (1985), p. 431.
148. The largest creditors were the Carron Co. (steel producers), Taylor Tunnicliffe Ltd (instrument-makers), Babcox & Wilcox (engineers), Thomas Bolton & Sons Ltd (copper suppliers), and G. Schulz & Co. (instrument-makers). They were owed sums ranging between £4,000 and £200, and the total debt was £56,099.
149. As a director of Thomas Bolton & Sons Ltd, Henderson was appointed as a representative of the creditors.

Notes to Chapter 4

1. Report of the Receiver-Managers to Creditors of Ferranti Ltd, Sept. 1903.
2. Ferranti Ltd, Balance Sheet Ledger No. 1.
3. FBM, Dec. 1903.
4. No record of this loan survives, but the Ferranti family assure me that this is how the patents were acquired.
5. For a history of J. & P. Coats Ltd, see Cairncross & Hunter (1987), Clapham (1951), p. 244, and Wardley (1991). According to the latter, Coats was the twelfth largest company in the UK by 1907, measured by market value, and the second largest manufacturing concern.
6. For a detailed history of this work on textile machinery, see Ponting (1963).
7. Clapham (1951), p. 177.
8. Evidence given in application for an extension to patent 18047, 1917. Ferranti Agreements.
9. By 1903, Oldham had 11,603,000 spindles at work, compared to 1,325,000 in Blackburn and 5,035,000 in Bolton. Ponting (1963). See also Farnie (1979), pp. 277–93.
10. Byatt (1979), p. 91.
11. For a detailed analysis of the cotton industry at this time, see Farnie (1979), especially pp. 277–323.
12. See Farnie (1979), pp. 277–323.
13. Ponting (1963), p. 19.
14. In 1903, J. & P. Coats recorded a profit of almost £3,000,000. Clapham (1951), p. 224.
15. Letter from the Coats Board to VZF, 16 Jan. 1963.
16. Ponting (1963), p. 19.
17. Ponting (1963), p. 20.

18. Reminiscences of A. W. Edwards.
19. See Parsons (1939), and Dickinson (1903), for a full history of the turbine and Parsons' work.
20. 'Electrical developments of the future and their effect upon everyday life', 1894.
21. Byatt (1979), p. 138. The Parsons master patents were also extended by five years in 1898, as a result of legal difficulties arising from a disagreement with his original partners, Clarke, Chapman & Parsons, in 1889.
22. These experiments are described in detail by Hall (1932), as well as in the James Watt Lecture Ferranti gave in 1913, entitled 'Prime Movers'.
23. See Trebilcock (1977), ch. 5.
24. Wardley (1991) estimates that, by market value, Vickers was the 29th largest company in the UK by 1907.
25. Ferranti to Vickers, May 1904.
26. See Ferranti Sketch-Books in FA.
27. This figure has been reached by conjecture, because Ferranti was paid £22,679 as salary and out-of-pocket expenses (Expenses Ledger (Turbines)), while the cost of building the experimental turbines and the two used by Vickers would at least double this figure.
28. The two Ferranti turbines were a 3000 kW unit used at the River Don Works, and a 1000 kW unit for the colliery owned by Vickers at Grimethorpe.
29. Irving (1975), p. 168.
30. Ferranti Note-Books (Turbines).
31. April 1913.
32. Quoted in a letter from Sir Henry Guy to the *Engineer*, June 1934.
33. Hannah (1979), pp. 33–5.
34. Ferranti Correspondence Books, FA.
35. Hall (1932).
36. *Engineering*, 29 June, 1906. This article was later printed as a catalogue by Hopkinsons.
37. Expenses Ledger (Stop-Valves).
38. C. C. Carlow to F. Bailey, 21 Nov 1930.
39. See de Ferranti & Ince (1934), pp. 151–6, for a description of this house and their lifestyle at this time.
40. de Ferranti & Ince (1934), p. 178.
41. Letter from the family chauffeur, J. Brocklehurst, to VZF, 9 Nov. 1972.
42. Correspondence between Ferranti, the Watsons and Dunlop, in Ferranti Letter Books, FA.
43. I am indebted to Mr E. V. Morgan for bringing this evidence from that company's board minutes to my attention.
44. This information was passed to me by Mr S.Z. de Ferranti.
45. Information culled from Ferranti Scrap-Book, evidently kept by Ferranti on interesting contemporary engineering developments. FA.
46. For a full history of this project, see Hughes (1971), pp. 103 *passim*.
47. SZF to the *Engineer*, 7 June 1913.
48. See King (1985), p. 2.
49. Ferranti Letter Books, FA.
50. RAE Report, FA.
51. See Chandler (1990), pp. 389–92, for confirmation of this view.
52. Hannah (1979), pp. 25–35.
53. Expenses Ledger (Consultancy).
54. See Appleyard (1939), pp. 215–7.

55. *Electrical Review*, 72 (1913), 6 June, p. 946.
56. See *Journal of the IEE*, 46 (1911).
57. Hannah (1979), pp. 34–5.
58. Hannah (1979), pp. 427–8. A gWh is one million kWh.
59. *Electrical Review*, 55 (1904), 12 Aug., p. 241.
60. 60 (1907), 18 Jan., p. 85.
61. 66 (1910), 25 Feb., p. 289.
62. Byatt (1979), p. 141.
63. Monopolies & Restrictive Practices Court (1957), para 687.
64. For a detailed history of this company's early history, see Jones & Marriott (1970), p. 43.
65. Byatt (1962), p. 375.
66. *Electrical Review*, 60 (1907), 15 March, p. 434.
67. Byatt (1979), pp. 170–83.
68. Kennedy (1987), pp. 134–57.
69. Anderson Correspondence Book.
70. Meter Pricing Agreement.
71. Report by A. B. Anderson to Ferranti Ltd board, Oct. 1906.
72. Aldcroft (1964), pp. 125–6.
73. Nicholas (1984), pp. 489–506.
74. V. Anderson, the Copenhagen agent, had patented a temperature correction device for DC meters, while E. G. Waters, a British representative, had patented a protective device for switchgear. Anderson Correspondence Book.
75. Anderson Correspondence Book.
76. *Electrical Review*, 67 (1910), 19 Aug., p. 290.
77. The history of Ferranti Canada is related in full in Ball & Vardalas (1994). The start-up phase is covered in pp. 82–120. See also Schofield (private notes).
78. Meter output rose from 31,381 units (£95,097) to 102,816 (£164,656) in 1912.
79. FBM, Sept. 1903.
80. See *Clothier* (1933), pp. iii–x.
81. *Electrical Review*, 63 (1908), 24 July, p. 38.
82. *Electrical Review*, 62 (1908), 3 April, p. 577.
83. *Electrical Review*, 69 (1911), 24 Nov., p. 885.
84. *Electrical Review*, 66 (1911), 25 Feb., p. 289.
85. *Electrical Review*, 67 (1910), 7 Oct., p. 587.
86. *Electrical Review*, 64 (1909), 29 Jan., p. 171.
87. *Electrical Review*, 69 (1911), 20 Oct., p. 638.
88. Byatt (1979), p. 140.
89. The shares in the new company were allotted as follows: the first and second mortgage debenture-holders received a similar holding in the new company, together with interest arrears; the unsecured creditors received an equivalent holding in preference shares; the preference shareholders received a similar holding in ordinary shares; and Ferranti was allotted 10,000 Deferred shares. In total, 112,911 shares were distributed. See Appendix C, Table 1.
90. In 1909, meter department staff were paid a bonus of one week's wages for working constant overtime. FBM, Sept. 1909.
91. Ferranti organised what became known as the 'Point Fives' scheme to standardise the safety rules for domestic appliances. *Electrical Review*, 72 (1913), 6 June, p. 946.
92. Reported in a letter from A. B. Anderson to SZF, 3 Nov. 1913.

Notes to Chapter 5

1. Landes (1977), p. 231.
2. Schumpeter (1939), p. 412.
3. See de Ferranti & Ince (1934), pp. 189–91, for an insight into this difficult period.
4. Management decided initially simply to reduce output by cutting the working week by ten hours, but employees objected so vigorously to this move that within a month the board was forced to restore production to its pre-War levels. Nevertheless, by January 1915 the workforce had fallen to 1,216, compared to 1,432 in January 1914.
5. *Electrical Review*, 74 (1914), 5 June, p. 956.
6. SZF to R. H. Schofield, 6 August, 1914. Schofield had joined Ferranti in 1912 as the head of the London sales office.
7. Clapham (1951), p. 335.
8. Reported in FBM, 2 Sept. 1914.
9. *Electrical Review*, 78 (1916), 28 Jan., p. 107. For the general level of anti-German feeling amongst British businessmen, see Davenport-Hines (1984), pp. 135–9.
10. SZF to R. H. Schofield, 6 Aug. 1914.
11. See Scott (1962), p. 97.
12. de Ferranti & Ince (1934), p. 191.
13. See FBM, 1914–15 for reports of these negotiations and debates.
14. Pollard (1992), p. 19.
15. SZF to VZF, 25 March, 1917.
16. Pollard (1992), p. 30.
17. The first representative had been Oliver Winder. Captain Thomas served on the board until 1929.
18. Information derived from Ferranti photographs of the munitions workshops. The board minutes for this period are silent on the issue of productivity.
19. The most important product was the six inch high explosive shell (£514,727), followed by 100-pounder forgings (£441,990), and fuzes (£421,088). Information gleaned from correspondence between Ferranti and War Office.
20. See de Ferranti & Ince (1934), pp. 179–82, for an insight into this atmosphere.
21. SZF to VZF, 15 Sept. 1915.
22. de Ferranti & Ince (1934), pp. 183–4.
23. SZF to VZF, 10 Oct. 1917.
24. SZF to VZF, 25 March 1917.
25. SZF Private Notes, Vol. I.
26. de Ferranti & Ince (1934), p. 191.
27. *Electrical Review*, 78 (1916), 7 April, p. 410.
28. Meter department statistics, 1914–18.
29. FBM, 20 Dec. 1915.
30. FBM, 21 Jan. 1915.
31. FBM, 1916–18.
32. See section 2.2.
33. Hannah (1979), p. 427.
34. Ballin (1946), p. 95.
35. See section 4.4.
36. For more detail on these issues, see Hannah (1979), pp. 22–35.
37. A detailed discussion of 'The Years of Indecision' is contained in Hannah (1979), pp. 36–74.

38. Quoted by Garcke at the 1922 IEE Commemorative Meeting.
39. Byatt (1979), p. 170.
40. SZF to VZF, 13 May 1918.
41. Dr Werner Lulops was a Dutch engineer living in Amsterdam.
42. *Electrical Review*, 91 (1922), 20 Oct., p. 557.
43. See *Ferranti News*, June 1974.
44. Sanderson (1972), p. 107.
45. FBM, 1920–22.
46. *Electrical Review*, 96 (1925), 20 March, p. 465.
47. Transformer department order book, 1920–26.
48. Sanderson (1972), p. 107.
49. For the early history of the Canadian venture, see Ball & Vardalas (1994), pp. 65–81.
50. For a practical example of this theory in action, see Boyce (1995), pp. 2–4.
51. This section is heavily dependent upon Ball & Vardalas (1994), pp. 89–120.
52. Casson (1991), pp. 3–21.
53. Nicholas (1983), pp. 504–6.
54. Dunning (1993), pp. 76–86.
55. Taylor (1994). pp. 152–4.
56. Buckley & Casson (1989).
57. Jones (1986), pp. 13–18.
58. Stopford (1974), pp. 316–17.
59. Nicholas (1989), pp. 138–9.
60. Jones (1986), pp. 265–7.
61. Interview with SZF.
62. Ball & Vardalas (1994), pp. 112 & 120–45.
63. Information supplied by the Ferranti family.
64. A. Whittaker to A. W. Tait, 28 Nov. 1918.
65. FBM, Dec. 1918.
66. Chairman's statement at 1921 AGM.
67. By 1921, the board was composed of A. W. Tait (chairman), A. Whittaker, Captain P. D. Thomas, R. W. Cooper, and S.Z. de Ferranti.
68. Information derived from BEAMA (1928), p. 32.
69. Report of the Engineering Trades (New Industries) Committee, Cd. 9226, 1918. R H Schofield represented Ferranti and BEAMA on this body.
70. Marrison (1996), pp. 246–8.
71. Byatt (1979), p. 170.
72. The pre-1914 figures are taken from Byatt (1979), p. 139, while the inter-war data can be found in Catterall (1979), p. 254. While some allowance for war-time inflation should be made here, one must remember that, as we shall see, after 1920 prices of most electrical products fell by up to sixty-five per cent.
73. Jones & Marriott (1972), pp. 96–120.
74. Hannah (1983), p. 111.
75. F. A. Szarvasy to A. W. Tait, 6 May 1919. Berry had been one of the leading transformer manufacturers since the 1890s, having patented many improvements to their design.
76. Hannah (1983), pp. 88–9.
77. Catterall (1979), p. 251.
78. MRPC (1957), appendix 13.
79. BEAMA (1927), p. 43.

80. BEAMA (1927), p. 57. The other ten companies were GEC, Metro-Vic's, BT-H, English Electric, Bruce Peebles, Lancashire Dynamo, Johnson & Phillips, BET, Reyrolle, and Ferguson, Pailin.
81. BEAMA (1927), p. 42.
82. The post-War government wanted to return to a pre-War parity of $4.86. Keynes argued that this overvalued the pound sterling by at least ten per cent. Pollard (1992), pp. 137–8.
83. *Electrical Review*, 93 (1923), 7 Dec., p. 863. See also Marrison (1996), pp. 246–8.
84. *Electrical Review*, 95 (1924), 10 Oct., p. 541. This movement was led by Forbes Mackay.
85. *Electrical Review*, 96 (1925), 13 March, p. 435.
86. *Electrical Review*, 96 (1925), 20 March, p. 465.
87. E. T. Norris to VZF, 9 Nov. 1931.
88. For a comprehensive review of this legislation, see Hannah (1977), pp. 209–11 and (1979), pp. 105–149.
89. Hannah (1979), p. 427.
90. Returns to the Electricity Commissioners, 1926.
91. *Sunday Chronicle*, 30 March 1919, found in JSB.
92. Weir was the head of a marine engineering firm in Central Scotland.
93. Harrop (1966), Ch. 2.
94. This section is based on Hannah (1977), pp. 209–11.
95. See the collection of press-cuttings in JSB.
96. This story has been provided by SZF.
97. FBM, 1929–31.
98. Catterall (1979), p. 254. Employment in electrical engineering also continued to rise, from 150,610 in 1924 to 195,450 in 1933.
99. Quoted in *Electrical Industries*, 30 April 1924.
100. *Electrical Review*, 84 (1919), 25 April, p. 466.
101. They had bought a second home at Deganwy, North Wales, to provide some solitude away from the bustle of Manchester. de Ferranti & Ince (1934), pp. 218–9.
102. 103 (1928), 19 Oct., p. 139.
103. See de Ferranti & Ince (1934), pp. 193–7, for a description of this scheme.
104. Private Notes, II.
105. See, for example, *Electrical Review*, 101 (1927), 2 Sept., p. 406.
106. *Electrical Review*, 99 (1926), 31 Dec., p. 1085.
107. Wilson (1976), p. 205.
108. Corley (1966), p. 109.
109. For details on Marconi's early career, see Jolly (1972), pp. 1–16.
110. See Maclaurin (1971).
111. Pocock (1988), pp. 103–7.
112. Sturmey (1958), pp. 138 *passim*.
113. This story is told in Hall (1926).
114. Holmes had won the King's Prize in mechanical engineering at Manchester College of Technology in 1903, and in the 1920s he designed ammeters and voltmeters which proved popular with radio 'hams'.
115. See Baggs (1947).
116. Hall (1926).
117. Beardsall (1948).
118. FBM, March-Nov. 1926.
119. *Electrical Review*, 101 (1927), 30 Sept., p. 339.

120. *Wireless World*, 25 (1929), 20 Nov., p. 27.
121. *Electrical Review*, 101 (1927), 30 Sept., p. 339.
122. *Wireless World*, 25 (1929), 2 Oct., p. 7.
123. C. P. Beardsall to R. H. Schofield, 14 Jan. 1929.
124. *Wireless World*, 1929–31.
125. A. B. Cooper to VZF, Dec. 1929.
126. Private Notes, II.
127. In 1930, according to the figures produced by BEAMA, Ferranti could claim thirty-four per cent of house-service meter production, and fourteen per cent of transformer production.
128. Gregory (1936), pp. 14–21
129. Dr Ferranti received 32,000 of these shares, and Vincent 8,000.
130. Chairman's Report to 1930 AGM.
131. Harris (1933).
132. Reader (1979), pp. 221–5.
133. Schein (1985), pp. 3–21.
134. Davenport-Hines (1986), p. 433. Davenport-Hines incorrectly states that Tait had given up his chairmanship of Ferranti in 1918.

Notes to Chapter 6

1. A volume of obituaries was collected by Gertrude and they have been preserved in the Ferranti Archives.
2. This quotation from the *Electrical Review* of 1910 is part of a collection gathered together by JZF.
3. Hannah (1979), pp. 12, 28–9.
4. See above, p. 76 & 92–4.
5. *Electrical Times*, Dec. 1932. See also de Ferranti & Ince (1934), pp. 234–6.
6. See Chandler (1990), pp. 276 and 285 for a negative view of British electrical manufacturers.
7. de Ferranti & Ince (1934), p. 174.
8. This was part of his speech to the IEE in 1924, when he was presented with his Faraday Medal.
9. Sanderson (1972), pp. 210.
10. de Ferranti & Ince (1934), p. 75.
11. J. Brocklehurst (the Ferranti chaufffeur) to VZF, 21 Nov 1972. By 1926, Dr Ferranti possessed an American Cole, an Alfa Romeo, an Austin Brooklands Swallow, a Morris Oxford two-seater, a Salmson dead-back axle, and the two-seater Standard Nine.
12. de Ferranti & Ince (1934), p. 202.
13. Letters to VZF in 1918.
14. FBM, 1918–19.
15. For the general scene, see Wilson (1995), pp. 157–63.
16. FBM, 1917–20.
17. de Ferranti & Ince (1934), p. 191.
18. Schein (1985), pp. 3–21.
19. de Ferranti & Ince (1934), p. 179.
20. de Ferranti & Ince (1934), pp. 202–227.

Notes to Chapter 7

1. Evidence to the Television Committee, 12 July 1934. Full transcript in FA.
2. Keynes by the 1940s was advocating an approach based on 'Capitalism wisely-managed' as an essential element of economic policy.
3. Correspondence between VZF and GZF in 1930, FA.
4. I am indebted to Sebastian de Ferranti for this information. The graphs still survive in FA.
5. See Wilson (1995), pp. 175–9, Hannah (1983), p. 88, and Chandler (1990), p. 390.
6. VZF to A. Lawton, July 1935. I am indebted to Tom Lunt for an insight into personnel policy at Ferranti.
7. In 1930 the CEB had given out orders worth £11 million, but in 1932 this had fallen to just £2 million. Seward (1961).
8. Hope (1949), p. 162
9. MRPC (1957), App. 13.
10. Imperial Economic Committee (1936), pp. 21, 33, 64 & 78.
11. Information gleaned from VZF correspondence with *Electrical Industries and Investments*, 1930–34.
12. Information gleaned from FBM, 1930–38.
13. MRPC (1957), p. 229.
14. R. H. Schofield to VZF, 9 May 1931.
15. Information supplied by Sebastian de Ferranti.
16. MRPC (1957), pp. 229–30 and App. 13. See Wilson (1995), pp. 176–80, for a review of trade association activity in this period and its deleterious impact.
17. See Jones & Marriott (1970), chapter 9.
18. Report to the board, FBM, July 1934.
19. Reported in *Electrical Review*, 113 (1933), Sept. 22, p. 405.
20. Private Notebook, Vol. 21.
21. FBM, 1928. For the Marconi licensing system, see Sturmey (1958), p. 171.
22. The number of licences issued by the GPO increased from 1,645,000 in 1925 to 3,412,000 in 1930. Coase (1958), p. 199.
23. Ferranti had established a subsidiary in New York in August 1926, Ferranti Incorporated. Little success was achieved in selling Ferranti products in the well-protected American market, but the agent, G. F. Chellis, was a valuable source of information on the latest technological developments.
24. For a review of the radio industry at that time, see Sturmey (1958), pp. 138ff.
25. *Wireless World*, 28 (1931), Jan 14, p. 40.
26. Maclaurin (1971), p. 123.
27. Maclaurin (1971), p. 127 & 179.
28. Reported in the *Daily Dispatch*, 1 July 1931.
29. See p. 231.
30. Fleming (1930), pp. 331–3.
31. See chapter nine for more on this trend.
32. This story is best related in Beardsall (1946), p. 40.
33. This work included experiments on new types of valve, cathode-ray tubes and X-ray tubes. Dr Darbyshire to VZF, 20 Sept. 1938.
34. *Wireless World*, 33 (1933), 27 Oct., p. 345.
35. *Wireless World*, 31 (1932), 25 Nov., p. 477.

36. *Wireless World*, 31 (1932), 8 July, p. 12.
37. See Pocock (1988), pp. 111–14.
38. T. H. Morris to VZF, 4 Nov. 1933.
39. Wilson (1995), pp. 141–56, and Hannah (1983), p. 34.
40. The information on these visits and the consequent reports are contained in FA file C/34. For evidence on the Bedaux consultancy, see Littler (1982), pp. 99–116.
41. FBM, 1935.
42. Taylor (1972), p. 6.
43. Vincent noted in a letter to an acquaintance, that: 'We are running a considerable risk in the radio industry'. VZF to H. C. Lamb (chief engineer to the Manchester Corporation electricity department), 28 March 1935.
44. *Wireless World*, 39 (1936), 18 June, p. 582.
45. *Wireless World*, 40 (1937), 18 June, p. 582.
46. C. P. Beardsall to VZF, 2 Feb. 1938.
47. FBM 191, 19 Dec. 1934.
48. FBM 171, 16 Nov. 1934. These vans cost £1,250.
49. Coase (1958), p. 199.
50. Wilson (1958), p. 137.
51. See Pocock (1988), pp. 111–14, for an analysis of the radio industry at that time.
52. Dr Darbyshire to VZF, 20 Sept. 1938.
53. Eckersley (1962), p. 197.
54. Sturmey (1958), p. 191.
55. This story is to be found in Sturmey (1958), chapter 10.
56. Information gleaned from VZF correspondence with Scophony.
57. *Scophony's Part in Television*, a 1938 catalogue. FA.
58. Taylor (1972), pp. 4–7.
59. Scophony Correspondence File.
60. *Electrical Review*, 119 (1936), 11 Sept., p. 340.
61. W. Adkin to VZF, 22 Dec. 1937.
62. M. K. Taylor to VZF, 13 Jan 1936.
63. Taylor (1972), p. 8.
64. Ferranti Agreements, 1938.
65. Chandler (1990), pp. 390–92. Information on capital expenditure from FBM, 1931–35.
66. Information gleaned from departmental reports to VZF, 1930–38.
67. Information gleaned from departmental reports to VZF, 1930–38.
68. Corley (1966), pp. 19, 34 & 48.
69. *Electical Review*, 110 (1932), 18 April, p. 513.
70. Reported in the *Goldsmiths' Journal* in an article about Dr Ferranti entitled 'A genius came to Clerkenwell'.
71. Information gleaned from departmental reports to VZF, 1930–38.
72. Trebilcock (1977), p. 3.
73. J. H. Whibley to VZF, 6 Dec. 1933.
74. This story is found in Beardsall (1946), p. 1.
75. Roberts (1984), pp. 93–104.
76. FBM, 1936.
77. Taylor (1972), p. 11.
78. Sir R. Henderson to VZF, 24 March 1937.
79. Beardsall (1946), p. 2.

NOTES

80. Beardsall (1946), p. 2–3.
81. J. N. Toothill to VZF, 3 April 1937.
82. Beardsall (1946), p. 2–3.
83. Beardsall (1946), p. 8.
84. Jones (1978), Part I.
85. Snow (1961), p. 29.
86. Burns & Stalker (1961), pp. 15–21.
87. Snow (1961), pp. 29–38. See also Buderi (1996), pp. 64–97, for an American perspective on this British work.
88. This story is told in Watson-Watt (1957) and Postan, Hay & Scott (1964), chapter 15.
89. W. G. Bass to VZF, 26 Oct. 1936.
90. War Office to VZF, 31 Jan 1938.
91. Vincent had married Dorothy Wilson in 1919. R. P. Wilson was a successful engineering consultant who was later awarded the CBE for services to his industry.
92. Fleming (1921), pp. 340–1, and Sturmey (1958), chapter 6.
93. SZF to R. P. Wilson, 21 June 1927.
94. W. Tyldesley to SZF, 15 Aug. 1928.
95. *Manchester Evening Chronicle*, 7 Nov. 1930.
96. Galletti Report to RAE, 1930.
97. Reported in a letter from S. Atkinson to A. B. Cooper (general manager of Ferranti Canada), 6 April 1931.
98. L. S. Palmer to VZF, 8 Aug. 1928.
99. This effect was recorded in the Galletti Report to the RAE in 1930.
100. Taylor (1972), pp. 8–10.
101. Bowden would later join Ferranti, firstly in radio development and later as a computer salesman. See chapter 9.
102. Postan (1975), p. 539.
103. Beardsall (1946) p. 30.
104. This story is recounted in Beardsall (1946) p. 30.
105. Snow (1962), p. 9, and Postan, Hay & Scott (1964), pp. 378ff.
106. This story is recounted in Beardsall (1946) p. 30.
107. Taylor (1972), pp. 10–14.
108. This story is recounted in Beardsall (1946) p. 24.
109. Beardsall (1946), pp. 24–5.
110. This story is based on an interview with Sydney Jackson in 1981.
111. J. L. Miller (chief research engineer at Ferranti) to VZF, 8 Sept. 1941.
112. Beardsall (1946), pp. 20–24.
113. Postan, Hay & Scott (1964), pp. 117–20.
114. McCallum (1987), p. 15. The story of Crewe Toll's origins can be found in many sources, but the most reliable is the collection of taped interviews made by Jack Toothill and Tom Neal in the early 1960s.
115. Beardsall (1946), pp. 30–32.
116. Toothill interviews.
117. Postan, Hay & Scott (1964), p. 120.
118. MAP to VZF, 20 July 1944.
119. Fuze department's total output between 1939 and 1945 was worth £7,305,498, peaking in 1941/42 at £1,765,585.
120. Beardsall (1946), p. 35.

121. In 1944/45, central services cost £328,701 to run, or 5.5 per cent of turnover.
122. H. W. Kolle died in 1943.
123. See Wilson (1995), pp. 175–81
124. This story is told in F. W. Taylor, 'The research department', *Ferranti Journal*, June 1943.

Notes to Chapter 8

1. Interview with SZF. For a survey of Basil's life, see Wilson (1996), pp. 133–4.
2. British business training techniques are examined in Wilson (1992), pp. 1–15, and Wilson (1995), pp. 218–22.
3. See Appendix E for a full analysis of the family shareholdings.
4. See Wilson (1995), pp. 180–97.
5. Interview with T. J. Lunt.
6. Interview with L. George.
7. This correspondence and associated files fills a dozen volumes in FA.
8. For a survey of post-War economic circumstances, see Pollard (1992), pp. 235–41.
9. Hannah (1979), p. 428 and (1982), p. 292.
10. Prophet (1950), pp. 7–9.
11. Interview with A. K. H. Thomas.
12. *Electrical Review*, 146 (1950), 30 march, p. 373.
13. Denis had a 17.9 per cent holding of Ferranti equity. See Appendix E.
14. W. C. Pycroft to VZF, 24 Jan 1951.
15. Interview with SZF.
16. W. H. McFadzean to VZF, 11 Jan 1949. One of the 1960s acquisitions was Aron Meters.
17. A. W. G. Tucker to VZF, 26 Oct 1946.
18. Hannah (1979), p. 309. See also Zeitlin (2000), Ch. 10, for an overview of the industry's post-1945 progress.
19. FBM for 1947–51.
20. *Electrical Review*, 144 (1949), 25 Feb, p. 330.
21. Hannah (1982), pp. 41–74.
22. *Electrical Review*, 142 (1948), 30 April, p. 649.
23. Speech to the 1945 AGM.
24. *Ferranti Journal*, Sept 1947 (article entitled 'Market research').
25. Interview with Sir Frank Rostron.
26. This story is related in a collection of letters and press cuttings in FA.
27. 27 Jan 1950.
28. 22 Jan 1950.
29. VZF to Seattle Council, 11 Jan 1950.
30. This story is based on information gathered during an interview with Sir Frank Rostron.
31. Interview with SZF.
32. Hannah (1982), pp. 60–72.
33. £105,071 had been invested in Ferranti Canada, while the Packard investment stood at £35,080. Ferranti Management Accounts, 1945.
34. Ferranti Management Accounts, 1945–60.
35. This section is heavily dependent upon Ball & Vardalas (1994), pp. 218–50.
36. Nicholas (1989), pp. 133–9.

37. Ball & Vardalas (1994), pp. 285–99.
38. Ball & Vardalas (1994), pp. 158–79.
39. Ferranti Management Accounts, 1945–60.
40. Ball & Vardalas (1994), pp. 180–217.
41. Ferranti Management Accounts, 1960–75.
42. Stopford & Turner (1985), pp. 8–10.
43. Interview with Dr N. Searby.
44. This section is based on a report from F. C. Aitken to VZF, 20 July 1949.
45. Wilson (1958), p. 138.
46. Quoted in F. C. Aitken to VZF, 20 July 1949.
47. Wilson (1958), p. 138.
48. F. C. Aitken to VZF, 20 July 1949.
49. P. R. Taylor, 'Ferranti House', *Ferranti Journal*, Christmas 1955.
50. Pollard (1992), p. 235
51. Ferranti press release 4 Sept 1955.
52. Pollard (1992), pp. 235–41. See also Zeitlin (2000), Ch. 10.
53. Interview with Dr N. Searby.
54. Ferranti paid £40,000 for Gem Mill. FBM 3673, 12 Sept 1952.
55. Wilson (1958), pp. 138–50.
56. Interview with S. Jackson.
57. E. Grundy to VZF, May 1954.
58. *Electrical Review*, 135 (1944), 17 Nov, p. 705.
59. Corley (1966), p. 148.
60. B. Z. de Ferranti, 'The heat pump', *Ferranti Journal*, April 1954, p. 39.
61. Quoted in correspondence between VZF and GZF during 1956.
62. Interview with SZF.
63. FBM 4402, 25 Oct 1956.
64. F. S. Allen to VZF, 15 Nov 1956, and E. K. Cole to VZF, 31 Dec 1956. In fact, the £300,000 was not paid in cash, but through a royalty of 2.5 per cent on sales of Ferranti radios and televisions, and it was 1964 before Ferranti received the full sum.
65. See Jones & Marriott (1972), pp. 200–39, and Zeitlin (2000), Ch. 10, for insights into manufacturers' strategies at ths time.
66. Interview with S. Jackson.
67. Quoted from E. Grundy, *The Role of the Instrument Department*, private notes written in 1981.
68. E. Grundy to VZF, 28 June 1955.
69. Quoted from E. Grundy, *The Role of the Instrument Department*, private notes written in 1981.
70. This story is related in I. D. Roxburgh, 'The FH7 miniature artificial horizon', *Ferranti Journal*, Spring 1959. See also *Aeroplane & Aeronautics*, 26 August 1960, for a full history of aircraft equipment department's early development.
71. FBM 4791, 4 March 1959.
72. This story is based on interviews with J. N. Toothill, D. N. McCallum, J. B. Smith, and McCallum (1987), pp. 15–18.
73. Letter from D. N. McCallum to the author, 7 Oct 1982.
74. McCallum (1987), p. 16.
75. M. K. Taylor, 'The applications laboratory', *Ferranti Journal*, March 1948.
76. J. N. Toothill to VZF, 14 Jan 1947.

77. McCallum (1987), p. 4. McCallum also recalls how Toothill refused to grant him the annual salary of £495, offering instead £490!
78. The activities of the four laboratories are described in *Ferranti Journal* for March 1948.
79. McCallum(1987), pp. 6–10. See also Taylor, op. cit.
80. Watson-Watt was also the government's scientific advisor on telecommunications matters from 1946.
81. *Wireless World*, 58 (1951), p. 414. See also McCallum (1987), pp. 16–7.
82. J. N. Toothill to VZF, 16 May 1946.
83. Interview with J. N. Toothill.
84. This section is based on McCallum (1987), pp. 19–29.
85. Tape made by Mal Powley for the *Scottish Record*.
86. Letter from D. N. McCallum to the author, 7 Oct 1982.
87. Tape made by J. N. Toothill for the *Scottish Record*.
88. McCallum (1987), p. 22.
89. McCallum (1987), pp. 23–9.
90. L Pascoe-Martin, 'The Ferranti Flying Unit', mimeo, 1979.
91. *Aeronautics*, 1 Sept 1959.
92. For a survey of the 1950s aircraft industry, see Gardner (1981), pp. 13–41, and Hayward (1980), pp. 45–82.
93. McCallum (1987), pp. 30–2.
94. Interviews with J. N. Toothill and M. Powley. See also McCallum (1987), pp. 36–9.
95. P Wimbush, 'Terrain-following radar', *Ferranti Journal*, Christmas 1958.
96. This section is based on an interview with M. Powley and McCallum (1987), pp. 47–50.
97. Drury (1962).
98. Tape made by J. N. Toothill for the *Scottish Record*.
99. Quoted in Langrish, Gibbons, Evans & Jevons (1972), p. 250.
100. Tape made by J. N. Toothill for the *Scottish Record*.
101. Burns & Stalker (1961), pp. 56–7.
102. Burns & Stalker (1961), p. 48. See also Toothill Tapes.
103. Sir Steven Bilsland to VZF, 19 June 1948.
104. See Corley (1966), pp. 14–21, and Jones & Marriott (1972), pp. 200–39.
105. In 1963 special components was responsible for developing Europe's first commercially-available gas laser, but this was a rare civil development at that time.
106. For a review of the emergence of NC technology, see Hamilton (1999). Tape made by J. N. Toothill for the *Scottish Record*.
107. D. T. N. Williamson, 'Automatic control of machine tools', *Control*, 1954, p. 19.
108. McCallum (1987), pp. 59–63.
109. Williamson, *op. cit.*, p. 19.
110. Interview with D. T. N. Williamson.
111. Langrish, Gibbons, Evans & Jevons (1972), p. 258.
112. Layton (1972), p. 84; Hamilton (1999), pp. 94–107.
113. R. H. Davies to J. N. Toothill, 15 August 1956.
114. In 1956 Sir Vincent was in detailed discussions with Giddings & Lews, a machine tool company in Fond du Lac, Wisconsin. E. L. McFerren to VZF, 16 July 1956.
115. H. Kirkham to VZF, 1 June 1956. This report provided a full breakdown of profitability in the civil and defence departments.

Notes to Chapter 9

1. I am deeply indebted to several people for helping me understand the Ferranti mainframe computer story, especially Harry Johnson, Peter Hall and Peter Dorey of Ferranti. Friends in the academic world like Geoff Tweedale, Martin Campbell-Kelly and John Hendry have been equally instructive. All errors remain my own.
2. These criticisms will be reviewed in this chapter, but for information see Hendry (1989) and Tweedale (1992).
3. For a detailed review of the early history of computers, see Campbell-Kelly and Asprey (1996), pp. 9–28 and 53–78.
4. This paper was entitled 'On computable numbers, with an application to the Entscheidungs-problem', *Proceedings of the London Mathematical Society*, 42.
5. Tweedale (1992), pp. 3 & 7–21.
6. For more on the role of Turing in developing this early software, see Lavington (1980), pp. 28–30 & 44–6, and Tweedale (1992), p. 98.
7. Lavington (1980), p. 1.
8. Babbage also built a 'difference engine', but the 'analytical engine' possessed much greater potential. Lavington (1980), p. 2, and Campbell-Kelly and Asprey (1996), pp. 10–20.
9. See Evans (1978), and Lingren (1990).
10. See Freeman (1982), p. 83, and Lavington (1980), p. 7, and Tweedale (1990), p. 21.
11. Lavington (1980), pp. 8–12.
12. The development of these devices will be examined later. See Lavington (1980), pp. 18–9.
13. Lavington (1980), pp. 16 & 24.
14. Lavington (1980), pp. 23–30.
15. Lavington (1980), pp. 54–6.
16. Lavington (1980), pp. 31–6 & 68–77, Bird (1994), and Caminer, Aris, Hermon & Land (1996).
17. This story is based on Lavington (1975), pp. 1–45, and *idem* (1980), pp. 18–9 & 36–43, and Swann (1974), pp. 1–4, and *Computer Weekly*, 10 April, 1969.
18. Lavington (1980), p. 36.
19. Hendry (1989), pp. 16–7.
20. Hendry (1989), pp. 8 & 42.
21. F. S. Barton (Director of Communications Development, MoS) to VZF, 25 Oct 1948.
22. This story is taken from Swann (1974), pp. 1–4. Porter was later to work for Ferranti, and in 1950 was sent to Canada to assist in the development of an electronics division at Ferranti Canada. Ball & Vardales (1994), p. 226.
23. Hendry (1989), p. 41.
24. Swann (1974), pp. 1–4, and *Electronic Equipment News*, March 1963.
25. For a misinterpretation of this issue, see Hendry (1989), p. 42.
26. Swann (1974), p. 5.
27. After his initial investigations, Dr Prinz had been moved to the guided weapons development team, and we shall examine in the next chapter how this work progressed.
28. Hendry (1989), p. 89.
29. Sir Ben Lockspeiser to E. Grundy, 26 Oct. 1948.
30. Hendry (1989), p. 89.
31. This institution's early development and Lord Halsbury's choice as its managing director is traced in Hendry (1989), pp. 9–11.

32. Hendry (1989), p. 171.
33. Hendry (1989), pp. 165–7.
34. Information supplied by VZF to S. C. Robbins (MoS), 7 December 1948.
35. Swann (1974), p. 10.
36. V. Bowden to VZF, 2 July 1951.
37. Lavington (1980), p. 37.
38. Lavington (1980), p. 40. The first German machine, the Z3, was not delivered until 1953.
39. Tweedale (1992), p. 99.
40. Swann (1974), p. 15.
41. Hendry (1989), pp. 89–91.
42. This story is related in great detail by Hendry (1989), pp. 47–59.
43. These discussions are recorded in a series of letters collected by M. E. Sions in 1957. The most crucial are those from VZF to Lord Halsbury, 22 Nov 1951, and from W. G. Bass (the Ferranti London office manager and head of government contracts) to Lord Halsbury, 22 Nov 1951. See also Hendry (1989), pp. 89–91.
44. V. Bowden to VZF, 15 July 1953.
45. Tweedale (1992), p. 100.
46. Lavington (1980), pp. 118–9.
47. These negotiations are described in Hendry (1989), pp. 88–104.
48. B. Swann to NRDC, 17 Dec. 1953, and NRDC to B. Swann, 2 Feb. 1954.
49. Quoted in Tweedale (1992), p. 104, and analysed in greater detail by Hendry (1989), pp. 95–6.
50. For a survey of Elliotts' history, see Lavington (1980), pp. 57–61
51. See Hendry (1989), pp. 74–87 for a detailed history of this project.
52. Strachey was the most influential member of the NRDC's computer sub-committee. See Hendry (1989), pp. 14–15. For a full review of Strachey's achievements, see Campbell-Kelly (1985), pp. 19–42.
53. NRDC to Ferranti Ltd, 2 Feb. 1954.
54. Hendry (1989), pp. 80–2.
55. Hendry (1989), pp. 98–100.
56. Hendry (1989), p. 102.
57. V. Bowden to VZF, 15 July 1953.
58. I am indebted to Harry Johnson for this information.
59. Hendry (1989), p. 101, claims that no drum store had been developed by early–1956, but Elliott claims otherwise.
60. VZF to W. Elliott, 22 May 1956.
61. C. H. Devonald, 'The Pegasus computer', *Ferranti Journal*, Summer 1957, p. 10.
62. The Elliott 402 was sold at £27,000, and the BTM 1201 at £37,000. Lavington (1980), p. 119.
63. Tweedale (1992), p. 106.
64. Tweedale (1992), pp. 103 & 118.
65. Tweedale (1992), p. 103.
66. Hendry (1989), pp. 56–9.
67. Hendry (1989), p. 101.
68. Interview with Harry Johnson.
69. Hendry (1989), p. 51.
70. Quoted in Swann (1974), p. 16.

71. Bowden had been hired in 1945 to spot new ideas, having been closely connected to many of the major technological developments of the previous decade.
72. For more material on the Canadian subsidiary and its computing work, see Ball and Vardalas (1994), pp. 222–33. See also Swann (1974), p. 4, and Williams (1994), pp. 4–12, for material on FERUT.
73. Tweedale (1992), p. 99.
74. Tweedale (1992), p. 99.
75. Swann (1974), p. 15. Tweedale (1992), p. 101.
76. V. Bowden to VZF, 15 July 1953.
77. FBM 3907, 14 Jan 1954.
78. FBM 3824, 17 June 1952.
79. E. Grundy to VZF, 6 March 1956.
80. P. R. Taylor, 'Ferranti House', *Ferranti Journal*, Christmas 1955.
81. Hendry (1989), p. 92–3.
82. Tweedale (1992), p. 106.
83. Swann (1974), p. 15.
84. Tweedale (1992), p. 106–7.
85. Hendry (1989), p. 91.
86. Hendry (1989), p. 196. As a further point of contrast, by 1960 165 computers had been installed in France and 300 in West Germany.
87. Freeman (1965), p. 45.
88. Quoted by Tweedale (1992), p. 118.
89. In fact, only one of the computers used by Ferranti was employed in product design (a *Pegasus* I for the transformer department), while the rest were part of the company's marketing and sales effort.
90. Hendry (1989), p. 10.
91. See Hendry (1989), p. 161, for further details on these contracts.
92. Freeman (1982), p. 88.
93. This section is based on an interview with Harry Johnson.
94. Perseus is mentioned in the lists of computers made by Ferranti, but the reader is not told why this machine was developed. Tweedale (1992), pp. 115 & 125.
95. The 1900 story is told in great detail by Campbell-Kelly (1989), pp. 225 & 234.
96. Conversation with Harry Johnson.
97. The two companies were AB Datacentralen of Stockholm, and the South African Mutual Life Assurance Association of Cape Town.
98. Computer Department Quarterly Report (April-June 1958).
99. Swann (1974), p. 27.
100. Hendry (1989), pp. 54–9.
101. For a complete history of these two firms, see Campbell-Kelly (1989), pp. 24–33 for BTM and pp. 34–46 for Powers-Samas.
102. Campbell-Kelly (1989), pp. 126 & 145.
103. Hendry (1989), p. 60.
104. Campbell-Kelly (1989), pp. 245–64.
105. E. Grundy to VZF, 25 March 1950, and conversation with Harry Johnson.
106. Hendry (1989), pp. 60–6.
107. Lavington (1980), pp. 62–4.
108. Campbell-Kelly (1989), pp. 168–9.
109. Campbell-Kelly (1989), pp. 169–70.

110. Swann (1974), p. 75.
111. Swann (1974), p. 61.
112. *Scope*, December 1958.
113. Conversation with Harry Johnson.
114. Tweedale (1992), p. 105.
115. Campbell-Kelly (1989), p. 179.
116. Campbell-Kelly (1989), pp. 187–90.
117. Campbell-Kelly (1989), pp. 171–4.
118. Campbell-Kelly (1989), pp. 201–5.
119. Freeman (1982), p. 90.
120. Swann (1974), p. 41.
121. Lavington (1980), pp. 43 & 119.
122. *Mercury* was purchased by atomic energy research establishments in Norway, France, the UK, Switzerland, Sweden and Belgium.
123. Lavington (1975), pp. 30–1.
124. Evans (1979), pp. 49–59.
125. The government establishment which commissioned STRETCH was the Los Alamos nuclear weapons station. Hendry (1989), p. 121.
126. This comment was made in a speech at the opening of the new Ferranti laboratory at Silverknowes in Scotland. *Electronics Weekly*, 18 Oct. 1961.
127. Lavington (1980), p. 50. See also pp. 51–2 & 83–5 for a discussion of *Atlas*'s technical specifications.
128. Dr C. M. Wilson [manager of the Portland Place Centre] to P. D. Hall, 24 Aug. 1960.
129. This section is based on Hendry (1989), pp. 120–35.
130. Hendry (1989), p. 136.
131. Campbell-Kelly (1989), p. 218.
132. Hendry (1989), p. 136.
133. Campbell-Kelly (1989), p. 219.
134. Swann (1974), pp. 82–5.
135. *Electronics*, 16 August 1963. At Cambridge, *Atlas II* was known as *Titan*.
136. CDC (Control Data Corporation) was a spin-off from the merger between Sperry and Remington Rand, and it had acquired access to *Atlas* technology by attending a 1959 seminar given by Tom Kilburn in Paris. Swann (1974), p. 81, and Hendry (1989), pp. 163–4.
137. Lavington (1975), p. 32.
138. Hendry (1989), pp. 187–92.
139. British Petroleum provided one-quarter of the funds for this machine.
140. Tweedale (1992), p. 114.
141. Tweedale (1992), p. 116.
142. Campbell-Kelly (1989), p. 219.
143. Tweedale (1992), p. 104.
144. Hendry (1989), pp. 100–2.
145. This work is reviewed by A. R. Wilde in '*Sirius*', *Ferranti Journal*, Spring 1960.
146. This work will be reviewed in great detail in the next chapter.
147. This was reported in the *Oldham Evening Chronicle*, 19 May 1959, after Hall had made the initial announcement about its availability. In contrast, the Elliott 803 sold at £35,000, while the ICT 1301 was priced at £120,000. Hendry (1989), pp. 183–4.
148. Computer department quarterly report (January to March 1959).

149. This Australian agency had been opened in 1956 (FBM 4356, 1956), initially for the guided weapons trials. See the next chapter.
150. See Tweedale (1992), p. 114.
151. Campbell-Kelly (1989), p. 220.
152. This was part of the publicity launch for *Sirius* in 1959 reported in the *Oldham Evening Chronicle*, 19 May 1959.
153. B Pollard to VZF, 7 May 1957.
154. Interview with Harry Johnson.
155. *Process Control and Automation*, July 1960.
156. P. Dorey, 'Digital systems', report to the 1968 Ferranti management conference at the Gleneagles Hotel.
157. *Electronics Weekly*, 13 Dec. 1963.
158. Interviews with Harry Johnson and Peter Dorey.
159. E. Grundy to VZF, 15 July 1953.
160. *Sunday Times*, 4 Feb. 1962.
161. Losses of £684,043 had been made on *Orion* by 1964.
162. For example, see the *Financial Times*, 7 Dec. 1959.
163. Hendry (1989), pp. 183–6.
164. Computer department quarterly report, Jan. to March 1961.
165. Hendry (1989), pp. 186 & 197.
166. Campbell-Kelly (1989), pp. 202 & 218–9.
167. Hendry (1989), p. 185.
168. Campbell-Kelly (1989), p. 219. I am indebted to Peter Hall for his recollections of these negotiations.
169. Campbell-Kelly (1989), p. 219.
170. Quoted in Tweedale (1992), p. 116.
171. *Financial Times*, 8 August 1963.
172. Tweedale (1992), p. 96–7.
173. Campbell-Kelly (1989), p. 219.
174. *The Times*, 21 May 1963.
175. ICT paid Ferranti £1.5 million in cash and 1.9 million ordinary shares, of which 625,000 were to rank with the existing ICT ordinary stock. This gave Ferranti a 10.6 per cent stake in ICT. FBM 5395, 18 Oct 1963.
176. *Economist*, 10 August 1963.
177. This section is based on interviews with Peter Hall and Harry Johnson. See also Campbell-Kelly (1989), pp. 221–3.
178. See Ball and Vardalas (1994), pp. 251–74, for the story of the Canadian subsidiary's work on computers.
179. Campbell-Kelly (1989), pp. 232–5, for an insight into the 1900's development.
180. See Campbell-Kelly (1989), pp. 245–64, for the creation of ICL.
181. Lavington (1980), p. 85.
182. Report by E. Grundy of a tour of the USA and Canada, 21 April to 2 June 1954.
183. Hendry (1989), p. 186.
184. Tweedale (1992), p. 118.
185. Hendry (1989), pp. 165–8.

Notes to Chapter 10

1. This is the term generally used by the 1960s to describe the process control computer. For an excellent survey of the minicomputer industry's development, see Hamilton (1996), pp. 81–101.
2. This conclusion is confirmed in the detailed academic analysis of the *Bloodhound* contracts by Flower (1966), p. 34.
3. This section on the early history of guided weapon development is based on Divine (1966), pp. 276–91, and Adams (1976), pp. 1–3.
4. Divine (1966), p. 311.
5. This section is based on Adams (1976), pp. 3–5.
6. This section is based on information gathered during an interview with Dr Searby.
7. This section is based on information gathered during an interview with Dr Searby, and Adams (1976), pp. 5 & 19–20.
8. Adams (1976), p. 20.
9. W. G. Bass to E. Grundy, 23 March 1949.
10. *Daily Express*, 11 June 1949.
11. See Snow (1962), p. 9, and Postan, Hay & Scott (1964), pp. 378ff.
12. Interview with Dr Searby.
13. Adams (1976), p. 18.
14. Adams (1976), p. 23.
15. Adams (1976), p. 24.
16. Interview with Dr Searby.
17. Adams (1976), p. 40.
18. Adams (1976), p. 31.
19. Interviews with Denis Best and Dr Searby.
20. Interview with Dr Searby.
21. W. G. Bass to W. R. Cook, 11 May 1952. The Royal Navy Scientific Service was also involved in sponsoring some of this work, in order to assist the *Seaslug* project.
22. Interview with Dr Searby.
23. Peter Hall came to Ferranti in January 1951, having worked for much of his career in government development laboratories. He was later to be the computer department manager. See section 9.8.
24. J. J. Thomson to E. Grundy, 2 April 1952.
25. Raytheon bought Ferranti know-how in this field for $200,000. *Manchester Guardian*, 21 Jan. 1959.
26. Interview with Dr Searby.
27. The story and data can be found in a report drawn up by Dr Searby to brief the board of directors when the Wythenshawe laboratories were opened in 1954.
28. Adams (1976), p. 24.
29. S. S. C. Mitchell to VZF, 18 March 1953.
30. Interview with Dr Searby.
31. W. H. Wheeler to VZF, 3 June 1954.
32. The story and data can be found in a report drawn up by Dr Searby to brief the board of directors when the Wythenshawe laboratories were opened in 1954.
33. Adams (1976), p. 42.
34. This decision was made in September 1956. FBM 4384, 20 Sept. 1956.
35. See Hayward (1989), pp. 67–73, for a full discussion of this development.

36. Adams (1976), pp. 42–3.
37. Sir Cyril Musgrave (Permanent Secretary to MoS) to VZF, 9 October 1956.
38. FBM 4144, 12 May 1956.
39. The low returns made on *Bloodhound* development were used in evidence to the Lang Inquiry of 1964. See The *Bloodhound* File (1964).
40. FBM 4402, 25 Oct. 1956.
41. A claim reported in the *Financial Times*, 7 July 1961.
42. Quoted in Adams (1976), p. 168.
43. Adams (1976), pp. 52–5.
44. Adams (1976), p. 55.
45. Adams (1976), pp. 54–6.
46. Divine (1966), pp. 311–15.
47. *Electronics Weekly*, 25 March 1965.
48. *The Observer*, 19 April 1964.
49. Divine (1966), p. 315.
50. Sir Richard Way to VZF, 15 Oct 1963.
51. Cooper Bros. to E. Grundy, 18 Nov 1963.
52. Interview with Alf Lawton.
53. Reported in SZF to Sir Richard Way, 28 July 1964.
54. FBM 5395, 18 Oct 1963.
55. SZF to Sir Richard Way, October 1963.
56. E. Grundy to SZF, 16 Jan 1964, reporting a meeting with Sir Richard Way.
57. Oral evidence of SZF to Lang Inquiry, June 1964.
58. This section is based on advice tendered generously by Sir Richard Way, and interviews with SZF.
59. Report of the Comptroller and Auditor-General on the Civil Appropriation Accounts, 1962–63.
60. Lang Inquiry Report, Cmd 2428, 1964. Assisting Sir John Lang were J. D. Russell (a member of the Council of the Institute of Chartered Accountants) and H. W. Hobbs (Deputy Controller of the Royal Ordnance Factories).
61. For an insight into the political atmosphere in 1963–4, see Morgan (1990), pp. 190–97.
62. The government won this censure debate on 14 February. *Guardian*, 15 Feb. 1964.
63. *Hansard*, 14 Feb. 1963. Sir Richard Way is convinced that his brief had provided the actual figures, and clearly Amery simply made a mistake in the heat of the moment.
64. Reported in the *Oldham Evening Chronicle*, 1 April 1964.
65. Second Report from the Committee of Public Accounts (hereafter PAC) (1963–64), reported in *Hansard*, Vol 694, No 99, col 408–546.
66. PAC, pp. iv–vi.
67. PAC, pp. iv–vi.
68. Lang Inquiry, para 44.
69. Civil Appropriation Accounts, p. xv.
70. Flower (1966), p. 34.
71. *Hansard*, Vol 694, No 99, col 408–546.
72. The *Bloodhound* File (1964).
73. Ferranti press release, 16 April 1964.
74. Interviews with Dr Searby and with Alf Lawton.
75. See especially Lang Inquiry, para 44. For a contemporary view, see Flower (1966), p. 34.
76. Lang Inquiry, para 5–7.

77. The *Bloodhound* File (1964).
78. Lang Inquiry, para 13.
79. *Hansard*, Vol 699, No 154, p. 1813.
80. Interview with SZF.
81. SZF to E. Grundy, 20 March 1964, and interview with Peter Dorey.
82. In fact, after deducting the tax paid on this profit, Ferranti was requested to pay £2,048,708, and Sebastian managed to persuade MoA to take this in five instalments, starting in June 1965. SZF to Sir Richard Way, 28 July 1964.
83. Interview with Dr Searby.
84. Second Lang Inquiry, 1967, Cmnd 2582.
85. *The Times* (2 May 1964) reported how the Minister of Defence, Peter Thorneycroft, had started tightening up procedures by May 1964.
86. *The Times*, 25 March 1967. The Bristol-Siddeley profit had actually come to light in 1964, but in view of the *Bloodhound* revelations the MoD managed to keep it out of the limelight.
87. *Financial Times*, 27 March 1968.
88. Lavington (1980), pp. 80–1. Maurice Gribble provided invaluable help with this section.
89. This section is based on interviews with Maurice Gribble, and R. A. Morley, 'Automation systems from Wythenshawe', *Ferranti Journal*, Spring 1961. See also J. Mullaly, 'Argus computers for industrial control', *Ferranti Journal*, Summer 1964, p. 15.
90. For an insight into the development of what was regarded as the minicomputer industry, see Hamilton (1996), pp. 81–101. The ICI *Argus* was later bought back by Ferranti for the RAF, which installed it in the Newton technical school for use in training *Bloodhound* launch control post operators.
91. I am indebted to Albert Dodd for this information.
92. Freeman (1965), p. 47.
93. This section is based heavily on Hamilton (1996), pp. 81–101.

Notes to Chapter 11

1. This section has benefited enormously from interviews with Sebastian de Ferranti.
2. For a general review of business developments in this period, see Wilson (1995), pp. 181–204.
3. Interviews with Harry Kirkham, Lester George and Tom Lunt.
4. In fact, Sebastian held 28.3 per cent of the equity, and Basil held 22.9 per cent. See Appendix E. Turner(1969), p. 431.
5. Interview with SZF in the *Manchester Evening Chronicle*, 11 April 1958.
6. Article on Ferranti entitled 'Third generation takes over', *New Scientist*, 13 August 1959.
7. Interview with SZF in the *Observer*, June 1964.
8. Interview with Lester George.
9. Interview with Lester George.
10. Tragically, W. C. Pycroft committed suicide.
11. He became President of the Chamber in 1956.
12. The other new director was T. Edmondson, from the Canadian subsidiary. See Ball & Vardalas (1994), pp. 176–9.
13. Interview with Tom Lunt.

14. Interview in *New Scientist*, 13 August 1959.
15. Such questions were certainly asked at the two senior management conferences held in 1965 and 1968 (at the Gleneagles Hotel), a debate we shall assess in Section 11.8
16. For a review of these debates, see Golding (1971), pp. 126–39, McCalman (1988), pp. 23–7, and Langlois *et al.* (1988), pp. 153–4. Morris (1995) provides an overview of the whole story, including on pp. 117–21 an insight into the Ferranti contribution.
17. For a general history of this 'revolution' in electronic components, see Golding (1971), pp. 60–85, Abelson & Hammond (1980), pp. 16–41, Langlois et al (1988), pp. 8–16, McCalman (1988), pp. 3–11, and Evans (1979), pp. 49–59.
18. Interviews with Dr Searby and Peter Hall, and S. S. C. Mitchell to W. G. Bass, 9 Feb. 1952.
19. This section is based on Golding (1971), pp. 61–9, and on Langlois et al (1988), pp. 8–13. See also Sciberras (1980), pp. 282–95. For a detailed study of the emergence of semiconductors, see Hempstead (1977), especially pp. 259–69.
20. Golding (1971), p. 292. Braun (1980), pp. 72–4, describes how the early Bell Labs products were not entirely reliable, holding up progress for several years until more effective production processes could be developed.
21. Correspondence between Dr Searby and W. H. Wheeler, February/March 1952.
22. W. G. Bass to VZF, 6 March 1952. Golding (1971), p. 292, claims that Ferranti did not attend the 1952 Symposium, but the Ferranti records state otherwise.
23. Dr Searby to W. H. Wheeler, 28 Sept. 1953.
24. Interview with Peter Hall, and Dr Searby to VZF, 9 March 1954.
25. Interview with Dr Shepherd.
26. Dr Searby to VZF, 9 March 1954.
27. Interview with Peter Hall, and Dr Searby to VZF, 9 March 1954.
28. This section is based on interviews with Dr Shepherd and Peter Hall.
29. Interview with Peter Hall.
30. See A. A. Shepherd, 'Ferranti semiconductor development', *Ferranti Journal*, Autumn 1957.
31. P. D. Hall to VZF, 3 Feb. 1955.
32. Golding (1971), p. 210.
33. P. D. Hall to VZF, 3 Feb. 1955.
34. P. D. Hall to VZF, 23 Jan. 1956 and 8 March 1957.
35. By 1957 they were also producing silicon power rectifiers. P. D. Hall to VZF 8 March 1957.
36. E. Grundy to VZF, 23 Oct. 1956.
37. Interviews with Peter Hall and Sydney Jackson.
38. FBM 4437, 10 Jan. 1957.
39. M. E. Sions to VZF, 29 August 1957.
40. *Instrument Practice*, May 1958, *Financial Times*, 7 Jan. 1960, and 'Ferranti at the International Transistor Exhibition', *Ferranti Journal*, Autumn 1959.
41. T. C. Fry (Vice-President of Bell Labs) to A. A. Shepherd, 23 Jan. 1956.
42. For a review of these process innovations, see Abelson & Hammond (1980), pp. 16–41, and Golding (1971), pp. 74–7.
43. *Electrical Journal*, 12 Feb. 1960; *Oldham Evening Chronicle*, 27 Jan 1960; *Engineer*, 5 Feb. 1960; *Electronics Weekly*, 19 April and 7 June 1961.
44. Golding (1971), p. 210.
45. Gem Mill had made losses of £469,000 in the previous four years. Ferranti Management Accounts, 1955–61.

46. Interviews with Dr Searby, Peter Hall and Dr Shepherd.
47. *Financial Times*, 12 Feb. 1961.
48. This section is based on Golding (1971), pp. 78–81, and on Braun (1980), pp. 76–8.
49. *Electronics Weekly*, 5 and 19 Sept. 1962; Golding (1971), p. 210–11.
50. *Financial Times*, 24 April 1963; *New Scientist*, 23 May 1963; *Industrial Equipment News*, July 1963.
51. Golding (1971), p. 210.
52. Interview with Dr Shepherd.
53. Interview with SZF.
54. Golding (1971), p. 152. Texas Instruments was also very competitive in this market.
55. P. J. Bagnall, '*Micronor II*', technical memo circulated to senior management, 12 June 1965, FA.
56. FBM 5686, 21 Dec. 1965; *Economist*, 20 Jan. 1966; *Daily Mail*, 20 Jan. 1966; *Electronic Components*, Dec. 1966.
57. *Financial Times*, 31 Jan. 1966.
58. *Economist*, 20 Jan. 1966.
59. Golding (1970), p. 134.
60. Interview with Dr Shepherd, and Golding (1971), pp. 265–72.
61. Golding (1971), pp. 329 & 369.
62. Golding (1971), pp. 136–43; Freeman (1965), p. 42; Sciberras (1980), pp. 288–9.
63. *Daily Telegraph*, 19 Oct. 1967; *Electronics Weekly*, 24 Jan. 1968.
64. Interview with Peter Hall. Hall had become computer department manager in 1959, and John Pickin had replaced him as manager at Gem Mill.
65. FBM 5831, 3 Feb. 1967; *Electronic Components*, Feb. 1967.
66. Interview in the *Financial Times*, 16 March 1966.
67. The title of his 1967 address to the Institute of Radio & Electronic Engineers, Australia, was 'Develop Technology – To Survive', and in 1963 (after selling the mainframe computer business to ICT) he had demanded a 'Buy British' policy in the computer market.
68. Golding (1971), pp. 146 & 178–80. See also a document submitted in 1971 by Ferranti, *Proposals on Maintaining a UK Microcircuit Capability*, to the Department of Trade & Industry (hereafter referred to as 'Ferranti 1971 Proposals').
69. For a survey of this trend, see McCalman (1988), pp. 30–5. See also Sciberras (1980), p. 284–6.
70. Interview with Peter Hall, and *Electronics Weekly*, 6 Aug. 1969.
71. Golding (1971), p. 179; *Microelectronics*, Oct. 1969; Sciberras (1980), p. 286.
72. This section is based on information supplied by Dr Shepherd.
73. For a review of the manufacturing process, see Oldham (1980), pp. 42–61.
74. McCalman (1988), p. 25.
75. For a review of this period, see Morgan (1991), pp. 239–76.
76. *Financial Times*, 9 Nov. 1966.
77. Over this period, sales had been worth £3.3 million, rising from £498,000 to £1.35 million. Ferranti Management Accounts, 1966–70.
78. This section is based on an interview with Dr Shepherd.
79. For Heath's own thoughts on this issue, see Heath(1998), pp. 325–53.
80. Sciberras (1980), pp. 284–6.
81. Interviews with SZF, Lester George, Donald McCallum and Dr Shepherd.
82. This section is based on an interview with Dr Shepherd.

83. Sciberras (1980), p. 289.
84. FBM 6557, 9 Nov. 1972.
85. Sciberras (1980), pp. 291–2.
86. The two exceptions were 1963/4 and 1967/8.
87. Ferranti Management Accounts, 1955–70.
88. Sciberras (1980), p. 284.
89. For a review of the Labour government's strategy, see Graham (1972), pp. 178–217.
90. McCallum (1987), pp. 41–2, describes how the American doctors had diagnosed a heart attack, but on returning to Edinburgh his own doctor quickly corrected this misinterpretation.
91. This reorganisation is described by McCallum (1987), pp. 40–3.
92. There was also a trials and installation operation at Prestwick airport, run by H. G. Hinckley, but this was never given trading department status.
93. McCallum (1987), pp. 42–3, and interviews with Sir Donald McCallum and J. B. Smith.
94. Gardner (1981), pp. 13–34. Other avionics firms involved in this project were EMI (sideways-looking radar), Decca (Doppler system), Smiths Instruments (air data system), and Elliott-Automation (flight control station).
95. Hastings (1966), p. 54. Gardner (1981), p. 112, does note that some problems were encountered during the early testing stage, but by early–1965 *TSR–2* was virtually complete.
96. Hastings (1966), p. 44, and BAC (1964), p. 4.
97. McCallum (1987), pp. 37–9.
98. This section is based on Gardner (1981), pp. 106–13.
99. Healey (1989), pp. 270–7.
100. *Daily Mail*, 20 June 1964.
101. Gardner (1981), pp. 98–105.
102. Healey (1989), pp. 270–1.
103. Gardner (1989), pp. 105–12.
104. Reported in the *Scotsman*, 10 Feb. 1965.
105. Hastings (1966), p. 106.
106. For Wilson's version, see Wilson (1971), pp. 42–3 & 91–2.
107. See Gardner (1981), pp. 114–20.
108. Reported in the *Scotsman*, 16 March 1965.
109. See Gardner (1981), pp. 98–120, for a comprehensive BAC view of the story, and Hastings (1966) for a strong anti-government view. Healey (1989), pp. 270–7, attempts to defend his department's actions.
110. *Aviation Week*, 12 July 1965.
111. McCallum (1987), p. 56.
112. Gardner (1981), pp. 125–6.
113. Gardner (1981), p. 126.
114. Gardner (1981), pp. 127–39.
115. Interview with Sir John Toothill.
116. Interview with Sir Donald McCallum, and Toothill report to the 1968 Gleneagles Conference.
117. This section is based on McCallum (1987), pp. 54–8.
118. Quoted in McCallum (1987), p. 57.
119. For a criticism of Toothill's strategy, see Burns & Stalker (1961), pp. 16–21.
120. *Electronics Weekly*, 1 March 1961.

121. *Electronics Weekly*, 26 June 1968, claimed that inspection times could be reduced by between sixty and ninety per cent using the Ferranti equipment.
122. This is apparent from McCallum (1987), p. 59.
123. Williamson went on to develop the Molins 'System 24', which Freeman (1982), p. 72, describes as 'an early forerunner of the complete automation of machine shops which is now being realised by a growing number of Japanese firms, based on a combination of computers, NC and robotics'.
124. The repayments on this loan did not start until 1966, and they were spread over five years. Ferranti Accounts, 1966–70.
125. In fact, the Sheffield Corporation was acquired by Bendix in 1963 and the Ferranti licence was transferred as a result.
126. For a detailed analysis of this business, see McCallum (1987), pp. 59–63.
127. *Machine Tool Review*, Oct. 1969.
128. Report to the Gleneagles Management Conference, 1968.
129. Report to the Gleneagles Management Conference, 1968.
130. *Sunday Times*, 6 July 1969.
131. *Technical Publications*, Nov. 1968.
132. For a detailed history of the IRC's intervention in the NC field, see Hamilton (1997), pp. 85–92. For further analysis of the NC sector, see Hamilton (1999).
133. *Sunday Times*, 6 July 1969, and *Financial Times*, 25 Oct. 1969.
134. See Turner (1969), pp. 81–5 & 379–88.
135. McCallum (1987), p. 61.
136. *Financial Times*, 2 Oct. 1969.
137. McCallum (1987), p. 61, and conversations with SZF.
138. FBM 6196, 13 Nov. 1969. Although the deal was valued at £2.2 million, Ferranti actually received £800,000 on completion of the deal and an annual payment of £600,000 over the following four years.
139. FBM 6343, 14 Jan 1971. This deal cost Ferranti £30,000.
140. I am indebted to Peter Dorey and to Harry Johnston for providing much of the information which is included in this section. See also Peter Dorey's report to the Gleneagles Management Conference, 1968.
141. See also H. Johnston, Digital Systems Division, mimeo of the chief sales manager's recollections, 1971.
142. *Electronics Weekly*, 14 Sept. 1966.
143. This is the view of both Dorey and Johnson.
144. *Bracknell News*, 5 Dec. 1968.
145. Ferranti Management Accounts, 1960–69, and Gleneagles Management Conference, 1968.
146. Interviews with Lester George, Sir Donald McCallum, and reports from the Gleneagles Management Conference, 1968.
147. Reported in the *Guardian*, 18 June 1965. Ferranti also managed to persuade the MoA that no annual payment should exceed one-third of the company's consolidated net profit.
148. FBM, 5867, 11 May 1967.
149. *Financial Times*, 23 Nov. 1967.
150. In April 1965 these ICT shares were provided as security against extensions of the overdraft. FBM 5612, 26 April 1965.
151. Campbell-Kelly (1989), pp. 255–63.

152. H. Kirkham, 'Long term financial forecast', Gleneagles Management Conference, 1968.
153. Interview with Lester George.
154. Interviews with Lester George and SZF.
155. This was not in his report to the conference, but Lester George remembers how in private Nash was convinced that closure was the only rational action.
156. Interview with SZF.
157. Quoted in Turner (1969), p. 339.
158. Interviews with Lester George, Tom Lunt and Albert Dodd.
159. This section is based on McCallum (1987), pp. 70–1.
160. L. George to SZF, 20 Oct. 1965.
161. Turner (1969), p. 340, and interviews with SZF.

Notes to Chapter 12

1. For a review of the anti-monopoly legislation of this period, see Mercer (1995). See also Zeitlin (2000), Ch. 10.
2. MRPC (1957), pp. 227–33.
3. *Ibid.*
4. I have relied considerably over the following pages on a series of interviews with SZF.
5. *Electrical Review*, 13 June 1969.
6. Interview with SZF. For a review of these trends, see Wilson (1995), pp. 194–201.
7. See Jones & Marriott (1969), pp. 368–80.
8. For an analysis of this debate, see Brummer & Cowe (1998), and Aris (1998).
9. On these developments, see Hannah (1982), pp. 193–217, 289.
10. Hannah (1982), p. 286.
11. This section is based on J. D. Carter, 'Meters', paper presented to the 1968 Gleneagles Hotel Ferranti Management Conference, and interviews with SZF.
12. Ferranti Management Accounts, 1965–75.
13. *Electrical Review*, 26 July 1968.
14. Bruce Calveley in *Ferranti News*, Feb. 1975.
15. Ferranti Management Accounts, 1965–75.
16. Interview with SZF, and R. W. Nash, 'Transformer division', paper presented to the 1968 Gleneagles Hotel Ferranti Management Conference.
17. R. W. Nash, 'Transformer division'.
18. 15 December 1967.
19. Richardson (1968).
20. Negotiations reported in *FBM*, 1965–70.
21. This section is reliant upon a series of interviews with SZF, along with discussions of the transformer story with Bob Campbell.
22. He left to join another former Ferranti transformer engineer, R. McDowell, at MK Electric.
23. Interview with Bob Campbell.
24. Ferranti Management Accounts, 1965–75.
25. Interviews with Dr Searby and John Pickin.
26. This section is based on interviews with SZF, Sir John Toothill, Sir Donald McCallum, Dr Searby, Harry Kirkham, John Pickin, Lester George and Tom Lunt.

27. Interview with J. B. Smith and Sir Donald McCallum.
28. See Sawyer (1991), pp. 158–75.
29. Reid (1982).
30. This scenario can be followed in *FBM*, 1970–75. Interviews with SZF, Charles Scott, Lester George, Harry Kirkham and Tom Lunt have also proved useful.
31. Interview with SZF.
32. As section 11.8 has described, the two de Ferranti brothers had accrued considerable debts because of the struggle to ensure that their uncle, Denis de Ferranti, did not gain control of the firm in the late–1960s.
33. This story is well told in McCallum (1987), pp. 71–7.
34. FBM 9774, 23 Aug. 1974.
35. Interviews with SZF, Sir Donald McCallum, and McCallum (1987), pp. 73–5.
36. FBM, Sept.–Dec. 1974.

APPENDIX A

The Genealogy of the Ferranti family

1010	–	Gianni Zani
1050	–	Gianni Zani
1090	–	Giraldo Zani
1130	–	Gianni Zani
1160	–	Gianni Zani
1200	–	Gianni Zani
1240	–	Giraldo Zani (Consul)
1280	–	Giraldo Zani (Proconsul)
1310	–	Duccio Zani (Officer of the Toschi di Bologna Cavaliere)
1340	–	Giraldo Zani (Proconsul in Florence)
1380	–	Duccio Zani
1466	–	Duomenico Zani
1522	–	Andrea Zani (created a Count of Palatine by Pope Pius IV)
1571	–	Andrea Zani (Doctor of Laws and Academics)
1647	–	Giovanni Zani (Count of Bologna)
1673	–	Giulio Cesare Zani (Count of Bologna)
1712	–	Giovanni Battista Zani (Count of Bologna)
1736	–	Marco Felice Filippo Zani (Chancellor under Legate Archetti to Pope Pius VI)
1783	–	Giovanni Battista Zani (de Ferranti, through an inheritance)
1801	–	Marco Aurelio Zani de Ferranti

FERRANTI: A HISTORY

Family Tree from 1801

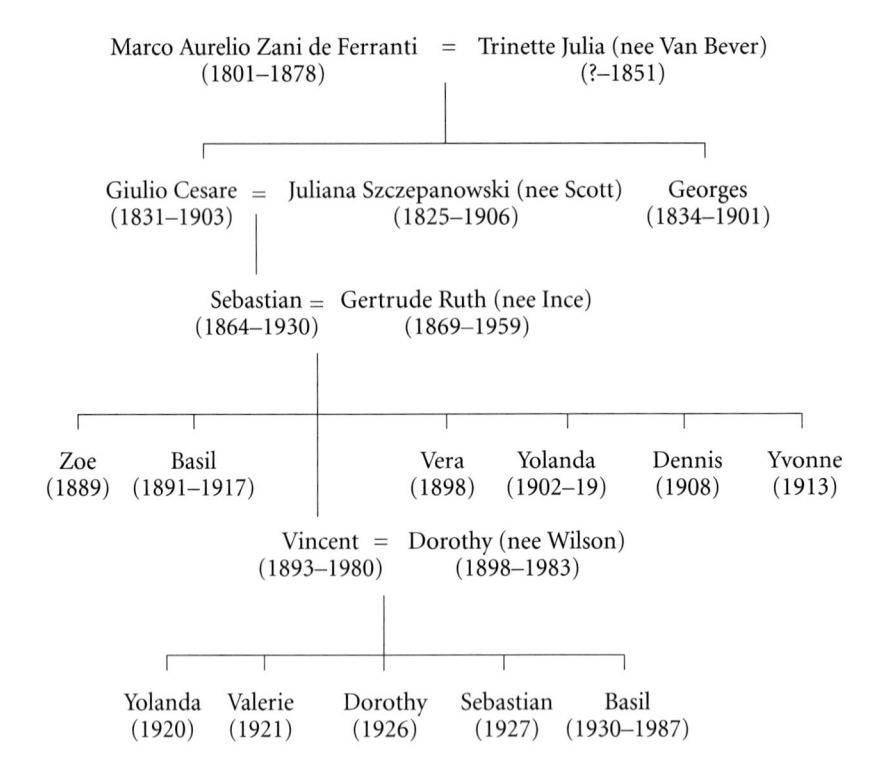

Marco Aurelio Zani de Ferranti = Trinette Julia (nee Van Bever)
(1801–1878) (?–1851)

Giulio Cesare = Juliana Szczepanowski (nee Scott)   Georges
(1831–1903)   (1825–1906)   (1834–1901)

Sebastian = Gertrude Ruth (nee Ince)
(1864–1930)   (1869–1959)

Zoe   Basil   Vera   Yolanda   Dennis   Yvonne
(1889)   (1891–1917)   (1898)   (1902–19) (1908)   (1913)

Vincent = Dorothy (nee Wilson)
(1893–1980)   (1898–1983)

Yolanda   Valerie   Dorothy   Sebastian   Basil
(1920)   (1921)   (1926)   (1927)   (1930–1987)

APPENDIX B

List of patents taken out by Sebastian Ziani de Ferranti, 1882–1930

A. *Electrical*

1882	3418	Arc lamp and regulator [a]
	3419	Alternators [a]
	3950	Dynamos [a]
	4596	Meters and regulators [a]
1883	36	Dynamos
	1371	Dynamos [b]
	3702	Dynamos [a]
	5132	Dynamos
	5929	Mercury disc dynamo and meter
	5927	Incendescent lamp and vacuum pump
1884	5335	Mercury connections for alternators [c]
1885	3587	Switches (spring-assisted)
	14917	Transformers (speech) [d]
	15141	Converters (transformers)
	15251	Distribution (high tension AC)
1887	700	Induction furnace
	701	Meters (mercury motor)
	702	Alternators (field magnets and coils)
	12418	AC systems and synchronous motors
	12419	Electric traction
1888	2313	Motors (AC)
	2313A	Smoothing commutated DC
	2314	Safety fuses
	2315	Electrical mains (flexible cable)

577

	2316	Dynamos (construction)
	12289	Electric traction
	12505	Electrical mains (flexible joints)
	13621	AC meters
	13622	AC meters
	15249	Displaceable field magnets
1889	915	Switches
	7275	Arc lamps
	7976	Arc lamps
	16237	Electrical mains (paper insulated)
	18361	AC meters
1890	2653	AC meters
	3096	Meters
	9061	AC meters
	12713	Electrical mains (manufacture)
1891	1049	Dynamos
	1050	Distribution system
	1051	Transformers
	1051A	Transformers and dynamos (testing)
	4682	Safety fuses
	6660	Distribution (Deptford system)
	10554	Transformers
	17220	Rectifiers
1892	3112	AC meters
	3113A	Distribution
	22923	Cables
1893	14000	Meters
	21324	Cables
1894	207	Transformers
	6458	Dynamos
	10917	Safety fuses
	11022	Rectifiers
	17065	Overhead cables (traction)

APPENDICES

	17066	Cables (air insulated)
1895	4065	Traction
	4490	Dynamos
	5003	Condensers
	5137	Transformers
	13091	High tension switches
1896	1888	Dynamos
	3481	Dynamos
	7195	Dynamos
	17557	Dyanmos
	17558	Dynamos
1897	2818	AC meters
	3363	Cables
1900	16664	AC meters
1901	18895	Switches
	25426	Surge absorbers
1902	5997	Surge absorbers
	6233	Switches [f]
	7039	Fuses
	10231	DC dynamos
	10800	Electrostatic instruments
	10899	Electrostatic instruments [g]
	18765	Switches
	18766	AC meters [h]
	24643	Traction systems
1906	774	Induction instruments [i]
	13949	Induction furnace
	13949A	Induction furnace
1911	3422	DC meters
1915	7826	Transformers
	7827	Transformers [j]
1918	131725	Transformers
	133727	Transformers

	133933	Transformers
	135515	AC meters [k]
	137090	AC meters [k]
1919	141285	AC meters [k]
1920	165133	AC meters [k]
	166500	AC meters [k]
	166869	AC meters [k]
	166870	AC meters [k]
1921	188979	Transformers
1923	217772	AC meters
1924	123210	DC meters
	234424	DC meters
	234425	DC meters
	235267	DC meters
	239940	DC meters
	242702	AC meters
	244807	Radio transformers
	246545	Transformers
	247248	AC meters
	248429	Radio transformers
1925	248925	Radio transformers
	259288	Radio Transformers
1926	273498	Loudspeakers
	278406	Loudspeakers
	281454	Meters
	281743	Meters
	287200	AC meters
1927	281543	Meters
	297563	Radio condensers
	299998	Transformers [l]
	300565	Fires
	302256	Fires
1928	322995	Meters

	322996	AC meters
	323499	Transformers[l]
	324919	Fires
	328955	AC meters
	329349	AC meters
1929	321363	Meters
	328561	Fires
	329984	AC meters
	330235	Fires
	333148	Transformers[m]
	338164	Meters[n]
	343905	Fires
1930	369959	Meters
	374057	Meters

B. *Engines, turbines and boilers*

1885	4505	Engines
1889	1902	Engines
1895	2565	Turbines
1896	5525	Gearing
1898	2374	Corliss valves
	7701	Engines
1900	3536	Engines
1902	22846	Air compressors
	24781	Turbines
1903	7685	Turbines
	11921	Turbines
	13199	Turbines
	15186	Turbines
1904	1409	Turbines
	4556	Turbines
	4556A	Balancing high speed rotating blades
	4556B	Turbines

	9495	Gas turbines
	28301	Turbines
	29495	Turbines
1905	19912	Turbines
1906	4694	Turbines
	8886	Gas turbines
	14692	Turbines
	15154	Turbines
	15154A	Turbines
	18413	Turbines
	28951	Compressors
1907	5538	Turbines
1909	530	Turbines
	531	Turbines
1910	5035	Thrust bearings
	5169	Turbines
	7089	Turbines
1911	14268	Turbines
	9968	Boiler superheater
	29683	Boiler superheater
1913	20561	Roller bearings
1918	131013	Heat engines
1919	185763	Boilers
	185765	Steam power installations

C. *Valves and fluid control*

1888	4115	Valves
1889	7276	Tubular mains
1891	2052	Tubular mains
1904	21032	Valves
1906	8887	Valves
1907	6097	Valves
1908	5344	Valves

1909   28193   Valves
1919   147256   Valves

D. *Processes*

1892   6009   White lead º
        23572   White lead º
1893   20236   White lead º
1894   3372   Oxides of lead º
1906   13965   Nitrogen fixation
1907   8255   Steel
       20697   Nitrogen fixation
1918   121818   Press forging of shells

E. *Cotton Spinning*

1903   18047   Textile spinning
1904   11558   Ring flyers
       18260   Supporters
1905   16716   Air turbines
       16716A   Turbines drives
       16716B   Air bearings
       16717   Pure couple drive
1906   11271   Bobbins
       24941   Braking
1933   416717   Flyers [p]
       416718   Spindles [p]
       416719   Brakes [p]

F. *Tyres*

1896   11799   Tyres
1897   9667   Bicycle drives [q]
1906   26080   Tyres
1907   10977   Tyres
       21726   Tyres
       26175   Tyres

1908	13375	Tyres
	14504	Tyres
1921	181842	Nail catchers

G. *Miscellaneous*

1884	4584	Spectacles
	16127	Spectacles
1909	24112	Gyroscopic control

Key: Patents taken out with

a. Alfred Thompson

b. Vincent Szczepanowski

c. Sir William Thomson

d. G. L. Addenbrook

e. Arthur Wright

f. H. W. Clothier and C. C. Garrard

g. C. C. Garrard

h. W. Hamilton

i. M. B. Field and C. C. Garrard

j. Jan Roothan

k. George Hall

l. John Turner

m. Joseph Whibley

n. Harry Pownall

o. J. H. Noad

p. Taken out in his name by Gertrude Z. de Ferranti

q. C. W. Atkinson

APPENDIX C

The financing of Ferranti, 1890–1993

Table 1. *Company capital, 1890–1990*

	Issued capital [1]	Bank overdraft	General reserve
1890 [2]	100,000	—	—
1891	100,000	—	—
1892	100,000	—	—
1893	100,000	—	—
1894	104,300	424	1,993
1895	122,300	1,500	2,987
1896	143,000	3,000	6,251
1897	149,100	18,100	8,412
1898	150,000	34,000	50,317
1899	179,600	20,400	39,771
1900	184,600	20,400	7,484
1901 [3]	160,000	—	6,255
1902 [4]	220,000	NA	—
1903	320,000	37,498	—
1904	NA	NA	NA
1905 [5]	123,281	NA	NA
1906	224,520	21,789	—
1907 [6]	128,514	21,597	—
1908	241,724	21,077	—
1909	241,724	20,609	—
1910	241,724	20,149	—
1911	244,886	19,632	—
1912	259,846	19,091	—
1913	267,774 [7]	28,562	22,000 [8]
1914	247,574	25,209	22,000
1915	245,328	20,976	22,000
1916	241,728	19,236	22,000
1917	238,478	23,439	22,000
1918	231,018	12,066	22,000
1919	231,018	20,000	22,000
1920	226,343	40,609	72,000
1921 [9]	222,243	2,717	102,630

	Issued capital [1]	Bank overdraft	General reserve
1922	190,543	—	152,630
1923	206,166[10]	—	90,000
1924	206,166	—	125,000
1925	206,166	—	165,000
1926	206,166	—	200,000
1927	206,166	—	235,000
1928	206,166	31,974	270,000
1929	246,166[11]	96,806	270,000
1930	446,166[12]	171,649	110,000
1931	696,166	—	105,000
1932	800,000	—	105,000
1933	800,000	—	107,070
1934	800,000	—	117,070
1935	800,000	—	120,000
1936	800,000	103,347	120,000
1937	800,000	248,218	130,000
1938	800,000	234,729	145,000
1939	800,000	—	145,000
1940	800,000	293,254	145,000
1941	800,000	513,021	145,000
1942	800,000	853,112	145,000
1943	800,000	1,852,370	145,000
1944	800,000	2,279,370	145,000
1945	800,000	2,356,037	300,000
1946	800,000	688,615	340,000
1947	800,000	149,592	400,000
1948	800,000	521,573	536,000
1949	800,000	801,360	950,000
1950	1,500,000[13]	1,069,599	450,000
1951	1,500,000	1,389,731	900,000
1952	1,500,000	2,438,632	1,200,000
1953	2,500,000[14]	3,085,974	719,235
1954	3,000,000[15]	1,607,240	1,050,000
1955	3,000,000	1,978,246	2,300,000
1956	3,000,000	4,393,112	2,750,000
1957	3,000,000	3,561,245	3,050,000
1958	3,000,000	2,936,454	3,650,000
1959	4,500,000[16]	2,301,290	3,100,000
1960	4,500,000	232,045	4,850,000
1961	4,500,000	390,074	6,150,000

APPENDICES

	Issued capital [1]	Bank overdraft	General reserve
1962	4,500,000	1,367,761	5,903,465
1963	4,500,000	2,302,074	5,953,465
1964	4,500,000	5,752,070	6,373,465
1965	4,500,000	6,352,304	4,549,757
1966	4,500,000	7,906,068	7,935,346
1967	4,500,000	9,944,940	9,385,346
1968	4,500,000	11,799,000	11,052,000[17]
1969	4,500,000	11,408,000	11,739,000
1970	4,500,000	9,038,000	13,392,000
1971	4,500,000	10,424,000	12,974,000
1972	4,500,000	4,373,000	13,534,000
1973	4,500,000	4,093,000	15,016,000
1974	4,500,000	9,645,000	18,083,000
1975	4,500,000	16,911,000	17,993,000

Key: NA signifies that the information is not available.

1. This includes ordinary shares, preference shares and debenture capital. For the voting stock see Appendix E.

2. For the period 1890–1907 the financial year ran from January to December.

3. Authorised capital raised to £400,000 by the creation of 200,000 £1 ordinary shares and 200,000 six per cent cumulative preference shares of £1. Dr Ferranti was given ninety-seven per cent of the ordinary shares, and 100,000 of the preference shares were issued, but only 60,000 taken up.

4. A further 60,000 preference shares were sold publicly.

5. The new company was registered with an authorised capital of £130,000, made up of 60,000 six per cent cumulative preference shares of £1, 60,000 £1 ordinary shares amd 10,000 £1 deferred shares, all of which carried a vote.

6. The financial year was changed to run from July to June.

7. The issued capital fell from 1913 because the board instituted a policy of redeeming the debenture stock.

8. £22,000 was placed in the general reserve account from the profit and loss account.

9. In this year Dr Ferranti was allowed to convert his deferred shares into ordinary shares, and the other ordinary shareholders had their stocks converted into voting preference shares. £69,300 was also taken from the reserves to write down goodwill and patent rights to £1.

10. The authorised capital was raised to £300,000 by the creation of 170,000 new shares. £82,792 of the general reserve was capitalised to purchase 50,000 of the new ordinary shares, 17,792 of the new six per cent cumulative preference shares and 15,000 of the new seven per cent non-cumulative second preference shares, all of which were distributed among the Ferranti family.

11. £40,000 of the general reserve was capitalised to purchase the 40,000 ordinary shares not issued from the 1923 scheme, and again allocated to the Ferranti family.

12. The authorised capital was raised to £900,000 by the creation of 300,000 seven per cent cumulative preference shares and 600,000 ordinary shares, all valued at ten shillings (50p). All the existing shares were also split in two and valued at ten shillings, to rank with the new shares. £200,000 of the general reserve was capitalised to purchase 400,000 of the new ordinary shares, to be allocated to the Ferranti family, and the new preference shares were sold publicly over the next two years to bring the issued capital up to £800,000.

13. The authorised capital was raised to £2,500,000 by the creation of 500,000 seven per cent cumulative preference shares of £1, one million five per cent second redeemable cumulative preference stock of £1 and one million ordinary shares of ten shillings (50p.). £700,000 of the general reserve was capitalised to purchase 400,000 of the new ordinary shares and 500,000 of the new second preference stock, to be allocated to the Ferranti family.

14. The authorised capital was raised to £3,500,000 and £1 million from the general reserve was capitalised to purchase 500,000 of the newly-created 5.5 per cent third cumulative preference stock and one million of the unissued ordinary shares, all again allotted ot the Ferranti family.

15. 500,000 of the second redeemable cumulative preference stock was issued for public sale.

16. The authorised capital was raised to £4,500,000 by the creation of two million ordinary shares, and £1.5 million was capitalised from the general reserve to purchase all of these as well as the balance of the third cumulative preference shares, and allotted to the Ferranti family.

17. The general reserve leapt so impressively in this year because all reserves (including the balance in the profit and loss account) was consolidated into what was called 'Retained Earnings'.

Table 2. *Profitability and return on capital employed, 1892–1993*

This table is an attempt to gauge the annual rated return on capital employed, as measured by gross profits. The *gross profits* are stated after the deduction of depreciation, directors' fees, auditors' fees and interest charges. The *net profits* are the funds available to the equity shareholders and could either be paid out in dividends or retained for future investment in the reserve accounts (see Table 1 above). It is important to stress that the gross profits were never given in the balance sheet until the 1960s, and because the figures shown here are unaudited, having been supplied by the accounts department for an internal assessment, there are several discrepancies with the final column, especially in the 1930s.

	Gross profit £	Capital employed £	Return on capital employed %	Net profit or (loss) £
1892[1]	NA	NA	NA	(2,802)
1893[2]	NA	NA	NA	1,218
1894	NA	106,717	NA	1,118
1895	NA	128,437	NA	3,964
1896	NA	133,201	NA	3,561
1897	NA	157,814	NA	771
1898	NA	192,413	NA	7,915
1899	NA	200,948	NA	17,635
1900	NA	224,371	NA	15,275
1901	NA	263,109	NA	25,160
1902	NA	328,755	NA	3,875
1903	NA	NA	NA	(58,557)
1904	NA	NA	NA	(40,114)
1905[3]	NA	NA	NA	(7,334)
1906[4]	NA	246,320	NA	(169)
1907	NA	250,115	NA	2,092
1908	NA	265,155	NA	3,275
1909	NA	263,853	NA	307

APPENDICES

	Gross profit £	Capital employed £	Return on capital employed %	Net profit or (loss) £
1910	NA	262,824	NA	2,991
1911	NA	263,519	NA	4,166
1912	NA	278,937	NA	7,129
1913	NA	305,337	NA	10,062
1914	NA	295,918	NA	1,598
1915	NA	296,721	NA	(1,022)
1916	NA	299,395	NA	3,546
1917	NA	254,928	NA	7,650
1918	NA	266,002	NA	35,174
1919	NA	279,362	NA	18,251
1920	NA	339,824	NA	36,622
1921	76,269	403,489	18.8	36,269
1922	36,372	384,087	9.5	24,371
1923	49,765	392,969	12.7	36,362
1924	72,105	416,526	17.3	55,546
1925	87,587	438,212	20.0	67,644
1926	75,557	485,120	15.6	59,766
1927	39,180	561,455	6.0	35,982
1928	76,531	606,610	12.6	54,616
1929	97,791	741,321	13.2	66,976
1930	89,076	868,921	10.3	68,749
1931	59,161	856,678	6.9	60,689
1932	45,182	930,750	4.9	54,905
1933	43,660	858,308	5.1	57,869
1934	67,335	853,654	7.9	68,245
1935	42,589	1,058,451	4.0	55,902
1936	51,611	1,166,039	4.4	57,438
1937	83,830	1,374,543	6.1	64,923
1938	106,177	1,372,783	7.7	68,263
1939	172,340	1,212,603	14.2	79,383
1940	496,874	1,939,026	25.6	78,159
1941	562,383	2,365,688	23.8	79,282
1942	683,366	2,796,765	24.4	63,467
1943	480,644	3,471,508	13.8	71,285
1944	647,981	4,196,115	15.4	96,237
1945	748,351	4,268,619	17.5	95,678
1946	1,870	2,609,691	0.1	—
1947	348,895	2,590,655	13.5	105,293

	Gross profit £	Capital employed £	Return on capital employed %	Net profit or (loss) £
1948	374,367	3,314,737	11.3	143,388
1949	320,672	3,575,372	9.0	178,818
1950	550,996	4,290,841	12.8	262,581
1951	1,227,601	5,781,679	21.2	507,930
1952	1,320,164	8,221,590	16.1	376,303
1953	1,284,033	9,423,585	13.6	362,170
1954[5]	1,446,649	9,107,835	15.9	531,955
1955[6]	1,193,364	11,012,429	10.8	720,038
1956[7]	1,311,223	14,857,770	8.8	626,366
1957	1,495,322	14,731,649	3.4	72,822
1958	1,252,971	14,087,722	8.9	575,971
1959	2,419,865	14,693,167	16.5	1,104,572
1960	4,014,890	14,123,074	28.4	2,123,390
1961	3,401,023	16,021,105	21.2	1,661,023
1962	2,170,517	20,658,318	10.5	913,017
1963	1,670,698	23,998,043	7.0	778,772
1964	1,824,151	24,666,412	7.4	980,665
1965	2,750,906	24,457,105	11.2	1,123,524
1966	2,848,275	24,983,595	11.4	1,702,372
1967	3,257,610	27,987,759	11.6	2,268,969
1968	1,530,840	30,461,757	5.0	1,184,000
1969	1,475,535	31,270,423	4.7	982,000
1970	1,591,498	33,258,710	4.7	935,000
1971	(826,590)	33,816,411	(2.4)	(348,000)
1972	1,188,483	32,626,098	3.6	915,000
1973	2,710,675	33,348,777	8.1	1,810,000
1974	53,880	42,871,749	0.1	373,000
1975	(488,006)	49,716,438	(1.0)	11,000

Key: NA indicates that the information is not available.

1. For the six months ending in December only.
2. For the calendar year hereafter.
3. For the six months to June only.
4. Year beginning in July to June.
5. For the nine months to March only.
6. Year beginning in April to March.
7. The figures from this year are for the consolidated Ferranti group, including overseas subsidiaries.

Table 3. *Turnover and employment at Ferranti, 1890–1993*

	Turnover £ million	Labour force (at 31 March)
1890	0.09	NA
1891	0.03	NA
1892	0.04	NA
1893	0.04	NA
1894	0.05	NA
1895	0.06	NA
1896	0.10	NA
1897	NA	NA
1898	NA	NA
1899	NA	NA
1900	NA	NA
1901	NA	NA
1902	NA	NA
1903	NA	NA
1904	NA	NA
1905	NA	556
1906	NA	653
1907	0.13	762
1908	0.13	656
1909	0.14	797
1910	0.16	869
1911	0.23	1168
1912	0.26	1584
1913	0.29	1752
1914	0.27	1432
1915	0.22	1216
1916	0.30	1880
1917	0.26	2555
1918	0.21	2994
1919	0.46	2014
1920	0.80	1872
1921	0.67	2190
1922	0.49	1783
1923	0.57	2056
1924	0.83	2340
1925	0.92	2492
1926	0.99	3321

	Turnover £ million	Labour force (at 31 March)
1927	1.11	3728
1928	NA	4009
1929	1.21	4200
1930	1.11	4773
1931	1.19	4322
1932	1.16	4666
1933	1.20	3672
1934	1.10	3823
1935	1.37	5394
1936	1.46	5160
1937	1.51	6170
1938	1.89	NA
1939	1.64	5703
1940	2.57	NA
1941	4.10	NA
1942	4.97	NA
1943	4.84	NA
1944	4.98	NA
1945	5.69	NA
1946	3.54	NA
1947	4.47	NA
1948	4.44	NA
1949	4.23	NA
1950	5.04	6926
1951	6.81	8468
1952	9.28	10677
1953	11.12	9390
1954	10.34	10560
1955	13.80	11642
1956	17.66	12943
1957	18.66	12390
1958	18.50	12277
1959	21.44	12681
1960	25.24	13649
1961	27.81	15917
1962	31.17	18809
1963	35.31	20849
1964	35.24	18865
1965	40.9	19272

	Turnover £ million	Labour force (at 31 March)
1966	46.2	19097
1967	47.2	19565
1968	50.1	19261
1969	51.6	17720
1970	54.7	17859
1971	57.2	16559
1972	63.7	16042
1973	65.1	16453
1974	70.2	16688
1975	86.3	16079

Key: NA indicates that the information is not available.

APPENDIX D

Chairmen and Directors of Ferranti Ltd, 1905–75

Chairmen:

A. W. Tait	(1905–28)
Dr S. Z. de Ferranti	(1928–30)
Sir Vincent de Ferranti	(1930–63) *
S. Z. de Ferranti	(1963–82) *
B. Z. de Ferranti	(1982–87) †

Directors:

A. W. Tait	(1905–30)
A. Whittaker	(1905–33) †
J. M. Henderson	(1905–22)
A. B. Anderson	(1908–14) *
R. W. Cooper	(1913–63)
O. Winder	(1916–17)
P. D. Thomas	(1917–29)
Sir Vincent de Ferranti	(1924–63)
H. W. Kolle	(1930–43)
D. Z. de Ferranti	(1933–51)
R. H. Schofield	(1934–35)
J. W. Davies	(1942–57)
W. Tyldesley	(1942–43)
W. A. G. Bass	(1943–60)
C. W. Bridgen	(1943–46)
W. C. Pycroft	(1943–58)
A. B. Cooper	(1947–54)
S. Z. de Ferranti	(1954–82) *
B. Z. de Ferranti	(1957–87) †
Sir Frank Rostron	(1958–68)
J. H. Thomson	(1958–71)

594

Sir John Toothill	(1958–75)
E. Grundy	(1959–71)
O. M. Robson	(1959–68)
J. Prince	(1959–68)
R. M. Hobill	(1961–69)
Dr N. H. Searby	(1962–75)
F. W. Hardstone	(1963–73)
T. Edmondson	(1963–76)
A. J. Gray	(1968–76)
Sir Richard H. Davies	(1968–76)
Sir Donald M. McCallum	(1970–87)
J. R. Pickin	(1970–87)
J. J. Ratcliffe	(1970–83)
P. F. Dorey	(1973–88)
G. Boyd	(1975–89)
H. W. Broad	(1975–86)
Sir Derek Alun-Jones	(1975–89) *

Key:

* indicates that this person was also a managing director at some stage in their career with Ferranti.

† indicates that at some stage this person was also deputy chairman of Ferranti

APPENDIX E

Family holdings of shares in Ferranti Ltd., 1923-1982

Year to July/March	Total Ordinary's Issued (No.)	Total Voting Stock [a]	Dr SZF	VZF	VZF Trusts	DZF
1923	60,000	206,166	48,000	12,000	–	–
1929	100,000	246,166	80,000	20,000	–	–
1930	600,000	1,100,000	–	306,000	180,000	–
1945	600,000	1,100,000	–	231,000	77,000	154,000
1950	1,000,000	1,500,000	–	231,000	79,999	170,666
1953	2,000,000	2,400,000	–	116,898	187,498	384,999
1959	4,000,000	4,500,000	–	3,495	–	769,983
1963	4,000,000	4,500,000	–	4,812	–	1,036,644
1968	4,000,000	4,500,000	–	–	—	826,654
1974	4,000,000	4,500,000	–	–	–	–
1975	8,000,000	8,000,000	–	–	–	–
1979	21,333,332	21,333,332	–	–	–	–
1980	21,333,332	21,333,332	–	–	–	–
1981	46,000,000	46,000,000	–	–	–	–
1982	58,000,000	58,000,000	–	–	–	–

a) First preference shares also held voting rights until 1973.
b) This was a trust set up with VZF's shares.
c) Without DZF hereafter. (DZF is Dennis de Ferranti, the youngest son of Dr Ferranti)
d) Both SZF and BZF placed their holdings with Control Nominees Ltd.

APPENDICES 597

SZF	SZF Trusts	BZF	BZF Trusts	Charter Consolidated	N.E.B.	N.P.B. Ltd & W.C.Pycroft [b]	Votes (% held by Family)
–	–	–	–	–	–	–	29.1
–	–	–	–	–	–	–	40.6
–	–	–	–	–	–	114,000	54.5
–	–	–	–	–	–	114,000	51.3
–	–	–	–	–	–	163,333	60.9
307,070	–	307,070	–	–	–	349,999	50.7 [c]
763,254	350,000	763,254	250,000	–	–	699,999	62.9
770,562	362,980	660,187	259,250	–	–	873,732	65.1
749,703	374,183	748,489	373,469	500,000	–	369,583	58.1
719,037	405,330	717,342	404,135	508,400	–	–	56.1
1,000 [d]	406,280	1,000 [d]	409,585	508,400	6,666,666	–	N.A.
1,077,965	940,560	1,364,378	947,159	1,666,665	10,666,666	–	20.3
929,965	940,746	1,156,378	897,159	–	10,666,666	–	18.4
1,611,242	1,411,430	1,609,506	1,518,688	–	426,666	–	13.4
1,682,000	2,146,000	1,580,244	1,478,088	–	–	–	11.8

APPENDIX F

The Ferranti Product Range, 1882–1975

The years mentioned in parentheses indicate roughly over what time period a particular product was made by Ferranti.

Alternators (1882–1904)
Arc Lamps (1882–83)
Avionics:
    Accelerometers (1948–90)
    Airborne Radar Systems (1945–90)
    Artificial Horizons (1953–93)
    Battery Chargers (1955–90)
    Onboard Computer Systems (1951–90)
    Gyrogunsights (1943–58)
    Gyrostabilisation Systems (1913–14 and 1943–90)
    Head-up Displays (1968–90)
    Inertial Navigation Systems (1955–90)
    Moving Map Displays (1970–90)
    Predictors (1950–93)
    Sighting Systems (1956–90)
    Turn and Slip Indicators (1950–70)
Bulbs, Incandescent (1883–84)
Cable, High Tension (1889–91)
Camera Controls (1939–48)
Capacitors (1950–65)
Cathode Ray Tubes (1935–87):
    Plasma Displays (1969–87)
    Specialised Tubes (1950–87)
    Standard Tubes (1935–60)
Cold Cathode Tubes (1945–54)

Computers:
- Command, Communications and Control Systems (1956–91)
- Computer Graphics Systems (1968–93)
- Digital Systems (1955–93)
- Display Systems (1958–87)
- Hospital Care Systems (1970–90)
- Mainframe Computers (1949–63)
- Naval and Air Defence Systems (1956–90)
- Police and Fire Service Systems (1970–90)
- Power Station and Electricity Distribution Control Systems (1965–90)
- Printing Systems (1975–93)
- Process Control Computers (1959–93)
- Simulation Platforms (1958–93)
- Sonar Control Systems (1955–93)
- Tape Recorders (1950–63)

Domestic Appliances:
- Clocks (1932–57)
- Cookers (1910–14)
- Fires (1910–14 and 1927–59)
- Fridge-heaters (1954–60)
- Immersion Heaters (1929–59)
- Industrial Heaters (1950–60)
- Irons (1910-14)
- Water Heaters (1928–59)

Electroencephalogarph System (1955–56)

Fire Control Systems (1948–90)

Foundry Castings (1897–1980)
- Malleable cast iron (1896–1980)
- Mouldings, High Precision (1960–75)

Fuzes, Explosive (1915–18 and 1936–90)

Gramophones (1930–36)

Guided Weapons (1949–65)
- *Bloodhound* system (1949–65)

>   Launch Control Post (1949–65)
>
>   Radar Systems, Ground-based (1949–65)
>
>   Spares and Maintenance (1949–90)

Gyroscopic Stabilisation Systems (1943–90)

Instruments:

>   Ammeters (1905–14)
>
>   Testing Equipment (1905–14)
>
>   Viscometers (1955–90)

Lasers:

>   Cutting Equipment (1962–90)
>
>   Marked Target and Seeking Equipment (1968–90)
>
>   Navigation Systems (1973–90)

Magslips (1938–90)

Meters:

>   AC Meter (1885–1975)
>
>   DC Meter (1885–1935)
>
>   Metering Equipment (1930–39)
>
>   Prepaying Equipment (1930–70)
>
>   Station Meter (1885–1975)

Microwave Links (1965–87)

Nail Catchers (1925–28)

Navigation Systems (1968–75)

Numerical Control:

>   Inspection Systems (1959–90)
>
>   Measurement Systems (1961–90)
>
>   Machine Tool Control Systems (1956–69)

Pirn Winders (1946–49)

Radio (1929–57)

Radio Components (1924–57)

Semiconductors:

>   Diodes (1955–87)
>
>   Integrated Circuits (1961–87)
>
>   Microprocessors (1973–90)

        Opto-Electronic Devices (1961–87)
        Transistors (1957–87)
Shells (1915–18 and 1939–45)
Steam-Alternator (1889–1905)
Steam Engines (1895–1905)
Switchgear (1886–1915)
Tapchangers (1955–85)
Television (1936–57)
Textile Machinery (1901–05)
Transformers:
        Audio-Frequency Transformer (1923–37)
        Distribution Transformer (1920–69)
        Instrument Transformers (1912–90)
        Insulation (1885–1980)
        Power Transformer (1929–79)
        Rectifier (1894–1914)
        Speech Transformers (1885–86)
        Surge Absorbers (1926–39)
Travelling Platforms, Bofors (1940–45)
Turbines (1901–05)
Valves, Steam Pressure (1903–05)
Valves, Thermionic Emission (1929–56)

Bibliography

Abbreviations

FA   Ferranti Archives
IEE   Institution of Electrical Engineers

Primary Sources

The Ferranti Archives

Over the course of the last twenty years, this rich set of family and corporate records has both expanded considerably and moved regularly. Today, it is housed in the archives section of the Manchester Museum of Science and Industry, Castlefield, Manchester, where the records are professionally indexed and secured. It was not always thus, because from the early–1960s they were cared for by a senior employee, Arthur Ridding, who was instructed by Sir Vincent de Ferranti to bring all the records together for the first time. Ridding performed an impressive job, indexing what must have been one of the largest set of company records in the country. He was succeeded by Charles Somers, who continued Ridding's work with a most able assistant, Edith Walsh. They, in turn, were succeeded by Cliff Wimpenny, undoubtedly the most able Ferranti Archivist. Cliff Wimpenny contributed enormously to the development of a truly company-wide archive, extending Ridding's interests from Hollinwood and Chadderton to Edinburgh, Bracknell and the increasing number of overseas subsidiaries. By the time the company's crisis in 1989 had brought an end to the archives department, the collection had expanded substantially in size and breadth. Indeed, a new premises at Moston was acquired for the archive, after spending several unhappy years in the former transformer department drawing office. I am confident that at the Manchester Museum of Science and Industry the archive will become a major source of information for historians of every ilk.

The principal sets of records are:
Family Papers: correspondence, diaries and scrapbooks.
Technical Notebooks: including over thirty bound volumes of the work of Dr. Ferranti.

Corporate records

Minute books
Correspondence
Patents
Account books
Agreements
Annual Reports
Photographs
Films
Ferranti News

Personal recollections and notes

Addenbrook, G. L. (1930), 'Ferranti and my connections with him', FA.
Alun-Jones, D. (1982), 'My business experience at Burmah Oil and Ferranti', paper presented to the Business History Unit, LSE.
Beardsall, C. P. (1946), 'The Ferranti War Record, 1939–1945', privately printed, FA.
Hall, A. R. (1932), 'The mechanical experiments of S. Z. de Ferranti'.
IEE Commemorative Proceedings (1922) [A collection of speeches given by a host of British electrical pioneers at a dinner to celebrate the industry's evolution since 1872.]
King, A. D. (1985), 'Ferranti gyro technology. A historical view', privately produced by Ferranti plc, FA.
McCallum, D. N. (1987), 'Forty years with Ferranti', mimeo, FA.
Negri, A. (1903), *The Ziani de Ferranti Family*.
Prophet, A. E. (1950), 'The FM meter', *Ferranti Journal*, Feb., FA.
Schofield, A. (1951) 'Ferranti Canada, 1911–1951'.
Swann, B. B. (1974), 'The Ferranti computer department'.
Taylor, M. K. (1972), 'An industrial biography', FA.

Secondary sources

(Where just the name of a town is given, this indicates a university press. Otherwise, publishers' names are given for reference, and the place of publication is London unless another town's name is provided.)

Abelson, P. H. & A. L. Hammond, (1980), 'The electronics revolution', in T. Forester (ed.), *The Microelectronics Revolution. The Complete Guide to the New Technology and Its Impact on Society*, Basil Blackwell.
Adams, A. R. (1976), *Good Company*, BAC.
Aldcroft, D. H. (1964), 'The entrepreneur and the British economy, 1870–1914', *Economic History Review*, XCII.
Appleyard, R. (1939), *The History of the IEE, 1871–1931*, IEE.

Aris, S. (1998), *Arnold Weinstock and the Making of GEC*, Aurum.
Bailey, F. (1932), *The Life and Work of S. Z. de Ferranti*, Electrical Power Engineers' Association.
Ball, N. R. & J. N. Vardalas (1994), *Ferranti-Packard. Pioneers in Canadian Electrical Manufacturing*, McGill-Queen's University Press.
Ballin, H. (1946), *The Organisation of Electricity Supply in Great Britain*, Electrical Press.
BEAMA [British Electrical & Allied Manufacturers' Association] (1928), *The Electrical Industry of Great Britain*, BEAMA.
Bird, P. J. (1994), *LEO: the first business computer*, Masler.
Black, R. M. (1972), *Electric Cables in Victorian Times*, Science Museum.
Bone, A. J. (1954), *The Guitar and the Mandolin*, Pitman.
Boyce, G. H. (1995), *Information, Mediation and Institutional Development. The Rise of Large-Scale Enterprise in British Shipping, 1870–1919*, Manchester.
Braun, E. (1980), 'From transistor to microprocessor', in T. Forester (ed.), *The Microelectronics Revolution. The Complete Guide to the New Technology and Its Impact on Society*, Basil Blackwell.
Brummer, A. & R. Cowe (1998), *Weinstock. The Life and Times of Britain's Premier Industrialist*, HarperCollins.
Buckley, P. J. & M. Casson (1989), 'Multinational enterprises in less-developed countries: cultural and economic interactions', University of Reading Discussion Papers in International Investment and Business Studies, Series B, No. 126.
Buderi, R. (1996), *The Invention that Changed the World. The Story of Radar from War to Peace*, Little, Brown & Co.
Burns, T. & G. M. Stalker (1961), *The Management of Innovation*, Tavistock.
Byatt, I. C. R. (1962), 'The British Electrical Industry, 1875–1914', Oxford D. Phil.
Byatt, I. C. R. (1979), *The British Electrical Industry, 1875–1914*, Oxford.
Cairncross, A. K. & J. Hunter (1987), 'The early growth of Messrs. J & P Coats, 1830–83', *Business History*, Vol. 29, No. 2.
Caminer, D., J. Aris, P. Hermon & F. Land (1996), *User-Driven Innovation: The World's First Business Computer*, McGraw-Hill.
Campbell-Kelly, M. (1985), 'Christopher Strachey, 1916–1975. A biographical note', *IEEE Annals of the History of Computing*, 7, No. 1.
Campbell-Kelly, M. (1989), *ICL. A Business and Technical History*, Oxford.
Campbell-Kelly, M. & W. Asprey (1996), *Computer. A History of the Information Machine*, BasicBooks.
Casson, M. (1991), *The Economics of Business Culture: Game Theory, Transactions Costs and Economic Performance*, Oxford.
Catterall, R. E. (1979), 'Electrical engineering', in N. K. Buxton & D. H. Aldcroft (eds), *British Industry between the Wars*, Scolar Press.
Chandler, A. D. (1990), *Scale and Scope. The Dynamics of Industrial Capitalism*, Harvard.
Clapham, J. (1951), *An Economic History of Modern Britain*, III, Cambridge,
Clark, R. (1977), *Edison, the Man who Made the Future*, Chapman Hall.

Clothier, H. W., (1933), *Switchgear Stages*, Newcastle.
Coase, R. H. (1958), *British Broadcasting: a study in monopoly*, Macmillan.
Collins, M. (1991), *Banks and Industrial Finance, 1800–1939*, Macmillan.
Corley, T. A. B. (1966), *Domestic Electrical Appliances*, Macmillan.
Cotrell, P. (1980), *Industrial Finance, 1830–1914*, Methuen.
Cox, C. J. & C. Cooper (1988), *High Flyers. An Anatomy of Managerial Success*, Basil Blackwell.
Crompton, R. E. (1928), *Reminiscences*, Pitman,
Davenport-Hines, R. P. T. (1984), *Dudley Docker, The Life and Times of a Trade Warrior*, Cambridge.
Davenport-Hines, R. P. T. (1986), 'A. W. Tait', in Jeremy, D. (ed.), *Dictionary of Business Biography*, Vol. 5, Butterworths.
de Ferranti, G. Z. & Ince, R. (1934), *The Life and Letters of S. Z. de Ferranti*, Williams & Norgate.
Dickinson, H. W. (1903), *A Short History of the Steam Engine*, Ernest Benn.
Divine, R. (1966), *Broken Wing*, Batsford.
Drury, J (1962) 'Inertial navigation', *Journal of the IEE*, July.
Drury, T. (1982), 'Finance Houses – Leasing', *Journal of the Institute of Bankers*, 103, Pt. 1.
Dunning, J. (1993), *The Globalisation of Business*, Routledge.
Eckersley, P. P. (1962), 'The achievment and failure of John Logie Baird', *Journal of IEE*, April.
Electricity Council (1982), *Electricity Supply in the United Kingdom. A Chronology.*
Electricity Council (1984), *Handbook of Electricity Supply Statistics.*
Evans, C. (1979), *The Mighty Micro. The Impact of the Computer Revolution*, Victor Gollancz.
Everard, S. (1949), *History of the Gas, Light & Coke Co.*, privately printed.
Farnie, D. A. (1979), *The English Cotton Industry and the World Market, 1815–1896*, Clarendon Press.
Finer, H. (1941), *Municipal Trading. A Study in Public Administration*, George Allen & Unwin.
Fleming, J. A. (1930), *Fifty Years of Electricity*, Allen & Unwin.
Flower, J. F. (1966), 'The case of the profitable *Bloodhound*', *Journal of Accounting Research*, Vol. 4, No. 1, Spring, pp. 16–34.
Foreman-Peck, J. & Millward, R. (1994), *Public and Private Ownership of British Industry, 1820–1990*, Oxford.
Freeman, C. (1965), 'Research and development in electronic capital goods', *National Institute Economic Review*, 34, Nov.
Freeman, C. (1982), *The Economics of Industrial Innovation*, Frances Pinter.
Gardner, C. (1981), *British Aircraft Corporation. A History*, Book Club Associates.
Golding, A. M. (1971), 'The semiconductor industry in Britain and the United States: a case study in innovation, growth and the diffusion of technology', unpublished D. Phil, Sussex.
Goold, M. & A. Campbell (1987), *Strategies and Styles. The Role of the Centre in Managing Diversified Corporations*, Oxford: Blackwell.

Graham, A. (1972), 'Industrial policy', in W. Beckerman (ed.), *The Labour Government's Economic Record: 1964–1970*, Duckworth.
Gregory, T. E. (1936), *The Westminster Bank Through a Century*, Vol. II, Westminster Bank Ltd.
Hamilton, R. (1995), 'Despite Best Intentions: The Evolution of the British Minicomputer Industry', *Business History*, Vol. 38, No. 2, pp. 81–104.
Hamilton, R. (1997), 'Continuous Path: The Evolution of Process Control Technologies in Post-War Britain', PhD Thesis, unpublished, University of Warwick.
Hamilton, R. (1999), 'Early British machine tool automation: the road to numerical control', *Journal of Industrial History*, Vol. 2, No. 1.
Hannah, L. (1977), 'The CEB and the national grid', in B. Supple (ed.), *Essays in British Business History*, Oxford.
Hannah, L. (1979), *Electricity before Nationalisation*, Macmillan.
Hannah, L. (1982), *Engineers, Managers and Politicians. The First Fifteen Years of Nationalised Electricity Supply in Britain*, Macmillan
Hannah, L. (1983), *The Rise of the Corporate Economy*, Methuen
Harris, R. E. (1933), 'A re-analysis of the 1928 new issue boom', *Economic Journal*, 4.
Harrop, J. (1966), 'New growth industries in an era of stagnation and depression, 1919–39', Liverpool MA.
Hastings, S. (1966), *The Murder of TSR–2*, Butsford.
Hayward, K. (1989), *The British Aircraft Industry*, Manchester.
Healey, D. (1989), *The Time of My Life*, Penguin.
Heath, E. (1998), *The Course of My Life. My Autobiography*, Hodder & Stoughton.
Hempstead, C. A. (1977), 'Semiconductors 1833–1919. An Historical Study of Selenium and some Related Materials', Unpublished Ph.D., Durham.
Hendry, J. (1989), *Innovating for Failure. Government Policy and the Early British Computer Industry*, Massachussets Institute of Technology Press.
Hope, R. (1949), 'Profits in British industry, 1924–1935', *Oxford Economic Papers*.
Hughes, T. P. (1962), 'The British electrical industry lag, 1882–1888', *Technology and Culture*.
Hughes, T. P. (1963), 'The bold conception of S. Z. de Ferranti', *Consulting Engineer*
Hughes, T. P. (1971), *Elmer Sperry, Inventor and Engineer*, Baltimore Press.
Hughes, T P (1983), *Networks of Power*, Baltimore Press.
Hunter, P. V. & J. T. Hazell (1956), *The Development of Power Cables*, Science Museum.
Imperial Economic Committee (1936), *Survey of Trade in Electrical Machinery*, HMSO.
Irving, R. J. (1975), 'New industries for old? Some investment decisions of Sir W. G. Armstrong, Whitworth & Co., Ltd, 1900–1914', *Business History*, Vol. 17.
Jeremy, D. J. (1990), *Capitalists and Christians: Business Leaders and the Churches in Britain, 1900–1960*, Oxford.
Jolly, W. P. (1972), *Marconi*, Constable.
Jones, G. (1986), 'Origins, management and performance', in G. Jones (ed.), *British Multinationals: Origins, Management and Performance*, Gower.

Jones, R. V. (1978), *Most Secret War*, Coward, McCann & Geoghegan.
Jones, R. & O. Marriott (1972), *Anatomy of a Merger*, Pan.
Kennedy, W. P. (1987), *Industrial Structure, Capital Markets and the Origins of British Economic Decline*, Cambridge.
King, J. (1985), 'The Ferranti gyroscopic platform', Ferranti Electronic Systems.
Landes, D. S. (1977), *The Unbound Prometheus*, Cambridge.
Langlois, R. N., T. A. Pugel, C. S. Haklisch, R. R. Nelson & W. G. Egelhoff, (1988), *Microelectronics. An Industry in Transition*, Unwin Hyman.
Langrish, J., M. Gibbons, W. G. Evans, & J. R. Jevons (1972), *Wealth from Knowledge*, Macmillan.
Lavington, S. (1975), *A History of Manchester Computers*, National Computing Centre Publications.
Lavington, S. (1980), *Early British Computers. The Story of Vintage Computers and the People Who Built Them*, Manchester.
Layton, J. (1972), *Ten Innovations*, Macmillan.
Lingren, M. (1990), *Glory and Failure: the Difference Engines of Johann Mulles, Charles Babbage and Georg and Edvard Schentz*, MIT Press.
Littler, C. (1982), *The Development of the Labour Process in Capitalist Societies*, Heinemann.
Lovering, J. (1995), 'Opportunity or crisis? The remaking of the British arms industry', in R. Turner (ed.), *The British Economy in Transition*, Routledge.
McCalman, J. (1988), *The Electronics Industry in Britain: Coping with Change*, Routledge.
Mackechnie-Jarvis, C. (1966), 'Some Victorian electricians', *Consulting Engineer*.
Maclaurin, W. R. (1971), *Invention and Innovation in the Radio Industry*, Macmillan.
Marrison, A. (1996), *British Business and Protection, 1903–1932*, Oxford.
Melling, J. (1980), 'NCO's', *Social History*, Vol. 6.
Mercer, H. (1995), *Constructing a Competitive Order*, Cambridge.
MRPC [Monopolies & Restrictive Practices Court] (1957), *Report on the Supply and Export of Electrical and Allied Machinery and Plant*, HMSO.
Morgan, K. (1991), *The People's Peace*, Oxford.
Morris, P. R. (1995), *A History of the World Semiconductor Industry*, Peter Peregrinus.
Musson, A. E. (1959), 'The Great Depression in Britain, 1873–1896: a reappraisal', *Journal of Economic History*, XIX.
Nicholas, S. J. (1983), 'Agency contracts, institutional modes, and the transition to foreign direct investment by British manufacturing multinationals before 1939', *Journal of Economic History*, 43.
Nicholas, S. J. (1984), 'The overseas marketing performance of British industry, 1870–1914', *Economic History Review*, XXXVII.
Nicholas, S. J. (1989), 'Locational choice, performance and the growth of British multinational firms', *Business History*, 31 (3), July.
Oldham, W. G. (1980), 'The fabrication of microelectronic circuits', in T. Forester (ed.), *The Microelectronics Revolution. The Complete Guide to the New Technology and Its Impact on Society*, Basil Blackwell.

Owen, G. (forthcoming), *Modernisation Delayed*.
Parsons, R. H. (1939), *Early days of the Power Station Industry*, Cambridge.
Passer, H. (1953), *The Electrical Manufacturers*, Cambridge, Mass.
Payne, P. L. (1967), 'The emergence of the large-scale company in Britain, 1870–1914', *Economic History Review*, XX.
Plummer, A. (1937), *New British Industries in the Twentieth Century*, Pitman.
Pocock, R. F. (1988), *The Early British Radio Industry*, Manchester.
Pollard, S. (1982), *The Wasting of the British Economy*, Longman.
Pollard, S. (1992), *The Development of the British Economy, 1914–1967*, Edward Arnold.
Ponting, K. G. (1973), 'The textile experiments of S. Z. de Ferranti', *Textile History*, 4.
Postan, M. M., D. Hay. & J. D. Scott (1964), *Design and development of Weapons: Studies in Government and Industrial Organisation*, HMSO.
Postan, M. M. (1975), *British War Production*, HMSO.
Reader, W. J. (1979), *A House in the City. A History of Foster & Braithwaite*, Macmillan.
Reid, M. (1982), *The Secondary Banking Crisis*, Cambridge.
Richardson, G. B. (1968), *The Future of the Heavy Electrical Plant Industry*, BEAMA.
Roberts, R. (1984), 'The administrative origins of industrial diplomacy: an aspect of government-industry relations', in J. Turner (ed.), *Businessmen and Politics. Studies of Business Activity in British Politics, 1900–1945*, Heinemann.
Sanderson, M. (1972), 'Research and the firm in British industry, 1919–39', *Science Studies*, 2.
Saul, S. B. (1970), 'Introduction', in S. B. Saul (ed.), *Technological Change: the United States and Britain in the Nineteenth Century*, Methuen.
Sawyer, M. (1991), 'Industrial policy', in M. Artis & D. Cobham (eds), *Labour's Economic Policies, 1974–1979*, Manchester.
Schein, E. H. (1985), *Organisational Culture and Leadership*, Tavistock.
Scholey, R. (1897), 'S. Z. de Ferranti', *Cassiers' Magazine*, Oct.
Schumpeter, J. A. (1939), *Business Cycles*, I, Oxford.
Sciberras, E. (1980), 'The UK semiconductor industry', in K. Pavitt (ed.), *Technical Innovation and British Economic Performance*, Macmillan.
Scott, J. D. (1962), *Vickers: a history*, Weidenfield & Nicolson.
Seward, S. F. (1961), 'British electrical manufacture in the national economy', paper given to the British Electrical Power Convention, FA.
Snow, C. P. (1961), *Science and Government*, Harvard.
Somers, C. (1975), 'Ferranti's proposed hydro-electric scheme at Laufenberg', *IEE History Weekend*.
Stopford, J. (1974), 'The origins of British-based multinational manufacturing enterprises', *Business History Review*, XLVIII.
Stopford, J. & L. Turner (1985), *Britain and the Multinationals*, John Wiley & Sons.
Strange, P. (1977), 'S. Z. de Ferranti and C. N. Wordingham', IEE History Weekend.
Sturmey, S. G. (1958), *The Economic Development of Radio*, Duckworth.
Surtees, V. (1993), *Coutts Lindsay, 1824–1913*, Michael Russell.
Taylor, G. D. (1994), 'Negotiating technology transfer within multinational enterprises: perspectives from Canadian history', *Business History*, 36 (1), January.

Thompson, J. L. (1993), *Strategic Management. Awareness and Change*, Chapman & Hall.
Thompson, S. P. (1910), *The Life of William Thomson*, Ernest Benn.
Trebilcock, C. (1977), *The Vickers Brothers: Armaments and Enterprise, 1875–1914*, Macmillan.
Turner, G. (1969), *Business in Britain*, Eyre & Spottiswoode.
Tweedale, G. (1990), *Calculating Machines and Computers*, Shire Publications.
Tweedale, G. (1992), 'Marketing in the Second Industrial Revolution: a case study of the Ferranti computer group, 1949–63', *Business History*, 34, No. 1.
Wardley, P. (1991), 'The anatomy of big business: aspects of corporate development in the twentieth century', *Business History*, Vol. 33, No. 2.
Watson-Watt, R. (1957), *Three Steps to Victory*, Odhams.
Whyte, A. G. (1930), *Forty Years of Electrical Progress. The Story of the GEC*, Ernest Benn.
Wiener, M. (1981), *English Culture and the Decline of the Industrial Spirit, 1850–1980*, Cambridge.
Wigham, E. (1972), *The Power to Manage*, Macmillan.
Williams, M. R. (1994), 'UTEC and FERUT: the University of Tornoto's computation centre', *IEEE Annals of the History of Computing*, 16, No. 2.
Wilson, D. A. (1976), 'The strategy of sales expansion in the British electricity supply industry between the wars', in L. Hannah (ed.), *Management Strategy and Business Development*, Methuen.
Wilson, H. (1971), *The Labour Government 1964–1970. A Personal Record*, Little, Brown & Co.
Wilson, J. F. (1985), 'A strategy of expansion and consolidation: Dick, Kerr & Co, 1897–1914', *Business History*, 27.
Wilson, J. F. (1988), *Ferranti and the British Electrical Industry, 1864–1930*, Manchester.
Wilson, J. F. (1991), *Lighting the Town: A Study of Management in the North West Gas Industry, 1805–1880*, Paul Chapman.
Wilson, J. F. (1995), *British Business History, 1720–1994*, Manchester.
Wilson, J. F. (1996), 'de Ferranti, Basil Reginald', *Dictionary of National Biography 1976–92*, Oxford.
Wilson, T. (1958), 'The electronics industry', in D. Burn (ed.), *The Structure of British Industry*, Cambridge.
Zeitlin, J. (1983), 'The labour strategies of British engineering employers, 1890–1922', in H. F. Gospel & C. Littler (eds), *Managerial Strategies and Industrial Relations*, Heinemann.
Zeitlin, J. (2000), *Between Flexibility and Mass Production. A Study of the British Engineering Industry*, Cambridge.

Index

Addenbrook, G. L., 68–9, 72, 85, 217, 584
Admiralty Signals & Weapons Establishment (ASWE), 385–6, 486
AEG, 97, 106, 134, 169
AEI –204, 222, 352, 362, 390, 502, 508, 509
Aircraft Equipment dept., 321–2, 328, 330, 331, 332, 334, 386, 458, 516
aircraft industry, 158–60, 276, 279–80, 400–1, 421, 473, 474–6, 477, 482, 483–4, 515
airpass radar (AI23), 326–9, 332, 336, 472–3
Alun-Jones, Sir Derek, 531, 533, 599, 600
Amalgamated Society of Engineers (ASE), 17, 117–8
Anderson, A. B., 6, 7, 120, 121 127, 129–30, 131, 132, 133, 134, 139, 140, 144, 166–9, 171, 173–5, 177, 179, 180–1, 194, 202, 221, 223, 230, 236, 247, 599
Argus, see 'process control computers'
Armstrong-Whitworth, 182, 268, 401, 417
Aron Meters, 294, 503, 558
artificial horizons, 320–1
Atherton, J. B., 103–4, 545
Automation Systems dept., 1, 399, 429 *passim*, 435–8, 458, 516
Avenue Works, Chadderton, 13, 298–9, 302–3, 305, 443, 499, 506–10, 512, 513, 525
avionics, 1, 9, 12, 13, 20, 281, 282, 318 *passim*, 322, 325, 332, 334, 427, 441, 449, 471 *passim*, 476, 480, 529, 530, 533

Babbage, Charles, 342–3
Babcock & Wilcox, 74, 84, 144, 243, 430, 436
Baird, J. L., 263–4
Barings Bank, 124
Barrow factory, 443, 463
Baslow Hall, 156, 213–4, 236–7
Bass, W. G., 269, 271, 280, 284, 402, 448, 599

Beardsall, C. P., 143, 145, 161
Bedaux, 257–8
Bell Telephone Labs, 416, 449–53, 454, 456, 458
Bendix Aviation Co., 337–8, 480, 572
Benn, Anthony Wedgwood, 465, 527–8
Benson, Lord Henry, 394, 418, 419, 421–2, 423, 425, 426
Best, Denis, 403–6, 407, 410, 412, 415, 429 *passim*, 434, 436–7, 458–9
Berry Electric Transformer Co., 190, 204, 209, 552
Blackett, Lord Peter, 346, 349, 364
Bletchley Park, 343, 344
Bloodhound guided weapon, 20, 317, 320, 403 *passim*, 438, 465, 477–8, 485–6, 487, 488, 489–91, 515–6
exports, 415, 416, 417, 423–4, 429
impact on company liquidity, 427–8, 429, 432, 438, 440, 471, 485, 489–91, 497, 529–30
Lang Inquiries, 420–1, 422 *passim*, 428–9, 477–8, 485–6, 489, 515
testing, 405–7, 416
Blue Parrot radar, 328–9, 332
Blue Study bombing system, 326, 329
Boulton, Matthew, 143, 145, 161
Bowden, Dr B. V., 274, 353, 363–4, 365–6, 397, 563
Bracknell factory, 11, 12, 306, 321, 360, 384 *passim*, 399, 430, 443, 485 *passim*, 489, 530
Bridgen, C. W., 284, 599
Brighton power station, 55, 70, 72, 106
Bristol Airplane Co., 399, 401–2, 404, 405–6, 407, 410–1, 415, 417, 421, 428, 429, 473
British Aircraft Co. (BAC), 421, 473, 474, 484
British Broadcasting Corporation (BBC), 179, 215–6, 220, 263–5, 311

British business:
  'personal capitalism', 2, 3, 4, 95, 101–2, 103, 106, 116, 121–2, 124, 140, 242, 245, 449
  'managerial capitalism', 2, 16, 140, 242, 291, 445
British Electrical & Allied Manufacturers' Association (BEAMA), 162, 163, 174–5, 177, 181, 204–5, 212, 230, 246, 248–50, 293, 500–1, 509–10
British Insulated Wire Co., 13, 103–4, 105, 119, 131, 145, 158
British Tabulating Machine Co. (BTM), 351, 370–2, 373, 393
British Thomson-Houston (BTH), 84, 110, 128, 132, 134, 138, 167, 190, 204, 209, 221, 559, 313, 408, 451
Brown, Ken, 330–1, 479
Brown, Boveri, 79, 92, 288
Bruce, Peebles & Co., 113, 137, 508, 510, 553
'Brush Bubble', 45–6, 47, 49, 50, 51, 54, 56, 59, 70, 71, 124
Brush Electrical Engineering Co., 36, 45, 46–7, 49, 50, 51, 55, 70, 105, 110, 111, 128, 138, 139, 165, 548

cable, high tension, 1, 13, 85–7, 103–4, 228, 229
Cairo Mill, Oldham, 386, 443
Calveley, Bruce, 512, 573
Carter, Jim, 348, 504–5
Cataract Construction Co., 96
cathode ray tubes, 13, 264–5, 277, 312–4, 318, 453, 455–7
cathode ray tubes, specialised, 318
Centimetric Revolution, 275–6, 403
Central Electricity Board (CEB), 163, 179, 208–12, 241, 246, 249, 250, 266, 298, 501
Central Electricity Generating Board (CEGB), 430, 431, 501, 502–3, 504, 506–7, 508, 509–10, 511
Chamberlain & Hookham, 167–8, 173–4
Chandler, A. D. C., 93, 95, 121, 122, 135, 265–6
Chilcot, A. L., 254, 277–8, 324, 335
Clothier, H. W., 110, 121, 172, 173, 231, 584

Coats, Ernest, 145, 148, 149, 153
cold cathode tubes, 277–8
computers, mainframe, 1, 12, 13, 18, 278, 306, 319, 335–6, 340, 341 *passim*, 351–2, 409, 439, 441, 461, 466, 484, 485, 491, 493, 506, 529, 530
  Atlas, 359, 368, 377–80, 382, 384, 388–9, 391, 397
  'baby', 344, 350
  conservative market, 363–5, 366–7, 370, 396–7
  FP6000, 394–6
  government funding, 341–2, 367, 368
  London Computing Centre, 355, 364–6, 369, 383, 385, 393
  Manchester University team, 344–8, 349–51, 375, 402
  Mark I, 350–3, 363, 364, 368, 371, 376
  Mark I*, 354–5, 356, 363, 364, 365, 368, 372
  Mercury, 354, 355, 356, 360, 368, 374, 375–7, 378, 388–9, 564
  merger talks, 372, 374, 381–2, 390–4, 395–6
  Orion, 368, 380, 383–4, 388–9, 391, 395, 397, 430
  Pegasus, 355–9, 360–1, 365, 368, 369, 373, 374, 375, 378, 384, 388–9, 395, 420, 429, 466, 485
  peripherals, 370–2
  Perseus, 368, 369–70, 374, 376, 382, 385, 389
  Pluto, 372–4, 376, 382
  Prinz, Dr D., 347, 561
  sales and marketing, 361–5, 369, 370, 372, 374, 275, 381–2, 392–3
  Sirius, 368, 380, 381, 382–3, 384, 388–9, 391, 395, 430
  transistors, use of, 373, 377, 379–80, 382–3, 385
  US developments, early, 343–4, 345–6, 347, 351, 397
  West Gorton, 360, 365, 373, 379, 382, 388–9, 391–4, 412
Concorde, 476, 477
consulting engineers, 116, 122, 126–7, 132
Cooper, A. B., 194–9, 222, 305–6, 307, 309, 599

Cooper, Major R. W., 176, 226, 242, 296–7, 448, 599
cotton industry, 115–6, 146–7, 149, 173, 212, 235
Crawford, Earl of, 64, 67–8, 69, 78, 83
Crewe Toll, Edinburgh, 11, 12, 278–81, 285, 287–8, 291, 306, 322 passim, 327–8, 331–2, 333–4, 335–8, 362, 427, 443, 471 passim, 477, 485, 489, 494, 516, 517–9, 521, 530
Crompton, R. E., 37, 46, 51, 55, 62, 70, 71, 81, 105, 111, 124, 128
Crown Works, Hollinwood, 5–6, 7, 10, 12, 18, 113–6, 118, 119, 120, 123, 130–1, 132, 133, 134, 137, 138–9, 140, 143, 171, 182, 184–5, 192–3, 202, 212, 219, 241, 273, 284, 294, 298, 443, 472, 489–90, 503–5, 506

Dalkeith factory, 443, 481–2, 483, 484, 492
Darbyshire, Dr J., 255, 262, 265, 278
Davies, J. W., 17, 234–5, 246, 284, 448, 599
Davies, Sir Richard H., 337, 452, 514, 519, 600
Davy, Sir Humphrey, 37
Day, Charles, 121, 132, 133
de Ferranti, Basil (1891–1917), 102, 156–7, 185–7, 200, 233, 236, 426
de Ferranti, Basil (1930–1987), 288–9, 297, 315, 394, 423, 426, 445, 491, 514, 525, 599
de Ferranti, Denis (1930–1999), 237, 243, 288, 292, 296–7, 316, 324, 339, 394, 574, 599
de Ferranti, Gertrude (nee Ince), 79, 100, 102, 115, 123, 156–7, 186, 212, 230, 232, 236–7, 244, 584
de Ferranti, Dr S. Z. (1864–1930), 1, 3–4, 6, 7, 15, 16, 599
  'All Electric' Ideal, 3, 34, 52, 57, 112–3, 156–7, 162–3, 189, 208–9, 212–5, 227 passim
  ancestry, influence of, 21–2, 26, 57, 230, 575–6
  artistic skills, 26, 31, 32, 35, 37
  birth (Havelock Buildings, Liverpool), 30–1
  death, 8, 227, 237, 241

delegation skills, 6, 7, 107–8, 120–1, 139, 140, 197, 235–6
diverse engineering interests, 228, 231–2
education, 5, 32–4, 36, 37–9, 40
electro-mechanical experiments, early, 32–4, 36–7, 40–1, 90
exile from Crown Works, 140–1, 225–6, 242
family finances, 3, 21, 39–40, 42, 57, 102–4, 123, 155–7, 164, 236–7
Faraday Lecture, 212, 230–1
Ferranti Research Scholarship, 231
founder's aims, 1, 3–4, 19, 20
freelance engineer, 143 passim, 156, 160–1
health problems, 31, 115, 214, 237
honours, 163–4, 230–1
individualism, 60, 103 106, 116, 117–8, 119, 130, 133, 135–6, 139, 140–1
IEE President, 162–3, 173–4, 230
intuitive thought process, 34–5, 54, 72, 93, 227, 231–2
'Manufacturing Engineer', desire to be, 3–4, 37–40, 43, 51, 57, 59
marriage and honeymoon, 79
mother, relationship with, 31–4, 37–40, 73
patents, 575–84
paternalist, 16–17, 18, 19, 117–8, 232–3
perpetual motion machine, 36, 213
persuasive skills, 4, 43, 46–7, 48–9, 69–70, 76, 93, 145–6, 152
power station work, 4, 59, 69, 84, 109–10
public speeches, 106, 112–3, 137, 143, 150, 159–60, 162–3, 189, 207, 208, 212–3, 228, 446
research assistant, Siemens, 41–2
self-taught, 5, 33–4, 39
'Senior Statesman', 161–2, 164, 227 passim
speed, love of, 157–8, 232
team-work, 72, 139–40, 144–5, 153, 184–5, 192, 220, 231–2
Technical Director, 7, 140–1, 192, 201, 231–2
university education, 37, 38–40
Venetian and Bolognan ancestry, 21–2, 23–5

de Ferranti, Sebastian (1928-), 1, 2, 10, 12, 13, 15, 16, 18, 19, 113, 133, 136, 199, 244, 288–9, 377, 391
  BEAMA President, 509–10
  chairman, 10, 12, 19, 393, 394, 418, 438, 439–41, 445–6, 485, 492, 497–9, 529, 599
  diversification, attitude to, 10–11, 12, 13, 15–16, 432, 437–8, 457, 459, 467, 470, 491–4, 514–5, 529
  engineering-led strategy, 1–3, 388, 421, 449–51, 467, 491, 523–4
  government contracts, attitude to, 399–400, 418–20, 421–2, 464–5, 480
  loyalty to workforce, 16–19, 392, 418, 423, 439, 510, 513, 514, 521
  management ethos, 20, 445–9, 490, 494–6, 497–9, 504–5, 508, 513, 514–7, 520–1, 523–4, 526, 527, 529–31, 533, 535
  managing director, 10, 379, 414, 418, 531, 534, 599
  shareholdings and dividends, 289, 297, 445–6, 491, 534
  training, 288–9, 418
  transformer experience, 288–9, 303–4, 510–1
de Ferranti, Sir Vincent (1893–1980), 1, 5, 8, 14, 15, 16, 17, 18, 19, 113, 133, 156–7, 177, 182–3, 194–5, 196–9, 199–202, 209, 225, 233, 241–2
  balancing civil and defence businesses, 13, 287–8, 316, 317, 318, 332, 334–5, 338–40, 341, 387–8, 391
  government contracts, attitude to, 269–71, 278, 287–8, 341–2, 349, 352–3, 356, 358–9, 399–400, 418, 421, 480
  Denis, relationship with, 243, 244, 296–7
  diversification, attitude to, 9–10, 12, 13, 15–16, 280–1, 304, 309–10, 331, 332, 410, 439–42, 451, 497
  dividend policy, 339, 491, 534
  external activities, 249, 293
  graphs, 9, 244–5, 270, 283, 291
  knighted, 286
  management style, 5, 8 *passim*, 12, 13, 20, 199, 224, 242 *passim*, 260, 270, 281, 283–6, 291–2, 306, 309, 316–7, 323, 533, 535
  managing director, 244, 599
  retirement, 414, 418, 439–41, 445
  transformer manager, 8, 199–200, 209–12, 242, 298
  wartime service, 19, 185–7, 200, 276–7, 286, 426
de Forest, Lee, 253
Del Rivo, George, 121, 132, 133
Department of Scientific and Industrial Research (DSIR), 192, 272, 351, 354
Department of Trade & Industry (DoTI), 466–7, 491, 525–6, 527, 528
Deptford, 4, 5, 59, 74, 76, 79, 81, 83, 84–5, 89–90, 91–2, 94, 96, 98, 99, 100, 101, 105, 108–9, 145, 163, 228, 229, 230, 243
  chisel test, 87
  'Ferranti Effect', 90
  steam-pipe explosion, 82–3
Dick, Kerr & Co., 128, 132, 134, 138, 165, 190, 204
Digital Equipment Corp (DEC), 436–7
Digital Systems department, 336, 357, 379, 382, 385 *passim*, 427, 449, 485 *passim*, 489, 494, 516, 530
  Apollo, 383, 385, 395, 488
  FM1600, 486–7
  naval, 13, 386–7
  Poseidon, 386–7, 486
displays, electronic, 385, 433–5, 437–8
distribution transformers, 194, 196, 303–4, 510
Dodd, Albert, 407
domestic appliances dept., 8, 9, 13, 14, 176, 188, 214–5, 250, 266–7, 270, 282, 287, 289, 294, 314–6, 317, 333, 338, 361, 412–3, 414, 439, 441, 490
Donner, H., 71–2
Dorey, Peter, 357, 386–7, 427, 485 *passim*, 489, 495, 514, 519, 524, 600
Drury, J, 330–1, 472
Duffy, W. N., 215, 266
Dundee factory, 335, 443, 481
Dunlop Rubber Co., 158, 197, 232

Edison, Thomas A., 33, 45, 51, 60, 70, 71, 81–2, 95, 227, 230, 253

Edison & Swan Electric Light Co. (EdiSwan), 45, 53, 78, 108, 253, 255
Edmondson, Tom, 307–9, 514, 568, 600
Ekco (E. K. Cole & Co.), 313, 315, 317–8, 327, 332, 559
Electric Construction Co., 105, 111, 128, 138, 548
Electric Plant Manufacturers' Association, 126–7
Electrical Association for Women, 212–3, 230
Electrical Development Association, 208–9, 212–4, 230
EMI, 263–5, 276, 311, 352, 362, 378–9, 390
electrical and electronics industries:
  cable industry, 103–4
  competition, 6–7, 12, 13, 15, 55, 95, 105–6, 125–7, 134–5, 141, 164 *passim*, 204–5, 173–5, 246–7, 340, 449, 497–8, 503
  conservative market, 13–14, 95–6, 153–4, 160–1, 287–8, 338, 341, 441, 482
  DC versus AC, 51–2, 57, 62, 66, 80–1, 82–3, 106, 108–9
  early development, slow, 4–5, 36–7, 40–2, 45–6, 47–8, 50, 55, 70–1, 93–4, 95–7, 105–6, 121, 135, 153–4, 160–1
  electricity sales, 125, 132, 135, 161–2, 163, 188–9, 203, 207–8, 214, 266, 294, 299, 303, 503
  exhibitions, 37, 42, 45–6, 53–4, 62, 64, 66
  export markets, 205–6, 246–7, 294 *passim*, 507, 511–2
  finance, lack of, 96, 124, 125, 135–6, 165, 225
  gas versus electricity, 4, 42, 45, 47, 51, 56, 60, 70–1, 76, 93, 163, 176, 212–3, 214, 503
  German industry, 4, 41–2, 55, 93–5, 106, 122–3, 124, 127, 135
  grid network, 179, 207–12, 237, 298–9
  import penetration, 123, 125, 203, 215
  mergers, 204, 483, 501–2, 509, 510
  multinational subsidiaries, 4–5, 95, 125, 127–8, 130–1, 134–5, 164–5, 172, 174, 222, 441, 464–5, 470
  municipal control, 49–50, 125–7, 134, 164–5, 189–90, 208

  price-fixing, 7, 106, 108, 126–7, 134–5, 144, 162, 165, 174–5, 204–5, 230, 247–50, 302, 500–1, 508, 509–10
  traction, 105–6, 123, 125
  US industry, 4, 51, 55, 70, 71, 81–2, 93–5, 106, 122–3, 124, 127, 135, 154, 160–1, 301–3, 325, 336–7, 362, 464–5, 466
electricity supply legislation, 4, 227
  1882 Act, 49–50, 51, 55, 56, 66, 70, 71, 80
  1888 Act, 80–1
  1919 Act, 189–90, 207–8
  1926 Act, 208–9
  1936 Act, 294–5
  Cross Committee, 189
  Marindin Inquiry, 80–1, 82–4, 93
  nationalisation, 299, 304, 501, 503
Electronic Components dept., 250–1, 262, 265, 276–7, 278, 282, 312–4, 414, 430, 438, 439, 441, 449 *passim*, 462–3, 470–1, 489, 493–4, 514, 515, 516, 529, 533
Elliott, W. S. (Bill), 357 *passim*, 360, 366, 370, 382, 385, 386
Elliott Bros, 279–80, 357–8, 359, 361, 371, 383, 390, 391, 393, 478, 479, 486, 487, 562
Engineering Employers' Federation (EEF), 117–8
engines, 1, 84–5, 88, 114–5, 129–31, 138–9
English Electric, 127, 153, 204, 209, 222, 322, 327–9, 344, 354, 358, 371, 375, 390, 401, 404, 415, 417, 421, 473, 492, 502, 508, 509, 510, 553

Fairchild, 449, 456, 458, 459, 463, 469, 470
Fairey Aviation, 336–8
Faraday, Sir Michael, 37, 111
Felten & Guillaume, 97, 104, 544, 545
Ferguson & Pailin, 188, 231, 553
Ferranti Canada, 169–71, 194–9, 222, 273, 303 *passim*, 364, 511
  electronics dept., 305–6, 364, 366, 395–6
  Ferranti-Packard, 306–8, 395–6
  Packard Electric, 198–9, 304–5, 306–8
Ferranti Ltd. (1901–05), 132–3, 134–5, 137–8, 139

crisis (1903), 3, 6–7, 19, 135–6, 143, 199, 497–8, 531
Ferranti Ltd. (1905–1993), 7, 140
  academic consultants, 220, 231, 253–5, 262, 273–4, 276, 452
  accounting system, 6, 7, 8, 9, 10 12, 15, 16, 120–1, 140–1, 166–7, 201, 235–6, 244, 256–9, 446–7, 472, 494–6, 498, 508, 513, 514–5, 520–1, 526, 529
  acquisition strategy, 297, 502, 510–1
  agencies, 7, 98–100, 168–71, 194, 196, 202, 205–6, 230, 260, 294, 299, 437, 481
  aircraft, 200, 273, 516, 518
  apprentice scheme, 246, 333–4, 411
  bank finance, 6–7, 14–15, 104, 224, 283, 316–7, 339, 413–4, 420, 490–1, 499, 517, 522 passim, 526, 529–31
  'barons', 10, 447–9, 495, 520–1
  board of directors, 10–12, 176, 202, 225–6, 242–4, 288, 447–9, 514, 519–20, 527, 529, 530, 552, 559–600
  Central Services, 284, 286–7, 292, 495, 520–1, 523, 529
  cost accountants, 9, 258–9, 270, 283, 291, 494
  defence business, 12–13, 14–16, 251, 267 passim, 278–8, 331–3, 338–40, 394, 398, 426–9, 438, 449, 465, 471, 477–8, 485, 489–91, 500, 515–6, 518–9
  departmentalisation, 6, 120–1, 197, 201, 235–6, 284–6, 290, 292, 340, 362, 387, 442–5, 446–7, 499–500
  divisionalisation, 10–12, 340, 447–9, 472, 495, 515, 520–1, 530, 533
  economist, 9, 285, 292–3, 447, 492
  engineering-led strategy, 1–2, 3, 5, 7, 9, 10, 12, 13, 15–16, 19, 20, 54–5, 57, 98, 102–3, 113, 121, 128, 130, 180, 192, 201, 206, 219–20, 222, 223, 231, 235–7, 242, 253, 261, 265, 291–2, 334–5, 339, 351, 356, 363, 391–2, 393, 438, 439–41, 446, 482, 494–6, 497, 514–5, 516, 529–31, 533–5
  family firm ethos, 2–3, 7–8, 9, 101–2, 284–6, 291–2, 351, 444–5, 449, 491, 492, 494–6, 497–9, 528

'Ferranti Spirit', 223–4, 231, 235–6, 237, 241–2, 275, 288, 291, 340, 533, 535
  finance and capital structure, 1–2, 3, 4, 5, 6, 7, 8, 9, 14, 15–16, 19, 20, 95, 101–3, 119, 125, 129, 132–3, 135–6, 140, 175–6, 199–202, 206, 224–5, 244, 247, 265–6, 270–1, 282–3, 297–8, 441, 516–7, 522–3, 585 passim
  geographical dispersion, 12, 278–81, 283–4, 409–10, 441–4, 516
  Gleneagles Hotel conferences, 491–4
  Inventors' Dinners, 2, 518
  lady supervisors, 17, 187, 233
  liquidity problems, 1, 2–3, 19–20, 438–42, 444–5, 449, 490–1, 492–4, 496, 497–9, 513, 515–7, 521–2, 523–5, 529–31
  London office, 168, 271, 311–2, 364–6, 423
  management consultants, 257–9
  management training, 19, 244–5, 288–9
  market-led strategy, 7, 13–14, 144, 164 passim
  mathematician, 9, 285, 286, 292–3
  organisational ethos, 2, 3, 5–6, 8, 9–10, 107–8, 120–23, 284–6, 360, 387, 442–5, 446–7, 449, 491, 494–6, 520–1, 529–31, 533
  patent purchases, 123, 190, 192, 231, 322
  paternalism, 16–18
  sales and marketing, 19, 52, 53–4, 55, 98–9, 168–9, 171–7, 220–2, 247–8, 260–1, 294 passim, 300, 563
  staff development, 19, 245–6, 288–9, 293
  succession, 8, 19, 288–9, 529
  toolroom, 116, 277, 504
  women workers, 17, 117, 233, 281
  workforce and industrial relations, 2, 14, 16–19, 116–8, 133, 180, 187, 212, 232–5, 246, 281, 528, 534, 551, 595–7
  works committee, 232–3
  works manager, 17, 234–5, 246, 528
Ferranti Electric Inc, 337, 519
Ferranti Hammond Electric Light Co., 51–2, 54, 55, 57
Ferranti, Thompson & Ince Ltd, 46, 49, 51
  Appold St. works, 44, 49, 51, 52, 54

Finch, Professor G. I., 220, 254–5, 262
fire control systems, 275, 319–20, 473
Fleming, J. A., 92, 253
foundry, 116, 123, 298
Forbes, James S., 78, 82, 88, 91–2
Forbes, Olivia, 187, 233–4
Foster, Carey, 39
Foster & Braithwaite, 225
fuze production (see also *'munitions'*), 265 *passim*, 271, 280, 282, 341, 352, 516

Galletti, R., 273–4, 278
Garrard, Dr C. C., 172–3, 584
Gaulard & Gibbs, 66–8, 73, 75, 79–80
Gem Mill, 276–8, 312–4, 318, 324, 359–60, 452, 453, 455 *passim*, 469–71, 489, 493–4, 514, 515, 528
General Electric (US), 106, 122, 154, 169, 221, 301, 308, 544
General Electric Co. (GEC), 45, 108, 128, 138, 165, 172, 176, 193, 204, 222, 294, 313, 314, 352, 362, 390, 391, 401, 408, 436, 451, 470, 483, 502, 509, 513, 527, 553
generators (see also *'steam-alternators'*), 1, 111–2, 125, 134, 137–9
  Deptford, 84–5, 90, 92
  Grosvenor Gallery, 74–5
  'zig-zag' (Ferranti-Thomson) alternator, 43, 48, 49, 53–4, 57, 60, 74, 81, 157
George, Lester, 293, 447, 492–3, 494–6, 514
Goodman, Lord, 527, 534
Gramme, Z. T., 40, 539
Gray, Archie, 514, 519, 600
Gribble, Maurice, 377, 383, 385, 415–6, 430–1, 433, 458, 460
Grosvenor Gallery, 63–4, 66–8, 69–70, 71, 72, 73, 74–6, 80, 83, 85, 86, 87, 88–90, 93, 99, 101, 110, 228
  fire at, 89–90
Grove, R. C. (Bob), 404, 406–7, 414–5, 419–20, 427
guided weapons, 13, 18, 20, 278, 319, 330, 340, 399 *passim*, 415, 417, 452, 453
gyrogunsights, 279–81, 322–3
gyroscopic stabilisation, 143, 158–60, 279, 319–22, 330–1

Grundy, David, 467, 469, 493–4
Grundy, Eric, 210–11, 279–80, 317–8, 319–22, 340, 346–8, 349, 363, 397, 412, 421, 447–9, 452, 515, 516, 519, 600

Hadley, A. E., 121, 132, 133, 248
Hall, Albert, 144–5, 155, 217, 220, 251–2, 253, 256, 259, 260, 275
Hall, Peter, 313–4, 318, 379–80, 382, 386, 388, 390–1, 392–4, 395–6, 408, 430, 451–3, 454–5, 456–7, 463, 467, 570
Halsbury, Lord, 342, 344 *passim*, 362, 366–7, 371, 373, 382, 396–8 436, 439
Hammond, Robert, 44, 45, 46–8, 49, 51, 52, 53–4, 55, 70
Hammond Electrical Engineering College, 52–3, 71
Hawker-Siddeley, 508, 513, 515
Hazeltine Electronics, 252–3, 255, 262, 265, 326
Hebbert, R. J., 17, 19, 215, 245–6, 293
Hegarty, W. F., 107, 120, 121
Henderson, J. M., 140, 175, 599
Hick, Hargreaves Ltd, 74, 84, 101–2
high voltage test laboratory, 498, 506, 508
Hinckley, H. G., 480, 481, 482
Hobill, R. M., 447–9, 519, 600
Hollinwood, 115–6, 146, 212
tram depot, 269, 277
Holmes, Sydney, 210, 217, 266–7, 279–81, 553
Hopkinson, Dr John, 67, 92
Hopkinson & Co., 154–5, 160
Hughes, T. P., 59, 70, 92–3, 94
Hughes Aircraft Co., 326

IFF systems, 272, 274–5, 325, 326, 345
Imperial Chemical Industries (ICI), 430, 436, 456
incandescent bulbs, 45, 53–4, 55, 108, 230
Ince, Francis, 5, 6, 42–3, 44–5, 46, 48, 51, 54, 57, 60, 71, 79, 80, 82, 96, 99, 100, 101, 102, 103, 106, 118, 119, 120, 121, 123, 125, 129, 130, 131, 132, 136, 139, 141, 187, 199, 231
Industrial Reorganisation Corporation (IRC), 483–4, 492, 502

Industrie Electtriche di Legnano, 308–9, 437, 511
inertial navigation platforms, 321–2, 330–1, 477–8
Institution of Electrical Engineers, 64, 71, 81, 96, 106, 113, 144, 159, 162–3, 173–4, 189, 207, 212, 230, 231, 293
Instrument dept., 7, 8, 9, 137, 172, 190, 211, 267–8, 279, 319, 346–8, 349–51, 467–8
International Business Machines (IBM), 334, 341, 346, 360, 362, 367, 371, 374, 375, 377, 378, 380, 381, 384, 389, 390–1, 392–3, 394, 395, 436, 461
International Computers Ltd (ICL), 361, 369, 395–6, 430, 464, 483, 492, 517
International Computers & Tabulators Ltd (ICT), 18, 374, 379, 383, 384, 389–94, 395, 396, 397, 461, 421, 463, 466, 491, 511

Jackson, Sydney, 277–8, 313–4, 456
Jarman, A. J., 34, 36, 37, 40, 41, 43, 46, 48
Johnson, Harry, 369–70, 385–6, 392, 395–6

Kilburn, Professor Tom, 344, 345 *passim*, 375–6, 377–8
Kirkham, Harry, 283, 291, 419–20, 447, 490, 492, 494–5, 513, 517, 521, 525
Kolle, H. W., 72, 86, 87, 243, 545, 599
Korean War, 316, 325–6, 405, 410, 515

laser-cutting equipment, 481, 560
Laufenburg project, 97, 104
Lawton, Alf, 419–20, 426
Lightning aircraft, 327–9
Lindsay, Sir Coutts, 63–5, 67, 69, 76, 78
Lings, Scott, 6, 133, 135, 547
Lockspeiser, Sir Ben, 346, 348–9, 351, 354, 401–2
Lodge, Oliver, 39
London Electricity Supply Co. (LESCo), 75 *passim*, 77, 78, 80–1, 82, 83–4, 85, 88–90, 91, 93, 95, 97, 101, 103, 104, 110, 189
Lunt, T. J., 19, 245, 286, 292–3, 360, 449
Lyons & Co., J. (Leo), 344, 390

McCallum, Sir Donald, 280, 324, 326 *passim*, 472, 473, 478, 479, 483–4, 514, 515, 517–9, 520, 524, 525, 527, 600
magnetrons, 276, 408
Manchester, University of, 42, 67, 344–6, 349 *passim*
Marconi, 215–6, 217, 218, 251–2, 253, 263–4, 273, 313, 390, 460
Massachussetts Institute of Technology (MIT), 330–1, 335–7
Mather & Platt, 105, 111
Merz. C., 163, 173, 189, 208–9, 228
Meter dept., 1, 5, 6, 7, 8, 9, 13, 60–64, 98, 106–8, 111, 115, 116, 119, 120, 129, 132, 134, 137, 138, 167–9, 171, 172, 173, 183, 187–8, 198, 202–3, 210, 229–30, 266, 276, 282, 287, 293–6, 297–8, 309, 334, 338, 362, 441, 449, 499–500, 503–5, 512
Metropolitan-Vickers Electrical Manufacturing Co. (MetroVic's), 153–4, 204, 209, 246, 272–3, 274, 275, 553
microelectronics, 1, 12, 20, 456 *passim*, 461–3, 465–7, 484, 486, 493–4
F100-L, 462
government support, 465–7, 469
Micronor, 458–60, 486
ULA concept, 467–71
Midmer, K., 268
Ministry of Aircraft Production (MAP), 277, 279–80, 282–3, 320–1, 329, 331, 332, 399–400, 413, 417 *passim*, 478, 485–6, 487, 488, 490, 529
Ministry of Defence (MoD), 428, 474, 475–6, 478, 486–7, 525, 530
Ministry of Munitions, 182–3, 184
Ministry of Supply (MoS), 277, 282–3, 320, 326, 333, 338, 348, 351, 385, 388, 398, 401–2, 404–5, 408, 409–11, 413–4, 415–6, 451–3
Ministry of Technology (MinTech), 436, 465–6, 469, 471, 483
Morrrison, Charles, 136
Moston factory, 11, 13, 259–61, 269–71, 275, 276, 279, 284, 287, 292, 310, 313, 317–8, 319–22, 335, 339, 346–9, 407, 408, 409, 411, 412, 414, 419–20, 423, 425, 427, 428, 443, 467, 472, 491, 516, 519, 528

Motorola, 463, 469
Mullard's, 253, 255, 313–4, 318, 407, 416, 455–6
munitions, 7–8, 180, 181 *passim*, 222, 267

Nash, R. W. (Bill), 494, 509, 510, 511, 512–3
National Research Development Corporation (NRDC), 348 *passim*, 361, 367, 371, 378–9, 380–1, 382, 388, 396–8, 420, 427, 436, 465–6
National Westminster Bank (*see also 'Parr's Bank' and 'Westminster Bank'*), 14, 15, 499, 519, 522 *passim*, 526, 529, 531
Neal, Tom, 280–1, 322, 330
Negri, Augustine, 21, 25
Nelson, George (Lord), 153
Newcastle Electricity Supply Co. (NESCo.), 154, 162, 163, 173, 189, 228
Niagara Falls, 76, 96–7
Nicholson, Rupert, 525, 526, 528
Norris, E. T., 191–3, 231
numerical control, 13, 332, 335–8, 430, 441, 449, 480 *passim*, 492, 493, 516, 517, 519, 530
   inspection machines, 480, 481, 484, 572
   IRC involvement, 483–4, 493, 502

Palmer, Professor L. S., 220, 273–4
Parr's Bank, 6–7, 118–9, 123, 133, 136, 137
Parsons, Charles, 112, 138–9, 145, 150, 152, 153, 508, 545–6, 549
Parsons, R. H., 145
Pickin, John, 408, 467–8, 570, 467–8, 513, 514, 518, 519, 527, 600
Platt Brothers, 147, 246
Plessey, 376, 380, 483–4, 486, 487, 492, 519
Pollard, Brian, 348, 351 *passim*, 363, 369–70, 376–7, 379, 382, 385, 388
polyphase AC, 97, 105, 123, 132
Portsmouth power station, 108–11, 119, 150, 173, 243
Powers-Samas, 351, 370–2, 373–4, 375, 393
Powley, Mal, 324, 326–9, 330–1, 478
Preston, Lindley, 507, 511–2
Prince, Jack, 294–5, 447–9, 503–4, 519, 600
process control computers, 399, 403, 415, 429 *passim*, 441, 458–9, 463

Argus, 383, 385, 395
protectionism, 203, 205, 215, 248, 252, 266, 500
Pycroft, W. C., 283, 285, 448, 599

radar, 271–4, 275, 278
Radar Research Establishment (RRE), 326–9, 332, 385, 407–8, 416, 427, 458, 478
Radio dept., 8, 9, 13, 18, 69, 215 *passim*, 224, 230, 250 *passim*, 270, 282, 287, 294, 309–11, 315–6, 317–8, 412–4
Raytheon, 415, 566
rearmament (1930s), 241, 267 *passim*, 271–2, 274, 278, 282, 310, 316, 319
rectifier, 110–11, 115
research establishments, Government, 13, 272, 278–9, 325–6, 399–401, 402–3
Reyrolle, 110, 172, 173, 174, 188, 193, 510, 513, 553
Robinson, J. E. L., 298–9
Robson, Murray, 289, 444, 448, 519, 600
Rolls Royce, 115, 169, 525
Rostron, Sir Frank, 247–50, 294, 299–302, 366, 448, 519, 600
Rowntree, F. W., 169–71
Royal Air Force (RAF), 281, 321, 401, 411–2, 413, 416, 417, 428, 474, 475, 478, 479, 488, 568
Royal Aircraft Establishment (RAE), 160, 273–4, 279, 281, 324, 325, 326–9, 330–1, 332, 385, 401–2, 427
Royal Navy, 13, 386–7, 474, 479, 485–6, 487, 488–9
Royal Scottish Society of Arts, 112–3, 137
Royal Society, 230
Royce, G., 169–71, 176, 214

St. Augustine's, Ramsgate, 32–4, 36
S. Z. de Ferranti (partnership, 1885–1890), 57, 60, 63, 86, 101–2
   agencies, 98–9
   Hatton Garden works, 57, 62, 97
S. Z. de Ferranti Ltd. (1890–1901), 102–3, 104, 105, 106, 108, 110, 111, 115, 117, 119, 120, 121, 122, 123, 125, 127, 128, 129, 131, 132, 134, 137

B. I. Wire merger, proposed, 131–2
Charterhouse Square works, 97–8, 100, 101, 103, 107, 110, 113, 115, 116, 117, 119, 133, 183
Patin, Oliver, 99–100
Schofield, R. H., 81, 202, 203, 205, 243, 247, 248, 250, 551, 599
Science Museum, 35, 41
Scophony, 262–4
Scott, William, 26, 27, 30, 57
Searby, Dr N. H., 255, 276, 278, 310–11, 347, 401, 403–4, 407, 408–9, 410–1, 412, 414–5, 426, 427, 428, 429, 447–9, 495, 513, 514, 600
Selsdon Committee (1934), 242, 263–4
semiconductors, 9, 20, 314, 317–8, 373, 377, 379, 382–3, 415–6, 429–30, 441, 449 *passim*, 453–5, 468
Shepherd, Dr A. A., 430, 450, 452 *passim*, 467–71, 493–4
Siemens, 36, 37, 41–2, 43, 45, 46, 48, 49, 55, 66, 70, 71, 75, 101, 105, 106, 111, 127, 138, 165, 505
Sions, M. E., 254
Silverknowes factory, 331, 443
Smith, J. B., 324, 472, 495
Sparks, Charles P., 6, 57, 71, 72, 73, 85, 100, 101, 103, 119, 120, 121, 130, 131, 132, 145, 231, 540, 547
speech (audio frequency) transformer, 69, 216–9, 220
Sperry, 33, 159–60, 279, 331, 401
Stalybridge factory, 219–20, 251–2, 254, 256–7, 259
steam-alternator, 5–6, 100, 109–10, 113–4, 127, 128–9, 132, 134–5, 137–8, 145, 167, 229, 230
steam valves, 1, 143, 154–5, 156
Stewart, J., 324, 325–9, 416, 472
stock exchanges
    London, 15–16, 46, 49, 96, 124–5, 133, 501, 534
    Manchester, 6, 133
    Wall St., 96, 159, 225, 241, 246, 469
Sutton, R. W., 254–5
Swan, Joseph, 45, 62
Swann, B. B., 364–6, 369, 372, 373, 374, 375, 392–3, 395, 397

switchgear, 1, 110–11, 112, 115, 123, 132, 133, 137, 171, 172, 188, 219, 228
Szczepanowski, Vincent, 27, 31–2, 35, 71–2, 114, 584
Szczepanowski, S., 27–8, 30, 40

Tait, A. W., 7, 8, 136–7, 138, 139, 140, 143, 144, 166–9, 171, 172, 175–6, 177, 179–81, 184, 188, 199–200, 201, 202, 204, 206, 222–3, 225, 231, 232, 235–6, 242, 599
Taylor, M. K., 254, 259, 260, 262–4, 274, 276, 278, 305–6, 323–4
Telecommunications Research Establishment (TRE), 276, 325, 326–7, 344, 345, 350, 364, 408
television, 13, 262–5, 282, 287, 315–6, 317–8, 412–4
terrain-following radar (FLR), 329–30, 473, 475
testing transformers, 8, 192–3, 507–8
Texas Instruments, 449, 458, 462, 463, 464, 467, 473
textile machinery, 139, 143, 144–9, 152, 160–1, 184, 217
Thomas, Captain P. D., 184, 201, 242, 551, 599
Thomas Bolton & Sons, 119, 548
Thompson, Alfred, 42, 44, 46, 48, 51, 584
Thompson, Jim, 418, 419, 421, 423, 448, 600
Thomson, Sir William (Lord Kelvin), 48–9, 54, 60–2, 81, 85, 96, 584
Tizard, Sir Henry, 272, 273
Toothill, Sir John, 258, 280–1, 322 *passim*, 340, 426, 447–9, 472, 474–5, 478–9, 495, 514, 515, 519, 599
    Crewe Toll strategy, 323–4, 332
    networking, 327, 335
    Scottish industry, work for, 333–4
Trafford Park, 128, 165
Transformer dept., 1, 8, 9, 13, 18, 66–9, 80, 106, 108, 137, 188–93, 198, 202–3, 204, 205, 209–12, 243, 248, 250, 266, 282, 287, 298–303, 304, 309, 334, 338, 362, 366, 441, 449, 494, 499–500, 501, 506–10, 511–3, 515, 518–20, 530–1, 533
transformer technology, 66–9, 209–10, 299, 507

TSR–2, 329, 331, 465, 472 *passim*, 505
Tucker, A., 145, 191–2
turbines, 34, 109, 112, 138–9, 143, 144, 145, 150–4, 160, 161, 184, 228, 229
Turing, Alan, 342–3, 344, 346
Tyldesley, W., 258, 284, 599
tyres, rubber, 143, 157–8, 160, 232

University College, London, 5, 37–9, 40

valves, thermionic emission, 219, 253–5, 262, 275–7, 312–4, 317–8, 407–8, 416, 451, 452, 455, 457
Varley, S. A., 37, 538
Vickers, 145, 151–4, 155, 158, 160, 182, 183, 197, 204, 373, 421, 473
Vickers, Douglas, 152, 153

Wantage, Lord, 77, 78, 92, 101
Watson, Robert & William, 145, 158
Watson-Watt, Robert, 272, 273, 274, 325
Way, Sir Richard, 418, 419–20, 421–2, 567
Weinstock, Lord Arnold, 502, 527, 534
Weir, Lord, 208
Western Electric, 273, 449, 451–3, 469, 470
Westinghouse (including British Westinghouse Co.), 71, 106, 122, 128, 132, 134, 138, 165, 167, 169,171, 190, 191, 204, 227, 252–3, 301, 308, 544
Westminster Bank, 6, 14, 15, 224, 244, 270, 283, 316–7, 413–4, 441–2, 448, 529

Whittaker, Arthur, 7, 8, 136–7, 138, 139, 140, 143, 144, 166–9, 171, 172, 175–6, 177, 179, 181, 184, 188, 200–1, 223, 225–6, 232, 235–6, 242, 263, 269, 276, 599
Wilde, Henry, 37, 48, 538
Wilkes, Maurice, 344, 346, 351
Williams, F. C., 272, 274, 325, 343, 344 *passim*, 354, 364
Williamson, D. T. N., 324, 335–8, 472, 480, 482, 572
Wilson, R. P., 273
Wilson Electric Transformer Co., 308–9, 511
Windsor Mill, Hollinwood, 172, 219
Wood, H., 274, 278, 311–2, 313, 345, 347
World Power (Energy) Conference, 153, 230, 293
World War One, 7, 17, 153, 161, 179 *passim*
World War Two, 282 *passim*, 286, 287, 339
Wright, Arthur, 106–7, 584
Wythenshawe, 399–400, 408–11, 412, 415–6, 420, 423, 428, 429 *passim*, 443, 452–3, 457, 513

Ziani de Ferranti, Cesar, 28, 30, 32, 35, 37–8, 39–40, 43, 57, 102, 236
Ziani de Ferranti, Juliana (nee Scott), 27–30, 34–5, 36, 37–40, 41, 68, 69, 73, 102, 236
Ziani de Ferranti, Marco Aurelio, 25–6, 28